Shadows over Anáhuac

SHADOWS
OVER
ANÁHUAC

An Ecological Interpretation
of Crisis and Development
in Central Mexico, 1730–1800

Arij Ouweneel

University of New Mexico Press
Albuquerque

To Arij Ouweneel, Sr. (1925–87),
who was unable to witness
the completion of this book.
It could not have been written
without his support.

© 1996 by the University of New Mexico Press
All rights reserved.
First edition

Library of Congress Cataloging-in-Publication Data
Ouweneel, Arij, 1957--
[Onderbroken groei in Anahuac. English]
Shadows over Anahuac : an ecological interpretation of crisis and
development in Central Mexico, 1730-1800 / Arij Ouweneel. — 1st
ed.
        p.   cm.
"Partly based on the large manuscript of the translation of . . .
Onderbroken groei in Anahuac"—Introduction.
Includes bibliographical references and index.
ISBN 0-8263-1731-6 (cl.)
1. Meseta Central (Mexico)—Economic conditions.
2. Meseta Central (Mexico)—Environmental conditions.
3. Meseta Central (Mexico)—History.
4. Indians of Mexico—Mexico—Meseta Central—
   Economic conditions.
I. Title.
HC137.M4O9513 1996
333.7'09725—dc20
95-41814
CIP

Contents

List of Figures, Maps, and Tables

Figures

Maps

Tables

Acknowledgments

This book is partly based on the large manuscript of the translation of my 1989 prize-winning Dutch publication *Onderbroken groei in Anáhuac. De ecologische achtergrond van ontwikkeling en armoede op het platteland van Centraal-Mexico (1730–1810)*. Because of some very substantial start-up costs, no English or American publisher could afford to embark on such a large undertaking in a period of general recession. At the suggestion of the editor of this present book, David Holtby, the original text was divided into two pieces: one dealing with the ecological approach and the other with the hacienda. The reader will find the second text in a separate publication, issued by another publisher. I thank David wholeheartedly for tackling the difficult task of splitting a complex analysis, and I hope that the public finds two books by one author, both published within such a short period of time, worth reading. The present book is still lengthy, but such amplitude is needed for a comprehensive study of the issues confronted in this work.

At first I concentrated on agricultural aspects, particularly the hacienda. Soon, however, it became clear that it was impossible to study agriculture or the hacienda in isolation. Since then, most of my research has concentrated on the functioning of the rural economy as a whole; and on both the *pueblos de indios* and the haciendas in particular. I visited archives in Mexico (1981–82, 1983–84 and 1986, and later on again in 1988 and 1990, partly for another project, partly to check some findings) and in Spain (1985, 1986, and 1987, and later again in 1989) to collect the necessary material. The research was initially rounded off in 1987, making it virtually impossible now to take recently published studies into account. I have tried to integrate a number of these where the original text permitted it. This additional material is contained in some paragraphs and the endnotes. The book was published in Dutch in 1989 by the Center for Latin American Research and Documentation (CEDLA) in Amsterdam. The English translation by Peter Mason is based on a revised version of that text, carried out in 1990; and as will be clear, I shortened the text in 1993.

It is customary for a preface like this one to include a statement that the book is the product of a "collective endeavor." However, monographs are often written in total isolation, during which the author's social life is at a (temporary?) low ebb, and I remember sitting for hours at my desk in solitude. All the same, a number of individuals and institutions contributed, of course, to make the final product what it has become. I received financial assistance for the project from the *Fundatie van de Vrijvrouwe van Renswoude* in The Hague; the *Vereniging Algemeen Studiefonds* in The Hague; the *Secretaría de Relaciones Exteriores* in Mexico City; the *Stichting voor Wetenschappelijk Onderzoek van de Tropen* (WOTRO) in The Hague; the *Nederlandse Organisatie voor Wetenschappelijk Onderzoek* (NWO) in The Hague, which financed the translation; the *Stichting het Unger van Brero Fonds* in Wageningen; and the CEDLA in Amsterdam.

I owe a great debt to Professor Richard Garner of Pennsylvania State University, who came to Amsterdam in the summer of 1990 to combine discussions of the economic trends in Bourbon Mexico with enjoyable meals in the city's restaurants. I took the opportunity to ask him about the unpublished manuscript of his book *Economic Growth and Change in Bourbon Mexico*. It is a sign of his dedication to scholarship that he sent me a copy soon afterward. I am very grateful to him for putting his trust in my use of his work. Although the Dutch-language version of my book had already been sent to the translator, I have been able to benefit from his insights in editing the final draft. Surprisingly enough, our individual research complement one another like red and green or yellow and blue. Inevitably there will still remain differences of interpretation—the tithe data!—but on the whole we arrived independently at the same conclusions. In fact, in some passages he had even followed the same line of argument as I had. All the same, there is still one unbridgeable difference, which lies in the research object itself: Garner's analysis of trends is mainly aimed at the public sector and the "Spanish" side of economic activity, while my normative, rural approach devotes a good deal of space to the "Indian" side of the economy.

Writing the book would have been much more difficult and certainly less inspiring without patient reading of the first drafts by Peter van der Meer and Jos Damen. Professor Bernard Slicher van Bath—my tutor for many years—Professor Hille de Vries, and Professor Raymond Buve furnished extensive comments on the final Dutch version. At a critical phase in the writing of that book, the thrust of the argument in some chapters benefited from discussions with Professor Frans Schryer. I have derived great pleasure from the presence of Rik Hoekstra, Frank Schenk, and recently, Juultje van der Valk of CEDLA— all of whom engaged in continual discussions with me about the development and character of the Indian communities in New Spain. Our agreement on many points is due in no small measure to our common allegiance to Slicher van Bath. Finally, I would like to add a word of thanks to professors Geert A. Banck, David Bushnell, Reinhard Liehr, Frédéric Mauro, Magnus Mörner, and Hans-Jürgen Puhle for their support in the preparation of this publication. Nor should I fail to mention the members of the board and the secretariat of the CEDLA. They were the ones who provided all the facilities for bringing this research project to a rapid and successful conclusion.

Besides Slicher's tutorial role, mention should be made of the great personal support provided by Raymond Buve, who introduced me to the CEDLA. I must also thank Patricio Silva and Berry Bock, who were prepared to give up their valuable time to assist me during an important scientific ritual ceremony on 6 April 1989. I received invaluable assistance in Mexico from Henriette Stevens; Arjen van der Sluis and his wife Mariana Yampolsky—whom we joined for our weekly excursions into the world of Mexico—Don Juan Faustino Juárez Vázquez and his family; Martha Zertuche; Bernardo García Martínez, his wife, Takako Sudo, and son Alex; and the unforgettable help and close friendship with Ricardo Rendón, Cristina Torales Pacheco, and Luis Vergara from the Universidad Iberoamericana. Later on, Professor David Brading of Cambridge, England, untiringly corrected errors of substance in my analysis of some of the topics introduced in the final text. His letters—one began with "I am sorry to be so bothersome"—led to both fundamental rewriting and a deepening of our friendship. I have a special relationship with Professor Eric Van Young in San Diego, California, who sends me his offprints and manuscripts so that I can rectify my own work. Although I have tried to find an answer, in chapter four, to its slight *tapatío* character—where is the *repartimiento* trade?—his work appeared extremely inspiring to me. I have a similar relationship with Professor Horst Pietschmann, who not only sends me all his publications, but has also given me words of encouragement when they were most needed. At first I was surprised at his generosity, since I am well aware that the theme of this book is, in the last resort, an elaboration of some lectures that he published years ago in the journal *Comunicaciones del Proyecto Puebla-Tlaxcala*. I hope that my interpretation squares to some extent with his profound knowledge of Spanish-American government.

This book is also dedicated to my mother, Magdalena Ouweneel-Lucas, who bears a great loss with fortitude. Virginie Rozemeijer deserves admiration, too, though of a different kind, for her incredible patience toward a husband hidden behind his books, papers, and word processor. It is a commonplace in prefaces of this kind, but it really is impossible to write a book without the unselfish support and confidence of a loving partner. She accompanied me on almost all of my trips, visited all of the villages and haciendas that I wanted to see, and even uncomplainingly helped me decipher some documents in the Archivo General de la Nación at a time when we could hardly hold our pencils because of the cold winter. The successful accomplishment of this book is due to her.

—Amsterdam, January 6, 1994

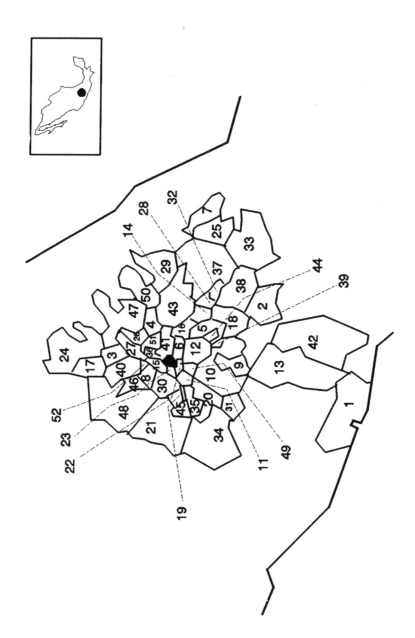

Map 1 The provinces of Anáhuac, late eighteenth century

1. Acapulco
2. Acatlán-Piastla
3. Actopan
4. Apan-Tepeapulco
5. Atlixco
6. Coatepec
7. Córdoba
8. Cuautitlán

9. Cuautla-Amilpas
10. Cuernavaca
11. Coyoacán
12. Chalco-Tlalmanalco
13. Chilapa
14. Cholula
15. Ecatepec
16. Huejotzingo
17. Ixmiquilpan
18. Izúcar
19. Lerma
20. Malinalco
21. Metepec-Ixtlahuaca
22. Mexicalzingo
23. México
24. Metztitlán
25. Orizaba
26. Otumba

27. Pachuca
28. Puebla-Amozoc
29. San Juan de los Llanos
30. Tacuba
31. Taxco
32. Tecali
33. Tehuacán
34. Temascaltepec-Sultepec/
    Zacualpan
35. Tenango del Valle
36. Teotihuacán
37. Tepeaca
38. Tepejí de la Seda
39. Tetela del Volcán
40. Tetepango-Hueypustla
41. Texcoco
42. Tlapa
43. Tlaxcala
44. Tochimilco
45. Toluca
46. Tula
47. Tulancingo
48. Xilotepec
49. Xochimilco
50. Zacatlán
51. Zempoala
52. Zumpango de la Laguna

[The list is somewhat arbitrary, because in the map the province of Tlapa is included, while the northern province of Xalapa—bordering provinces 29 and 37 to the northeast—is left out; in other maps the situation is sometimes reversed, depending on the data. Also the province of Acapulco is sometimes left out for this reason.]

xiii

And one of the hallmarks
of contemporary life
is what I perceive to be
a conspiracy against
conscious thought.

—Frank Vincent Zappa

Prologue

The Ongoing Problem of the *Chiaroscuro* Century

Introduction

In view of the broad scope of this book, it seems best to introduce the theoretical spectrum with two short examples from documentary evidence. The first brings us to Huayacocotla, a province north of the valley of Puebla in central Mexico. In 1784 the *alcalde mayor*, or Spanish provincial officer, refused to ratify the election of a certain Miguel Mérida as Indian governor of the principal Indian village.[1] Mérida was unacceptable to the Spanish authorities because he had carried out robberies on the exit roads from Mexico City as a bandit for seven years and was wanted by the officers of the Tribunal de Acordada. Mérida, a *tributario* (Indian taxpayer) from the province, hoped that his election would be a means of exchanging his profitable but dangerous life of robbery for an attractive position in Indian government. His popularity among a few leading families in the village was due to his promise to reduce the tribute if he were elected *gobernador* and to settle the dispute with the Conde de Regla involving a plot of land that was adjacent to the village in the latter's favor. Feelings ran high in the village: the Conde had won an official case in court because he was able to show that the disputed land had been in his use for years. Mérida's support in the village was the *mulato* Manuel Rojo, who had borrowed a large sum from the village treasury to register an appeal against this decision in Mexico City. However, Rojo had spent the money during his journey on excessive food and drink in the taverns. All the same, Mérida thought he would still be useful as a pawn in the village and loaned him money to buy votes from the leading villagers by organizing and financing festivities. Mérida's strategy paid off because the alcalde mayor was confronted with the election of Mérida. Of course, the alcalde mayor saw which way the wind was blowing in advance and did not fail to register his displeasure. When he refused to ratify the election, he was driven out of the village with stones, knives, and sticks by a crowd of some five hundred men, women, and children. Cursing, shouting, and throwing stones, they pursued him almost two kilometer past the village, and he had barely had time to mount his horse.

In dealing with the case, the authorities recognized that the *tumulto* was

essentially the result of the Audiencia's refusal to grant the disputed fields to
the village. This was a mitigating circumstance, so the army, which had been
called in to restore order, was instructed to go to work carefully and only to
arrest Mérida, Rojo, and a third ringleader. The Audiencia supposed that these
rascals had misled the Indians. The military ostentation—the alcalde mayor
received the support of two hundred dragoons—was due to the fact that Miguel
Mérida had been a wanted criminal for a long time. However, the rebellious
peasants fled with Mérida to the impenetrable Sierra Norte. An assistant of the
former gobernador, designated as the village representative, was sent to per-
suade them to resume their normal life without any risk of being prosecuted.
His mission was successful, but it proved impossible, he reported, to trace the
three ringleaders. After the cavalrymen had left, a new gobernador was chosen. This was a victory for the alcalde mayor, but his authority had still sustained a blow. The Audiencia advised him to move his residence to nearby
Chicontepec, for the peasants had acquired a taste for rebellion—an official
stated in the government report on the case—and they would continue to
disobey his orders.

The second example comes from a village not far away, Huasca Zaloya in
the province of Tulancingo, where, in 1803, the young Lazaro Antonio Huerta
asked *not* to be obliged to assume office. Huerta, who was only twenty-eight
years old, was a simple migrant laborer who lived in a hamlet in the mountains. The post in Indian government was not at all attractive to him. In fact,
it could mean his downfall, just as his predecessors had ended up in jail because they had not been able to transfer the village tribute. His own father
had been gobernador, had spent four years in prison, and had been released
before his sentence was complete, only to die. The problem here was that
Huasca Zaloya had been a brainchild of the Conde de Regla, founded in 1760
to provide the Indian laborers in the Conde's silver mines with a village of
their own, primarily as a form of pension. Most of the official residents did
not pay a cash tribute to the gobernador because they worked in the mines
and were therefore absent when the tribute was collected. Those villagers who
did not work in the mines consisted of those who had retired, of cripples, and
of invalids with black-lung disease. These men were exempt from tribute
(*reservados*). The rest were mestizos. There was hardly anyone answering to
the description of tribute payer in Huasca. The Juzgado de Indios decided on
a new tribute assessment, in which the tribute would only be required from
those Indians who were present in the village. New elections were held as
well, so that someone with experience could assume responsibility. The candidate was Don Luis Paulino Pérez del Castillo. He accepted on the explicit
condition that he would be held accountable exclusively for the Indians on
the new list, and not for the others who owned a house in Huasca but were
never there or were exempt. In addition, the village was granted a protected
area of land and the Spanish and mestizo rancheros, who lived within the
new boundary, had to leave; and eventually they did leave, two years later.[2]

Our encounter in both villages with Don Pedro Ramón Mariano José

Romero de Terreros, the Second Count of Regla, will be taken for granted. The reader will remember the part played by his father, Don Pedro, in Doris Ladd's beautiful book on the Mexican silver workers' strike in Real del Monte, 1766-75.[3] The Second Count was throughout his lifetime less prosperous and less fortunate than his father. Shortly before his death in 1809, at the age of forty-eight, he was even forced to sacrifice a good deal of his landed property to satisfy his creditors.[4] What really interests me in Huayacocotla and Huasca is the implication of tribute payments. It seems that governorship in the Indian communities was only worthwhile for the Indians if there were sufficient tributarios. In Huasca the number of tributarios was obviously too small, while in Huayacocotla the number must have been quite attractive for a governor's candidate to present himself. In fact, Miguel Mérida thought to live from the tribute revenues! Our central question, then, must concentrate on the background of the seemingly high level of revenues in the Indian villages in eighteenth-century central Mexico. Although the Indians did not keep any books to support a well-developed historical analysis, I think that sufficient evidence can be presented to argue in favor of a hypothesis concerning the active and profitable participation of the Indians in the economy of eighteenth-century central Mexico.

The examples suggest that population density is the major analytical tool for historians tackling the problem. It is well known that population density played a key role in the analysis of the agrarian history of early modern Europe. Presumably, an increase in population density meant an increase in the specialization of labor and a greater diversity in the range of economic activities. A core of economic activities can be discerned in the most densely populated areas. But the further one moved from this core, the more the population density decreased and the smaller the range of economic activities became. Population density was low on the periphery, and *consequently* economic differentiation was small because of that. This rule is an extension of the model devised by the nineteenth-century German geographer and agronomist von Thünen.

The response to the problem will be found in the functioning of the economy of a region in Latin America during the period 1730–1810. I shall try to improve our historical knowledge and historical insights in three areas:

1. The role of geographical conditions in the economy, such as landscape and precipitation, combined with the development and composition of the population;
2. The functioning of the regional economy and the integration of the indigenous communities within it;
3. The micro-level of the social and economic organization.

In short, I hope to present the hypothesis on the economic integration of the Indian population in the colonial Mexican economy in the form of a description of the various aspects of that economy.

The new perspective that will be formulated in the course of the volume is a "translation" of an *ecological approach* to the Mexican situation. This approach, which was formulated by the economist Wilkinson in 1973 and elaborated further by the historian Skipp in 1978, deals with the interaction between population density, landscape, climate and culture in economic development.[5] It is concerned with the success and failure of resource management on the local level. The objective of this management is adaptation to a natural environment by the application of means of production. Resource management is usually defined in agricultural terms. Wilken, for example, writes that there are three elements involved: the crop plants; the environment, including solar energy in its various transformations; and the farmers who, with their knowledge, tools, and institutions, actually manage the modifications and maintenance of the ecosystem they are living in.[6] This final point is most important for my investigation, because there is no question of seeing the effects of the environment on human society as a one-way process. In adapting to the natural environment, human beings modify it continuously, and this in turn has an impact on the human process of adaptation. The two-way interaction plays an important part in the development of human behavior in society. The social psychologist Leonard Berkowitz writes:

> The person's society has arrived at certain modes of adjustment to the ecological pressures confronting it, and these adaptive techniques are exhibited in many aspects of his culture, including the tools that are available to him and how he has been brought up and educated.[7]

It is the merit of Wilkinson to have incorporated these important cultural and psychological factors in the theory of economic history.

The book reflects my viewpoints on the position expressed by other writers, as well as my reading of the documents. Both activities are inspired by the ecological approach. For Wilkinson the major variable for investigation is the relation between the volume of the population and the production of basic needs. This relation gives the ecological approach its typical heuristic value. The ecological problem only arises when a population is confronted by the features of *relative overpopulation* and tries to find a way out of the impasse by reaching a new ecological equilibrium. Although all this sounds rather "green," as if the work under scope has any relevance for the so-called "green movement" in world politics, I never intended to write "green history," despite my sympathies.[8] To me, the analysis of historical ecology concerns the features that indicate relative overpopulation and the solutions which have been devised. In fact, in reading Malcolm Chase's 1992 commentary "Can History be Green?,"[9] I was rather surprised to find the names of the writers I follow closely—Skipp and Wilkinson—acting prominently among the most successful "green" historians. Skipp's book is even described as a "notable, but rare exception" to the generalization that historical ecology remains a branch of topographical, even a kind of paleobotanic, history in Britain. And Chase found no other ecologically informed study of English industrialization in his library save Wilkinson's. Chase's frustration is fed by the observation that against a general intellectual background which is increasingly preoccupied with environmental issues, British historical scholarship remained largely impervious to "green" issues.

The answer of John Sheail was published in the form of a more optimistic review of environmental history in England.[10] However, Sheail ranks ecology apparently as a branch of natural science only, and advocates the historical research of the complex interplay between technical and policy considerations, like the question of how the two preoccupations of "habitat" protection and pollution control have become focused as a single, central concern in the minds of government, industry and environmental organizations alike. This truly is the history of "sustainability," the history of environmental degradation,[11] and it sounds, to me, far from the purposes of the ecological approach. The observation of environmental degradation might be the outcome of the research to the interaction in the past between human societies and their natural habitats, which the ecological approach fosters, but it is certainly not its main goal. In fact, the ecological approach should not be misunderstood as another all-explaining format of theoretical thinking that everyone henceforth should adopt. It is a heuristic tool only, and in this case, one to use in clarifying the problems—and the solutions to these problems—in one region of colonial Mexico during a specific period of time. The approach is merely a way of gathering a body of research material, published or not, and looking at it in a particular way. Nevertheless, it is possible and worthwhile to look more generically at the elements of the approach in studying other regions, or other periods.

However, most writers of the "New Ecological History" focus upon the history of environmental degradation resulting from the forces of political economy. Because these writers originate in traditional Marxian currents, they look for the cause of environmental degradation in the development of the capitalist world order, since, as Martínez-Alier has put it, "the large exosomatic consumption of energy and materials by rich people" implies a great ecological burden on the environment, especially in the countries of the South. Stressing the notion that *production* is *extraction* former "Reds" turned "Green" and the "New Ecological History" became the "green current" of traditional political economy. Therefore, to them the New Ecological History is at the same time the history of local or indigenous movements against this "extraction." But ecological history should be much more than this. The very word *ecology* should address the historian to local ecosystems and the different forces shaping or transforming it. The ecosystem was described by Tansley, some sixty years ago, as an interaction system comprising living things together with their nonliving habitat. Here, to analyze this interaction, the *nonliving habitat,* more or less absent or of secondary importance in political economy, should receive the attention it requires. In a mature ecosystem, the nutrient supply is

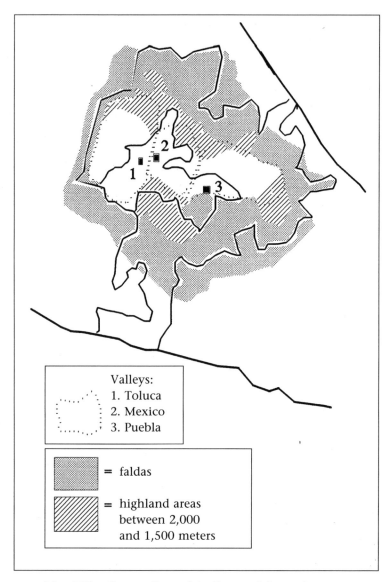

Map 2 The three valleys of Anáhuac, eighteenth century

in equilibrium; there is little loss. Such a situation suggests a static view, but, indeed, transformation of the ecosystem is the rule: increase or decrease of animal or human population, climatic change, greater knowledge of agriculture, and the like. Of these, climatic change is the most powerful force belonging to the nonliving habitat.[12]

People were capable of improving the local ecosystem by introducing new agricultural methods. A growing number of people might even have, in some cases, beneficial consequences. So changes within the ecosystem, or ecology, need not always be environmental degradation. Nevertheless, the main threat to the ecosystem, of course, is population growth. This would cause the search for reestablishing the ecosystem, by modifying the land to improve its farming potential. Precisely this inspired historians to emphasize the destructive role of man in the development of agro-ecosystems. It points to forces *from within* the ecosystem, which have little to do with political economy. And besides political economy, the New Ecological History should address itself to these forces of change.

Despite the regional emphasis, my study might be viewed as a break with the conventions of Latin American historiography because it is a thematic study, not a regional one. The issues will be discussed from a theoretical point of view as far as possible, using published and unpublished source material and academic studies of specific aspects of the economic system in the region. The region selected is central Mexico. An optimal research situation demanded a limited region without great differences in physical geography and one where a uniform settlement pattern existed at the time. The Mexican highlands— referred to as the *Llano,* or the *Mesa de Anáhuac* by Humboldt[13]—meet this requirement. It consisted of three large valleys—the valley of Toluca in the west, of Mexico in the center, and of Puebla in the east (see Map 2)—which were enclosed by rugged and impenetrable mountains, referred to as the *sierra* or the *faldas,* and volcanoes. With their high population density and the presence of the two large cities of Mexico and Puebla, the highlands provide a suitable field of investigation. In addition, it was an area with a strong central government and a well-integrated market. Because the term *central Mexico* generally refers to a region stretching from coast to coast (from Veracruz to Acapulco and from Tampico to Mazatlán) and might cause misunderstanding in the following chapters, I will follow Humboldt in using the designation *Anáhuac.*

The arguments defended in the book might bring us to choose sides in the well-known controversy over the impact of the Bourbon Reforms on the colonial economy. No doubt, the economy of Anáhuac underwent a disruption between 1780 and 1810. I would like to call this the *shadow that fell over Anáhuac.* In fact, *three* shadows fell over Anáhuac:

1. The first was demographic: relative overpopulation in the peasant communities.
2. The second was climatological: a wave of droughts in May and June.

3. The third can be traced to the administrative reforms of the Bourbon regime: the abolition of the *repartimiento de comercios,* which reinforced a crisis in the economy of the Indian communities.

There were responses. The Indian peasants could put pressure on the elites, both Spanish and Indian, to alleviate the greatest suffering by acts of charity and by intervening in the price mechanism or by underpinning traditional community coherence. Another solution demanded from the governing elites was the acquisition of more land. The Indians also tried to find a way out of the difficulties by themselves, like the switch to proto-industrial activity. The changes—and the lack of changes!—that can be discerned in the wake of the disruption of the economic system are explained in terms of the ecological approach. The concept of *ecological ethic,* derived from the theory of the normative economy, is introduced here. It is the expression *par excellence* of the politico-cultural component in economic analysis that we will be looking for.

Times of Dearth

The Trends

The hypothesis will probably not be considered a progressive one. According to recent literature, we are to meet an impoverished population in the Mexican countryside, for the decades prior to the Hidalgo/Morelos revolt of 1810–16 are generally seen as edging toward a kind of Malthusian crisis. The historian Eric Van Young introduced the "chiaroscuro" image to describe the era metaphorically:

> In a period of Baroque splendor—witness those sumptuous monuments to the Churrigueresque style: Santa Prisca, Tepotzotlán, La Valenciana—the *lépero* became a familiar figure on the streets of the viceregal capital. . . . In terms of the overall social distribution of wealth, then, the eighteenth was a century in chiaroscuro—a pattern of light and dark, of vivid contrast and contradiction.[14]

According to this position, the once-defended option of generalized prosperity, increasing territorial integration, and economic growth of New Spain in the late colonial period has now given way to an image of growth and impoverishment occurring at the same time.

Indeed, the period demonstrates an increase of wealth in the hands of elite groups and a continued transfer of resources from the countryside to the city, going hand in hand with growing poverty of the indigenous and mestizo population. The last point, especially, has been made quite often, most recently by well-known authors like Brian Hamnett and John Tutino, and has resulted in a dark picture of rural development.[15] That sense of crisis, however, might well be overstated. In his recent discussion of economic growth and change, Richard Garner concluded that the Mexican colony was not developing in a Malthusian direction, and no significant long-term inflation could be deducted from his data. Moreover, Garner estimates that the Indian population may have needed 175,000 tons of maize per year during the first decades of the eighteenth century, and some 265,000 tons a century later. If maize output across the whole of New Spain grew at rates between 0.8 and 1.2 percent per year—rates calculated from data of the Michoacán area—then the supply of maize could have met these needs, though with little to spare.[16] In general terms, the economic measurements that are made in the mentioned controversy are to be seen as not always well specified. Some data are even real historical elephant traps, like the ecclesiastical tithes, given in values that do not reflect actual market transactions, nor represent a consistent and well-defined commodity.

This is not the place to address an alternative picture of the late eighteenth century. Most of the data have been discussed and the problems involved set out in the open, however, without emerging general agreement. Nevertheless, some trends might be presented, although these are still to be understood as very tentative because of inconsistency. In the years after the 1770–80 decade, for example, prices of meat, maize, pulque, sugar, tobacco and beans all rose in New Spain. The trend was upward, and little evidence for a compensation in living standards for the mass of the rural population could be found in the archives. It is known that even a modest inflation in a preindustrial economy could have a disruptive effect on the consuming public. A first approximation by John TePaske of the workers' wages revealed a slight decline of per capita income between 1742 and 1806 (thirty to twenty-eight pesos, respectively), but a steeper decline if the view is limited to the much shorter period of 1793 and 1806 (forty-one to twenty-eight pesos). Van Young asserts that it seems fair to say that any working person who received more than about 25 percent of his total income in cash was likely to have experienced a perceptible drop in his living standard during that period.[17] But, of course, these authors are prudent in expanding this conclusion to the peasants in the villages, who would have gained very little in the wage-market. In fact, as producers of market commodities they might have profited from rising prices.

Using Florescano's figures of the Mexico City maize prices,[18] I have made a similar estimate. An average family of four to five persons required around twenty-five *fanegas* of maize a year, that is, a little more than two fanegas a month. The average wage of an ordinary laborer—the lowest paid workers—in Mexico City was three to four pesos a month. This is the most pessimistic estimate, since wages were between 50 and 100 percent higher in the factories or in agricultural companies. Around 1730 a wage of three to four pesos a month was just enough to buy the two fanegas required each month. The situation even improved after 1730 with the fall in maize prices, but spending power was reduced dramatically after 1780:[19]

This means that a ration in 1800 was half of what it had been in 1765, but the same as a ration in 1730 (the period shortly before the massive epidemics of 1736–39). However, taken on the whole, it was a considerable deterioration for the nonagrarian population in thirty-five years. The presumed drop in

Table 1 Maize prices in Mexico City,
1730–1810

year	maize price (in reales)	spending power per month (in fanegas)
1730	15	1½ – 2
1765	9	3 – 3
1785	40	½ – 1
1800	18	1½ – 2
1810	36	½ – 1

living standards affected the poor in the suburbs to a lesser extent because they had their own plots of land where they could grow maize, beans, chili peppers, and other vegetables. Besides, the maize price on the other markets of the city was probably not the same as on the grain exchange.

All this is based on the assumption of impressive population growth, especially in the Indian villages. The assumption was correct. Fortunately, there is no need to go into it in great detail, because the data of the main demographic changes that took place in central Mexico were described in a paper contributed to a professional journal.[20] Again, one must recognize that the data are problematic because of their origin: they came from the government's tributario accounts (for example, those of the tribute payers). There were always people who escaped registration and officials who reclassified people, made different classifications per province, copied previous counts, or simply counted wrong. And, of course, one struggles with the thorny problem of the "coefficient": most researchers, for example, always put the number of tributarios at between four and five members per family-head, without investigating the changes in family size through time. Although all this is bound to arouse suspicions about the overall rhythm of any curve derived from population data, as well as about the competence of cross-checking methods at the provincial level, I have demonstrated that some conclusions can be drawn. For the central Mexican highlands, two periods of population increase stand out: the 1720s and from the 1780s onward (see Figure 1). Between these peaks, the number of tributarios for all provinces of Anáhuac stagnated or fell. Overall totals grew by 45 percent between 1720 and 1800, for an average increase of 0.6 percent per annum. This low rate is the result of the drop between 1730 and 1765, reflecting the severe *matlazahuatl* epidemic that plagued the highlands in 1736–39. The great number of deaths combined with out-migration to create a general decline in the number of residents of the Indian townships, which lasted until roughly 1765. This was a decline of about 20 percent (an average of 0.5 percent per annum). However, the falda provinces experienced a slight decline, suggesting that the residents of the highlands could have left

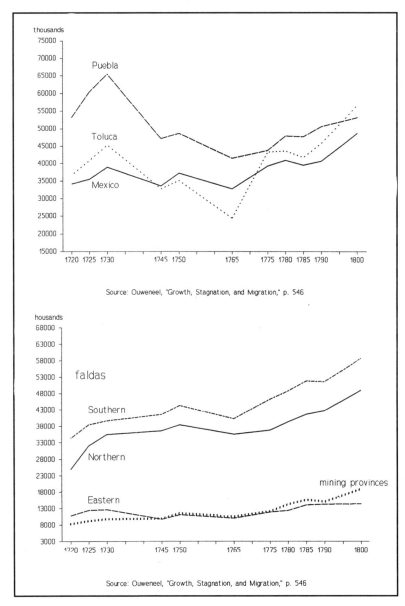

Source: Ouweneel, "Growth, Stagnation, and Migration," p. 546

Figure 1   Number of tributarios in seven subregions
of Anáhuac, 1720–1800

for these provinces in the faldas, where it was apparently possible to accommodate the migrants.

After the crisis of the 1760s, including another epidemic, the population in the "pueblos de indios" of Anáhuac began to increase again, with a growth of 52 percent (an average of 1.5 percent per annum) between 1765 and 1800, but it is not clear whether this increase was initiated by a wave of births or by remigration. There were incidental fluctuations, such as the notable growth in 1750 and a decline after the crisis of 1785–86. Growth between 1765 and 1785 had risen at a moderate 22 percent, or about 1.1 percent per annum. After 1785 the rise in the number of tributarios continued almost uninterrupted until 1800, first increasing by almost 19 percent or 1.2 percent per annum, and during the 1790s by 1.4 percent per annum, an average that was not unusual for the eighteenth century. The number of residents in the Indian townships around 1800 was much higher than it had been in the middle of the century, thanks to a continuous increase during the latter decades, an increase as substantial and widespread as that in the 1720s and 1730s. And to conclude, as I have shown in the 1991 essay, the available figures of 1805 indicate still further growth.

Despite a recognizable general pattern, notable differences exist between the subregions. The decline in the number of residents in the pueblos de indios after the epidemic of the late 1730s was particularly dramatic in the valleys of Puebla and Toluca in the highlands, as well as in the eastern falda provinces (Orizaba, Córdoba, and Xalapa). The figures for the valley of Mexico do indicate a period of stagnation after the 1730s, but certainly no dramatic decline. The falda provinces to the north and south even showed a modest growth (of 0.2 and 0.3 percent per annum). It is striking here that even the stagnation that followed upon the epidemic was soon turned into a growth in population figures. The growth of the pueblos de indios in the northern and southern faldas was caused by an increase in the inhabitants of six silver-mining provinces that formed part of these faldas (Zimapán, Taxco, Pachuca, Tetela de Xonotla, Temascaltepec-Sultepec, and Cuautla Amilpas). These mining provinces witnessed an almost uninterrupted increase in the number of residents in the pueblos de indios, especially in the second half of the century. The interruptions in 1765 and in 1790 were caused by epidemics and the famine of 1786, less notable in the highland provinces.

The population of the valley of Mexico represented between 16.2 and 17.7 percent of the total number of tributarios in Anáhuac. It had a regular development, with no dramatic declines, no spurts. The percentage corresponding to the valley of Puebla fell from about 27.5 in the early eighteenth century to about 20 around 1800. Relatively speaking, fewer Indians were living there, especially since the 1740s and 1750s. The Indian part of the valley of Toluca had grown in 1800 to 20.2 percent of the number of tributarios in Anáhuac. Although the percentage of 1720 was somewhat lower, 18.9, by the middle of the eighteenth century it had fallen to about 16, also indicating a decrease during the 1740s and 1750s. The population increased here again during the

1770s. The Indian population of the faldas increased relatively more in the middle of the eighteenth century, stabilized for a while, but experienced another spurt during the 1780s. The population rates of the northern and southern faldas, in particular, marched to a different drummer than those in the valleys.[21]

On the topic of migration David J. Robinson recently published a collection of essays dealing with migration in Parral and northern Mexico, in Guadalajara and western Mexico, in Guatemala, Costa Rica, Peru and Upper Peru, as well as the in-migration into major metropoles of colonial Mexico and Peru.[22] This pioneering study was given a very warm welcome by the community of historians. However, none of the essays deals with the region of Anáhuac, by far the most densely populated region of colonial Spanish America. (About 30 percent of all Spanish- American Indians lived in this region; about half of the Mexican Indians.) A good migration model of Anáhuac could be drawn up using parochial data, but I did not have sufficient time to carry this out, since it would take years to do so. Hence I entered the office of the tribute counters once again.[23]

Although the relationship is not inevitable—think of natural increase, better counting—it is possible that a drop in one subregion was connected with a rise in another. In other words: with migration. But, as I have discussed in the 1991 article, the use of net population change between the provinces of Anáhuac is known to be beset with problems.[24] Nevertheless, and despite the restrictions, the figures were analyzed in a hypothetical way to discuss the usual two kinds of migration. A superficial examination of the data showed the effect of some of the above-mentioned epidemics, especially the matlazahuatl epidemic of the late 1730s, and agrarian crises, like the 1785–86 crisis, as heavy fluctuations, caused by migration and remigration. The remigration of people who left only temporarily explains why tribute populations sometimes recovered in only ten to fifteen years.[25] Some individual provinces provided evidence of considerable fluctuation. Metztitlán, for instance, had a rapid increase followed by a rapid decrease, and Tetepango saw people come, then go, and finally return again; the reverse was the case in the province of Orizaba (eastern faldas). The in-migration provinces of the first decades of the eighteenth century were located in the northern faldas. Also Ecatepec and Otumba on the central highlands were in-migration provinces. Possible out-migration occurred in Apan, Texcoco— where in 1729 a measles epidemic was reported[26]—Xochimilco and Taxco.

The upheaval that an epidemic like the matlazahuatl epidemic of 1736–39 could cause can be seen from the numerous requests for a postponement of tribute payment, which are to be found in the archives in Mexico City and Seville. These petitions were supplemented with testimonies and included a statement by the alcalde mayor. It is enough to cite one example for the purposes of illustration. The epidemic of 1736–37 resulted in the loss of the harvests in the province of Ixtlahuaca (Toluca), which formed an alcaldía mayor together with the province of Metepec. Both the peasants in the pueblos de indios and the hacendados had left the maize standing in the fields, the former because they had left to escape the calamity, the latter because they were unable to recruit enough farmhands, even though they were offering higher wages (of 50 percent). Moreover, there was a severe night frost in 1739, which had dried out much of the maize in the fields. The Indian peasants had left their homes to look for food and work. The ones who stayed behind plundered the abandoned houses to get their hands on the loot in order to exchange it for food.[27]

In the second half of the century, the spotlight again shines on the faldas more than on the central highlands. Nevertheless, more indications of possible in-migration occur in the valleys of Mexico and Toluca, while the Indian population might have left the valley of Puebla, the northeastern faldas, and the dryer provinces in the valley of Mezquital around Actopan. An agrarian crisis in 1771 would have led to such a westbound migration. During the 1770s and early 1780s, the valley of Toluca and provinces like Actopan experienced decreases in the tributario population, probably caused by epidemics.[28] The literature suggests the last quarter of the eighteenth century as one of the most disastrous apart from the epidemics of the 1730s.[29] The year of hunger, 1786, led to mortality and out-migration in the provinces of the northern faldas; perhaps to migration into the valley of Mexico. Indeed, Anáhuac was much less affected by the harvest failures than its western neighbors, the regions of Michoacán and Guadalajara.[30] Possible in-migration from Michoacán can be recognized in the results of the 1790 counting, with its overall increase and the provinces on the northwestern fringes of Anáhuac standing out.

To summarize, we may note first the confirmation of the consequences of epidemics and subsistence crises. Beyond this, the faldas have a strong profile as an overall in-migration area and the valley of Puebla as an out-migration area, especially in the second half of the eighteenth century. If, by further research, this pattern could definitely be established as migration, I think the people who left their Indian communities were integrated into another officially recognized Indian community, although sometimes only temporarily, and began to pay their tribute there. I suspect, but cannot prove this at the present stage of research, that even in years of crisis the Indians showed a preference for the communities where the indigenous languages were still spoken and popular Catholicism still flourished: those in the faldas. These tributarios remained tributarios and their migration should therefore be considered as originating from *push factors:* epidemics and harvest failures.

Urbanization

Another demographic trend stood out during the eighteenth century, for apart from the route from one Indian municipality to another—inside the Anáhuac area or outside—there was an alternative—migration to the non-Indian towns and cities. I think one might say this migration encompassed a change in *calidad,* in sociojural status: people left the *república de indios* to move into the non-Indian categories of mestizos, mulatos, and other casta groups. The well-known and often discussed jural segregation of the two repúblicas kept on playing an important part during the late eighteenth century. In practice, the Indians were the residents of villages in the countryside and special districts in the colonial cities: the so-called pueblos de indios. These pueblos were legal persons in the legislation, and might looked upon as municipalities. Every inhabitant of a pueblo had the rights and duties laid down by law, including the usufruct of village plots. I will discuss this in later chapters. In return for this juridical protection and agricultural benefits, the crown collected an annual amount, the *tributo*. This obligation applied to the male head of the family and, since 1786, also to his adult sons: each male member of the república de indios between the ages of eighteen and fifty years, head of a household or not, was eligible to pay this tribute every year and paid it collectively with his fellow villagers. In the late eighteenth century several changes were proposed but never fully implemented, and the tribute data I found were based mostly on the older classification.[31]

A small percentage of the tributarios worked as factory hands or manual laborers in the urban centers. In such cases the employer paid the tribute in advance to the treasury.[32] The same applied to tributarios who lived on the haciendas, and the hacendado paid the tribute in advance, with the consequence that the tributarios on the haciendas were also included in the accounts of the Spanish fiscal authorities. Throughout the eighteenth century, the number of tributarios and their families amounted to roughly 80 percent of the total population. Most of these people—some 85 percent—lived in pueblos de indios. "In the Spanish conception," Taylor writes,[33] "Indians in the colonial system were inseparable from their pueblos." If they moved house, the tributarios could be transferred from one list to another. That is the background of the conclusions expressed above, and it is why I prefer to speak of "Indians" instead of "indigenous" or "natives": we are dealing with a fiscal, thus sociojural classification, and not primarily with an ethnical group.

This definition of the ethnic term *Indian* is not unusual according to eighteenth-century standards. On the contrary, it is based on contemporary European tradition after centuries of conquest and reconquest. Historian Robert Bartlett finds it worth stressing that while the language of race in Europe was biological, its medieval and modern reality was almost entirely cultural.[34] An ethnic group differed at the time in descent or assumed descent, customs, language, and law. The criterion of "descent"—real or assumed—seized on biological markers, not unlike modern forms of racism, but seems to have been relevant in speech only. The other criteria were much more significant and emerged as the primary badges of "ethnicity," especially law, which was "personal" and sometimes also "autonomous," as in medieval "orders" (*états*). All three criteria of law, customs, and language share one important common characteristic: they were malleable and could be transformed from one generation to the next, and even within an individual lifetime. In this respect, "ethnicity" at the time was a social-jural construct rather than a biological datum. Studying and discussing "race relations" means analyzing the contact between various juridical, linguistic, and cultural groups—in medieval and modern Europe as well as in New Spain—and not between breeding stock.

Included, therefore, in the "Indian order," the group of tributarios, were people from other "ethnic" origins. One can easily produce a large number of examples from the archives of mestizos or even Spaniards who were registered on the tribute lists and were therefore eventually regarded as members of the república de indios. Taylor cites evidence of pueblos de indios in the region of Guadalajara. Already in the sixteenth century, one village was founded with black slaves and its residents were routinely called *indios* in official records even though nearly all were mulatos and "afromestizos." In the late colonial period, according to Taylor, in the region of Guadalajara "Indian" meant "village tributary." In order to increase the number of contributors to village fiestas and other public expenses, some pueblos allowed mestizos, mulatos, and Spaniards to register as Indian members, live within the village, and share in the lands assigned to Indian families. Also in the Sierra Norte de Puebla, in Anáhuac's northeastern faldas, analyzed by the Mexican historian Bernardo García Martínez, groups of runaway slaves of West African descent formed pueblos de indios with the recognition of the crown.[35] I think, this situation was also typical for other regions in New Spain.

The social system discussed here made use of an ethnic terminology and was called the *régimen de castas,* or *sistema de castas.* The concept of casta originates in the sixteenth century as a Spanish classification of a group descended from a common ancestor, or from two ancestors with different ethnic backgrounds. As such, the term can be found in the etymological dictionaries. However, over a period of time the term came to be used by Spanish officials to classify urbanized non-Indians who were also non-Spaniards, thereby ordering a hierarchy of "ethnic" groups according to their proportion of Spanish "blood." Therefore the castas were not part of any legalized order. The Spaniards formed a separate *état,* or order, from the Indians, and, in fact, possessed a Spanish birth certificate, which can be seen as a sort of "passport" of their order. This order, however, comprised two groups: the *europeos,* who were born in Spain—although a few came from other European countries—and the *criollos,* who were born in New Spain. Although these orders were jural categories, it was not difficult to change one's order.[36] There were Spaniards, for instance, who entered Indian villages, started to pay tribute, and therefore later were registered as Indians. Other Spaniards led a threadbare existence on the margin of society. Of course, the elite looked down on these impoverished Spaniards and tried to establish a distinction between the group to which they themselves belonged as *gente decente,* on the one hand, and their impoverished "peers" as *plebe,* on the other.[37]

In general, from the seventeenth century onward, all the groups not included among the Spanish or the Indian orders were referred to as the castas. This plebe consisted of variously named subgroups: the commonest were castizos, mestizos, and mulatos, but in official documentation other names like *moriscos, lobos,* or *negros* were frequently used as well.[38] But despite the division into two orders, it was the case that legally each main stratum other than the Spanish and Indian also had distinctive civic and fiscal rights and obligations. For instance, the members of the mulato category, which was quite important in western New Spain, had slave ancestry, paid tribute, and were prohibited from entering certain professions. The result was that many mulatos tried to "cross over" into another category, which in the cities would have entailed becoming a craftsman. Marriage was a suitable instrument for attaining or maintaining a higher position on the social ladder, or, indeed, for a step down, because, for example, where the sex ratio was unfavorable, women readily married down the ladder.

Changing one's order assumed such proportions that the vagueness of the criteria as to who belonged to which category was exacerbated in the course of the eighteenth century. In fact, all the distinctions meant only that, despite legal restrictions, in practice any combination of factors could affect one's "ethnic" label, called *calidad:* the color of one's skin, the purity of one's descent, one's profession and standard of living, and one's personal worth, integrity and place of birth. An investigation of the criteria for determining the "ethnic" labels in Mexico City in the second half of the eighteenth century revealed a kind of individual assessment. For instance, a tailor who married a mulata was regarded as a castizo by the church, while a government official classified him as a Spaniard. The priest concerned wanted to reduce the social distance between the man and woman by degrading the man, because he had married beneath his calidad. Another document introduced the Spaniard Vicente García, who had settled as a ranchero in the province of Cuernavaca. He was married to a mestiza and was also regarded as a mestizo by his neighbors because of his relatively low social status as a ranchero. The author of the document, a Spanish official, described him as "de calidad español, aunque corre por mestizo" ("a Spaniard, although he goes as a mestizo"). His profession did not yield a sufficient income for García to maintain the standard of living that matched his original calidad. He worked as a muleteer in the company of two other rancheros (*de calidad india*) and the tribulations he met with on his travels left him looking somewhat the worse for wear, since he was referred to *as a mulato* in the villages through which he passed. Humboldt states that European muleteers were called *pezuñas* by the people he had met; Indian muleteers were called *poscos,* and black muleteers *grajos.* He was told that the Mexicans were able to distinguish between these muleteers from different casta origins in the darkness of the night according to their smells, because they thought that the castas of Indian and African descent had retained their peculiar bodily odors.[39] The example of García shows that Humboldt's statement was not true.

More evidence of this kind indicates that the ethnic terminology no longer reflected the original and legal distinction between different sociojural orders. In fact, Seed demonstrated that deviation in occupation from expected norms would lead to a reclassification of the calidad nearer social expectations.[40] The poorer groups in the cities and towns of Anáhuac's central provinces did not care very much whether they were seen as mestizos, mulatos, or castizos. A census taker in Tepeaca reported that the non-Indian plebeian groups of the province left it up to those who asked them to decide which calidad they belonged to. They were only concerned not to be classified as tributarios, for, as I will show in the next chapters, paying the tributo held no advantages for them outside the pueblos de indios. However, as revealed by Aguirre Beltrán some time ago, even "ethnic Indians" in villages could claim non-Indian status if their economic occupation had shifted impressively. He presents an observation of a census taker writing a report of the inhabitants of Tepetlaoztoc, a pueblo de indios in the province of Texcoco. This official had recorded the calidades of Spaniard, Indian, castizo, mestizo, and the like based on the declarations of the people themselves. This pueblo de indios was therefore recorded as *a town full of Spaniards*.[41]

It is clear to me that the calidades reflected an ideal of social stratification and the main indicators of social status, especially for the rich and prosperous; a way for this economic upper crust to distinguish itself. Historian Robert Cope argues:

> By imposing a strict hierarchy on Mexico's welter of [ethnic] divisions, the sistema assured that the "cream" would rise to the top: since poor Spaniards took their place at the apex of plebeian society, all Spaniards ranked higher than all castas.[42]

Although, the "sistema de castas" provided a structuring of interaction between castas and Spaniards, it was particularly important for the elites, for by moving into the "Spanish" order, elite members not only gained a higher prestige in society, but also access to the institutes of higher learning as well as to the most important and profitable occupations in the colony. The rest of society, the overwhelming majority of whom did not belong to the social climbers, adopted an attitude of wait and see.[43]

What interests me in the calidades is not so much the precise way of defining stratification criteria, but the acknowledgement of the fact that the "régimen de castas" mirrored, in one way or another, the social and economic strata in New Spain. It is obvious that the terminological system had become more complex by the late eighteenth century. According to Chance, this was not a consequence of the system becoming more rigid: "it meant only that the elite was making a belated effort to maintain its position as a dominant . . . minority."[44] Such an attitude would only show up in New Spain during periods when growing numbers of people could claim belonging to the "non-Indian order." Several writers, including myself, found indications of a growing number of castas and a further process of differentiation between the castas. This may be considered evidence of social mobility and an extension of the social ladder during periods of population growth. This, of course, meant that by 1800 the face of Anáhuac had changed: migration within the highland itself, from pueblo to town, had caused a growth in the urban population.

The arrival of the poor from the pueblos de indios had led to considerable disruption in Anáhuac as their share of the urban population increased, especially among the old status groups there. The plebeians who had mainly been living in the countryside until then had now reached the suburbs of the towns.

The Sequence of Adaptations

Arden and the Veluwe

The data discussed here, I admit, mirrors the crises in the countryside of eighteenth-century Anáhuac. The obvious conclusion of overpopulation, an established reply to the big question addressed here, leaves me unsatisfied, because inspection of the trend led me to the interesting observation that the available figures of 1805 indicate still further growth. Therefore, if there had been a Malthusian crisis, it would probably have been in the matlazahuatl period, earlier in the century and not in the last decades. A number of historians point to the ecological problems that underlay this pressure. Since not much on this exists in Latin American historiography, the point of analogy I adopt in this study is the situation in early modern Europe. The questions on the population breakthrough, and on the subsequent absence of widespread dearth and starvation, posed by the historian Victor Skipp are central for my research as well:[45]

1. Why was it possible for the population of Anáhuac to break through the 1730 barrier in the 1790s?
2. Why was there no widespread dearth and starvation in Anáhuac around 1800, despite the 1785-86 crisis in Michoacán?

These "Skipp-questions-transferred-to-Anáhuac" lead us to follow a route of abduction to Skipp's Forest of Arden in the English seventeenth century.

Abduction means that we should start from the facts, without having any particular theory in mind.[46] Induction seeks for facts, determines a value, deduction evolves the necessary consequences of a pure hypothesis based on theoretical discussion, but abduction suggests a hypothesis that seems to recommend itself, coming from the facts. Therefore, the route we take is not deductive, for I had gathered the material before seeking this European analogy in my writing; but the route is not inductive either, for I was educated partly in European agrarian history. And there I found the concepts and tools to enter the archives. I prefer to understand the eighteenth-century villagers of Anáhuac by listening to their contemporaries in Europe.

How do I know I am doing that? There is no need to recall that the eighteenth-century peasants were substantially different from us, which, of course, might also have been the reason for the economy to follow a different course from the one in our age. Take the following example from Alain Corbin concerning the emotions of our ancestors; an example that particularly moves me because it involves the fight of the Dutch against the sea.[47] Dykes were already so normal for the Dutch in the seventeenth and eighteenth centuries that they no longer had any emotional force. The same goes for the French of our own age, Corbin claims. But when the French philosopher Diderot visited Holland in 1773 and observed the construction of the dykes, he was confronted with an unprecedented courageous activity and his reaction was one of astonishment: the sea level in that country was often higher than the land. He recorded with surprise that the Dutch population could sleep in a situation that would cause the French *"to shiver."* Since emotions of this kind are basically different from what we experience today, it is therefore essential to lay bare the emotions of our ancestors if we are to understand their economic development. Corbin rightly concludes that there is hardly a more serious error than a calm, blind assumption that the past can be grasped unproblematically on the basis of our own experiences. And the big stumbling block in the analysis of historical data remains the impossibility in conducting experiments, for the historian cannot fail to register events and compute a correlation on qualitative or quantitative grounds, or sometimes on both. The convergence of several independent lines of investigation should substantially reduce the possibility of erroneous abductive hypotheses.

The ecological approach points to the interdependence of three such independent lines: research in the relations of social power, in the structure of production, and in the cultural dimension. This is best explained by the example of Skipp's work. His *Crisis and Development* (1978) is an investigation of the relation between population growth and economic development in five English parishes in the Forest of Arden between 1570 and 1674. He discovered that population growth did not result in appalling misery there; on the contrary, it promoted economic development in the form of an increase in production in both the agrarian and the manufacturing sectors. The population growth was due to both natural growth and immigration. The price increases that followed bad harvests proved to be a major source of incentive, since an intensification of agricultural technique and an expansion of metal manufacturing took place. Skipp even calls the price increases a form of capital injection for the agrarian sector, although this was only to the advantage of those farmers who were producers themselves, and not to that of the agricultural laborers or small-scale artisans. The result of this development was a concentration of income in the hands of a minority. The *nouveaux riches* who had been dirt farmers shortly before, now reinvested their profits, so that they were indirectly responsible for the avoidance of a Malthusian crisis in the region. These reinvestments led to technical improvements in the agricultural cycle, calling for increased labor. Since it was possible to take on more hands, the number of consumers with increased spending power grew. Moreover, the more well-to-do farmers provided loans to finance technical improvements of this kind on other farms.

However, there is another side to this development in the Forest of Arden: it also resulted in increased social inequality. The wealthier farmers enjoyed a higher income at the expense of the smallest farmers. The latter had to give up their farms and join the landless. It is also remarkable that not every village followed the path of modernization. Some of them opted for the classical solution: increasing the area under cultivation by bringing the poorer land that had not yet been used under cultivation. Skipp therefore distinguishes between *high-pressure solutions,* the modernization discussed here, and *low-pressure solutions,* the bringing under cultivation of marginal territory. It now appears as though the need in the villages which adopted low-pressure solutions was not pressing enough. The implementation of both solutions in a small region like the Forest of Arden led simultaneously to development and underdevelopment. Landless, mainly young peasants left the villages that had adopted the path of the low-pressure solution for those parishes with increased employment opportunities. The capacity of the "modern" farmers to control their own economic development could be increased by stimulating the spending power of the agrarian population through an intensification of labor. The modernization of agriculture and the escape from the ecological straits in which the increasing population of the Forest of Arden found itself depended on radical improvements in the agricultural scheme—which were implemented at a fast rate by the farmers and peasants themselves—and on the reinvestment of capital. Agrarian communities with a surplus of wasteland will be more likely to opt for an extension of the area under cultivation, a low-pressure solution. The ecological straits have to be dire before radical changes are implemented.

The critical equilibrium between population growth and means of survival thus calls for drastic adaptations of the economic activities of a region. Roessingh, another historian working in the European field, indicated what these adaptations might be. It is worth looking at this example more closely, because the area of Roessingh's investigations, the Veluwe (Netherlands), resembled Anáhuac in that it suffered from relative overpopulation. The farmers lived on sandy soil, apart from a small tract of clay on the banks of the Rhine and the IJssel and on the Zuiderzee, an open bay. Nevertheless, this formed no obstacle to a strikingly uninterrupted population growth in the region from the middle of the sixteenth century. The population tripled from about 36,000 to over 106,000 *capita* between 1526 and 1839. This population growth was marked by two periods of accelerated growth: 1650–1749 and 1815–29. In the first of these periods the growth was primarily in the rural areas.[48] The urban areas were not affected by growth until later. This process was accompanied by a drop in the size of the family from seven members per family in 1526 to around four at the beginning of the nineteenth century. Roessingh characterizes the Veluwe in 1526 as an unsophisticated agricultural society.

Although 75 percent of the inhabitants of the Veluwe still lived in the countryside in 1795, life had changed drastically. In the seventeenth century the population growth was accommodated by improving manuring and by the introduction of buckwheat cultivation in rotation with oats. With the eradication of weeds, the yield increased and the same land could feed more mouths. This was a major intensification of the economic system; Roessingh speaks of a radical change in the agrarian structure by comparison with the preceding period. After 1650, however, it was not sufficient. The growth of the population proceeded at a faster rate than the new land could be brought under cultivation. The solution this time was once again a radical one: a rapid, high specialization in the cultivation of tobacco, a cash crop that could provide small farms in particular with good returns. At the same time, whole communities switched to the manufacture of paper. The paper mills sprang up like mushrooms. It was this "industrial" revolution that was responsible for the drop in the size of families, which is hardly fortuitous in a situation of this kind. However, employment dropped again after 1750, when many firms went out of business under competition from abroad. The dirt farmers in the rural areas now opted for the potato, a new crop with high yields and a high nutritional value, to meet the growing shortage. Potato cultivation was combined with migrant labor and—once again—the bringing under cultivation of marginal territory. The solution to further population growth in the region, however, was emigration. Roessingh correctly states: "This is a common occurrence in a rural area where there is little agricultural expansion and no other means of subsistence arise."

Wilkinson's diagram

Wilkinson summarized the sequence of such adaptations with the help of a diagram, see Figure 2.[49] Population growth and environmental change causes ecological disequilibrium and ushers in a resource scarcity which would be dealt with in two different ways, or by a combination of both of them. One way is an attempt to fill the gap, caused by the breakdown in local self-sufficiency, by importing materials and by producing special commodities for export. The other way consists of the introduction of new substitute resources or the exploitation of the scarce resource more intensively. In either case the productive process is likely to become more complicated and difficult, imposing increasing demands. The possible results of this are given below in the diagram: more tools and equipment are required, as well as additional sources of energy. In the end labor saving methods are inevitable, including a division of labor, even regionally, and mechanization. These are all high-pressure solutions, according to Skipp's standard. The low-pressure solutions like out-migration, urbanization and the expansion of the area under cultivation for traditional agriculture should be included in the diagram as well, of course.

In Anáhuac all variants might have occurred at the same time, or in a sequence, one after another, as it had in the Dutch Veluwe. Indeed, out-migration and urbanization took place in Anáhuac. But the population growth around 1800 also suggests high-pressure solutions. I shall try to tackle this question by using the work of authors like Mendels, Fischer, Medick, Gutmann, and Levine. The increased employment in the manufacturing sector could have caused a new population growth because of a drop in the age of marriage

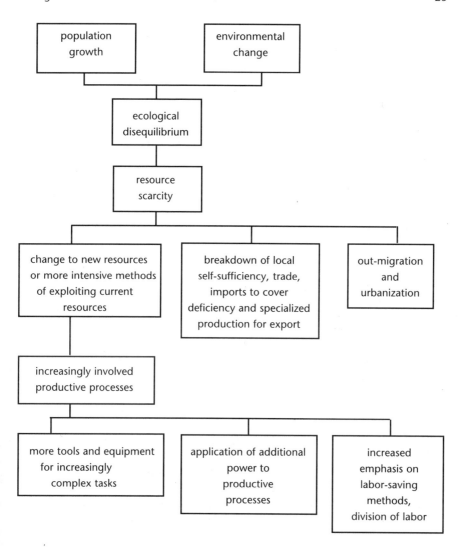

Figure 2 The course of adaptation to ecological problems,
based on Wilkinson

and a slight increase in marital fertility. A change in mentality can have had the same effect. For example, in his study of the contemporary Mexican Tlayacapan (in the federal state of Morelos), anthropologist Ingham provides examples that are not directly related to a drop in the age of marriage, but which nevertheless resulted in population growth: changes in the norms, values, and customs of the peasants' culture that resulted in the disappearance of traditional forms of sexual abstinence. All such changes combine modernization and the introduction of a capitalist mentality. Levine draws the same conclusion from his investigation of a number of early modern villages in England, referring to the eighteenth-century writer Arthur Young:

> The evidence . . . supports the argument that the acceleration of
> economic activity after 1750 was the prime agent breaking down
> those traditional social controls that previously maintained a demo-
> graphic equilibrium in which population size was kept in line with
> resources.[50]

I will hypothesize that the same conclusion may apply to Anáhuac for the 1780s and 1790s, although we do not know what the birth and mortality rates were in the different parishes of the region. At any rate, we are set on the track of profound economic changes in the countryside of Anáhuac. In Europe, the connection between these phenomena led to the important conclusion that they must have formed the foundation there for the *wave of proto-industrialization* that hit the continent at that time. I certainly think that some of the same phenomena can be described in eighteenth-century Anáhuac, especially during the 1790s: a wave of proto-industrialization may have hit this region too. If so, the rapid population growth around 1800 can be explained.

Such, in brief, is the subject matter of the following chapters. Although no foolproof method can be found, we have identified the central problem as one resulting from the interaction between population density, landscape, climate, and culture in economic development. Chapter One is conceptually important because it discusses the theoretical position I held before entering the archive and justifies the ecological approach as a heuristic tool for historical analysis. Here, I will go somewhat further than Wilkinson, because of the special features that guided the course of Mexican colonial history. Chapter Two shows in detail how the ecological disequilibrium in Anáhuac was reinforced by environmental change. The crux of the argument focuses on droughts in the months of May and June, during the period of 1770–1810, causing failures in maize production. These droughts hit the small producers harder than they hit the large wheat farmers. Chapter Three is concerned with the paternalistic response of appealing to the governors and lords in the colony. Charity, the regulation of prices and stocks, and the securing by law of land for traditional agriculture were its main features.

Chapter Four is the first to present the basic dynamics of change. It provides a structural description of the nonagricultural production in the pueblos, showing that a special system of trade and production, the so-called "repartimiento de comercios," could be used to introduce proto-industrialization. Chapter Five outlines the adaptive response made by the Indian elites to transfer of power from their lordship, or *cacicazgo,* to the Indian municipalities or "pueblos." The argument here is not without both political-economic and ethnographic implications. Chapter Six, which combines the insights of the two preceding chapters, is highly tentative and theoretical. In fact, the a priori arguments here might overwhelm the data. But because of the hypothetical nature of my approach, to foster further research, a chapter indicating the road I would like to follow in the coming decades is, to my mind, inevitable. The epilogue advocates a rethinking of the economic participation of the Indians in New Spain. It argues that the approach I took, indeed, inspired me to break away from traditional, Black Legend conceptualizations.

1

Enfolding the Ecological Approach

Introduction: On Heuristic Instruments

"Analogical inference," writes D. H. Fischer in a well-known seminal work, "plays an important, and even an indispensable, part in the mysterious process of intellectual creativity."[1] Analogy: if two or more things agree in one respect, they might also agree in another. Analogies are an epistemological tool in the articulation of ideas and the formulation of explanations and interpretations; in short, of the communication (or discourse) of historical understanding. The language of epistemological analogies is metaphorical, and historians use metaphors all the time. Most analogies are diachronical ("Augustan age," "feudalism"), pointing, usually, to the historians' own era: the past needs to be "explained" in images of the present, or in "past images" fixed to a specific content in the present. Indeed, it is only possible to "understand" the past, that is, to write history, if one can "understand" the present: not the whole of present-day society, but one's own position in society, particularly with respect to ideology.

This is all rather pedestrian. All historians are well aware of the "fact" that their own worldview influences or perhaps guides their work.[2] There is no past waiting to be interpreted or explained with the assistance of a rigorous scientific method. Historical data have no meaningful existence and truth independently of the historian. It is the historians themselves who introduce meaning and coherence in their presentations: they work with data they have been able to gather and render intelligible to themselves. The double subjectivity hidden in the historians' craft—the subjectivity of the historical objects and that of the historians themselves—makes some pessimists claim that the picture presented is nothing more than a construct of the writer. Some conclude that the French Revolution, for example, does not exist: there are as many French revolutions as studies of the history of France in those turbulent years.[3] And indeed, it seems an illusion to suppose that there will ever be a definitive account of the French Revolution, because there are no objective criteria allowing us to determine the truth or falsity of representations of the past. In fact, historian Simon Schama wrote a novel, *Dead Certainties*, to play with the idea that even fiction can reveal some historical "truth" by narration alone.[4] He invites the historical community to contemplate once more the difference between an historian's and the novelists' imagination. Though readers may find in this work an echo of Derrida's postmodern sentiment—a text is a text—Schama brings us nevertheless back to the "truth-value" of the historians' arguments, for where most literary narrative is nothing but text, not all texts are fiction.[5]

These more or less banal remarks cannot be repeated often enough, I fear, not only in our postmodern age, but particularly if the object is the rural history of a continent that has been told in the form of a myth for centuries. The mythical, epistemological analogy referred to here is, of course, the widespread myth of the oppressed Indian, the slaughtered noble savage. It is as unconscious and inchoate as it is simply a conscious inference that is still defended or promoted by many historians working in the field. "The psychological power of analogical explanations is dangerous both to logic and to empiricism," Fischer concludes, for "many bad ideas have had a long life because of a good (effective) analogy."[6] And indeed, Las Casas's message has already been repeated for five hundred years. Even the postulated virtue of the historian, a lack of "prejudice"—objectivity is too strong a term anyway—can hardly be expected in such a context. Where the "self"-consciousness of the historian is one of the essential elements of his work—by observing himself performing in dialogue with the texts he reads, the historian "discovers" the historical reality he studies—the reflection upon such a successful and "effective" analogical inference like the Black Legend is unavoidable.[7] Therefore, in interpreting my research data, I have constantly tried to bear in mind this mythical origin of Latin American historiography.

Because historians use analogies widely as heuristic instruments for empirical inquiry, I will not be able to avoid this mythical origin as an explanatory device in the present text unless I develop an alternative. As the reader will remember, I have found an analogical reference or conjecture in the course of European agrarian history: I entered the archives with concepts from that field in mind, and much less, for example, from research on contemporary twentieth-century Indian townships, so often appearing in colonial historiography and, sometimes, also loaded with Black Legend inferences.[8] Because the European concepts may be unknown in the Latin American field, I felt the obligation to explain my abductive position beforehand. As a writer, I have the obligation to navigate for the reader. The present chapter serves this purpose for the theoretical foundations of my research. It is acknowledged that the interactions addressed in the ecological approach necessitate complexity. Ecology is the study of the interactions of organisms with their physical environment and with each other. As a science, it seeks to discover how an organism affects, and is affected by, its environment and to define how these interactions determine the kinds and the numbers of organisms found in a particular place and time. I will try to find my way through the historical elephant traps of historical ecology. I will apply some ecological metaphors, like "ecological succession" and "climax community," and introduce my tools on the subsistence line, on the demography of the ecological approach, on the ecological ethic, on reciprocity and power, on the community, and on *Herrschaft* and the cultural factors behind the question of population density and the economy.

The chapters that follow invite the reader, indeed, to sign up for a long voyage, which, of course, should not be uncharted, leaving too many discussions of definitions scattered throughout the text. I would like to start with the migrants. Step by step, we will reach the heart of the matter: high-pressure solutions. The factor of migration should not be underestimated. Steve Hochstadt claims that the static picture of rural development in France presented by French historians is distorted by the lack of research on migration in the French countryside during the *ancien régime*.[9] He casts doubts on this static picture, which is inherent in the structuralist approach: his own research on the situation in a few regions of Central Europe at that time has shown that a rural population is extremely mobile when it comes under pressure from population growth and bad harvests. If there are prospects of improvement, its members are prepared to leave for the cities. The result will be the familiar pattern of population growth and increasing economic differentiation, which many historians have recently established for agrarian Europe.

To describe the process leading from low-pressure to high-pressure solutions, I need to introduce the concept of the *subsistence line*. As a rule, in a situation of population growth, the number of persons above the subsistence line increases at a slower rate than that of the number of persons below it. Where it is possible to discuss social stratification and demographic development together, there should be an indication of what the theoretical consequences might be. It is assumed that population growth linked with an "extended" social ladder reflected "economic development":[10] intensification of economic activity, probably resulting in (proto)industrialization. The relation between patriciate and plebs has been transformed, and what emerges is a virtually landless proletariat of day laborers, impoverished dirt farmers, weavers, and the like. This group, below the subsistence line, will experience acute difficulties unless a way out is found through the intensification of economic activity. In fact, an intensification of this kind did take place in such areas as the Eastern Netherlands, the Ardennes, Flanders, Switzerland, Burgundy, Languedoc, Saxony, and parts of Sweden and Germany. The Mexican region of Anáhuac was probably no exception to this rule, densely populated as it was.

Within the ecological approach, this should be metaphorically referred to as *ecological succession*. According to ecology, communities of living organisms replace one another in a predictable and orderly sequence. This process is carried out by the living organisms themselves, which define themselves as "temporary," for the population is always changing and no static situation will ever be reached. During the adaptational sequence, each "temporary community" changes the local conditions in the attempt to find an optimum situation, but in the process sets up favorable conditions for the next "temporary community." Nevertheless, when the site has been modified as much as possible—here the limits are set by the environment—succession ceases for a while, or at least slows down considerably. This "community," which inhabits and interacts at that moment, is known as the *climax community*. But, in a sense, the climax community is in a state of constant change as well; individual organisms die, and their places are taken by new individuals. In the end, the situation will be taken over by a new kind of interaction, starting the process of adaptation over again. The metaphor serves to describe the change from agrarian societies into proto-industrial and industrial societies during periods of severe population pressure. But under what conditions is such a climax community to be recognized?

Stratification

The Subsistence Line

The adaptation of "organisms" to their local environment does not develop according to egalitarian principles. In fact, a process of stratification is constantly going on. Take the migration pattern as described in the prologue. Eighteenth century central Mexicans saw people moving from the eastern provinces (the valley of Puebla) to the central and western provinces of Anáhuac and even beyond, to Michoacán. The pattern makes one curious to know the reason for moving, the background of the push factor. Why did relative overpopulation result in migration on this scale? It is known that the migrants belonged to the poorest inhabitants of the area they left, those who suffered most from rising prices, landlessness, and disease.[11] It brings us to consider the question of the social stratification of the farming population. Generally speaking, this can be ascertained according to size of farm, farmland surface area, number of cattle or horses, and income or capital. It is known that population growth hardly affects the number of family farms of "normal" size, but results in a strong increase in the number of smallholders and a rise in the proletariat of day laborers and workers in rural industries. Since agriculture, unlike industry or trade, barely offers any scope for social climbing, population growth in rural areas has the effect of extending the social ladder downward. It is important to include the artisans in the stratification. This makes it clear that the group of producers is relatively much smaller than that of the consumers. In view of the analogical reference between agrarian Europe and agrarian Anáhuac in this period, I discuss the effects on social stratification, as Mörner suggested a few years ago, in terms of a specific model of social stratification.[12]

The producer strata in the rural societies of preindustrial Europe consisted of:

1. producers who were not self-sufficient;
2. producers who were just self-sufficient and only turned to the market as consumers in bad years;
3. producers who supplied the market with an annual surplus and

hardly operated as consumers;

4. producers of the same kind who used seasonal labor in production;
5. producers of the same kind who employed permanent staff;
6. producers who produced exclusively for the market and little for their own consumption.

The subsistence line passes between groups 2 and 3: the line dividing those farmers who could support themselves from those who were unable or barely able to do so. Although no research has been conducted for Anáhuac, I believe that group 6 corresponds to the sugar haciendas, with group 5 corresponding to the wheat and maize haciendas and the larger rancheros.[13] Group 4 corresponds to the smaller rancheros and the larger farmers in the villages, including many Indian elite families, as we shall see. Groups 1 to 3 consisted of peasants. In eighteenth-century Anáhuac, groups 3 and 4 were much fewer in number than in the rest of New Spain, and the vast majority of Indians belonged to groups 1 and 2. Once again, this accentuates the gap between elite and dirt farmers or crofters.

The consumers can be classified in three main groups and eleven subsidiary groups as follows:

1. The agrarian consumers who produced part or all of the agricultural products that they consumed themselves. There were three subsidiary types of those who consumed their own produce, namely, (a) those who did not produce enough to support themselves; (b) those who produced just enough to support themselves; and (c) those who produced slightly more than enough to support themselves. A fourth type (d) produced nonfood agrarian crops and was heavily dependent on the market. Members of the fifth type (e) worked as wage laborers for agrarian companies and were paid in cash or in kind.
2. Those who were not agrarian producers, but whose income was partly or wholly derived from agrarian production. These were in the first place (a) landowners, who received their rent in kind. The second type (b) received their rent in cash.
3. The nonagrarian producers whose income was derived from artisanal production or wage labor. These were the villagers and urban dwellers who did not work on the land and who were entirely dependent on the market.

The first three groups of producers—the peasants, the smaller renters, and the rancheros—belonged to the first group of consumers. So did the agricultural laborers who received part of their wage in kind. It is striking that those plantations which were dependent on the market belonged to this group as well. This scheme does not include propertied/landless status. We should be careful not to overemphasize this distinction in preindustrial rural stratification.[14]

Table 2 Differential effects of price increases

Benefit from price increases	Suffer from price increases
1. hacendados	1. plantation owners
2. landlords (paid in kind)	2. landlords (paid in cash)
3. big rancheros (Indian elites)	3. small peasants
4. small rancheros	4. agricultural laborers
5. peasants with a surplus	5. artisans and laborers

This model of producer and consumer strata guides me toward making an important point for the historical analysis. An increase in the price of food-stuffs had a favorable effect for producer groups 3, 4, and 5, namely, the hacendados and rancheros. However, it was also beneficial to consumer group 1c, the ordinary villagers who brought their surplus product to the market, as well as to the landowners who rented their land, including the Indian elites and the church. Price increases were seriously detrimental to producer groups 1 and 6, consisting of poor peasants and plantation owners who could not maintain their laborers. As for the consumers, the groups hit hardest by price increases were those who depended on the market for their food supply, namely, 1a, 1d, 1e, 2b, and 3, consisting of agricultural laborers paid primarily in cash, the landowners who received their rent in cash (especially the church!), and the poor with no land to work. The differential effects of price increases can be illustrated as in Table 2.

The remarkable feature of this theoretical approach is the preliminary, tentative conclusion that the subsistence line must have drawn a "solidarity line" right through the middle of the Indian villagers, because the rancheros and—what is of crucial importance for the situation in Anáhuac, as we shall see—the Indian elites in the villages who produced a surplus benefited, while the small peasants in the villages could get into difficulties. The division within the Indian communities was accentuated in times of population growth, since it led to an increase in the number of nonagrarian consumers and the number of farmers who produced little for themselves. Although scant research has been conducted in this field in Mexico to date, it looks as though a phenom-enon of greater differentiation occurred. In other words, the problems of the late eighteenth century will have had negative consequences for the poor peas-ants, while the more well-to-do, such as the hacendados and Indian elites, profited from it. The subsistence line must therefore be an important variable in research on social stratification. It accentuates access to the means of pro-duction of the elite in preindustrial society, and suggests the motivation for out-migration for the poor or other low- and high-pressure solutions.

The Poorer Strata

Although we must be careful not to proceed in a deterministic way, European historiography confirms the picture outlined above. Since a very large percentage of the population was close to the subsistence line, there seems not to have been a way to avoid severe ecological pressure. What effect did relative overpopulation have on the economy in the preindustrial period? There was little difference between a dirt farmer in Europe or in New Spain. More than 80 percent of the French population in 1789 were peasants; more than 80 percent of the population of Anáhuac at that time were registered as Indians. As we have seen, this comparison is less strange than it seems. Prosperity during the ancien régime was generally the privilege of a small minority, whether one is talking about France, England, the Eastern Netherlands, Spain, or Spanish America. For the majority of the population, life was a constant struggle for survival with few prospects. Quesnay's dictum that prosperity only arises where it already exists applies to Anáhuac too. Those who got off to a bad start were certain to end that way. Another eighteenth-century French writer remarked that the sufferings of the poor seemed so interminable that awareness of suffering was accepted as something as ineluctable as death: it belonged relentlessly to earthly existence.[15]

The discussion of the relation between population and economy centers around the works of two authors. One of them, the classical figure of Thomas Malthus, wrote, at the end of the eighteenth century, a number of works in which the population was presented as the victim of agrarian society. Malthus argued that the growth of population, in particular, had an unfavorable effect on the agrarian system. In a situation of overpopulation, the holdings were divided and distributed among the many heirs. This resulted in fragmentation of the landholdings, a drop in real wages, and an increase in arable land as opposed to pasture and grazing land. The fragmentation of the land meant a drop in the average size of land under cultivation, so that there was an increasingly smaller surplus for the market. In the end, it was starvation and epidemics, in Malthus's words, which would violently restore the "natural equilibrium" in such areas. The remedy lay in an intensification of the labor process to provide work and food for a larger population. However, this did not usually occur, because the sizable labor reserve acted as a brake on the introduction of the new, labor-saving techniques that could have increased productivity. According to the other classical author, Ester Boserup (1965), constant intensification takes place during a process of population growth. As soon as a region is in danger of becoming overpopulated, new and more intensive agricultural techniques will be introduced to obtain a higher yield from the available land. In Boserup's view, the population is not the victim; on the contrary, the population is the driving force behind the agrarian development.[16]

The views of Malthus enjoyed pride of place in agrarian history for a long time. A well-known series of historical investigations of the French countryside (referred to above, in Hochstadt's criticisms) laid bare the mechanism of the Malthusian cycle. In doing so, the French historians were primarily interested in demonstrating the stagnation of agrarian society. In the meantime, modern demographers have rejected the theses of Malthus, and recent work by a few French historians is also critical of the Malthusian interpretation. The French historian Morineau, for example, goes so far as to claim that a Malthusian crisis never took place at all in France under the ancien régime. In his opinion, there was always room for growth in the level of production, even without the introduction of drastic changes in agricultural technique. It also implies that most of the epidemics should be regarded as independent variables in historico-demographic analysis and that they bear very little relation to a situation of overpopulation. The real cause of an epidemic lay in the condition of poverty of population. The agrarian crises, according to Morineau, were a result of the unequal distribution of incomes and the hierarchical social stratification. His findings were backed up by the work of Lis and Soly and that of Weir: neither marriage patterns nor birth and mortality statistics in France, England, and Germany during the ancien régime indicated a situation of Malthusian overpopulation. The family structure and social organization of society were not exclusively determined by the food supply. The behavior of relative prices—so often connected with the climate—was an indication of the market situation in a broad sense; it was not a specific index of problems in the food supply resulting from excessively high or low temperatures.[17]

Was Malthus wrong? In eighteenth-century New Spain, it was suspected that there was a connection between bad harvests and increased mortality, particularly in the periods of the worst droughts. The archival documents mention catarrhal fevers and more or less severe forms of dysentery. There is nothing remarkable about this connection. High temperatures and drought usually lead to a drop in the water level, which meant in the past that a large part of the population was forced to drink impure water at such times because there was no alternative to drawing water from marshlike pools, infected by bacteria originating from animal dung. Research by Titow revealed a connection between such impure drinking water, drought, and high temperatures and a dysentery epidemic. Precisely the same connection is made in documents from the archives in New Spain dating from the 1790s. In general the Mexican agrarian population therefore preferred to drink a mildly alcoholic drink, *pulque*, instead of water. There was little else to drink in Anáhuac besides pulque, made from the *maguey* cactus. The drought meant that this drink was of poorer quality than at other times and that it contained more bacteria than usual; the bacteria contained in pulque were already a source of intestinal infections in good years.[18]

The historian James C. Riley discovered that insects can also play a role in the spreading of epidemics. Dysentery, paratyphus, and smallpox spread by means of physical contact, through the air, or through the consumption of impure water. It should be added that the peasants had to work every day to earn a living, so that they could not take time off when the first symptoms of infection broke out. The fate in store for them was terrible: severe stomach cramps, bilious and bloody evacuation, a furry tongue, pain in the head and loins, an urge to vomit, thirst, fever, rapid debilitation, hiccups, and thrush. The number of victims of severe dysentery could rise dramatically. There were also milder forms of the disease in which the symptoms only lasted a week. A lot depended on the physical condition of the patient at the time of the attack. The cause of these epidemics and plagues was, above all, social: the meager standard of living of a large part of the population and the excessively hard work they had to perform to guarantee a marginal existence.[19]

However, epidemics could also occur in times of relative plenty. For instance, there was no risk of night frost in the province of Iguala, which lay on the southern flanks of the Anáhuac highlands, nor was this province hit by a succession of droughts. The water supply was regularly replenished by the rains, and the entire region of the southern faldas contained a copious supply of streams and rivers into which the water from the highlands flowed. The small peasants cultivated their maize in *chagües,* a sort of paddy cultivation with permanent irrigation. There were no haciendas. When all the maize in the highlands was frozen in August 1785, stocks in Iguala were sufficient to supply the hungry in Anáhuac as well as in the province itself. However, this hardly occurred at all, because the region was plagued by the *peste bola.* This epidemic was probably spread by flies that infected the food supply. Eyewitness accounts present an appalling picture of the epidemic. People suddenly dropped dead at work or in the street, clutching their stomachs because of the severe cramps. Others died a few hours or days later; a priest mentioned a group of people who stood silently against the church wall, "until they dropped." Unable to eat, they awaited the end. At least twelve people died each day in the small village. The final mortality figure totaled one-third of the village population. It is hardly surprising that the harvest was left standing in the field during this period.[20]

In other words, this foray into the literature leads to the conclusion that starvation and a shortage caused by overpopulation—a Malthusian crisis—are heavily influenced by a combination of biological, social, economic, and political factors. Of course, in most cases, bad harvests were preceded by a period of catastrophic weather. Grain products were the main staple for the majority of the population in Europe, and there was not usually any alternative kind of food available on a large scale. The relatively poor transport communications meant that trade could not remedy the situation. The relatively steady demand on grain caused an enormous increase in grain prices in lean years. The demand for somewhat more expensive products like meat or manufactured items dropped drastically, so that the economy entered a deep crisis. At the same time, employment fell. This pattern could be repeated every few years. The great menace was precisely the awareness on the part of the peasants that people had to face this cycle, and the expectation of starvation was itself enough to increase tension.[21] The climax community, then, must have been the one living prior to the situation of relative overpopulation, before a critical development of the subsistence line. We should consider it as the optimum situation.

Caging

The Ecological Ethic

Saving the optimum situation was the object of intensified activity by the elites. In fact, this was their duty: the members of government and church, the landlords, and the rich had the obligation to adopt various measures in order to alleviate tensions resulting from temporary drawbacks or nascent relative overpopulation. Because it is sometimes possible to predict a bad harvest months ahead, this meant buying up and requisitioning food supplies for distribution among the poor, the prohibition of food transport to areas where there was no shortage, and a prohibition on price increases. However, the government always acted later than the peasants would have liked, and the first priority of the landlords was to make a profit by speculating on food stocks. At these moments, the agrarian community was infected by a collective tension before the actual crisis hit. This tension found its expression in aggression at the first opportunity. Dirks refers to people's loss of control of their situation on two counts: the shortage of food led to physical exhaustion, reducing the vitality and level of endurance of their bodies; and the tension that had been building up for months in some cases disrupted the social order and drove people to deviant, violent behavior.[22] Moreover, when disaster struck eventually, large groups of people left their homes for a while, increasing their vulnerability to disease because of the lack of hygiene and the arduous physical demands of life on the road.

The duty to avoid escalation had a moral background. In preindustrial Europe, access to the means of production was potentially the object of bitter disputes between the elite and the peasants. An important concept to be used as an essential instrument in comprehending the economic system was introduced by historian R. H. Tawney in 1912, but it was elaborated extensively by another historian, Edward P. Thompson: this was the concept of *the moral economy of provision,* also known as *the moral economy of the poor,* which was an instigator of peasant revolts (*collective bargaining by riot*) and government policy at the same time. The term *provision* here refers to the character of the economic transaction, while the term *poor* refers to the ethic of the poor. In fact, the two terms can be seen as both sides of the same coin. It was developed to make a distinction with the *political economy* of capitalism. This concept was also applied by the historian George Rudé, in his essay on the ideology of popular revolt, as well as by many other European researchers, to interpret various aspects of the transformation to capitalism, from Giovanni Levi interpreting the story of an exorcist in a tiny seventeenth-century village in Piedmont, Italy, to Joyce Appleby's discussion of economic thought and ideology in seventeenth-century England. Latin Americanists Phelan, Larson, McFarlane, Stavig, Langer, Tutino, and Schryer have all recently pinpointed "moral economic" aspects in discussing the *Comunero* revolt in Colombia (1781), the social structure of colonial Bolivia, the ethnic conflict during the revolt of Tupác Amaru II in Peru and Bolivia, the resistance of hacienda laborers to modernization, or the peasant revolts during the Mexican Revolution and afterward. Vanderwood, in criticizing such discussions of relative deprivations, would clearly like to stimulate more research on the *mentalidad* of the poor. However, I think that this is precisely what the original Thompson thesis is about. It is, above all, the ecological ethic, as I would like to call it, that provides the key to understanding the normative economy of *pre-political-economic* Europe, Asia, or Latin America, including Anáhuac in the eighteenth century. Or, to paraphrase Joyce Appleby, the persistent ecological ethic dominated rural ideology until the principal director of agricultural production became an individual rather than a group of villagers coordinating their farming activities.[23]

In European medieval studies, a more specific terminology is chosen to indicate the transition from moral economy to political economy. This terminology points to a transition from personal social relations to a legal and fiscal system based on territorial criteria: the transition from *Personenverband* to *Territorialverband*. Personal relations were dominant in a system of Personenverband. The political relations of the moral economy were structured in accordance with the characteristics of a Personenverband. The well-known European system of vassalage was based on this principle: the relations between liege man and liege lord, between vassal and feudal lord, were of a personal nature; there were separate jurisdictions for clerics, nobility, peasants, and, later, urban residents. An interesting observation of a transition like this was made by Heide Wunder for Germany. She spoke of *Herrschaft mit Bauern*, rule with peasants, and *Herrschaft über Bauern*, rule over peasants. The crux of her argument can be gleaned from these phrases, for she used them to entitle the two main sections of her book.[24] In the Middle Ages, German peasants were able to develop a relatively autonomous collective life. Because the manorial and territorial lords needed the cooperation of the peasantry in order to secure their own control over the land, they had to allow the formation of communities with a distinct sphere of local control. The rule "with peasants" declined when the territorial state grew in organization and effectiveness, from the sixteenth century onward. The transition gave birth to increased modern "professionalized" legal practices, which removed one of the primary props of local authority. The result was discipline from above: dominance "over peasants." In other parts of Europe, a similar process began as early as the thirteenth century.

The moral economy becomes manifest in times of deprivation, dearth, and changing ecological circumstances centering on the relationship between population and resources. The latter, above all, force societies to exploit their environment in new and often more difficult ways. Economist Richard Wilkinson concludes: "When the economic system can no longer bring [human needs and the environment] together satisfactorily it shows how individuals are motivated to change the economic system."[25] For that reason, he calls it a human theory, not highly abstracted and removed from the feelings, experiences, and problems facing real people. I would like to refer to this stage

of intensification of economic activity as the *Great Leap Forward*. It provides
more people with security, but it can only be taken after considerable difficulties have been overcome. The changes in the economic system—the "economic development"—are implemented reluctantly. What is new involves,
first and foremost, insecurity. The balance that guaranteed everyone a living
is gone, and no one knows whether the changes will lead to its restoration.
Slicher van Bath provides a good illustration of this setting in his overview
essay on the Dutch Republic in the seventeenth century:

> As the population increased it became necessary to work the
> limited land at one's disposal more intensively. . . . In particular, the
> small farmers with only a small plot of land tried to secure the
> highest yields. Intensive agriculture was not the result of wealth; it
> was a bitter necessity.[26]

Second, Wilkinson claims, the implications of what is new are often seen as
regressive, whether they lead to a greater degree of security or not. He put it
simply as follows:

> We now regard plastics as an inferior substitute for leather in shoes
> and handbags, and primitive societies of hunters and gatherers no
> doubt thought that much more work was involved in cultivating the
> crops they needed than in gathering those that grow naturally. . . .
> Poverty stimulates the search for additional sources of income and
> makes people willing to do things they may previously have avoided.[27]

Development creates employment, but at the expense of leisure time. Leisure
time was reduced to a minimum in the European process of development
described by Wilkinson. At the same time, there was an increasing dependence on those who controlled the labor market. In this environment, the
moral economic ethic inspires peasants to react, mostly to state officials and
lords in person.

The reaction of these "lords" was predictable: they tried to bring the peasants under increased control (*Herrschaft über Bauern*). Developing a similar
argument, the English sociologist Mann speaks of *caging*. He claims that human evolution was a protracted and slow affair because every new step needed
to keep population growth in check made a new, more differentiated organization inevitable. This step meant a loss of autonomy; with every Great Leap
Forward, as I call it, the rural and urban population grew more dependent on
the owners of the means of production: the social elite. The plebeian sector of
the population found itself caught up in the political, economic, and cultural
network woven by the elite. Combining in an eclectic way these concepts, I
would conclude that every *Leap* meant the construction of a *social cage*. As its
"building process" continued, the bars of the cage became irreplaceable. Inside the "cages" was a process of stratification and the formation of economic
power, in fact, of a struggle for ideological and cultural positions of power.
Military and political power groups were formed. Mann describes a virtually

linear process of impoverishment, increasing dependence of the poor and increasing power of the rich, although he does indicate that the developmental phases may undergo setbacks. These hypotheses, formulated by Mann after the perusal of empirical historical research, can be regarded as an extension of the Wilkinson model. So, the rhythm of development was determined by population growth and the acquisition of and access to the means of production.[28] This also shaped the relation of exchange between the elite and the poor. As I shall proceed to demonstrate, this relation of exchange determined the tempo in which the process took place.

It will be obvious that there was considerable reluctance to accept the changes: people were aware of the disadvantages of this *"caging* into *political economy."* Opposition assumed various forms, depending on the perception of the way in which the economy was expected to function. Nowadays people are convinced that the proper functioning of the economy improves employment. This conviction is based on knowledge of how the economy functions objectively *(positive economics)*. The question as to how the economy *ought* to function *(normative economics)* is answered by drawing on elements of positive economics: positive economics and normative economics are fairly closely related in our eyes.[29] This is a situation typical of twentieth-century society, but there was a wide gulf between the two in the past: *normative economics* was determined by the ecological, biblical ethic, which rested upon powerful social assumptions undergirded by God's injunction to Adam to work by the sweat of his brow and not to "swallow up the needy."[30] The characteristics of this ethic may explain the sluggishness of the process of development discussed by Mann and Wilkinson. In general, the ecological ethic of the small farmers in Europe, their view of the normative economy and the way in which they had to maintain themselves, was sustained by what Rudé calls the "mother's milk ideology," "based on direct experience, oral tradition or folk memory, and not learned by listening to sermons or speeches or reading books." Thompson's well-known description is more precise. He remarks that although views of this kind emerged during periods of unrest and rebellion, they formed a substantial component of popular ideology, a consensus as to what were legitimate or illegitimate practices in social and economic performances. An offense to these moral assumptions was the usual occasion for direct action. This is therefore a sociocultural pattern of values that has grown historically, based on the necessity of survival in ecologically difficult circumstances, which directly affects the operation of the economy. It is a pattern of values that adapts to the needs of the times and may be labeled as characteristic of agrarian economy which has not yet been penetrated by industrialization or some proto-agrobusiness; for example, of the agrarian "climax community."[31]

Therefore, the background to the moral economic and ecological ethic is directly related to, in fact formed by, the economic conditions of the era before the Industrial Revolution, when the necessity of survival and hard work was a daily preoccupation. Of course, people do not choose their ideas freely, but rather share in a socially constructed reality. It is well known that in his infancy man learns a way to perceive the material world and acquire a set of concepts that explains his society's invisible world of values and truths. During his adulthood, these ideas are being reshaped through an intellectual response to new experiences, and after that, they are continuously exposed to reworking. Until around 1830, Europe began to wrest itself from the limitations imposed by nature for good; this conglomerate of ideas, or ideology, was shaped and reshaped by ecological circumstances. Before this time, a bad harvest could seriously affect the life of every rural family as a direct catastrophe, especially if it had been preceded recently by another bad harvest. In most cases farmers worked their tiny allotments from sunrise to sunset. In the poorest regions of Europe this was not enough to avoid chronic malnutrition. Many small farmers under the French ancien régime, for instance, were only able to survive if everyone made an effort. Rural families were an economic unit: the parents worked on the land, while the children collected wood, tended the herds, fetched water, or begged. There was a very slight dividing line between poverty on the farm and beggary or vagrancy. If the harvest failed, there was often no alternative to trying one's luck elsewhere. The French countryside was full of migrant, roaming farmers (sometimes entire families) at that time. Work had to be carried out as a communal labor as far as possible in order to attain a level of food production that was higher than what an individual could achieve. All the same, this meager existence was based in the first instance on the minuscule fields encircling the farmhouse.

Mutual dependence, hate, and conflicts meant that the majority of French peasant communities were anything but miniature paradises. In the eighteenth century, 45 percent of all infants failed to reach the age of ten. Death was always just around the corner of every farmhouse. Although the situation in France, which was extremely impoverished, may not be taken as the norm for all of Europe, the situation in most parts of England at the time was not appreciably different: poverty, illness, hunger, and sudden disaster were "familiar features of the social environment of this period," as Thomas puts it. The world of the ancien régime was a world of broken families, dead parents, stepmothers and stepfathers, grandparents and orphans—a world that can be recognized in the traditional tales. For example, Tom Thumb belonged to a family of seven children, which was unable to make ends meet. The parents decided to get rid of their children by abandoning them in a wood. The children had to find a way of saving themselves. In fact, they found the way back home again, but the welcome they received was far from warm. In his analysis of French tales like this one, Darnton sees a thread running through them all: "To eat or not to eat, that was the question peasants confronted in their folklore as well as in their daily lives."[32]

It is therefore understandable that in agrarian society the attitude of peasants to all aspects of life was by and large determined by anxiety. By anxiety psychologists mean the unpleasant emotion characterized by terms like "worry," "apprehension," "dread," and, of course, "fear" that humans—and, indeed, animals—experience at times in varying degrees. Any situation that threatens the well-being of the organism is assumed to produce a state of anxiety and find its way into a "discourse of anxiety." Freudian psychologists see anxiety as an unconscious conflict. It will be clear from the discussion above that I join the behaviorist or learning approach in focusing not on internal conflicts but on ways in which anxiety became associated with certain situations via learning. The stimulus outlined here is starvation. Recurring bad harvests did not mean simply a shortage of food. In these cases the farmers were forced to sell their means of production, such as livestock and land, which entailed a considerable reduction in expectation of improvement during the following year, and even created the fear of prolonged starvation. In general, once established, a fear or "anxiety discourse" is difficult to eradicate because it produces avoidance behavior. Consequently, the person hardly has an opportunity to learn that the conditioned stimulus might really have lost its danger and he tends to make continuous withdrawal responses to situations that may no longer be harmful. Because starvation is a *state anxiety*, a transitory response to a specific situation, people are bound to develop a collective ideology to canalize or avoid such withdrawal responses. Of course, being with others who are also fearful about a forthcoming danger like starvation helps to alleviate fears. Therefore, the central collective tenet of the ecological ethic is the "right to live." With the trauma of starvation in the background, the main problem became how to materialize this tenet and introduce into society a system of obtaining the basic necessities of life. The problem tended to be solved rationally, that is, by taking into account the evidence, the alternatives, and the consequences of each of the alternatives. That is why the peasants, for instance, treated collective security discourse as the main "defense mechanism" and tried to materialize this discourse in attempting to achieve a maximal income from the household to avoid risking the food supply. But logical decision making was hampered by the person's own emotions and the uncertainty of the future. There were always anxiety-producing unknowns and risks that had to be taken.[33]

Reciprocity and Power

Reciprocity is an important form of cooperation to improve the chances of survival. Services are exchanged for fixed norms in a system of reciprocity: one farmer spent a day working for another farmer in return for a day's assistance, sometimes with a horse or ox. The intensity of the activities was usually included in the calculations; for instance, two days' ridging in return for one day's ox traction. The guarantee that services of this kind would be performed was of prime importance; a day's labor was performed in the expectation that the same service would be returned. This mechanism was closely linked to the social relations within the peasant community: kinship relations, friendships, ritual kinship, and relations of fraternity. Reciprocity was one of the major elements binding the mud farmers to one another in a structure of service for services in return, gratitude and obligation. The incentive for mutual assistance is of major importance in reciprocal exchange relations.

The basis of the exchange relations lay in the social stratification and in the different developmental phases in which the various peasant households found themselves. Reciprocal exchange was a way of obtaining resources that were otherwise unavailable. This means that the mechanism excluded the penetration of generally applicable market and price relations. The acquisition of factors of production and the organization of production were regulated by relations of scarcity and not by those of the market. However, it is not clear who was involved in the cycle of reciprocity. Were these relations located exclusively within a community, or were they to be found outside of it? Historians have recently demonstrated that in preindustrial Europe reciprocal services were above all relations between related peasant households; village boundaries were irrelevant. In addition, there was also an intensive exchange relation with the government and the large landowners, which can be called reciprocal.[34]

Therefore, one should not link reciprocity with some kind of egalitarian community structure. Anthropologist Brian Juan O'Neill concluded from his research in a Portuguese hamlet community—a kind of community, by the way, that was formerly described as egalitarian in social structure—that an egalitarian ethos was invented only to hide existing "social inequality." He found out that beneath apparently egalitarian structures of turns and rotations would lie significant differences in the ownership or use rights of landed properties, especially when such turns and rotations are related to specific agricultural tasks. "For instance," he writes, "at threshing it is obvious that helpers producing less grain on their own landholdings will work more hours for villagers with larger harvests than the latter will in return." Also, Orlove, for rural Peru, noted that certain individuals were able to use social forms of reciprocal exchange for their personal advantage: they received more than they gave away. According to O'Neill, reciprocal turns only momentarily unite individuals who may pass the entire year without ever cooperating at any other task. The peasants knew it and realized it, but did nothing to change the situation. He suspects—and this is revealing—that it is the location of "corporate property" that provides the basis for rotating systems. It is his hunch that villagers within corporate, communal units do not entirely "control" certain key elements within their system of production, but that it is these elements that control them. In other words, rather than dominating their own form of property—like any large-scale farmer would—it is the unit itself, through the mediating systems, which dominates them, and at the expense of the poorer members of the community. Reciprocity, then, should be viewed as a hiatus of theoretical equality in an otherwise unequal system of social and productive relations; it is a discursive act of temporary suspension of inequality.[35]

Nevertheless, reciprocity might work to confirm both social inequality and the "right to survive." It is curious to recall Giovanni Levi's account of reciprocity and the land market in the tiny seventeenth-century Piedmont village of Santena (Italy). Property here was extremely fragmented and of little value. Each peasant family had such small quantities of land at its disposal that every minute parcel was of significance. In analyzing the living allowances left to widows, Levi found out that the land market was entirely subordinated to family ties and reciprocal assistance and that the prices involved were relative values determined in conformity with characteristics of the concrete social situation, and thus not just the results of an impersonal interplay between demand and supply of scarce goods. The documents display a constant succession of proprietors, exchanges, arguments, and confiscations. Prices of one particular type of land were of a high level in transactions between kin, of a medium level in dealings between neighbors, and of a low level when outsiders were involved. Because satisfaction of basic material needs was tied to land, Levi acknowledges that ownership of land and its rapid change of hands were a central part of this community's value system, and in particular, among the poorest peasant families. Buying land from a relative was an act of "reciprocity": it was unacceptable to profit from his misfortune to leave him with little money. High prices could not only serve the seller with some short-run purchasing power, but also, for instance, it could cancel out his debts. Sometimes sales went without direct payment in coin because they consisted of an exchange for several forms of assistance received in the past. Outsiders were hardly connected with this social fabric and simply bought the land at its intrinsic value; usually at a low price. In short, kinship, vicinity, friendship, clientage, and charity had altered prices, and solidarities and conflicts within the community had contributed their bit, working not so much to prompt transactions as to determine their prices: a price scale that tended to decline the farther one moved from close kinship and as the market became more impersonal.[36]

The relations of exchange, reciprocal or not, that involved peasants on an informal, individual or collective basis were fed by the ecological ethic. The society in which one lived was expected to support the struggle for survival. In times of need, direct support was expected from the more well-to-do villagers, the landlord, and the government representatives. The power of the members of the elite in a specific region was based on their control of important means of production that the residents of the region needed. According to Mann, their powers "derive from their ability to mobilize the resources of that collectivity."[37] The social balance could depend on the extent to which this group was prepared to meet the peasants' demands. In times of shortage, it was the duty of the lord—including the king—to implement a food policy, starting with the control of market prices and culminating in free handouts of food. The peasants accepted a higher market price, but there were limits: they demanded a fair price. This gave the economy the character of a simple, guided economy. In the relation of exchange, the lord guaranteed the existence of the community in return for payment. This transfer of income was a form of insurance against crises, and the peasants regarded it as an inevitable necessity. The relation of exchange legitimated the rule and social prestige of the elite, but this legitimacy immediately collapsed if the guarantee of subsistence was no longer forthcoming. The relation of exchange was thus marked by a reciprocity of obligations.

The ecological ethic determined the attitude of the peasants, the "crofting" mud farmers, and the agricultural workers toward what was regarded as exploitation and what was not. The peasants concluded informal patronage agreements with the local elite in order to remain within the limits of what they viewed as acceptable. It could even happen that their standard of living dropped while the exchange relation with the lord improved. This was the case after a bad harvest, for example, when the lord (or the state) doled out food to the hungry peasants. In view of the extremely precarious nature of the agrarian economy, with the enormous fluctuations in prices due to the unstable quality and quantity of the harvests, the legitimacy of the social prestige and rule of the elite, the lord, and the state was permanently open to discussion. It was accepted at the outset that the exercise of power and the accumulation of wealth were, to some extent, arbitrary and had only been surrendered by the peasants under the pressure of necessity. The peasants constantly checked the rich and those in power in the abuse of their position.

Precisely because so little was laid down by law—the normative economy was usually based on informal agreements—there was an incessant conflict over the nature of this exchange relation. The government, the elite, and the lords defended the legitimacy of the relations of patronage and their rule at every available opportunity with the assistance of patronage activities and the use of religion as an ideological basis. Every change in the agreements led to resistance. In Würtemberg (Germany), for example, the peasants refused to take part in the usual routine of church services and communion as long as the government failed to tailor its policy of modernization to suit the usual practices in the village. Changes of this kind were inevitable, since the needs and desires of the lords, the elite, the state, and the peasants themselves changed in the course of time:

> In the dialectic between arbitrariness and legitimizing lies one of the central mechanisms for the continual forming of historical consciousness. . . . Within the lord/subject relationship, new "needs" are continually being generated and old "needs" denied.[38]

Needs as defined by the lords were uninterruptedly at conflict with needs felt by subjects, so that most of the costs of legitimacy were to be found in the continual round of redefinition of needs or their suppression. Therefore, one should argue that "lords" and "subjects" formulated discourses about legitimacy, rights and duties, and power relations.

Lords and Subjects

Community

In the endless struggle with their "lords," the peasantry needed cohesion and a kind of solidarity. In the Latin American case, this cohesion is traditionally found in the so-called "closed corporate community." Leaving the "closed" or "corporate" designations apart for the moment, the conclusion above should warn us about making an uncritical use of the word "community." In general, in historical writing this word is used in a wholly descriptive manner to refer to the population under consideration, a synonym of "village," "settlement," or "neighborhood." It should be stressed here that in case the reader wishes to see a more precise and refined description, I include the fact that the constitution of community boundaries was linked to the development of a discourse on "belonging," on the "Us and Them," not just on some physical, structural setting. In fact, the construction of this might neglect the sharing of several structural links between the "Us" and "Them" villages, like ties of kinship, membership in the same congregations, or owning collectively a certain area of land. Migrants were included in the discourse, but residence alone did not automatically make one a village member: the sociocultural processes constituting a collectivity in the same time served to make the collectivity exclude certain people who were physically present in its spatial domain, but who failed to signal interest in the community discourse or to exhibit the "proper" behavior linked to it.

Both the "lord/subject" discourse and the "Us" and "Them" discourse served as the cohesion in identifying and constructing "natural units," as anthropologist Peter Mewett prefers to call them, a category relevant to the local conceptualization of spatial organization and discernible only through local "knowledge" and without affecting structural links. The "natural unit," constructed in sociocultural space, was symbolic. It did not have an independent existence and was considered "natural" because it was perfectly normal and proper, reflecting the feeling of "that's the way things are."[39] This means that it is a mistake to search only for structural reasons for the existence of such "natural units," because they above all *served a purpose*: other than the discourse with the "lords," it served subjects to define who belonged to their "community," who was involved in precisely that discourse, and who did not. The "boundaries" of the "community" were implied in the contextualization of everyday life. Though the knowledge of where the boundaries were—manifested in a way that could be perceived by the physical senses and reified as a territorial phenomenon—was publicly available, participation in the discourse that produced it remained restricted and legitimated by the "members of the community." This means that the "Us" and "Them" discourse had to be *self-limiting*, central to the process of "boundary construction" and setting the criteria of eligibility for inclusion, usually resulting from some or several issues between "community members" and "others." "It is the cultural stuff of everyday behavior," writes Mewett, "which in turn is embedded in the local social organisation." "But," he continues, "it should not be thought that this implies any 'corporateness' on the part of the villagers." It only suggests that *within* a certain constructed "area" different people discussing issues associated with the integrity of the "area" would have addressed them from a similar perspective. The boundaries could take on the *appearance* of a territorial phenomenon, but were a symbolic manifestation of people interested in a "lord/subject" discourse.[40]

But what about the "closed" and "corporate" designations? Generally, the inhabitants of rural communities are seen as "peasants." The use of the term *peasants* assumes the perception of a certain category of agrarian producers who operate collectively in a certain sense and who tend to shut themselves off from the outside world. Members of the elites outside the communities tried to get their hands on the economic surplus produced in the communities; according to a significant number of researchers, this brought the members of the communities into a continual class struggle with the elite outside the village. The concept of class is viewed as something static in this perspective; it is a component of the social structure, in which various social strata form "classes." The peasants formed the lowest class. This entire constellation is seen as the source of both an alleged group attitude of joint defense, and an alleged high level of social equality among the members of the community, which should be regarded as typical of the closed corporate peasant communities.[41]

However, I have to be careful here, because the concept of "peasant" is vague. Anthropologists, sociologists, and economists recognize that the theory-forming stage is still in full swing. At any rate, the term refers in a wide sense to the inhabitants of the countryside, whose economy, operating on a small-scale and using what modern researchers regard as primitive tools, is a unit of production and consumption combined. The peasant, it is supposed, is assisted by relatives in an attempt at self-sufficiency. His method of operations is supposed to be based primarily on a survival strategy, that peasant economy, dominated by distrust of change, innovation, or investment. As the lowest class in capitalist society, the peasants form a residue of the past. The chance of transcending this status is not rated very highly by sociologists, anthropologists, or economists, although the introduction of innovations by the more well-to-do on a limited scale is not out of the question. A few theorists realize that the peasantry cannot be regarded as an undifferentiated whole. According to the anthropologists Wasserstrom and Schryer, the socioeconomic stratification *within* the group of peasants is probably not different from the Marxist class antagonisms. This led certain scholars to propose the term *petty commodity producers* instead of *peasants*. As a commodity producer, the argument goes, the peasant can be included in the standard Marxist theories of political economy. I see no essential difference, because despite this claim it is still assumed that "peasants" or "petty commodity producers" live together in a kind of corporate community.[42]

Interpretations of the peasant economy constantly draw on the observations of the economist Chayanov at the time of the Russian Revolution. The translation of his work from Russian has made a deep impression on European and North American scholars. According to historian David Sabean, this is because Chayanov's model shares the same romantic framework with most of the views on peasants. Chayanov's followers look at the peasant community as a group of family households working exclusively for their own exist-ence. The aim of the domestic economy was to feed, clothe, and shelter every member of the family, as well as to finance spending for village feasts and religious ceremonies in the village—which symbolically underpinned its co-hesion—and state taxes. The peasant economy was characterized by a preoc-cupation with the ratios of family to family labor to increase global income rather than by a maximization of revenue per family worker, or any other concern for capital investment; a noncapitalist logic. Other characteristics included its social properties stemming from the importance placed upon patriarchal authority, and, of course, the egalitarian ideal of working for the good of the family group instead of developing individualistic aspirations. One might argue, therefore, that the "Chayanovians" regard the peasant house-holds as the cells out of which the "closed corporate community" was con-structed. In a situation of overpopulation, all these demands could only be met if so much family labor was employed that a situation of "self-exploita-tion" arose; with labor being an overhead rather than a variable cost, the true family farm did not contract wage payments with its own members. Strictly speaking, a rigid interpretation of Chayanov's peasant concept excludes any Great Leap Forward, so often verified in European agrarian history. No won-der historical research brings doubts. The historical demographer Richard Smith concludes from material concerning the English "peasant economy" that it was the forces of the market economy that tended to produce social differen-tiation. And in this case, "only a minority of the rural populace were able to maintain what we can term a Chayanovian equilibrium." Jacek Kochanowicz concluded that for the Polish economy of the eighteenth century, "family size and structure were mainly determined by the productive capacity and the amount of land under cultivation," thus standing Chayanov on his head. In interpreting the peasant economy of the Irish parish of Killashandra, histo-rian Kevin O'Neill states that the attempt to provide a single model for peas-ant society, like Chayanov's, is indeed "a particular risky business."[43]

In Latin America, the closed corporate peasant community is usually con-trasted with other types of peasant communities, including the more open mestizo villages, which are supposed to work along capitalist lines of produc-tion. The closed communities are said to be a product of European colonial-ism. Although created by the Spanish conquerors, many institutions of the closed corporate community were subsequently modified or redefined by the Indians themselves as part of a set of defensive strategies to mitigate the im-pact of external forces. They would have restricted membership to fellow vil-lagers, enforcing endogamy. The internal structure should have been egalitarian, with effective leveling mechanisms that prevent or at least at-tenuate the emergence of significant wealth differences or internal exploita-tion. The wealthier members, it is said, are expected to sponsor village costs and communal public life, especially *fiestas*, to ensure the equal redistribution of surplus wealth and to reinforce and maintain the egalitarian social struc-ture. To Wolf and others, the Indian communities of Mexico possessed all the hallmarks of the closed corporate peasant communities such as restricted membership, communal jurisdiction over land, a religious system of notable endurance, and the leveling mechanism from the early colonial period onward, and they maintained barriers against the entry of goods and ideas from outside. The members of these communities were socially and culturally isolated from the larger society in which they existed. One would not expect internal class differences to develop as long as the corporate institutions persisted. If such differences did emerge, the closed corporate community would disappear.[44]

Although the model of the closed corporate peasant community has become widely accepted, Eric Wolf, after reading the most recent historical studies of colonial Mexico, has stated, in a recent review of his own work,[45] that his original idea "now seems overly schematic and not a little naive." And indeed, several characteristics of the model of the closed corporate peasant communities can no longer be properly defended. In fact, the question of whether such closed and harmonious communities ever existed at all, or at any time, in the European and Latin American past might in itself be regarded as doubtful. Historians know of Le Roy Ladurie's description of an extraordinary variety of relationships between villagers in the French Pyrenees in the late thirteenth century. The internal structure of one of these mountain villages under study, Montaillou, was anything but egalitarian. Anthropologists have not only confirmed a similar inequality in modern Mexican Indian townships, but have even challenged the idea of the egalitarian ethos of the villagers. They noted a lack in emphasizing conformity and denied any workings of a leveling mechanism.[46] Other writers, like Friedmann or Bernstein, noted that the most usual distinction between "peasants" on one side, and "farmers" or agrarian "entrepreneurs," on the other, was the ratio of subsistence to commodity production, a distinction that is purely quantitative.[47]

It will be clear that I consider a more general definition of the term, but at the same time, it would be desirable to follow a classical writer in doing so. I find it in R. H. Hilton's description of the peasantry as rural dwellers who possess and sometimes own the means of agricultural production. Peasants support, through their agricultural production, not only themselves but superimposed classes and institutions, such as landlords, churches, and towns that dominate them politically and skim off surplus profits. But the peasantry should not be considered a "lumpen" class, historian Barbara Hanawalt declares, for some possessed considerably more than others.[48] The anthropologist and historian Alan Macfarlane, who feels suspicious of the arguments used in the peasant debate in general, stresses the romantic background of the traditional attitude toward peasants and their communities, present not only in Latin America, but also in studies focusing on Africa, Asia, and even Europe:

> The belief that stable and tightly knit communities have existed in
> the past and still survive in distant lands is an important myth for
> industrial and highly mobile societies. It's therefore no coincidence

that it was in the turmoil of late nineteenth-century industrialization that the idea of "community" as opposed to modern "society"
was developed extensively, ... It was felt that society was changing, values were being undermined, an older closeness was being
lost. This powerful myth both influenced, and seemed to find
support in, the work of historians and anthropologists during the
first half of the twentieth century.[49]

In England, for example, after the 1950s, which were the highpoint of similar
local community studies in British sociology, there followed a waning of this
research activity during the 1960s and 1970s as skepticism grew about the
applicability of the idea of "community." Until then, the tradition of community studies had assumed that the boundaries of territory, social interaction,
and culture coincided with one another. In fact, by studying an administra-
tively defined unit it was assumed that one was studying a "community."
Abroad, many researchers were disappointed to find so much exploitation
and poverty in past or in Third World societies: European capitalism had robbed
the peasants of their innocence. The term *corporate community* may therefore
be considered a relic of the simplistic thinking of nineteenth-century and early-
twentieth-century writers seeking in history or anthropology an emotionally
satisfying alternative to their own socially mobile and industrial-urban age.
Macfarlane concludes that the peasants will only be truly emancipated in historical and anthropological research when historians and anthropologists have
overcome their romantic visions. Underpinning this, anthropologist O'Neill,
in studying a community in Portugal, argues that "the most essential task at
this moment is to provide solid empirical data which will serve to banish
once and for all the myth of the egalitarian . . . community."[50] These are comments made to stress the fact that the concept of community requires careful
investigation and that we have to abstain from any egalitarian characteristics.
It is true that common usage of land provided a ready basis for the sentiment
of community. Even in this case, however, a small group of rich or powerful
peasants might have exploited the mass of the poor. In Europe, the commons
were all too often neither close, compact, nor collectively owned. Gross inequalities of provision, as between sections, and of access, as between individuals, ensured that common usage of land remained a source of perennial
conflict rather than consensus.

How to interpret the word *community* in the following chapters? The word
reflects a temporal or spiritual juridical organization, like parishes and neighborhoods. Or one might find seigneurial units like manors, households, marks,
and communautés at the origins of community organizations. But most important practically, the word *community* is used in a simple juxtaposition with
such terms as "village" or "rural settlement." This stresses the physical context of the community, and, indeed, many historians and anthropologists
would argue that the sense of community can only develop in conditions of
geographical proximity. The temporal and spiritual authorities merely conse-
crated this identification by turning the village into a unit of fiscal and paro-

chial administration.[51] Jones introduced a major point of criticism that cannot easily be neglected. If the rural community is viewed primarily as a by-product of an agglomerated settlement pattern, he writes, its existence in thinly inhabited regions lacking a well-ordered landscape must be questioned. He found traces of kinship in such surviving communities in southern France. Henry Kamen wrote in his book on European societies between 1500 and 1700, however, that neighborliness may have been a stronger bond than kinship, especially if the "ties that bound" had been formed mainly by discourse on land-tenure rights. Kinship might have been a *consequence*, not a cause of community formation. The same argument can be found in Laslett's influential *The World We Have Lost*,[52] which argues that to "the facts of geography, being together in the one place, were added all the bonds which are forged between human beings when they are permanently alongside each other; bonds of intermarriage and of kinship, of common ancestry and common experience and of friendship and cooperation in matters of common concern." Members of communities would have been linked together by bonds of administrative, jurisdictional, biological and psychological cousinhood. Thus, without returning to the Chayanovian analysis, a simple solution to the problem of community in the countryside, according to Jones and Laslett, would be to assert the primacy of the household units cooperating in matters of common concern.

In my view, these remarks on the common ancestry and common jural, social, economic and political experience and of friendship and cooperation in matters of common concern of households, living within a certain unit, might be the most useful definition of communities. It is not necessary to pronounce on either the open or closed nature of the community, or upon its corporate character. Anthropologists like O'Neill even provide native linguistic evidence of distinct internal hierarchies of occupational, economic, and social groups. Villagers did *not* paint a self-portrait of some kind of Arcadian democracies. If they allowed the traditional anthropologists to begin their sketches of them in such tones, it is because these authors' work, in Jacob Black's famous words, are "skewed by the tenacious legend that such societies are fundamentally egalitarian in outlook and structure."[53] Such a definition has moved away from traditional class analysis.[54] Particularly interesting for my argument is the conclusion of this kind of theoretical critique: there exist in each individual multiple subject positions corresponding both to the different social relations in which the individual is inserted and to the discourses that constitute these relations. In short, all these relations are the basis of subject positions and every social agent is thus the site of many subject positions and cannot be realistically reduced to one.[55]

Herrschaft

This brings me to the concept of reciprocal dominance and the introduction of lordship—the Personenverband—within the concept of "community." The focus upon a changing legitimacy in time, as well as the constitution of communities in sociocultural space, point to personalized and concrete relationships of authority and power. This should not be confused with the more abstract and impersonal structures of domination in a modern state. Sabean recalled the German term *Herrschaft* here, referring to specific relationships of power, rooted in customary law—or sometimes written down—and entailing reciprocal obligations. Such domination was understood concretely, that is, for instance, as Herrschaft over land, over serfs, over manorial economy, or courts. In short, as Robisheaux affirms, although with each of these authorities came the right to extract certain surpluses, like rents, dues, labor services, or the right to command obedience and loyalty from those under a jurisdiction, "lords had always to provide protection (*Schutz und Schirm*) in exchange for these rights, or their authority could be called into question."[56] The legitimacy of Herrschaft is embodied in specific historical symbolic public forms and discourses; thus, in acts as well as in speech. Where legitimacy broke down, the subjects developed a discourse of resistance based on these same particular historical forms and discourses, but this time expressed in rumors, in unflattering folktales and stories about the lords, in "up-side-down" festivities like carnival, and eventually, in open, violent rebellion.

There is an outsider and an insider view of communal development, and much of what is discussed in this chapter is an attempt to analyze the notions from the frontier between what was conceptualized as "inside" and what was viewed as "outside." The rural community, Jones writes, evinced a Januslike character: explored from within, it resembled nothing so much as a nest of vipers; but as soon as an external threat loomed over the horizon, internecine strife ceased and ranks closed behind the broad shoulders of the village dignitaries. The crucial element, it follows, lies in the answer to the question of what comprised matters of common concern. Ties of kinship were only partly important. Some years ago, Sabean argued that what was common in community was the fact that members of a community were engaged in the same argument, the same *raisonnement, Rede,* or discourse, in which alternative strategies, misunderstandings, and conflicting goals and values were threshed out. Insofar as the individuals in a community might all have been caught up in different webs of connection to the "outside," no one was bound in his relations by the community and in addition to this particular boundary situation, people would simply pass each other by. Cousinhood or not, people would emigrate to the other side of the world if they thought matters were better there. This means that community relationships between the family units were formed every time a problem of common interest occurred, mostly from outside the fabric of household relationships. This might originate in climatic changes: a bad harvest was a strong incentive to join hands.[57]

Here we are back at a statement made earlier: the rural community was a *construction* by different peasants and farmers, perhaps even landholders, to serve some kind of political, economic or social struggle with "outsiders," as a matter of mediations and political reciprocation. What made community possible was the fact that it involved a series of mediated relationships that changed over time. A community existed not as an actual cluster of institutions within a defined locality, but as an ideological construction used by a group of people to give meaning to some aspects of their lives. Their place of residence is, theoretically, not important. In English sociology, Anthony Cohen, who began his research in the "community" of Whalsay, a remote Shetland fishing island, in 1973, was a major figure in the reorientation of locality studies. The social psychologist Tajfel was another one, stating that social groups are "cognitive constructions shared by the individuals involved, and/or result from a perception of shared interests." A social group like a rural community comes "to life when [its] *potential* designations as such [has] acquired a psychological and behavioural reality."[58] Such a situation occurred during the struggles experienced by the people involved, when mediation about basic production factors—such as usufruct, use right or ownership of land—was urgent. Another form of mediation could be found within the spheres of production and exchange. A third form would be found in the sphere of social value and religion. These forms included both sharing and conflict. In short, community existed where not just love but frustration and anger also existed, providing a psychological outlet to vent feelings. Villagers grasped community most centrally within the terms *envy* and *hate*, *struggles* and *clashes*.

Since we know that villagers were constantly altering their structural relations as the nature of state and church institutions changed, it is clear that there were as many communities as there were mediated relationships. One item stood out, however. Two groups were involved in community discourse: the ones that had easy access to the means of production and the ones that had no access, or hardly any. Here different communities were formed. In the case of usufruct of land, for example, one might see Mexican villagers join to form communities that negotiated with their chiefs to share in the distribution of township lands. For that purpose, commoners and elites might also have formed clientelistic coalitions against other groups inside the township. But in case of danger of losing communal lands, all—including the chiefs—would join hands against the outsiders.

The language of these conflicts was highly and predominantly religious and moral. Although this is not to deny that both lords and subjects actually believed in the moral doctrines, every kind of morality is composed of rules, and rules are subject to change. For example, the wish of the ruling minority to strengthen labor discipline and thereby stimulate production resulted in attempts to increase its hold on the normative economy. This meant getting the peasants and workers to abandon community life and related self-sufficient production. Muchembled describes the process by which a gradually widening gulf grew up between the elite and the peasants in modern France, from the sixteenth century on. During this process, the elite tried to impose its views on the peasants, while the peasants resisted as best they could. Their culture was a *culture de survivre,* a culture of anxiety—fear of hunger, pain and death—and change disturbed the balance that they claimed to have found.[59]

The translation of the German term *Herrschaft* as reciprocal dominance and lordship brings another, very important, and elementary feature to the surface. The offer of protection in the form of clientage, justice, general tranquility, order, or military protection was just as central to the institution. The sum total of all forms of Herrschaft was viewed as offering protection and guaranteeing the reproduction and survival of the rural household units, thus making it unnecessary to question any single form. But precisely because of the changing relationships through time, most forms of Herrschaft appeared to be very unbalanced. Subjects sometimes put one or another form of Herrschaft into question because it did not offer any correlative service any longer. The specific factor of time resulted in a vision of Herrschaft as always partially arbitrary, not always correctly balanced by an adequate return, too costly, and sometimes maintained by a degree of violence. This necessitated a continuing process of legitimization.

Indeed, when one examines the daily practice of reciprocal dominance, it becomes clear that legitimization was integral to it. Villagers demanded a just treatment from colonial, religious, or local magistrates. It was accepted at the outset that the exercise of power and the accumulation of wealth by magistrates and elite members were to some extent arbitrary and thus its arbitrariness had either to be justified or masked: Herrschaft as the evocation of obedience, the satisfaction of mutual interests, and the fulfillment of needs. As stated above, the arbitrariness and legitimizing of wealth and power should be considered as one of the central mechanisms for the continual formation and reformation of historical consciousness. It is good to repeat that new "needs" were continually generated and old "needs" denied. Needs, as defined by the officials and lords, were uninterruptedly in conflict with needs felt and defined by subjects, so that the costs of Herrschaft were not just to be found in the payment schedule of, for example, tributes and rents, but also in the continual round of redefinition of needs or their suppression.[60]

More than a decade ago, Foucault wrote that discourses are not once and for all subservient to power or raised up against it, "any more than silences are."[61] On the contrary, he continued, "we must make allowance for the complex and unstable process whereby discourse can be both an instrument and an effect of power, but also a hindrance, a stumbling block, a point of resistance and a starting point for an opposing strategy." Mexican Indians and Indian leaders were well aware of this. In eighteenth-century New Spain, I will argue, there were important advantages in the everyday exercise of power, which attracted Indian elites to accept administrative posts in the political or religious hierarchy of the pueblos de indios and wait for opportunities to perform as the village governor. But the exercise of power could also have its costs of isolation, risk, fear, dishonor, and ridicule.

Conclusion

This chapter is the result of an attempt to present some thoughts on the current state of the art in modern historical research in order to avoid confusing the reader about my abductive position. All attention was focused on the heuristic value of the consequences of *relative overpopulation*, the problems it might cause and the solutions that could have been devised for these problems. The inquiry in the following chapters is concerned with the character of the possible disruption of the ecological equilibrium—which I detected in the problematic of the "chiaroscuro century" in Anáhuac—and the possible search for a new one. In the end, after reviewing all the data coming from literature and archival study, the hypothesis is launched that in late-eighteenth-century Anáhuac the new ecological equilibrium, despite its temporary nature, was of a proto-industrial kind. This means that possibilities of finding a way out for problems within the agrarian circumstances were exhausted by then. The climax agrarian community had been left behind. Agriculture had obviously been tied to a limited framework, and the population had encountered its limits. These points lead to the question of how ecological factors like landscape, climate, and population growth affected economic activity and the organization of the economic system in Anáhuac. The factors determined whether population growth in this region was to lead to a Small Leap Forward or to a Great Leap Forward.

Wilkinson explains to what extent the normative economy stood under pressure at a time of rapid population growth:

> Both individuals and societies will give priority to the maintenance of subsistence activities at a level at least adequate for survival. This is a cultural imperative. The importance of basic production gives it a key role in initiating cultural change. If the demands which basic production imposes on society change, then the rest of the cultural system will have to change to meet them. The demands of production have a preeminent position which allows them to ridge roughshod over other elements of a culture.[62]

It is obvious that a process of this kind coincided with the growth of the monetary economy in the countryside. The development of the market economy and market relations in this region were regarded as an *"unchristian economy"* by lords and peasants alike. The peasants in the Hohenlohe district in southern Germany, for example,[63] increasingly demanded "just prices," and the lords gladly met their demands by stepping up their paternalism. The lords did not take advantage of the economic expansion simply as calculating landlords bent on extracting an economic rent from scarce land and resources. The political and social relations between lord and peasant in Hohenlohe made it impossible for lords ever to separate material wealth from the social relationships that produced it. Efforts to control the marketplace and to distribute grain to the village poor suggest that they sought social and economic stability even if it cost the state dearly. The threat of chaos and disorder if the consensus were to be lost—Robisheaux refers simply, and correctly, to "order"—drove the elite to pay great attention to the demands that arose from the *culture de survivre*.

Where the maintenance of subsistence activities prevailed, the bargaining position on the part of peasants must still have been strong, especially when these peasants lived in an agrarian society that was relatively sparsely populated. The effect of population growth in this context can be expressed by a formula.[64] Since it is known that the collective mentality adjusts to changes in socioeconomic circumstances, in a situation of population growth or a relatively high population density we can state:

$$\text{a) } P\uparrow = pl \rightarrow b > pb \rightarrow l,$$

where P stands for the volume of population ($\uparrow$ = growth or high population density; $\downarrow$ = decrease or low population density), p stands for "power of," that is, a dominant bargaining position, l stands for "'the lords, elite and state," and b for the "peasants"; the $\rightarrow$ sign indicates who exercises power over whom. This formula indicates that in a situation of population growth or high population density, the bargaining position of the lords, the elite, and the state with respect to the small peasants is better than that of the peasants with respect to the lords, and so forth. The small peasants will have to modify their demands. In a situation of low population density or a decrease in population, in which more land is made available to the small peasants, the situation is the reverse:

$$\text{b) } P\downarrow = pl \rightarrow b < pb \rightarrow l.$$

This is an important point for the interpretation of labor conditions in the countryside and for dealing with the question of the coherence of the economic system. The relations of exchange within the normative economy changed considerably when there were changes in the variable "population."

Of course, this compels me to connect the social stratification with the variable of population density. The p in the formula refers to what Mann defines as *economic power* and can naturally be reduced to "the satisfaction of subsistence needs through the social organization of the extraction, transformation, distribution, and consumption of the objects of nature."[65] The ensuing stratification means that few people have direct and full access to the means of production, while many only have limited and indirect access. A high population density may result in an extension of the social ladder as intermediate groups arise in a process of economic development. In that case, of course, more people will have less access to the means of production. The members of the elite, however—the upper crust of society—try to make sure that they do not lose their dominant position in the stratification—and thereby in the economy—and will try to recover the old balance that existed before the increase in population took place. This is a complex situation in which the various social groups have conflicting interests.

The modern period saw not just the ideological triumph of political economy. According to Macfarlane, we deal with the triumph of a new culture: the ethic of endless accumulation as an end, not as a means, was gaining momentum over the subsistence ethic. The development forced the peasant communities to describe the features of their ecological ethic more precisely. The horizontal links in the communities had to be reinforced in order to resist

the increasing pressure of the elite and the state. The vertical links were strengthened too, for it could sometimes happen that both the landlord and the peasants saw their wishes satisfied within a system of patronage. The precise way
in which this was regulated varied from state to state, from region to region.[66]
The striving for consensus appears to be of vital importance; in the *culture de
survivre* it was group interests that counted, not those of the individual. In the
case of such a group spirit, the role of religion must be taken into account as a
cement binding individuals together. This relation was formulated more than
forty years ago by Theodor Adorno and his associates, who established a connection between authoritarian power and obedience.[67] However, their explanation is also applicable to relations of reciprocity in agrarian societies, as
Barrington Moore indirectly showed.[68]

At any rate, it is clear that this *culture de survivre* leads to the difficult
terrain of the history of popular culture and social behavior. The English historian Peter Burke modestly calls this terrain "an elusive quarry," while Mitzman
refers to research on the human "cultural superego"; Frijhoff sticks more closely
to the historian's task and emphasizes the heuristic aspect, underscoring a
remark made by Burke during a conference on cultural history held in
Amsterdam: "Cultural history is the study of attitudes, norms, values, and
images as they are embodied in artefacts, texts, and other sources." Cultural
history is not treated here as a separate subdiscipline, but as a way of approaching the symbolic element in the history of human behavior. This is
relevant to my research because historiographers of Latin American history
will also have to investigate the connection currently being made in European historiography between the socioeconomic features of agrarian society
and the *mentalité* of various groups within that society.[69] Nevertheless, research
has been started only relatively recently in Latin America.

By stressing the normative background of economic activity, it is almost
inevitable that the "vision of the participants" (Dumont) comes to the fore;
the voice of the "other," to use a fashionable phrase.[70] Indeed, it seems to be
of decisive importance for the application of an ecological approach to economic development. All the same, we should be wary of overemphasizing the
sociocultural aspects of the normative economy. The balance of the analysis
should not swing toward a pure history of mentalities, for this runs the risk of
regressing to a very old style of interpretation that assigns so much importance to the cultural factors that there is no room left for recognition of economic changes in agrarian society. Socioeconomic research has provided such
insights that the notion of a completely static agrarian structure will not hold
water. Despite their cultural norms and values and the ethological ethic, small
peasants were prepared to take risks and to introduce new techniques if they
were guaranteed or likely to lead to improvement. Many innovations were
only incorporated in the process of production much later on, because they
could not be introduced immediately at the time of their discovery without
an element of risk. If modernization was likely to result in overproduction, it
would have been economic suicide to adopt it. Besides, it was safer to exploit

the flexibility of the existing techniques first. Modernization, innovation, and development are typical of a situation in which the old methods are considered to be absolutely and definitively insufficient to meet the demand of subsistence.

To conclude, the chapters that follow start from the knowledge of an intense relation between the physical environment and human socioeconomic organization. The theme has stirred up acrimonious debates for decades, which has warned the researcher to be careful, even prudent. That is why I have chosen the ecological approach for my analysis as a heuristical tool only. There is no definitive answer to the ongoing problem of the "chiaroscuro century." This book is intended to stimulate new research, to move away from traditional interpretations like Wolf's or Chayanov's.

2

A Lower Ceiling

Introduction: The Purest Air

Demographic pressure on agricultural resources in Anáhuac at the close of the eighteenth century did not develop by an increase of the number of inhabitants only: droughts in the months of May and June acted as a kind of catalyst. The term *catalyst* is used by chemists to describe any substance that regulates the rate of a chemical reaction but itself remains unchanged. Catalysts do not cause reactions to take place that would not otherwise be possible; for example, those that are not in accord with the principles of equilibrium. It is the purpose of this chapter to underscore the ecological emphasis of my text by showing that this is the correct metaphor to use, in this particular case. The early summer droughts affected the maize producers of Anáhuac (Indian villagers) more than wheat farmers (hacendados). This suggests, obviously, that the social structure itself was easily infected by the forces liberated by the catalyst. However, it has proved difficult to devise a theory that can indicate the extent of this influence, precisely because of the complex interactions of a large number of determinants.

A geographical area is not just a color on a map, of little relevance to human lives—to borrow a phrase from Flaubert—and mentioned by historians only to give the reader an impression of what the region under scrutiny looks like.[1] One might entertain doubts about acquiring information about an agrarian society before investigation has been conducted concerning which factors could have influenced agriculture. The historian Patch is aware of this and explicitly draws attention to the geographical, social, and economic factors that *combined* to determine in a complex way the agrarian development of the Yucatán peninsula (his object of research) in the colonial era. It was precisely the specific topography, nature of the soil, and climatological conditions that had a major impact on the historical development of the peninsula.[2] Similarly, specific geographical conditions are very important in formulating the prior conditions of the regional economy of the Mesa de Anáhuac.

There are few studies of Anáhuac that explicitly focus on the geographical component. An important reason for this absence is the assumption that the negative effects of this component, in particular, must have been relatively minor. Despite the uneven rainfall, the climatological conditions of the highlands are generally considered to be favorable. The Mexican essayist Alfonso Reyes realized how little Europeans knew about Latin American geography. During a stay in the old mother country, he told his Spanish audience about an American Castilia, at a higher altitude than the Spanish one, more harmonious and less rugged, where the air is as clear as a mirror and where people enjoy an eternally green autumn. "Ours in Anáhuac," he wrote, "is more resilient." He praised the exceptional purity of the air and quoted the simple words of Fray Manuel de Navarrete:[3]

> una luz resplandeciente
> que hace brillar
> la cara de los cielos.

Anáhuac is the area where the air is purified: this was how Reyes endorsed the words of the traveler Alexander von Humboldt, who visited New Spain in the early years of the nineteenth century.

Many historians would like to agree with him, but unfortunately appearances are deceptive. The failures of the maize harvests indicate a climatic force behind economic development that is still underrated today.[4] Of course, it is difficult for outsiders to assess the vagaries of Anáhuac's climate properly. European and North American visitors to Mexico—and most of the members of the scientific community of Latin Americanists are nothing but visitors—soon become confused, accustomed as they are to green and fertile landscapes. If they encounter the Mexican highlands during the dry period, for instance, they are astonished at the arid scenery surrounding them. Can the maize for which Mexico is famous grow in an area like this? If they come to Mexico in the summer, however, when the torrents of rain can be heard beating down in the wet season, they wonder why the maize is not completely crushed beneath such natural violence. They are reminded of their house plants at home, which need watering. Subject to the climatic conditions of Europe, these plants are watered once every few days all year round. In Mexico, however, the annual water supply falls on the plants at one go and they have to manage without water for the rest of the year. With mild disapproval, these visitors will therefore recall the works of authors like Humboldt and Alzate, who, during the late colonial period, wrote about the potential of Mexican agriculture in glowing terms, calling it the basis of a great future for the country.[5] In theory, these classical writers were quite right: this landscape, plagued by drought and downpours, still produced wheat harvests with a yield per unit of sowing seed many times the European equivalent, despite the fact that the Mexican highlands were cultivated in the same way. Where differences arose, the specific geographical conditions of the highlands proved to be the decisive factor in Mexico.

The problem lies in the location of this American Castilia. It is situated at an altitude between 2,200 and 2,600 meters above sea level, and extends 180

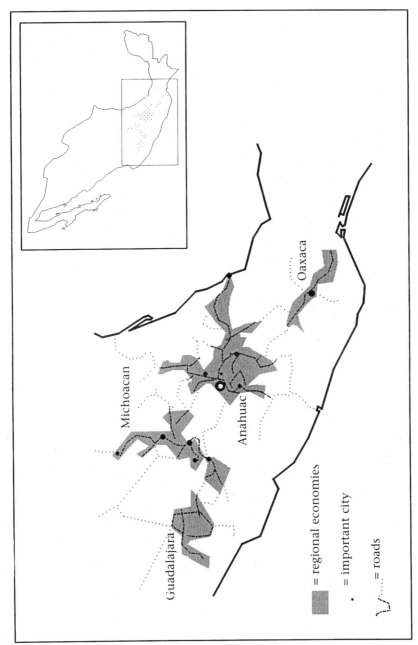

Map 3 Four regional economies of New Spain in the eighteenth century

kilometers in an east–west direction and 160 kilometers in a north–south direction. Most important, it is surrounded by mountain ridges formed by the so-called neovolcanic axis, which cuts Mexico into two along an east–west axis. The problem is that these ridges deflect the rain clouds from the plains, so that the precipitation mainly falls directly in this mountain area and is less frequent on the larger plateaus in the highlands. This is the first difficulty the farmers face. The second is that the flat plateaus from which four enormous volcanoes majestically rise are generally fertile precisely in the valleys *between* the mountain ridges and the highland volcanoes. Consequently, an expansion of agricultural territory to cater to the high population density was already out of the question in the eighteenth century. The third difficulty was the fact that the natural irrigation channels, fed by streams running off Mexico's largest volcanoes, were dry for a large part of the year.

It would be out of place here to attempt an in-depth account of the changes in the agricultural landscape between around 1730 and about 1800, as has been done by Trautmann.[6] However, such an account is not necessary if we adopt the ecological approach, because attention will be devoted primarily to the *consequences* of these changes, in other words, to the ways in which people reacted to them. Nevertheless, the conclusion of this chapter will be that the drought of the late eighteenth century stimulated the relative overpopulation by reducing the basis of nutrition. In fact, the "pure air" that Reyes wrote about was too dry for the peasants.

Anáhuac

A Structural Typology

First of all, Anáhuac itself must be defined. Here, my research did not start from scratch. The structural typology of the region under study is based on work by Professor Bernard H. Slicher van Bath.[7] My plans to carry out my own research took shape during the period when he was attached to the History Department of the University of Leiden, a special chair maintained by the Leiden University Fund. In 1974 he and Adriaan van Oss had begun a joint, large-scale holistic investigation of the social, economic, and cultural development of Latin America. In 1981, Slicher published a large historico-geographic and demographic survey of New Spain, which determined the characteristics of a number of regional economies. However, most of his work is published in Dutch, and because it is essential for my regional focus I will discuss the results of Slicher's work shortly.

According to the Slicher–Van Oss model, there were four concentrations of population in eighteenth-century Mexico. Anáhuac was in the center, the most densely populated area of New Spain. They referred to the area as "Central Mexico." It included the large cities of the country: Mexico City and Puebla de los Angeles. The second center of New Spain, the region of Michoacán, was on Anáhuac's western border. This area also included a few large cities, such as the silver city of Guanajuato and the textile center of Querétaro, but the number of Indian communities was smaller than in Anáhuac. Further to the west was the region of Guadalajara, whose capital (of the same name) only became one of the large cities of the viceroyalty after 1750. The fourth region, centered on the valley of Oaxaca, was in the south of New Spain. Unlike Guadalajara or Michoacán, this was an area with many Indian communities whose roots went back to the pre-Hispanic period. It is this division into four regions that I follow throughout this book (see Map 3), though I shall repeatedly refer here to the borders of the modern states of the republic of Mexico, which often bear the same names. The area between these centers of population was practically uninhabited and barely cultivated. Only a few almost impassable roads wound their way through the desolate mountainous landscape to the next valley or plateau, where a significant concentration of population had been formed. According to the criteria introduced here, sparsely populated areas like the so-called *Mixteca*, between Anáhuac and Oaxaca, or the dot of villages around Tlapa to the south of the Anáhuac highlands are not referred to as "regions."

The pattern of settlement of the four regions of New Spain can also be determined by reading historical studies published to date. Taylor, Pastor, Hamnett, Romero Frizzi, Chance, and Carmagnani emphasize the small-scale character of the rural economy of Oaxaca, consisting mainly of Indian communities. Van Young, Lindley, and Serrera devote most attention to haciendas and ranchos in Guadalajara. Morin, Tutino, and Brading do the same for Michoacán. As far as the last two regions are concerned, hardly any research has been conducted on the Indian communities of the period. On the other hand, there is considerable literature on the urban economy of mining and handicrafts in these regions. The available literature on Anáhuac, such as the work of Gibson, Osborn, Tutino, Riley, Konrad, Kicza, Taylor, Liehr, Nickel, Trautmann, Von Wobeser, García Martínez, Wood, Haskett, Thomson and Martin, focuses on the towns, villages, and haciendas, but there is very little discussion of the ranchos.[8] The idea is clear: in Michoacán and Guadalajara the haciendas and ranchos dominated; while in Anáhuac and Oaxaca, the villages were predominant.

Van Oss and Slicher van Bath were able to identify the demographic and economic characteristics of the four regions and to specify their boundaries with greater precision. The result was a geographical pattern divided into centers, intermediate zones, and peripheries. The centers were characterized by labor-intensive agriculture and gardening, handicrafts, commerce, and wheat cultivation. The production of food crops (wheat and maize) predominated in the intermediate zones. There was also livestock breeding, and in Anáhuac and Oaxaca *maguey* was cultivated, from which the light alcoholic drink *pulque* was made. It is striking that the mining provinces, with their own hinterland for the production of food crops and livestock breeding, formed separate enclaves and did not belong to the core areas mentioned. The only development of a large city in a mining province was that of Guanajuato, in the region of Michoacán. Mining was hardly integrated into the four regional economies of

New Spain. Of course, considerable overlap existed between the sparsely populated areas in western and northern Mexico, including Michoacán, Guadalajara, and the mining enclaves of Zacatecas and Parral. Domestic textiles, livestock, tobacco, wheat, and sugar were transported through deserted landscapes from enclave to enclave.[9]

Introducing a division into eight categories, Slicher presented a clear overview of 1,280 separate important economic activities in the 129 provinces of the *gobierno* of New Spain. The production of food crops accounted for a quarter of the economic activities. These food crops were cultivated close to the concentrations of population. Handicrafts were an urban activity. It was not profitable to transport low-priced foodstuffs over long distances in New Spain because of the difficulties raised by the mountainous geography of the area. Beasts of burden were expensive. With a simple pair of compasses, Brading declares,[10] a historical geographer can draw a series of concentric circles around each urban market and thus determine the price of maize as the market's supply zones expanded, contracted, and overlapped. Farming with large animals like cattle, horses, and mules, however, did not take place in the centers of population. The cultivation of plantation and cash crops was typical of the peripheral areas. To indicate with precision which economic activities predominated in specific areas, Slicher divided the provinces of New Spain according to population density. Combining his data, he distinguished five zones of intensity. The zone with the greatest population density and the largest cities was dominated by handicrafts, commerce, and the cultivation of vegetables. The second zone was a typically agricultural area: food crops, small livestock and horses. Here haciendas dominated the rural scene. The third zone was similar, but with more emphasis on maize, beans, plantation products and cash crops, cattle, and fruit. The fourth zone was characterized by minerals, some handicrafts, and natural gathering. The fifth zone was characterized by cacao, coconut palms, and docks.[11]

Combining economic data and population density, the provinces were classified in terms of their economic activities as the *many-sided economy*, the *supportive economy,* and the *one-sided economy.* The categories of handicrafts, commerce, vegetables, and fruit—the labor-intensive economic activities we would expect to find in areas with a high population density—belong to the many-sided economy. The supportive economy was characterized by the production of food crops, on a more extensive scale, and small livestock, which were supplied to provinces with higher concentrations of population; in some cases, they supplied the mining provinces (the enclaves!). The one-sided economy is composed of plantation products and cash crops, large livestock, minerals, and natural products. Overviewing this, one is immediately struck by the connection between large livestock breeding and the extraction of minerals. These activities went hand in hand in Europe as well, because of the large demand for leather as well as animal power in mining. It is also striking that the many-sided economy and the one-sided economy did not have much contact with one another. There was, indeed, no relation of dependence in

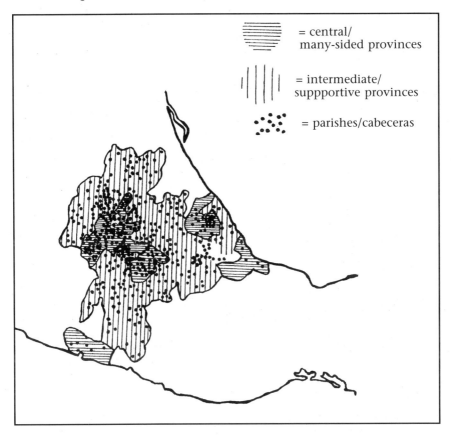

= central/
many-sided provinces

= intermediate/
suppportive provinces

= parishes/cabeceras

Map 4   Division of Anáhuac by structure of production into central and
intermediate provinces based on data from Van Oss and Slicher van Bath

this respect, despite the center-periphery models devised by the developmental economists or Wolf's famous remarks in his *Europe and the People without
History*, which describe a "political economy . . . in which each lower level
yielded surplus to the level above it."[12] The provinces with a supportive
economy supplied the other two economies with basic food crops.[13]

The correspondence between the geographical model devised by Slicher
and Van Oss and that of the German geographer von Thünen is remarkable.
Other scholars also have been able to demonstrate that the distance to be
covered in order to bring a certain product to the market could have a decisive
effect on its production. The high transport costs of the early modern era
meant that it was not long before high prices adversely affected the demand
for the products concerned. During the ancien régime transport by land was
very expensive because of the poor conditions. The large-scale use of wagons

and carts did not get under way in England until the end of the seventeenth century, and this phenomenon occurred in Castilia late in the eighteenth century. Cheap transport by inland waterways was an eighteenth-century phenomenon in some parts of Europe, and in other parts of the continent major canals were not created or rivers made navigable until the nineteenth century. The only alternative, beasts of burden, had a limited capacity. In New Spain the weight (*carga*) of a load that could be carried by a beast of burden was between 100 and 140 kg, sometimes as much as 170 kg (flour). Large-scale transport was carried out by caravans of mules. Agricultural producers will have tried to keep transport costs down as much as possible in order to remain competitive. Fresh products with a short life span were produced not far from the market. That is why market gardening, vegetable farming, and the production of other food crops took place as close as possible to the urban centers in economies with large cities. There was a direct correlation between distance from the towns and the intensity of land use. Extensive livestock breeding, with a high market value, was thus forced to the periphery of the economic system. The animals could cover the distance to the market by themselves. Von Thünen's concentric circles were also affected by the road network. Provinces with major roads had a more intensive economy than those without them.[14]

The categories introduced by Van Oss and Slicher can be combined to yield an economic structural typology of Anáhuac (see Map 4); a scheme in which, in general, the central provinces correspond to the provinces with a many-sided economy, the intermediate provinces correspond to those with a supportive economy, and the peripheral provinces correspond to those with a one-sided economy. From now on, I shall follow Van Oss in referring to *central provinces* and *intermediate provinces*. By combining these two types of provinces, we arrive at the economic units to which I refer as regions. The peripheral provinces accounted for the sparsely populated zone between the centers of population, and are therefore excluded from the regional division. There is a strikingly unambiguous pattern according to which the central provinces and the intermediate group form contiguous areas. Looking at the parishes included on the map (the black dots), it is immediately striking how densely populated the central provinces were.

The Anáhuac region was only one of the identified four economic units of the viceroyalty. The most important variants affecting this typology were the density of population, the ecological configuration, and the distance from the market. Changes in these variables led to changes in the pattern detected. The interaction between haciendas, ranchos, and townships undoubtedly were affected by population density and the settlement pattern. In view of their characteristic features, it is plausible to assign the provinces with a many-sided economy a larger number of townships than those with a supportive economy. The "supportive" provinces, on the contrary, were characterized by hacienda agriculture. That is why the interaction in an area with a many-sided economy may differ from the interaction in an area with a supportive

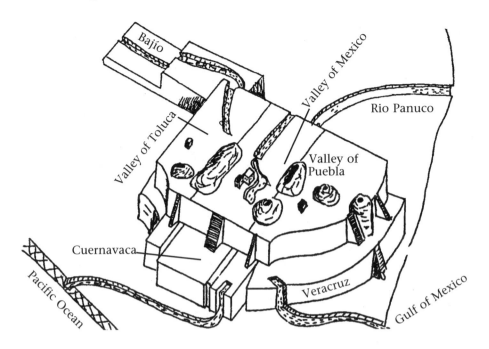

Figure 3   Diagram of Anáhuac's physical appearance.
Elaborated from a drawing by P. F. Gallagher, published in E. R. Wolf,
Sons of the Shaking Earth (Chicago, 1959), p. 7.

economy, while it may even be entirely absent in an area with a one-sided economy. The difference between these three kinds of economy will recur time and again in the following chapters.

Three Main Valleys

The plateau region of Anáhuac was the highest major agricultural area in Mexico, for the three other regions of New Spain—Michoacán, Guadalajara, and Oaxaca—were at a lower altitude. The surrounding volcano ridges made the trip to Anáhuac seem like a mountain climb. The route from the eastern harbor of Veracruz, where the ships from Spain, Cuba, Yucatán, and other Caribbean places were unloaded, was hardly passable. A climb of two thousand meters had to be accomplished in one hundred kilometers or so, and the last part of the journey was shrouded in thick mist because of the low clouds that always hung there. At the time, the only way to do it was to use mules. This led Humboldt to suppose that all kinds of export goods would never be able to compete on the export markets because of the high transport costs. Indeed, this was why Mexican wheat had lost the competition with Philadelphian wheat in La Habana, Cuba, in the late eighteenth century.[15] At the same time the difference in altitude favored autarky, because it promoted internal—for example—intraregional, trade. All imports were regarded as luxury items because of the high transport costs.

No illustration is clearer than the diagram of the central highlands drawn by Patrick F. Gallagher (see Figure 3), published more than thirty years ago by Wolf.[16] Since the volcanoes formed an extra barrier for transport in the highlands, I have added them to the diagram. A particular detail is furnished by the steps leading to the highlands. The roads from the surrounding mountains were as steep for the transporters who used mule transport as houses on the canals of Amsterdam, where it is an enormous task to get large items of furniture up to the second or third floor. All reports of the time contain dramatic narratives of the transport to and from the highlands. The climb from Veracruz was extremely dangerous. In 1783, Don Diego Panes y Abellán, an officer commissioned to assess the roads between this harbor city and Mexico City and to suggest improvements, regarded the *Cuesta del Soldado,* or Soldier's Mountain, near the city of Xalapa as the main obstacle. The mountain track was so narrow and slippery here that every caravan lost a few mules as they crashed down to the bottom. At this point, ropes and pulleys were used to haul not only the load up the slope, but the mules as well.[17]

There is another difference with the European visitor's homeland. In Europe, agricultural potential is mainly determined by temperature and rainfall. In Mexico and other tropical countries altitude is much more important. In fact, temperature and rainfall depend on altitude in these cases. That is why the commonest division of Mexico into climatological zones is in terms of altitude. The torrid zone, the *tierra caliente,* rises up to 600 meters above sea level and has an average annual temperature between 23° and 26°C. Between the 600-meter and 2,800-meter levels is the temperate zone, the *tierra templada,* with an average temperature between 17° and 24°C. This is the altitude of Anáhuac. Humboldt warns that the name *tierra templada* may be confusing for Europeans, because despite the temperate climate European crops grow more slowly at this altitude than in Europe.[18] The cold zone, the *tierra fría,* starts at an altitude of 2,800 meters and has an average temperature below 17°C. At around 4,000 meters (the timber line in Mexico) this zone gives way to the ice zone, the *tierra helada,* where the daily temperature rarely exceeds 10°C.

The quality of the soil is important for agriculture, because, of course, good agricultural ground is scarce. A densely populated region like Anáhuac was faced with the major difficulty that the best ground was already permanently under cultivation. According to the German geologist Werner, this already had led to large-scale erosion in the pre-Hispanic period. It is striking that Sherburne F. Cook came to the same conclusion in 1949 on the basis of a combination of fieldwork and documentation from 1540: the valley of Teotlalpan, an extension of the valley of Mexico in the north of Anáhuac, was already heavily eroded in the middle of the sixteenth century. Erosion had also taken place there before the arrival of the Spaniards, as a result of overpopulation and exhaustion of the soil in the valley in the fifteenth and six-teenth centuries.[19] In general, bringing new land under cultivation was only a short-term solution. After reasonable results were achieved at the initial stage, the yield on such land started to fall after a while. This can be deduced from the yield ratios of the products, which dropped sharply in such cases.[20] The yield falls as the ground becomes exhausted because the main nutritional ele-ments—the minerals—are used up; although the presence of these nutritional elements varies from one kind of soil to another.

In general, the younger soils in the temperate zones of the world are more fertile than the older ones in the tropics. The highlands of Anáhuac, however, have a combined alluvial and volcanic origin and are therefore relatively young. The best and most expensive agricultural land was land that could be well irrigated, called *pan llevar* in New Spain. This Spanish name is based on the production of grain on such soil: pan llevar was more or less a guarantee that good quality bread (*pan*) could be made from the grain. In New Spain land of this kind was used virtually exclusively for wheat. *Pan coger* was an inferior-quality soil that would at least sustain a harvest (*coger*). This soil was provided with plenty of water in the rainy season, but it could not be irrigated. The lowest-quality soil was called *pan sembrar,* whose general fertility was called into doubt. Farmers could sow (*sembrar*) on this land, but they must not ex-pect much of a harvest. The infertile soils had special names, too, most of them deriving from the pre-Hispanic period. The most well-known were *tequisquite*, brackish soil, and *tepetate*, a sort of consolidated tuff.

The highlands of Anáhuac consist of three large valleys: the valleys of Toluca, Mexico, and Puebla. The westernmost of these is the valley of Toluca, which has the most inclement climate of the three. It is situated at an altitude of 2,600 meters, an average of 200 meters higher than the valley of Mexico and 400 meters higher than the valley of Puebla. Toluca is therefore generally assumed to have twice as many days of night frost—more than half of the year—than Puebla. This is a negative factor in agriculture, indeed, one of its most terrible dangers. The main crops on the better soil here are maize and barley. The strip of agricultural land is relatively narrow; it is no wider than 60 kilometers and most of it is unusable because of the marshes (then, in the eighteenth century, more than now). The very poor drainage means that a lot of water is collected in the more central, lower parts of the valley in the rainy season. This marshy "lake" is the source of the river Lerma. Nevertheless, there were many settlements in the valley of Toluca during the pre-Hispanic period. The provinces that comprised the valley in the Spanish period were all very small and can be classified as central provinces with a many-sided economy. The forty or so Indian townships were very close to one another and faced competition from, especially, the extensive Atengo hacienda complex, which was owned by the rich count of Santiago Calimaya. The problem particularly affected the smaller peasants. And all this, in a situation in which population density was relatively high: excluding the faldas and using a conversion factor of 4.5 per tributario, the pueblos in the valley had about thirty inhabitants per square kilometer in 1730 and about forty per square kilometer in 1800. Of course, these figures are nothing but mere speculations; not including lakes and some mountainous areas, for example. But nevertheless, a contemporary claimed that it was as if the peasants in this valley had to squeeze three feet into one shoe.[21]

The central situated valley of Mexico has fewer night frosts, which in itself is enough to offer farmers more scope. The strip of agricultural land is about 60 kilometers wide and 100 kilometers long, but does not have natural drainage either. This resulted in the formation of large lakes: Chalco, Texcoco, Xaltocan and Zumpango. Before the arrival of the Spaniards, these lakes formed an elongated unit stretching from the north to the south of the valley. The *Mexica* had built their capital, Tenochtitlán, on the western bank of the largest lake. During the Spanish conquest, this city was destroyed and rebuilt in Spanish style within a few decades, when most of the canals of this pre-Hispanic Venice were filled in. The city was plagued by muddy streets and inundations far into the eighteenth century. A specialist from abroad was called in to improve the drainage artificially, but the channel that he designed was not completed until the end of the eighteenth century. In the meantime, the city was protected against the lake by embankments. These efforts were not in vain, for the level of the lake began to drop in the late eighteenth century. The natural link between the four lakes seemed to disappear. In the 1790s, the commentator Alzate was struck by the fact that the point where water was regularly to be found at the peak of the rainy season in the 1760s was completely dry twenty years later. The banks of the lake were in danger of becoming brackish because of evaporation, which entailed a loss of fertility. Alzate wrote:

> I remember that not so long ago a lot of people gathered in
> Candelaria in the east of the city to make a trip on the canals in the
> afternoon. Nowadays the water level of the canals has dropped to
> such an extent that nobody is to be found there because of all the
> dust that is blown about.[22]

Incidentally, Alzate wondered whether this was due to the drainage works. Deforestation had proceeded at such a pace over the years that the result was a drop in rainfall, for it is the woods that retain rain clouds. He may have been right.

Lake Chalco was a freshwater lake, and its shores were very suitable for agriculture. The villages of Xochimilco and Ixtapalapa had laid out their fields and vegetable gardens (*chinampas*) here on the shore. In 1825 the Englishman Mark Beaufoy saw more ducks and other waterbirds here "than in Holland." The Spanish priest Ajofrín, who visited New Spain in the 1760s, imagined that the addition of a few more trees would have made this region look like paradise. The adjacent lake of Texcoco, which had already been separated from Lake Chalco by a wall for a long time, though there were channels between the two lakes, was a saltwater lake because of the alkaline minerals there. Alzate noted the difference in flora and fauna between the two lakes. He even claimed that the fish in the two lakes had a different taste and color. The fish from Lake Texcoco were small and their flesh was yellowish, while the same fish from Lake Chalco had white flesh, were fair-sized, and could be used as a tasty main course. Alzate preferred the Chalco restaurants to the Texcoco ones; nowadays, the only places where one can get the same fresh fish are the cafés beside some small breeding lakes in the federal state of Morelos, to the south of Mexico City. Lake Texcoco is now practically dried up and has been turned into a sort of alkaline desert, although plans exist to revive it. The alkaline minerals already created problems for agriculture in the eighteenth century, because alkaline storms on the shores of the lakes in the spring spread the brackish dust from there, over the more fertile areas surrounding the lakes. These storms were caused by changes in the air currents in February and March. On the other hand, the process of becoming brackish had its advantages too, for there was a lot of salt extraction on the banks of the lakes, an economic activity mainly carried out by Indian commoners here, sometimes by their chiefs.[23] Nevertheless, this series of unfavorable circumstances did not discourage the farmers. Human labor produced a flourishing agrarian culture in the valley of Mexico. Like Toluca, it had a many-sided economy in the eighteenth century, but population density was considerably lower: about twenty-nine inhabitants per square kilometer in the *pueblos* around 1730 and some thirty-six per square kilometer in 1800; or double that ratio, if the lakes themselves are included in the calculations.[24]

The easternmost of the three valleys of Anáhuac is the valley of Puebla. It is more than 150 kilometers long and a good 100 kilometers wide. Of the three valleys, that of Puebla is a little below 2,000 meters. The drainage of the valley is better than in the others because of a riverbed in two of its appendages to the south, and especially because of the river Atoyac. (These extensions, or subsidiary valleys, are the smaller valleys of Atlixco and Tehuacán.) The valley of Puebla is at its widest in the eastern half. Here, in the eighteenth century, the provinces of San Juan de los Llanos and Tepeaca provided considerable opportunity for large-scale agriculture and livestock breeding. There were relatively few Indian communities. It is therefore understandable that in terms of the classification presented in the previous chapter, most of these provinces are labeled intermediate and generally had a supportive economy. The only area with a many-sided economy was a narrow strip in the western half near the cities of Puebla and Cholula, which included the province of Tecali and the southern part of the province of Tlaxcala. The central provinces also included the gently sloping valley of Atlixco, where the landscape was determined by a thriving wheat cultivation. In the seventeenth century, this valley was known as the granary of Anáhuac. These "many-sided provinces" are situated at the foot of high volcanoes. In all, this valley was significantly less populated than the two other valleys. And what is more, population density in the pueblos decreased between 1730 and 1800, from about nineteen Indians per square kilometer to about sixteen.

Besides the three large valleys with their relatively extensive agricultural area there are also a few smaller, narrower valleys on the borders of Anáhuac. These valleys are mainly situated in the northern foothills of the valley of Mexico. The brooks and streams that flow there and the ease of communication with the center of the region gave these valleys a certain popularity as immigration areas in the eighteenth century. However, the climate was already drier and hotter at that time, which could be a major obstacle to agriculture. Drought was a relatively recent phenomenon here, for the semiarid valleys were not always so dry. It is not rainfall that is the crucial point here, for it can never have been very much in any case. It is *ecological drought* that grew alarmingly over the years as a result of erosion. The overpopulation that took place before the arrival of the Spaniards was responsible for deforestation and erosion, resulting in the loss of the fertile layers of soil on the slopes of the valleys. Later on, this degradation seems to have been increased by the rapid expansion of cattle breeding, which would have radically changed the structure of the local flora and fauna. This seriously affected the capacity of the soil to retain enough water for the intensive agriculture upon which so many depended up to that time.[25]

Around the plateaus and their appendages is a gradually sloping mountain landscape, the faldas or sierra. Population density here was lower in the eighteenth century than on the highlands and agriculture was extremely difficult because of the slopes, which could be very steep at times. The faldas include the agricultural land on the edge of the plateaus. Despite the fact that these areas had a somewhat autonomous development, their economy was connected with the highland economy. The townships on the flanks supplied the highland markets with tropical fruit, cotton, coffee, cacao, baskets, mats and other handicrafts. As has been shown,[26] the villages on the flanks exerted a clear attraction to the poor population of Anáhuac in times of scarcity, especially in the major drought years. But even then, one notes that the agricultural land in the region of Anáhuac was generally so limited in size that the inhabitants were in danger of rapidly running up against a situation of relative overpopulation.

Weather

Rainfall and Climatological Zones

As we have seen, it is above all the precipitation in Mexico—or lack of rainfall—that strikes the foreign visitor as extraordinary. Ajofrín wrote in his travel account that the rain did not form small brooks, as it did in Europe, but enormous rivers at times. The fact that the streets of Mexico City were turned into canals during the rainy season enabled him to gain a picture of what the old city of Tenochtitlán must have looked like. During Ajofrín's visit to Mexico in 1763–66 the city was practically inaccessible for long time. It was a miracle, he thought, that the city was not flooded by the rising current of Lake Texcoco. According to the priest, the water level usually dropped after an impressive

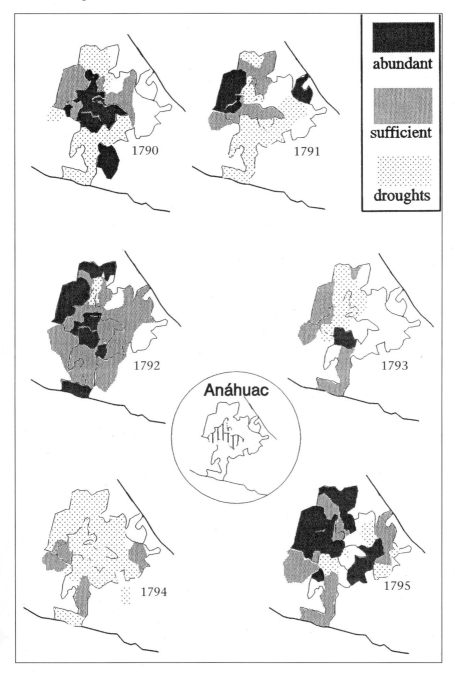

Map 5   The pattern of rainfall in some provinces of Anáhuac, 1790–95

procession had passed through Mexico City, but he was still unable to account for where all that water had come from in such a short time. The situation in Puebla was often pretty much the same. The Italian Gemelli, who
visited the viceroyalty in 1697, saw houses and animals being borne away in a
strong flood current that surged through the city. He later discovered that
four men and two women had drowned in the flood on the same day. He too
had gazed at the spectacle in astonishment. The chaos that the rains can cause
is portrayed in an inimitable way in the first paragraphs of Juan Rulfo's "Es
que somos muy pobres" from the collection *El llano en llamas,* where the rain
is responsible for a massive inundation within three days and wreaks enormous havoc. It is also worth comparing the description of an incredible flood
in García Márquez's short story "Monologue of Isabel Watching it Rain in
Macondo."[27]

The rain falls in Mexico between May and October. There is a brief rainy
period in the early spring, usually in February or March, in the valley of Puebla.
This is used for the sowing of the summer crops. The rains that fall throughout the country from May on are not isolated showers: it is as if, starting with
the first drizzle in May, the rainfall increases every day in volume and duration. This development reaches its climax in July, when it pours for days on
end. After this, the rainfall drops off. It is remarkable that despite these beating downpours and the floods, there is not an excessive amount of rainfall
over the year as a whole. With an average rainfall of 700 to 800 mm per annum,
Anáhuac has less rain than France, for example, which has an annual average
of 1,030 mm. Other tropical regions, such as Tabasco (south Mexico) or Java
(Indonesia) have an annual rainfall that is five times as much (3,800 mm in
Tabasco, 3,500 mm on Java). The effect of the rainfall in Mexico is also less
than a European might be inclined to suppose. The many hours of sunshine
and the more rarefied and drier air reduce the beneficial effect of the water.
This led a Mexican geographer to conclude that his country is "thirsty." However, this thirst is not shared by everyone equally. In general, it can be stated
that the mountainous areas and the volcanoes attract the rain clouds and
retain them. Irrigation is possible on the plateaus surrounding the volcanoes.
The water streams down the slopes in broad channels, which have been there
for a very long time and have acquired their shape and course from the repetition of the same cycle over the centuries. In the winter, these riverbeds are
dry, but in the summer it is usual for an impressive volume of water to pour
down. Of course, the locals are familiar with this phenomenon and try to
collect the water in reservoirs so that they can irrigate during the dry winter
months.[28]

Rain arrives from the northeast. The landscape relief guarantees a decreas-
ing intensity of the showers as they move towards the southwest. One would
therefore expect the supportive-economy provinces in the valley of Puebla to
have a higher rainfall than the economically more many-sided provinces in
the two other large valleys. The volcanoes I mentioned earlier exert an influence here. The beautiful valley of Puebla is, in fact, the land between the

volcanoes. On a clear day five volcanoes can be seen from the city of Puebla: Popocatepetl (5,452 m) and Ixtaccihuatl (5,286 m) in the west, Malintzi (4,461 m) in the north (Tlaxcala), and Citlaltepetl, also known as Pico de Orizaba, (5,747 m, the highest point in Mexico) and Cofre de Perote (4,282 m) in the east. Popocatepetl and Ixtaccihuatl, which form the natural boundary between the valleys of Mexico and Puebla, can also be seen from Mexico City. There is also a volcano in the valley of Toluca: Xinantecatl, or Nevado de Toluca (4,680 m). The volcanoes of Puebla are relatively close to one another and therefore form a center of attraction for rain clouds.

However, the expectation of a high rainfall intensity in Puebla is not borne out by the facts. The volcanoes and mountains attract as many clouds as possible. As far as the eighteenth century is concerned, this can be seen from documents from the period 1790–95 that describe the rainfall and the harvests and link the two together. The data illustrate the general pattern of rainfall, particularly in the western part of Anáhuac (see Map 5). The period covered here is that extending from May to August, that is, the *first half* of the rainy season. This period is exceptionally important for the success of the maize harvest. The map clearly indicates where the scarcity made its presence felt if the rainy season began late. During this period, there was sufficient rain in 1790 and 1795 and too much in 1792. In 1791, there was enough rain for the maize in some of the central provinces, but other provinces experienced a drought. A sharp reduction in rainfall prevented a good maize harvest in 1793. The year 1794 was one of absolute drought; the only places to receive sufficient rain were the central provinces of Anáhuac situated between the volcanoes. The data also indicate that during this six-year period the most rain fell in the provinces adjoining the western mountain ridge of Anáhuac (Ixtlahuaca-Metepec and Xilotepec), which formed the boundary with the Michoacán region, and the provinces of Chalco and Huejotzingo at the foot of the two volcanoes in the heart of Anáhuac. There was also sufficient rain in the flat areas between the two relief accents mentioned here: the provinces in the valleys of Mexico and Toluca. Unfortunately, the data on the valley of Puebla are incomplete. The impression that one gains is that there was enough rain there, but not so much as in the two western valleys of Anáhuac. In Puebla, irrigation appears to be essential for good agriculture in periods when Chalco, Huejotzingo, and Toluca can do without it.[29] Map 5 suggests a relation between rainfall and the intensity of economic activity that cannot be ignored. During this six-year period, the provinces with a many-sided economy in the center of Anáhuac received more rain than those marked by a supportive economy. This link, though obvious, should be stressed: people had settled in the most favorable areas.

The German geographers Lauer and Klaus have described how rainfall in Puebla is stimulated by the sun. The cycle of the sun and the altitude of the plateau landscape operate as a duo. In the rainy season, the sun rises around 5:00 hours. It takes about an hour for it to warm up the valleys. The rise in temperature is accompanied by wind on the plateaus. After noon they increase in tempo, and in the course of the day they blow rain clouds over the highlands with great force. They group the rain clouds around the volcanoes. If the temperature is lower, as it is after midnight or in the spring and autumn, the rain clouds cannot rise high enough to water the highlands. In this case, they come up against the faldas. Hence the Sierra Norte de Puebla in the north of the province of San Juan de los Llanos and the provinces of Huachinango, Huayacocotla, and Sochicoatlán on the northeastern flanks receive rainfall all year round. As the temperature starts to drop in the afternoon, the rains begin to fall on the highlands. In the rainy season the sun sets at around 19:00 hours, but the wind circulation continues for a few hours longer because the landscape, which has received such intense light from the sun during the day, is still releasing warmth. This phenomenon is reinforced by the warmth released by the low-hanging clouds, which are already present, and the humid air. The air circulation continues to attract clouds from the northeast. The rainfall reaches its highest frequency at sunset, between 17:00 and 18:00 hours. In the higher volcanic regions it can keep on raining deep into the night.[30]

The most obvious place for an Indian township to settle in the relatively dry valley of Puebla was thus on or close to the slopes of a ridge of hills or of a volcano. This was already the case in the pre-Hispanic period. After the invasion, some townships (referred to as *congregaciones;* see next chapter) were founded in the center of the valley in the early seventeenth century, it is true, but these were exceptions. The village of Tecamachalco, for example, was situated on the southern slope of a hilltop that attracted a lot of rain. In fact, rainfall was so heavy in the early spring and the first months of the summer, in particular, that the streets of the village were regularly inundated. Nobody minded, however, because the vegetable gardens and fields behind the houses were irrigated by channels which ingeniously dispersed the flood of water from the streets. Tecamachalco was therefore a garden center in the province of Tepeaca, dominated as it was by wheat and maize haciendas. There was even enough water left to irrigate the wheat fields of the Spanish entrepreneurs and to drive a few grain mills.[31]

On the basis of the combination of altitude and rainfall, Anáhuac as a whole can be divided into three types of climate in accordance with the generally accepted classification of Köppen (see Map 6). The expansive center of the plateau has a so-called China climate. This type of climate corresponds to the temperate maritime climates and is characterized by a dry winter. The three valleys of Anáhuac are of this type, with the exception of the southeast of the valley of Puebla (the province of Tehuacán) and the northern part of the valleys of Toluca and Mexico (the provinces of Ecatepec, Teotihuacán, Pachuca, Tetepango, Actopan and Ixmiquilpan). These areas have a semiarid climate with a long, dry winter (steppe climate). The southern flanks, including a small "sugar plateau" in the provinces of Cuernavaca, Cuautla Amilpas, and Izúcar, have a subtropical climate with a dry winter. The transition from the northeastern plateau to the Caribbean embraces all three climatic types: a temperate climate, with rainfall all year round on the edge of the plateau; a

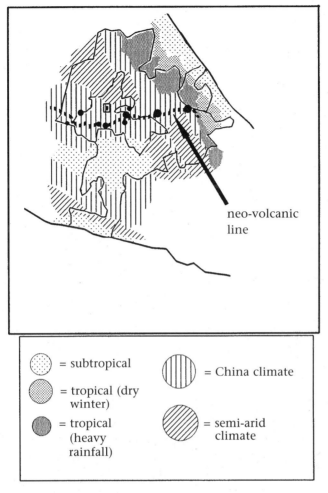

neo-volcanic
line

◌ = subtropical   ▥ = China climate

◍ = tropical (dry
        winter)

● = tropical   ▨ = semi-arid
        (heavy   climate
        rainfall)

Map 6   The five types of climate in Anáhuac, Köppen classification

tropical climate, with heavy rains in the summer; and a tropical climate, with
dry winters in the lower regions. This means that it is only the higher parts of
the northeastern faldas that receive rainfall in every season; this is the area
lying in the route along which the summer rains are driven and where rain
clouds hang all year round. It will be obvious that the division of the plateau
into a temperate maritime climate and a semiarid climate is particularly important for the theme of the present inquiry, since agriculturalists in the regions with a semiarid climate have to manage with little water.

Anáhuac as a whole can be classified as tierra templada, but primarily it is
the two dominant types of climate mentioned here that have affected agriculture. The regional differences emerge clearly from an overview in which the

Table 3 Rainfall in seven cities of Anáhuac (1976)

Cities	altitude (m)	rainfall (mm)	average annual temperature (Celsius)
Toluca	2,675	800.2	12.7
Tlaxcala	2,552	802.3	16.2
México	2,240	720.8	15.1
Puebla	2,209	822.9	17.1
Pachuca	2,435	386.8	14.2
Cuernavaca	1,529	1,061.0	20.7
Xalapa	1,487	1,514.8	17.9

Source: *Nuevo Atlas Porrua de la República Mexicana* (Mexico City, 1980)

rainfall for seven different settlements in Anáhuac is given in millimeters (see Table 3). The highland cities of Mexico City, Puebla, Tlaxcala, and Toluca have roughly the same amount of rainfall and differ from the dry city of Pachuca, situated in an area with a semiarid climate; subtropical Cuernavaca in the southern faldas; or the very humid city of Xalapa on the northeastern flanks. Despite these differences, however, the highlands of Anáhuac have the advantage of forming a relatively large geographical unit, which makes it easier to interpret and compare the data in the archives of haciendas and villages, which were scattered over the highlands. Although they formed part of the domestic market of Anáhuac, the provinces in the faldas cannot be included in this analysis because of the large discrepancies in density of population, pattern of settlement, type of climate,' and characteristics of the landscape.

A Selection from Weather Reports

Of course, the weather obeys its own rules, but not according to a day-to-day fixed plan. At this point, the possibility of a shortcut emerges to specify the alternation between rainfall and drought. I have scrutinized 3,650 weather reports for the years 1775–85 in order to gain some idea of this alternation. Gibson published data based on the daily reports of Don Felipe de Zuñiga y Ortiveras, a publisher, covering the preceding period of 1763–73 on the weather in Tacubaya. The astronomical bureau of Mexico City, in Tacubaya, kept records of the position of the planets and the course of the weather from 1595 on (!), though most of the data seem to be lost.[32] From my experience of the area and from having combed through a sizable number of weather reports, I feel on almost familiar terms with Don Felipe. The following account is a selection from the notes Don Felipe made in Tacubaya, with some particular attention to 1775 (a bad agricultural year) and 1781 (a good year). The account shows how variable the climate could be and gives us the foundation to discuss the consequences of climatic changes.

The records I consulted open in January 1775 with the clear sky of New Year's Day. There was a flash of lightning in the afternoon and a shower of rain. Tacubaya can be very unpleasant at moments like this. The town is closer to the mountains that surround the valley of Mexico than Mexico City is, and the rainfall is higher there. The first week in 1775 was rainy and very cold. Don Felipe records that the volcanoes on the outskirts of the city were covered with ice. There was even ice and heavy night frost in the city from 7 to 12 January. Although the weather cleared up afterward to some extent, by the end of the month he was still noting overcast afternoons and even days when it never stopped raining (exceptional weather for Mexico for the time of year!). January 1781, the first month of a good year for the harvest, also began with clear skies and cold temperatures, and there were showers at the end of the month.

February and March 1775 were better than January had been. The cold was over and Don Felipe recorded more clear mornings. All the same, it was very windy and it rained in the afternoon. The peaks of the volcanoes remained covered with a layer of ice during the month of February, but it melted once the temperature began to rise at the end of February. Don Felipe even recorded a few hot days in the middle of March, which were immediately followed by thunderstorms. This was not unusual for the time of year. It was the time for night frost and north winds (*nortes*), an inheritance of the North American winter. There were heavy rains during this period in 1776, although the following year was a very dry one. In 1777, when the population of the city was hit at precisely the same time by a typhoid epidemic that not even the members of the elite were spared, the spring was a very dry one. The pattern in other years (1778, 1779, 1780, 1781) followed that of 1776: thus, bad weather in March was not the rule in Tacubaya. It was particularly bad weather for people like Don Felipe, who complained that it was very difficult to move about in the city during the downpours. That is still the case, although the streets are not flooded so quickly anymore. Of course, the farmers never complained, because this weather was favorable for sowing the crops.

The temperature usually rose in April. The *nortes* had passed and the chilly and sometimes rainy days were followed by a hot period. Nevertheless, during the hot noons of 6 to 13 April 1775 (Maundy Thursday) there were still strong gusts of wind. Don Felipe noted that during this period the population succumbed to epidemics of a special eye virus, with stitches in their side and fever. The same was true for 1777, 1781, and 1784; a striking sequence. In 1784 it was extremely cold until late in April, with an unusual degree of night frost and extremely low temperatures. The month of April was not always completely dry. Downpours were noted for this month in every year between 1775 and 1785. In 1777, the heat alternated with thunderstorms in the afternoon, and on 2 April a church was struck by lightning. The sky was dull at the beginning of April 1777, but heavy clouds gained the upper hand around the twenty-fifth. There had even been storms on the sixteenth and seventeenth. In 1781, March and April were months of clear weather, overcast at times, and later followed by the first summer showers.

The rainy season was due to begin in May. That was the case in 1776, 1778, and 1779 (although it did not amount to more than drizzle in both years), and in 1780 and 1785. In 1777 and 1783, the rainy season began in April, marked by overcast skies, downpours, and thunderstorms with lightning. Don Felipe recorded a lot of hot days; he did not like it at all. In 1775, 1781, 1782, and 1784 the rainy season began late, and on 19 May of that year the image of the *Virgen de los Remedios* was carried through the city and placed in the cathedral to call for rain, which was a usual measure. To this saint, a statue of about thirty to forty centimeters, was devoted a small church in the mountains to the west of Mexico City, and she had to be carried down some twenty kilometers. The first rainstorms (*aguaceros*) began the next day. In 1785, the Virgin was placed in the cathedral on 14 May and removed on the twenty-third, once it was realized that the rainy season had begun. The manager of the Hacienda Molino de Flores near Texcoco reported a heavy hailstorm on the twenty-second of that month, but not the end of the drought.[33] Sometimes there was night frost in May: this was the case on 15, 16, 29, and 30 May 1777. There were reports of epidemics in 1779 (smallpox) and 1784. In 1781, there were afternoon showers on 1, 2, 6, 7, 9, 10, 13, 15, 18 (evening), and 19 May, and from 24 May the rainy season had begun.

However, the rains of May did not always continue, and that was a cause for much concern. In 1775, for example, the rainy season was delayed. May was too dry and too hot, and June was overclouded into the bargain. There were occasional showers. The manager of the Hacienda Molino de Flores complained bitterly about the drought in June. He was relieved when work on the land could finally begin in July after a few showers had fallen, although the storm on 11 July, which blew off the storehouse roof, was too much of a good thing. August was hot too, with showers in the afternoons accompanied by thunder and lightning. On 28 July, someone died after being struck by lightning in Coyoacán, one of the eight victims that month. The rainy season had now begun in earnest, and sometimes heavy torrents fell for days on end. The complaining had stopped now in Molino de Flores. The intensity dropped at the end of September, and Don Felipe reported more clear days again in Tacubaya, with occasional frost at night. The weather had turned cold. At the end of the year, he noted that the late arrival of the rainy season had damaged the harvests, although things had not been so bad in the provinces of Chalco and near Toluca. This was not unusual. Droughts in May and June and rains out of season were reported by Don Felipe in 1768, 1770, 1771, 1772, and 1773, with shortages of all grains but above all in maize in 1768, 1771, and 1772 (wheat in 1768, 1769, and 1770), while 1773 saw immature ears in some areas.

Because this was an extremely important period for agriculture, I have investigated rainfall for a number of years in succession. In 1776, the downpours of May were not followed by regular rainfall. In fact, it was a dry year, in which the rainy season did not really get under way until July. The Virgen de los Remedios was transported to the cathedral on 16 June in the hope of rain. The first shower followed soon afterward, on 2 July. It coincided with the birth of quintuplets. The inhabitants of Mexico City saw a clear connection between the two events and many of them visited the five girls, who were all to be baptized Maria Isabel. The babies were overwhelmed with presents. However, the rain kept on pouring from the sky for the rest of the month. Don Felipe does not mention whether the quintuplets continued to enjoy their popularity later on, but most of the people caught a cold from the heavy, cold showers of July and August.

In 1777, the rainy season was late in starting as well. The drizzle of May was not followed by increasingly showery weather in June. The showers did not come until July, and after a few weeks of heavy showers at the end of August and the end of September, October marked the end of the rainy season for that year. In 1778, most farmers were pleased with the heavy rains that fell in June. The Virgen de los Remedios had been transferred to the cathedral on 7 June as a precautionary measure, but she could be removed again on the sixteenth. It rained continuously on 11, 12, 13, and 14 June (so that the Virgin had to stay longer in the cathedral than had been intended). In fact, the stormy weather continued right up to the middle of October, when the sun began to appear regularly again. Don Felipe counted fourteen fine mornings in July, nine in August and eight in September. He also recorded that it was a very good year for the rains. Moreover, the first night frost and ice did not come until 30 October, an unusual occurrence. The agriculturalists were guaranteed a good harvest. The stormy weather was accompanied by heavy outbursts of thunder and lightning. On 29 July, the choir of the Carmelite monastery *El Desierto de los Leones* in the mountains to the west of Mexico City was struck. There were many monks present at the time, and three were killed. The monks were still getting over their shock a few weeks later, when a church in the city was struck on 21 August. Not much damage was caused this time, but three people were fatally struck by lightning on an unspecified street corner in Mexico City that day.

In 1779, Don Felipe de Zuñiga's record was overshadowed by the serious epidemic of measles and smallpox in the city. He first mentioned this epidemic in May 1779, and tried to connect it with the position of the planets, though without success. Once again, it was exceptionally dry. The Virgen de los Remedios was carried to the cathedral in a large procession on 13 June and stayed there until the twenty-second. The procession was larger than usual because of the epidemic. People hoped for a miracle. The rain fell in showers in the afternoons—although the rainy season did not start properly until August—but the epidemic spread. Reports of victims came from Puebla and Veracruz as well. Now Don Felipe claimed to have discovered certain irregu-

larities in the position of the planets. It was decided to ask the Virgin to inter-
cede again on 17 October. The entire patriciate of the city joined in the procession. However, no sooner had the procession left the church on the way to
the cathedral than it was overtaken by such a heavy shower that people were
forced to shelter in the nearest church. It cleared up immediately, but the
people did not venture to continue the procession to the cathedral until a few
days later. Hospitals were opened and reopened, including the hospital of San
Andrés, which had been in Jesuit hands until 1767. The epidemic was not
over until February 1780. Don Felipe gives a figure of 12,345 fatalities, but he
noted with satisfaction that 44,990 people had been cured.

The rainy season was also late in 1780. The Virgen de los Remedios was
taken to the cathedral on 4 June. The first rain clouds appeared on 18 June,
followed by downpours a few days later. July was dry, despite a thunderstorm
on the eighth. The altar of Saint Joseph in the basilica of Guadalupe was struck
by lightning at exactly 16:30 hours. The first real shower of the rainy season
fell on 18 September and caused a massive inundation in the city in the brief
period between 17:00 and 20:00 hours. Although the showers decreased in
October, the farmers were hit by severe night frost on the fifteenth and seventeenth, which affected all the crops that had been sown late. Don Felipe recorded the menace of a bad harvest because of the late start of the rainy season
and the night frost in October. He was already afraid that there would be
famine, and he was right. The manager of the Hacienda Molino de Flores,
who had shown concern over the bad weather for years, reported striking
grain and livestock losses for that year. The drought had even caused the death
of seventy-one of his oxen. However, the damage caused by the night frost in
October was less than expected, and the maize that had been sown late could
still be harvested.

As an example of a good agricultural year, it comes as no surprise that
1781 was a rainy year in Zuñiga's records. It rained every day from morning to
evening during the periods 10–16 and 26–31 July. There were only six afternoons in August when there were no heavy showers. Although the intensity
of the rains dropped in September and October, the weather remained wet. As
usual, the rainy season ended with the arrival of night frost, which began on
5 October. Surprisingly enough, the good harvests were not reflected in the
prices of agricultural products. Don Felipe attributed the high level of prices to
the war in the Caribbean, which was absorbing large quantities of wheat, beans,
chick peas, and ham.

The autumn was chilly and cold almost every year, according to Don Felipe.
The weather was often fine, although there were occasional reports of night
frost, ice, and hail storms (if there was any precipitation at all). In fact, such
frosts could cause a lot of damage, before the maize had reached maturity.
During the preceding decade of 1763–73, this had occurred in 1771 and 1773,
but then only in some areas. The last months of the year were not completely
dry. Although the mornings usually remained dry, clouds, cloud banks, and
heavy rain clouds made their appearance in the afternoon. In 1775, there was

rain on isolated days: 2, 9, 18, 27, and 28 October; 9, 18, 25, and 28 November; and 26 and 27 December. In 1776, the rainy season continued until late in September, which was extremely favorable for the maize that had been sown late. The delayed arrival of the night frost was a very important compensation for the late arrival of the rainy season. The following year, the rainy season extended into October. November and December were completely dry. The major event during these months was the serious earthquake in Veracruz on 9 October, which will be discussed later in this chapter. In 1778, the rainy season appeared to have ended prematurely on 18 September, but there were a lot of overcast and very rainy days in early October and at the end of November. The autumn of 1779, the year of the smallpox epidemic, was dry but very cold, just as in 1780. In 1781, it rained regularly in October, but in November there were more clear days than overcast ones. December 1781 was a month of clear and cold weather, although there were heavy thunderstorms on 21, 22, 23, 24, and 25 December. The autumn of 1782, 1783, 1784, and 1785 was much the same.

Don Felipe de Zuñiga's records demonstrate the increasing dryness of the months of May and June. Besides 1768, 1771, and 1772, the years 1775, 1776, 1777, 1778, 1779, 1780, and 1785 were too dry for maize producers in the valley of Mexico in the late spring; ten years—and almost in a row! The main problem facing the farmers of Anáhuac was not the rainfall, even though it was excessive at times, but the absence of rainfall. The regular recurrence of drought was particularly catastrophic during the important weeks of the growing season, a point to which I shall now turn.

Implications

Harvest and Climate

Generally speaking, the growing season starts with the last night frost of the spring and ends with the first night frost of the autumn. The daily minimum temperature is above 5.5°C during this period. Wheat requires a minimum temperature of 3° to 4°C if it is to germinate properly. It was possible to sow the wheat before the end of the period of night frost by irrigating the fields during the night; this was the only remedy against the night frost, which dries out the plants on the surface of the soil. This extended the wheat growing season and was even necessary for a good harvest of summer wheat. The farmers who had the right to carry out irrigation at night were at an advantage; during daytime it would have evaporated on the fields too fast. Not all hacendados had this right, however. They were compelled to collect water during the daytime and store it for night irrigation. Maize needs at least 10°C if it is to germinate properly; that is why it was not sown on the highlands of Anáhuac until March. The conditions for germination of the Mexican beans are identical. European beans, on the other hand, such as broad beans and peas, can stand lower temperatures during the germination period. In fact, peas do not produce any seed if the temperature is too high.

Table 4 Rainfall and the wheat and maize situation in thirty Anáhuac provinces, 1790–1797

Provinces	1790 SA/FH	1791 SA/FH	1792 SA/FH	1793 SA/FH	1794 SA/FH	1795 SA/FH	1797 SA/FH
			Wheat				
1 Chalco	aa/ag	gg/gg	ag/gg	-p/-p	pp/gg	-a/-a	p-/p-
Coyoacán	aa/gg	pg/pp	aa/pp	-p/-g	pp/gg	-a/-g	p-/p-
Xochmilco	aa/pp	gg/gp	gg/gg	-p/-p	pp/pp	-a/-p	p-/p-
Tacuba	aa/gg	pg/pp	gg/gg	-p/-a	pp/gg	-a/-a	p-/p-
Cuautitlán	ga/gg	pp/pp	gp/gp	-p/-g	pg/gg	-a/-a	g-/p-
Otumba	ga/pg	pg/gg	aa/gp	-p/-p	pp/pp	-g/-g	p-/p-
Teotihuacán	aa/pp	pg/gp	gg/ap	-p/-p	pp/pa	-a/-g	g-/p-
Texcoco	aa/ag	pg/gp	gp/gg	-p/-g	pg/gg	-g/-g	p-/p-
2 Lerma	ga/ga	gg/gg	gg/gg	-g/-a	pp/gp	-a/-g	p-/p-
Metepec	ga/gg	gg/gg	ag/gg	-p/-g	pp/gg	-a/-g	p-/p-
Toluca	aa/ag	gg/gg	ag/gg	-p/-g	pp/ga	-a/-g	g-/p-
Ixtlahuaca	ga/ag	ga/gg	aa/gg	-g/-a	pp/gg	-a/-p	p-/a-
Tenango V.	aa/ag	gg/gp	gg/gg	-g/-g	gp/gg	-a/-g	a-/p-
Malinalco	ga/ag	pp/gp	aa/gg	-p/-p	pp/ga	-g/-a	p-/p-
3 Actopan	pg/gp	pp/-p	pp/pp	-p/ p	pp/p-	-g/-p	p-/p-
Ixmiquilpan	pa/-p	ga/gp	gg/gg	-p/-p	pp/pg	-g/-g	p-/p-
Metztitlán	pa/-p	pp/-p	ag/g-	-p/—	pp/—	-a/-p	p-/p-
Tulancingo	pg/ag	gg/pp	gg/gp	-p/-p	pp/gg	-a/-g	p-/p-
4 Pachuca	gg/ii	pg/ii	pp/ii	-p/ii	pp/ii	-g/-p	p-/p-
Tetepango	aa/-p	gp/gp	ag/gp	-p/-p	pp/pp	-a/-p	p-/p-
Tula	gg/gg	gg/gg	ag/gg	-p/-g	pp/ga	-a/-g	p-/p-
Zumpango L.	aa/gg	pg/pp	pp/pp	-p/-p	pp/pp	-a/-p	p-/p-
Ecatepec	aa/ag	pp/pp	gp/gp	-p/-p	pp/pp	-a/-g	p-/p-
Zempoala	pg/-g	pg/gp	gp/pp	-p/-p	pp/pp	-p/-p	p-/—
Apam	aa/gg	gg/gg	ap/gp	-p/-p	pp/gp	-a/-g	p-/p-
5 Yahualica	pa/ii	pa/ii	aa/ii	-g/-i	pp/ii	-a/-i	p-/p-
Cuernavaca	aa/gp	pp/-p	aa/pp	-a/-p	pg/ii	-p/-i	p-/p-
Chilapa	pg/ii	pa/ii	ga/ii	-g/-i	gp/ii	-g/-i	p-/p-
Taxco	pg/ii	pg/ii	gg/ii	-p/-i	—/—	-a/-i	p-/p-
Temascaltepec	pa/ip	gg/gp	gg/gp	-g/-p	ga/gg	-g/-g	g-/g-

Table 4 (continued)

Provinces	1790 SA/FH	1791 SA/FH	1792 SA/FH	1793 SA/FH	1794 SA/FH	1795 SA/FH	1797 SA/FH
				Maize			
1 Chalco	aa/ag	gg/gg	ag/ga	–p/–p	pp/pp	a–/g–	pp/–a
Coyoacán	aa/ag	pg/pg	aa/gg	–p/–p	pp/gp	a–/g–	pp/–g
Xochmilco	aa/ag	gg/gg	gg/gg	–p/–p	pp/pp	a–/g–	pp/–p
Tacuba	aa/ag	pg/gg	gg/gp	–p/–a	pp/pp	a–/g–	pp/–g
Cuautitlán	ga/gg	pp/gp	gp/gg	–p/–p	pg/pp	a–/g–	gg/–a
Otumba	ga/ag	pg/gg	aa/ag	–p/–p	pp/pp	g–/g–	pp/–p
Teotihuacán	aa/ag	pg/pg	gg/gg	–p/–p	pp/pp	a–/g–	gg/–a
Texcoco	aa/ag	pg/pg	gp/gg	–p/–p	pg/pp	g–/p–	pp/–p
2 Lerma	ga/ag	gg/ga	gg/gg	–g/–g	pp/pp	a–/g–	pp/–g
Metepec	ga/ag	gg/ga	ag/gg	–p/–p	pp/pp	a–/g–	pp/–p
Toluca	aa/ag	gg/ga	ag/ga	–p/–g	pp/gp	a–/g–	gg/–p
Ixtlahuaca	ga/ag	ga/gg	aa/gp	–g/–p	pp/gp	a–/g–	pp/–p
Tenango V.	aa/ag	gg/gg	gg/ga	–g/–g	gp/gp	a–/p–	aa/–a
Malinalco	ga/ag	pp/gp	aa/pp	–p/–p	pp/pp	g–/g–	pp/–p
3 Actopan	pg/gg	pp/gg	pp/gp	–p/–p	pp/pp	g–/g–	pp/–p
Ixmiquilpan	pa/ag	ga/gg	gg/gg	–p/–p	pp/pp	g–/g–	pp/–p
Metztitlán	pa/ag	pa/ga	ag/gg	–p/–p	pp/pp	a–/g–	pp/–p
Tulancingo	pg/ag	gg/gg	gg/gg	–p/–p	pp/pp	a–/p–	pp/–p
4 Pachuca	gg/pp	pg/–p	pp/pp	–p/–p	pp/pp	g–/g–	pp/–p
Tetepango	aa/ag	gp/gg	ag/gg	–p/–p	pp/pp	a–/p–	pp/–p
Tula	gg/gg	gg/gg	ag/pp	–p/–p	pp/pp	a–/g–	pp/–g
Zumpango L.	aa/ag	pg/pp	pp/pg	–p/–p	pp/pp	a–/g–	pp/–p
Ecatepec	aa/ag	pp/gp	gp/pp	–p/–p	pp/pp	a–/g–	pp/–p
Zempoala	pg/gg	pg/pa	gp/gp	–p/–p	pp/pp	p–/p–	pp/–p
Apam	aa/ag	gg/gg	ap/gg	–p/–p	pp/pp	a–/g–	pp/–p
5 Yahualica	pa/a–	pa/pp	aa/pp	–g/–i	pp/ii	a–/g–	pp/–p
Cuernavaca	aa/ag	pp/gg	aa/gg	–a/–g	pg/ii	p–/p–	pp/—
Chilapa	pg/gg	pa/ga	ga/gg	–g/–g	gp/ii	g–/g–	pp/–p
Taxco	pg/gp	pg/gg	gg/gp	–p/–p	—/—	a–/g–	pp/–g
Temascaltepec	pa/ap	gg/gg	gg/gg	–g/–g	ga/gg	g–/g–	gg/–a

Legend:

1. valley of Mexico
2. valley of Toluca
3. northern valleys
4. semiarid provinces
5. faldas

Rainfall:

S = spring
A = autumn

Harvests:

F = fields sown
H = harvest

Quality:

a = abundant
g = good/sufficient
p = poor/meagre/or bad
i = imported
– = unknown

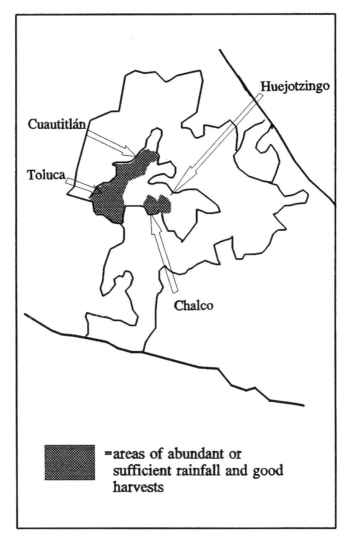

Map 7   Area of repeated good harvests in Anáhuac, 1790–97

There are also differences in the amount of water required by each crop. Wheat cannot tolerate an absence of water during the initial period of growth, nor can maize tolerate it in the late period of growth. The critical phase for wheat is in the winter, but it was usually possible to get around this problem by irrigation. The critical period for maize is in the late spring, from April to July. As indicated above, this is precisely the period when the rainy season is due to begin. In the eighteenth century, maize was usually cultivated without irrigation (*de temporal*), but even if irrigation was possible—as it was on most of the haciendas—there was a good chance that all of the water saved for irrigation had already been used up at this stage in the dry season. Any delay in the onset of the rainy season was thus usually an omen of a bad maize harvest. If one bears in mind that maize was the main product of the Indians, while wheat and some irrigated maize were the main product of the hacendados, a probable cause of social tensions emerges: if the summer rainy season was delayed, the peasants had a bad harvest; but the haciendas had already harvested their main crop by then and could probably harvest most of their maize as well without losses later in the year.

This set of problems can be further illustrated by information from the documents already mentioned, recording the rainfall and the state of the harvests for the period 1790–97. These documents, which provide information about a geographically larger area of Mexico than the reports of Don Felipe, are part of an inquiry conducted by the Spanish government into the background of the general failure of the maize harvest in 1785 and the famine year of 1786. The intendants were instructed to report on the agricultural situation in their *intendencias* over a ten-year period. In 1799, these reports were sent to the central government in Madrid. They contain detailed information on the effects of the weather for the cultivation of wheat, maize, barley, and seeds in the various intendancies for the years 1790–95 and 1797. They also contain some information on 1789, 1796, and 1798, but not for the intendancies of Mexico and Puebla. The most detailed of the usable reports is the one by the intendant of Mexico. Table 4 contains the data from the report, grouped by crop and province (though there is not a report for each province).[34]

The regional classification has been made on the basis of the criteria of landscape and climate featured in this chapter so far. The quality indices— abundant (a), good/satisfactory (g) and poor/meager/bad (p)—are in relation to the condition of the fields sown (F) and the harvest (H). Reporting occurred twice a year, in the spring (S) and in the autumn (A). A first glance at the survey reveals a regional distinction in wheat cultivation: the wheat produced in the highlands (groups 1 and 2) was generally more successful than the wheat grown in the arid northern provinces (groups 3 and 4). This was clearly the case in 1794, when the harvests in provinces like Chalco, Coyoacán, Tacuba, Cuautitlán, Texcoco, Metepec, Ixtlahuaca, and Tenango del Valle were good, while they were unsuccessful in provinces like Actopan, Tetepango, Zumpango, Ecatepec, and Zempoala. Hardly any wheat was grown on the faldas. A few mining provinces (Pachuca and Tasco) imported wheat from the neighboring provinces. This regional distinction does not apply in the case of maize, however.

For the period 1790–97, there are two and a half wheat harvests and three maize harvests that can be regarded as failures. Those of 1793 and 1797 were general disasters, despite the reasonable wheat harvest in the valley of Toluca. The year 1794 was also very poor, especially for maize, though in this case too an exception is formed by a few provinces in the valley of Toluca and the province of Chalco, which still managed to achieve a reasonable result. Rainfall was plentiful only in the faldas, so that the provinces situated there might be expected to compensate for the deficit to some extent. The wheat harvest in 1791 and 1794 was especially poor, but there were provinces with good harvests, such as Chalco, Cuautitlán, Otumba, Tula , and the valley of Toluca. On the other hand, the maize harvest was either a success in all provinces at the same time or it was a general disaster. Nevertheless, the 1792 harvest seems to have been inferior to that of 1790, which was considered to have been reasonable in a number of provinces. As for 1795, all the factors were favorable in the middle of the year.

It is remarkable that not a single crop yielded a generally abundant harvest during this period. Only in some areas was the result of a certain year considered better than normal; such was the case with the wheat harvest of 1794 in Teotihuacán, Malinalco, and Toluca, or the wheat harvest of 1795 in Chalco, Tacuba, Cuautitlán, and—once again—Malinalco (wheat was grown in Malinalco in a narrow, low-lying strip of the province). There were abundant maize harvests in 1792 and 1797 in Chalco and Tenango del Valle, as well as in Toluca in 1792 and Cuautitlán and Teotihuacán in 1797. The constant factor in this very diversified range of harvests is a strip of provinces from Teotihuacán and Cuautitlán to the easternmost part of the valley of Toluca and the province of Chalco, which lies to its east (see Map 7). These provinces situated between the volcanoes stood up to the heaviest climatic conditions like an ocean breaker. One disadvantage, however, was that the quality of the wheat and maize from Toluca was held to be considerably inferior.

The three reasonable-to-good harvests of 1790, 1792, and 1795 are the result of plenty of rain. In a number of provinces, especially in the valley of Mexico (group 1), there was even too much rain, as in the autumn of 1790 and the spring of 1795. This rainfall implied a serious menace, for direct drainage had to be implemented right away to prevent the formation of marshy land. Since the capacity of the relatively small reservoirs was not able to cope with such a volume of water, it was sometimes necessary to reinforce the dikes to prevent the nearby plots from being inundated.[35] After drainage of surplus water, of course, there did not remain sufficient water for irrigation in the following year. The unsuccessful wheat harvest of 1791 in the highland provinces of Coyoacán, Tacuba, Cuautitlán, Teotihuacán, Texcoco, Tenango del Valle, and Malinalco, as well as in all of the semiarid provinces, was in most cases due to the delay of the first rains. It would have been possible to fight the drought if the reservoirs had been full; since this did not take place, it may be surmised that there was not enough water in the reservoirs. There seems to be a clear connection with the surplus rainfall of the previous autumn. The intendant's report, in fact, makes a connection between some of the wheat harvest failures and the occurrence of the *chahuistle*, a kind of grain rust that often occurred during periods of excessive rainfall. However, closer inspection of the data in the report indicates that this plague was not necessarily connected with an excess of rain. The chahuistle in Coyoacán and Huichapan (Tetepango) in 1791, and in Ixmiquilpan, Malinalco, and Tulancingo in 1793, occurred precisely in periods of drought. The unsuccessful harvests in Teotihuacán, Tenango del Valle, Tulancingo, and Tetepango in 1795 were certainly preceded by overabundant rains in the spring, but a note in the report mentions that, at that moment, the harvest had already dried up after a night frost.

This is the other main reason for bad harvests. It is the same problem to which Don Felipe de Zuñiga repeatedly drew attention during the period 1763–85. The modest harvest of 1791 was caused by the drought, and above all by the night frost that occurred during this drought. In 1793, the first of the two general harvest failures in the seven-year period under discussion, there was too little rainfall everywhere (except for Toluca). The rainy season was too late in coming in the other two disaster years (1794 and 1797). In 1794, the only areas to receive a reasonable volume of rain were Temascaltepec, Cuautitlán, Teotihuacán, and Tenango del Valle. It is noteworthy that the 1794 wheat harvest was not ruined. There was an opportunity to reap a plentiful harvest before the outbreak of the very dry summer. The 1795 harvest was not a disappointing one either, so despite the dry summer of 1794, sowing generally took place as usual in the autumn. The only explanation seems to lie in irrigation: the haciendas where the wheat was produced had been able to save the July or August rainwater that had fallen in their reservoirs.

The dependence on rainfall and reservoirs is striking. However, eighteenth-century sources hardly ever mention wells. In 1777, the only village with a well in the falda province of Tehuacán, for example, was La Magdalena, near Chiapulco. The rest of the area was dependent on the river whose source was located there. The Hacienda San Francisco Xavier Chiapulco had sunk a well of its own for irrigation, which provided nine thousand liters of water a minute. Sinking wells was no easy matter. The Indian alcalde of Tlayacapa, a jurisdiction that formed part of the province of Chalco, wrote in 1743 that his village had nothing except the rainwater that the villagers had tried to save in reservoirs. The natural lake near the village was brackish and only suitable for cattle. There had been many attempts to sink wells, but each time they encountered the impenetrable volcanic ground at the deeper levels. The only alternative in Tlayacapa was the morning dew in the rainy season, which was regarded by the alcalde as extremely fertile. The dew provided enough water for the plants, as well as for the fennel and pomegranates cultivated by the farmers in their farmyards. But he was forced to admit that they soon ran into difficulties when the rainy season was late in coming.[36]

Most of the data presented so far on harvests and rainfall in the 1790s refer to the intendancy of Mexico. The intendant's report on Puebla yields more or less the same picture. It reveals the pattern of fair to good harvests in 1790, 1791, 1792, and 1795 (including the failure of half the wheat harvest in 1791), bad harvests in 1793, 1794, and 1797, and a total write-off in 1799. The results for 1796 and 1798 are not known. This means a total of four harvest failures in eight years, which was a high average. And the good harvest of 1790 was not achieved without difficulties either. The excessive rainfall of the spring was followed by a forty-day drought. In the highlands, this was interrupted in time by the last remnant of the rainy season, which brought enough water to fill the reservoirs. In some provinces, people were already talking about a result "which we have not had for a long time." However, the drought lasted too long in the faldas of Puebla. It was usually possible to harvest maize twice a year in this area because of the faster cycle of the crop there. One of the two harvests was in a critical phase during the forty-day drought and was in danger of being ruined. The result is unknown. At any rate, the number of reports of night frost in the log of the intendant of Puebla is higher than that of his Mexican colleague. The same goes for the number of reports of chahuistle; it remains obscure how much damage it caused.

The harvests in Puebla were endangered by other threats. The intendant regularly mentions a maize worm, which menaced the maize fields (*milpas*) and reduced the quality of the harvest. In 1795, the fruit harvest in the province of Chiautla, on the southern flanks of the highlands, was ruined by a plague of unidentified flying insects. Two years earlier, the province had been alarmed by a plague of scorpions, which preyed particularly on the older oxen and mules. Not far away, in the province of Tepeji de la Seda, locusts were a great nuisance. Although the farmers killed many of them, it proved impossible to get rid of the insects. In Huayacocotla, to the north, there was a plague of rats in 1791. Things got so bad there that the farmers had difficulty in bringing in the harvest because the laborers stayed away in fear. There were problems with wolves in Tepeaca in the same year. The numerous mule caravans passing through the main road from the harbor city of Veracruz to Puebla and Mexico City were regularly attacked by wolves, and many of the mules were killed. The intendant reported that he had already seen many sacks being carried into the city smeared with blood. As a result, the cash crops, mainly consisting of grain, vegetables, and other food items, were unsalable. All the same, claimed the intendant of Puebla, the many plagues of various kinds should not detract attention from the connection between the drought in the spring and the poor quality of the maize harvest the following December.

There was fear of a repetition of 1786 twenty-three years later. Time and again, it was determined that the food reserves in 1809 were far less than they had been in 1786. The big drought of 1809–11 also cost the lives of more livestock than had been the case in 1786. In Anáhuac, the provinces hit the hardest were those in the valley of Puebla and the drier area northwest of the valleys of Mexico and Toluca, but the losses to the maize harvest were great in the other provinces of the region as well. The result is predictable: increases in the price of food, a reduction in the transport of goods, a shortage of raw materials for industry, and no work for weavers, spinners, or dyers. The hardest hit were the regions of Michoacán and Guadalajara, where there was no rain until mid-June 1810. The hopes that the 1811 harvest would solve the problem were already dashed by then. Although Hamnett, Tutino, and Van Young indicate that the revolt led by the priest Miguel Hidalgo in these regions was not exclusively the result of such ecological factors, the harvest failures of 1808–10 certainly were a reason for the population groups affected in the countryside to resist the state, if they thought that it did too little to remedy the situation at the time.[37] It is noteworthy that the situation was less critical in the valleys of Toluca and Mexico, due to the successful harvests in Toluca and the imports from the southern falda provinces, particularly Cuernavaca and Cuautla, which made it possible to avoid another general year of famine.

The harvest failures of 1793 and 1797 had been accompanied by high mortality among the population. The peasants died of smallpox, high fever, or diarrhea. The reports of both the Mexican and the Pueblan intendant establish a direct connection between the climatic conditions, the quality of the harvest, and the deaths among the peasantry. The same applied to reports of good harvests, as the following example indicates: "There have hardly been any illnesses in Xalapa as a result of the very favorable weather conditions from 1 January to 1 June."[38]

Of course, it is debatable whether the scale of epidemics of this kind should be attributed to weather conditions or also to the socioeconomic organization of the society. Is the shortage of food cause or effect? The examples of the years 1775–85, 1790–95, and 1797 suggest the former. After all, the bad harvests were the result of drought and night frost, to which maize was particularly susceptible. But the differences between 1791, 1793, and 1794 in the wheat harvests suggest that irrigation might have provided a solution. In that case, the disaster was to be attributed to bad organization; this could have been the case in the other years as well.

In all, the data on climatic conditions in Anáhuac in the eighteenth century point toward an increasing drought and night frost, especially during the second half of the century. This followed a period of excessive, and thus sufficient, rainfall from 1740 to 1765. The big drought began in the period 1768–73, years of a poor or modest harvest. As noted before, according to Don Felipe de Zuñiga, ten years were too dry for the farmers. The entire maize and bean harvest of Anáhuac was destroyed by a severe night frost on 27 August 1785, which had accompanied earlier droughts. The weather did not pick up, and this led to a drastic shortage of food: 1786 has gone down in the history of Mexico as the year of famine. It is striking that bad harvests were reported in Europe and Bolivia during the same period. The problems of the 1790s, three more years of late spring droughts, have just been discussed in detail. They were followed by the long drought of 1808–11, which recalled the trauma of 1786, especially because after some decades of population growth more mouths had to be fed. Swan recorded shifts in the rainy season in her data: the rainy season in Texcoco shrank from July–November to August–October during the 1770s and 1780s. Although the rainy season was extended between 1799 and 1808 from May–August to April–August in the small valley of Mesquital (Tetepango), there were many dry weeks during the rainy season itself. The situation was particularly critical in the early months of the summer. To sum up, at least *fifteen* years out of a total of *forty* were too dry![39]

Finding a Way Out

One solution to the drought was to obtain more access to the water rights. The documentation indicates that the intensity of the fight for water rights rose with the number of years of drought. This is not the place to go into this issue in detail, but it is clear that in the drier provinces the villages tried to gain control of more water for irrigation, especially for the critical period when the night frosts could strike. These drier provinces are situated in the semiarid areas, such as the provinces of Actopan and Ixmiquilpan in the northwest of Anáhuac and the province of Tehuacán in the southeast, but we also encounter a remarkable degree of litigation in the generally drier central provinces of the valley of Puebla. This includes townships that did not depend entirely on rainfall; they were settled in areas provided with rivers, perennial or simple streams which flowed mainly during the dry season. Nevertheless, most Indian townships, situated upstream as they were, did not face any problem of water disputes.

The litigation resulting from real fights over sufficient water resources amount to only a limited number of cases in the General Indian Court or in any other Court of the Audiencia. A large number of these proceedings instigated by the villagers were concerned with recovering water rights they had once leased or even sold to hacendados and Indian elite members, called *caciques*, members of the old or renovated Indian aristocracy.[40] They could resort to rights as recorded in old *mercedes* and *composiciones*. The allocation of the water—which largely if not predominantly flowed to the haciendas and the ranchos belonging to *cacicazgos*—entailed a considerable technical and legal administration. In addition to the natural riverbeds, there were also artificial riverbeds, canals, and aqueducts in the valleys to get the water where it was needed. The haciendas and the villages had the right to tap this water at certain times of the day and week. In most cases, a lock and small water tower (*caja de agua*) had been constructed for this purpose, and the lock gate was ceremoniously opened at the appointed time. Officially, the villages had the first right to tap water because their documents were the oldest, but in practice it was often the person who could tap water the farthest upstream who had the advantage because he could exercise his rights to the full—this was usually someone from an Indian township—while at drier periods the farmers further down the stream—usually hacendados—were often faced with dry channels. This resorted in legal proceedings, of course, but in most cases the verdict came too late to put the matter to rights. In one of the few areas of Anáhuac where commercial agriculture expanded in the late eighteenth century, the sugar province of Cuernavaca, some hacendados tried to construct more aqueducts upstream, in the mountains, but in most cases villagers damaged or sabotaged these constructions, even making additional apertures to divert still more water to their own crops.[41] And, of course, some litigation occurred where feeder canals had been constructed near rivers and waterbeds to irrigate the central valley lands for hacienda wheat cultivation. These lands were usually used by the Indians for pasture. In any case, I have come across hardly any enduring proportional distributions, and they could not be put into practice either. The water simply followed its course or the Indians would make it do so.

That is precisely what makes analysis of the struggle over water rights so pointless. In fact, closer investigation reveals that many villages fought their battles in the context of a general attempt to acquire rights over their own facilities. I shall return to legal disputes about land and the process of "secessions" later on, but disputes over water rights have not been very different or were even part of this process, or part of the struggle that the villagers waged with their former caciques who had possession of such rights in a person (belonging to their cacicazgos). This was at stake in the province of Tehuacán, for example, where many villagers disputed the rights of the caciques. Precisely because of this background, most of the litigation dates from the period 1700–20, the years of the composiciones, and from the post-1780 period, the years of the "secessions." The droughts sometimes had not only preceded the increase in litigation, but the increase itself was caused by the leaders of subordinated pueblos, who wanted to secede from their *cabeceras* or municipal headtowns, as well as from the caciques reigning there. This included a splitting up of communally owned land and water rights.

It is therefore questionable to what extent litigation reflects the drought of the period. The leaders in the villages certainly did complain about the increasing shortage of water, especially if these villages were situated in the middle of a valley and not at the foot of a hill. The residents of the village of San Juan Bautista Ajalpan, situated in the semiarid area to the southeast of the valley of Puebla, noted a reduction amounting to a quarter of a *surco* in 1783, as against the official grant dating from 1689. Although the increasing drought was confirmed by the residents of the nearby villages of San Diego Chalma, San Gabriel Chilac, and San Sebastian Zinacantepec, there are problems in accepting the statement at face value because the villages of Ajalpan and Zinacantepec had been at loggerheads with one another for a long time about the payment of tribute and land use, and water rights were a part of this political-jural dispute. The large number of disputes concerning the use of water from the Atotonilco River in the province of Izúcar is also striking, litigation that time and again involves the same villages and haciendas. However, this litigation seemed to become an end in itself. In 1789, the women from one of these villages asked the government to put a stop to the interminable squabbles among the men. Their households suffered from absenteeism, since the men were constantly lodging in Mexico City to plead their case. It was precisely in these two areas that there existed major problems between the Indian leaders and their subordinates in the villages. In fact, most of the struggles—some violent, others in court—had started in the early colonial period and can therefore not be introduced to discuss a "new perspective on Puebla's eighteenth-century agrarian decline," as Lipsett pretends to have done.[42] Moreover, the problem was not even typical for Puebla, because for both of the other valleys of Anáhuac the same amount of litigation can be found in the archives. It is interesting to note that Martin discusses cases in which a simple rumor that Indians in the province of Cuernavaca were about to rebel was enough for the hacendados to reach compromises regarding irrigation. In fact, deviation of water streams and sabotage of waterworks were more effective strategies than litigation. And, as said before, most Indian townships were located upstream.[43]

There was thus no practical solution to fight the droughts. As has already been indicated, a lot of energy and capital were spent on religious measures. Prayer sessions and processions were organized, both in the vicinity of the lands of the haciendas and in the villages and towns. The aim was to invoke the aid of the Virgen de los Remedios, Saint Teresa, or the Virgin of Guadalupe. A simpler and more preventive measure was to ask a priest to bless the crop after the sowing had taken place. Priests were also called in to divest certain plots of land of "demonic powers" that might bring down rain, hail, drought, or night frost on the fields. In 1784, the manager of the Hacienda Molino de Flores was convinced that the damage caused to his neighbor's fields by a hailstorm was the result of his own negligence: the neighbor had failed to have his crops blessed, unlike what had taken place on Molino. The high investment of twelve pesos a month to pay the priest thus proved its worth. Besides, the neighbor could have had his crop blessed for nothing because the hacienda belonged to a monastery. Sometimes joint activities came up with results, too. In July 1800, a mass was held in the chapel of the Hacienda Tulancalco to pray for rain after six weeks of drought. Every member of the staff and every laborer on the hacienda was there. When the mass was over and they were leaving the chapel, it started to rain cats and dogs. Everyone went home contented.[44]

Epilogue: Summary and Speculation

Summary

In surveying the features discussed so far that may have had an effect on the characteristics of the economic system of Anáhuac, it can be concluded that there is a connection between the character of economic activity—for instance that of the many-sided economy in the valleys of Toluca and Mexico and in a few provinces in the valley of Puebla—and the pattern of precipitation. The agriculturalists settled between the volcanoes because that was the area the rain clouds were attracted to. It was much drier in the valley of Puebla, with the exception of the provinces near the city of Puebla. However, these drier provinces had the advantage of the short spring rains, so that they could fill reservoirs and the crops could be sown. In this respect, the hacendados enjoyed an advantage because they had the money to pay for large-scale capital investments like reservoirs with irrigation systems. The haciendas in the highlands were mainly wheat farms. The wheat in Toluca, nevertheless, was a less important product than it was in the other two valleys. The wheat in Toluca suffered from too many days of night frost. Moreover, Toluca was much higher than Mexico or Puebla. Crops grow slowly in the highlands; foreign crops like wheat or barley grow at a slower pace than in Europe or Asia. Even in periods with a good rainfall, it was not possible to harvest more than once a year, whether the crop was wheat, barley, or maize. Economic life in the country-side was based on this fact. Only the highlands of Anáhuac displayed an even distribution into haciendas and villages, although the haciendas dominated to a certain extent in Puebla. The falda provinces possessed a different out-look.

Any changes in the economic system may be influenced to a large extent by the excessive drought in the second half of the eighteenth century. There were fifteen years of insufficient rainfall between 1768 and 1808. The greatest danger at times of drought was night frost, which occurred when the seasons changed in the late spring and in the early autumn. This caused damage if the crops were affected by a delay in the onset of the rainy season during the critical phase of the growth process between May and the end of July. It was equally disastrous if the young seedlings were affected by frost in October. It is precisely this constant factor in the crises, consisting of the combination of night frost with drought, that posed a threat to the existence of the commu-nity. An occasional bad harvest could be borne by the agrarian society, but a *succession of bad years* reduced it to misery. Factors that normally led to a suc-cession of crises included the use of too little seed or seed of a poor quality, a disturbance in the agricultural schedule, or a shortage of labor power because of migration.[45] The additional factor in Anáhuac was the persistent bad weather. At the end of the eighteenth century, people nostalgically recalled the time before the bad harvests and the drought. Alzate called it a golden age of "bumper harvests, a total absence of epidemics. People managed to obtain a genuine Octavian peace, so typical for that kind of era."[46] After around 1780, Anáhuac, the heart of Mexico, had become too dry to support a population which remained stable. This is why the drought aggravated the relative over-population. But the problems grew worse when the population started to rise sharply as well.

On the Causes of the Droughts

What was responsible for the climatic problems? A number of historians, in-cluding Florescano and Swan, seek an explanation for the unusual behavior of the weather in the theory of the Little Ice Age, which is supposed to have held the world in its grip between 1450 and 1850. During this period, tem-peratures were an average of 2°C lower than they are today. There are other interpretations of the reason for the wavelike pattern in the development of the temperature, ranging from excessive volcanic activities and earthquakes to the effects of sun spots. The theory of the Little Ice Age was developed on the basis of climatological phenomena in Europe and the behavior of Euro-pean grain prices. This was particularly significant in the seventeenth cen-tury, while in the eighteenth century temperatures rose again and the winters became less cold. In his analysis of the prices of maize on the official corn market in Mexico City in the eighteenth century, Florescano compared them with European wheat prices. He concluded that the pattern of the two series was the same. However, it is debatable whether the comparison is justifiable. Wheat and maize are compared with one another, while the discussion of the harvest results in the period between 1790 and 1797 (presented above) led me to conclude that the demands made on the climate by wheat are not the same as those made by maize.[47]

There have already been justified warnings in the historical literature against the determination of climatological cycles on a world scale and in particular the attempt to measure them by using grain prices. Grain prices could only be affected by meteorological conditions at a regional level, especially if the market was not very large and the stocks could not be replenished easily and cheaply from outside. The consequences for the physical harvest can be complicated too. A good example of the latter is provided by Baars's investigation of agriculture in the Beijerland polders in the Dutch province of South Holland.[48] Baars noted a clear correspondence between the yield of the crops in the polders and the winter rainfall: periods of reduced rainfall were responsible for increased harvests; and vice versa, an increase in rainfall depressed the harvests. However, the connection that he was looking for could not be demonstrated in a direct way because there was a certain lag with respect to the winter rains. The decreased rainfall in these polders between 1737 and 1747 resulted in increased harvests between 1740 and 1750. On the other hand, increased rainfall in the period 1748–56 brought about smaller harvests between 1752 and 1760. There was a time lag of some three or four years. The longer such a wet or dry period lasted, the longer its effects could be felt. Minor fluctuations in the winter rainfall, however, were not immediately reflected in the yield. Moreover, the effect of the rainfall on the harvests could only be seen clearly in polders with poor drainage in winter. In the better organized polders it was possible to counteract this effect. Thus, once again, it can be stated that technical resources could be utilized to control the effects of changing weather conditions.

Although, to me, the theory of the Little Ice Age appears to be overambitious, most historians tend to agree on a general cooling between roughly 1500 and 1800.[49] Recent years have seen a flurry of activity in trying to understand the dynamics that "drive" global weather. True, global weather patterns do reflect a global atmospheric and oceanic system. While parts of the world may be separated geographically by vast distances, the weather in one area does not exist in isolation. For example, the large-scale, worldwide wind circulation can be viewed as a single huge convection system, whereby the atmosphere is busily conveying heat and moisture toward the poles. It is the unequal heating of different zones of the earth that sets the system in motion. Besides this, one can surely leave out of account the notion of a "long, slow process of climatic change," for climatic change include steplike, *abrupt* changes. Sudden changes of the wind regime produce periods of perhaps ten to fifty years of great prevalence of blocking patterns, changing, among others, the course of the winds around the world and resulting in, for example, a reduction in the frequency of mobile westerly situations. The temperatures prevailing at the surface of the Arctic ice adjust themselves within a few years, at most, to either a calmer regime than before or to one with stronger winds and ocean currents that import more heat from other latitudes. Of course, the climate of some places is clearly more sensitive to changes in the prevailing winds; England is such a place, and Anáhuac another.

There are signs of a repeating pattern in southwesterly surface winds above Europe, which may be related to other evidence of a cyclic process of about two hundred years in length. This frequency shows low points around 1400, 1600, and 1800, and around the year 2000 another seems to be reached; there were high points around 1250, 1670, 1730, and 1920. What interests us most is the severe drop in wind frequency after the 1750s, which lasted until the 1810s. In addition, the cooling trend and climatic deterioration all over the earth, from the late Middle Ages onward, brought wet summers and mostly wet springs and autumns as well. The sixteenth century saw the sharpest change resulting in the coldest regime at any time since the last major ice age. The winters from the 1750s to 1780s were, on average, colder than before; the summers from about 1760 to the 1780s were much wetter. After the 1790s another change set in, bringing drier summers and warmer winters to Europe. This sequence seems to parallel the droughts in New Spain, which should lead us to conclude that the end of the Little Ice Age was favorable for Europe but a disaster for New Spain. Anthropologist Lewis Messenger confirms the idea that a cooler global climate is to be desired by Mesoamerican peasants.[50]

Nevertheless, the general cooling was accompanied by notably great variations from year to year and from one group of a few years to the next in all parts of the world. This considerably hinders historical analysis. In fact, Lamb, the English historian of the climate, does record the predictable dry winters in the 1730s in North America, but not in a later period. He attributes the deviation in the pattern of the weather—which was repeated in the late eighteenth century and appeared to have taken place on a worldwide scale, marked by another *drop* in temperatures—to a few volcanic eruptions. The most serious of these occurred in Iceland in 1783, but there was another eruption that year in Japan as well. As a result of these eruptions, a thick layer of dust and ash entered the stratosphere, spreading into an increasingly uniform veil, which for years interfered with the sunshine on the earth. Generally, the greater the height to which the exploded material is thrown by the eruption, the longer the veil will last. The two eruptions of 1783 must have had that effect, for various European reports of the period referred to "weak sunshine" and the presence of a "sulphuric-smelling mist." Shortly after the eruptions the sun could not be seen in the south of France until it was 17° above the horizon. There were also major eruptions of Vesuvius in southern Italy in 1737, 1774, and 1794. In April 1816, the Tambaro volcano in eastern Asia was immediately responsible for "a year without a summer" in Europe and a remarkably cold winter in North America with a lot of snow caused by the thick layer of dust in the stratosphere. The weather was out of joint for years.[51]

Other evidence supports these findings, for volcanic eruptions may be connected with earthquakes and earthquakes were recorded at various times in eighteenth-century New Spain. Some people in the eighteenth century were aware of the congruency and mentioned it in their observations. Of course, they had not failed to notice the situation of repeated bad harvests and, in particular, the Mexican commentator Alzate looked for the cause of the bad harvests in a series of earthquakes:

> Even more than in Europe, where the 1755 earthquake in Lisbon disturbed the weather for a few seasons—though still leaving them more or less intact—the post-1768 earthquakes, which could be felt until 1776, are the reason why our country is no longer the New Spain that Cortés conquered; there is no pattern in the years any more: night frost out of season, drought in the atmosphere. Excessive rains in certain areas and at the same time a shortage of rain in others: this is the dangerous result (because it menaces the harvests) from which the inhabitants of New Spain suffer.[52]

Curious are the daily earthquakes that plagued the village of Nopalucan in the province of Tepeaca for three months in 1740. The villagers saw in this a sign of divine wrath and a reason to leave the village. They returned when the earthquakes were over.[53]

I have been able to trace a few of the earthquakes mentioned by Alzate in the notes of Don Felipe de Zuñiga, the government official who kept a daily record of the position of the planets and of the weather, and in some other published and unpublished texts.[54] The precision of these observations is surprising. There were several earthquakes in the eighteenth century before the droughts began: severe *temblores* were registered in 1729 (16 and 28 March), 1753 (12 February, 29 and 30 June, and 1 July), 1754 (30 August, 1 September, 14 November), and 1768 (30 March, 3 and 4 April). But the sequence became intenser after 1770. There was a severe earthquake in 1773, 2 August at 6 in the morning. The first report from Don Felipe is from 29 May 1775, when the earth moved slightly a few times at 7:45 hours. The next quake brought the clocks to a standstill on 23 November at 17:30 hours. The damage was minor in both cases. Don Felipe received very different news on 21 April 1776. There had been earthquakes the whole day, including a few very heavy ones, in the southern harbor city of Acapulco, where the link was maintained with the Philippines. A wave that must have been caused by the earthquake flooded the harbor town and destroyed all of its houses (many of which were made of wood). There was a heavy tremor in Mexico City for four minutes at 16:15 hours. Observers claimed that it passed through the city from west to east. The damage was enormous. Next morning there was another quake at 7:05 hours, this time passing from the northeast to the southwest of the city, and fifteen minutes later another passed through the city from north to south. A few days later, on 24 April, heavy earthquakes at 13:00 hours and at 15:35 hours destroyed a very large number of buildings. The tremor at 7:38 hours the next day was slightly less severe, but the temblores lingered on until the twenty-ninth.

Everyone who can remember the earthquake that hit Mexico City on 19 September 1985 can imagine the chaos these earthquakes must have caused in the city. On 28 April, one day before the last quake of 1776, the archbishop organized a large procession, which was joined by practically every resident of the city, all carrying candles. Next day, a total of twenty processions set out from the smaller churches. However, the earthquakes were certainly not over yet. There were tremors on 12 May at 22:58 hours, on 30 May at 10:45 hours, and on 3 June at 15:15 hours. Don Felipe noted reports of later earthquakes on 9 October 1777: at precisely 24:00 hours on the east coast in Veracruz, during which a few churches collapsed; on 3 November 1777 in Xalapa near Veracruz at 8:30 hours; on 21 May 1782 at 13:45 hours in Mexico City (a slight tremor); on 16 January 1784 at 8:00 hours; on 26 June 1785 at 2:45 hours; and on 4 December at 8:00 hours. The next sequence took place between 28 March 1787 and 6 July 1789; with strong quakes particularly on 30 March; 3, 8, and 17 April; and 7, 8, and 13 November 1787.

How should we view the connection between these earthquakes and the unsuccessful harvests? It would be very presumptuous for a historian to try to solve a problem that still leaves meteorologists and geologists puzzled. All the same, reports like those mentioned above are very valuable if we follow the modern publications about El Niño, or Christmas Child, because, as noted above, it is the unequal heating of different zones of the earth that sets weather systems in motion. The El Niño current reflects this phenomenon, originating in a peculiar deviation in the weather pattern above the Pacific, which modern views attribute to the combination of a change in the temperature of the sea water and the atmospheric pressure above the equator. Each time this phenomenon occurs it can last for a few years. In this case, the air pressure above the Indonesian archipelago rises in the autumn and the water in the western part of the Pacific reaches an unusually high temperature. The high atmospheric pressure drives the low air pressure eastward. This creates problems for the system above the mainland of Mexico, Central America, and the Andes. The winds that normally blow from east to west and drive the water in the direction of Asia decrease sharply in force or shift direction. The oceanic currents that usually move westward are driven eastward by this shift and reach the coast of Peru around Christmas. It is this date that provides the unusual warm current with the name of El Niño. The Christmas Child is not particularly welcome because the fish which live from the cold water off the coast of Peru, an area rich in food, are driven southward by the warm water, which does not contain so much food, and all to the dismay of the fishermen.[55] El Niño manifests itself once every four to seven years in a mild form, but at certain times it can reappear with a higher frequency and in a more serious form than at other times. This leads to very severe climatological disturbances, not only in Peru but, because of the global connection of weather systems, all over the earth.[56]

Each sudden change in the atmosphere may be enough to excite El Niño. Meteorologists suppose that a few serious disturbances in rapid succession lead to a more long-term disruption of the climate. The consequences are familiar, especially after a turbulent bout of El Niño: rain instead of expected drought, drought instead of expected rain. Only a few years ago, in 1982–83, the warm Gulf Stream upset the climate of the whole world, resulting in unexpected floods and exceptional drought. Harvests were unsuccessful everywhere. The renovated Peruvian fishing fleet went bankrupt straightaway. After the effects had worn off, there was another serious disturbance in 1986. There can be no doubt that El Niño was also active in the eighteenth century, probably in connection with the volcanic eruptions noted by Lamb. Although meteorologists and geographers are still in the dark as to the precise cause of this shift in the ocean currents, there are increasing indications that the rise in water temperature is the result of underwater volcanic activity, in which eruptions led to the flow of a huge mass of lava over the ocean floor at a temperature of around 1,000°C. The amount of heat conducted by the water in a brief period was sufficient to bring about a disruption of the oceanic circulation.[57] This may have been an important factor in the activation of an unusually forceful El Niño. It is no speculation that findings in Mexico and the oceanic volcanic activity are connected with the shifts in the earth's crust under the Pacific, which has been in a state of violent upheaval for centuries. This is where the continental plates are splitting apart. Plates that slide toward the east cause earthquakes in America, and upwelling magma from the asthenosphere fills the void left by separating plates around the Indonesian archipelago. That is where El Niño arises. Could this be an explanation for the drought in Mexico in the 1780s and 1790s?

3

A Good Tree Is a
Good Shelter

Introduction:
Between the General Good and the Theft of Time

A mild irritation, though perhaps a serious one: I fear that this may be the state of mind of the reader who works his or her way through this complicated chapter. It contains a critique of a traditional model of interpretation, combined with the text of what may be a new interpretation, all mixed up with a historical exposition of the Indian municipality, and presented almost from scratch again, which is inevitable in view of the relatively low level of understanding of this unit. There is a sketch of the growing *de jure* landownership of the pueblos (that is, municipal government). The altepetl will be introduced as a "demesne," subjected to Indian seigneurial rule, for the Indian townships are *not* seen as a form of corporation in which collective responsibility was predominant, but, on the contrary, as municipalities. This is bound to meet with criticism, which obliges me to counter my critics in this and the following chapters as much as I can in advance by presenting a large number of examples to buttress my hypothesis.

But this chapter starts with a discussion of rulership and government on the crown level, including viceregal policy adopted during the 1786 disaster. The population of Anáhuac did not just stand by and watch its world collapse within the space of a few decades. According to ecology, "organisms" control the survival of their coexistence themselves. Also people try to devise solutions to the problem. In eighteenth-century Anáhuac, the first response was a cultural one connected with the ecological ethic. It included a short-term solution aimed at combating acute poverty, which had grown to enormous proportions in the countryside, with charity. And it included a long-term solution aimed at securing Indian landownership. Both solutions implied intensive contacts between the Spanish government, Spanish elite families, and the Indian populations in the rural areas. The response involved, above all, the duty of the monarch, who, like God whom he represented on earth, was seen as the father of his people. The monarch owed justice to the inhabitants of the realm, tempered by mercy, in return for unquestioning obedience. It had to be recognized, of course, that the monarch, being human, might err, and that there could be bad kings as there were bad fathers. Nevertheless, the authority of the monarchs was justified by the same kind of arguments that were used to justify parental authority in both the former Aztec society and post-conquest Spanish times. This means that the fiction that parents must necessarily love and promote the interests of their children was maintained in relation to the rulers: no father could wish to harm his children, no monarch could wish to harm his subjects.[1] This was known as *buen gobierno,* good government, in the Spanish realm. Offering "buen gobierno" was metaphorically viewed as offering the shade—protection—of a good tree.

And offering "shade" was inevitable around 1800. Baron Alexander von Humboldt, who was in New Spain in 1803, learned from the Spanish administrators that many villages had burst at the seams. He noted the existence of newly constructed cottages all over the countryside, as well as the complaints of the clergy and local government that this expansion was occurring at the expense of agricultural land in the villages. He took this to imply that the Indians did not produce enough maize and he perceived what he saw as signs of undernourishment. He concluded that the hacendados should cultivate more maize and that the potential of the land, as well as the development of manufacture, must be utilized better.[2] These remarks are a cause for reflection, for the prosperity of New Spain before 1780, of which he had heard, had apparently become a thing of the past by 1803.

Nevertheless, the year of hunger, 1786, did not repeat itself around 1800 because of "buen gobierno": from generally good entitlements to food distribution, perhaps the existence of poor relief, and certainly the securing of lands under Indian plows. This "buen gobierno" response should be understood as "charity," an important response, though one that has not received much attention in historical discussions. In his investigation of health care, education, and welfare in Europe and the United States of America in the modern era, sociologist De Swaan summarizes extensive historical and sociological research that shows how local charitable institutions could serve to prevent the outbreak of violence in such situations.[3] It is understandable that these responses were for the poor to draw on the relations of Herrschaft in which they were enmeshed: the reciprocal dominance of hacendados, Spanish entrepreneurs and officials, and the leaders of their villages. It was a complicated solution containing diverse elements.

But the attitude of the governing strata of New Spain was not limited to charity only. If the Indians had possessed sufficient agricultural space, charity would not have been necessary. This means that the relations of Herrschaft between the royal government and the Indians resulted in "looking for shade" at two sides of the "powerful tree" of the governing groups: charity and land tenure. Indeed, to preserve human resources for Spanish exploitation, Wood endorses,[4] royal policymakers took steps to protect and preserve Indian towns by ordering a safe distance to be kept between them and obtrusive settlers, and legislating limits on the number of laborers drafted and the length of time workers spent outside their pueblos. However, the question should be raised about whether "exploitation" was the main or even the sole ground for such charity policies. Once again, I would like to stress the fact that the elite, with its exclusive access to the means of subsistence, and the poor stood in a complementary relation to one another. It was in their joint interests to maintain this relationship, to canalize the process of never-ending change. They found, especially, the Indian gobernadores at their side. Whereas in medieval Germany the lord was expected to provide his subjects with *Schütz und Schirm*—"in the lords shadow," as in the shadow of a tree—Haskett stresses that the duty of the gobernador in New Spain was described by using the same metaphor: *in pochotl in ahuehuetl*, or "like silk cotton trees or cypress giving shade." This symbolizes the patriarchal and legal responsibility of the gobernador.

Charity

Food Entitlements

Charity was a Christian obligation, of course, but this should not be seen in terms of individual motives of altruism or as a matter exclusively concerning the dispenser and the recipient of charity. Charity was a collective affair in which the elite's interests were involved. The great menace to the elite was theft, arson, revolt and murder. This threat could be deterred by lending an ear to the complaints of the poor and propertyless on recurrent problems and by providing gifts of charity after short-term setbacks and disasters. The main collective function of charity was to appease the threat posed by the poor, while for the other party it involved a kind of collective insurance against future setbacks.

Present-day economists are usually puzzled by collective voluntary altruism. After all, the performance of Christian obligations is mainly sought in the church and in religious institutions like confraternities. It is assumed that many traders were not convinced of the need for overgenerous deeds of charity, since charity costs money. The problem with this approach, as De Swaan points out, is that these welfare economists and neo-Darwinian ethologists base their assumptions on theories in which the central role is played by the individual economic agent. Thus they opt for the smallest composite element as the agent in the theory. As soon as the concept of a collectivity or group is introduced into the picture, a paradox results. De Swaan therefore argues for an analysis based on the group dynamics of a structured process of competition and interdependence, which he calls "figuration sociology." This approach is very close to the ecological approach advocated in the present volume, and the correspondence absolves me from the responsibility of examining De Swaan's model in more detail. It is sufficient to underline his conclusion that a collective charity of this kind can only be understood as a transitional phenomenon, "a phenomenon that occurs during the development of a combination of interdependent but uncoordinated persons to form a coordinated association able to impose an effective policy on the members of which it is composed."[5] In other words, we can situate this as a transitional phenomenon between Personenverband and Territorialverband.

Access to the food market plays a key role in poverty. This raises an analytical problem, for ever since the publication of Florescano's *Precios del maíz* (1969) we have known that maize prices remained at a constantly higher level after the crisis of the 1780s, which suggests that the poorest inhabitants of the city suffered a loss of entitlements. In view of the harvest failures in the countryside, this phenomenon seems not to have been confined to the city. At this point, it is appropriate to refer to the consumer-orientated *entitlement approach* of the developmental economist Amartya Sen, which pays particular attention to "entitlements to commodity bundles" by the consumers. The trade in manufactures and the food market coincide at this point:

> The entitlement approach to starvation and famines concentrates on the ability of people to command food through the legal means available in the society, including the use of production possibilities, trade opportunities in the society, entitlements *vis-à-vis* the state, and other methods of acquiring food. . . . Ownership of food is one of the most primitive property rights, and in each society there are rules governing this right. The entitlement approach concentrates on each person's entitlements to commodity bundles including food, and views starvation as resulting from a failure to be entitled to a bundle with enough food.[6]

Poverty was certainly on the increase in New Spain, but there was no famine. The situation with regard to "entitlements to commodity bundles including food" therefore seems to have been a favorable one.

Why? According to Sen, it is not only the exchange relation on the market that is important, but also the exchange relation which determined the political system of the region in question. This explains his interest in the entitlements of the poorest sectors of society vis-à-vis the state: the provision of social security. The data themselves suggested to me that it is likely that the poorest members of society in the Anáhuac region successfully demanded access to sufficient commodity bundles, including food, in times of need and on the basis of their ethological ethic, thereby guaranteeing their survival.[7] There is no need to adopt a romantic position here. Systems of charity and large-scale relief do not arise because people care so much about one another. The basis of these systems lies in suspicion and interest. Fear of others, mistrust, and enlightened self-interest have been responsible for the rise of institutionalized solidarity on a large scale. This is the motivation behind the concern of the Spanish government and of Spanish private individuals, which will be discussed below. After all, the elite of New Spain lived in Mexico City, surrounded by a sea of peasants and cottagers who could engulf the prosperous Spaniards in their midst. Charity was a "compulsory coordinated activity" that could be sanctioned physically, financially, religiously, or in other ways by a central body or by the collectivity as a whole. The reaction of the "rich man," the "lord," the member of the "elite"—or however I have referred to these individuals so far—was to guarantee the chances of survival of the poor.[8]

Theft of Times

The entitlements of food had found a reflection in the ideology of state officials during this era. Despite the Bourbon Reforms, which would revolutionize government in New Spain, crown policy at the lower level was still based on the need to subject economic activities to the supervision of civil servants. This was clearly a noncapitalist logic. The attitude of the elite and the state toward intermediate trade was crucial. Within the ecological ethic, intermediate trade, for instance, was seen as a disturbing factor, or even as a menace to the divinely ordained state of things. Middlemen were difficult to distinguish from usurers, it was claimed, because they speculated on stocks and derived their profits from differences in prices. In fact, all they sold was the intervening time between the moment at which they bought their goods and the moment when they marketed them. As the contemporary documentation and literature show,[9] it was then generally believed that producers should sell the means of subsistence as close to home as possible, and that they should do so on public markets under crown control. Bakers, millers, and carriers were regarded as civil servants who were supposed to work for the common good. Price agreements, sale well in advance of the harvest, and speculation with stocks were regarded as sinful; intermediate trade was taboo in a market system where one was expected to sell directly to the public. Authors of the period "found retail traders difficult to fit into their concepts of social harmony. They did not earn their keep by praying, they did not protect others with their weapons, they did not engage in productive labour."[10]

Although the fundamentalist, orthodox Catholic arguments of the thirteenth century had lost much of their force by the eighteenth century, the time during which both middlemen and usurers traded was still considered as the property of God. Thus the middleman was a thief of time. Thieves were expected to give back the time they had stolen, but naturally this only occurred on a minor scale. According to the French historian Le Goff, who has conducted a detailed analysis of ideas about the usurer in medieval society, the attempt to get the usurer to make repayment—and putting this intention into practice—was much more common than is generally supposed: it found expression in charity. And where intermediate trade was considered a "sin," the only argument in favor of the theft of time was that of the "common good."[11]

However, as is well known, economic development, enterprise, and even the food supply in the cities owed their existence to intermediate trade. In Europe, the economic development of the eighteenth century resulted in a reappraisal of intermediate trade, but in Anáhuac little of this reevaluation was to be seen. In general, the people at large as well as the elite continued to regard intermediate trade as a moral evil—at most, a *necessary* moral evil in the eyes of a few—and as an activity that was basically immoral. This is hardly surprising in light of the success of the Counter-Reformation in Spanish America. The church had a very direct influence on the daily life of the population of New Spain, not only through the sacraments of baptism, marriage, and funeral rites, but also through the provision of education, science, and art, and the exercise of important government positions, ranging from alcalde mayor to viceroy. The traces of orthodox Catholicism, based on the ordinances of the Council of Trent, can be found even in the simplest symbolism:[12] thousands of villages and haciendas are named after Saint Joseph, probably hundreds of thousands of girls have been named after Teresa of Avila since the eighteenth century, and the same goes for boys named after Thomas Aquinas. The names of the new saints of the Counter-Reformation occur constantly in the baptismal registers of the parish churches throughout the continent.

What is far more important, however, is that the ideology of the Counter-Reformation inspired the church to assist and manage the state in the practical affairs of government and to advocate the preservation of order and tranquillity. It also encouraged preaching submission to the divinely appointed government, a message picked up and put into action by members of the elite. One of the important instruments of the reformers, of course, was the church monopoly in education. In theory—following European developments—the elite moved toward a genuine *innerweltliche Askese*. The English historian Peter Burke explains the success of both the Reformation and the Counter-Reformation in Europe in terms of the sharp rise in the educational level of the elite; it was these two movements that made intensive use of the printed word. Van Oss also referred to "an increasingly educated clergy" in the framework of his research on book-printing in Central America. The situation in New Spain was not very different. Although this led to a widening gulf between popular and elite elements in popular culture through labeling its pagan and corporal aspects as sinful, it should not be assumed that the elite turned its back on the popular classes. In addition to the fear of popular revolt and the repayment of the "theft of time," the reformers' urge to make conversions motivated them to show considerable charity toward the poor. I think these three aspects determined the behavior of the elite in the famine year of 1786, for example, and during the difficult fifteen years of drought at the turn of the century.[13]

A good example of the motivation of the government in intervening in the economic structure and economic activity is found in the exceptional situation during the famine year of 1785–86. A request by the inhabitants of the city of Toluca in January 1786 for tax exemption on flour sold in the city for the duration of the shortage throws some light on the ambiguous form of argument that was used. The request was directed to the king through the alcalde mayor. The residents of Toluca informed him of the misery which the food shortage had created in the city. The poorest residents now had to make their tortillas from bran and barley because there was hardly any maize available. The city was in a state of great tension, exacerbated by the robberies that took place on the city's arterial roads. The citizens appealed to the king's paternal affection: nothing moved the Father King (*El Rey Padre*) Charles III more, they suggested, than the profound care for the welfare of all of them. They added that the viceroy's government must be guided by the same motives as the king's, so that they were sure of being able to count on unselfish support in times of need. In their particular case, they argued, this support should consist of an exemption of the tax on trading wheat flour in order to prevent a rise in the price of bread. Their request concluded by pointing out that otherwise there was a danger that the price of bread would rise to unjustifiable proportions. The government official in the capital who had to submit the request to the viceroy added that compliance with their wishes would indeed alleviate the distress in Toluca. In turn, he pointed out to the viceroy that he expected El Rey Padre to offer support to his children in need by this means. The viceroy himself signed the request with the words: "So be it."[14]

The arguments put forward by the citizens of Toluca are important in light of the polemic conducted within the viceregal capital precisely on the measures to be taken in such circumstances. Many civil servants pointed out the justness of the petitions from the provinces: prices had to be checked and, at any rate, must not be allowed to rise to unacceptable levels. One of these men was Don Francisco Fernández de Córdova, who contributed to the debate with a long document in 1787. Córdova was a top-level civil servant in Mexico City and closely associated with the viceregal policy. He claimed that the scale of the disaster in 1786 was a policy error. If the crown had paid more attention to religious morality—which represented the common good—the price of maize would not have risen to such a level and fewer people would have suffered as a result. In his opinion, it was particularly in New Spain that the government had a very important economic task to perform, because although the scale of the famine could be limited in Europe by importing stocks from elsewhere, the poor transport conditions in New Spain made this impossible. The free economy that he had seen emerging in Europe could only be tolerated in Spanish America, Córdova stated, if it was not allowed to put "public health" at risk.[15]

Córdova considered that this danger was very acute because generally a bad harvest was followed by a contracted market. At such times, farmers appeared on the market who usually grew their own food. Demand increased and pushed prices up. But, Córdova argued, that these consumers were not the main cause of the inflation. In his opinion, the disaster of 1786 was due to the excessive freedom given to the middlemen in New Spain to increase prices. There was already legislation on price thresholds for beans, meat, and bread, but why did it not exist for maize? It is maize particularly that soon became scarce, he remarked, if one considered all those who appeared on the maize market as consumers after a harvest failure: first, there were the hacendados, who came to buy maize for their workers' rations; next, the *trajineros* (peddlers), who bought maize to sell on the weekly markets at a higher price; then, the *pulperos*, the grocers in the villages and suburbs, who bought maize to sell in their shops at a higher price; and last but not least, the *tocineros* (pork butchers), who needed maize for the pigs in their sties in the cities. Córdova believed that these groups should be excluded from the market after a harvest failure because they drove the poor away from the market. The poor were then left with no alternative to religious or secular relief. Besides, he added, the effect of high prices was structural because the cottagers and peasants would be forced to sell their donkeys, oxen, ploughs, pigs, sheep, and chickens in order to obtain cash. This meant that they no longer possessed the means of production required to survive the following year. Another consequence was migration, because many Indians would leave their farms to look for work and food elsewhere. Córdova considered it the responsibility of the crown to prevent this distress. The peasants must be protected according to the divine commission with which the government officials were entrusted.[16]

Writers like Fernández de Córdova accused the middlemen of exploiting crises. Córdova made it clear that society could live without trade or commercial activity, which he regarded as a luxury. The real world was not like this, as Fernández de Córdova also pointed out. Every "sin" that could be committed in this respect was committed, especially in periods of prosperity. The hacendados collaborated extensively with the middlemen in selling their products. In fact, the entire structure of trade provided many poor peasants with a living in the manufacturing sector or in transport. However, it is clear from the documentation that hacendados and alcaldes mayores had an aversion to intermediate trade on moral grounds; a *labrador*, as the hacendado called himself,[17] should not meddle with usurers. At times of crisis, most of them strikingly kept out of the picture if peasants marched to the homes of the buyers to burn them down as a reaction to allegations of speculation. At such times, the middlemen were treated as scapegoats and could count on having to face the fury of the popular masses. And the hacendados did not miss an opportunity to display their religious sentiment and to actively support poor relief in times of need, as if all this made good their sinful commercial activities.

In fact, and this will be very important for my argument, the documentation I have seen confirms the picture of an ecological ethic among many hacendados. At times of great famine, they were prepared to abandon their commercial policies—including speculation with stocks—and to provide the peasants with food at low prices, or even free of charge. In such cases they resigned themselves to losing the profits to be made by speculation. Even the large-scale entrepreneurs followed this line. Swan quotes examples from the correspondence of the proprietress of the Tulancalco hacienda, who lived in Mexico City, with the manager of the hacienda. Each time there was danger of a shortage, the manager of the hacienda was instructed to stop the storage policy that he usually followed. In August 1799, after years of bad harvests and famine, the proprietress of the hacienda wrote to him that the price of 5p4 (five pesos, four reales) per fanega of maize was still a fair price at that time, but higher prices could not be allowed because "that would be to the detriment of the poor, for whom this food is a basic necessity of life." She repeated her command to control the prices in 1800 and 1801, and did the same later on in 1809, 1810, and 1811. At such times, the servants were also prepared to exchange their weekly rations for a daily wage in reales in order to release maize for the starving urban population.[18]

On the other hand, and equally important, there were those in the state apparatus, and particularly among the members of the elite, who advocated doing away with state intervention in the economy. The idea that letting supply and demand run their unobstructed course would serve the common good better than the imposition of controls on prices and the food supply was clearly gaining ground. Within this conception, the middleman was an essential link in the market process. Its theorists argued, for example, that if the price of grain were relatively low shortly after the harvest because of the large supply, the middlemen could buy up various stocks at exceptionally low prices in order to put them on the market again later on for a higher price—more or less coinciding with the large-scale agrarian producers—once the small and medium-sized farmers had sold their harvest. The result, it was claimed, was that food stocks would be available on the market all year round. Moreover, the buyers were assumed to be responsible for a more even geographical distribution of the food stocks because they were offered on markets where the demand was high. The process was thus seen as a way of preventing general famine, and the "theft of time" was in fact a form of "saving for the common good." The state's role in this process was a limited one, confined to encouraging intermediate trade, for the latter could best be realized if the state abandoned its own regulatory function. Various royal families in Europe used these arguments in an attempt to abolish state control of the economy in the eighteenth century. The relative laissez-faire policy of the House of Bourbon, which held sway in Spain from the beginning of the century, was no exception. All the same, it can be supposed that the civil servants and merchants in New Spain were torn between the views of the old moral economy and the new proto-liberal views of laissez-faire.[19]

The Disaster of 1786

The reader of these pages will agree that a shift in weight was possible here—from food entitlements protected by the crown to protection by hacendados and merchants. However, even though we have many documents from the hacendados that adopted a strongly favorable tone in line with the Tridentine ideology, for a long period the crown's officers in the colonies often still adhered to the old ideology as well. It is true that during the 1786 crisis, government officials, merchants, priests, and big landowners wanted both to profit from the rise in maize prices and to provide assistance to the victims of the famine, but a large proportion of this kind of assistance appears indeed to have been "disinterested," despite the fact that civil servants and hacendados were urged to take such action by those in need on the basis of the reciprocal claims of the Herrschaft relation. It is known that small farmers and manufacturers generally resorted to legal channels for the expression of grievances or to demand specific measures in the first instance.

Traditionally, the most natural persons to whom to appeal were the provincial officials and the priests. After the harvest failure of 1785, many villages in Anáhuac had to send a letter to the government in Mexico City, containing a call for assistance by a village priest or an alcalde mayor. This call for help was usually backed up by an appeal to the crown to come to their aid, to reduce prices, to combat the intermediate trade, and to prevent many people from starving to death. The authors had no qualms about adding force to their request with heart-rending illustrations. For instance, the alcalde mayor of the province of Apan wrote his letter after being threatened by a crowd of peasants from his province, who had thrust a young woman forward with a dead baby in her arms. She was unable to breast-feed her child any longer because of the shortage of food. This scene was related to the metropolitan government in full detail. Since the letter meant the promise of assistance, the alcalde mayor wrote it to save his own skin. The civil servant who was later sent from Mexico City to solve the problems "discovered" that there was still maize on some of the haciendas in the province and requisitioned it on royal authority. The maize was later distributed to the starving population.[20]

Apparently, there were still ample stocks of food in some parts of the highlands in spite of the general shortage. This was certainly the case in the sparsely populated marginal areas of Anáhuac, where the crisis did not pose a threat until late in 1786. One of these areas was the province of Cadereyta, in the western border region. No rain fell there throughout the summer of 1786. On 1 September, the local hacendados met to pray for rain at a special mass. Their prayers were in vain and no rains fell. All the same, the hacendados closed their stores two weeks later to prevent the rations for their own workers from running out. The alcalde mayor of the province, alarmed by the measure, instructed a respectable citizen of the provincial capital to buy maize elsewhere. This was readily carried out, to the delight of all. Its success was due, to a large extent, to the assistance of two merchants from Cadereyta, who were prepared to pay for the transport of the maize out of their own pockets. Although the first danger had been averted, the next harvest threatened to be a failure as well. On 20 September, the alcalde mayor issued a decree prohibiting all trade in maize and beans. A few days later, a sort of soup kitchen was opened in the town hall, with contributions from all the merchants of the town (including hacendados): six hundred meals were served there each day. The morning meal consisted of a well-seasoned and roasted piece of meat weighing half a pound (*una ración de carne media libra bien condimentada*); the midday meal was a bean dish. The meat was provided by a local hacendado, a stock farmer who usually sold his meat to the *obligado de abasto*. Some tortillas were distributed during meals as well. Although it continued to pour with rain after 29 September, it was decided to keep the soup kitchen running until the following harvest, which was due soon.[21]

More cases can be cited of assistance rendered to the alcaldes mayores by hacendados and merchants in the performance of this duty in this respect. On the initiative of the alcalde mayor of Tulancingo, for example, the hacendados in the province were prepared to sell maize at cost price at the hacienda entrances in 1786. They sold exclusively to poor peasants, not to retailers. The consumers came from over the provincial borders. This example was followed later the same year by the hacendados, who had originally wanted to hold on to their stocks for their own servants. Since it had become obvious by then that their next harvest would be a good one, they proceeded to sell the stocks they still held. Their own servants could get by on lower rations for a few weeks. A few hacendados offered the maize for sale at a low price on the weekly markets in the province. This brought about a fall in the price of maize in the area. Another hacendado, in the province of Teotihuacán, also assumed a leading role in curbing price increases directly after the harvest failure. He bought maize from fellow hacendados—including two hundred cargas from the Masapan hacienda in the province of Texcoco—in order to offer it for sale at a low price on the Monday market in Teotihuacán. On the other days of the week, he sold the maize for the same low prices in his shops in Teotihuacán and Tepexpan.[22]

Of course, the alcaldes mayores also received considerable support from the church. This support consisted of direct assistance with aid in the countryside and financial contributions from the bishop. An example of direct aid is provided by the town of San Luís, where processions were held on a number of occasions in 1786. The image of the Virgin of Guadalupe was carried three *leguas* by the townsfolk. After one of these processions, the priest organized a soup kitchen in the girls school, which provided a meal for five hundred of those in need every day. In combination with this, the bishops provided large sums of money to finance extra harvests in the tierra caliente, where the maize ripened three times as rapidly as in the highlands. The main provinces involved were Cuernavaca, Cuautla Amilpas, Tasco, Malinalco, Zacualpan, and Temascaltepec, as well as the southern faldas, where it was not as humid as in the northern sierra. But the priest of Huejutla, in northern Metztitlán, had also received four thousand pesos from the bishop to grow maize in the tropical parts of his parish that could soon be put on the market. The production of the maize proceeded without any difficulties, but there were serious problems during the transportation to the big cities in the highlands. For example, the road through the valley of Metztitlán was washed away by the rains in the summer of 1786, so that the bishop's carriers were unable to get the heavy sacks with the precious maize from the faldas to their destination. Humboldt points out that maize has a greater volume than wheat, which creates transport problems. The bishops had to decide on such a *préstamo gracioso* without delay, because it only took four months before a general harvest failure started to claim its victims.[23]

To conclude, the government officials and commercial entrepreneurs did not fail to do their duty within the framework of the ecological ethic. As soon as the need among the poorest strata of society grew acute, they gave up the large profits that could be made by speculation and engaged in poor relief on a large scale. Although to a large extent this came in response to the demands of the poor themselves—there was the danger of revolts if the starving were left to their fate—the church and religion still exerted sufficient influence to compel the members of the elite to observe their obligations to dispense poor relief.

The Maize Trade

While no problems for the entitlements to food appeared in the short term, in the long run considerable changes took place, particularly in the distribution of maize, the food of the people par excellence. During most of the colonial period, the government tried to maintain strict control of this distribution during ordinary years as well as attempting to prevent the existence of the poorest strata from being threatened by high prices resulting from speculation. More than half the population lived on a daily diet of a combination of tortillas, chili peppers, and other vegetables, some dried meat, ham, beans, and fruit. The main meal was prepared with lard (*manteca*), then sold in the village stores and by peddlers on the weekly markets. This meal, which was usually eaten around three o'clock, was accompanied by pulque, hot chocolate (cacao made by using boiling water) or *atole* (maize flour mixed with boiling water). The evening meal was lighter and included less meat. There was a larger demand for maize on feast days when tamales were consumed and more atole was drunk. People preferred to leave their own stocks intact for these feast days, buying extra maize on the market or from a store or hacienda.

Here political-economic opportunities arose. In this period of failing village harvests, the haciendas could try to expand their maize production for the market. However, looking in hacienda archives, I have not been able to discover traces of bringing fresh land under cultivation in Anáhuac like those mentioned by Brading and Morin for the Bajío district in the region of Michoacán.[24] We can gain an idea of how large the share of the haciendas in the maize market was around the turn of the century from the example of the parish of Tepozotlán in the province of Cuautitlán. Seventeen agricultural enterprises (most of them were ranchos, but the haciendas produced the biggest harvests) produced more than 2,950 cargas in 1807. There were eight Indian pueblos in the parish, with a joint harvest of 1,620 cargas, 1,000 of which were the produce of Tepozotlán alone. This means that 64 percent of the maize harvest in the parish was under commercial cultivation. Besides the hacendados, the rancheros also offered maize on the free market, but these will not have been large quantities. This can be illustrated from an example of a few rancheros in the province of Otumba during the late eighteenth century. There were fifteen rancheros in the village of Axapusco at the time, who sowed a total of fifty-five fanegas with maize, that is, an average of around five fanegas per rancho. The neighboring village of Ostoticpac only had five rancheros, who had sowed seventeen fanegas, that is, an average of slightly more than three per rancho. There were nine rancheros in the village of Otumba itself, each of whom had sowed an average of three fanegas. By comparison, the Hacienda San José Acolman alone, which virtually bordered on these villages and produced maize as a secondary product in addition to wheat and pulque, sowed around forty fanegas at this time. Like the Indians from the villages, the rancheros sold their maize on the many street markets in town or supplied the groceries (*pulperías*).[25]

On the basis of the accounts kept by the hacendados, there are, theoretically, in addition to the extension of the area under cultivation, two other ways of investigating whether hacienda production increased in the eighteenth century: an increase in the yield in units of weight per hectare, or an increase in the yield ratios (ratio of sowing seed to harvest).[26] However, too little documentation has been preserved from haciendas over a long enough period to carry out the detailed analysis that this would require. In the case of only a few haciendas, I have seen documentation covering a period of more than ten years. Moreover, there are exceptionally few statistics available for the most interesting period, that of 1770–1810. The yield ratios of a few haciendas in Anáhuac are presented in Table 5, and those specifically relating to the Hacienda San Martín (Tlaxcala) and the Hacienda San José Acolman (Otumba) are presented in Table 6. The maize yield was somewhere between 80 and 100 units per unit of seed. The top scorer in Table 5 is the Hacienda Sotoluca in the valley of Mexico, with a yield ratio of 290:1 for 1791. The maize harvest on the Hacienda Acuicuilco was very good as well, with a yield ratio of 215:1 in 1768. The Hacienda San José Acolman harvested 207:1 in 1776, and Palula harvested 142:1 in 1766. In general, the yield of the haciendas are said, by a number of civil servants in the viceroyalty, to have been lower than that in the Indian townships. Curiously, this fact brought them to advocate the division of the haciendas as a remedy for the food problem, though this plea for land reforms was not heard in Madrid.[27]

Incidentally, the yield ratio of wheat was naturally much lower: it ranged between 6 and 17 units for each unit of seed, although judicious sowing meant that the wheat harvest in Anáhuac was at least twice that in Europe in the same period. The Hacienda San Diego Pinal in Tlaxcala was an exception in this respect, producing a yield ratio of 21:1 in 1762. The Hacienda Acuicuilco (Huejotzingo) had a yield of 19½:1 in 1768, and the Hacienda San Antonio Palula yielded 13:1 in 1766. As shown in Table 6, there were extremely large fluctuations and differences between the yield ratios. The yield ratios for maize on the Hacienda San Martín fluctuated between 30:1 and 177:1 in a period of barely four years! All this was due to the differences in the soil and climate with which every hacendado was confronted, as well as to the different climatological circumstances, which varied from year to year. The material is too scanty and heterogeneous to support any hard conclusions. It is therefore impossible to use the accounts to determine whether production on the haciendas actually did expand in the eighteenth century.

On the other hand, the documents do allow a picture of the hacendados' customers. The hacendados grew their maize primarily to feed their servants and not for commercial purposes.[28] Besides, they could sell their surplus to

Table 5 Some maize and wheat yields on selected haciendas and one pueblo in Anáhuac (three periods)

WHEAT

1700–40		1740–80		1780–1810	
Texomulco	9	Los Reyes	10	Chichimapan	3
San José	8	Acuicuilco	12	Bautista	7
		Acolman	6	Acolman	8
		Pinal	12	Pilares	7
		Palula	13		
		Santa Agueda	14		
		Mixco	8		
		Aragón	15		
		Pueblo Tlalmanalco	10		
average	8		17		6

MAIZE

1700–40		1740–80		1780–1810	
Texomulco	16	Acolman	125	Acolman	93
Xaltipan	62	Ozumba	78	Sotoluca	290
		La Noria	40	Chichimapan	39
		Pinal	90	Bautista	105
		Acozac	81	Pilares	35
		Acuicuilco	139		
		San Martín	99		
		Aragón	38		
		Los Reyes	40		
		Pueblo Tlalmanalco	50		
average	47		78		112

peddlers and shopkeepers on the local markets. For example, a good 70 percent of the maize in the province of Texcoco was consumed locally in 1819 by both the population of the province and the pigs on the pig farms. Most of the average annual production of five hundred fanegas in the province of Tulancingo was consumed by the inhabitants of the province themselves around the year 1785. In the first instance, maize production in the province was accomplished by the twenty or so haciendas situated there at the time. It was necessary to grow maize for the servants, a hacendado wrote at the time, to prevent them from looking for another employer. The surplus was sold in the villages of the province, in most cases through stores in the hands of the hacendados themselves. These stores were rented out to relatives. An inspector from Mexico City noted that the maize in these stores was usually sold below the market price and often on credit, too, through a *tienda de raya* (a

Table 6 Yields of maize and wheat on two selected haciendas

ienda San Martín (Tlaxcala)				Hacienda San José Acolman (Otumba)						
	maize				maize				wheat	
	seed	harvest	:1		seed	harvest	:1	seed	harvest	:1
–51	27.0	2,650	98	1776	16.5	3,424	207	253	2,075	8
–52	24.5	3,000	124	1777	28.5	3,760	132	253	2,265	9
–53	26.5	3, 730	141	1778	28.5	1,321	46	254	2,483	10
–54	28.5	860	30	1779	20.0	1,896	95	317	2,016	6
–55	27.5	3,580	130	1780	20.5	1,370	67	259	1,651	6
–56	22.5	910	40	1781	20.0	2,800	136	248	3,184	13
–57	23.5	2,540	108	1782	20.0	1,560	78	288	2,281	8
–58	21.5	3,770	177	1783	20.5	2,000	98	294	1,639	6
–59	25.5	2,250	88	1784	22.5	940	42	264	981	4
–60	29.5	3,540	121	1785	19.0	890	47	268	2,151	8
–61	25.5	750	30	1786	—	—	—	274	3,129	11

[maize in fanegas, wheat in cargas]
Source: AGET 1761, Leg.2, Exp.6; AGNM, Colegios, Vols. 12, 30, 31, and 33.

store where purchases could be made on credit). This was also the case with the maize that the hacendados put on sale each week in a market stall in the town of Tulancingo, for example. A few hacendados in the province sold maize to middlemen from outside the province; a buyer from Mexico City or the owner of a silver mine in neighboring Real del Monte (Pachuca). The hacendados only sold at the granary door (troje) in times of shortage.[29]

After the selection of the maize seed and the donation of the bad ears to the church (for the tithe), part of the harvest was reserved for the peons' rations (about one-quarter of the harvest). A hacienda like Acolman produced a lot of maize for the pig farms, and part of the harvest was also destined for the donkeys and mules, but the majority of the haciendas sold the maize to a handful of customers each year for consumption in the towns and villages. From the figures for the Hacienda San Diego Pinal (Tlaxcala) covering the years 1754 to 1762, we know that it sold 5 percent of the 1,827 cargas (28 percent of the harvest yield in the period) at the granary door—14 of these cargas were sold to the Indians from Ixmiquilpan, 200 km away from the hacienda!—5 percent to the granary of Puebla, and the rest to seven merchants. Most of the maize produced on the hacienda was for the pigs there. The Hacienda San Antonio Xala (Apan) sowed 3 percent of the harvest (380 fanegas of maize) in 1786; 25 percent was for the rations. The rest was sold: 27 percent to the company servants, and 44 percent to a pig farmer in the neighborhood. In 1735 the Hacienda Xaltipan in Tlaxcala had five buyers from Puebla de los

Angeles, who were prepared to buy 322 cargas, 113½ cargas, 26 cargas, 20 cargas, and 9½ cargas, respectively; the price varied between fourteen and eighteen reales per carga. The maize involved in this transaction accounted for 75 percent of the harvest. In 1780, the Hacienda Acozac (Chalco) harvested 1,000 cargas; 10 of these were selected as sowing seed, 3 cargas of poor seed were used as horse fodder, the senior members of staff of the hacienda received 10 cargas, and 877 cargas (88 percent of the harvest) were sold. The farmhands of the hacienda paid for their rations themselves. This accounted for 100 cargas, sold to them at a price of sixteen reales per carga. The remaining 777 cargas were sold to seven customers at prices ranging between eighteen and thirty-six reales per carga. Two customers who bought 500 cargas were able to bargain for the lowest prices, while the five other customers had to pay much higher prices. The prices of these consignments were far above those of the *alhóndiga*, the urban central grain exchange, in the same year. The Malpais and Sotoluca haciendas (Apan and Otumba) sold almost 72 percent of the 1791 harvest to the *encomendero de alhóndiga* José Manuel de Arechaga; 6 percent was for the workers' rations, 6 percent was sold to the workers separately on credit, 1½ percent was sold to peddlers, ½ percent was reserved as sowing seed, ½ percent was used in the hacienda kitchen, and 13½ percent was left unsold. The accounts reveal that the smaller quantities were sold husked (*desgranado*) to passing traders, while the large amounts of corn on the cob (*mazorcas*) were kept back for the encomenderos de alhóndiga after an order (*encomienda*) had been placed well in advance. These stocks were delivered in Mexico City and in Puebla de los Angeles or Tlaxcala City.[30]

In sum, I have not been able to find much information bearing on the question of an expansion of the maize market through an increase in hacienda sales. It is therefore necessary to retrace our steps to Mexico City and the statistics for the grain exchanges found there. The main feature of the grain exchange was the large government influence on price determination.[31] The cities had a special board, the Tribunal de Fiel Ejecutoria, which was entrusted with the duty of supervision. The Tribunal was active in three main areas: the determination of the maximum prices for a few major subsistence articles; the inspection of workplaces and markets, intended to encourage and supervise the observance of the regulations; and the regulation of the maize market by obliging the producers to sell their maize to the alhóndiga. Since it was not obligatory in New Spain for the inhabitants of the Indian pueblos to sell their maize through the alhóndiga, virtually all the maize that was traded came from the hacendados. The exemption from the obligation to sell on the alhóndiga also applied to those rancheros with the *calidad de indio*. These restrictions make the alhóndiga figures suspect: would it not be advantageous for any hacendado to have his maize sold freely in the city by one of his Indian dependents? Anyway, the alhóndiga was able to affect the maize prices inside its buildings thanks to the stocks that the exchange itself had stored in a granary (*pósito*). The maize for the pósito was bought in the provinces close to the city and offered for sale on the alhóndiga if prices rose too rapidly.[32]

Most of the hacendados who did actively supply the grain exchange had their hacienda in the province of Chalco. This province accounted for almost a quarter of all the maize cultivated commercially in the diocese of Mexico in the eighteenth century. One-third of the maize in this diocese came from the provinces of Texcoco and Cuautitlán, and one-fifth from the valley of Toluca. The maize from Texcoco and Cuautitlán was more expensive because it had to be transported by mule. Moreover, this maize had a bad reputation. The maize from Toluca had a similar bad reputation and proved to be harder to keep. The transport advantage of the producers in Chalco was considerable. This province southeast of the city was linked to the capital by means of a network of canals. The produce could be transported almost directly from the haciendas to the entrance of the grain exchange by canoe. In 1743, the price for the transport of thirty-five cargas of maize by canoe was 4p2, as against a price of 26p2 for the transport of the same cargo over the same distance by mule! Between 70 and 150 canoes arrived in Mexico City every day. The cargo was brought to the granaries of the alhóndiga or to those of the merchants in the city by porters. An example from 1811 shows how cheap transport by canoe was in comparison with the price of these porters. The Hacienda San Nicolás Buenavista in Mexicalcingo had sent eighteen cargas of straw to a merchant in Mexico City in that year, a distance of a good thirty kilometers. The transport cost 2p2 for hiring a canoe and 0p2 to pay the rowers. The price for the same cargo to be transported a few hundred meters within the city itself by the porters was the same: 2p2. More than forty haciendas were involved in the production of maize in Chalco.[33]

The supply to Puebla de los Angeles was arranged with haciendas in the province of Tepeaca. They supplied maize of the same quality as that produced in Chalco for the capital, but they lacked the transport advantages. The alhóndiga in Puebla therefore had built larger granaries in the city, where the producers could store their maize for twenty days before proceeding to sell it, though the producers were allowed to order it to be sold earlier. Thomson has published a precise and detailed description of the development of the public granary in Puebla.[34] As in Mexico City, trading took place both "inside" the premises, by the hacendados, and "outside," in the patio, by the small producers. In addition, maize was also sold (illegally) at other points in the city. Thomson shows that the regulations were even treated lightly in the granary itself, so that the hacendados were able to secure higher prices. The result was bound to follow: the government intervened in 1800 to assist the small retailers "outside" the premises. The hacendados were left with their maize on their hands, which was left to rot in the granaries. After the harvest failures of 1809–11, which particularly affected the smaller producers, the city had no maize.

The volume of maize traded in Mexico City probably matched the city's demand. In fact, if the production of the small farmers is included in that of the grain exchange, there was probably something of a maize surplus. According to the 1790 census, Mexico City had a population of 112,926, of whom

25,603 inhabitants were registered as of the *calidad de indio* (under the authority of specific pueblos that were districts of the city). The rest of the population consisted of the Spanish (some 61,000) or the casta. It may be assumed
that the maize in the city was only consumed by the "indios" and perhaps the
majority of the 7,100 mulatos, resulting in an estimate of about 33,000 potential maize consumers in 1790. The indios in the suburbs had their own agricultural land, however, so that the number of people who depended on the
alhóndiga was much lower.

The literature usually refers to the figure of twenty-five fanegas of maize
as the annual requirement of a colonial Mexican family comprising 4½ individuals. This corresponds to one *cuartillo* per person per day (roughly eight
tortillas). According to the estimates of Cook and Borah, this provided enough
calories per person: each cuartillo provided more than 80 percent of the average daily requirement of calories in New Spain. The rest came from the beans,
chili peppers, and vegetables mentioned at the beginning of this section. Cook
and Borah consider that consumption was even one-third in excess of the
actual requirement of the time. Approximately 700 fanegas would thus have
been required each day in Mexico City in 1790 (= 21,000 fanegas a month).
The monthly import of maize into the city in 1709, when the population was
50 percent less than it was in 1790, was 8,100 fanegas. The corresponding
figure for 1773 is 10,000 fanegas, which was probably too low. In 1796, 9,179
fanegas were sold each month, which is obviously not enough when compared with the 21,000 required.[35] If this reflects a trend, it indicates a moderate increase of sales in the city, a process that was under the control of the
producers.

However, this is pure speculation, because the peaks in trade and prices
should lead us to cast doubt on it. Since Florescano regards the alhóndiga
prices as a reflection of maize production, he uses price trends as the basis for
the reconstruction of an annual cycle, in the first place, and of ten agrarian
cycles in the eighteenth century, in the second place. Closer examination indicates that a number of annual peaks coincide with the main religious holi-
days of Easter and Corpus Christi. Thus, there is little need to follow Florescano
in assuming that the increased demand on the grain exchange at these times
is an indication that the stocks of the Indians were exhausted. It seems more
likely that people were reluctant to touch their own stocks during feast days
so as to avoid shortages later in the year, especially when the maize would
have been paid by the confraternities in the townships. Moreover, the monthly
fluctuations in the maize trade were much higher than the annual averages of
Florescano's general series. No two years were alike in this respect. When the
harvests were good, the trading rates were well below the average he gives of
8,000 fanegas per annum, while in bad periods they were far above the average. The statistics even reveal a difference of 13,339 fanegas in May 1741 and
457 fanegas in February 1767. This difference is far in excess of the difference
mentioned of three times as much trade in bad years. It is therefore tempting
to suppose that the alhóndiga was not the major market, because very many

Indians sold maize freely on the streets.[36] In that case, the maize sold on the alhóndiga was probably of secondary importance, and may even have been of inferior quality.

According to Florescano, the high prices were the result of speculation—which he never tires of berating—which hit the poor hard. Low prices like those of the 1760s led to speculation in stocks in the commercial maize trade. We know that the small producers had already sold their surplus before the hacendados appeared on the market with their harvest later in the year. Indeed, the seasonal fluctuation in prices on the alhóndiga fell during the summer because the hacendados were able to maintain the price at what they considered an acceptable level for a few months thanks to their storage policy.[37] At the time this procedure was regarded as no more than a sensible policy to guarantee one's survival. This storage policy is also familiar from European agrarian history, and it was regarded by both the large-scale agrarian producers and the middlemen as the best way of covering high production and transport costs. A Mexican writer of the period, however, described it in 1773 as a risky business, for the hacendados could not delay too long in putting their maize on the market; otherwise, the seeds would soon sprout or start to go moldy in the rainy season. He saw a partial remedy for this problem in building trojes, or barns, with very thick walls to reduce differences in temperature and increases in humidity. In fact, hacendados did build such barns and the thick walls gave the trojes the menacing appearance of impregnable fortresses. Moreover, he claims, it was essential to leave the maize as long as possible in the field so that it could dry properly in the warm winter sun. This all means that the hacendados had to match their retail policy to the quality of the maize in storage and to what the demand in the city allowed. All the same, I suspect that the storage policy in New Spain was only profitable for those hacendados with large financial reserves: the elite merchants. Producers who depended on the sale of their harvest for the greater part of their income did not have the economic backing to keep the lock on the granary door for long. The producers from the villages and the ranchos belonged to this group, as did the agricultural companies of smaller entrepreneurs and, surprisingly enough, of the Jesuits.[38] They opted for rapid sales and gained information on local differences in prices. Speculation was beyond the liquidity of the Jesuit companies, so this market policy offered them a good alternative.[39] This was also true of smaller hacendados. Apparently, regional price differences were large enough to make it worth their while.

The value of the price of maize as an index of the rhythm of production is called into question even more if we turn to data recorded by the hacendados. It appears that the sales by the hacendados to the alhóndiga displayed the same fluctuations, but that prices remained stable. The encomenderos de alhóndiga were private middlemen, who had placed their orders (encomiendas) with the hacendados well in advance. This trade was illegal, but the authorities were prepared to turn a blind eye under pressure from the producers. Like the merchants, each encomendero had his own network of customers. The hacienda accounts reveal that *fixed prices* were agreed upon, which were only altered if there were large price differences. In general, the prices agreed upon between the hacendado and the encomendero were, of course, stable for months, and only rose at times of extreme scarcity (as in the autumn of 1780 and after February 1785). Some tentative research into these price differences suggest that at least until 1780 the maize prices in Mexico City were lower than in the surrounding areas, with the exception of the "maize granary" of Chalco, which had the same price level as the city.[40] What is important is the rising trend that had set in after the recovery of the market from the famine of 1786. There is every reason to suppose that the average price level after 1786 was higher than before that year. This may be an indication of a monetary inflation, but it may also point to poorer sales on the free market in the city. Since the latter would be due to bad harvests in the villages, it may be concluded that the price level on the free market must have risen too.

Florescano himself indicates that the rise in prices in the late eighteenth century can be attributed to the disappearance of state control. In the late eighteenth century the functioning of the alhóndiga and pósito came under pressure. The pósito, the main instrument of price control, was dependent on the budget granted by the city administration, in which the major merchants and agrarian producers were well represented. One result was that the pósito preferred to buy from friends who were hacendados or from hacendados who held a position on the city council. The biggest encomenderos on the grain exchange were the ones who placed their orders with the very same hacendados. In other words, the grain exchange assured the elite in Mexico City and Puebla de los Angeles of a good trade in the city. However, this trade was inevitably bound by price limits. The population growth in the cities in the late eighteenth century gave many producers the idea of bypassing the buyers on the grain exchange and looking for ways of obtaining higher prices. From then on the practices of the grain exchange were felt to be acting as a brake on these alternatives. The resistance to the pósito was expressed by cutting its budget.[41]

These factors took their toll. The city administration no longer had a granary. After the harvest failure of 1785, for instance, the pósito of Puebla hardly had any reserves to feed the hungry, let alone to prevent price increases. It had to borrow fifty thousand pesos from the archbishop in order to replenish stocks. A few years later, the pósito had become virtually extinct in Puebla. The same was true of the pósitos in the smaller provincial towns. The function of this government body continued to exist in Mexico City, but its effectiveness was seriously impaired. At the turn of the century it was possible to speculate with maize much more than it had been in the past. These events took place in a period of reasonably successful harvests on the haciendas and harvest failures in the villages. The influence of peddlers, shopkeepers, and other middlemen in the economy of Anáhuac increased considerably as a result of the drop in self-sufficiency in the villages. The abolition of the pósito can be regarded as a pregnant sign of the times, comparable to the problems faced by the manufacturing guilds in the same period. The data reviewed in this section indicate a higher maize price after the 1780s, which may have resulted in an increased share of the haciendas in the maize market. The haciendas may have produced more maize, but I do not believe that any revolution took place in this field. However, the abolition of the pósito was a step in the direction of a freer market. It meant a loss to food entitlements for the poor in their relation with state officials.

Such entitlements had not been formed in the wheat trade, the other staple, because wheat had always found relatively few Indian consumers in the rural areas, and even in the cities of Mexico.[42] The market was much smaller, since only 20 to 30 percent of the population of Anáhuac consumed bread on a regular basis. It is true, though, that wheat was the main crop for the haciendas in the highlands; it was an expensive main crop, because it required irrigated soil. This meant that the haciendas had to demand high prices to cover their expenses. Spanish interests in the wheat trade were much larger than in the maize trade, and a government institution like the pósito, to ensure low consumer prices, was extremely undesirable in the eyes of the wheat producers. It is hardly surprising that the pósitos set up throughout the country in the sixteenth century, in regions with a relatively high percentage of non-Indians, soon went into decline or disappeared altogether. The regulatory function of the government was apparently irreconcilable with the need of the producers to obtain as high a price as possible for the main product of their agricultural companies. Commercial arguments in this sphere thus gained the upper hand over charitable considerations at an early stage.

But competition ran high. The documentation contains indications supporting the claim that there was an overproduction of wheat in Anáhuac well into the nineteenth century. In the eighteenth century it was the wealthy middlemen, the millers, or molineros, in Mexico City, who ensured that the price remained high. They had a majority share in the metropolitan flour market and were able to win the bakers over to their way of thinking. The situation in Puebla de los Angeles, according to Thomson, was the opposite. Wheat farmers and bakers, together with the millers, constituted a powerful economic group in the city, persuading the city council to supervise the production and sale of bread. Despite the wishes of the bakers, the producers successfully lobbied for the introduction of a wheat assize to set prices in slump years above their free-market price in order to guarantee them a profit above the high cost price. The wheat assize was temporarily suspended in 1767, but the unstable conditions facing wheat agriculture in 1769, 1777, 1789 and 1802 led to the introduction of regulation again. It was not abolished for good until 1813.[43]

It should be added that the Tribunal de Fiel Ejecutoria saw little reason to rejuvenate the declining wheat pósitos. Supervision was limited to control of the quality of the bread and ensuring that the bakers adhered to the guild regulations. In fact, they appear to have observed them closely. Contraventions were punished with a stiff fine, and the guild's wishes were complied with by preventing an increase in the number of bakeries in the course of the eighteenth century. This stability is remarkable in the light of the rapid population growth in Mexico City around 1800. It is highly probable that the new immigrants generally followed their traditional diet and continued to consume maize. Therefore it was neither desirable nor profitable to increase the amount of flour that was processed in the city. The wheat flour market does not enter discussions of the bargaining position of the poorest strata, because they could not afford bread anyway. The case for the overproduction of flour seems to have been proved if the flour could hardly be sold in the large cities.[44] It is thus unlikely that further research in the archives will produce evidence for an impressive increase in wheat production, similar to that of the Bajío.

To conclude, the wheat trade was commercialized at any early stage, but in the late eighteenth century it was in a state of overproduction. The only influence exerted by the state was through the bakers in the cities, while the intermediate trade itself was monopolized by the molineros. The maize trade in Mexico City was under strong government control, but here too the crown was unable to prevent the intermediate trade from determining price levels. In all, if my argument is correct, this means that in the "lord"/"subject" relationship one important transformation *did* occur: the "subjects" did lose "entitlement to food" vis-à-vis the state, precisely because the state gave up the regulation of the food market in Anáhuac. In a period of increased political economy, the role of the state was taken over by hacendados and other entrepreneurs. As we have seen, however, they too were still prepared to answer appeals to charity in the outgoing colonial period and sell to the poor for low prices in times of dearth. Consequently, in general, the entitlements of the rural population were not bad.

The Six Hundred *Varas*

Land Tenure and Vassalage

The role of the state did not decrease on the other "charity road" the Indians could follow: securing the community's landbase. The expansion of cultivable land is a low-pressure solution, considered before emigration or other high-pressure solutions are chosen. In theory it is an individual, private question for each peasant household, hardly a "corporate" one.[45] Curiously, in Anáhuac the task of acquiring more land was in the hands of the community officers in the Indian townships. If this "solution" was indeed sought in a "corporate" way, the question of the increase of the area of land under cultivation raises questions about how the pueblos were organized internally and about the scope of their landownership. Therefore, again, before discussing the relevant data, I need to clarify the pre-Hispanic and early colonial heritage considering pueblo land tenure. This involves the introduction of the concept of vassalage.

As we have seen, there was very little good agricultural land in Anáhuac, and what could be kept under the plow was already cultivated by a great number of pueblos de indios, some rancheros, and many hacendados. Consequently, one could suppose that the Indians were trying to acquire or purchase more land. From the viewpoint of the twentieth century, the land market looks like the most obvious place to pursue such a quest. But such was not the case in the eighteenth century. In a capitalist economy, land is primarily a commodity, in which the right to work the land is transferable. In such a case, land is free of all kinds of claims that might be made on the basis of custom, claims described by Thompson as "the grid of inheritance." According to the historical geographer Butlin, the erosion of these customs is the last phase in the penetration of the countryside by a capitalist mentality. Previously, it was land use and the rights to parts of the harvest, not landownership, which was important, including the right to decide on land use and its terms. In a small-scale, simple economy, access to land was theoretically open to all. It was not the field, but the crop that belonged to the peasant, and after the harvest the field reverted to common ground again—to be used as a stubble field, for example. If the user showed no signs of intending to sow the same field again, his right to work it passed to someone else. This free access to fertile land raised difficulties when the population density increased. Good agricultural land was scarce, and the technology for improving it was limited. The community of peasants created institutions to determine the right to use the land (and the water as well), or left the decision to a landlord. Village leadership was also required to maintain the community's external contacts.[46]

For heuristic reasons, it can be useful to remain in Europe for a little while longer. In medieval and modern Spain, for example, common land was exploited by the legal residents of the municipalities. Every member was assured of a free right of use as permitted by the number of residents in the population. The municipal council settled external matters in particular, including the defense of the municipal borders and the transfer of taxes that the peasants were obliged to pay to the church and state. The municipal authorities were usually well-to-do persons, who cultivated more land than the poorest residents because of their status as "more equal than the rest." This was acceptable as long as they were prepared to meet the demands of the ecological ethic. If the population continued to expand, the municipal council was also empowered to regulate the use of land. Vassberg discovered a high degree of uniformity in this Spanish—Castilian—practice from the thirteenth century on, with only a few variants: each taxable resident of a municipality was allocated a plot of land by the municipal council; and in some cases lots were cast. Villagers could refuse land and retain the right to another plot. The allocation procedure was carried out each year in many municipalities, but the trend was toward one allocation per family, leading to the more permanent "possession" (that is, use right) of plots of land by families. They came to regard the land as their own "property." Vassberg notes that the richer families, who divided the functions of the municipal council among themselves, allocated the plots of land in a way that was extremely favorable to themselves.[47] The transition indicated here, which had such a profound effect on the character of the village administration, passed from Personenverband to Territorialverband, which took place all over Europe in the thirteenth century.

Although the Indian lords rapidly adapted the Spanish urban rules—the Indian lords of, for example, Tlaxcala, Tehuacán, or Cuernavaca pleaded in Mexico City for their pueblos to be recognized as cities—Indian society as a whole—including the lordships of the mentioned lords—had not yet reached this stage. Borah draws attention to an important comparative point:

> For the Indians land was essentially a means of production, held by the community or clan and allocated to support certain offices or functions. Tenure was fundamentally conditioned and subject always to the requirement of use. Indian conceptions of the nature of landholding most closely approximated those of the feudal linkage of land tenure to service or office. It is unlikely that aboriginal Indian society had any conception of the owning of land in the sense of Roman law, that a man could be the master of land which was his to allow to remain idle, destroy, or till as he chose, subject only to the right of the sovereign to tax or take for public use on due compensation.[48]

I read this as use rights, within a Personenverband. If that is correct, one can imagine the consequences. Ethnohistorians already detected factual ownership of land in pre-Hispanic times. Does our modern sense of property—the "grid of inheritance" of our own scientific community—stand in the way of analyzing Indian society with *their* eyes? Indeed, it may be that we engage too often in retrojection, as twentieth-century Indian community life, centered around a village *cabildo* and communal land tenure, and known through anthropological research, is projected onto the colonial or even pre-Hispanic past. Anthropological and ethnohistorical research, however, only presents the final stage, the situation within a Territorialverband. It is undoubtedly more logical to start with the *altepetl* or indigenous demesne, which is bound to be closer to the Personenverband in theoretical terms alone, and then to proceed to the analysis of the pueblo by means of comparative hypotheses.

However, in-depth analysis of the pueblos in Anáhuac runs up against difficulties caused by the lack of a considerable body of research. I would have preferred to present a carefully wrought text with a large body of evidence, as in some of the other chapters of this volume. A large number of references to other literature or to archive material is usually the result of caution and scientific wariness. However, such caution is not a sign of insecurity, but of tactics, because daring or generalizing claims sound less explosive if they find an echo in a library or archive. It could have led to some demoralization of the reader, which usually sets in when every sentence involves a discussion with the views put forward by those to who the notes in the text refer. The same applies to texts in which every sentence is derived from, and thus can only be understood by reading, the books mentioned in the notes. I would have been prepared to run the risk of demoralizing the reader in this way.

Nevertheless, I hope to be sufficiently convincing with the only alterna-tive left open to me: a view of the Indian community in Anáhuac based on some hypothetical assumptions. And these are somewhat different from the traditional view, for the publications on the Indian townships available to students of Mexico today form an implicit or explicit twentieth-century pro-jection.[49] This forces me to make a choice: the point of reference of what follows is not the usual mass of ethnographical, anthropological, or archeo-logical literature with which students of Mexico are most familiar, but the European literature on communities and relations of authority in the coun-tryside before the Industrial Revolution. As already expressed, I try to under-stand the eighteenth-century Indians by listening to their contemporaries in Europe instead of to my own contemporaries in twentieth-century Indian town-ships, because otherwise I am afraid that I will hear nothing but an echo of my own times.[50]

Order, "Ethnicity," and Indian Lordship

What was a "pueblo de indios"? Recently James Lockhart took a seem-ingly neutral position by defining the pueblo as a "Spanish term for an altepetl, but also applied to any identifiable indigenous settlement." An altepetl, then, was "any sovereign state; in central Mexican conditions, generally the local ethnic states the Spaniards were to call 'pueblos' [sic!]. They became munici-palities after the conquest and are occasionally called 'towns'." This defini-tion has a Derridaen deconstructive quality ("Il n'y a pas de hors-texte."[51]) that makes it difficult to work with. But the notion is not at all "inabordable," I think, and Lockhart also seems to understand it outside this deconstructive context and shows a preference for political geography ("ethnic states," "iden-tifiable indigenous settlement"). Curiously he pays little attention to the ju-ridical and administrative origins of the pueblo. Lockhart continues:

> The entity was partially defined by its tradition of ethnic distinct-ness, partially by its possession of a certain territory, and partially by its dynastic ruler, the *tlatoani*, whom the Spaniards immediately and correctly recognized as such, terming him the cacique.[52]

Though Lockhart states that there was much more continuity after conquest than presupposed, this definition of the pueblo seems to me too imprecise, too personalized, too static, and, as mentioned, too deconstructive, as if no change occurred between the pre-Hispanic period and the late eighteenth cen-tury, or between the altepetl and the pueblo. Therefore, I seek something more solid. After all, during all of its different stages, both Spaniards and Indians knew exactly what a pueblo was, and could give it a firm administrative and juridical foundation.

However, even this approach is far from generally accepted. Most writers concerned with the Indian villages defended the traditional stance of exploi-tation and destruction. If we follow a simple and elegant theory of looking at reality, what we see often seems to confirm the theory by that fact alone. The personal views, cultural background, and education of the observer are just as important as what is observed. A perception that does not match the theory often does not take place at all, or it is explained away, disguised, or only mentioned without being integrated into the observer's perceptions. It is therefore strange that present-day Mexican ethnohistorical studies rarely deal with the question of their roots. It may well be difficult to find a serious scholar nowadays who still subscribes to the Black Legend, but that does not mean that it has had its day. Was it not barely a decade ago that—in a survey of the history of the hacienda—Van Young referred to the major proposition in colonial research as "the continued seizure of Indian resources by non-Indians" and "its effect in undermining the integrity of the traditional landholding Indian community"?[53] In full agreement with Eric Wolf's position in 1959, or Charles Gibson's in 1964, I find two elements of the Indian community that were supposed to be historically and indissolubly under fire: the integrity of the Indian community and its land resources.

It will be clear that a discussion of the character of the altepetl should concentrate on its land base. Nevertheless, in translating terms like altepetl or pueblo, the first problem I encounter is a semantic one. If we are to describe a specific situation in colonial Mexico in the English language, we must watch what we say. Are words like *town* or *village* correct? We—the author and the reader—are well aware that each country has its own history, of course, and that certain historical situations may be comparable. However, it is clear enough that I have not found a good translation or description of German terms like *Herrschaft* and *Personenverband*. We have to start on a quest in British history if we are to approximate as closely as possible the meaning that words like *town* or *village* possessed at the time. In a recent survey of the origins of the English village, Christopher Dyer defines the village as "a compact rural settlement containing at least six households and exercising some collective control over surrounding land." The households concerned need not live next door to one another in a street or around a central square; somewhat isolated units scattered over the land are also allowed. But there is a difference with a countryside dominated by single farmsteads. It was long supposed in English history that such compact villages were combined by feudal lords in the course of the development of feudalism to form manors; a sort of *reducción* within the walls of a hacienda. However, this traditional model has been revised to such an extent that it has now been reversed. "We can contemplate," Dyer writes, "the thought that lords made villages." First came the lords, then the manor, and finally the villages.[54]

But what is a "manor"? Is it synonymous with the word *hacienda,* as sociologist Cristóbal Kay claimed some twenty years ago? Certainly not, because Kay followed not only the traditional view of the hacienda, but also the traditional view of the manor.[55] For a long time, historians have advanced the idea that the Roman villa was the precursor of the medieval manor in England, as well as in France and Germany. A new version pushed the origins of "estates" back into Celtic, Saxon, Frankish, and Germanic prehistory, and argued that they were large and complex organizations, with specialized functions assigned to different parts of a "federated" structure. At this point, Dyer comes up with a second definition that is important for present comparative purposes: the manor is defined as the unit of lordship, divided between land reserved for the lord's own use (demesne) and that held by peasants, through which the peasants provided the lord with an income directly by paying rents—in cash or kind—or indirectly by laboring on the demesne. In fact, the British manor had its roots in what has been called a "multiple estate." In England and Wales, for example, dairying would be pursued in one place, barley grown in another, horses bred in a third. Each part of the "multiple estate" owed dues and services to a center, whose lord was thereby able to satisfy all of his requirements. The "estate" was rooted in a period of transition from a tribute-collecting regime to one based on demesnes and labor services. The word *estate* might be expected to describe a single block of land, as it currently does, as well as the scattered units subordinated to a single lord, that is, land *and* people. During the development of the medieval period, these "multiple estates" broke down into smaller units that would become the manors. The great attraction of the "multiple estate" as an idea, Dyer says, is that it gives precision to the archeological perception of societies exploiting resources, and provides the opportunity to visualize at an early period those intangible institutions of tenure, boundaries, obligations, and lordship.[56]

In the end, the manor could well develop into a modern farming "community," despite absentee lordship. The large manor of Havering, in the English southwest of Essex within thirty kilometers of London, is a peculiar example. It enjoyed certain special legal and administrative privileges, as a parcel of the royal ancient demesne. This freedom from central authority—to me, as will be argued, certainly similar to the status of the pueblos in Mexico—enabled the inhabitants to develop their own economic lives without restriction or serious exploitation by a manorial lord or the government. At first glance, the inhabitants show great political collectivism, above all during the 1381 revolt and in the manorial court. But in scrutinizing the peasants' lives inside the manor's borders, Marjorie K. McIntosh, who conducted research among the manorial documents, discovered an early appearance of a large wage-laboring force and crafts or industrial employments as early as the fourteenth century. McIntosh chooses the term *individualism* to describe this local social order and concludes that the environment was favorable for personal effort to maximize action and reward.[57]

Dyer's attraction to the definition of manorial rule appeals to me as well. But it breaks with any traditional conceptualization of the Indian community. It would mean that lords and lordship were integral parts of the "Indian community" of New Spain. In fact, it assumes that the colonial Indian villages were the product of lordship, and the pre-Hispanic altepetl as well. It is generally agreed that any description of colonial land tenure must begin with the inheritance of the period before the coming of the Spaniards. Although there can be hardly any doubt about the existence of communal landholding in the seventeenth and eighteenth centuries, historians, ethnologists, and anthropologists are increasingly uncertain as to its existence or importance in the sixteenth century. The sources most often used agree upon several categories of land, like lands assigned to the support of temples, office holders, the army, or the rulers (in this case, patrimonial lands). Most of them existed well into the seventeenth century, and designations in Nahuatl, the indigenous lingua franca, can be found until the end of the eighteenth century.[58]

The term *altepetl* was translated by the Spaniards as *señorío*, that is, a seigneury or lordship. Central to lordship was the liege of the "subjects." Theoretically, a specific group of individuals, probably a tribe originally, belonged to the lord's personal retinue. This lord received his seigneury from the monarch, the highest lord in the hierarchy. The Aztec monarch had held this prerogative by divine right; he was the gods' vassal or *macehual*. The lord lower down in the hierarchy could, in turn, transfer his seigneury to the lords below him, his vassals. Ethnicity and kinship did not need to play a part when the sociopolitical organization of a monarchy was based on personal relations of this kind, as, for instance, among the Franks of early medieval Europe. In such a situation, everyone could owe allegiance to the lord and thereby belong to the seigneury. Usually the lord's seigneury included rights to an income from domains. Although seigneurial domains such as a county and a barony—also known as a "benefice" or a "fief"—had specific territorial boundaries in the late Middle Ages, those people who belonged to the lord's seigneury were bound to their lord not because they lived on his land, but because they had a personal relation with him; they were his vassals. Seigneuries below the level of a kingdom or domain did not have specific boundaries, and it was possible for two neighbors in the same demesne to fall under the jurisdiction of different lords, while spiritual affairs fell under the jurisdiction of the church.[59]

Here we encounter the second theoretical difficulty that cannot be evaded: if the altepetl is to be viewed as a "seigneury" or "benefice" of this kind, how are we to define the relations within the altepetl? The most attractive course, in view of the striking analogy, is to choose a terminology acceptable in European medieval studies to indicate the transition from personal social relations to a legal and fiscal system based on territorial criteria: the transition from Personenverband to Territorialverband. Personal relations were dominant in a system of Personenverband. The Herrschaft discussed in chapter one was structured in accordance with the characteristics of a Personenverband. The well-known European system of vassalage was also based on this principle: the relations between liege man and liege lord, between vassal and feudal lord, were of a personal nature; there were separate jurisdictions for clerics, nobility, peasants, and later, urban residents.[60]

To me, there can be no doubt that the description of peasant life under a Personenverband and the corresponding symbolism, familiar from medieval studies, also applies to the period immediately preceding the Spanish invasion of 1519–21. The term *altepetl,* "mountain and water," was a metaphor for "the place where people can live." For the Nahuas, "mountain" and "water" were the two complementary elements necessary for the creation and continuation of life. The pyramid, *coatepetl* or serpent mountain, stood in the center of the altepetl like a man-made mountain and symbolized the triumph over the forces of nature. It was surmounted by a temple with a statue of the tribal deity, the divinity who guarded the independence of the altepetl. The leading men of the altepetl had subjected themselves to this deity and hereby had become his vassals. In return, or as a token of gratitude, the deity had delegated his power to them. Thus the power of human beings to triumph over nature was thus held from the gods in vassalage, like a seigneury. The lords, in turn, transferred this power to the lower nobility, who thereby were the vassals of the leading men. The lowest rung of the hierarchy was occupied by those who lacked nobility. Vassals owe a debt of tribute, recognition, and assistance to the powers that be. In the Aztec era this tribute consisted of the attributes of the altepetl: water and firewood. Everyone who was obliged to pay tribute also supplied "his" lord with his specific skill or "commission in life"; his *tequitl.* For the peasants, this meant a share of the harvest and manual labor. For the merchant, it included his artisanal products and his services. For the nobility, it meant the performance of duties in the civil and religious administration and military protection. Moreover, the lord of the altepetl offered the gods an extra blood sacrifice when he assumed power. When an altepetl was conquered, the first act was to evict the supernatural "lord," the tribal deity, from his throne and to make the lord himself a vassal of a new god. The temple was burned as a symbol of this fact.

In practice, the altepetl consisted of a group of peasants and a few aristocrats, led by an elected military chief—or prince—the *tlahtoani.* He ruled until he died, whereupon his brother, one of his cousins, his son, or, if no member of his family was deemed suitable, a male member of a different noble family was elected prince. In theory, the tlahtoani held rule on behalf of the gods, but in practice he had to take into consideration the wishes of the other aristocrats, who were sometimes united in a council of elders. He supervised the division of the agricultural land among the non-nobility, the nobles vassals or *macehualtin.* Land was allocated on a periodic basis and depending on the number of households in the retinue. He also guaranteed political and military protection for the peasants and arranged the religious ceremonies in the temples of the altepetl. In return, he received tribute through the intermediary of a so-called *calpolli,* the larger household within the altepetl (*calpolli* literally means "large house"), or of another sub-unit, the *tlaxilacalli,* a unit very similar to the calpolli.

Incidentally, it should be borne in mind that these terms are based on Aztec documentation, which is mainly derived from the central authorities, and reflect the situation in the capital Tenochtitlán and its immediate surroundings. Other terms were used as synonyms or variants in the provinces, and other linguistic groups naturally would have translated the terms into their own languages. Aztec organization, directed from above, had been much stronger in western Anáhuac than in the valley of Puebla, for instance, where the smaller noble's houses, referred to as *teccalli,* had kept their relative independence. In the *relaciones geográficas* of the early sixteenth century, all eastern nobles considered themselves allies of the Aztec king, not as his vassal. This was not without reason. I read Aztec history as a attempt to "bureaucratize" the "empire," from the capital to the outer provinces, on a step-by-step basis; and by 1520 the Aztec lord had succeeded in including the local household organization in the valleys of Mexico and Toluca, but not the one on the eastern side of the volcanoes. In the western part of Anáhuac, the nobles acted as the heads of the calpolli units of local society. The noble titles seem to have been related directly to these units, as if they were appointed by the central authorities regardless of the continuance of a line of nobles. In the eastern part of Anáhuac, the lords seem to have kept their lordly lines, their "houses." This might explain why researchers find the usage of calpolli more in western Anáhuac, and teccalli more in eastern Anáhuac.[61] But in both cases, the lord/subject relationship followed the altepetl organization as described in this chapter.

After the "bureaucratization" of the altepetl in western Anáhuac, the step toward a Territorialverband was not taken, however, because the nobles lived from tribute revenue and not from landownership. This is typical of the nonmonetary economy. The term altepetl as a "benefice" or "fief" should therefore be translated as "domain" or "demesne" rather than as "town"; in fact, the historian García Martínez even speaks of a *tlahtoanate,* a Mexican pendant to the Arabian emirate.[62] Consequently, it is incorrect to regard the altepetl strictly as a landholding settlement or as a "town." Today, the anthropologist Herbert Harvey claims, the evidence is mounting to show that the altepetl did not own land. In his description of the estates of the aristocrats, known as *pillalli* or sometimes as *tlatocatlalli,* Haskett remarks that "before the conquest pillalli and tlatocatlalli seem to have been lands of the altepetl held by the ruling class by right of rank or status but which had not yet become true private possessions."[63]

After the fall of Tenochtitlán in 1521, the tribute from the native population was to be paid to the Spanish crown and not to autonomous lords as the tlahtoani. For that purpose, a separate legal world with its own legal apparatus, independent of that which applied to the Spaniards, was created for the Indians. The institution of the two *repúblicas* bore such a close resemblance to the medieval system of orders and in so many ways that it is justifiable to regard them as such. Of course, the Indians were allowed to retain their old laws within their order, provided they did not come in conflict with those of the crown or with what the crown regarded as good and proper; for an order was self-governing and had a jurisdiction of its own. However, one order, the Spanish, was considered to unite *gente de razón,* civilized and educated people; the other order, the Indian, united people "to be educated" as such. As a result of this legislation for the two orders a juridical father/son relationship was installed; thus paternalism was institutionalized, though it was a paternalism that offered the Indian peasants several advantages, which they managed to exploit throughout the entire colonial period.

As has been remarked above, New Spain was not special in applying "ethnic" terms to designate social orders (états), but was, in fact, rather common. Conquest and colonization had created all over medieval Europe societies where different ethnic groups lived side by side according to the principle of "personality by law." Individuals had their own "ethnic" law regardless of the territory they inhabited or the lord they served. Precisely because ethnic groups often lived in a state of chronic mutual suspicion, most of these were marked out by their own legal regime, including special provisions and privileges. Fears of being framed led to reassurance that a person could not be judged by, or convicted solely on the testimony of, members of another "ethnic" group. Several kingdoms organized a wide-reaching dualism, in which different and parallel systems of courts and substantive law existed for each of the "races." In case the kingdom endured, a single system of courts and a single body of substantive law was to be avowed, but not without incorporating procedures and legal capacities that varied according to orders based on "ethnic" groups. In Spain itself, the dualistic type was found in cities like Toledo, where even *three* separate judicial regimes were installed (Castilian-Christian, Mozarabic and Frankish-Christian). Despite the social and economic inequalities between the three groups, as well as the irreversible domination of the Castilian group, the legal ideal in Toledo was that of separate but equal ethnic and jural communities. In fact, Bartlett argues, recognizing the jural autonomy could be one way of trying to reconcile the conquered to their lot. All over medieval Europe, submission included provisions safeguarding jurisdiction and legal procedure, and apart from this, the groups were not closed. It was possible for men living under a particular "ethnic" law to acquire another by grant or purchase.[64]

After centuries of conquest and reconquest in Europe, the Spanish crown was quite experienced in incorporating the conquered peoples. No wonder, when the altepetl was transformed into a "pueblo de indios"—the basic territorial unit of the "república de indios"—during the period of administrative and legal reforms at the end of the sixteenth century, the idea of the demesne was left intact, at least at first. The indigenous settlements inside the pueblos became not jural enclaves, islands of ethnic-legal particularism within a wider, different, and hostile world—as Eric Wolf wanted us to believe—but equal jural, autonomous *municipalities*, enclosing the wide majority of the population, subordinated to a mixture of Spanish law, indigenous law, and indigenous customs, all protected by the law on the repúblicas and gradually modified over the course of Spanish rule from pluralism to jural homogeneity. The land outside these settlements, but still belonging to the altepetl, was recognized as the lordly domain. It is therefore difficult to translate the term *pueblo* as "village" or "township." It was easier to do so for the eighteenth century, though, as is clear from the development toward jural homogeneity.

Although all common macehualtin and *pipiltin* (nobles) in the native lordships enjoyed the status of indios from now on, the term altepetl was used by
the Indians to refer to a pueblo until late in the eighteenth century.[65] At any
rate, the new system could not operate without involving the former tlahtoque,
now known as *señores naturales,* or caciques, in view of the persistence of lordship and its sociopolitical practice. This is not the place to discuss the extent
to which the caciques became impoverished or disappeared in the sixteenth
and seventeenth centuries. In any event, as I will argue later, cacicazgo as an
institution remained intact or reproduced itself within the pueblos; sometimes within the same old families, sometimes under the authority of nouveaux
riches such as *principales* (lesser nobility; all nobles were later on called the
"principales"). Although the pre-Hispanic lords continued to hold office in
the pueblos, their relatively high position had become a thing of the past. The
new pueblos were administered by *gobernadores de indios,* Indian mayors who
officially held office for one year, but in practice did so for several years. Deviations from the rule were allowed for the time being, but nonetheless they
were regarded as anomalies.

The distinction persisted between the tlahtoani/cacique and the rest of
the nobility (pipiltin): the cacique received the official title of *Don,* the others
did not. This was a sign on the part of the Spaniards that they regarded the
caciques as gente de razón; and, *de facto,* as belonging to the Spanish order,
who, de jure, had to govern the Indian order. They allowed the children of the
caciques to attend special schools and gave them important political posts in
the administrative apparatus of the "república de indios." The caciques received a material compensation for the loss of their old position; they were
allowed to collect a tribute of their own in the pueblos, in the form of a prearranged regular sum or as special labor services. If they held the position of
gobernador, this office would bring in extra revenue as well. And even though
the tribute and the extra sum were expressed in monetary terms, the Indians
could pay them in kind or in labor services, just as they had done in the pre-
Hispanic era to prevent the burden from becoming too heavy.

For these reasons and to stress its origins in the Personenverband, I prefer
to see the altepetl as a "seigneury" or "benefice." In fact, there is little evidence that, as a rule, the altepetl was located around a specific center, and the
area belonging to it was somewhat undefined. Harvey declares that one important deficiency in the general descriptions of land tenure in the sixteenth
century is that there is rarely a mention of the locality or region to which a
description applied. No wonder, García Martínez responds in his book on the
Sierra Norte de Puebla—indeed, one of the best introductions to the altepetl
and its subsequent development—because the issue of landownership by the
lords was of considerably less importance than the several kinds of tribute
payments and labor services they received from their subordinates.[66]

Here we return to the "multiple estate" discussed earlier. Therefore, one
should argue: the altepetl not only had a demesne, but *was* a demesne, a "multiple estate," a certain area of land cultivated by the people who were linked

to its lord. They did so in smaller unities described as a calpolli or a tlaxilacalli.[67] But over the course of time, something changed: the Spaniards were "enclos- ing" the lordships more and more, restricting them to certain and specific lands. This looks like—and it is a speculative thought—the quick transforma- tion of a "multiple estate" to a "manor." The last center of the altepetl was founded as the headtown, or cabecera, of a pueblo on a fixed place: the church was built there and became the center of the parish; the town government had to reside there; and the hamlets, often former calpollis or tlaxicallis, be- came *pueblos sujetos*, for example, subordinated townships or satellite settle- ments of the central township or municipal headtown, or they formed part of a "cabecera" or "sujeto" as a barrio. To note the difference from a "pueblo sujeto," the greater unit became known as the *pueblo-por-sí*. The terminology of pueblo-por-sí, a legal, full-fledged pueblo, is used for the cabecera-sujeto- unit; sujetos also preferred to present themselves as pueblos ("pueblos sujetos"), without legal recognition of the status of "pueblo-por-sí." I will try to use the word *pueblo* in the sense of "pueblo-por-sí," and as juridically correct as I can manage; "pueblos sujetos" are generally referred to as "sujetos."

A Suggestive Picture

It was to their traditional lords that the common Indians turned to seek protection against usurpation of their milpas by intruders. And these lords made use of the jural autonomy imposed by law, thereby accepting Spanish policy to form municipalities within their domains. Critical in this develop- ment was the period of the Great Death, which started directly after conquest, when the old villages ceased to exist. The introduction of the germs of un- known diseases like smallpox, measles, or influenza killed many Indians and forced others to leave. It was a period of despair, of suicides, out-migration, and profane drunkenness,[68] when the Indian world adopted the paternalistic policy of regrouping the survivors. Thus far, the Indians had been living in big cities like Tenochtitlán or Texcoco, or they had been scattered over the coun- tryside, although probably some compact rural settlements had already been formed as well. During the congregations, Spanish policy was generally suc- cessful in creating, with the help of the Indians themselves, new townships out of the remnants of a depopulated altepetl. However, population density and the resulting complex jurisdictions of Indian lords, the old Personenver- band, introduced immense problems, because most congregations generally had to be implemented with due respect for the integrity of the legitimized native polities, and without any intention whatsoever of disturbing cacique jurisdictions, demesne boundaries, personal dependencies, or lordships. Espe- cially around 1600 several small pueblos or barrios, of a few dozen Indians at most, were congregated into one pueblo.[69]

It was the intention of the Spanish crown to create an administration based on territorial divisions, to build a system with more effective justice under the supervision of Spanish officials, and to ensure more effective Christianization under the Catholic clergy, first the regular and later the secular. The juridical, administrative, or ideological background of the *congregaciones* (also referred to as reducciones) is neglected or brushed aside too often. Hoekstra argues that the principle aim of the congregaciones was not to resettle the Indian population, but to record the division of landownership between Indians and Spaniards.[70] By recording this—the Territorialverband!—the authorities hoped to be able to settle the many conflicts over land and over jurisdictional authority, and to protect the Indians in their legitimate property. After all, it was important to diminish litigation and unrest and to restore public order. Indians could apply for mercedes, but this had happened incidentally. In fact, possessing a merced was an important condition for Spaniards to prove landownership. Thus the mercedes were complemented by the congregation documents. The concentration of the Indian households was a means to attain this purpose.[71] For the small peasants, it became important to have their names on a tribute list. Every tributario was entitled to a municipal plot, or, as it was expressed at that time, a share in the *común repartimiento* (the distribution of land among the inhabitants of the pueblo). On this plot, they were supposed to build their hut and to cultivate maize, beans, and other basic foodstuff, but could not leave it idle.

After several decades, the Personenverband began to give way to the institutions of the Territorialverband, but, nevertheless, with a wave of litigation as a result, because the lords did not give in without resistance, attempting to make legally their own the lands now claimed by their subordinates. Already, in early colonial period, the creation of municipal politics caused some cabeceras and sujetos to ease themselves away from their former lords or caciques and to own lands more or less independently of them. Also macehuales were fortified in their rights to land. Previously, during Aztec rule, between 30 to 50 percent of the rural population, as serfs, servants, or slaves, seem to have had no access to use right of land for their own households. As "indios," these people did possess such access; they were settled in townships and given use right of municipal plots. Dyckerhoff mentions a plot of 0.92 ha. per peasant in Huejotzingo in the mid-sixteenth century; Williams plots between 0.5 to 2.1 has. per household in Tepetlaostoc (Texcoco, in the late sixteenth century). Menegus, in describing this process, gives the impression of a kind of agrarian reform instituted by the Spanish authorities. The consequences of the reforms were disastrous: they left most of the caciques without income—if we may believe Spanish lawyer Alonso de Zorita: "quedan los pobres señores más pobres que los pobres" ("leaving the poor lords poorer than the poor"). Many nobles did indeed lose their rights to tribute, and as a result, they became impoverished. Hoekstra supposes that the sense of noble status must have inhibited many of them from being realistic and taking up the digging stick.[72] Inside the municipal boundaries, Aztec manorial rule was over, but the lords refused to recognize it.

The acquisition of municipal "property" rights by the pueblos was completed around 1700, when a series of composiciones recorded all land tenure in Indian Mexico. The term *composición* referred to the process of legalization of land possession through payment of a fee. In order to extract abundant funds for its American territories, as a contribution to the Caribbean Fleet, the crown issued a series of revenue measures (in 1591, 1635, 1643, and 1709–17). The law called for anyone who held land without proper title to make a donation to the royal treasury to obtain a clear deed. It was not very successful, so in the seventeenth century the crown really began to force individuals and corporations (including the church) to verify their holdings, and finally, regional programs, the *composiciones generales*, were proclaimed and executed. The resulting document of confirmation was also called "composición." However, despite all efforts, it appeared that the pueblos rarely applied for these programs, mainly because of exemption. They were considered to be too poor to pay for land titles, although barely a generation later, in the end of the eighteenth century, these communities in fact could spend hundreds of pesos in claiming land tenure rights. García Martínez, Hoekstra, Wood, and Torales show that the Indians started to participate in the programs during the 1710s and 1720s—and according to crown planning, no doubt. And nearly two decades ago, Osborn demonstrated its adequacy as a definitive entitlement for Indian landholdings. The documents served as the material evidence of landownership—that is, in the sense of Roman law so important in our own age—necessary to win litigation in land tenure.[73]

It is interesting to note that pueblos always asked to "compose" lands, which were called *demasías*, or surplus. These demasías consisted of land "owned" in the municipal sense by the pueblo, besides 2½ *caballerías* of land (1 caballería equaled 42.8 has., so this townsite involved 101 has.) around the church. The 2½ caballerías formed the equivalent of what came to be known during the era of the Bourbon Reforms as the *fundo legal* of the municipality, but it had been a municipal entitlement since the early colonial period. The demasías could involve quite an interesting quantity of land, especially in the faldas. To give an idea of this, I will mention some randomly chosen cases of composiciones of the demasías by Indian municipalities in Anáhuac. All cases *exclude* the fundo legal townsite of about 101 has.! The pueblo of San Ildefonso in the district of Huichapan (northwestern Anáhuac), to begin with a regular example, composed some *suertes* of land (house lots) near the Hacienda Santa Clara (1710). The barrio Santa María, a sujeto of the pueblo San Andrés Chalchicomula (Tepeaca) comprised some 556.5 has. in 1716. In 1717, the pueblo of Santa Cruz Tlacotepec (also Tepeaca) composed 7,150 has. near the village, excluding, of course, the 101 has. townsite *and* some 2,341 has. of land already recognized as theirs on an earlier date. The pueblo of Santiago Tlacotepec, in the province of Metepec-Ixtlahuaca, comprised some 86 has. in the same period; the pueblo of Santa María Tulpetlac (Ecatepec) included some 171 has.; both pueblos can be found northwest of Mexico City. In the southern faldas of Anáhuac, in the early decades of the eighteenth century, three pueblos in the province of Tlapa comprised the areas of land as indicated in Table 7.

Tlapa was a province of some twenty-four thousand Indians in 1720, all over the province. Each pueblo, of course, had considerably fewer inhabit-

Table 7 Three pueblos in Tlapa, early 1700s

San Nicolás Tolentino
  Soyatlan, sujeto of Tlapa
	comprised 1,884 has.	apart from 101
		  has. fundo legal;

San Miguel Metlato,
  sujeto of Tlachinola
	comprised 3,511.3 has.	apart from 101
		  has. fundo legal;

San Juan Amatlichan,
  sujeto of Olinalá
	comprised 3,940.24 has.	apart from 101
		  has. fundo legal
		  and 427.9 has.
		  already
		  acknowledged

Table 8 Three pueblos in Izúcar, early 1700s

San Diego Chiconcoa,
  barrio of Izúcar
	comprised 171.2 has.	apart from 101
		  has. fundo legal
		  and 42.8 has.
		  already
		  acknowledged

San Luis Chalma,
  pueblo
	comprised 64.2 has.	apart from 101
		  has. fundo legal

San Lucas Colucan,
  pueblo
	comprised 5,267 has.	apart from 101
		  has. fundo legal

ants. In another falda area, the province of Izúcar, the surface belonging to Indian municipal rule could be identically impressive in the first decades of the eighteenth century; see Table 8. Some Indian confraternities (*cofradías*) were also created out of these lands. For instance, the Cofradía de Nuestra Señora del Rosario, founded in the pueblo of Xilotepec, had titles of 86 has. of land on the borders of the pueblo. In 1710, the Cofradía de San Simón y Nuestra Señora de la Concepción, in the pueblo of Yehualtepec (Tepeaca) comprised 3,506.1 has. But usually the confraternities did *not* own that amount of land—indeed, if any at all!—and most of the pueblos in densely populated areas—the provinces of the many-sided economy!—could only claim some "suertes" or even not more than 101 has. fundo legal.[74]

The state revenues from the composiciones indicate their success.[75] The sum paid on each occasion varied from ten to one hundred pesos—sometimes more, sometimes less, depending on the size of the land. Most surveys were carried out between 1711 and 1715, especially in the densely populated highlands. Considerable sums were also received in 1717 and 1718 from a few pueblos in the falda provinces of Huichapan-Tetepango, Tula, Yahualica,

Huauchinango, Zacatlán, Tulancingo, Tehuacan, Izúcar, Taxco, Igualapa and Temascaltepec; the more central provinces of Atlixco, Otumba, San Cristóbal Ecatepec, Tenango del Valle, and Metepec; and elsewhere. The relatively high number of municipalities in the provinces of Metepec and Tehuacan is particularly striking. The sums corresponding to the Indian pueblos were, on average, around 10 percent of those of the individual Spaniards, who had to pay a much higher price for their titles. Later, the number of payments from the Indian townships was much smaller, though there were some exceptions. For instance, the gobernador of Chiautla de la Sal in the southern faldas paid sixty pesos in 1734, and I discovered new payments from the same township in 1735, 1738, and 1739. There were also revenues from Indian townships in Ecatepec in 1743, some confraternity lands in Aculco (Huichapan-Tetepango) in 1742, water rights from Santa Isabel Tecali in 1744, municipal lands of Calimaya and Tepamachalco (Metepec) in 1757, and more pueblo lands in the regions of Oaxaca (Villa Alta in 1737), Michoacán (for instance, the two hundred pesos from Pátzcuaro in 1734), and Guadalajara after 1734 until the late 1750s. In 1757 composiciones were performed in Calimaya, Milpa Alta (Xochimilco), Chalchicomula (Tepeaca), Axapusco (Otumba), and Santa Catarina (Acatlán); all on the basis of *manifestaciones de títulos,* or communal titles. Composiciones to Spaniards in the far north of the Mexican colony dominated the 1740s and 1750s. It is evident that Anáhuac and Oaxaca were the first to receive their composiciones; apart from a few exceptional cases, the turn of the "less Indian" regions came later.

The overall, though relatively late, participation of the Indians in paying for composiciones was only partly, I think, a consequence of Spanish imperial policy in financing its fleet. Another reason may be found in the growing awareness of the Indian leaders that it was essential to acquire official legal titles. In her dissertation, Wood shows that the Indians did not hesitate to step forward and obtain as many confirmations as were necessary to protect or enlarge their communal holdings.[76] Impressive demographic recovery occurred in the late seventeenth century. The times of despair, suicide, and profane drunkenness were not only over but long forgotten. Around 1700, the number of inhabitants in the municipalities started to apply pressure on available land and all land possessions of the community needed to be secured. Using the occasion by reacting positively to the measures of the crown, the majority of the pueblos, like the haciendas, had composiciones at their disposal by around 1720. The Indians had almost completed their transformation toward the system of Territorialverband.

During the period of the composiciones, this mental adaptation to the new rules of the game acquired a specific form in addition to the familiar documentation like the mercedes and composiciones. At least, that is my view of the so-called Techialoyan Codices and the *títulos primordiales,* which generally date from the late seventeenth and early eighteenth centuries.[77] These are documents written in Nahuatl, sometimes in the style of old codices, which claim to provide "authentic" documents for the existing landbase of a pueblo that had lost them, or more probably, never had them in the first place. The most important object is the description of the territorial boundaries in an attempt to *re*-substantiate the old altepetl or a part of it. That is why this documentation should be regarded as community discourse. The fact that the caciques, who were probably the ones behind this documentation, realized that they must give up at least part of the traditional oral discourse in exchange for a discourse on paper is of great importance for later developments. It reveals something of the mental world of these caciques: the desire to retain the pueblo as an integrated territory, one resembling the surface of their old domain. Of course, these documents were false, and were recognized as such, but they indicated that the Indian pueblos of the late seventeenth and early eighteenth centuries had a traditional right *as a unit within a specific territory.* The "títulos primordiales" were no doubt intended to compensate for what was lacking: paperwork.

Thus, the caciques knew that possessing composiciones was not enough, and they set out to get legal possession of the rest of their demesne. As has been indicated, besides the demasías, the township was entitled to 2½ caballerías of land (101 has.) around the church, the so-called "fundo legal" of the municipality, the official legal base or townsite to which the villagers were entitled since, first, the royal decree of 1567, which established the town base at 500 *varas* (a *vara* being 84 centimeters or 33 inches) in the four cardinal directions from the last houses, and later on, in 1687, at 600 varas. In 1695 a decree was issued which ordered the 600 varas to be measured from the principal church in each town. Claiming these 2½ caballerías was obviously no problem: first, the demasías had to be legally entitled to the township by the composiciones; then the villagers turned to the task of securing their townsite or the fundo legal itself. The eighteenth century is the epoch of fundo legal, with hundreds of villagers acquiring their corporate titles in this manner; and it was to have far reaching consequences for the old "pueblo-sujeto" relationship.

In measuring the 600 varas in each of the four cardinal directions, a square was constructed by measuring 1,200 by 1,200 varas, that is, 1,440,000 square varas (= 101 has.). It was therefore assumed that the sides of the square should be twice 600 varas. Even the Indians always referred to the 600 varas as the standard for their land entitlement: the *común de 600 varas.* However, this only added to the confusion. Wood has discussed how many difficulties the concept of the fundo legal initially created.[78] It may be that the idea of a square measuring 1,200 by 1,200 varas was not immediately clear to everyone. After all, it was possible to construct lines directly connecting the axes of the measurements in each of the four cardinal directions with one another, resulting in a smaller square of 600 by 600 varas, or 720,000 square varas; but this interpretation foundered on the fact that the difference from the original plan of 500 varas *from the last habitation* would be too great. According to decrees of 1573, 1628, and 1713, the fundo legal was supposed to provide a pueblo with sufficient water, agricultural land, wood, and uncultivated land.

This could only be attained by means of the larger variant. Even this variant was not clear to everybody, however, since some still claimed that the fundo legal was primarily agricultural land, that the farms of the Indians must therefore be disregarded in the measurements, or that the size of the fundo should depend on the number of households, at the rate of forty-eight households per fundo. Although Wood cites cases in which such demands were actually made, it is clear enough that the 1,200 by 1,200 standard was the rule, measured from the church doors and including the dwellings of the "indios." As soon as the villagers grew short of land, as in a period of population growth, a request was submitted to the Audiencia to plot a fundo legal in order to obtain the documents of ownership for the corresponding 101 hectares. This procedure was followed on an increasing scale in the course of the eighteenth century.

The fundo legal could not be sold once it had been officially granted, for it fell under the authority of the municipal government. The villagers treated the land with a certain religious awe, regarding it as a sacred gift of God that must not be disturbed. All the same, this does not mean that the municipality did not have any other holdings. The fundo legal was usually the minimum landholding of the township. Many villages owned more land, which was not covered by the legislation on the fundo legal. Of course, individual Indians could also have the use of land outside the fundo legal, whether rented or purchased from their caciques. In addition, a municipality was expected to have an extra piece of land to pasture the livestock and for the collection of brushwood and firewood: the *ejido* (seventeen square kilometers). In reality, only cabeceras were entitled to claim an ejido, but the majority of the cabeceras in Anáhuac did not have one. Wood provides an example of an ejido outside the town of Toluca; Dyckerhoff mentions an ejido in Huejotzingo, which formed part of the municipal territory and thus did not reach the norm. I have not found any myself. Of course, the legally determined ejido was much too large for this densely populated area. Villages in the sparsely populated semiarid provinces and in the faldas sometimes had ejidos. In order to provide the highland municipalities with uncultivated land outside the fundo legal without having to satisfy the seventeen-square-kilometers norm, a different term was used: *propios*, which will be discussed later.[79]

Disputed Possession

In general, struggle for land—the agrarian question—is obviously the result of overpopulation in the countryside. Modern historical literature indicates that the haciendas in the sixteenth and seventeenth centuries were set up on land that had been abandoned by the pueblos as a result of the population decline, or had been unused lands, which were in the hands of the Indian aristocracy. It was not until the eighteenth century that the pueblos applied to the Audiencia with claims to these lands. It has been agreed among agrarian historians that the number of court cases involving land, which were held over the years in a specific region, can be regarded as a good index of the

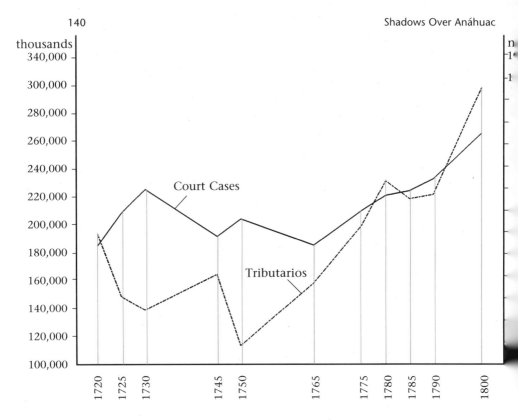

Figure 4   Number of court cases involving land disputes in Anáhuac, compared with the number of tributarios, 1710–1809. Source: Ouweneel, "Growth, Stagnation, and Migration," p. 546 and Ouweneel and Bijleveld, "Economic Cycle," p. 525–526.

shortage of land there. Using lists of the contents of archives in the Archivo General de la Nación in Mexico City, I have taken up one of Tutino's ideas and compiled a series for the period 1710–1809. They are court cases in provinces that now belong to the federal states of Mexico, Hidalgo, and Puebla; only the small federal state Tlaxcala and the falda regions of Morelos and Guerrero are missing. I have counted all the cases involving both haciendas and pueblos de indios. The external point of view is important, because cases involving pueblos and caciques have a different character and do not always reflect a shortage of land, as we shall see in chapter five.

Nevertheless, totals based on the archives are not without their uncertainties. It is unlikely that the Spanish government kept such good records of cases that *every* dossier is still to be found in the archives. The figures for the number of cases involving land cited in these archives are therefore only reliable if the data correlate well with other, more reliable statistical material. I have shown elsewhere that this is the case, at any rate, as far as the demographic development in the pueblos is concerned.[80] Figure 4 indicates the fluc tuations in the number of legal cases in the course of the eighteenth century. The number of cases around 1710–20 was extremely high; it then dropped until the middle of the century, and did not pick up again until late in the eighteenth century. As can be seen in Figure 4, there is a connection between the increase in the number of land disputes after around 1750 and the growth in the population of the pueblos. The rapid increase just before the turn of the century is certainly striking and should be explained. The decrease after the turn of the century seems to be the result of a lack of resources to sustain legal proceedings of this kind any longer.

In looking at this development in more detail, I shall confine myself to a sample from a few provinces. There is no room to discuss all of the fifty-one provinces of Anáhuac, so the following remarks will be limited to the situation in the provinces of Chalco, Huejotzingo, Tepeaca, Malinalco, Izúcar, Metztitlán, and Actopan. The choice is arbitrary, and the most that it has to recommend it is its wide geographical range within the region. There are two points that stand out in a first perusal of the archives. There is hardly a backslider to be found among the mass of villages and haciendas that were brought before the magistrate in this connection. Only a few were repeatedly involved in land disputes. However, this means, at the same time, that in view of the large number of cases, the majority of the pueblos and haciendas in any province must have been confronted with the Audiencia in the course of the eighteenth century. Second, most of the cases date from after 1770, the period of protracted drought and an increase in relative overpopulation.

The province of Chalco has been chosen because it tallies with the cases mentioned elsewhere in the book. At least thirty cases involving land were tried there between 1710 and 1809.[81] Seven of them date from before 1740, the caesura of the matlazahuatl epidemic. Six cases were recorded for the period between 1740 and 1770; for the post-1770 period—after 1779 in fact—I counted seventeen cases (57 percent of the cases that I counted over the span of a century). In twenty-nine cases a pueblo called upon the Audiencia to arbitrate. The only hacienda calling for arbitration—San Andrés, alias La Retana (1782)—did so because it was dissatisfied with an earlier verdict that had been passed on a dispute over land in 1711. The township of Temamatla was the only one to address more than one request to the Audiencia (1712, 1713, and 1782). In eighteen of these thirty land cases, it was in the hands of a hacienda; in four cases it was held by a municipality; and on six occasions a request was submitted for the plotting of a fundo legal to be carried out. In two cases, the hacendado was also cacique (one of them was a certain Don Luis Páez de Mendoza, whom we shall meet later); in the others the cases were submitted, and probably initiated as well, by the gobernadores.

The municipality of Tepeaca, which is listed separately in the archives for the province of the same name, was the site of at least nineteen conflicts in the period under review. Five of them antedate 1740, while the rest occur after 1770. In eighteen cases the matter had been brought before the courts in Mexico City by a gobernador; the nineteenth case was a request by a group of hacienda hands for a fundo legal, thereby indicating that they wanted the status of a "pueblo de indios." The village of San Agustín de Palmar crops up twice in the list, in 1794 and 1797. In eleven cases the disputed land was in the hands of a hacienda, in four cases it was in the hands of another pueblo. Six cases, almost a third of the nineteen, took place between 1797 and 1807. The eight cases from neighboring Huejotzingo—a hacienda province like Chalco and Tepeaca—which I was able to find in the archive all date from after 1783, and almost all of them were requests for a fundo legal, instead of requests for a specific piece of ground belonging to a hacienda.[82]

The provinces of Malinalco and Izúcar, which were partly situated on the highlands and partly in the southern faldas, did not have as many haciendas as the provinces mentioned above. All the same, the situation in these provinces was more or less similar. The archives contain nineteen cases of land disputes in Malinalco (south of the valley of Toluca) during the period under review. Five of them antedate 1740, two belong to the 1740–70 period, and twelve (63 percent) date from after 1777. Once again, it is the 1780s and 1790s that are a peak period, accounting for almost half of the cases. In ten cases the party taken to court was a pueblo; in the other seven cases it was a hacienda. The proportions were the same in the province of Izúcar (Puebla), although there were many more legal proceedings there: forty. It is striking that only three of them date from before the matlazahuatl epidemic. There were twenty-six land conflicts after 1778 (65 percent of the forty), with a peak period between 1787 and 1810. The party taken to court by a village was a hacienda in fifteen cases (37 percent) and an Indian pueblo in twenty cases (50 percent). The remaining cases involved requests for a fundo legal of 101 hectares because of overpopulation.[83]

As I read and classified these documents on land conflicts between municipalities and haciendas or between municipalities and other municipalities, I was struck by two remarkable cases: Metztitlán and Actopan in the northern outskirts of the highlands.[84] The majority of court cases in Actopan were from the middle of the eighteenth century; only five dated from before 1740, and seven from the period before 1770. This is not unusual, but what was striking was that only one case dated from a later period. The lack of an increase in the number of court cases cannot be explained as a result of a drop in demographic pressure, because Actopan was also very densely populated after 1770. A closer inspection of the sources revealed that the growth in the number of cases had shifted to a series of conflicts between residents in the pueblos and the caciques there! This suggests that the caciques in Actopan had seen the legitimacy of their authority crumbling drastically. Elsewhere, if a township instigated legal proceedings against its neighbors, this was usually an attempt to reinforce this legitimacy. I conclude from the work of Hamnett and Taylor, and from Ladd's book, that the labor conditions in the silver mines of Real del Monte in Pachuca were responsible for this situation. The silver mines there had a permanent labor shortage, and it was not uncommon for peasants to be sent to the mines against their will by the caciques. In 1756, this situation had already led to a violent revolt in this region by a handful of pueblo residents going against the governing caciques and the owners of the silver mines; in 1766, the miners even resorted to strike action against the working conditions, which has been described with verve by Ladd.[85]

The province of Metztitlán is interesting because of the apparently classical picture of a clash between haciendas and an Indian municipality, in which the Indian leaders asked for the land taken from their pueblo. Half of the court cases in this province date from after 1770; only two of them antedate 1740. All those taken to court were haciendas, and in six of the thirteen cases the plaintiff was the Indian municipality of Metztitlán itself. Osborn's monograph on this valley presents the picture of a feud between the caciques from the pueblo and the hacendados, who also lived in Metztitlán. Although there was plenty of land in this mountainous province, it was extremely sparsely populated. The population was mainly concentrated in the narrow valley of the Metztitlán river, which flowed into a large lake. There were only a few townships and haciendas here. According to Osborn, the gobernadores wanted to exploit the special situation in the valley. According to him, the thirty-one or so residents in the province, 90 percent of whom were "indios," held more than enough land at the time because of the extremely high maize yields. He gives harvest–sowing seed ratios of between 400:1 and 600:1! Osborn estimates that only 1,710 hectares of agricultural land were required to feed everyone, while there were actually 3,500 hectares available. This relative prosperity weakened the position of the hacendados, because the peasants had less need for seasonal labor on the haciendas. Thus the hacendados were relatively accommodating to claims by the caciques from Metztitlán, so as not to endanger the willingness to engage in migrant labor.[86]

All of these examples suggest that it was certainly possible to obtain an expansion of the area of ground under cultivation. At any rate, it is clear that the Spanish hacendados were not sure of their land, because overpopulation meant that the neighboring pueblos were in the same boat. Nevertheless, villagers engaged in bitter disputes with one another over land in provinces where there were few or no haciendas. I do not consider that expansion of the area with uncultivated marginal land took place very often, if at all. These marginal territories were either in the hands of the hacendados, who used them as pastures, or they were so dry or eroded that there was no point in trying to cultivate them. Thus it was with envy that the Indians viewed the fertile lands of the haciendas, often located close to their own townships. The simplest way to gain possession of that land was by means of the fundo legal. Indeed, during the course of his research on the documentation pertaining to the Juzgado de Indios, Borah found that the increase in the number of court cases involving land consisted mainly of requests for a fundo legal.[87] The process probably ran its course, as Wood supposed: the success of one town inspired the next, with word of mouth and sighting of survey teams in the valleys surely contributing to the enthusiasm for making the trip to Mexico City.[88] The Indians involved were frequently the municipal leaders, the gobernadores.

Here, the metaphor of the "tree" providing "shade" recurs, because the gobernadores, as I will argue later, were the Indian lords.

Measurements of Land: The Hacendados on the Defensive

Since this impression is the opposite of the picture traditionally presented, there is sufficient reason to include a section on the position of the hacendado in the fundo-legal process. After all, various scholars, such as Gibson in his *Aztecs under Spanish Rule* and Florescano in his essay in the *Cambridge History of Latin America*,[89] consider that the pueblos lost land to the haciendas rather than gaining possession of it.[90] A square construction like the fundo legal created problems if the church was not situated in the middle of the village, as was often the case. Good agricultural land or a few village farms might fall outside the township boundaries; on the other hand, land that was useless for agriculture because of erosion, rocks, or gorges, or even plots belonging to an adjacent township or hacienda that might be included within the municipal boundaries. In practice the Spanish government meticulously corrected this by subtracting useless or undesirable land from the square that had been drawn up and seeking compensation elsewhere to bring the desirable land or excluded farms back inside the boundaries of the fundo legal. I noted many of these readjustments in the course of my investigations. This brought the municipality into conflict with other landowners, such as caciques and hacendados, as well as with neighboring pueblos.

One of the maps (recently published by Wood)—in this particular case that of the pueblo San Juan Atzcualoya in the province of Chalco—indicates what the ideal fundo legal looked like (see Map 8).[91] It reveals the roads through the village, the church, the farms, the fields and the uncultivated land. The fundo legal has been measured from the church in the middle of the map. There were more than eighty households in the township, which was, in fact, a precondition for obtaining the status of pueblo, all grouped more or less around the church. It is not the neat street plan of a model Spanish village, but it does come close to it. Every outsider knew exactly where the boundary ran, because boundary marks (*mojones*) were placed on the corners of the fundo legal with an ostentatious ceremony, to which the neighbors were invited.

It is not certain that the resulting tract of land was sufficient to meet the needs of the eighty or more households. Dyckerhoff does not think so. Compare the figure of 101 hectares—she writes—with the amount of land considered necessary to feed the family and pay tribute or rent, plus house lots of about 15 x 15 meters, a central plaza, and church with churchyard. The fundo legal might not have been sufficient to feed more than seventy-three households. The author of a document from 1809 on the fundo legal of a township in the province of Teotihuacán claims that a fundo legal was sufficient to feed a maximum of forty-eight families, because there was only enough room for 11½ cuartillos of sowing ground: one fanega de sembradura, or 3.57 hectares. He did not indicate, however, the number of family members involved. The rest of the land would have been needed for the farms, stables, church, street, and church-

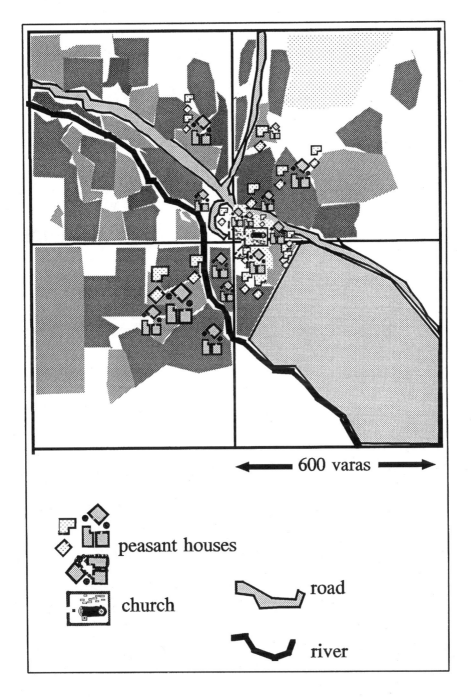

Map 8   The fundo legal of San Juan Atualoya (Chalco-Tlalmanalco), 1799

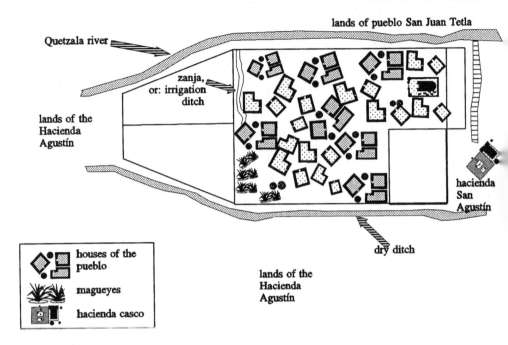

Map 9   The fundo legal of San Agustín Atzompan (Huejotzingo), 1784

yard. The author of the document argued for a change in the law by which a fundo legal would correspond to fifty families. He did not secure a hearing in Madrid.[92] In fact, his argument depended to a large extent on the maize yield ratios. However until the 1790s most of the townships in Anáhuac did not consist of as many as fifty families.

The square fundo of Atzcualoya was a very tidy solution, of course, but things did not always run so smoothly. It was usually necessary to make adjustments and alterations. San Agustín Atzompan (Huejotzingo), for example, which requested its fundo legal in 1784, lay between two gorges and the most fertile land of a hacienda. The plotting of the 101 hectares was complicated by the two gorges, which converged 1,200 meters west of the village church, and by the Hacienda San Agustín. In particular, a major problem was the fact that the village church was a stone's throw from the hacienda. Plotting a fundo legal would bring the hacienda within the village boundary and exclude two-thirds of the farms. The solution was to plot the fundo legal on the land to the west of the village (see Map 9). In exchange, the hacienda possessed the right to a small square of land south of the village church and to a few plots of land to the east. The 56 tributarios (36 heads of families and 20 adult sons, many of them married) could divide half of the 101 hectares among themselves as good agricultural land (approx. 1½ hectares per tributario). With a yield ratio of 300:1 (maize) and a (generous) average family size of 4½ persons, this land was sufficient to feed 124 families at most, though this number dropped to 41 families if the yield ratio was only 100:1. The fundo legal thus offered the people of Atzompan room for growth,[93] but the tribute figures from the province of Huejotzingo suggest that this potential was soon used up, since the population of Atzompan may well have doubled between 1784 and 1794.

In almost all cases, of course, the plotting of the fundo legal came at the expense of the neighbors. This was less serious if the neighbor was a cacique or hacendado, but it was more complicated if the neighbor happened to be another pueblo, with its own right to the "600 varas." The case of a village survey in the province of Cholula, carried out in accordance with a request made in 1730 by the township of San Bernabé Temoxtitlán, indicates how accurately this could be done (see Map 10).[94] The request was for the village farms to be included within the boundary of a fundo legal. The map, executed in various colors, reveals an elongated settlement lying at the foot of a ridge in an east-west direction and bordering on two haciendas to the north and northwest. The township consisted of sixty-two independent farms, with their land directly adjacent to the farmyards, according to the draughtsman. They had also planted fruit trees there, a specialty of the Puebla valley. The township was intersected by dry ditches, which carried the water from the nearby hills in the rainy season. There were a few bridges connecting the districts of the township. There was a barrio called Tlalistaca among the fruit trees in the southwestern part of the valley, which kept somewhat aloof from Temoxtitlán and was not involved in the request for a fundo legal. The church, the starting point for the surveyors, was in the northwestern exit of the valley. The fundo legal initially marked out excluded thirty-six of the sixty-two farms. This was sufficient reason to deduct one-quarter from the square formed by this fundo legal and to give it to the adjacent hacienda; some land was also given to the hacienda in the northwestern part of the square (the hatched area in Map 10). In exchange, the hacienda had to relinquish its claim to the land where the expansion of the township had taken place. This expansion was illegal at first, because the peasants had simply squatted on land belonging to the hacienda. The thirty-six farms were brought within the boundary of the fundo legal by precise measurements (there are nineteen corners on the map!). Some land to the north was also left unallocated for a communal plot near the church. In this way, the squatters of Temoxtitlán acquired the right to stay put.

The hacendados had little choice. Of course, they put up resistance whenever they could, but as Wood describes, it was usually in vain. She gives an example of a hacendado from 1746, in which the man was confronted with a survey that would cost him his best land. He proposed to give the pueblo another plot of land instead, comprising six caballerías, that is, almost three times the size of a fundo legal! But the disputed area that the Indians wanted

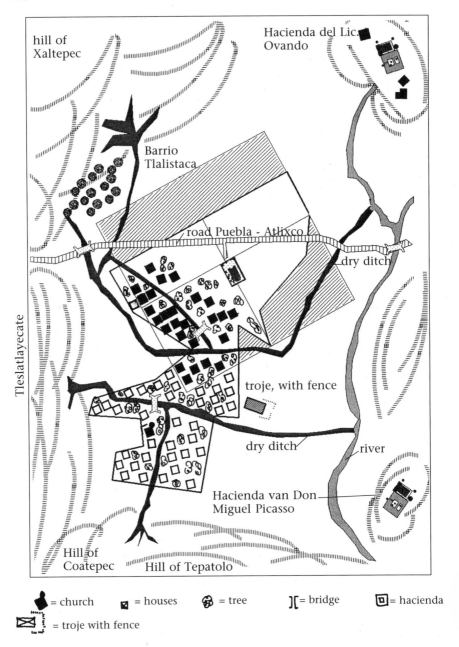

= church   = houses   = tree   ][= bridge   = hacienda

= troje with fence

Map 10 The fundo legal of San Bernabé Temoxtitlán (Cholula), 1730

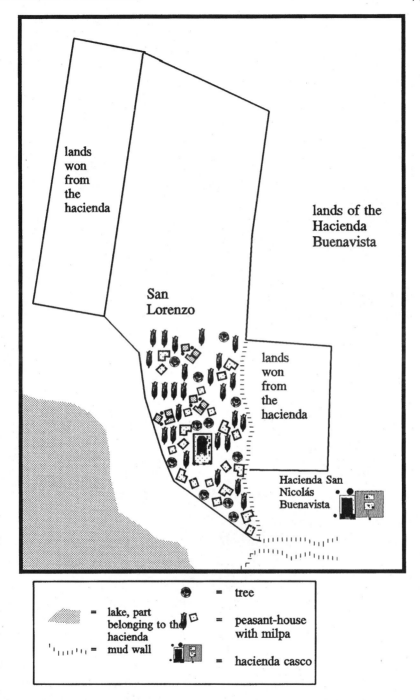

Map 11 The fundo legal of San Lorenzo Tezonco (Mexicalzingo), 1806

to cultivate was of better quality. The Indians, Wood writes, "not only refused the swap, but threatened to seek additional legal endowments for each of the two barrios adjoining the town."[95] However, if they set their sights so high, the villagers had to come up with a good claim; otherwise, they lost their case. This is what happened in Chicoloapan (Coatepec). This municipality disputed the entitlement of a piece of land that was in use by the Hacienda Huatongo. Chicoloapan had a composición dating from 1709, which clearly indicated that the land belonged to the village.[96] The heads of the municipality of Chicoloapan—two brothers!—applied to the representative of the Audiencia with this composición in 1766 and asked him to restore the land right as indicated.[97] They added various statements by inhabitants of the township who testified that the hacendado worked land included in the composición as if it belonged to the hacienda. As a result, the pueblo no longer had sufficient agricultural land for its one hundred or so families. Nine families had already resorted to rental agreements with the Hacienda Xocuatlaca, twenty-eight couples with young children and twenty-seven single persons lived in the township without being able to sow plots of land, and fifteen couples worked an extremely small strip of land. Of course, the hacendado refused to acknowledge that this was the case. The legal fact finder from Mexico City complained about the man's "arrogant attitude" toward the Indians. The hacendado also used "insulting language" toward them. Although this figure could have been a model for Eisenstein's well-known film ¡Qué viva México! of 1931, it transpired during the inquiry that he had right on his side: the pueblo had sold the disputed land to him in a legal transaction.

Perhaps this hacendado was so uncompromising because he knew that he had right on his side. Elsewhere, the behavior of hacendados tended to be moderate, almost friendly, and they showed a readiness to negotiate. This can be seen, for instance, from the proceedings brought by the pueblo of San Lorenzo Tezonco (Mexicalcingo) against its neighbor. This township was entirely surrounded by the fertile lands of the Hacienda San Nicolás Buenavista, owned by Don Francisco Arteaga, a civil servant from Mexico City. The villagers worked on the hacienda to supplement the meager takings from fishing in Lake Chalco. They also fished in water belonging to Arteaga, and paid him for the right to do so (1½ real per week). In 1806, there were twenty-nine families in San Lorenzo, too many for the amount of agricultural land available.[98] Besides the peasants' milpas (see Map 11) situated between the houses, more land was needed for the future families and young couples. There was uncultivated land near the church, but it was boulder clay (tepetate), and could not be used to grow anything. The Audiencia declared this tepetate to be barren soil, so that a new fundo legal had to be mapped out. To his great anger, Arteaga had to relinquish two large plots to San Lorenzo. This decision is all the more remarkable because Arteaga worked on the General Indian Court of the Audiencia, which dealt with matters of this kind and usually showed preference to the pueblos. He could have got his way with the assistance of an internal lobby. The fact that this did not occur may serve to underscore the force of the letter of the law in New Spain in cases of this kind.

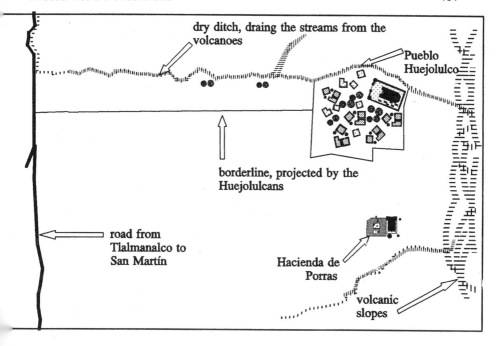

dry ditch, draing the streams from the volcanoes

Pueblo Huejolulco

borderline, projected by the Huejolulcans

road from Tlalmanalco to San Martín

Hacienda de Porras

volcanic slopes

Map 12 The fundo legal of Santa María Huejolulco (Chalco), 1750

Another case in which a hacienda had to give up land took place in 1750 (Map 12). There were twenty-five families in the township of Santa María Huejolulco (Chalco-Tlalmanalco) in that year, including three Otomí-speaking ones. Each family sowed its own plot of land in the township, but wheat was grown on the communal land to pay the tribute. The harvest due that year was not enough to feed the villagers, and the low price of wheat was an ominous sign as far as the tribute payment was concerned. Most of the families also engaged in wood crafts (*arte de madera*), but the money they brought in was not enough to compensate for the bad harvest. The Indian gobernador of the municipality, Don Bernardo Velázquez, asked the Audiencia to transfer a narrow strip of land from the Porras hacienda on the gorge beside the township. This plot of around fifteen hectares would be sufficient to provide the township with enough in the way of harvests for a few years. Velázquez's claim was deliberately very moderate, because he realized that in this case the hacienda was not legally obliged to relinquish the land. The Audiencia proved to be receptive to this strategy.[99]

However, friction between villagers and hacendados could escalate, as in the provinces of Toluca and Cholula, where a number of conflicts on landownership remained unresolved. In the municipality of Toluca, the main town in the valley of Toluca, the various Indian municipalities beside the road to Mexico City were so close to one another in the eighteenth century that

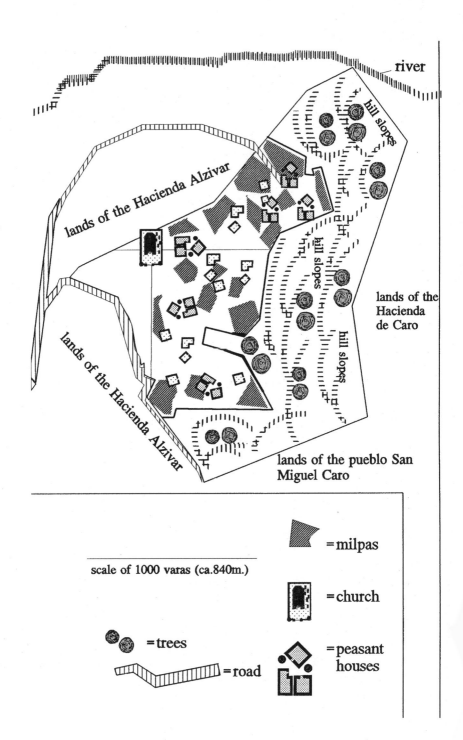

river

hill slopes

lands of the Hacienda Alzivar

hill slopes

lands of the Hacienda de Caro

hill slopes

lands of the Hacienda Alzivar

lands of the pueblo San Miguel Caro

= milpas

scale of 1000 varas (ca.840m.)

= church

= trees

= road

= peasant houses

Map 13 The fundo legal of Santa María Sitindeje (Ixtlahuaca), 1805

there was not enough room for a fundo legal for each of them. There had been a population increase of a good 250 percent between 1706 and 1809, including a doubling between 1771 and 1809. The pueblos wanted to be allocated hacienda land, but these haciendas were able to show the court good deeds of property. Even the villagers had to recognize that the plots in question were essential to running the haciendas. After a verdict was delivered in favor of the hacendados, they constructed wide ditches to protect the fields, but in vain because the villagers carried out land invasions on the haciendas until at least 1825, causing considerable damage to the harvests.[100]

The same problems arose in the small province of Cholula, where there were already forty-three townships and fifty-eight haciendas (can a hacienda be called large-scale landownership in such cases?) and ranchos on a surface area of around seventy square kilometers in 1743. In view of this, it is hardly surprising that these peasants carried out land invasions at a fast rate during the last decennia of the colonial period. In 1809, for example—a difficult year, when many harvests failed—the villagers of Chalchoapan invaded the Hacienda Portezuelo. The intendant from Puebla, Manuel de Flon, warned the Audiencia in Mexico City not to behave in an accommodating fashion this time, because if the Indians in this area—or, indeed, in the rest of New Spain!—were to engage in land invasions with the same fanaticism as that with which they engaged in court proceedings, there was a danger of a general uprising. An example must be set! It is not known if that actually happened, but the viceroy did support Flon's advice.[101]

In 1805, Santa María Sitindeje (Ixtlahuaca) did not go as far as her counterparts in Toluca or Cholula. There were still legal methods for trying to get the Audiencia to carry out a partial expropriation of the neighboring Hacienda Santa María Alzivar (see Map 13).[102] The request was formulated in menacing tones, however. It was claimed that a fundo legal was not at the Indians' disposal; and in any case, the villagers managed to make it clear that the land which could be considered their property consisted of extremely steep slopes on the adjoining ridge, without much land suitable for agriculture. It could not be used for the township livestock either, because the slopes were too steep for the animals. As usual, the agricultural land in the township was situated between the houses (see the hatched areas in Map 13). The holdings amounted to around 77 hectares, while they justifiably claimed the right to have 101 hectares of agricultural land. The hacendado put up a spirited defense. He declared that the township had more than enough land, perhaps even too much. The "indios" could secure high yields thanks to the protected situation of the township. In that year (1805), the December maize harvest would certainly bring in seventy or eighty fanegas. Besides, there was room to grow broad beans on the milpas. There were even barley fields in the township. According to the hacendado, the steep slopes were well covered with sturdy plants, so the village goats could easily climb them and large livestock could graze there without difficulty. The township replied that sixteen farms contained twenty-two tributarios, with a total of 101 persons, that is, 6 per family; that was far too many and led to considerable tension between the villagers themselves. Various couples had already rented land elsewhere, but they had difficulty in paying the rent. There had been a revolt against the hacienda in 1799, the gobernador reported, when stones and sticks were thrown at the head of the hacendado. The gobernador, who was naturally the mouthpiece of the municipality, added meaningfully that history could easily repeat itself. Unfortunately, we do not know the outcome, but in this case the township must have stood a good chance.

Finally, the hacendados noted that Indians also came to live on their land in a different way, by squatting land belonging to the hacienda. Since this was the most direct consequence of the rapid growth in population, there were two waves of squatting actions in Anáhuac in the eighteenth century. The first occurred in the years immediately preceding the matlazahuatl epidemic of 1736–39; but in examining documentation of this period, it is difficult to make a distinction between this and the surveys conducted for the composiciones, which were taking place at the same time. The second was concentrated in the period between 1770 and 1800. The settlement pattern in Anáhuac, particularly at the end of the eighteenth century, was so overcrowded with haciendas and pueblos that the pueblos expanded along the municipal boundaries. If these also lay beyond the limits of an already existing fundo legal, the peasants had no choice but to pay rent to the haciendas. This is how sharecroppers and tenants emerged on a small scale in Anáhuac, a phenomenon detected on a large scale in the regions of Michoacán and Guadalajara in the late eighteenth century by Brading, Morin, Tutino, and Van Young. I suspect that many young sons for whom there was no longer any room in the pueblos of Anáhuac eventually ended up in these and other regions in New Spain. The peasants who continued to share the life of the townships, but settled on the haciendas as squatters, were outside the sphere of influence of the gobernadores. The village council of San Agustín Tlaxco (Tlaxcala), for example, was already aware, in 1731, that 51 of the 109 farms were outside the fundo legal, on territory belonging to the Hacienda Xalostoc, San Juan Bautista, and San Miguel, to whom they paid rent. The attempt of the gobernadores to obtain an expansion of the surface area of the fundo legal was in vain, because the hacendado was in possession of the appropriate documents.[103]

Thus there was little scope for the expansion of the surface area within the boundaries of the pueblo in Anáhuac, and the external expansion of the surface area was problematic because of the dense settlement pattern in the highlands. Consequently, a low-pressure solution ran up against serious difficulties. Most of the Indian pueblos, especially the new ones that followed the secessions, had barely more than the fundo legal at their disposal. Those who lived in the pueblos sujetos could do little except request a fundo legal if they did not yet have one, or to try to obtain plots of land from the haciendas. An alternative was to squat land owned by hacendados, who accepted the squatters as tenants because of their inability to evict them peacefully, especially if the plots of land in question were not so important for the hacienda. Population growth increasingly set the Indian villagers outside the sphere of pueblo's influence, and literally so if the peasants settled on hacienda territory and no longer paid tribute to the village, if they emigrated to the city, and if they could no longer pay the tribute at all. The only remedy for this loss of power was for the caciques to profile themselves as the champions of the Indians and, in this way, try to maintain the growing number of tributarios within their sphere of influence. They therefore formed the connecting link between the peasants and the state; in fact, they could be said to personify the "Indian community."

In the event of a negative Audiencia verdict, the village could consider buying land, but endeavors of this kind had little chance of success. Ewald mentions a few typical examples of Indian pueblos in the valley of Puebla that wanted to buy a hacienda or a rancho. These attempts foundered on the Real Hacienda's reluctance to guarantee a loan to these villages. An official commented on the refusal that the pueblos would simply have to save the money required for the purchase. In other cases, the Audiencia tried to reach a solution by assessing a fundo legal that encircled the land of the ranchos which had caught the eye of the villagers. Incidentally, the argument regarding the creditworthiness of the villagers was not far off the mark: they really were impoverished in the late eighteenth century. Osborn refers to peasant households in Metztitlán which had gone deeply into debt and proceeded to sell their property both inside and outside the fundo legal.[104] Metztitlán was certainly no exception in this respect.

The sale of land within the boundaries of the fundo legal was against the law, of course, unless it was sold to Indians, since the law prohibited all sales to non-Indians. The Indians who were able to buy land from poor tributarios were mainly caciques, though the confraternities were important buyers too. Unlike the caciques, they sometimes allowed the common Indians to use the land. The Mexican anthropologists Loera and Pérez Rocha discovered a connection between the sale of land to caciques and to Indian confraternities in crisis years, reaching a miserable climax in the late eighteenth century. The tributarios in Calimaya (Tenango del Valle) gave up their land on a large scale during the decennium, before the outbreak of the War of Independence in 1821. The plots concerned varied between 0.8 and 1.5 hectares per peasant before 1776, and between 0.3 and 0.8 hectares per peasant in the subsequent period. This provides an indication of the fragmentation brought about by population growth within the común.[105]

Sales of this kind did not alleviate the problem. Rural poverty was extremely high around 1800. An official inspection of the province of Tlaxcala in 1803 revealed that the failure of the tributarios in the province to pay the tribute for years was the result of poverty after the fragmentation of the land within the común. It was evident to the government that the caciques/ gobernadores could easily live off what they worked or engaged others to work, while two-thirds of the Indians in the villages could barely keep their heads above water, and one-third did not take part in the común repartimiento and were to be considered landless.[106] The situation in other provinces was similar. It was certainly possible to obtain more land for the pueblo with the assistance of the *gobernadoryotl,* but this had its price, since the gobernador decided how it was to be divided. In Anáhuac, the gobernadores laid down the social rules in the pueblos, in the first instance taking account of the legislation of the Spanish system of orders, and in the second instance following their powerful position in the village. They tried to run the Indian pueblos like households in which they themselves occupied the position of *patrones.* In this role, they guaranteed the use of land and protection to the members of the "family," in return for reserving the economic benefits for themselves. They were well aware that it was not to their advantage for the peasants to obtain a greater degree of autonomy, and I suspect they took this into account in their land-allocation policy. The boundaries of the fundo legal were primarily their responsibility. In this chapter, then, we have obtained a glimpse of the consequences of the population pressure around 1800: the growth in the number of peasants below the subsistence level increased the influence of the gobernadores if these peasants could be allocated an extra plot of land. As important mediators, the gobernadores exercised particular control over the poorer inhabitants of the townships, since the better-off could settle elsewhere or adopt a more independent position.

Many visitors to Mexico at the time claimed that the haciendas could certainly afford to miss some of their land, even though they did not have much land that was not under cultivation. State officials agreed with such views. A number of them were already infected with a "proto-land-reform-virus": they claimed that smaller peasants were more productive than large landowners. There were supporters of a policy of expropriating the holdings of big landowners and dividing the land among the peasants of New Spain, like their counterparts in Spain (where the crown had implemented far-reaching land reforms in the eighteenth century). This idea may lie behind the relative success of the fundo legal, the mediocre success of the resistance put up by the haciendas, and the rise in the number of secessions. By the last decennia of the eighteenth century the hacendados already had been driven into a defensive position. Others with some knowledge of the situation countered that it was thanks to the effective exploitation of their land that the haciendas supplied the cities with raw materials. This debate was interrupted by the events of 1810 and 1821—which is a pity for historians, because it would be interesting to know whether the crown would have announced the program of land reforms in New Spain that had already been implemented in Spain.

Conclusion

In this chapter, I discussed the "charity-system" of Anáhuac, in which the inhabitants of the pueblos could guarantee their subsistence after years of harvest failures. First of all, there was the strategy of appealing to direct charity. This appeal could be made to the hacendados, the priests, and the alcaldes mayores, or later on, the subdelegados. The requests were for favorable terms of lease, the opening of field kitchens at times of extreme scarcity, the reduction of food prices after bad harvests, and so on. This strategy assumed a violent character if the person to whom the appeal was addressed refused to cooperate.

The population pressure constituted a threat to the economic and social privileges, since more and more peasants found themselves outside the borders of the fundo legal. Therefore, there was the second strategy of the participation in vertical relations in the pueblos to which they belonged. The caciques and "caciques y principales," who dispensed the administrative and religious positions in their villages through governorships, made the necessary juridical efforts to expand the area of land available to the villagers when the population pressure rose in their villages. The Audiencia in Mexico City was flooded with requests from the pueblos, written by the gobernadores, right up to the 1790s. The Indians living in urban areas and dependent of the alhóndiga or the pósito lost entitlements to food redistribution in their relationship with state officials, because the state itself lost its hold on the food market in late eighteenth-century Anáhuac, or gave it away. In the rural areas, this kind of "entitlements" were not lost, for hacendados and other entrepreneurs continued to avoid excessive prices, although they did demand a higher average price for maize and wheat.

In short, the farming population of Anáhuac was assured of its right to subsistence. First, the attitude of the caciques must have played a part. Their proto-indigenista rhetoric, their unflagging efforts to get the "village issue" discussed in court, and their readiness to lead violent action if necessary must have created the impression that the way out of the crisis was near at hand. Their prosperous position and the legitimacy of their authority depended on the maintenance of this image, which was in no way hindered by the increased income that they derived from their manipulations in the villages. Second, the attitude of the hacendados must have been important. They created the impression that they made available to all in need the limited opportunities for increased employment. Their charitable image was likewise maintained intact, despite the fact that in the late eighteenth century (when maize prices had become so high) this was an economically advantageous way for them to evade the high costs attached to the facilities of the hacienda. Moreover, many hacendados were prepared to open field kitchens in bad years or to sell their maize for lower prices at the door of the hacienda.

Anáhuac was probably a special case, because around 1800 the two strategies were combined, resulting in relative tranquillity in the countryside on the highlands, while other regions, especially Michoacán and Guadalajara, and some falda or semiarid provinces around the highlands of Anáhuac (Tetepango, Actopan, Metztitlán, and the Cuernavaca valley) saw a lot of violence. Of course, the attitude of the church and government, especially that of the lower-ranking government officials and priests, must have had a calming effect. Many priests, bishops, and government officials were often prepared to make efforts to mitigate the immediate needs of the poor at a relatively high cost. So fear of a peasant revolt, a *"miedo a la revolución,"* encouraged the elite to maintain their charitable activities.

Thus we find an interdependence between gobernadores/caciques, government officials, and hacendados, on the one hand, and more common Indians, on the other, which confirmed the conviction that the old, consensus-based order should not be disturbed. New Spain was a highly religious and "traditional" colony. The ecological system of values, backed up by church regulations, guaranteed the continuing existence of the economic system of Anáhuac. Although the bargaining power of the poorest sectors involved in the economic process had deteriorated by 1800, what Sen calls the "entitlement to subsistence" had not. The claims to self-sufficiency were commanded, to some extent, by the poorest sectors. But another argument arises if we look more closely at the documents: the active integration of the pueblos in the economic functioning of this central Mexican region would mean that the entrepreneurs could not abandon the "indios" without suffering an economic loss. To this possibility, I turn now.

4

Every Cloud Has a Silver Lining

Introduction

Another "Shadow"

There was a commercial alternative to a more intense exploitation of the moral and economic "charity system" in Anáhuac. This alternative found its way through a mechanism called the repartimiento de comercios. Since the colonial period, repartimientos had evoked controversy. Following the famine of 1786, alarming reports continued to issue from the Indian villages. On some ordinary day in 1792 in the headtown of Tenancingo in the valley of Toluca, the subdelegado of the province, Juan Francisco Fernández, who had recently replaced his predecessor (the former alcalde mayor), wrote a concerned letter to the central government in Mexico City:

> Since the Indians are forced to miss this revenue, many of them
> have left their villages to spread out into other provinces. They abuse
> the distance from their village to avoid paying tribute and church
> contributions. As a result, those who stay behind now have to
> furnish these heavy contributions by themselves.[1]

To make matters worse, while most of the Indians who stayed behind tried to drown their despair in drink and gambling, the "poor governors" had to pay the tribute out of their own pockets instead of receiving it from their subordinates.

Fernández referred to the prohibition of the repartimientos, and he was certainly not the only civil servant to see in this measure a catastrophe for the pueblos. For one, Vicente Velázquez de León, the subdelegado of the province of Otumba, reported on 23 September 1792 that with the repartimiento gone, the Indians had lost their jobs as artisans, wandered aimlessly around without work, abandoned their villages to look for work, and were no longer able to pay their tribute, nor sell products on the local weekly markets. Confraternities, the lay brotherhoods in the villages to which every Indian belonged, experienced difficulties because their members were no longer able to pay the contribution. The subdelegados of Taxco and Pachuca added that the Indian villagers in their provinces were not the only ones suffering, noting also the

hardships of miners, because they had without exception made use of muleteers from the villages, who had no beasts of burden now that the prohibition
had been introduced. The subdelegado of Chalco also claimed that the
hacendados were hit hard because their wheat harvest was now unnecessarily
expensive, for because of the shortage of cattle, they found it difficult to hire
ox teams with their drivers from the Indian villages. In 1790, some hacendados
paid 7½ reales per ox team instead of the usual price of 2![2]

The subdelegado of Coatepec, a Spanish immigrant who noticed the grum-
bling among his colleagues but did not know what the problem was, called a
meeting of the Indian village leaders. This meeting concluded that the prohibition of the repartimiento should be lifted because the villages had sunk into
poverty since the province's last repartimiento, more than fifteen years earlier. In 1794, this plea was underscored by the creole regent of the high court
of justice, Baltazar Ladrón de Guevara, who explicitly stated that the
repartimiento trade was necessary for the Indians and the poor to avoid the
increase in their misery, "since they will lack the most necessary things to
exist such as their poor clothing, oxen for the cultivation of their fields, and
mules for the transport of their goods."[3]

The subdelegados were right. The prohibition of the repartimiento was a
disaster for the economy of the Indian pueblos. It took only a few years to
destroy a commercial structure that had been carefully constructed during
150 years of Spanish rule. In this chapter, I describe the repartimiento trade as
I encountered it in the archives. The description seeks not only to reveal the
workings of the mechanism or to find out if the repartimiento trade might
have been used for a Great Leap, but also to deal with the controversy that the
repartimientos had evoked among historians. I will therefore start with the
image of the repartimientos in historical literature.

Repartimiento Trade

Because of the repartimientos, around the middle of the eighteenth century
an exceptionally large number of Indian villages had taken on a nonagrarian
character. The economy of the pueblos in Anáhuac was marked by the artisanal
production of utilities, from yokes for ploughs and crockery to luxury items
such as wood carvings and enameled dishes (the *lacas de Olinalá*, for example).
To mention another example, Tepetlaoztoc, in the province of Texcoco, was
mainly inhabited by muleteers, called *arrieros*; Chiconcuac, in the same province, was the home mainly of weavers and small wool merchants. They were
all petty merchants, but nevertheless belonging to the Indian order. It is difficult, however, to estimate the scope, and few statistical data have been preserved of the kind on which modern meticulous analyses of historical change
are so often based. Officially, this commerce was illegal, so sometimes the
information was deliberately excluded from the accounting records. The enormous importance of this repartimiento trade thus could come as a surprise to
historians who strongly trust statistical records. None of the recent surveys of

the economy during the last decades of New Spain—such as Richard and Linda Salvucci's essay on economic growth and productivity change between 1750 and 1895, Garner's book *Economic Growth*, Brading's chapter in the *Cambridge History of Latin America*, or Van Young's Chiaroscuro essay—contains an extensive discussion of the effect of the prohibition in the Anáhuac region, nor of the mechanism of the repartimiento here. Only the rather particular cochineal industry in Oaxaca is discussed under the repartimiento heading.[4]

In theory, it is not difficult to explain this fact. The abolition of the repartimiento was interpreted as a positive measure by modern standards ever since its proclamation as one of the Bourbon Reforms. In 1804, Humboldt praised King Charles III for his resolute and wise decision to prohibit the repartimiento. As far as Humboldt was concerned, this was reason enough to confer the title "benefactor of the Indians" on King Charles. In fact, the German scientist even claimed that the measures embodied in the Bourbon Reforms heralded the onset of a memorable period of Indian prosperity.[5] This interpretation of the prohibition as the termination of a criminal and exploitative regime was echoed almost 150 years later by C. H. Haring, who, in 1947, set the tone for the contemporary academic interpretation of the repartimiento in precisely this terminology:

> Under cover of this concession [the privilege of commercial monopoly within his jurisdiction] called repartimiento, [the state official] introduced goods to double or triple the amount allowed by law and through the native cacique forced upon the Indians objects which were often unnecessary or entirely useless to them.[6]

Authors like Haring were indignant at the "fact" that the Indians were forced to buy products against their will. Haring, for example, repeated his conclusion that under cover of this privilege the state officials "imposed upon their Indian charges excessive amounts of unwanted articles at arbitrary prices." All the same, the activities of the corregidor or alcalde mayor were understandable, since their salaries were only small, sometimes amounting to no more than a percentage of the local revenues. It was tempting for the alcalde mayor or corregidor in a province to use his position to increase his income from illegal sources. As Haring noted, the most obvious way of doing so was through the economic exploitation of the Indians:

> And in spite of laws and royal injunctions making it the special responsibility of the corregidores to defend the lives, property, and general well-being of the natives, this was the very function in which they were most delinquent.[7]

This delinquency, however, was not in principle the exclusive preserve of the Spaniards, as Haring pointed out in a footnote—or have we forgotten the colonial practices of the Belgians in the Congo or of the British in East Africa (Kenya)?[8] There, too, the natives were the victims of the European oppressors.

A milder form of this critique of colonialism is also found in the work of

Gibson, whose *Aztecs under Spanish Rule* (1964) was the first well-known and widely read ethnohistory of Mexican Indians. Gibson tried not to let the rhetoric of the Black Legend affect his work. All the same, he described the common procedure followed by the officials as "to buy cheaply, often from Indians themselves and then to make a forced distribution or repartimiento to the Indians at inflated prices, resulting in profits of several hundred per cent."[9] His identification with a group that he regarded as oppressed and exploited is clearly betrayed in stressing what he perceived as proof: the Indians were forced to buy not only intoxicants, but also luxury goods, including silk stockings. He even presented the international community of historians, anthropologists, and ethnographers with a typical villain of the Spanish administration: Phelipe Díez de Palacios, alcalde mayor of the province of Chalco in the early 1720s. Since this case will crop up repeatedly in the present chapter, it is necessary to cite Gibson's comment, almost in full, on how this villain operated:

> His principal economic activity was the forced distribution of animals. He maintained a ranch for cattle and horses, demanded the unrecompensed service of three Indians per week in caring for the herd and equipment, and disposed of the animals by compulsory sale to Indians at prices imposed by himself. His procedure of sale was to issue an order to each pueblo in the jurisdiction whereby individuals and groups were required to accept cattle, mules, and colts. Following the distribution, he sent Indian subordinates to collect the money, often approving in advance their use of extortionist methods, which included the imprisonment and kidnapping of Indian women. . . . Animals costing five pesos were sold at twelve. Mules costing from six to twelve pesos were sold at twenty-eight and thirty pesos.[10]

Gibson, like Haring, was also bound to deal with this alcalde mayor from a legalistic point of view, which led him to treat the contradiction between practice (see his remarks on the *derrama*) and legislation in an almost twentieth-century fashion. Nevertheless, according to Gibson, villains like Díez de Palacios were certainly not isolated cases.

This point of view was adopted by researchers like Pastor for the Mixteca in southern Mexico, MacLeod and Lovell for Central America (Guatemala), and Larson for the Cochabamba region in Bolivia. Here, too, we find characterizations like "a mechanism of forced sale and compulsory acceptance," which worked "regardless of whether or not the merchandise was desired by the recipients in the first place" (Lovell), or "whether they wanted them or not" (MacLeod).[11] However, MacLeod pointed out the proto-industrial aspect of the system, presenting the state official as "an illegal manufacturer, or rather a cottage industry supervisor" who had set up a local-level textile industry.

The most extensive discussion of the repartimiento in the early 1970s was provided by Hamnett and Brading. They preferred to use neutral terms as free as possible of the Black Legend rhetoric, which was so popular at the time. Both Hamnett and Brading described the discussion held in the court in Madrid on the value of the repartimiento for the state treasury, pointing out the economic importance of the system for the villagers. At stake was the plan by the Minister of the Indies, José de Gálvez, to prohibit the repartimiento. The effects of the implementation of the plan were also discussed. Hamnett claimed that those responsible for abuses were not the state officials, but their trading partners in Mexico City, who supplied or bought the products the alcalde mayor traded with the villages. Nevertheless, Brading indicated the results in no uncertain terms:

> Judicial authority was thus exercised, not to say prostituted, in the pursuit of commercial profit. The natural victims of this system were the Indians. . . . Defaults in payments frequently resulted in whipping and imprisonment.[12]

Despite the image of "delinquent officials" (Haring) who "prostituted their authority" (Brading), the main point in Brading's analysis is the emphasis on the propaganda element in the documentation. He refers to the philosophy of the Enlightenment, the uniformity of human nature, and the power of the state to bring about economic progress. Precisely how this economic progress was to be achieved was the object of the heated debates in the court in Madrid. Considerable documentation was deliberately created by Gálvez's officials in order to win the political dispute at court: "What encomiendas were to the missionaries of the sixteenth century, repartimientos became for the eighteenth century reformers."[13] This approach to the problem has been followed by Pietschmann, Borah, Dehouve, Farriss, and Wasserstrom.[14] While Dehouve demonstrated the value of the repartimiento for the economy of the province of Tlapa and Farriss came up with scanty evidence for the forced sale of goods to the Indians in Yucatan, Pietschmann conducted a closer scrutiny of the background of most of the documentation as propaganda. He made his case clear: modern authors have blindly followed Gálvez in their eagerness to condemn the Spanish officials.[15] A curious situation thus arises in which the officials of the Great Reformer, José de Gálvez, who wanted to emphasize and extend the colonial character of the overseas territories, are cited with approval by scholars in texts which were aimed at a condemnation of that very "colonial situation."

It hardly comes as a surprise that a critical reappraisal of this documentation leads to different conclusions. Brading somewhat modified his position in acknowledging that in certain areas, especially in South America, Indians found it difficult to obtain credit for any production aimed at the market, since merchants were reluctant to risk their monies without the sanction of a magistrate's authority. Borah and Wasserstrom, for instance, also understood that the Indians accepted the system, and in their survey of the economic development of New Spain MacLachlan and Rodríguez eventually concluded that the system was beneficial to the natives and other small farmers because it provided a source of credit and a means of marketing local products.[16] Nevertheless, these scholars do not dismiss the negative assessment of the

repartimiento. They dispense with the reports on the forced sale of silk stockings and other remarkable and useless items to the Indians as pro-Gálvez'
propaganda, but the notion that the repartimiento was a "forced sale" remains intact, supported by the words *por fuerza*, which crop up in the documentation. We are thus left with the question of how it was possible to impose
a system based on force on more than 90 percent of the population in regions
like Anáhuac and Oaxaca. Where does this leave the "independent" Indian
peasants (introduced in the early chapters above) as vigorous opponents of
exploitation? Before continuing my argument on the high-pressure solutions
found in late eighteenth-century Anáhuac, this question urges me to discuss
the "historical reality" of the repartimiento. Of course, I realize how much the
terminology of "historical reality" is besieged by postmodern philosophy nowadays, but I will leave this point aside until the last chapter of the book.

Understanding *Repartimiento* Roots

Herrschaft and Repartimiento

The repartimiento trade had indigenous roots, namely, the payment of tribute in kind to the rulers of Tenochtitlán. Although after the invasion of 1519–21
tributes were expressed in monetary terms, the "indios" could continue to
pay them in kind or in labor services, just as they had done in the pre-Hispanic era. The practice of obligation and privilege made vassalage and
Herrschaft the key to repartimiento trade, as they had been to indigenous
lordships. In accordance with the principles of Herrschaft, the administrative,
legal, religious, and military activities of the tlahtoani were recompensed with
the right to make demands on his vassals as laborers in times of need or for
public works, beside the hands whom he may already have employed on his
own farm. The *repartimiento de labor* of the colonial period had its origins in
this "snake work" or *coatequitl*, that is, the work for the gods. Coatequitl, which
was later called *servicio de tezquiz* or *el tequio* in Spanish with respect to certain
activities, was based on the service obligations of the macehualtin and was
therefore connected with tribute obligation. It was this tribute obligation that
also brought the common macehualtin into contact with the economic power
of the nobles, for they paid the tribute in kind: the fruit of their labor. Thus
the tlahtoque could come to own more products than they could consume. In
that case, they could begin to trade these products on the local and interlocal
markets through vassals described as "merchants" by modern archeologists.
Eventually, as Hoekstra has shown, the nobles were able to channel the tribute transfers, determine their character, and operate as entrepreneurs *avant la
lettre*. Thus the tribute was supplied in raw materials, such as cotton, which
was spun for the tlahtoque by women who had to fulfill their labor services,
before it was brought to the market by the nobles as cloth.[17]

The term *repartimiento* is thus connected with the reciprocity of rights
and obligations that the nobility had agreed on with their vassals (Herrschaft).
Although both of the repartimientos under discussion here (*de labor* and *de*

comercios) involved obligations of the common macehualtin—or *macehuales*, as they became to be called in the colonial period, a term which became then more or less to be synonymous with "indios" or "naturales"—toward the caciques, the common macehuales had an important right granted to them in return, one that may be seen as a kind of "benefice": the común repartimiento, the division of the village land among the tributarios. Although it is not made explicit by all authors on the Aztec era, in reading their work I have the feeling that the indigenous nobles likewise were to deliver a kind of tribute to their superiors. This included, no doubt, labor-service—administration!—military assistance, and even products in kind. A similar type of economy for Europe was described by the Dutch economic historian Slicher van Bath. He labeled it "the time of direct agrarian consumption."[18] This coincided with the hey-day of feudalism in the central regions of Europe, in particular, and with the Personenverband in general (500–1200). Modern economists would refer, perhaps a bit anachronistically, to *imperfect markets*, where the free and full exchange of goods could not take place. Government supervision, for instance, was inevitable and the laws of supply and demand played an extremely minor role. The striking feature is that the task performed by the nobility continued into the Hispanic era, from the moment when the role of the tlahtoque was officially confined to the municipal boundaries of the pueblos.

Nevertheless, the alcaldes mayores and corregidores would take over elements of the old tlahtoanate as well, and thereby would inherit aspects of the "direct agrarian consumption," even though their limited periods of office would prevent them from establishing direct personal authority in the provinces. An important traditional tlahtoanate privilege was that of food and lodging during the period of office.[19] This privilege, like all such privileges called "repartimiento," consisted of a number of Indians who performed domestic chores without payment. A woman came to grind maize and to cook it, both for the tortillas and for the atole (a maize porridge eaten for breakfast). It meant, by the way, an Indian meal for the Spanish officials. The villagers who were under the Herrschaft of the official brought him maize stalks (*zacate*) or barley for the horses and beasts of burden of the alcalde mayor. During the case against the "villain" Díez de Palacios in 1722, the Indians of Tlalmanalco stated that in their province it was customary to send each week three *topiles*—low-ranking Indian constables—to the town hall (this service was called *tequio de topiles*) to fetch water, tend the horses, and clean the residence of the alcalde mayor. They also delivered the alcalde mayor's correspondence, for which they received a few reales to cover food and travel expenses. In addition, the six villages affected and the seven barrios of the cabecera sent each week a chief—for instance, an *alguacil mayor*—to ensure that the three topiles did their work properly from sunrise to sunset and that the villages complied with their obligation to supply coal and fodder (zacate). Each day, it was the turn of a different village to supply a tercio of coal and twenty-four *manojas* of fodder. If the village whose turn it was could not supply any coal, it had to provide a carga of firewood or pay 1½ reales in cash. In fact, they could pay another 2 reales instead of the zacate. Finally, the villages also sent a cook (*india tezqui*), usually a widow without any young children, and were responsible for supplying the alcalde mayor's kitchen with 12 reales each week to pay for the meals. All of these servants themselves had the right to receive food and lodging from the alcalde mayor. They slept in the town hall, or *Casas Reales,* and took their meals there, which were estimated to cost 2½ reales a day. The right to food and lodging also included providing everything required by the alcalde mayor when he visited the villages in his province on the *visitas* that he carried out once during his period of office.

While they really had the most exclusive opportunity to do so—for Díez de Palacios was then in a very weak position—none of the Spanish or Indian witnesses questioned in Tlalmanalco accused the alcalde mayor of exploiting this situation personally. Don Phelipe Díez de Palacios had enjoyed the same rights as his predecessors upon assuming office. The Indian gobernador of Tlalmanalco, Don Salvador de Gúzman, even claimed that the obligation was not so burdensome because the servants who were expected to turn up once every fortnight belonged to a specially formed team (*caudrilla*) of sixteen Indians. Four of them—three servants and a foreman—served one month in every four in the official residence of the alcalde mayor. The distribution of these "repartimiento tasks" was organized in such a way as to preserve the traditional principle of equal subdivision of rotating functions in Indian governmental operations, which is so well known from the pre-Hispanic era (the four cardinal points!). According to Bernabé Santiago, one of the Indian "alguaciles mayores" who served for the villages of San Mateo and San Lorenzo, the expenses were shared among the villages: San Juan, San Lorenzo, and San Mateo contributed 5½ to 6 reales each month to the collective fund for the topiles; San Mateo and San Lorenzo contributed every twenty days with the double (the number twenty was also customary for such services prior to the Spanish invasion); San Martín, San Marcos, and Santa María provided zacate and coal; San Pablo, Tlapala, and Ixcahuacan each contributed between 6 and 20 reales in cash each month, in addition to small supplies of zacate; and Tlailotlacan paid 5 pesos into the kitty. This was a better solution than to saddle each of the villages and barrios involved with these labor obligations twice a year, for a total of four weeks. A few villages were given heavier burdens with the appointment of Díez de Palacios, but that was because the barrios of Ocotepec and Tianguizpan had become so impoverished that they could no longer pull their weight. The Indians stated that the alcalde mayor found everything to his liking and did not personally interfere with the arrangement in any way.

The situation was different in Yahualica, a province in the northern faldas where the recently appointed alcalde mayor, Don Juan Mejía, demanded similar repartimiento privileges of the local population.[20] As mentioned above, the alcalde mayor in general received hardly any payment for his work, so he tried to obtain the usual revenues in the province for his judicial and administrative activities. He visited all the villages in the area and demanded the traditional daily supply of three almudes of maize and specific quantities of chili, salt, beans, and similar items. He also expected the usual two servants to turn up to collect the zacate, two widows to prepare the meals, and two topiles to do the household chores in the official residence every week. The villagers acknowledged that they had supplied such services in the past, but such practices had become obsolete for some time. They added that the "servicio de tezquiz" was now rendered to the priest because of the importance of the church and religion. This particular "servicio de tezquiz" was not to be sneezed at: traditionally it amounted in Yahualica to 40 pesos for the six main festivals of the year, 12 pesos for the wine, 4 *ilacaziques* or *mantas* (a cotton cloth, part of the caciques' dress) per month, more articles of clothing, 20 turkeys (*gallinas*), meat, and foodstuffs, as well as 3½ almudes of maize each day. In addition he was attended by 21 topiles and received 48 *faros* of cotton, plus 103 pieces of material every two months. The gobernadores added that the priests had agreed to a reduction in 1722: from then on, his tribute was reduced by 3 *mantas*, 4 turkeys, 34 *faros* of cotton and 29 pieces of material. The number of topiles who attended him was reduced to 15: 3 *sacristanes*; 2 *teopantopiles*, or church constables; 1 *teopantlapixque*, for the upkeep of the church and the collection of tithes; 4 topiles in the kitchen; 2 women to grind the maize; 1 cook; and 2 hands for the zacate. The villages had become much poorer, the gobernadores claimed, because of the complete failure of the cotton and maize harvests in 1715. Of course, a crisis would occur every five to seven years because of the slash-and-burn technique used by the Indians in Yahualica: the old milpas would be exhausted and they would not have yet slashed and burned a new piece of jungle. All the same, there was enough to provide a surplus for the priest. This was not really extravagant, however, because the priest did not secure as much as his colleague in Mazatenango, Guatemala, for example, who received, in 1812, enormous rations of salt, maize, hay, firewood, pears, lime, green peppers, garlic and onions, 234 dozen eggs, 728 hens, 104 dozen fish, and 5,840 bananas every year.[21] But it is evident that the priest of Yahualica held a more important economic position than the alcalde mayor, and the same is probably true of his political position.

In the meantime, the alcalde mayor of Yahualica did not receive anything. He begged Don Antonio Cortés, the Indian gobernador of Huazalingo, one of the pueblos in the province, for a loan of one thousand pesos to pay off a debt he owed to a merchant; but his pleas were in vain. In desperation, he decided to resort to repartimientos and increased the tribute in kind to the old level of one thousand pesos worth of cotton and maize. He also demanded a small amount of brown unclayed sugar (*piloncillo*) from the sugar producers in the province, Indians and non-Indians alike. Furthermore, he imposed a new customs duty, which consisted of rating the products offered on the market far below their real price, buying them up himself, and then reselling them at higher prices. The price difference per product amounted to one peso. He also tried to gain access to the village treasury, which the pueblos controlled in order to cash in on the tribute revenue. In addition, he obliged the villages to sow six fanegas of maize on their land (twenty-one hectares), which had to yield at least thirty fanegas to deliver to him. This order would imply a yield ratio of 5:1, ridiculously low I think, because the actual yield ratios were usually around 100:1 and could even rise to as much as 300:1. The ratio of 5:1 meant that the Indians could share a large part of the real harvest among themselves in return for their labor. Nevertheless, this right of the alcalde mayor could become a real burden after a bad harvest, because the same volume still had to be supplied to the Casas Reales. Finally, he reinstated the traditional "flower service" (servicio de xuchil), which obliged the villages to supply him with a certain amount of cotton cloth every year. The villages refused and applied to the magistrate in Mexico City, where they won their case. Don Juan Mejía had to earn his income in a legal way. When a later successor of Mejía, Don Santiago Pardiñas, tried the same tricks again in 1773, the procedure was repeated and the villagers won their case once again. The Indians had abolished "Herrschaftliche" services and repartimientos to state officials in Yahualica, and there was little that an alcalde mayor could do about it.

However, the local assistants of the alcalde mayor, such as the alguacil mayor or teniente, were more involved than the alcalde mayor himself in the integration of the traditional privileges (and obligations) of the tlahtoanate in the Spanish administration. This is easily understandable if we bear in mind that these lower-ranking officials were not outsiders, as their provincial superiors were, but usually owned a hacienda or ranch or ran a trading center in the provincial cabecera, in addition to their official duties. They generally belonged to the Spanish república, although Indians could be appointed to the posts. As we shall see, these officials could implement repartimientos on a considerable scale without the alcalde mayor being able to intervene in any way. Hoekstra cites a case of such abuses in the repartimiento held in the province of Huejotzingo in 1619, when the corregidor of the province was instructed by the Audiencia to take action against his subordinate. The corregidor was not considered to be involved in the case by the Audiencia or by the Indians who had lodged their complaint.[22]

Be that as it may, the alcalde mayor was personally accountable for his subordinates. Pietschmann justifiably refers to this as, in principle, a case of a "rationalised bureaucratic Herrschaft in the Weberian sense."[23] Although we now know that, in practice, the state sold positions in the civil service to the highest bidder, the traditional principle of the Personenverband, by which the superior appointed one of his acquaintances, preferably a relative, remained in force so he would be able to exercise some degree of control. Personal ties were supposed to guarantee loyalty and prevent abuses. Moreover, the background of the state in the social orders meant that the nobility held the positions; and nobility, it was assumed, did not require payment in view of the income from feudal sources. Therefore, civil servants received extremely low salaries, if any. This was a blot on the concept of the "rationalised bureaucratic Herrschaft in the Weberian sense": civil servants who did not receive feudal incomes tried to earn a living from their official position, and in Latin America this rule applied to virtually every civil servant, including, of course, the Indian gobernador. Imbued as we are with terms that have become common parlance since Weber, we nowadays call it *corruption;* a civil servant should receive a decent wage from taxes that have been fixed and are open to public scrutiny, to prevent him from imposing his own arbitrary forms of tax. Haring and Gibson reacted in that way. However, these idiosyncratic forms of tax were endemic to a state based on the social-jural orders (*états*), and they were still in existence in New Spain. The repartimiento, in all its types, can be seen as such a form of private taxes.

The alcaldes mayores and corregidores ensured that this "Herrschaftliche" reciprocity was respected: private taxes by means of the various forms of repartimiento were levied in return for government and jurisprudence. Such taxes were obligatory—like modern forms of tax—and were universally accepted as long as the alcalde mayor observed the familiar rules of "buen gobierno." These rules usually coincided with the rules of the moral economy of provision discussed earlier on. That is why every Indian or non-Indian who was questioned replied that the repartimientos were imposed by force (*por fuerza*). It was the *compulsion* of reciprocity, symbolically reinforced every time the administrative staff (*vara*) was displayed or touched at a sale. Whether it was the vara of the alcalde mayor or that of his teniente or alguacil mayor, there could be no repartimiento without a vara.[24] Thus the Indians—and the Spaniards as well, for most of them took part in the "repartimiento de comercios" too—hardly ever complained about the repartimientos in principle; all they objected to was what they regarded as nonobservance of the reciprocal relations of Herrschaft. The only physical "compulsion" exercised was during debt collection: the debtor was imprisoned (held in custody, we should call it) if he was unable to pay his debts. At a time when the "civilizing offensive" had not advanced as far as it has in the present century, this could well be carried out violently. In fact, the predecessor of the modern fine is the whip. To paraphrase James Riley: the perceptions of just punishment differed from ours.[25] Custom condoned a certain amount of whipping or beating for laziness or errors.

There is a nice demonstration of this in the case of Don Manuel Estaban Sánchez de Tagle, alcalde mayor of Zacatlán, in the northern faldas, who was faced with a rebellion against "mal gobierno." However, this "mal gobierno" had nothing to do with the repartimiento; it was the reaction to his policy in the famine year of 1786 that cost him so much trouble.[26] As a province with a large subtropical tract, Zacatlán was suitable for the emergency harvest program drawn up by the viceroy and the church. Sánchez de Tagle had ordered the planting of 500 fanegas of maize on uncultivated land, or land that was lying fallow. The bishop of Puebla would cover practically all the expenses. A few months later, in June, this resulted in a harvest of fifty thousand fanegas. The harvest was taken to the Zacatlán corn exchange (alhóndiga) by some 1,500 Indians. The alcalde mayor was somewhat overzealous in collecting the harvest: the villages had to surrender all their maize. Sánchez de Tagle did not trust the Indian leaders. He suspected that the caciques were colluding with the priests in holding back maize from the previous harvest and were speculating on stocks. His deputies combed the province with squads of twenty-five armed militiamen to ensure the delivery of the grain that the church had paid for. Although the majority of the harvest was earmarked to alleviate the hardships in the highlands, some of it was sold to the residents in the region itself for 4½ pesos per fanega, an astronomical price. These actions involved two pieces of "mal gobierno": excessive prices and failing to leave any grain behind for the villagers. In a prosperous year, this would not have led to anything more than a few incidents, but with the almost hungry village population—or with fears of being in that position very soon—suffering from the price increases, it was the oil on the ever-smoldering fire of the "Herrschaftliche" relations of authority. A crowd consisting mainly of women stormed the alhóndiga on 5 July and sold the maize in a hilarious spectacle. They also harvested the communal milpa of Zacatlán and sold the proceeds in a similar way. Sánchez de Tagle sought asylum in the priest's house and fled to Mexico City four days later.

The argument put forward here does not depend on the background or particular course of this popular revolt. It is evident that the alcalde mayor was responsible for a classic example of "mal gobierno," and he had to pay for it without delay. Yet it was not as serious as all that, for once peace had been restored he was able to return to Zacatlán and resume his position. There is more of interest in his defense, which centered on the fact that he had observed the principles of "buen gobierno" throughout the rest of his period in office. Of course, he refused to recognize that he had been in the wrong in 1786, but when the magistrates were called in to pronounce on the situation, as they always were after a popular revolt, he managed to divert their attention from the issue. Apparently this sidetracking was successful, since his maneuver saved him from severe censure or even from a transfer.

Sánchez de Tagle's defense consisted of the dispatch of a number of dossiers from the previous period, in which he had applied the practice of "buen gobierno." Without exception this was concerned with the maintenance of the normative economy—such as supporting a petition from a few villages to the Audiencia for a postponement of tribute payment, the prevention of dissension in the Indian villages, and resistance to what he regarded as an abuse of power on the part of the village priests. (Several of these cases, such as those connected with the elections of the gobernadores of San Baltasar, Huitlapan, and Ahuacatlán, will be discussed in more detail in the next chapter.) He explicitly championed the cause of the Indians who had come to him to complain about their old gobernador, who was in league with the priest. In fact, the Indians showed that they knew that they could count on him for support, and he also dispatched as evidence a case concerning a village riot over the theft of a pig. On each occasion, the main opponents to his endeavor to practice "buen gobierno" were a small group of priests in the province. It was these very same priests, he claimed, who tried to discredit him after the popular revolt by making incriminating statements about his repartimientos. However, he argued, the repartimientos were regarded as the reward for his work, which is why they were accepted by the people. It was true that the repartimientos brought him 125 pesos a year from each village, as they had done for his predecessors in the past; but this was still less than what the priests were paid for performing weddings, baptisms, funerals, masses, and the blessing of the various village festivals. He was certainly right on this score. What annoyed him was the fact that the priests were allowed to demand such large sums from the Indians while the alcaldes mayores were not. He concluded his defense with the statement that the repartimientos were the just "wage" for "buen gobierno," and were recognized as such by both Indian and non-Indian in the provinces. There was no room here for the modern, rational state that pays its civil servants a reasonable wage.

The extent to which the traditional, personal practice of Herrschaft was still deeply rooted in the eighteenth century can be gauged from another case that Sánchez de Tagle adduced in his defense.[27] It concerned the rights of a group of Indians who had brought under cultivation a piece of jungle on the border with the province of Huauchinango. This tract was called Tlapacoya, and it belonged to the pueblo San Juan Ahuacatlán. The colonial regulations prohibited an act of this kind: each Indian was supposed to live in a "pueblo de indios," Indian cacicazgo—the estate of the caciques outside pueblo borders—or hacienda, so that his privileges and obligations were guaranteed. This resulted in three juridical types of tributarios: *indios de pueblo* enlisted in the pueblos, *indios terrazguerros* enlisted by caciques on their estates, and *indios gañanes* enlisted on the haciendas. It was uncertain to which type the Tlapacoyans belonged: they did not belong to any provincial headtown, nor to a specific cacicazgo; and haciendas would not be found in these mountainous circumstances. This unfortunate circumstance made them "vagrants." Again, European analogy can be clarifying. In the European medieval and early modern constellation, by statutory definition, a vagrant was a person able to labor who possessed neither land nor master, who worked at no recognized trade and refused to do so.[28] Outside these requirements, a man was not free to dispose of his own labor. People were settled legally in certain parishes or villages, or under manorial rule. Anybody needed a "lord" or "master." In New Spain the same legal basis was in order: the "subjects," mostly belonging to the "Indian order," needed a master—be he gobernador, cacique, hacendado, or any other—to secure "buen gobierno," the Catholic "education" of the Indians, and tribute payments.

Consequently, for the Tlapacoyans a master was being sought. The teniente of Ahuacatlán, an Indian civil servant, appealed to the alcalde mayor at the end of 1784 to resolve the dispute. After all, there was a danger that the pueblos would become ghost towns if such illegal settlements, which did not pay any tribute, were allowed to continue. Besides, the projected influence of the caciques of Chicontla, a neighboring pueblo, on these Indians was at risk.

However, further investigation revealed that most of them did in fact pay tribute: 60 to 70 families paid it to the government of the province of Zacatlán through various pueblos, and 313 families did the same to the government of the province of Huauchinango. There were also 20 to 30 nonpaying families in the settlement. The group from Huauchinango was the largest, and thus had the strongest claim to form an official "pueblo de indios." This implied a greater risk for the Spanish king than for the local caciques, the alcalde mayor stated, because the Indians of Huauchinango were not direct vassals of the king of Spain, but of the duke of Atlixco. Huauchinango was part of his tribute domain. If the Indians of Huauchinango were to receive village rights in the jungle of Tlapacoya, then Tlapacoya would belong to Huauchinango instead of Zacatlán. The border would be changed and this territory would be lost to the king! It was therefore an act of "buen gobierno" by Sánchez de Tagle on behalf of the king to give the tributaries of Zacatlán in Tlapacoya village rights. The Indians from Huauchinango had to claim their rights on the other side of the border. It is hard to imagine a clearer illustration of the fact that relationships founded on land had not yet fully displaced relationships founded on personal ties in eighteenth-century New Spain.

The Late Eighteenth-century Repartimiento

This brings us back to the repartimiento and the economic reforms of the eighteenth century. Don José de Gálvez, the special representative of the crown, must have been bitterly angered by the economic activities of his alcaldes mayores, and for that reason, he replaced them with subdelegados. The arrival of Gálvez as *visitador general* in 1765 heralded the "revolution in government" that King Charles III (1759–88) and his follower in Mexico, the count of Revillagigedo (1789–94) were to implement, and which has gone down in Mexican history as the *Reformas Borbónicas*.[29] Among other points, the visitador general opted for an administrative system in which the civil servants would be paid better, so that they would not feel the need to engage in commercial networks in their provinces. It was the state's responsibility to raise the funds for this purpose from taxation and to prevent the civil servants from imposing their own taxes.

Ever since Herbert Priestley's 1916 biography of Gálvez, the visitador general and his measures have been credited with improving administrative efficiency and combating corruption. Research, however, has indicated that the measures actually undertaken by the visitador have been somewhat overrated, and the new civil servants were only dedicated to the interests of the mother country to a limited extent. It has been shown that Gálvez's appointments betray a preference for friends and relatives from Málaga, his own place of birth. He helped them into lucrative positions in the colonies, so that they could increase their family fortune. Linda Salvucci has shown that historians too are children of their time, by demonstrating that the untarnished image of Gálvez was deliberately created by his first biographer because Priestley himself was at that time (1916) a civil servant engaged in campaigning for a civil service in the United States that would be free of corruption.[30] However, several of the civil servants appointed by Gálvez used their position to fill their own pockets. They married the daughters of the local elite and invested their fortune in haciendas. Curiously enough, their direct descendants supported the Creole party in the War of Independence twenty-five years later. Nevertheless, this is not to understate the extent of the Reforms, because the plans of Gálvez did result in legislation; it entailed a new army, the tobacco monopoly, a growth in the number of civil servants, the coming of the intendants, and the viceregal secretariat. That "revolution in government" was short-lived and often still corrupt does not affect its novelty. It doubtless increased the efficiency of the tax-collecting system and resulted in greater revenues for the treasury.

Gálvez was particularly irritated by the fact that the government officers acted as middlemen and therefore paid scant attention to the position of the treasury. The abolition of this "abuse" was hindered by a number of practical problems. First, the alcalde mayor was responsible for collecting the tribute, which was often paid in kind, while he was expected to transfer the payment to the state in coin. Since he had to convert the goods into cash, the civil servant borrowed the starting capital for his private business affairs from prosperous merchants; he did so soon after being appointed to a position for a number of years in a particular province, but before he actually started work there. Agreements were made with the money lenders as to the nature of his business activities: the supply of goods from pueblos within the jurisdiction of the government official to the merchants, and vice versa, the supply of goods from the merchants to the Indians. The merchant guaranteed that the payment would be made to the crown in cash, provided that the alcalde mayor ensured that the value of the goods supplied by the villagers would be higher than the amount he had to pay to the crown. This difference in price was the source of the profits for the merchant and the alcalde mayor.[31] An additional factor was that the alcalde mayor had often rented his position from the government and was obliged to obtain an extra loan to pay for it. This was not such an astronomical amount, and at any rate it was less than the turnover from the repartimiento trade.

The tribute was imposed on the Indian pueblos on a collective basis in proportion to the number of residents. In the case of pueblos which still paid in kind, the alcalde mayor fixed the nature and price of the goods that the villagers were to pay him as tribute. As stated above, this price was less than the market value of the goods, so that the villagers had to supply relatively more than the market value demanded. These goods were subsequently sold by the alcalde mayor to the merchants with whom he had made agreements. These merchants, in turn, sold the goods elsewhere in the country for the highest possible prices—and not back to the same Indians, as has been stated in the old literature. It is true, however, that soon it became common practice for the villagers to buy goods from the alcalde mayor or from his representative at a price above the market value, but this was different merchandise.

This practice sometimes culminated in a system of barter between merchants and villagers, with the alcalde mayor acting as middleman. However, as the villagers in particular purchased capital goods like livestock and looms, the Indians' debt outstripped their tribute obligation. This means that the alcalde mayor had to make a great effort to ensure that this debt was repaid. In all, these dealings between a pueblo and an alcalde mayor were free and open in principle. The Indians refused to pay for items they could not use and the alcaldes mayores naturally adjusted to these demands since they had very few means of actually forcing the Indians to accept items of trade they did not want. Besides, gross abuse entailed the risk of rebellion. This could pose a direct threat to the life of the alcalde mayor; after all, his residence might soon be set on fire. It is important to emphasize that, in the last resort, the pueblos in New Spain were driven to cooperate with the system out of economic necessity; unlike the situation in Peru, which should apparently be sharply distinguished from that in New Spain,[32] there seems not to have been any direct physical coercion.

If the Indians or non-Indians had nothing to gain from a repartimiento, it was not held or the tradition was brought to an end. For example, it was customary until late in the eighteenth century in the province of Actopan to buy pigs from the alcalde mayor for fattening on credit ("venta al fiado," as the repartimiento was also called there). However, in the course of the century the growth of the population in Actopan made it necessary to plow more land for maize, and pig-keeping disappeared from the Indian pueblos. From then on, the Indians bought beasts of burden through the repartimiento in order to earn an extra income in the transport sector—referred to as *arriería*— but these purchases were on a considerably smaller scale than that of the trade in pigs which had taken place earlier in the century. Elsewhere, the owner of the Real del Monte silver-mine complex in Pachuca, Don Pedro Romero de Terreros, received special permission from the crown to impose a labor levy— also called repartimiento—on the Indian villages near the mine, including those in the provinces of Actopan and Tulancingo, in the 1750s and early 1760s. The villagers in Tulancingo registered a protest with the magistrate, which resulted in official exemption for the villages from the labor levy in the mines. The Indians in Actopan rebelled in April 1757, when the men were expected to work at the time when the milpas had to be sown. This was in a period when poverty due to harvest failures and relative overpopulation had already increased drastically. The protest was heard in Mexico City, but the Indians were not granted exemption from their labor levy. We do not know whether many Indians from Actopan actually went to Real del Monte, but there were traces of peasant disobedience in Don Pedro's complaint some years later that he had never had more than one-twentieth of the agreed quota of laborers.[33]

It was customary in the province of Tulancingo for three of the ten villages to pay their tribute in cotton sheets. In view of the handling and retail costs, the sum was converted into pesos, 3p1, which was higher than the 2p1 official tribute due. With the recurrence of poor cotton harvests in the late 1760s, an appeal for a cessation of this repartimiento and a reduction of the tribute to 2p1 was granted in 1771. The Indians in the province of Tochimilco, on the eastern slopes of the Popocatépetl volcano, had already achieved something similar in 1711. When Don Antonio Rodríguez was installed there as alcalde mayor in 1710, he immediately implemented a cattle repartimiento, offering beasts of burden for 30 pesos, young bulls for 14 pesos, and horses for 20 pesos. He had already visited the province before taking up office to see how large the herd was supposed to be. He then proceeded to sell the Indians sandals for 20 reales, blankets for 20 and 32½ reales, hats for 12 reales, and other items of clothing at the same rate of three times the price on the free market. The goods were displayed in the meeting room of the Indian village council, which was thus prevented from holding meetings. All private sales were prohibited in this municipality; the alcalde mayor had even monopolized the trade in meat and candles. In addition he invited the villages to sow a milpa or maize field for him with seed supplied by himself, and to do the same in a few wheat fields. Instead of being paid in cash for this work, the Indians were to be allowed to keep a part of the harvest. The officer demanded additional money and goods for the visits to the villages in the province, and he even carried out more of these visits than was customary—performing two of them in 1710 alone! During these visits he collected fourteen pesos, one carga of maize, and twelve turkeys in the villages. The Indians who did the domestic chores in his official residence and prepared his meals as a work levy were sent home, and the villages were asked for money instead. Finally, he instructed the villagers to build a luxurious extra floor in the village hall for Don Tomás Serán de los Ríos, a merchant from Mexico City who had loaned him money for his business activities. After all, Don Tomás had to be given a decent reception! Don Antonio Rodríguez had clearly not grasped the principles of "buen gobierno" and he underestimated the resistance of the Indians. He was only saved from a disgraceful retreat because the crown reversed his measures and confiscated his belongings.[34] The Indians were allowed to distribute among themselves the harvest from the milpas already sown.

An alcalde mayor was thus aware of the rules of the game. There were fixed prices for the purchase of items from the villages and for the sale of livestock and other capital goods to the Indians; and as far as the sale was concerned, there were even fixed quantities, as Sánchez de Tagle, the alcalde mayor of Zacatlán, pointed out. The peasants in his province, both Indians and non-Indians, specialized in eggs. Although they were expensive, there was a large demand for eggs in Mexico City and in Puebla de los Angeles. A number of merchants sold eggs in these cities; I know of a case of a merchant from 1777 who needed three cargas of maize a year to feed the chickens he kept. However, most of the eggs on sale in these cities came from Zacatlán, supplied within a repartimiento arrangement. The producers were rancheros, most of whom were official Indian residents of pueblos in the province, who had made an informal contract with the alcalde mayor to supply eggs at the rate of twelve pesos per half carga (a *tanda*). At the request of the Indians, this price—which was actually an advance since the alcalde mayor had to pay it beforehand to the gobernador of each village—was independent of the market "since time immemorial."[35] Of course, in 1786 the alcalde mayor complained about the fixed nature of the advance and the terms of delivery:

> I believe that the contract is as old as the province. What it boils down to is that the alcalde mayor has to pay the indios 12 per half [carga], no matter whether he gets 8 or 16 from the sale of the eggs. In addition, the alcalde mayor may not refuse the monthly delivery from the villages, because the quantities were laid down in long-standing agreements. With each delivery the peasants have to be paid a fixed sum in advance for the next month's delivery, but it is common for money to be taken to the villages without the eggs being delivered. The villagers still owe me three or four monthly deliveries from last year.[36]

Some people in the province even claimed that the alcalde mayor's situation had deteriorated over the past few years, because Sánchez de Tagle had to pay an advance of twelve reales for each tanda, while his predecessors had only paid ten. He had been presented with this fait accompli upon taking office in the province; his direct predecessor had negotiated this unfavorable price increase with the Indians in 1781 (although Sánchez de Tagle himself stated that the price increase had already been in force for twenty-five years). Moreover, the Indians also had their transport expenses. Still, the alcalde mayor's complaints about the contract were particularly strong in the years unfavorable for him, while the Indians complained about it in the years when the repartimiento was unfavorable for them. We do not know whether the trade had become so important that it was impossible to ignore the alcalde mayor. Sánchez de Tagle himself stated in 1786 that no more than 10 percent of the eggs were traded through the alcaldes mayores.[37]

According to estimates of the time, between 240 and 320 cargas of eggs were supplied to merchants in Mexico City by means of the repartimiento, while an additional 120 to 160 cargas were supplied to traders in Puebla. The village of Huechutla alone supplied more than 50 cargas a month. The combination of these data suggests an annual production of at least 5 million eggs (the product of 25,000 hens, assuming 200 laying days per hen); and this figure does not include the eggs sold independently at the regional markets on behalf of the Indian peasants by women or confraternities from their villages. Furthermore, the priests and some traders also played a large part in the egg trade. With the assistance of the female personnel from the villages, they even competed as middlemen with the alcalde mayor. In other words, millions of eggs must have been involved, which lends probability to an estimate of between 50,000 to 100,000 hens in the province of Zacatlán at the time.[38]

Various witnesses in the Sánchez de Tagle case claimed that the alcaldes mayores would have preferred to abandon the egg trade because the losses could sometimes be steep. This was not just because the alcaldes mayores had to pay the full price for a carga despite the fact that a large number of the eggs arrived broken, crammed in straw-packed crates on the backs of the mules. To make matters worse, the Indians had developed a flair for the market and sold their eggs where the price was highest, so that the alcalde mayor sometimes had to wait months for his deliveries. In 1786 alone, the villagers were ninety-four tandas in arrears, with a market value of 1,128 reales (141 pesos). Most of these debtors, ten in number, lived in Aquixtla. It is also clear that the Indians generally did enjoy the most favorable terms of trade under the repartimiento, because the price in Mexico City or Puebla was usually lower than 12 reales per carga;[39] not to mention the fact that the middleman, the alcalde mayor, had to pay the transport costs too.

Another example of the importance of the repartimiento as a part of the exaction of tribute concerns the province of Tlapa, in the southern faldas of Anáhuac. The major article of trade here was the lacquerwork from the villages of Olinalá, Chavingo, Tlalapa, Tealocazingo, and Chipetlán. The villagers decorated dried and hollow pumpkins of various sizes with a lacquer made from the oil of the fruit of the *chía* tree. The wood and oil came from the tropical lowlands near the port of Acapulco, and the pumpkins were from the same region. This already indicates a far-reaching division of labor within the economy of the villages of the southern falda provinces, involving large numbers of pack animals. These beasts of burden were purchased from livestock breeders in Guadalajara, through the intermediary of an alcalde mayor. The lacquerwork was sold by the villagers themselves at every major annual market in the regions of New Spain; part of it was paid to the alcaldes mayores as tribute. The repartimiento of pack animals in exchange for lacquerwork (and also for cotton cloth later in the eighteenth century) took place twice a year. The alcalde mayor of Tlapa wrote that this exchange represented a trading value of five thousand pesos a year. The lacquerwork service was in great demand throughout the country, so he had set up a large storehouse in Mexico City for the decorated pumpkins that he collected. In 1743, the system provided work for eight thousand families in 105 Indian pueblos.[40]

The Indians did not only cooperate with the various repartimientos out of considerations of political reciprocity. The economic advantages that accrued to the Indians who participated in this system also provide an important point in the analysis. The villages actually stood to gain from the continuation of the repartimiento in view of the employment opportunities created by the system in numerous areas. The features of the repartimiento trade, as will be shown below, indicate the incipient characteristics of the emergence of proto-industrialization (which is discussed in another chapter). The skeptical reader may wonder how proto-industrialization could arise in a region lacking in good roads, canals, and rivers. After all, in Europe the good transport facilities were practically an essential condition for the growth of industry. The answer is obvious: this lack was compensated in Anáhuac by the repartimiento precisely because of the "imperfect markets" of New Spain. The commercial activities of the alcaldes mayores were responsible for a large part of capital transfer, commercial transactions, and transport in the viceroyalty. This system enabled the full integration of the residents in the Indian pueblos into the economic system. There is not a trace to be found of any economic separation between a "Spanish world" and an "Indian world," despite the claims of scholars like Wolf to the contrary.

Considerations of this kind led the subdelegado of Taxco, Don Fernando Mendoza, to bring up some confusing terminology in 1792.[41] He claimed that the repartimientos had been enforced under physical compulsion in the seventeenth century, but that this was no longer necessary in the eighteenth century because the Indians accepted the economic necessity of such "Herrschaftliche" taxes, and of course, because they had become economically dependent on the entrepreneurial activities carried out by the *repartidores*, both private individuals and civil servants. The initiative was therefore in the hands of the Indians and Spaniards who wanted to retain a traditional system as long as it was in their interests to do so. He had noted that the herds in Taxco used to be driven to the central square and that the alcaldes mayores themselves must ensure that the Indians and non-Indians did not buy too much livestock from the merchants or their agents, or else they would get in to repayment difficulties. Repayment was fixed at four reales a week in these parts. The last repartimiento in Taxco (of 4,090 mules) had been held in 1787, but this had not been repaid in full because the alcalde mayor was replaced before completing his term of office. The subdelegado had not been allowed— nor was he able—to recover the remaining thirty-six hundred pesos, amounting to more than one-third of the turnover. In the opinion of this subdelegado, the term *repartimiento,* which placed such a heavy emphasis on the initiative of the alcaldes mayores, should be replaced once and for all by the term *venta al fiado* (buying on credit).

The Scale of Repartimiento Trade

The Livestock Repartimiento

As we have seen, the alcalde mayor usually supplied the Indians in the villages with livestock, partly in exchange for other items. This part of the mechanism deserves a more detailed presentation in view of the enormous sums of money involved. In Zacatlán, it involved some eight hundred mules and five hundred bulls a year, even though Sánchez de Tagle only held one mule repartimiento and one bull repartimiento. He organized the first of these in the autumn of 1784.[42] The animals involved were mules, as beasts of burden the main product for the alcalde mayor. The herd roamed through the province for a few months in the direction of grazing land that had been earmarked for that purpose, watched over by twenty-eight cowboys who worked in shifts of seven at a time. Most of the cowboys earned eight reales a day, a very high wage indeed and usually paid in cash, although a few of them were paid in kind: they were allowed to take some of the animals. Sánchez de Tagle paid four times the rent to private individuals for grazing the bulls, while the mules were pastured in the meadows the villages made available to him. Once the animals arrived in one of these meadows, the residents of the villages, ranchos, haciendas, and towns were told that the sale was due to begin. This brought the Indians from the mountains and the non-Indians from their ranchos or haciendas to examine the animals and make their choice. The prices of the best livestock were naturally higher than those of the poorer specimens, so that the buyers in Zacatlán, the cabecera, paid higher prices—2 pesos a piece more—than the buyers in Tepetzintla, the last stopping place after the journey through the faldas. The cowboys also became aware of this price difference, because in the faldas they were paid only half of what they received in the highland part of the province.

The accounts reveal a vast number of buyers, who each bought one or two animals. Many Spaniards and other non-Indians were involved, and even priests, especially in the cabecera Zacatlán. Some of them bought as many as three or four animals. Don Lucas Wading, the previous alcalde mayor and now a trader in the region, bought thirty-two animals for 1,184 pesos; Don Joseph Ayansa Xavier, the priest of Amixtlán, Don Manuel Antonio de Arco y Castilla from Tepetzintla and Don Francisco Sandoval from the Paderon rancho each bought ten; and Blas González from Tepeixco bought eight. The Indians are recorded in the accounts as married couples (and only their first names were registered, of course, sometimes accompanied by a calpollilike toponym). In many cases, Indian and non-Indian alike, someone had to stand surety for the repayment. The takings from the cabecera Zacatlán and the neighboring pueblo of Tepeixco—where mainly rancheros showed an interest in buying— amounted to 16,231 pesos, of which 124 pesos were paid by Indians. The number of rancheros in the highland area of this province was unusually high; most of them were not registered on a tribute list and subsequently should not be regarded as Indians. This did not apply to the Sierra Zapoteca, the mountainous tract that extended throughout almost half of the province. The takings in the pueblo of San Juan Ahuacatlán and environs in that part of the province amounted to 8,741 pesos, of which 6,753 pesos were paid by Indians. In this area, the Spaniards paid 30 pesos for a mule, the Indians generally 29 pesos. In terms of the total turnover of this *repartimiento de mulas y machos*, no more than 30 percent was sold to individuals who were registered as Indians, while more than 70 percent was sold to non-Indians.

The Indian share in this repartimiento was thus strikingly small. Not only did they play a minor part in the amount of money involved, but the number of Indians among the total number of buyers was relatively low as well. Only 4 of the 216 buyers who turned up in Zacatlán to buy pack animals were registered on a tribute list. As for the others, 38 were allowed to call themselves by the title Don. Most of them, of course, were caciques and thus Indians in juridical terms. At any rate, this is true of Don Joseph Silva and Don Manuel Sánchez, who were gobernadores at the time or had been so in the past. Excluding the caciques, 219 of the 250 buyers were Indians from the following villages: San Juan Ahuacatlán (11), San Marcos (8), San Mateo (8),

San Andrés (2), San Francisco (5), San Antonio Tetepango (12), San Pedro Comacuautla (11), San Bernardino (1), San Bartolomé Coatepec (23), San Francisco Tapayula (3), Zapotitlán (18), Zongozotla (2), Huitzila (12), Nanacatlán (10), Tuxtla (6), Hueytlapam (24), San Antonio Chipahuatlán (7), Zitlala (13), Ixtepec (17), San Martinito (7), San Miguel Atlequezayam (6), La Concepción (4), San Juan Oselona Caxtle (5), San Francisco Caxuacan (6), Olintla (10), Huehuetla (10), Xopala (7), Amixtlán (1), and Tepetzintla (1), in the falda area of the province. Eight of the remaining 31 buyers bore the title Don; 5 of them were priests and 2 were gobernadores.

Of course, there were far more than 254 Indian households in the province. The number of tributarios in 1785 totaled 6,900.5. Although I do not have any other available statistical data, the 1803 figures of the *intendente* Manuel Flon are also interesting. After several decennia of population growth, his officials counted a population of 41,625 souls (*almas*) in the forty-nine pueblos, five haciendas, and sixty-nine ranchos. Flon described 3,701 of them as "Spanish," 2,464 as mestizos or other castas, and 35,460 as "Indians." Assuming an average family size of 4.5 persons, the latter figure yields 7,880 tributarios. Ten years earlier Carlos de Urrutia counted 49,625 "almas," without breaking the figure down any further. My records indicate that there were 8,228 tributarios in 1800.[43] Taken as a whole, it therefore seems that it was only a small sector of the population that was involved in this repartimiento. However, since the alcalde mayor carried out such repartimientos very regularly and the mules were used for a number of years, the actual intensity of this involvement could have been higher. How is one to find out? The answer depends on how long the Indians used a pack animal. Although it is tempting to suppose that they were only used for a few years (I shall return to this point later), I do not have any actual statistics. Even if we assume the worst variant, with only 254 buyers in 1784, it is impossible that *every* Indian was forced to buy a mule every year, or even a *majority* of the Indians. There is no trace of a repartimiento of mules in 1785 or 1786. But even if the alcalde mayor had held a repartimiento de mulas y machos every year in the same rhythm, and 254 *different* Indians had been forced to buy on each occasion, it would have taken 27 years (6900.5/254) before the turn of the buyers of 1784 came round again. An Indian must have decided to replace his pack animals of his own accord four of five times in the meantime.

The same goes for the second repartimiento, which Sánchez de Tagle held in Zacatlán, concluded in November 1784. On this occasion, he was offering young bulls to be castrated and used as plow oxen. He found 198 buyers in or near the cabecera Zacatlán. Although the independent rancheros dominated here as well, more of the highland pueblos were involved in the transaction, including 50 Indian buyers. Remarkably enough, they included individuals who bought bulls jointly, such as Domingo Cruz, María de los Santos, and Bartolo Felipe from Tlatempan, a barrio of Zacatlán, who bought two animals for thirteen pesos, or Pedro de la Cruz, Rosa María, Pablo Antonio, and Francisca María annotated with the toponym Tlaxlixtlipam, a barrio/calpolli of Tepeixco who bought one bull between them for fourteen pesos. The number of animals purchased varied considerably, and more than in the case of the mules, which were more expensive. Most buyers bought one or two bulls; some of them bought four to six. Don Manuel Venancio González, who bought nine, and Don Francisco Ricaño, who bought eleven, were exceptions. They were hacendados from Tepeixco. Once again, some people had to stand surety for repayment. The bulls were virtually useless in the mountainous faldas, where slash-and-burn cultivation was practiced, but all the same the alcalde mayor managed to find forty-nine buyers, each of whom bought a single bull, with the exception of Pedro Antonio and Miguel Antonio of San Andrés, who each bought four. This was the same Pedro Antonio who had previously purchased the large number of five mules. Upon closer examination, however, I was struck by the fact that most of the names differed from those in the first repartimiento (of mules). Nevertheless, a few of the same leading figures were also involved in the *repartimiento de toros*, such as gobernador Don Joseph Silva and the priest Don Juan García from Tepeixco. The sale of 413 bulls in the highlands and 55 in the Sierra Zapoteca yielded 5,590 pesos. The average price per animal was 12 pesos in the highlands (mainly Spanish/casta) and 10 pesos in the villages in the faldas (mainly Indians). The latter were offered the second-best bulls.

Of course, after the propaganda of Gálvez the alcalde mayor was accused of making a profit of more than 50 percent from these transactions. In a dispute with the tax office in Mexico City, Sánchez de Tagle claimed that his income amounted to 30,000 pesos. On the debit side were 25,940 pesos in expenses plus 900 pesos in alcabala taxes in accordance with the norm of 3 percent. The tax office, however, claimed 8 percent, that is, 2,400 pesos. The alcalde mayor's own estimate of the profit was 3,160 pesos, hardly 10.5 percent. According to the norm of the tax office, he should be left with only 1,660 pesos, or 5.5 percent. He had bought the mules for 20 pesos each and the bulls for 8p2 each: a total purchase price of 20.125p2. Another document relating to the same repartimientos, signed by Sánchez de Tagle's predecessor, gives an income of 30,562 pesos. The total purchase price of the animals was 19,906 pesos (836 mules at 20 pesos, bought in Alamo from the Marquis of San Miguel de Aguayo, and 482 bulls at 8p2). These figures included twenty-five dead mules and fourteen dead bulls. A further sum of 995p4 had to be included for the cowboys, plus a reserve of 3,000 pesos for any future nonrecoverable debts. The personnel who kept the accounts (repartidores) and collected the debts (cobradores) were paid 4 percent of the takings, that is, a sum amounting to 1,222p4. Finally, the alcalde mayor had been left with 49 mules that could not be sold, representing a loss to the value of 614p6. The remaining 17 bulls and 178 mules might be sold at cost price to other government officials in a different province. This all resulted in a total for expenses of 25,738p6, leaving 4,823p2 as profit. Nevertheless, the tax office still had to claim its alcabala of 3 percent (917 pesos) or 8 percent (2,445 pesos). The profit was therefore low by this estimate as well: 13 or 8 percent.

We do not know, however, whether the alcalde mayor actually received his money or not, and thus whether his reserve was too large (and therefore also included a fraction of the profit) or too small. The prospects were grim for Sánchez de Tagle after the bad harvests of 1784 and 1785 and with the famine year of 1786 in sight. The payment for the mules and bulls was to take place in two installments (*plazos*), at the end of April and the end of October 1785 (immediately after the extreme night frost of August). The alcalde mayor did not have any income other than this profit and what he made from the egg trade, because the previous repartimiento in 1780 had been carried out by his predecessor and he did not have the opportunity for another because of the crisis in 1785–86. Nonetheless, as pointed out before, he admitted that he received 125 pesos per village each year from the egg trade and from payments for minor legal cases, amounting to a good 6,000 pesos. The livestock repartimiento accounted for no more than 12 to 15 percent of this total.

As far as the collection of debts was concerned, this could create enormous problems, particularly when the debtors were Indians. Of course, the alcaldes mayores wanted to see their money as soon as possible. Although the documentation on Sánchez de Tagle extends far into 1787, it does not contain any details in this respect, neither material from his own hand nor complaints from his opponents, which certainly would not have been slow in coming otherwise. This can be seen from the other case that I shall present in detail: the repartimientos in Tlalmanalco in 1720 and 1721. Although Indians and non-Indians claimed that it concerned a repartimiento by the alcalde mayor, Don Phelipe Díez de Palacios, a closer examination of the documents reveals that the herds in the repartimientos of 1720 and 1721 were, in fact, the property of Don Pedro Gutiérrez de Prio and Don Joseph Gutiérrez de Castro, two immigrants from Spanish Vizcaya who had made their fortunes as merchants and hacendados in the province of Chalco.[44] They were also local money lenders and therefore had many debtors in the province. One of the latter was Don Pedro Velarde, the Spanish alguacil mayor or chief constable of the "república de españoles" in the province. They asked him to hold the repartimiento in 1720 and to carry out the negotiations with the buyers. The following year, the two hacendados asked another Vizcaíno, Don Manuel de la Torre, lieutenant of Ozumba in the south of the province and married to a niece of Gutiérrez de Prio, to help with the second repartimiento. The role of these two—Spanish[45]—subordinate civil servants gave the repartimiento an official coloring: it made it look like a repartimiento held by the alcalde mayor, which conferred legitimacy on the higher prices. This was not the only reason why the hacendados resorted to this sleight of hand. It would be difficult to get the Indians to repay their debts quickly if no official were involved in the transaction. In this case, moreover, Velarde's brother conveniently happened to be the village jailer. Anyway, as the other traders in the region complained, the Indians tended to treat the business negotiations laconically and to extend the repayment period endlessly.[46] The only alternative open to a merchant in such cases was to resort to legal proceedings, a time-consuming and expensive business.

The maneuver worked. The buyers, both Indians and non-Indians, believed that the repartimientos were held on the authority of the alcalde mayor precisely because Velarde and De la Torre were involved. The two hacendados were regarded as nothing more than frontmen (*tapadores*). Don Juan de Salazar, another immigrant from Vizcaya and a hacendado; Don Lorenzo de Urtiago, manager of the Hacienda and Molino de la Concepción; Don Francisco de Mendizabal, a shopkeeper in Tlalmanalco, Juan Sánchez Dávila, a miller in Tlalmanalco; Don Juan López de Contreras, a Spaniard from Tlalmanalco and manager of a cacicazgo (Indian estate) as the husband of the cacica Doña María Pérez; Francisco Madriaga, a shopkeeper from Atlautla; and a few other Spaniards claimed that the prices demanded by Velarde and De la Torre were sometimes exorbitantly high and that the repayment had to be made within an unreasonably short period. If the hacendados in the area had known, they said, they would never have cooperated. The mules cost 22 pesos each, and the bulls 10 pesos (a higher price than that asked in Zacatlán sixty-six years later!). Miguel de Estrada, a Spanish muleteer from Chalco, had even paid 25 or 26 pesos for his mules. Don Juan Bautista de Echagoian, a Basque farmer from Tlalmanalco, had bought his six mules at the high price of 25 pesos each, but he also purchased 12 bulls for the relatively low price of 8 pesos. Incidentally, he had not paid for any of the animals and managed to withstand the pressure put on by Velarde. Nevertheless, the price of a mule on the free market was 5 to 5½ pesos and that of a bull 12 pesos, but hardly anyone could, or would, pay for the animals with cash. The terms of payment offered by the alcaldes mayores were far more favorable.

This was precisely the element missing now that Velarde and De la Torre traveled nonstop through the Indian villages and haciendas to collect the debt little by little though rapidly, preferably within fifteen days. The debtors were threatened with imprisonment, and these threats were promptly carried out if they were unable to hand over the money. For instance, the mestizo Antonio de los Reyes from Xuchitepec paid off his debt in maize as usual, but when Velarde turned up one day and received no payment because the man only had enough for his family, he was taken to Chalco and imprisoned until his family would pay the debt. Various gobernadores from the villages in the province met with the same treatment. Velarde and De la Torre visited the church masses to get their hands on the debtors. Juan Sánchez Dávila, the miller, even had a debtor—who had purchased grain—who could not pay him because he was in prison for his repartimiento debt. Velarde and De la Torre also carried out confiscations. In addition to all kinds of minor confiscations in the villages, all the witnesses referred to the brutality against Don Juan Gil de Zalazar, a hacendado, as typical of the attitude of their creditors. Velarde accused this man of having got into arrears in paying off twenty-two mules and ten bulls. When Velarde failed to find Gil at home during one of his provincial rounds, and when no one on Gil's hacienda was prepared to give him the money, he confiscated thirty-two animals and took them back to Tlalmanalco, despite the fact that Gil had already repaid 226p6 of the 584 pesos! Of course, this was seen as a typical case of "mal gobierno" on the part of the alcalde mayor, and all of the witnesses uttered strong condemnations of Díez de Palacios. It is tempting to agree with them, for Díez de Palacios was responsible for the actions of his subordinates, even though he had nothing to do with the repartimiento. He defended himself with the remark that the repartimientos had been carried out before he assumed office, which was confirmed by all.

In fact, there was one Spaniard who knew that the repartimiento really had been by the two Gutiérrez hacendados. This was Don Luis Hareno de Alarcón, a merchant in the village of Ayamonte. He had made enquiries because the two of them had also assumed responsibility for the previous repartimiento in 1716, four years earlier. The Indians of Atihuacan, Tecomazusco, and Ozumba also knew that the two Gutiérrez hacendados were behind the transaction, because Velarde had given the game away in Atihuacan, De la Torre's wife had done the same in Tecomazusco, and De la Torre himself had blurted out too much in Ozumba. The gobernador of Tecomazusco only got wind of this when he spoke to De la Torre's wife to tell her that the repayment would have to wait a month. He explained that if he had known about it earlier, the villagers would certainly not have bought so many animals (twenty-two). Now there was no chance of getting round the alcalde mayor!

While the Spaniards bought relatively large numbers of animals—for example, Gil de Salazar bought twenty-two mules and ten bulls, De Urtiago bought thirty bulls, López Contreras bought ten bulls, Echagoian bought twelve bulls and six mules, and Madriaga bought as many as ninety-six bulls—the Indians only bought one or two animals each. When the herds had arrived in the grazing land, Velarde went round the villages in 1721, and De la Torre did the same in 1722 to tell the villagers to come and buy the animals. They were obliged to buy animals, Velarde and De la Torre both declared, "because it was a herd of the alcalde mayor." The gobernadores then asked the villagers who wanted a mule or a bull, and accompanied the potential buyers to the herds. Velarde sold 124 mules and 302 young bulls. Assuming that no Indians bought both mules and bulls (although this must have happened in some cases), this involved 426 Indians out of a population of 8,626 tributarios, hardly 5 percent of the Indian population. The market was immediately saturated, however, because a year later De la Torre got no further than 3 mules, 247 young bulls, and 27 foals. Although buying was done individually, the gobernadores were held accountable for repayment, which was normal practice here. Velarde and De la Torre thus threw a number of Indian gobernadores in jail later on, or sometimes their wives, when the repayment took too long. De la Torre displayed more mercy in this respect than Velarde. Several villagers, particularly those of San Martín Pahuacan and San Miguel Atlautla, emphasized the fact that De la Torre had generally not used coercion and that no violence had been used in the repayment procedure of the 1721 repartimiento.

The scope of these repartimientos at the village level can be gauged from Table 9, showing the sale of livestock to the Indians of Chalco in 1720 and

Table 9 The sale of repartimiento livestock to the Indians of Chalco in 1720 and 1721

village	number of families	*Repartimiento* of 1720		*Repartimiento* of 1721		
		mules	bulls	mules	bulls	*potros*
Temamatla	171	2	12	—	—	—
Atlihuacan	14	—	3	—	3	—
Tlapalán	33	—	6	—	—	—
Cocotitlán	94	8	8	—	5	—
Metla	25	—	7	—	—	—
Achacualoya	28	—	—	—	—	—
Huizilingo	34	—	—	—	—	—
Santos Reyes	?	5	—	—	—	—
Sn Gregorio	42	6	—	—	—	—
Cuauatlalpan	67	10	5	—	—	—
Sn Lucas	19	9	—	—	—	—
Sn Mateo	?	—	7	—	—	—
Sn Martín	?	9	5	—	—	—
Ozumba	239	6	12	—	8	—
Sn Mateo Ch.	16	—	12	—	14	8
Xuchitepec	161	8	24	2	28	—
Soyazingo	59	—	24	—	15	—
Ayapango	86	—	16	—	6	—
Zentlalpan	192	4	8	—	30	—
Pahuacan	23	2	10	—	14	—
Amecameca	491	12	14	—	—	—
Atlautla	163	—	14	—	22	—
Tepetlizpan	178	8	32	—	8	—
Chimalhuacan Ch.	150	8	24	—	22	—
Mamalhuazuacan	64	6	14	1	12	6
Quixingo	33	—	—	—	20	—
Tenango Tep.	62	—	—	—	6	—
Tepecoculco	16	—	24	—	—	—
Ecazingo	114	—	13	—	18	13
Tecomazusco	18	—	6	—	16	—
Ayozingo	105	13	2	—	—	—
Ixtapaluca	66	8	—	—	—	—
Totals	**2,763**	**124**	**302**	**3**	**247**	**27**

See note AGI, Indiferente General, Leg. 107, fs. 283–286; and, AGNM, Civil, Vol. 1690, Exps. 1,2, and 3.

1721. The figures for the repartimiento are based on payments made by the
Indians with receipts. The number of buyers is compared with an estimate of
the number of residents in these villages in these years. The point of reference
is the 1743 *relación geográfica*, with correction for population growth based on
the numbers of tributarios.[47] In 1721 the following villages chose the animals
they wanted and signed the contract of sale: Temamatla, Cocotitlán, Santos
Reyes, San Gregorio, San Martín Quautlalpan, San Lucas, San Martín, Ozumba,
San Mateo de Chalco, Xuchitepec, Soyazingo, Ayapango, Zentlalpan, Pahuacan,
Amecameca, San Esteban Tepetlizpan, Chimalhuacan Chalco, Mamalhuazucan,
San Juan Tepecoculco, San Pedro Ecazingo, San Marcos Tecomazusco, and
Ayozingo; the latter did so even *buenamente*. Of course, no physical coercion
was employed, and its use was stringently denied. One of the gobernadores of
Tepetlizpan, a thirty-seven-year-old man who spoke perfect Spanish, accepted
thirty-two young bulls and paid in a single installment. The head of the village of Chimalhuacán Chalco also paid in one installment. Most of the other
villages had still not paid for their livestock in 1722. In the case of the
gobernadores of Atlihuacan, Xuchitepec, Tenango Tepopulo, and San Mateo,
Velarde in 1720 and De la Torre in 1721 tried to get them to buy more livestock. Most of them refused; the village leaders of Atlihuacan took three young
bulls in 1721 instead of the proposed six, those of Xuchitepec nine instead of
twenty-four (although the local caciques also took nineteen animals for their
own use), those of Tenango Tepopulo six instead of twelve, and those of San
Mateo seven instead of ten.

Many villages did not participate in the repartimiento of 1721, let alone
that of 1722, because they had not yet paid for that of 1720 (see Table 9). The
Indians of Tlapalán added that they had not taken part in the repartimiento
of 1721 because they did not have any horses to take them to the hacienda
where the herd was. Tenango Tepopulo did not produce a single buyer in 1720
either. A few village leaders, such as that of San Mateo Huizilingo, did take
some livestock, but they had to return the animals later because the villagers
in their charge did not need any. Velarde and De la Torre had no alternative
but to accept. They threatened the Indians with imprisonment, but lacked a
police force to compel them, and the alcalde mayor naturally refused to lend
them his support. After all, no sale had been made and no contract was concluded in such cases. A number of villagers, such as those of Achaqualoya, did
not take any animals at all because they bought their livestock in repartimientos
elsewhere. This was also the case with Santiago de Chalco and La Visitación
Chalma in Xochimilco. Velarde was not prepared to do business with the Indians of San Martín Quixingo when they turned up at the herd, because he
considered them to be a bunch of "mountain dogs" who never paid their
debts. During a previous repartimiento some years earlier, Velarde had arrested
two of the villagers and handed them over to a hacendado to pay off their
debt with labor. De la Torre, however, was prepared to sell them twenty young
bulls in 1721, which was a large number for the thirty or so families who lived
there. There was no tradition of repartimientos in the villages of Chalco,

Ixtapaluca, Tlalmanalco, Tlaltengo, Ayotla, Tlapichahua, Xico, and Tlapacoya because they lived from fishing in Lake Chalco or grew their maize in *chinampas* and thus had no use for oxen. As mentioned in an earlier section, Tlalmanalco and its barrios provided labor services to the alcalde mayor, and one did not need to participate in more than one type of repartimiento at the time.

Repayments did not always have to be made in cash; labor services were common practice too. For example, a number of villages in the valley of Toluca had concluded contracts with the local hacendados for a repartimiento de toros. The hacendados were represented at the signing of the contracts by the count of Santiago Calimaya, and the villagers were represented by one of their caciques, generally called El Caudillo. The contracts state the number of bulls that the villagers would receive. It was very important that they should be supplied on time because they were intended for the village festivals, an important part of community life in the pueblos. The hacendados were aware of this. In most of the contracts, the "Caudillo" signed for more than one thousand pesos per repartimiento, but the hacendados were not alarmed by these sums. They were not out to force the "Caudillo" to pay off his debts quickly. On the contrary, they saw the repartimiento as an investment that would indirectly guarantee them migrant labor from the villages during the summer. Consequently, they aimed at strengthening the position of the Indian leaders in their villages.[48]

As with ordinary commercial contracts, dissatisfaction could be expressed about the quality of the products or the price agreed upon. Witnesses testifying during an examination of the alcalde mayor of Metztitlán in 1743 stated that a repartimiento had been held twice that year in the fields on the edge of one of the villages. The first repartimiento involved one hundred young bulls and forty-three mules. The livestock came from haciendas owned by the Jesuits in the neighborhood and was supplied at the rate of ten pesos per bull (current market value: five pesos) and twenty-four pesos per mule (current market value: twelve pesos). These prices were virtually the same as the ones mentioned above, although the price of a mule was 80 percent higher in Zacatlán in 1784, forty years later. The alcalde mayor paid part of the sum in kind with maize from the village stocks. The rest was to be paid with a share of the harvest that still stood in the fields and that the alcalde mayor was due to receive from the villagers as tribute. The witnesses stated that the three merchants who arranged the transaction for the Jesuits were from Metztitlán. The pueblo was represented by the alcalde mayor's brother-in-law and son, who had also made the business contacts. The second repartimiento that year was carried out by the alcalde mayor's assistant, a mulato, who usually collected the tribute. As seems to have been the usual practice, he delivered the short trousers, hats, and blankets that the villagers had ordered in Querétaro (where the factories were). The villagers were to give him thirty fattened pigs in return for this delivery. These pigs were delivered to a few pork butchers (*tocinerías*) from Puebla de los Angeles. The bargaining over this exchange was carried out by the alcalde mayor's wife. It is remarkable that at the last moment they were apparently unable to agree on the price because the alcalde mayor's wife returned to the village, pigs and all. A witness reported that, after his arrival in the village, the alcalde mayor had said that he was sure he could get a better price for the peasants from another trading partner.[49]

The alcalde mayor's involvement was not always as high as in the cases presented above. When Don Fernando de Retes was appointed alcalde mayor of Xochimilco in the 1720s, for instance, he thought that he could shelter himself behind his brother Joseph, alcalde mayor of Tecali at the time, who had to hold a repartimiento of 610 mules worth fifteen thousand pesos in 1725 as if it were a private deal. However, things immediately went wrong, because the person who was to do the actual selling, a minor civil servant from Tecali, innocently told everyone that Don Fernando was behind it. Don Joseph dismissed him as soon as he could, ordered him to hand over his accounts, and transferred the rest of the livestock, the collection of debts, and the bookkeeping to a few professional repartidores whose field of operations was located in the provinces of Xochimilco, Chalco and Cuernavaca. These repartidores, however, had bought a herd valued at twelve thousand pesos, and wrote off the proceeds in 1730. Most of this herd—299 bulls, 151 mules and 36 horses—were sold in Chalco for the sum of 7,712p4. There were between ten and twenty buyers in each village, which amounted to the same relatively low frequency that we encountered in the repartimientos described earlier. Almost every buyer purchased no more than one or two mules, though some of them bought four and a handful purchased more than four. However, when Don Fernando passed away unexpectedly and his creditors claimed the remaining repartimiento debts, great confusion arose as to which animals belonged to whom. In the end, it proved possible to distinguish the livestock by the brand markings.[50]

Most of the hacendados who stood to gain from the repartimiento were the stock breeders from the Guadalajara region. The livestock they sold to the Spaniards and Indians in this manner formed part of the largest internal trade of New Spain in the eighteenth century. A nice study by Ramón Serrera reveals that an unbroken stream of cattle, mules, and horses flowed from the hinterland of Guadalajara to Anáhuac, Oaxaca and the mining enclaves in the Michoacán region. The herds were driven to Anáhuac in the autumn, because the animals could be well nourished after the rainy season and green pastures were available on the way. Moreover, the farmers and peasants had an idea of how large the harvest would be by that time of the year, so that they could proceed to purchase livestock. The repartimiento was primarily responsible for the supply to Anáhuac and Oaxaca, the only regions in New Spain with a large number of pueblos. The annual production of livestock in Guadalajara in the late eighteenth century was between 300,000 and 350,000 head of cattle. Between 5 and 7 percent of them found their way to a village in Anáhuac. (These averages are based on eleven thousand head of stock between 1761 and 1770, fourteen thousand between 1771 and 1780, twenty-five thousand between 1781 and 1790, and fifteen thousand between 1791 and 1800.) The mule trade followed the same pattern.[51]

In Anáhuac, most of the livestock found its way to the cattle markets in Toluca, Tlaxcala and Puebla. That was where the cattle farmers met the merchants and civil servants who came to make their purchases for the repartimiento, but they also met the traders who were involved in supplying the towns with cattle, an urban monopoly (*abasto*) farmed out by the town councils to the highest bidder. A single example will suffice to indicate the following stages in the proceedings. It is taken from the repartimientos of Miguel de Pedraza, a small merchant in Zacatelco (Tlaxcala). In his will of 1767, the repartimientos are listed under outstanding assets, including the following items: 5,211p4 from the Indians in the municipalities of Zacatelco, San Gerónimo and San Pablo del Monte for the supply of oxen and clothing, of which 3,000 pesos had already been paid; and 500 pesos outstanding from the villagers of Santo Toribio, who had only paid 100 pesos from this repartimiento. His will stipulated that these assets could still be claimed provided the Indians did not suffer any setbacks. There were also assets (totaling 2,763p4) which would never be repaid because the peasants concerned had died or emigrated during the last epidemic.[52]

The system of repayment did not just apply to the Indians, for the merchants and traders themselves paid for the livestock long afterward as well. Miguel de Pedraza and his son Francisco, who took over the business in the small town of Zacatelco after his father's death, bought the livestock they sold in the villages from a hacendado friend of theirs, José Antonio González Ruíz, who also lived in Zacatelco and owned the San Antonio Palula and San Buena Bentura Tenexac haciendas in the municipality of San Pablo del Monte. In 1766, this González had bought 199 bulls for 5p6 each and 629 for 5p7 each on the Puebla cattle market. He sold 29 of them to Francisco Pedraza on 30 December 1766 for 8 pesos each. The contract states that they were intended for a repartimiento. It took Pedraza a whole year to pay for the bulls: he paid González 32 pesos in cash on 14 May 1767, 50 pesos in cash on 29 August, 15 pesos in cash during the annual market in Puebla on 5 September, 115 pesos through an exchange on 17 September and another 20 pesos during four visits to González's home. González sold most of the other bulls to Joseph Armas, a government official in Zacatelco. Armas sold 30 of these bulls for prices ranging between 10 and 12 pesos a head to the Indians in Santa Catarina and San Marcos, two villages that belonged to the municipality of Zacatelco, in 1768. Armas made a commission of 1 peso on each bull; the rest was for González. The hacendado also supplied the Indian pueblos with mules via Armas, with prices ranging from 11 to 19 pesos a head at that time. These were small-scale, individual transactions, involving only a few animals each time. González supplied another Zacatelcan merchant, Miguel Briones, with 43 bulls for 9 pesos each on 15 December 1767. These bulls were intended for a repartimiento in San Pablo del Monte. The payments for the bulls were to continue until March 1769, but the villagers felt that they had been cheated regarding some of the bulls. They refused to accept a number of the animals for this price because of their poor condition. In their stead they ordered bulls from a different trader who did not buy his stock from González.[53]

González Ruíz was not a stock breeder himself; his Haciendas Palula and Tenexac were wheat haciendas. His role in the transactions was that of a middle-man, and it comes as no surprise that he applied the same system of repayments which he observed in his own transactions to the purchase of the animals in Puebla. For instance, he had bought the 629 bulls mentioned above from Antonio de la Moza on 14 October 1766; it had cost him 3,734p5. González and Moza agreed that 1,000 pesos would be paid before the end of May 1767, and the rest of the sum before the end of October in the same year. González gave him an advance payment of 10 percent, rounded off to 400 pesos. A friend of his, who was also a merchant, Manuel Palacios, handed the 100 pesos over for him on 1 June 1767; González delivered the rest in person on 18 December 1767, presumably accompanied by excuses, because he was almost two months in arrears. The documents indicate that the payment of such large sums of money in one lump sum was exceptional; payment usually followed a more improvised course of exchange, small transfers and current accounts. A good example is González's purchase of 20 mules at 8 pesos each on 7 February 1767. He concluded a contract with Antonio Saez, who sold the animals for the sum of 160 pesos, less 40p5 that Saez still owed González in connection with a different transaction. González promised to pay half of the remaining 119p3 before the end of June and the rest before the end of September. In practice, events followed a different course, for Saez bought a con-signment of peppers from González on 11 March for 15p5, and deducted this amount from González's debt for the mules, which had been delivered in the meantime. González then supplied Saez, on the same basis, with 8 cargas of maize for the price of 20 pesos on 2 May, 2 cargas of sowing seed (maize) for 5p4 on 5 May, and 12 cargas of maize for 30 pesos on 10 May. After these deliveries had been made, Saez received goods worth a total of 120p1, and was thus forced to grant González credit in return.[54] Remarkably, neither of the parties charged interest on payments of this kind.

The remarkable feature of all the information in this section is that merchants like Pedraza arranged the repartimiento with individual residents in the pueblos and not on a collective basis, as was usually the case with the collection of the tribute, even though the village gobernador or alcalde usually had to stand as surety. The payment was also arranged on an individual basis with a duration of between six and twelve months, apart from the repartimiento in Tlalmanalco in 1721 and 1721, where the cobradores hoped to have their money within a month. The period within which payment had to be made tended to expand rather than contract. In Lerma (in the valley of Toluca), the individual peasants had an average of three years each in which to pay for their mules, and the transaction was regarded as concluded if they died in the meantime. Thus the debt was not transferable to the next of kin. In Ixtlahuaca (not far from Toluca), the peasants paid in two installments if their trade in timber—for which they used the animals—was successful; otherwise, they were given longer to pay. Even if the merchant were a government official as well, he lacked the means of calling the villagers collectively to account. After all, extended payments over a long period entailed the risk that it might prove impossible to recuperate the whole amount as a result of epidemics or of the rapid rotation of the village government responsible for collective expenses. As a result of the epidemics, the gobernadores often had to pay off large debts they had not incurred themselves, so that each new village council usually refused to assume responsibility for the expenses of its predecessor.

Repartimiento goods were traded on such a scale that the turnover far exceeded the value of the tribute. Therefore, it is preferable to refer to trade on a credit basis, since goods were supplied to the rural population, on the one hand, which had to be paid for within a set period, while, on the other hand, the Indian pueblos made down payments on the quantities of certain products they ordered. The merchants were responsible for settling the transactions and for transport, calling in the paid assistance of the local muleteers (arrieros) to help them. The turnover depended on the products in which the pueblos were specialized—specialized regional manufactures and agricultural items—and on the demand for these products in other pueblos, in the towns and in mining enclaves. The villages bought products they could obtain only with difficulty, if at all, on the market, including mules, oxen, and horses. For example, around 1780 the villages in the province of Tehuacán (valley of Puebla) placed orders each year for 300 mules at 32 pesos each, 50 horses at 12 pesos each, and 150 bulls at 12 pesos each. These prices were fixed for a reasonably long period and thus barely affected by fluctuations on the livestock market. The sum of 6,000 pesos was paid in this province in a variety of ways: part of it was paid in cash (1,000 pesos every All Saints Day), and the rest was paid in wheat (!) at the market price, in small livestock at 7 pesos each, and in specific quantities of clothing, mats, and salt at the market price. The original tribute figure was no more than a small fraction of this sum. The extension of repartimiento trade in this way generally provided commercial benefit for the village economy in a number of ways: the livestock and looms were used to supply goods to the merchants, to transport these goods, to transport other goods, and to produce crops, clothing, or consumer goods for the local markets. The villages that were more remote from the large trading centers, the towns, or the roads also ordered other products from the alcaldes, which might even include maize. In very remote areas, such as the northern faldas, the government officials even ran shops where the villagers could select from the wares on sale. No repartimientos were carried out in provinces where the villagers earned sufficient money with seasonal labor, for instance, and where virtually everything they needed could be bought on the market; they paid their tribute in cash.[55]

Regional Integration

One can imagine that large sums of money were involved in the repartimiento. Despite the existence of Pietschmann's innovatory and lucid 1973 article on the scale of the repartimiento trade in the intendancy of Puebla, it seems in-

evitable to repeat in detail some of the data contained in that extensive account of the mechanism of this trade, complemented with similar data from
the intendancy of Mexico. The German historian made statistics available for
the year 1776 from the valley of Puebla and the surrounding faldas. At that
time, around 4,600 mules, 7,000 oxen, and 1,300 horses were sold to the pueblos. The majority of the mules was sold that year in the provinces of Zacatlán,
Cholula, Tepeaca, Tehuacán, and Tlaxcala, provinces where many of the villagers worked as muleteers. The largest trade in oxen that year was in agricultural provinces like Huejotzingo, Tlaxcala, Cholula, and Atlixco. Pietschmann
calculated that goods were sold in the villages each year for a total sum of at
least 250,000 pesos, and that purchases were made in the villages for an annual average of 70,000 pesos. This yields an annual per capita turnover of
3p3, based on the number of residents in the provinces. This is a high figure.
The annual tribute from the whole of New Spain at this time provided the
state with an average of 800,000 pesos, or approximately 1p3 per tributario
per annum.[56]

Although the result would make demands on the reader, I propose to
present the complementary data nearly one province at a time. Starting with
the provinces with a many-sided economy, I move on to those with a supportive economy, following an east-west trajectory. For the purposes of comparison, this is followed by a few provinces in the tropical areas with a one-sided
economy. The data are derived from the statistics collected in the provinces
themselves in 1752 and 1788.[57] The 1752 statistics were collected by clergy,
those for 1788 by both clergy and civil servants. Not every province is included in this documentation. Some reports are no longer extant, or at any
rate, I have been unable to trace them. Flon provided Pietschmann with an
excellently organized survey from Puebla, which could be well illustrated with
a table, as the German historian did. The 1752 statistics, mainly from Puebla,
and the 1788 ones for Mexico are less tractable. Thus I have opted for a geographical approach, in which the documentation for 1752 provides the most
qualitative details and that for 1788 the most quantitative information.

The central provinces had a wide range of both agricultural and horticul-
tural products and commodities. The market economy was the least "imperfect" here, so that many products bypassed the repartimiento to reach the
consumer. Trade activities were so important—according to a priest in 1752,
"because agriculture in the villages did not yield enough to provide every
resident with an income"—that the Indians badly needed mules to be able to
travel to the markets or to service the towns and larger villages for the merchants. But the variety of repartimiento products extended beyond just mules.
Accounts were settled in cash, earned from muleteering, from the sale of local
handicrafts (artesanía), or from migrant labor on the haciendas. The Indians
in the provinces of Amozoc, Cuautinchan, Tecali, and Totomehuacan (Puebla)
bought cotton cloths, mules, bulls for agriculture (oxen), sheep (in
Cuautinchan), and horses. An important specialty here was charcoal, for which
the oxen and mules were purchased, partly in exchange. The repartimiento in

Totomehuacan was also paid for with palm mats, hats, and the supply of a specific herb that was found in the woods of a hacienda. (The hacendado allowed it to be plucked.) In Tecali, it was the practice to buy unworked wool from the merchants—usually for six hundred arrobas—and then to sell woven fabrics in various forms back to the same gentlemen. Each contract concluded by the local gobernadores with the traders in Puebla and Mexico City was for six months, and the Indians made a profit of six reales on each piece of cloth. In Toxtepec, which belonged to Tecali for a long time—the reader will meet the Toxtepecans later on in conflict with Tecali—there were so many indigenous weavers that the Indians even bought palm mats and maize (two hundred fanegas a year in deliveries of seventy-seven fanegas every fortnight) through the repartimiento.

Trade was more or less the same in the provinces with a many-sided economy, to the west of Puebla. In Atlixco, it was common practice around 1752 to sell two thousand bulls (to be castrated and used as draught animals), three hundred mules and three hundred horses, most of them going to the hacendados. The hacienda economy here collapsed in the 1760s because of the loss of the Havana market to farmers from nearby Louisiana, and around 1786 sales had fallen to only eight hundred bulls and no horses at all, although the number of mules, which were supplied to the Indian pueblos, remained the same (for which payment had to be made more or less straightaway). There was only a moderate amount of manufacture in Huejotzingo, where most of the Indians earned an income on the haciendas. They had little time left for the arriería in 1752, and consequently did not buy many mules. However, these Indians, as well as those in Atlixco, bought textiles. The priests claimed that there were far too many repartidores, who passed through the villages each week. A few villages in Huejotzingo bought oxen to transport the beams erected by the Indians on the slopes of the volcanoes. The animals were paid for in timber (exchange), leaving a profit of six reales per beam for the Indians. There were also a few villages on the slopes of Popocatépetl in Atlixco that supplied cochineal after receiving repartimiento credit, but the priest stated that their number was falling year by year. Weaving cotton was more interesting for them, although not many villages in Atlixco had gone over to cotton weaving in 1752. Another product that was supplied to order was salt.[58]

Naturally enough, trade and production on the other side of the volcanoes had the same structure. The situation in Coatepec, at the foot of Ixtaccihuatl, closely resembled that of Huejotzingo, although there was less hacienda labor and more Indians were involved in the arriería. They therefore bought more mules, with eight villages buying a total of around two hundred a year. The Indians paid for them in cash at the rate of two reales a week or one peso a month. Their fields were on the slopes of the volcano, so they had no need of bulls; the two hundred traded each year went to the hacendados. After 1769, the Indians bought the animals elsewhere on their own account, probably in the so-called Mixteca, the faldas of the region of Oaxaca, and no more repartimientos were held. As we have seen, mules, bulls, and horses were traded in Chalco, as they were in the provinces of Apan (the last repartimiento there was in 1784), Teotihuacán, Zempoala (for the last time in 1776, after which the alcaldes mayores in the province refused to cooperate any longer), and Texcoco (for the last time in 1783). In Chalco, payment was usually made in cash at the rate of ½ real a day for peasants who offered their services as ox drivers to the haciendas, or 2 reales a month for muleteers, who were usually on the road for long periods. Here too, particularly near Tlalmanalco, payment was also made in wooden beams and shelves.

The prohibition of 1786 hit the Texcocans hard, because they were waiting for a new repartimiento: the animals they had bought during the previous years had grown old or had died by then. The problem for the ordinary, private retailer, as the government official wrote in his 1788 report, was that the Indians could never scrape ten pesos together in order to buy on the free market. A reintroduction of the repartimiento would therefore mean a reintroduction of draught animals and beasts of burden in the province. The man who drew up the report from Teotihuacán wrote the same: the mules were necessary to revive the local pulque trade. The pulque trade in Zempoala could be given new life in the same manner. No governmental repartimiento was ever held in Otumba. The peasants and merchants bought their livestock in the same way and for the same prices as elsewhere, but this was always a question of private livestock trading. The alcalde mayor was only paid a commission for any assistance he might give in collecting debts. The compiler of the report claimed that the last large herd had been sold nine years earlier in 1782. The term of payment was one year. The merchant Don Diego Irigoyen had held a private repartimiento of clothing in the province in 1789, 1790, and 1791, which had to be paid for in two installments within a year.

Repartimientos were also barely mentioned on the other side of Lake Texcoco, where people spoke of buying on credit, a credit that was extended for a year. All the same, when the subdelegado of Tacuba made inquiries in 1790, he discovered that what had taken place were in fact repartimientos. In Ecatepec, the repartimientos were held by the alcaldes mayores until 1770. Immediately afterward, they were conducted by merchants, some of whom had interests in selling mules to the Indians since they dealt in pulque. The last repartimiento in Cuautitlán was held in 1785. Livestock was sold in Tacuba in the autumn, but in Ecatepec it was also done in the spring. The Indians in Tacuba and Cuautitlán bought the mules for their charcoal and timber trade with Mexico City, while others used them to transport salt, vegetables, pottery (Azcapotzalco in Tacuba),[59] chalk, barley, and other foodstuffs they sold in town. After repayment at a high rate and the deduction of all other expenses, a muleteer from Tacuba made seventeen reales profit a month. The bulls were castrated and then used both in the felling of timber on the mountain slopes (where mules were less suitable) and as draught animals. They could be put to work a week after castration, paid for within a year, and proved useful for a number of years. Payment was sometimes made in cash every three months, but it was usually made in artesanías, textile, wood, charcoal, or vegetables. Besides livestock, the Indians in Tacuba bought clothing from Villa Alta (Oaxaca) or Querétaro (in the Michoacán region) through the repartimiento; each Indian made annual purchases to the value of two pesos in 1753 and five to six pesos in 1790. Two reales of this debt were paid in cash every week (the equivalent of a daily wage for a hacienda field hand). The muleteers from Ecatepec paid for their mules in quantities of pulque, which they supplied to the outlets in Mexico City.

In the valley of Toluca, such repartimientos were conducted in Ixtlahuaca, one of the two large provinces of the valley. The trade in mules and bulls was similar to that outlined above, and the same goes for the use to which the animals were put in the villages. The alcaldes mayores held the usual repartimientos in Lerma in 1779, and they were also held in 1783 and 1784 on the same conditions by merchants (*repartidores particulares*). The official repartimientos in Tianguistengo continued until 1780, and in Metepec until 1783, when they passed into private hands. Payment was due within a year in these provinces just as it was everywhere else, provided the animals were still alive, because no buyer had to pay if their mule or horse died during the period of installments. If the debtor failed to meet his obligations, the repartidor took the animals away. The alcaldes mayores in Malinalco and Tenancingo organized the livestock trade, keeping the herds on the grazing land for the Indians and non-Indians to make their selection. The subdelegado's informants told him that the buyers were free to choose and to negotiate the terms of payment. Sometimes payment was made in cash, particularly by the Spaniards. The alcaldes mayores were not present during these transactions. Their role was confined to giving their approval and collecting a commission. After the abolition of 1786 there was hardly a mule to be found in the provinces, leading to a revival of the old practice of having the carrying done by special porters (*tlamemes*). However, they were only able to carry far less, so that the result was a shortage, especially of charcoal. In Xilotepec, the other large province in the valley, no repartimiento had been held since 1770 because the alcaldes mayores were no longer prepared to cooperate. This had led to an economic malaise because the Indians were now without draught animals and could no longer support themselves from the arriería. Before then, each family used to own three or four mules and five or six oxen for one yoke (*yunta*).

These details indicate not only the scale of the repartimientos, but they also show that purchases made by the Indians did not always have the character of an exchange. For example, there was the case of a peasant in the province of Chalco who bought oxen for ½ real a day and a few mules for 1½ reales a day from the alcalde mayor. Although he used the oxen to plow his own fields, this total daily spending of 2 reales was precisely the equivalent of a daily wage for a field hand, which forced him to hire himself out with a team to hacendados in the neighborhood. Although this could earn a peasant 7 reales a day between May and October, most Indians were content to work half-days on the haciendas. For example, a man in Tacuba, who bought two oxen for 24 pesos, used them to earn 62p4 on haciendas during the year, giving him a net income of 38p4 in the first year and 62p4 during the two following years (250 working days per year, 2 reales a day). Others were looking for timber production. Each head of a familia de indios in the province of Xilotepec had three or four mules in order to make extra earnings in the arriería, as well as five or six oxen for plowing. The purchase was made in cash in both provinces, because the peasants did not have any local manufactured goods to offer the alcaldes mayores. The repartimiento in Xilotepec was exclusively a sale on credit (venta al fiado).[60]

The arsenal of products traded in the repartimiento appears to have expanded as the distance from the main towns of the viceroyalty increased. This was particularly true of the provinces with a supportive economy. In the highland areas they were situated in the spurs of the highlands, such as Actopan, Ixmiquilpan, Tula, and Meztitlán in the northwest of Anáhuac, and Tehuacán in the southeast; others were situated to the north of the valley of Puebla, such as Pachuca, Tulancingo, and San Juan de los Llanos. Tepeaca also belonged to the supportive economy. Apparently, the market economy was so far less developed here than in the more centrally situated provinces that the repartimiento was seen as a way of resolving the difficulties. It was primarily a question of credit being provided by the alcalde mayor in return for a specific manufactured or agricultural product. Livestock repartimientos were not held in all of these provinces in the late eighteenth century. We have already seen that the situation in Actopan had changed. There were no repartimientos of mules and bulls in Ixmiquilpan and Tula around 1752; in Tula this was because so much timber had been felled that there was no more brushwood to be found, which made the mules redundant. The situation appears to have changed in Ixmiquilpan by 1791, for in that year the subdelegado mentioned *repartimientos de mulas*, though without adding any further details. Probably he was referring to a traditional practice rather than to contemporary events.

The Indians in Ixmiquilpan supplied small livestock in 1752. The alcalde mayor gave them four reales per animal in the months from August to December, with the understanding that the Indians would deliver a specified number of goats to his official residence the next May or a specific number of lambs in the following July and August. The alcalde mayor of the province thus received around three thousand head of livestock each year. Usually the arrangement was to the advantage of the Indians and to the disadvantage of the alcalde mayor, but if the number of new-born animals was lower than specified in the contract, the Indians had to pay a full peso instead, or twice the amount. Although the repartimiento trade in small livestock had collapsed in nearby Actopan, there was still a maize repartimiento, in which villagers received credit for a specific maize harvest. This maize was put on sale in the Actopan corn exchange. The alcaldes mayores followed the same procedure for giving credits to villagers in Actopan and Ixmiquilpan for the production of sacks (*costales*) made from *ixtle*, the fiber of the maguey cactus, paying two reales for each carga of sacks, and particularly for various materials and items of clothing made from cotton (the price of one *manta* was three reales) or from *ixtle*. The producer had to supply the item within a fortnight, and consequently he received enough credit to cover his production. Thus this system most favored the fastest *artesanos*. Indians usually earned an income of three reales in this way; nevertheless, they could earn four times as much, or twelve reales, by selling directly to peddlers without the intervention of the alcaldes mayores or their agents. However, there were not enough peddlers in the provinces to enable them to bypass the repartimiento. In the village of Cardenal (Ixmiquilpan), the Indians produced for the alcalde mayor twenty to thirty cargas of lead for each peso they received.

In Tehuacán, the alcalde mayor put 300 to 400 mules, 150 horses, and 50 to 100 bulls on the market each year in the period around 1752. These quantities were thus more or less the same as those from forty years later, but the prices were lower in 1752: twenty-five pesos for a mule as against thirty-two pesos forty years later; the price of a bull remained constant throughout the entire century at twelve pesos. This suggests that mules were more scarce by then, which could indicate increased transport activity in the late eighteenth century. The alcaldes mayores also provided credits for the production of goats and sheep on more or less the same terms as in Ixmiquilpan. In this case, however, the Indians could pay off their debt in kind with tallow and skins (one arroba of tallow for every three animals). The same procedure was followed in the neighboring province of Tepeaca. A number of Indian villages in Tehuacán asked for credit for the production of wheat (!), six pesos per carga, and other villages still produced some cochineal (twelve reales per pound), salt, a considerable number of mats (around four thousand a year), or cotton clothing woven from the unworked cotton they were given. Many villages, especially in the more remote areas, ordered digging sticks (*coas*), clothing, pieces of material, wax, and other goods from their alcalde mayor; they paid him two to four reales a week, either in cash or in articles of clothing. Enormous quantities of wax were purchased in Tepeaca—a province famous for the scale of its All Saints Day then and now—for the candles on the graves. Everywhere, each Indian decided whether to ask for credit or not. The alcaldes mayores were reluctant to grant it because their losses could be incalculable if the Indians proved unable to repay their debts, and thus they would certainly not press the Indians to accept "forced loans."

We shall close this section with a trip through semitropical falda areas. I hope that the reader is not exhausted yet and is prepared to join me in a quick tour through some mountainous provinces. We start in the north of Anáhuac, go eastward to the coast, passing through Veracruz and the tropical lowlands to the south of the central highlands, before ending up in the western province of Temascaltepec. The reader whose patience has already been taxed will be pleased to hear that I do not have full data for each of the provinces, so that the picture will only be presented in its general outline. Hardly any repartimientos were held in the mining province of Zimapán, where only the small group of charcoal burners (*carboneros*) bought mules for eighteen to twenty pesos each. In the province of Xochicoatlán, the peasants—Indians and non-Indians alike—produced raw cotton (every two years, though of poor quality) and brown, unclayed sugar (*piloncillo*) on a credit basis for the alcaldes mayores. The cotton was woven only to make cloth in the villages of Izhuatlán, Tlachichilco, and Sontecomatlán. Mules had not been sold for some time because there was not much transport in these provinces. Besides, the main road ran through such mountainous country that many animals fell into the ravines. Since the Indians were not obliged to pay for dead animals, the alcaldes mayores incurred such heavy losses that they stopped the repartimientos. They did not sell bulls either, because there were only four haciendas in the province where the Indians could find work. The alcaldes mayores did sell hats (for 1p2), clothing, soap and even bread, usually in exchange for the piloncillo. The situation was the same in the neighboring provinces of Huehutla and Yahualica—where piloncillo was also produced, again on a credit basis, as well as a purgative made from the root of a plant, and a few mats a year.

The provinces in the eastern tropical lowlands supplied the alcaldes mayores with vanilla and raw cotton on a credit basis. Humboldt described how repartidores particulares granted loans to the vanilla producers, but he claimed that payments were in kind rather than in cash: textiles, in particular, as well as alcoholic drinks and cacao beans.[61] The provinces in the higher altitudes—Xalapa, Córdoba, and Orizaba—also produced the purgative for the alcaldes mayores, a trade which was worth three hundred pesos a year in Xalapa alone. This *purga de Xalapa* was a particularly important product, and nearly all the Indians were employed in looking for it in the woods. The alcaldes mayores supplied various goods in exchange. In the province of Orizaba, where the feast of All Saints was also very popular, the main item supplied was wax for the candles. Since the Camino Real to the harbor of Veracruz ran through these provinces, the alcaldes mayores sold many mules each year (three hundred in Xalapa). The price of these animals, ranging from twenty-five to thirty pesos, was not exceptionally high if one remembers that there was no need to pay the full price of the animals if they fell into the ravine during the steep climb to the highlands. The alcaldes mayores were apparently unable to incorporate any further reserves in their prices. Many muleteers preferred horses to mules anyway, because they were more suitable in the mountains. The agricultural farmers and lumberjacks bought two hundred bulls a year from the tropical lowlands, because the bulls from the temperate highlands could not stand up to the climate. There were enough sugar haciendas in these provinces to provide work for the Indians who offered their services for hire with teams of oxen.

It was not common for the alcaldes mayores in the provinces to the south of the highlands to sell many mules. An annual figure of one hundred mules was only sold in Piastla, a jurisdiction within the province of Acatlán, and of course in the provinces of Tlapa and Chilapa, which have already been mentioned. Many mules were also sold in Cuernavaca and Cuautla Amilpas, where the Camino Real from Acapulco ran, which was important for the trade from the Philippines. Most of the Indians and non-Indians in Cuautla were involved with this transport in one way or another. In 1788, the subdelegados stated that no repartimiento had ever been held in the rest of Acatlán, further to the south, where a lot of timber was felled. The occasional repartimiento had taken place in Tepejí de la Seda in the past, but it had gone out of fashion by this time in the eighteenth century, suggesting that marketing products could be done better outside the repartimiento arrangement. The alcaldes mayores sold a large range of articles of clothing and hats on credit in these provinces. They also bought small livestock on credit: in Acatlán six thousand goats for the Puebla slaughterhouses (where tallow was manufactured) each year. However, this also included animals from the province of Tepejí. In these provinces, the Indians paid their tribute in goats alone. In this manner, the alcaldes mayores bought salt (fifteen hundred fanegas a year) and mats (eight thousand a year) in Acatlán. The neighboring province of Chiautla de la Sal was also highly specialized in salt, while Tepejí specialized in palm mats, selling three different kinds to the alcalde mayor. The production of palms for these mats accounted for most of the labor time in the villages of Tepejí.

Repartimiento sales were held in Cuernavaca, selling particularly to Spanish sugar estates. The repartimientos to Indian villagers were overshadowed by the unusually heavy labor services—also referred to, of course, as repartimientos—in the Taxco silver mines, especially after Don José de la Borda—known at the time as "the first miner of the world" and nowadays as the man who built the splendid Santa Prisca—had given mining in the province of Taxco a new lease on life.[62] The priest of Oaxtepec (near the eastern part of the province of Cuernavaca), who bore witness to the abuse of the workers in 1725 claimed that the Indians ought to be paid in cash for that kind of work. The neighboring pueblo of Tepoztlán had just refused the repartimiento de labor, which had been reintroduced in the 1720s. A crown inquiry to determine the exact number of Indians for such repartimientos and to investigate which geographical area should be covered by the compulsory labor, led to further refusals through legal proceedings. Some villages were held to their obligations; others saw their obligations reduced, or even completely abolished. Although Tepoztlán lay just outside the newly determined legal limit for the mining draft, it was exceptional because the Indians there had to go to Taxco. There was rioting, as in Actopan forty years later, but without much effect.

So we arrive at the provinces south of the Nevado de Toluca volcano: Temascaltepec, Sultepec, Zacualpan, and Taxco. There were a number of silver mines in this area, though most of them produced very little at the time. When one of the mines entered a temporary period of growth, considerable livestock was required, which was supplied through private trade or through a repartimiento. The villages where the miners lived did not have the status of pueblos (they were called rancherías, hamlets of small farms, and belonged to separate jurisdiction called a Real de Minas), but many mules were sold there around 1752 because the residents (castas) were hired to transport ore and timber. There were also a lot of charcoal burners. Some Indian villagers grew wheat, which required oxen. However, they were so slow in paying for them (sometime not until three years later) that the alcaldes mayores grew more reluctant to hold repartimientos every year. The last repartimiento in Temascaltepec was held in 1783. Besides this livestock, the alcaldes mayores or their agents also sold clothing and other utilities. This trade even replaced the livestock trade in the 1780s. In fact, twelve thousand pesos' worth of clothing was sold each year in Zacualpan alone. Finally, raw cotton was supplied to the villages by private traders and government officials for the local textile industry. In the course of the eighteenth century, the alcaldes mayores appear to have been replaced by repartidores particulares in the clothing industry. Payment was due within a few months in cash, local manufactures, or foodstuffs, such as maize from most of the villages, salt from Ixtapan and Ixcateopan, fruit from Tlalimaltenango, or baskets from Tonatico. These villages also received credit to make the artisanal products.

Salt was one of the main products in this area. Tribute had already become repartimientos in the sixteenth century, when villages producing salt had to deliver fixed quotas of salt to the neighboring mines. This was a substitute for the labor services of the villages, the repartimientos de labor. In the seventeenth century, Tejupilco and Ixtapan produced more than six hundred fanegas of salt each year for the mines in Temascaltepec and Sultepec. A teniente clearly overstepped the mark in 1720, in demanding both labor in the mines and salt, as well as prohibiting the Indians from selling on the market. The crown intervened in this case: the labor in the mines was not called for, and the salt could be traded freely on the market once the repartimiento had been completed. It is clear from the 1784 data that the average salt production in Temascaltepec never corresponded to the required repartimiento, but I have not been able to ascertain the consequences of this shortfall.[63]

To summarize: the repartimiento can be used as a guide to, and a tentative measure of, the Indian market economy. The classic repartimiento of mules, bulls, and horses to Indians and non-Indians played a particularly prominent role in the central highlands. It also took place in the regions with a supportive economy, but the provinces in the faldas were dominated by the credit system by which the alcaldes mayores and corregidores managed the production of certain items in the municipalities. As we have seen in previous sections, the introduction of a repartimiento of mules and bulls in these areas ran up against enormous difficulties. In absolute figures, more foodstuffs and utilities were sold than large livestock in these parts. This meant that to bind the members of the two repúblicas to each other, the moral economic mechanism of the "charity system" had included an important political economic component as well. Of course, the alcaldes mayores and corregidores made the largest profits from the sale of livestock to Indians and non-Indians. Large amounts of capital were involved in these transactions, so that business was less profitable in the faldas. Furthermore, the provision of credit for special agricultural products or artesanías was a risky business for the provincial officials, because the Indians took so long in supplying the products that were ordered.

Naturally, the alcaldes mayores had been aware of this.[64] It is highly paradoxical that in view of the great economic importance of the mule trade through the repartimiento, the volume of the capital turnover of these repartimientos provides a good indication of the extent to which Anáhuac was commercialized. Assuming that the market was more "imperfect" as the range of goods involved in the repartimiento trade widened, a high commercialization (in combination with the selling of many mules, but a restricted range of articles involved in the repartimiento trade) is to be found in the provinces with a many-sided economy, and a low commercialization (few mules, a large range of articles involved in the repartimiento trade) on the outskirts of the region. The latter phenomenon is striking from a regional point of view, because with the exception of cochineal production and livestock trade in Oaxaca (discussed by Hamnett and Chance), hardly any repartimientos were held in the Indian villages in the other regions of New Spain. The subdelegados from Michoacán and Guadalajara wrote to the court in Madrid that all trade with Indians in their region was private commerce, with the probable exception of a few shops run by the alcaldes mayores. However, their capital turnover was marginal when compared with the turnover of the repartimientos in Anáhuac and Oaxaca. The *tienda* operated in Michoacán and Guadalajara by the alcaldes mayores and which supplied a great variety of goods, not all of great value, seems to me to have been virtually absent in Anáhuac. The only places where a small-scale repartimiento was occasionally held were Pátzcuaro (originally Indian) and the other Purépeche villages in the surroundings. On the other hand, very large numbers of livestock were sold to Spaniards and castas, and this was sometimes done by means of repartimientos as well. In fact, the case of Pátzcuaro should be treated with circumspection. It was the only densely populated spot in the Michoacán-Guadalajara regions in the pre-Hispanic era. It looks as though the repartimientos could only take root where the Indians were accustomed to disposing of their products first of all by means of the tribute collection.

In that case, the official position of the indigenous nobility in the pueblos, the gobernadores, was of decisive importance. Where the gobernadores played a less prominent role, as in the majority of the Michoacán and Guadalajara regions, hardly any repartimientos took place in Indian villages. This went hand in hand with a greater performance of the "Spanish" economy and a reasonable sale of repartimiento cattle to non-Indians; the degree of commercialization was higher here. May one conclude from all this that as a result of the work by Brading, Van Young, Garner, and others, the image of these particular regions has affected the general historiography of New Spain, thereby accounting for the sparse attention paid to the repartimiento? William Taylor, for example, was probably writing under this tapatío influence when he referred to the repartimientos of eggs in Zacatlán as "unusually important."[65] I hope to have demonstrated that the repartimiento was equally important throughout the whole of Anáhuac, and that Zacatlán was by no means exceptional in this respect, although it was the only "egg province."

The Repartimiento and Local Politics

The enormous importance of what, in fact, was an illegal practice entailed a dangerous political risk for those who took an active part in it. The alcaldes mayores and corregidores were susceptible to blackmail after the prohibition was decreed. And this had been done repeatedly during the eighteenth century; see, for instance, the *Reales Cédulas* of 13 December 1721, 15 June and 17 July 1751 from Madrid; the *Plan de Intendencias* of Gálvez of 15 January 1768 and the New Ordinance of Intendants of 23 September 1803, part of the Reforms program; or the early decree of the Audiencia of Mexico in Mexico City of 22 December 1722.[66] It is this political background to the documentation that explains why we have so much information on the repartimiento at our disposal. I shall therefore return to a number of the cases already mentioned in order to comment on them in this light. Whether they were traditional or not, the pueblos naturally knew how illegal a repartimiento was, and on occasions, they tried to exploit their cooperation in the trade for political ends. As a number of cases have already shown, the principal victim was usually the alcalde mayor. However, if this political game went wrong, it could have serious economic consequences for the inhabitants of a pueblo.

The town of Santa María Toxtepec in the province of Tecali wanted political autonomy in the 1730s, instead of falling under the jurisdiction of Santiago Tecali, the provincial headtown. An ethnic problem lay behind this demand, for Toxtepec was Chocho-speaking, and Tecali was Nahuatl-speaking. Another factor of a general kind resided in the growing irritation in many subsidiary villages (pueblos sujetos) of the viceroyalty about the reservation of the economic advantage of, for example, the repartimiento gains to the caciques or gobernadores of the cabecera themselves. More specific, the Indians of Toxtepec were deeply involved in textile production through the repartimiento mechanism and might have wished to do without the middlemen in the cabecera. Dehouve has argued that pueblos sujetos experienced several such features of an unequal sharing in the communal organization in the late eighteenth century, like enforced residence in the cabecera for their own political leaders and double work for the construction of community houses and village churches, both in their own subsidiary village and in the headtown.[67] Furthermore Dehouve concludes, the growing number of "secessions" in that period should be understood as the result of the disappearance of the old relationships between the nobility of the pueblo and the Indian subordinates in remote villages. The hostility between Toxtepec and Santiago Tecali went back at least to the early period of Spanish government, because Toxtepec had been allowed to form a headtown of its own after the conquest, but remained subordinate to Tecali lordship.

In fact, the hostility probably went back even further in the pre-Hispanic era to the collapse of the kingdom of Cuautinchan in the twelfth century. The Indians of Toxtepec, who regarded themselves as a different "people" ("pueblo" in Spanish), had never accepted the Herrschaft of the lords of Tecali. The two parties were continually involved in law suits against one another. The request for a granting of the wish to secede was presented as an official petition in Mexico City; but yet another document was received from the province. After an appeal had been held, it was finally turned down in 1734.[68] The village council of Toxtepec, which, in line with common practice, consisted of caciques, decided to refuse any further cooperation with Tecali: it no longer paid tribute to the caciques of Tecali; other rents were no longer paid, and the payment for goods received under the repartimiento was suspended. The documentation gives the impression that this strategy was inspired by the village priest, who had been agitating for decennia against the practice of the repartimiento, just as priests elsewhere had been doing. A government official was not supposed to be paid for his services! Besides, he received his annual stipend from the cacique of Tecali and not from that of Toxtepec (a stipend, moreover, which was only one-third of what his counterpart in Tecali received). However, the political adventure cost the Indians of Toxtepec dearly. The corregidor of Tecali regarded this animosity between the two pueblos as a risk to his repartimiento investments. He did not budge an inch for the Chochos from Toxtepec; on the contrary, accompanied by the local cacique, Don Cayetano de Tovar, and hundreds of followers, he left for the rebel village in the dark of night to teach the villagers a lesson. The troops of the corregidor and cacique invaded the church and attacked those who were hidden there. Four people from Toxtepec were killed, a number of them were wounded, and a part of the village was burned down. The same day, the other villages in the parish of Toxtepec were given the same treatment. And the priest heard one of them snarling something like: "Well Padre, now you can see that there are still some fine fellows in this place!"

This escapade was naturally an embarrassment to the Spanish government. The enmity that had been smoldering in the small province of Tecali for centuries suddenly threatened to flare up and revive the old "caste war" between Nahuas and Chochos. The government therefore intervened firmly: the corregidor of Tecali and the cacique were arrested, and the priest of Toxtepec was transferred. The Audiencia let the corregidor feel that his action could certainly not be regarded as a piece of "buen gobierno," and that he might as well forget his future career. The peasants' complaint against the repartimiento was not accepted. There was nothing unusual in the situation, and more importantly, it was perfectly understood that this dispute was not a repartimiento question at all. The political game that had been played in Toxtepec was regarded as more serious than the illegality of the repartimiento in the eyes of the Audiencia. Nevertheless, the magistrates ordered the Indians of Toxtepec to pay off their repartimiento debts without delay, after which the Audiencia kept a close watch on the situation in the area—and with serious consequences indeed, for fifty years later, in 1788, the provincial administrator of Tecali reported that no repartimiento had been held in Toxtepec since the case of 1734. This had resulted in a marked backwardness in economic development and even in bitter poverty in a few areas. The residents of Toxtepec had been forced to abandon their artisanal production almost entirely, and their only alternative was to report to the haciendas in the area as seasonal laborers in order to earn enough to cover their communal expenses.[69]

It is not entirely clear to what extent the events of 1786 in the "egg province" of Zacatlán arose from a similar background. Taylor seems convinced by the complaint lodged by the Indians with the Audiencia, through the intermediary of the priest. However, closer examination reveals that the priests had probably pumped as much money out of the villages as the alcalde mayor had done, if not more. They therefore regarded the alcalde mayor as a competitor in the egg trade. Both the priest and the alcalde mayor traded in the villages through the gobernadores. The question of who was appointed as village head was thus of importance to them. The priests tried to get their candidate elected, often not only against the wishes of the alcalde mayor but also, remarkably enough, against those of most of the Indian nobles themselves. (This case will be presented in one of the following chapters.) At any rate, the controversy regarding the repartimiento flared up when Gálvez's prohibition of 1784 reached the province and was immediately nailed to the church door. From the pulpit, the priests urged their flock not to buy mules from the alcalde mayor any longer. The lieutenant of Tecoyuca, who acted as repartidor of the alcalde mayor, reported to his superior that he had heard the priest, Don Antonio de Nava, instructing the Indians to pay off all of their debts, particularly those due to the church and the confraternities, but not to buy any mules from the Spanish official (referred to as the corregidor here) because the priest saw him as an outrageous usurer. They could spend their money more profitably on their families. Don Antonio de Nava was indeed one of the few priests who had not bought any livestock himself from Sánchez de Tagle; other priests had done so extensively. After this sermon, the Indians had only smiled at the lieutenant in passing him by, without saying anything. After mass, he had summoned the debtors and told them that they only needed to pay what they had left over after the sale of their harvest, and the rest of the debt could wait. Sánchez de Tagle then visited the villages to tell the Indians that they were only obliged to obey the priest in spiritual matters. The priest, however, stated later on that Sánchez de Tagle had threatened the Indians with beatings and imprisonment in Mexico City on that occasion, which, by the way, was not at all unlikely. I do not know the outcome of the dispute, because all attention was focused on the events of 1785–86. Sánchez de Tagle had simply held his two repartimientos in the autumn of 1784 for a small group of Indians, as always, who had apparently cooperated of their own free will, again as always.

At any rate, politics were involved in the charges brought against Don Phelipe de Palacios in Tlalmanalco (Chalco) in 1722,[70] the case presented by Charles Gibson. Careful study of the documentation reveals that the ethnohistorian formed his judgment entirely on the basis of the statements made by the caciques. The charges against the alcalde mayor were initiated by Don Antonio Galicia, cacique of Ayapango. According to independent witnesses, who were picked from the street at random by an examining magistrate from Mexico City, Galicia had developed a dislike for the alcalde mayor because he suspected the alcalde of sidetracking him in a conflict in which Galicia was involved with the municipal council of Tlalmanalco. The cacique had rented land from the municipality, the rancho Tenayuca. The pueblo financed certain payments that it made to the church with its income from the rent. As a consequence of all kinds of problems, Galicia had run into difficulties in paying his rent, resulting in the municipal leaders being unable to meet their own obligations to the church. Galicia had proposed at the time to transfer the running of the rancho temporarily to a Spaniard, but this proposal was indignantly turned down: a Spaniard on Indian territory! Both "orders" should be kept separate! When the municipal council had terminated the rent contract, Galicia tried to gain a judgment in his favor from the alcalde mayor and later in Mexico City, though in vain. In the end, Galicia arranged with the gobernadores of Tlalmanalco to tear up the contract demonstratively during a ceremonial meeting in the pueblo square. This, indeed, did take place, but when the church demanded its money and the municipal council pointed to Galicia, who also owed money to the church, the church council decided to arrest the cacique until the money was forthcoming. In the meantime, the alcalde mayor was involved in the case as magistrate, but Díez de Palacios, portrayed as a wavering figure by these witnesses, did nothing except confirm the decision of the municipal council of Tlalmanalco. Although this may be regarded as an act of "buen gobierno" in theory, Galicia probably considered that he should have been backed up by the alcalde mayor in his bid to keep the rancho for himself.[71] Galicia, in fact, made no secret of his conviction that Spanish officials had to back up traditional caciques in their conflicts with gobernadores.

While Galicia was planning his revenge in prison, Velarde and De la Torre, the officials of Díez de Palacios, were overhastily and more or less violently collecting the debts due from the repartimiento of the two Gutiérrez hacendados in 1720 and 1721. They confiscated the animals of both Indians and non-Indians and even threw debtors into prison. Galicia found a supporter in Don Nicolás de Garate, the priest of Tlalmanalco, who had argued with the alcalde mayor over the latter's failure to practice "buen gobierno" in the case. Don Salvador de Guzmán, the gobernador of Tlalmanalco, who was also a cacique, had complained about the debt collection as well. One of his jailers stated that Galicia, while in prison, saw the priest show a letter to the alcalde mayor which he wanted to send to his superiors in Mexico City. The alcalde mayor snarled a reply at the priest, threw the letter to the ground, and left angrily. He saw himself powerless in the face of the dominion of the Gutiérrez hacendados. Now Galicia himself owed Gutiérrez de Castro 200 pesos from the repartimiento of 1716, and he did not have the means to pay off the debt quickly. Galicia probably summoned the priest after the incident and plotted with him to pin it on the alcalde mayor and wriggle out of his debt to the hacendado in one fell swoop. Galicia presumably also promised to pay as soon as he could the 120 pesos that he owed as his contribution for a church monument.

The first official step was to be taken by the priest: he submitted an official complaint on behalf of Galicia and Guzmán. He was then empowered by the Audiencia to collect statements from witnesses. In the first instance, he collected statements from notorious enemies of the alcalde mayor, including two figures who had wanted to be appointed as lieutenants by Díez de Palacios, but whom he had deliberately ignored, and one from a quack who called himself a doctor, who had been ordered to leave the area by the alcalde mayor. The two caciques then summoned all of the gobernadores of the province to the priest's house. Galicia addressed the first group in Nahuatl from the balcony on 5 October 1722: every debt would be abolished by the Audiencia if everyone was prepared to pin the repartimiento of the two Gutiérrez hacendados on the alcalde mayor. When the gobernadores came village by village to make their statements between 5 and 20 October 1722, Galicia stood by the door and reminded all of them to incriminate the alcalde mayor. They followed his instruction; all of the gobernadores issued nearly identical statements, whose content was brought to the Audiencia within a few weeks, and published by Gibson 242 years later.[72]

The Audiencia reacted as if it had been stung by a gadfly: all debts were declared null and void, and the alcalde mayor was to be questioned and given a provisional trial. Díez de Palacios was not bothered about the debt payment, since he had little to do with it anyway, but he was concerned about his reputation and summoned what were clearly randomly chosen witnesses in the second round to testify before the magistrates of the Audiencia that he had or had not organized the repartimientos. It was at this stage that the details of the case presented above emerged, and an investigation of De la Torre's accounts revealed that the livestock was from the Gutiérrez hacendados. The first condemnation of the alcalde mayor was revoked, but the Indians were not required to pay off the hacendados. The Audiencia still had not reached a definitive verdict in 1728, when Díez de Palacios had already been dead for some time. The Gutiérrez hacendados had started debt collecting in the pueblos again that year, which was once again forbidden on pain of a fine of two hundred pesos.

Díez de Palacios was doubtless a feeble and indecisive alcalde mayor. He may have been responsible for the problems connected with the collection of the repartimiento debts, but that was above all, I think, because of his failure to take action. All the same, he was certainly not the rogue portrayed by Gibson. The ethnohistorian's verdict did not take the statements by Díez de Palacios's followers and those from randomly chosen witnesses into account. Was Gibson influenced by the Black Legend, which still had not lost its grip in the early 1960s? Was that why he had already declared the alcalde mayor guilty as a representative of Spanish colonial rule? The conclusion of his book *The Aztecs under Spanish Rule* betrays an unambiguous sympathy for the Black Legend, despite the fact that the argument of the whole book maintains that Indian structures and vitality had survived the conquest in a major way. He demonstrated (first, by the way, in his 1952 book, *Tlaxcala in the Sixteenth Century*)[73] that these structures and the power of the Indian peoples affected or even corrected whatever measures the Spaniards planned. Gibson argued that they rejected everything that did not fit in with their sociocultural tradition and only accepted what guaranteed their interests and the preservation of their way of life, dressed up differently if necessarily. Though Gibson strangely denied it, I believe this was also true of the repartimiento. The obvious signs of a frame by Galicia and the priest of Tlalmanalco are in the same file as the cacique's protest. Gibson apparently deliberately ignored the relevant documents. This is just as remarkable for a critical historian as the uncritical acceptance of what Gálvez's officials in Madrid said about the repartimiento.

Conclusion

In this chapter, I have attempted to explain the mechanism of the "repartimientos de comercios" and, in doing so, to alleviate the curse of the Black Legend to some degree. Of course, abuse did take place, and I have presented a few examples. However, at least two cases of what are presented in the literature as abuses prove, on closer examination, to be nothing of the kind. I have engaged in a long search for more examples of abuses in Mexican and Spanish archives. After all, the mark of a true historian is a sufficiently skeptical attitude in handling evidence. Even if I only managed to gain a glimpse of half of the actual number of abuses—in the unlikely event that the Indians did not register a protest, although they continually did so the rest of the time—it remains true that the number of cases of abuse that I have managed to find is remarkably small. Supposing a four-year period of office for each alcalde mayor in these fifty-one provinces of Anáhuac during the period 1710–1800, there were 1,150 potential cases of abuse. However, many officials only held office for a couple of years. Chance estimated at least thirty officials in the province of Villa Alta in the Oaxaca region for the period 1710–1800.[74] If this figure was the norm for each province in Anáhuac, there were 1,530 potential cases of abuse. I have only managed to find a few, and in each of these cases firm measures were taken.

All in all, it must be evident by now that, above all, the rapid growth of livestock trade was bound to be interrupted by the prohibition of the repartimiento in 1786. This prohibition was extremely effective and resulted in a total freeze of the livestock trade for a number of years. Considering the trade was illegal, it was naturally very difficult to move such large herds across country without being seen. The prohibition particularly affected the Indians in the provinces in the highland valleys, who used the mules for transport of all kinds; here the livestock, including the bulls as plow oxen, had become the basis of their economic activities. However, since the mule was the only cheap means of transport in the colony and the mortality rate of mules had increased dramatically in the drought years of 1784 and 1785, trade between and within regions was seriously affected, and the peasants in the villages were no longer able to perform important agricultural operations because of the lack of draught animals. The situation was less catastrophic in the faldas (which is why such a large number of migrants poured in there in the late 1780s and 1790s), but it still meant an impoverishment of everyday life.

The intendentes of Puebla and Oaxaca refused to carry out the prohibition from fear of a popular uprising. They were afraid of a repetition of the situation in Yucatán in 1722, after the prohibition of the repartimiento there at that time. The Spanish administration was thrown into such a turmoil by the prohibition that the measure had to be revoked to preserve peace. After the lifting of the prohibition, which implied a de facto legalization of the repartimiento, trade picked up again in the 1790s. Since the production of livestock had not stopped, the market was flooded for a few years after the ban had been lifted, and the villagers were able to bring up the numbers of their draught and pack animals again at low prices.[75] It may therefore be concluded that what government officials, hacendados, caciques, and other Indian representatives wrote to the government in Mexico City at the time was correct: the structure of trade of Anáhuac would not have been able to function even in a broad sense without the repartimiento. The difference between the purchase price paid to the Indian pueblos and the retail price paid to the pueblos went some way toward compensating for the high cost of transport, enabling the small peasants in Zacatlán, for example, to travel more than two hundred kilometers to bring their eggs to Mexico City. The repartimiento also provided a solution to the problem of the shortage of coin, which usually complicated the collection of tribute. The Indians, like the non-Indians, generally cooperated with this trade on a voluntary basis, sometimes on their own initiative, and in any case, were usually motivated by economic considerations. The repartimiento meant extra income for the residents of the pueblos at a time of population growth, increasing drought, and a concomitant loss of security.

To conclude, then, the scholars of the ecological approach have analogically suggested to me that after 1780 or so "something" of a way out should have existed for the peasants in the villages of Anáhuac, because in a time of despair their number could increase without suffering from a Malthusian setback. This was what brought me, heuristically, to investigate the repartimiento trade and examine its data, which eventually did reveal more than just the crisis. The investigation of the mechanism of the repartimiento presented in this chapter leads me to think that the interregional trade that made use of the system must have increased in the course of the eighteenth century (with the exception of a province like Atlixco, where wheat production collapsed). That brings me to the second analytical feature of the repartimiento: although the prohibition in the late 1780s was another "shadow" that fell over Anáhuac, the restoration of trade in the 1790s was an important "solution" devised in the villages, at the same time, to put an end to the entire malaise. The data discussed in this chapter show that there was a commercial alternative to a more intense exploitation of the moral economic "charity system" in Anáhuac. And the prohibition brought crown officials, entrepreneurs, and Indian leaders together to disobey Madrid. This is why the governments in Mexico City and Madrid were forced to recognize the value of this trade. Because a subordinate in the colony was supposed to have the revenue of the state at heart instead of supplementing his own salary, the vigorous anti-repartimiento tracts written by many high-placed officials in Madrid did not meet with much response in either the court or the pueblos.

5

First Implication:
The Rise of *Gobernadoryotl*

Introduction

Intensive exploitation of charity systems, in combination with an increase of repartimiento trade, could not fail to have consequences for the functioning of local political-economic institutions. Not only was the commercial integration of Spanish and Indian "worlds" speeded up, but also the political-jural integration. The last decades of the eighteenth century witnessed the resultant decay of the traditional cacicazgos, and in the end, the emergence of new cacicazgos in the form of what I would like to call *gobernadoryotl*, or governorship, within the borders of the pueblo. It is important to remember that the pueblos were not created from nothing. Without going back to Adam and Eve, it is inevitable that this chapter starts with a tentative rehearsal of the characteristics of the traditional cacicazgo, linked with *tlahtocayotl* or "tlahtoani-ship." In doing so, I shall endeavor to be as succinct as possible, but this is barely possible in a field in which there is a lack of academic consensus concerning, namely, the character of the Aztec state and its economic foundation, as well as the post-conquest and even contemporary Indian communities.[1] I think the anthropological literature on modern Indian communities in Mexico and Guatemala is unsuitable for this purpose; the bias in these works has already been pointed out. Various contemporary scholars have already argued that the Indian communities of colonial Mesoamerica were less egalitarian than previously thought. Most of these scholars have also questioned older interpretations of a whole set of institutions associated with such communities, whether the "cargo-system," the role of the confraternities, or the *caja de comunidad*. In the present chapter, I argue that Indian communities in Anáhuac represented a de facto "feudal-type" demesne, thus representing a high level of continuity in lordship from the pre-Hispanic times until at least the early nineteenth century. The Indian pueblos were ruled by a small elite of caciques and "principales," who either traced descent from the pre-Hispanic nobility or took the place of that nobility by acquiring parts of early post-conquest grants in which pre-Hispanic demesnes were recognized.

In short, the pueblos go back to a pre-Hispanic corporation that we know as the altepetl. As previously expressed, an important cohesive element in liege to the altepetl was the personal relation with the lord. The altepetl is to be viewed as a "seigneury" or "benefice" of this kind, consisting of a group of peasants and a few aristocrats led by an elected chief or prince. I will return to the concept of Herrschaft, drawn from German historiography once again, a concept that already has made several appearances in the present volume. Since all history is comparative, I do not think we can get very far without a comparison with Europe. The sketch already given encompassed the reorganization from personal loyalties to the territorial principle of the municipality. This reorganization must be understood as a reworking of those personal loyalties *within* municipal boundaries. This indicates that we are not dealing with a black or white kind of problem, but with a matter of primary and secondary emphasis. The post-conquest worlds really consisted of "two worlds merged," to paraphrase Hoekstra's image: all original indigenous elements of the post-conquest society were touched by Spanish law and policy, but at the same time no institution or social-cultural component was without pre-Hispanic roots.

The Demise of the Old-style Cacicazgo

Counting Caciques

The traditional demesne of the caciques was situated geographically within the old altepetl boundaries, but in practice it lay between haciendas and pueblos. Its legal structure was modeled on the Spanish *mayorazgo*. This made the cacicazgos inalienable and indivisible, and legally subject to the rules of entail and primogeniture under Spanish law. Indians who lived on these estates were "indios" in legal terms, but they were called *terrazgueros* to distinguish them from "pueblo indios" and hacienda "indios" (the *gañanes*). The terrazgueros had obligations similar to those of European serfs or manorial servants, like *solariego* peasants of late medieval Spain—Taylor notes—who were bound to the lord's land and received use rights in exchange for labor services or tribute that were rarely spelled out in detail. The terrazgueros' settlements were often described in the sources as *rancherías*, but this term could also be used to describe any hamlet. The caciques' estates were worked by these terrazgueros, but the caciques also took on wage laborers from the villages, or allowed "pueblo indios" to pay their pueblo tribute to them in labor services on cacicazgo lands.[2]

This legal construction meant that a cacicazgo belonged to one lord, one cacique, but since this did not correspond to the indigenous manorial tradition, sons and daughters of caciques all successfully adopted the title and rights linked to it. Since the criticisms of Chevalier's book on the haciendas, we know that there can be a large discrepancy between the letter of the law and practice of this kind. It was the case here, too: at the local level, it was possible for not only all the children of the cacique to assume these rights, but brothers and cousins as well. This meant the collapse of the mayorazgo character of the cacicazgo. In short, a cacique was someone who could claim direct descent from pre-Hispanic nobility, or who had acquired titles of parts of lordly demesnes recognized as such in the early colonial period. In both cases, the caciques were tributarios, but exempt from factual payment of royal tribute. For this reason, they were allowed to call themselves Don.

If efficiently managed, in the cacicazgo archives were kept records of family transactions, but the heirs never stopped taking one another to court, resulting in an enormous fragmentation of the cacicazgo rights, from labor service to landownership. Some caciques tried to prevent this. The cacique Antonio Xihcotencatl in Tlaxcala, for example, determined in 1755 that his heirs must exercise the use right alternately for a year each to prevent such fragmentation. Others rented their land to tenants, or it was confiscated and sold by the royal authorities because the caciques were heavily in debt. The many ranchos acquired by the haciendas de facto or de jure in this manner came from a cacicazgo inheritance. The same goes for land held by rural confraternities. Sometimes a pueblo could acquire such rights, a juridical activity initiated on a universal scale, particularly in the late eighteenth century. This was done by applying for rights to the land before the court, as well as through inheritance. The pueblo San Dionisio Yauhquemecan (Tlaxcala), for example, was already assigned the cacicazgo land of the cacique Francisco Aquiahualtzin in 1717, because he had no heirs. Besides being extremely vulnerable to encroachment, fragmented cacicazgo holdings presented a myriad of problems of labor and utilization.[3]

All the same, despite this fragmentation, the cacicazgo retained its value. Taylor wrote on a similar development in Oaxaca:

> Heated disputes in the seventeenth and eighteenth centuries over
> the succession to . . . cacicazgos . . . testify to the enduring wealth
> and prestige of the caciques.[4]

The caciques considered themselves aristocrats on the Spanish model, and that is how their rights were protected as well. Aristocrats who did not hold such rights were mere "principales"; they were obliged to pay tribute and to contribute to the mass, and they were not allowed to assume the title of Don or to use a patronym. The principales, however, especially the ones living in barrios and sujetos, who were often linked to the old aristocratic families, tried to obtain such cacique rights through legal proceedings and political marriages. They were successful, too, since the documentation from the municipalities indicates that the number of individuals in Anáhuac who were entitled to call themselves *caciques y principales* in the eighteenth century was extremely large.

However, it is difficult to back up this impression with hard data apart from the hundreds of court cases involving cacicazgo rights. The tribute registers give figures for the number of caciques in a province, but they only do so occasionally and irregularly. There is a lack of systematization in the tribute figures until around 1800, but then they reveal a remarkably low number of caciques. It could be that these statistics were irregularly collected as well, or that they only reflect "genuine" caciques, that is, those families with documentation to prove their nobility and a family tree. One important source only provides caciques in four provinces in the valley of Toluca and its northern extremities: 9 in Ixtlahuaca, 9 in Tetepango, 26 in Tula, and 7 in Xilotepec. The corresponding number of provinces in the valley of Mexico and its faldas is six: 3 cacique families in Chalco, 3 in Coyoacán, 12 in Tacuba, 3 in Tasco, 2 in Teotihuacán, and 12 in Texcoco; for the valley of Puebla it is nine provinces: 241 (!) families in Tlaxcala, 7 in Atlixco, 3 in Cholula, 6 in San Juan de los Llanos, 29 in Tehuacán, 65 in Puebla (including Amozoc, Totmehuacán and Cuautinchán), 63 in the tiny province of Tecali, 5 in Tepejí de la Seda, and 11 in Acatlán.[5]

The striking cases are thus Tlaxcala, Puebla, Tehuacán, and Tecali, with a curiously high number of caciques. These provinces in the valley of Puebla ("eastern Anáhuac") were less influenced by Tenochtitlán's bureaucracy, resulting perhaps in a stronger accent on lordship in eastern Anáhuac, contrary to an emphasis on calpolli structure in western Anáhuac (the valleys of Mexico and Toluca). However, lordship in itself was as strong within the western calpollis as it was in eastern desmesnes.[6] This allows us to scrutinize the eastern situation in more detail. In the semiarid and poor province of Santiago Tecali the 1743 figures yield 479 households distributed among sixteen pueblos, 80 of which (17 percent) were "caciques y principales." The corresponding figure for 1800 is 63, which suggests that the figure in the tribute register of 1800 for this province is reliable. In the nearby pueblo of Cuautinchán, however, there were 87 caciques and 117 macehuales (commoners) in 1777, accounting for 43 percent of the township's Indian population. Of course, the various cacique families formed a closely knit network here through marriage politics: the source contains households of couples in which the names Luna, Torres, Quintero, Flores, Sánchez, Navarro, Rojas, López, Ximenez, Tapia, and Castañeda occur in various combinations. It is striking that a number of individuals with the same surnames are registered in the census separately from the caciques. They belonged to the *indios macehuales* or to the mestizos (there is even a mestizo couple named Flores-Sánchez). Perhaps the extraordinarily high number of caciques in this pueblo can be accounted for by its illustrious history, since Cuautinchán was the former center of a pre-Hispanic, and pre-Aztec, kingdom. The difference becomes striking when compared with other statistics from the valley. In 1743, Tochimilco contained 438 tributarios (Indian households) in eight pueblos, with only 19 caciques (4 percent). The 1800 tribute register does not mention a single cacique, though it lists 16 gobernadores. In 1743, there were 50 caciques in Huejotzingo out of a total of 540 Indian households distributed among eight townships, or 9 percent; in 1800 there was not a single cacique, but there were 58 gobernadores. In the province of Tlaxcala in 1779, there were many caciques concentrated within a radius of ten to fifteen kilometers from the capital of the province, though there were hardly any outside that area (there are no exact statistics available).[7]

According to the priest of Santiago Tecali in 1783, the large number of caciques in these areas was a heavy burden on the ordinary peasants.[8] He considered that many caciques obtained money illegally through the illegal acquisition of traditional privileges. This particularly concerned the rent obtained from the cacicazgo lands, which was paid to *soi disant* caciques by the Spanish hacendados from the region who rented the land. During his ten years in the province, the priest witnessed the common practice, when a cacique died without an heir, by which a rich third party, often an ordinary Indian or a rich cacique, appropriated both the rights and the title of the deceased. In this way principales, called ordinary Indians, became caciques, and rich caciques amassed three or four surnames. The priest accused some of these men of removing baptism and marriage registers from the parish to add their names to the old family trees. After continually pestering these men in connection with the fraud, he was eventually given back one of the baptism registers, while, in the meantime the land was used by hacendados instead of by the villagers. The best solution was to examine who had a genuine right to the cacicazgos in the province, to confiscate land that had been unlawfully acquired, and to add it to the pueblo holdings by means of a composición. The caciques would be required to show their entitlement papers. The alcalde mayor of Tepeaca was commissioned to carry out this investigation, but I was unable to find out the result. I suspect that it was in vain, for the 1800 tribute register for Tecali indicates that the province still had a large number of caciques—a significant fact, as we shall see.

It was certainly possible for the communities to put an end to a cacique's aspirations through the legal channels. Not far east of Cuautinchán and Tecali was the township of Santa Cruz Tlacotepec (Tepeaca), on the road to Tehuacán. The township was surrounded by a number of ranchos belonging to various cacicazgos. As a result, different families were continually at strife with one another and with the pueblo Tlacotepec. It is worth looking at one of these cases in more detail, because two maps have been preserved that illustrate well the difference between the traditional cacicazgo claims; one based on a large demesne with only an external boundary, and one on the modern landowning township, including mercedes, composiciones, and fundo legal—a splendid illustration of the contrast between Personenverband and Territorialverband. As far as the background is concerned, it should be mentioned that the rights to the cacicazgo of Tlacotepec were disputed in the first half of the eighteenth century between the Cortés de las Nieves and Rojas de Santiago Rojas y Mendoza families. In particular, Don Juan Cortés, gobernador of Tlacotepec on repeated occasions, was a dedicated litigant, although the cases mainly involved one rancho. He was unpopular with his family because he took his cousins and uncles to court one after another. Though Cortés had cacicazgo privileges, he had been poor until his marriage with the rich Doña María Martínez, a member of a third cacique family in the township. After her premature death, he married Doña María de Santiago Rojas, the daughter of Don Roque Rojas, from Tecali. In addition to his land, livestock, and labor privileges, Cortés also successfully derived an income from an inn (*venta*).

When he died and the estate had to be divided between his two children, there were still a few legal proceedings under way.[9]

The telling conflict here, to which I referred, took place between 1740 and 1745. The cacicazgo that was the object of such a bitter dispute between the two families went back to the privileges of the first cacique, Phelipe de Calzada y Mendoza.[10] It was now contested during this period by a third party, led by Don Domingo Sánchez on behalf of his wife Doña Nicolasa Flores Gutiérrez Alcazar, a descendant of the branch of the family that had found its way to Mexico City. (As we have seen, the names Sánchez and Flores occurred also among the caciques of neighboring Cuautinchán.) The striking feature of Sánchez's claim is that he demanded not only the land allocated to Cortés, but also land that officially belonged to the pueblo Tlacotepec. The cacique thus denied the pueblo's right to exist, as if history did not exist. Sánchez also claimed that Cortés's *venta* belonged to his own wife. Tlacotepec was represented in Mexico City by Don Luis Cortés, the son of Don Juan. Apart from the usual cacicazgo documents, including baptism and marriage records, wills and family trees, each of the two parties presented a map in 1743 at the request of the Audiencia. I have included both maps for the purpose of comparison (see Map 14). Don Domingo Sánchez came up with nothing more than a few roughly drawn boundaries, no doubt corresponding to those of the cacicazgo in the dim and distant past. Ranchos were mentioned by name, and the pueblo was included within the boundaries as well. On the other hand, Tlacotepec was able to present precise measurements following the Spanish model, with Spanish units such as mercedes, caballerías, and *sitios de ganado menor*. The case was decided in favor of the Tlacotepec Indians in 1745. In the first place, they had valid documents of possession, but, in addition, Sánchez and his wife were considered Spaniards and had even presented the court with a proof of *limpieza de sangre* to that effect, doubtless unaware that they were thereby disqualified since the cacicazgo belonged to the Indian order of society.

A similar case was situated on the other side of the volcanoes, in the province of Chalco, but there is something farcical about the problems faced by Don Luis Páez de Mendoza, the cacique of Panoaya, who lived in Amecameca (Chalco).[11] In January 1791, a group of representatives of the Indian township Santa Isabel Chalma appeared before the Juzgado de Indios in Mexico City. They had heard of the Juzgado's intention of giving every pueblo its right to 101 hectares of fundo legal, and asked for a survey to be conducted. They claimed to represent three hundred Indian residents. There was a shortage because of the population growth of the last few years, aggravated by the fact that a cacique, Luis Páez, refused to allow them to use his land. The Juzgado officials agreed that this was a scandal because as a high-ranking Indian nobleman, a cacique was expected to act in accordance with the wishes of his Indian vassals. The Juzgado therefore initiated the procedure for a survey of the fundo legal and asked the neighbors of Chalma to attend. They were the managers of the Hacienda Tequimilco and Panoaya, as well as the council of the

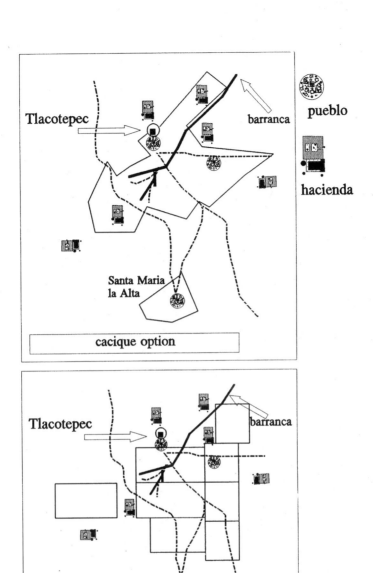

Map 14   The cacicazgo dispute of Tlacotepec in 1743

Indian pueblo San Antonio Tlaltecahuacan. The report was completed on 4 February. The township land was increased with a few plots from the Hacienda Panoaya and a few fields belonging to Don Luis Páez, who thereby lost a piece of his cacicazgo. No one interfered with the procedure on the spot.

The next day, however, the Juzgado received two letters of protest. The hacendado Francisco Bazo Ibañez, owner of the Hacienda Panoaya, wrote that his manager had no authority in matters relating to landownership and that he should never have agreed to the procedure. He demanded the restoration of the plots that had been confiscated. He claimed that the township did not have a leg to stand on in the case, since the Indians of Chalma did not have village rights. They lived with a mere sixty-five families on the cacicazgo of Páez de Mendoza and used his land. So they could be considered terrazgueros, but even if one would like to see Chalma as belonging to a pueblo it would be no more than a sujeto of the cabecera Ayapango, seventeen kilometers away. Don Luis Páez also protested. He had not been involved in the procedure either, and was unable to be present anyway because his wife had been very ill and had passed away that very day. Moreover, he also claimed that Chalma was too small to obtain village rights, unless it were to associate with the two other hamlets, San Antonio and Zentlalpan. The three hamlets had indeed regularly conspired against him and his family, and relations between the caciques Páez de Mendoza and the villagers were certainly poor. All the same, the land in question belonged to him. The Juzgado recognized the procedural mistakes and called upon the Indians of Chalma not to sow the newly acquired land.

This time it was the turn of the Chalma village council to issue a strong and indignant protest. No village rights? They satisfied all the criteria! There was a church with a baptismal font, where masses were held on every major Catholic feast. There was an elected village council. There were forty farms in the village, and if the Contla barrio was included, which belonged to Chalma, there were as many as eighty; exactly enough. Furthermore, some farms contained as many as three families. The village council claimed that there were thus four hundred Indians in Chalma. The Juzgado should conduct an inspection before starting a new procedure. Páez de Mendoza was only out to obstruct the Indians, it was said, and he had chosen a bad time for it, because the agricultural year had started and the land had to be sown. However, the sowing did not take place, because the official required for the inspection was busy for months in other villages. The inspection did not actually take place until 31 October. The Juzgado official found eighty-nine families in Chalma, including the Contla barrio. Chalma therefore had the right to a fundo legal. The judge also considered the other points raised by the village council to be correct and stated that Chalma could certainly claim village rights. The fundo legal procedure of 4 February had been in order. Confirmation of this report came from Madrid on 20 April 1792. It was decided to hold another survey. This time the cacique and hacendado must be in attendance. Everything went according to plan, and the case seemed to be closed.

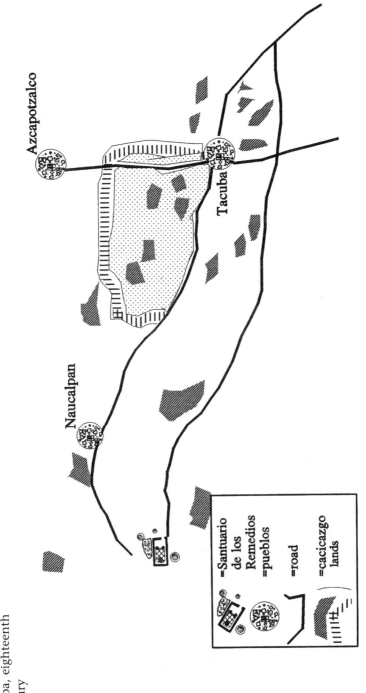

Map 15 The cacicazgo of Cortés Chimalpopoca in Tacuba, eighteenth century

Azcapotzalco

Naucalpan

Tacuba

= Santuario de los Remedios
= pueblos
= road
= cacicazgo lands

In the autumn of 1793, however, a few witnesses appeared before the Juzgado on behalf of Don Luis Páez, with the claim that the Indians of Chalma had carried out a deception during the inspection of 31 October 1791. The Indians had begun building all kinds of huts at night on the land of Don Luis Páez and the Hacienda Panoaya a few weeks before the date of the inspection. As a result, the village looked twice as large as it really was. They had asked Indians from other villages to come and stay with them for a few days—and they were paid for this!—in order to pull the wool over the eyes of the official from Mexico City. They had even invited blacks from Mexico City to occupy a few of the huts. The church was adorned and decked with items borrowed from other pueblos. Even the images of the saints were taken from elsewhere. The cacique stated that the request for a fundo legal had been incorrect because the three hamlets of Chalma, San Antonio, and Zentlalpan had more than one hundred hectares of land between them and carried out all their activities on a joint basis. Besides, many Indians worked as day laborers on the neighboring haciendas and had rented out the extra land which they had been allowed to sow since 4 February 1791, to a Spaniard.

These were serious charges. The Juzgado now ordered a full investigation, and a few months later the deceit perpetrated by the Indians of Chalma was confirmed. However, Don Luis Páez de Mendoza was not a sympathetic cacique either—the Juzgado's officers declared—and he had exploited the Indians on his land on more than one occasion in the past by forcing them to carry out extra labor services. That was more serious than the deceit carried out by Chalma. They proposed to give the village protected status. During the period of waiting for permission to be granted in Madrid, however, the Chalma village council had devised a different solution. The Indians had made a financial arrangement with Don Francisco Bazo Ibañez, by which they would officially relinquish their claim to the land in return for a donation of four hundred pesos to the village treasury. They intended to use this money to buy other land and to pay the tribute. Don Francisco accepted the offer, even though the land at issue was certainly not worth so much money. As the owner of the Hacienda Panoaya, he was afraid that there would be a shortage of hands during harvest as long as the conflict with Chalma continued. He also offered to pay their legal costs (fifty pesos) and gave them a field belonging to him and the right of access to the uncultivated land of the hacienda, where the Indians collected wood for their kitchen fires.

The Juzgado was evidently charmed by this move by the Chalma Indians, because the officers had grown despondent after so many false statements and all the reopenings of the case. Until now they had expected the affair to drag on and on. On 24 September 1795, Don Luis Páez was informed of the deal and he was asked to reach a similar agreement with the peasants. It was his son Diego who replied to the Juzgado, for Don Luis had died soon after the death of his wife. Diego Páez de Mendoza, the new cacique of Panoaya, was interested in the possibility, but he was not prepared to go as far as the neighboring hacendado had done. Don Diego considered one hundred pesos more

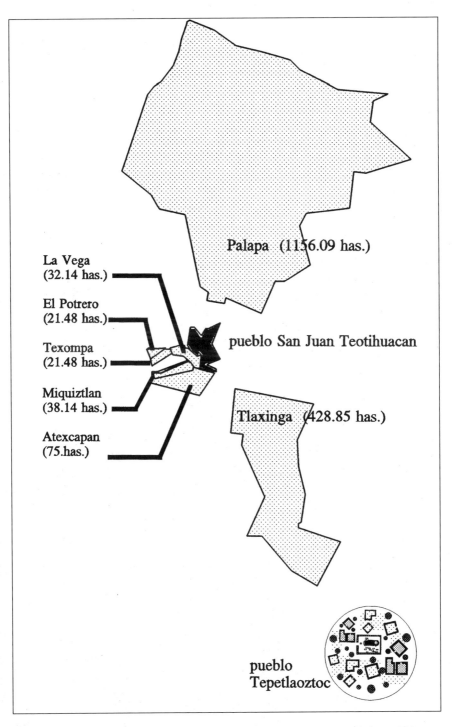

La Vega
(32.14 has.)

El Potrero
(21.48 has.)

Texompa
(21.48 has.)

Miquiztlan
(38.14 has.)

Atexcapan
(75.has.)

Palapa (1156.09 has.)

pueblo San Juan Teotihuacan

Tlaxinga (428.85 has.)

pueblo
Tepetlaoztoc

Map 16 The cacicazgo of Alva y Cortés de San Juan Teotihuacán in 1763

than enough. The Páez family had given the Indians sufficient money over the years. Apparently the peasants refused to give up their rights for this sum, because a new offer was made a few days later: besides paying the 100 pesos to Chalma, Don Diego would also give them a plot of land, and allow them the usufruct of a few fields of the cacicazgo, namely, the uncultivated land in the hills around the village. In addition, he offered the peasants of Chalma an attractive plot of land for twenty pesos. This time they accepted, cleared away the huts they had built on the land belonging to Páez and to the hacienda, and returned to their village. They then solemnly promised to relinquish their rights to a fundo legal and pledged themselves not to split up into more than one village. They also promised not to bother Don Diego in future. However, during the 1810 rebellion they would turn against him once again.[12]

Survivors

With the growth in the number of property rights of Indian pueblos, the trend indicated here resulted in considerable problems for the traditional landowning cacicazgos in the course of the eighteenth century. An example of such a cacicazgo is the one belonging to the Cortés Chimalpopoca family, which was already scattered among a good twenty ranchos and other small plots of land (*pedazos*) around the *villa* of Tacuba and the pueblo of Azcapotzalco (Tacuba province) in 1708 (see Map 15). This cacicazgo was described as typical, and as one of the most impoverished, by Gibson. He even claims that the cacicazgo lordship "had little meaning beyond family pride in the conditions of the late colony."[13] I tend to disagree concerning this last point, for the family still wielded influence in the villages precisely because they were caciques: thus, Don José Cortés Chimalpopoca was still gobernador of Tacuba. All the same, the history of this specific cacicazgo in the eighteenth century is dominated by the numerous legal disputes between the members of the family involving the rights of inheritance on the various ranchos, which were so typical during that time. Toward the end of the eighteenth century, a descendant of this family became so poor that he ended up as an ordinary Indian on the tribute list; only briefly, however, because he managed to have his descent confirmed and thus win back his privileges by law.

Nevertheless, a cacique could have considerable land under his control. The cacicazgo of the Alva y Cortés family, near San Juan Teotihuacán, encircling the famous pyramids northeast of Mexico City, was still sizable in the eighteenth century (see Map 16).[14] The area was not even one-quarter of the size of the province, but in 1763 the cacique still disposed of an area of 40.5 caballerías (1,725.23 hectares), worth 17,200 pesos. This was land that actually had passed into the possession of the caciques as estates, which were comparable to haciendas. The family also referred to haciendas, since according to them the cacicazgo consisted of the Tlaxinga, La Vega, and Palapa haciendas, as well as the Atezcapan, Miquiztlan, Texompa, and Tlapetoca ranchos. Most of these entities were wedged between the buildings in San Juan Teotihuacán and a few barrios. Some one thousand people lived on these estates. The cacique also had a hacienda and two ranchos, which did not belong to the cacicazgo, covering some 455.53 hectares. The cacique retained direct control of a few of these estates, but most of them were rented. The cacique's annual income from his cacicazgo was probably around eighteen hundred pesos, though he experienced the greatest difficulty in collecting his rent. There were constant problems with the pueblo of San Juan Teotihuacán, which had already obtained its fundo legal in 1695 and ever since had claimed an increasing number of rights. The cacique was able to put up a reasonable defense. Neither he nor his predecessors had exercised political influence in these villages.

I have not been able to find out how the rights of inheritance of the cacicazgo in Anáhuac were settled. That would require a close examination of all the documentation, including the different variants. The examples presented so far include cases of primogeniture, such as the case of Chimalpopoca and Alva y Cortés, but there were also cases of inheritance by a plurality of relatives, including cousins and brothers. Both the anthropology and the historiography of the European Middle Ages have shown that "families" need not necessarily always consist of direct biological kin. It is common for a family to incorporate a few outsiders into the household as "sons" or "daughters," especially in a period when the Personenverband is strong. Incidentally, the Personenverband terminology makes use of the terms *father, son, daughter, brother,* and so on. In a system in which primogeniture is dominant, it is thus possible for the oldest "son" to be a classificatory son rather than a biological one. The *patrón* of the family is then no more than a *primus inter pares*, like the medieval European nobles, who shared status and privilege with their lineage mates. Practices of this kind fall into disuse with the introduction of private ownership in the wake of the Territorialverband. Anthropologist Chance claims to have come across such traditional kinship patterns in the eighteenth-century Villa Alta in Oaxaca, and provides examples of the distribution of cacicazgo rights among diverse "brothers and sisters," with each individual receiving a portion for his or her own use. One cacicazgo was shared by a group of *primos* (cousins), all of whom received rent from macehuales who farmed part of the land. Although Chance suggests that this is different from the picture in the provinces of central Mexico, I prefer to see similarities with the picture sketched above, but I agree that much more research is needed. Without further information, it is difficult to determine just what sort of kinship groups existed among the Indian nobility of colonial Mexico.[15]

Of course, large aristocratic houses, with large numbers of biological or classificatory kin, were only to be found during periods when these families enjoyed a high status. This seems to have been increasingly less the case after the tribute reforms in the sixteenth century. Although the division of the estates was a general phenomenon, examples of the loss of status must be regarded as the exception rather than the rule: all gobernadores were caciques, precisely because of their status. We should therefore avoid making the old mistake of supposing that the demise of the cacicazgo meant the disappear-

ance of the caciques from the Indian world. In fact, as I suggested, a new
cacicazgo sprang up on the site of the demise of the old cacicazgo—in the
municipality itself! This was the result of the fundo legal, providing the pueblo
with lands outside cacicazgo rights.

After reviewing all of the documentation at hand, I begin to suspect that
the term of "gobernador" began to replace "cacique" in this respect. After all,
the rule was one gobernador per cabecera (pueblo-por-sí), or Indian headtown.
But there were 3 cabeceras in Tecali in 1800, for example, and 26 gobernadores
in addition to the 63 caciques. There were 6 cabeceras in the province of Puebla
at the time, but 35 gobernadores are listed along with the caciques already
mentioned. The same goes for western provinces: 40 cabeceras in Chalco
around 1800, but with 129 gobernadores; 19 cabeceras in Tacuba, but 82
gobernadores; 25 cabeceras in Texcoco, but 105 gobernadores; and 9 cabeceras
in Tula, with 49 gobernadores. Other figures are even more striking. There
were, for example, 18 cabeceras in the province of Metztitlán around 1800, but
277 gobernadores and no caciques. Or 7 cabeceras in Actopan and 71 gobernadores, with no caciques; 18 cabeceras in Malinalco and 40 gobernadores; 51
cabeceras in Tenango and 156 gobernadores. Or in the east, Acatlán had 10
cabeceras and 70 gobernadores; or there were 25 cabeceras in Tepeaca with
177 gobernadores and again no caciques. The exploration of the situation in
the provinces mentioned above suggests that the new cacicazgo was prepon-
derant, and with it the instrument available to them for the exercise of their
Herrschaft: the "gobernadoryotl," the exercise of the office of gobernador in
the pueblos.

The conclusion seems obvious. The Territorialverband was so successful
that caciques also had to turn to the residents of the pueblos, ranchos, or even
haciendas for their personal network of clients, and these were all residents of
territorial units. The new cacicazgo retained the characteristics based on personal loyalty, but on a much smaller scale and with much more modest claims.
As heir to the tlahtoque, the cacique had once been able to claim a demesne
of hundreds of Indian macehuales (vassals) in numerous settlements on the
basis of descent and "natural rule" (in this case, he was called *señor natural*),
and in this way, he could live from tribute revenue.[16] Before discussing the
principal elements of this new cacicazgo I wish to stress the fact that the transition from the first to the second kind of cacicazgo naturally occurred much
more gradually than this brief outline suggests. It is therefore possible that the
eighteenth-century caciques combined in themselves elements of the old
cacicazgo and the new cacicazgo.

In short, I find myself in disagreement with the tone of modern historical
research which suggests that the power of the caciques had come to an end.
As a result of the transition from Personenverband to Territorialverband, the
caciques were given a new look, or a new mask to hide the same old face. The
old-style aristocracy nearly died out, but the *institution* of cacicazgo reproduced itself, just as it was to do once more during the Mexican Revolution of
1910 (and probably also had done as a result of the Ley Lerdo in the nine-

teenth century). Each time, the *discourse of community* was borne by the same type of figure. It is the typical reaction of a traditional system of Herrschaft: under pressure from above (through legislation or government policy) ways were sought and bargains were struck to allow the traditional system to continue, with slight modifications in a modern form. Thus, in the eighteenth century, the caciques were no mirror of a distant past. It is precisely because of the capacity to reproduce itself that the Mexican cacicazgo is always modern, always typical of its time, and by definition, then, not exclusively traditional.

The Indian Governor

The Duties of the Gobernador

The cacicazgo made use of an official function of the Spanish administration: the Indian governor of the pueblos. To understand this, we have to turn to the precise juridical thinking of the time, which, by the way, was much stronger than it is now. The Spanish government only allowed cabeceras to call themselves full-fledged pueblos and to carry out their own administration in accordance with the basis of the legislation on the social orders (the repúblicas). The sujetos were under the authority of the cabecera, which was still called altepetl by the Indians themselves well into the eighteenth century.[17] Each "pueblo-por-sí" was supposed to be run by an elected gobernador, usually aided by a few assistants. They formed the village council (the *cabildo*, in accordance with Spanish usage). Without exception, the gobernadores in the Indian townships of Anáhuac were members of the cacique class. The gobernador controlled the use of all the communal lands, which were known as the *común*. According to the rules of play of the new cacicazgo, the control of the común was still in the hands of the caciques, even though such was the case only during their period of office. The land outside the común could be controlled by him as well, or be distributed among various families owning cacicazgo grants.

In one of his well-known annotated source publications, Luis Chávez Orozco referred to *instituciones democráticas*. There is the same danger of misunderstanding that we found in the case of Herbert Priestley's interpretation of the Bourbon Reforms (and Gálvez): the historian is eager to see something in the past that was probably only there on a limited scale, if at all. The gobernadoryotl cannot be discussed by using concepts from the nineteenth and twentieth centuries like democracy. It was an Indian adaptation of a Spanish administrative practice, connected with the traditional legislation on social orders and the Personenverband. Writing on the province of Cuernavaca, in the southern faldas of Anáhuac, Haskett comes to the conclusion that so much of the old hierarchical structure was still intact that the "power and authority of the . . . traditional ruling elite was . . . preserved rather than removed by the establishment of the cabildo system."[18] No doubt, this conclusion applies to all the provinces of Anáhuac. And its instrument was the gobernadoryotl.

What were the characteristics of the gobernadoryotl? Each year, as Christmas approached, a pueblo had to elect a new gobernador. It must be someone who had not held this office for three years. Initially, the pueblo was supposed to act without the intervention or supervision of the Spaniards, since an order is self-governing, in obedience to the crown. However, there were so many conflicts that during the Bourbon Reforms it was decided to assign the task of supervision to the subdelegado and the priest. Moreover, the crown wanted to supervise the expenditure of the caja de comunidad, the village treasury in which income from collective services and the tribute were deposited; it was to be used to pay the tribute, but the money disappeared in paying for village feasts. At this time, it was also decided that before the election of a governor the Indians first must put forward three candidates for approval. However, the letter of the law and its practice were not always the same thing: there simply were not enough Spanish officers in a province to supervise all of the elections under their jurisdiction. In such cases, the former practices were continued. The elections were originally held in the village hall of the pueblo (also known as the local community palace or *comunidadtecpan*) where the gobernador held sittings; later, they were held in the official premises of the subdelegado (the Casas Reales) in the capital of the province, or in the parish hall. In the event of conflicts between the leading families in the villages that supplied candidates, the provincial civil servants or the priests put up their own candidates, often in the framework of a reelection (which was prohibited). Of course, the case can be put in reverse, too: rival parties tried to win the support of the provincial officials or church administration for their bid for office. The priest's prerogatives, in this respect, were not done away with until 1803, but that did not mean that his influence in the village had been removed. The final approval—and authority to take decisions—rested with the viceregal cabinet, the Audiencia, which was supposed to scrutinize all the official election documents toward that end. The gobernadores and the other members of the cabildo received their insignia of office during a large village festival, the *feria de varas*, which was held around New Year.[19]

The interference by the Spanish officers in the late eighteenth century was sometimes a bone of contention between them. This can be illustrated with a case from the province of Zacatlán in the 1780s, when Don Manual Esteban Sánchez de Tagle was in control. It will be recalled that he had problems with the priest on the repartimiento trade and that he also ran into difficulties as a result of his unusual policy during the famine year. A popular tumulto led to an Audiencia inquiry into his rule, and in order to show that he had observed the rules of buen gobierno he sent the documents of a few cases in which he had championed the Indians' cause to Mexico City. One of these cases opened when two Indians, "caciques y principales" from San Andrés Hueytlalpan, reported to him on 20 January 1785, with the complaint that by now they had been obliged to carry out six years of service in the parish church as *fiscales de Santa Iglesia* (church stewards, the highest indigenous ecclesiastical officials in a pueblo—although pueblo boundaries were not always the same as parish boundaries). As a result of the manipulations of the priest, who kept on reinstating the incumbent gobernador, no elections had been held during all this time, and thus there had been no changes of office. They thought the time had come to be freed from their duties, and they were probably eager to assume a different position in the cabildo. They therefore stated that the village was fed up with the gobernador—of course he was called a "stranger," cruel, drunk, and despotic—and wanted to hold new elections. Their evidence was a document in Totonaco, dating from January 1783, written by four lower Indian officers from their pueblos sujetos, which showed that members of the común already had had enough of these practices two years earlier. The alcalde mayor ordered an investigation by the Indian gobernador of Zacatlán, who took enough statements from witnesses to convince him that the complaint was justified. Sánchez de Tagle summoned the priest to come to Zacatlán and to come up with three names of candidates for the position of gobernador, as well as a proposal for two new fiscales. The priest failed to comply, but since he sent a letter offering his excuses, Sánchez de Tagle considered himself authorized to hold new elections in the Casas Reales. They were held on 5 February 1785, remarkably soon after the date on which the Indians had lodged their complaint. He chose three candidates from the seventy-seven men in the común. Don Miguel Gabriel secured fifteen votes, Don Carlos Pérez twenty-one, and Don Antonio Bernabel forty-one. The latter received the official staff (vara), the insignia of all gobernadores and alcaldes, and could return to his township as gobernador.[20]

A year later, on 20 December 1786, problems occurred after the gobernador of Ahuacatlán had been reappointed for the umpteenth time by the priest. Some Indian nobles asked Sánchez de Tagle to summon the village's "caciques y principales" to their cabecera to hold an election independently of the priest. That could be done during the village feast, as in the past, because the priest would then be present to say mass. The priest offered his excuses; his letter to the alcalde mayor was not delivered as a result of a quarrel between neighbors involving the postman. When the election was finally held, the same names emerged as during the earlier elections in the priest's house. The común kept a level head. So did the "caciques y principales" of the cabecera of Zacatlán the following year, when they were confronted with a list of electoral candidates of whom they disapproved. Sánchez de Tagle had chosen one of them, Don Manuel Sánchez, as the number one candidate, an ex-gobernador for many years who had not held office for three years. The second was Don Joaquín de la Cruz, who had held every office at some time and had been fiscal mayor during the previous year, an office that Sánchez de Tagle regarded as "in fact equivalent to that of the gobernador." Number three was Don Simon de Huesca, who also had held every office at some time and whose last position had been alcalde, or barrio/sujeto official. The alcalde mayor considered them to be good candidates, but the majority of the común (thirty-three votes) chose Don Anastasio de la Cruz, who had never before held office. Sánchez de Tagle refused at first, because he regarded this man as leader of the tumulto in

1786, and claimed that he was ineligible because he saw him as a mulato. All the same, the común refused to give in, and Sánchez de Tagle had to back down. Moreover, the Audiencia investigation showed that De la Cruz was registered as an Indian.

It will be clear that the elections were fraudulent in our eyes. A group of prominent men met, so they claimed, and decided who was to be the new gobernador. There was little specific ballot-taking, since the Spanish inspectors did not insist on it unless there were conflicts and the case was brought before the Audiencia. Officially the gobernador was elected by the común de naturales. These, by no means, were all of the residents of a pueblo, but only those who had the voz activa y pasiva: the recognized "caciques y principales" of the pueblo and the former officers. According to the rules of the Personenverband, the aristocracy speaks on behalf of the people and is obedient to the monarch: the term macehuales in the documentation can be confusing. Since it often concerns documents addressed to the crown, the nobles presented themselves as "macehuales," the Nahuatl for vassals. Apart from the caciques, the "wise old men" of the village (huehuetque) could interfere in the elections, even if they were macehuales. Younger macehuales were excluded. In some cases, especially in the late eighteenth century, there were incumbent civil servants involved in the elections. All in all, this was a relatively small group. At the election held in Otumba in the valley of Mexico in 1775, 45 men (barely 8 percent) elected the gobernador of their community of 595 Indian households. Haskett estimated the corresponding figures for a number of pueblos in the province of Cuernavaca as follows: Cuernavaca 10 percent, Mazatepec 27 percent, Tetecala 14 percent, and Tepoztlán 7 percent.[21]

By law, a pueblo with less than 80 households of 100 Indians had the right to be represented by one alcalde, one regidor, and one fiscal; larger pueblos could have two of each office, with a maximum of two alcaldes, two fiscales, and four regidores. These were the so-called "higher offices," which were exclusively for "caciques y principales." This specific scheme, however, did not fit the practice of indigenous government, so that regional and local variants had already emerged in the sixteenth century. The problem was that two systems had to be combined: the Spanish cabildo tradition—for example, the formation of a town council made up of a finite number of elected officers— and the indigenous council of elders, a larger group of hierarchically selected rulers led by a cacique as primus inter pares. There seems to be a connection in eighteenth-century Anáhuac between the number of officers and the cabecera-barrios-sujetos proportions; "cabildo posts in Cuernavaca were apportioned among a town's internal subdivisions, wards, or districts," Haskett states.[22] The gobernador ran the pueblo, and I am positive that he appointed an assistant in every barrio and every sujeto. This choice would have been a compromise between the gobernador and the barrio or sujeto. An alcalde might have been the representative of one calpolli or tlaxilacalli, although it is not clear to me to what extent these unities survived into the eighteenth century. Although there are indications that some sujetos or barrios were allowed to appoint their own officer, the genuine elections were exclusively restricted to the officer of gobernador.[23] This mirrors full-fledged lordship.

There was plenty of variety. Summaries may be tedious to read, but since they can help one to understand the situation better, I shall present a summary of the cabildos in Tlalmanalco, a part of the province of Chalco, which was under the control of gobernador Don Salvador de Guzmán (we came across this figure in an earlier chapter) in 1722. In his proceedings against the alcalde mayor, he summoned all of the members of the cabildos under his jurisdiction to bear witness. Every village responded. In the following presentation of their cabildos, it should be borne in mind that *all* prominent men were described as "caciques y principales," with a couple of exceptions that I shall mention, and they often bore the same toponyms too. Temamatla and Metla each sent the current and the former alcaldes, as well as the *escribano*. Atlihuacan sent the current and the former alcaldes plus two caciques who did not hold any office. Zula sent the alcalde, a former fiscal and the escribano. Tlapale sent the alcalde and four caciques without office. Cocotitlán sent two alcaldes, one fiscal, the current escribano, and a former escribano. Huizilingo sent the alcalde, who stated that he previously had been escribano. Santos Reyes and San Lucas each sent two alcaldes. San Gregorio also sent two alcaldes, as well as the remarkable addition of two macehuales without office. The pueblo sujeto San Martín sent one alcalde and two regidores. Chalma—the demesne of the Páez family—sent one alcalde, one *teniente de alcalde,* and one former alcalde. Ozumba sent two alcaldes and one former alcalde. San Mateo Chalco sent one alcalde, three former alcaldes, one regidor, one ex-fiscal, one teniente alcalde, and one alguacil mayor. The pueblo of Xuchitepec sent the gobernador, three former gobernadores, three alcaldes and one former alcalde. Soyazingo sent the alcalde, three former alcaldes, three tenientes de alcalde, two former tenientes de alcalde, one regidor mayor, one former regidor mayor, the escribano, and his predecessor. Ayapango sent the alcalde, three former alcaldes, a former teniente de alcalde, the fiscal, and the escribano. Zentlalpan sent the alcalde, a former alcalde, two former regidores, one former fiscal, two former tenientes de alcalde, the current teniente de alcalde and the current regidor, who arrived later. The pueblo of Atlautla sent the gobernador, two former gobernadores, one regidor, and one escribano. The summary continues like this, with very many alcaldes and former alcaldes. An unusual place is occupied by the large pueblo of Amecameca, which sent a former gobernador, two former alcaldes, one *contado,* and five young macehuales who did not hold any office. The current gobernador was unable to attend because he was ill.[24] This example suggests that the cabildos were not exclusively manned by the official officers, but that ex-officers and some specific caciques played an active part in them as well. These men were called *pasados,* "former high-ranking officers."

I do not have any other comparative material of this kind, but I can provide a few election results. Of course, no details are provided on the other members, consisting of former officers (pasados), since it was only information on the official officers that was required. In Santiago Temoaya (Metepec) the new cabildo in 1740 consisted of a gobernador, Don Cayetano Cruz del Castillo, who, of course, was a cacique and had been in office for eight years; an alcalde; a regidor; an alguacil mayor; and an escribano. Don Cayetano was assisted by his son, Don Joseph Cruz, *teniente de gobernador.* The sujeto of San Lorenzo was represented in the cabildo by an alcalde and a regidor (the latter was not a cacique). The cabildo of Cuautinchán (Puebla) in 1756 was dominated by caciques from the Ximenes, Torres, and López families. Don Juan de Luna was the gobernador. The cabecera had an alcalde; a regidor; an alguacil mayor, who was sent as a representative to the Spanish authorities in Puebla; a *mayordomo mayor,* to lead a confraternity; a fiscal; and of course, the escribano. In addition, each of the seven barrios had its own regidor. According to the document, this cabildo was formed in consultation with the macehuales, who wanted more diversity in the council. These macehuales had probably been caciques or principales too—there were plenty of them in this village, from the same families, in fact—who were excluded from the común by the ruling faction. In San Juan Ahuacatlán (Zacatlán), the official cabildo in 1787 consisted of one gobernador, one alcalde, one regidor, one teniente de alcalde, one alguacil mayor, one fiscal, and one escribano. Two barrios and three pueblos sujetos each had one alcalde, one regidor, one teniente de alcalde and one alguacil mayor. Another barrio had only one teniente de alcalde and one alguacil mayor, and one pueblo sujeto had one regidor plus the teniente and alguacil mayor. In addition, there were three fiscales de Santa Iglesia, divided among these barrios and sujetos.[25]

In my opinion, the alcalde was the chief executive of the barrios or sujetos of the pueblo, the local representative of the gobernador or perhaps of the calpolli or tlaxilacalli constituting the barrios. The teniente de alcalde was his assistant. In addition, there were the regidores, based on the Aztec *huey calpixqui,* the economic managers. They performed general duties in the villages, such as the management of the municipal lands and funds, the regulation of the markets, the division of the repartimiento purchases, and the collection of tribute. A third office below the gobernador was that of the alguacil, the constable for secular and religious crimes, responsible for maintaining law and order, particularly during village festivals and elections. There was also an alguacil mayor, who performed similar duties on behalf of the pueblo or a group of pueblos in the Casas Reales of the Spanish officer of the province. The religious side was taken care of by the fiscal, also known as *alguacil de la Santa Iglesia* or fiscal mayor. Finally, another important "higher office" was that of the clerk of the pueblo, the *escribano de república,* who drew up electoral documents, wrote all declarations and petitions addressed to the Spanish officers or the Audiencia, and acted as interpreter (sometimes in addition to an official interpreter) in court proceedings. This man, the successor to the preconquest *tlacuilo,* or pictorial draughtsman, was knowledgeable about legal procedure and the rights and obligations of the Indians, and thus was of inestimable value. It is therefore understandable that some escribanos held positions in the cabildo all their lives.

In addition to the higher offices, there were a few lower positions intended for the younger members of the cacique kinship groups to learn the profession, or even for ordinary macehuales. The one that appears most often in the sources is the topile, a constable, who was sent to the Casas Reales of the alcalde mayor or subdelegado. It was his duty to apprehend criminals on the orders of alcaldes or gobernadores. Thus he was in the service of the Spanish authorities, and directly subordinate to the alguacil mayor. Assistants of this kind made their appearance in the preceding chapter in the household of Chalco's alcalde mayor, Díez de Palacios. They actually had *no* function in the townships themselves. This is one reason for viewing the many alguaciles mayores in Ahuacatlán (Zacatlán) as an exception. I suspect that only the alguacil mayor of the cabecera actually functioned in that capacity, and that the others were sent as a team of topiles to work in the Casas Reales. In addition to these lower civil offices, there were the *teopantopiles* or tenientes de fiscal, who did the same under the authority of the fiscal in the church. Also there was the *alcalde carcelero*, the jailer of the pueblos, who had plenty of work to do because men and women were continually being arrested by Indian officers.

Since there was a close connection between the collection of tribute and the possession of land by the Indian pueblos, it was in the interest of the gobernadores to ensure that this landownership was respected. Indeed, I believe, as indicated before, that without the fundo legal "explosion" this transition toward gobernadoryotl would not have occurred. The gobernadores managed the village treasury and collected the tribute: 1 peso per tributario per annum, plus ½ *real de ministros* (to pay the legal aides of the Juzgado de Indios); ½ fanega of maize, or its money equivalent; money for the hospitals; and *teopantequitl,* or "God's housework" to be paid to the parish church. They were also empowered to allocate the plots of land that the tributarios were given the right to use. The level of the tribute was usually above the legally determined norm. The gobernadores were expected to balance their books, and deficits had to be made up out of their own pocket (as was always the case with positions in the civil service during this era). They asked for a higher tribute in the village to build up a reserve fund. Since the gobernadores made the contracts with the alcaldes mayores, the situation was similar with regard to the repartimiento trade. Although many gobernadores went bankrupt during their term in office, it will be clear that the extra contributions from the tributarios ended up in the private savings of the caciques and were not repaid. This attractive incidental circumstance made the office of gobernador suitable for the accumulation of capital.[26]

In dealing with this characteristic, we should not forget to refer to the credo "*in pochotl in ahuehuetl,*" or "like silk cotton trees or cypress giving shade," mentioned earlier. The gobernador had to ensure the continuance of low market prices in periods of scarcity during his term of office and to guarantee a fair distribution of the available resources in the Indian pueblos. His duties also included keeping the market squares clean and maintaining roads and bridges. He could summon the villagers to carry out unpaid collective labor in the community's interest (*faenas*). He was also expected to prevent the residents of the municipality from neglecting their own agricultural land. Drunkards and layabouts could count on a reprimand and sanctions. Every Sunday or holy day the gobernador greeted his subjects at the church door, and he was expected to visit those who were not there and urge them to go. Of course, he was not allowed to force the villagers to perform faenas for his own ends or to benefit from his function in any other way, but this happened all the same. His powerful position lent itself eminently for abuse, or as a way of maintaining nobility.

The latter concern was certainly not unusual. Let us consider a Spanish example from the Andalusian *Aljarafe Sevillano*. The villages in this rural district to the west of Sevilla had their own village council in the seventeenth and eighteenth centuries, led by an alcalde mayor or gobernador—the same terminology as in New Spain. There were also regidores, an *escribano de cabildo*, and alcaldes. Some were in charge of the confraternities. There were also other minor offices, varying from village to village. The interesting point to emerge from this comparison with the hinterland of Sevilla is that this district was dominated by secular lordships (*señoríos seculares*). Here, too, the villages were part of a manorial structure. Here, too, the annual elections in the villages, which were held around New Year, were also dominated by a small group of villagers, including the more well-to-do, but the gobernador or alcalde mayor was *appointed* by the local lord. Only the minor offices were filled by "free elections" in the villages. However, in view of the tradition of appointments of gobernadores by the local nobles, it is hardly surprising that in their colonies the Spaniards allowed the caciques to appoint the officers in their jurisdictions, the pueblos.[27]

Though village officers were appointed by nobles, or, if not, directly by royal government, they always represented the wealthier families in the community everywhere in Europe. Several examples can be given, but I will restrict myself to that of seventeenth-century Entraigues, a village southeast of Grenoble and at the foot of the French Alps, described by Keith Luria—where two families stood out as antagonists.[28] The village assembly and communal offices were dominated by a handful of families. When they cooperated, the village displayed its solidarity despite whatever dissension may have existed between them and the powerless below, but when they clashed, the community suffered deep internal divisions. And this happened. Each of the two families must be considered not just as a household but as an economic enterprise, a political faction, and—writes Luria—a locus of cultural production for the village. Their rivalry endured at least three generations. Each successive *chef de famille*, generally the oldest male, took on the family feud as he took on responsibility for the family patrimony and the main house, which was the symbol of family continuity over the years. As the wealthiest, the two families sat atop a village social structure similar to that of many communities in the area. The social distinctions here were not based strictly on wealth, however, and the family competitiveness was not restricted to the economic realm, for political position and cultural contact with the outside world were often as important in determining the community leaders. Not surprisingly, the assembly was very selective in choosing its consuls, the chief executive of the village: between 1641 and 1703 only eighteen families provided consuls, and certain individuals held the post frequently. And of course, the elite manipulated village politics for advantage over their poorer, less-powerful neighbors.

To return to Anáhuac, we can now understand that the offices in the pueblos rotated among a few related families of noble origins. The Spanish state repeatedly instructed the alcaldes mayores to be on their guard for abuse and to declare such elections null and void, but many alcaldes mayores, and later the subdelegados, had an interest in keeping on good terms with the local caciques because of their involvement in the repartimiento trade, so that the Spanish state was powerless to do anything about abuses. Besides, it should not be forgotten that people were used to "appointments" in this field.[29] The prohibition on reelection was therefore widely ignored; in fact, reelection was the rule. Still, we should also consider the Aztec tradition, where the tlahtoani held his position for life. A prohibition on reelection was at odds with pre-Hispanic traditions. In 1754, Haskett notes, a governor of Cuernavaca even went so far as to claim that the governorship was his by right of inheritance! Of course, the monopoly of the gobernadoryotl in the hands of a few families generated conflicts with other families or with newcomers (nouveaux riches). Haskett describes the case of the cacique Don Antonio Hinojosa, gobernador of Cuernavaca for nineteen years in the late seventeenth century, seventeen of which were consecutive. Chance noted that Cayetano de Tovar, cacique of Tecali, was "reelected" for the ninth time in 1734. Tutino describes heavy factional conflict between caciques in Otumba and Acolman. It is possible to refer to large numbers of similar cases. Consider Don Vicente Toquet, who had been in office for eleven years (1747–58) in Malinalco. Toquet's subjects were particularly annoyed by the fact that he had received 150 pesos each year from the Jesuits in the Hacienda Xalmolonga for the village festival, although he had only organized one feast in the course of these eleven years. Toquet also asked each tributario for four reales more than usual, and he had never held elections. In combating such cases, their opponents resorted to descriptions of the clique in power as mestizos, mulatos, or Spaniards; drunkards, layabouts, or dictators; or as macehuales contesting the cacique descent of the incumbent gobernador. Elections were also declared null and void because, it was alleged, the electoral college did not consist of all of the caciques, but of macehuales, non-Indians, and others as well. All of these allegations were hard to corroborate. The important factor was whether there was still enough support for the ruling families. Factional strife, however, could also go down the wrong way with the rest of the villages. Sometimes opposition groups stayed away from the electoral meeting, so there was no quorum. In Tepoztlán (Cuernavaca), the factional strife was so endemic around 1725 that a third group of current and former officers organized itself and attempted to take control of the villa's council.[30]

The governors of the pueblo of Almoloya (Apan) were summoned to court by their opponents in 1786 on the grounds that they were not eligible for office because they were regarded as mulatos. Witnesses appearing on behalf of the complainant claimed that the incumbent gobernador, Juan Hernández, described as a mulato, had once been employed as a shepherd in the Hacienda Nanacamilpa, and that he was married in the village to an Indian commoner from the Sánchez family. The alcalde Felipe Neri, a charcoal burner (carbonero) by profession, was also seen as a mulato from Tlaxcala; he, too, was married to an Indian woman, who came from the Martínez family. The regidor Ignacio Juan was the son of a black, or so they said. The members of the Sánchez family were alleged to stem from blacks in the female line, with the family name Crespin Zapatero. The plaintiffs added that there had never been caciques in Almoloya, and that the persons in question were simply registered on the tribute list. Since 1778, however, the Sánchez, Martínez, and Avila families, to which the individuals mentioned above belonged, had suddenly presented themselves as caciques and demanded the corresponding rights from the tributarios, large sums of money in particular. In addition, they had connived with the priest, who was supposed to have made a false statement, to gain control of the gobernadoryotl. They had deprived the Indians in the village of their fields to distribute them among their relatives and other "mulatos." The Juzgado ordered an investigation of the case and concluded that the plaintiffs were in the right. The mulato in-migrants, who did not pay any tribute, were expelled from office and the fields were redistributed among local Indians.[31]

Tensions between a number of cacique families were common in practically every pueblo, even though these families had acquired mutual interests through judicial marriages. For example, in Tutotepec, a Tepehua community in the green faldas of the province of Tulancingo, the leading families around 1800 were the Tolentinos and the Guzmáns, who held office as gobernador in turns, alternating regularly. The two families were connected through arranged marriages, but they lived in different neighborhoods. Nevertheless, there were still conflicts, especially over debts owed to the village treasury and the division of the village lands. Feelings ran high on 13 and 14 April 1803, when the ex-gobernador Don José Guzmán was accused of letting the neighborhood of the current gobernador, Don Juan Tolentino, his father-in-law, burn down. A total of thirty-seven houses went up in flames. The subdelegado's deputy had to get to the bottom of the matter, but he only managed to find two potential culprits: Don José Guzmán, who could not specify where he was at the moment that the fire broke out—he claimed to be on the way from a liquor store which he had left at 20 hours to reach the wake of his uncle, where he arrived fifteen minutes later—and Cristina Toledo, the daughter of the sitting gobernador, who was believed to have had an argument with a lover and dropped a torch that she had carried to be able to see in the dark. Although both suspects denied the charges, the subdelegado initiated proceedings against the ex-gobernador at the instigation of Tolentino. When the Audiencia decided that there was not enough evidence to substantiate the charge, he initiated proceedings against Cristina at Guzmán's instigation, but the Audiencia eventually decided that there was not enough evidence for that either. In the end the two fighting cocks came to an agreement because there was no solid evidence for the arson and because further proceedings would have to be held before the Audiencia, which would involve both caciques in considerable expense. Don Juan Tolentino was prepared to pay one hundred pesos in compensation to his rival because the latter was obliged to go and live in Tulancingo at a certain point in the year, because his family was menaced by the Tolentinos. Guzmán accepted the proposal, though I doubt whether it actually put an end to the conflict or the feud. At any rate, Cristina would have been put through a grilling by her father for what she had been up to with the anonymous young man. In the meantime, the Tolentino neighborhood was rebuilt with the assistance of joint labor and tribute exemption.[32]

The rivals in San Esteban Axapusco (Otumba) were less prepared to forgive and forget. A small number of families waged a bitter struggle for power there from 1737 until 1778, with a peak period in the 1750s. Sometimes it came to blows, but, in most cases, the conflict was fought out in court with allegations of electoral fraud, embezzlement of community funds, and extreme favoritism in the allocation of land. The climax was reached after the alcalde mayor received a letter of protest on behalf of the común on 14 June 1755, calling for new elections because the present gobernador, Don Juan Santos, had been postponing them for years. The day for holding elections was approaching—they were always held in the month of July in this municipality—and this time it should not be allowed to pass by unnoticed. The request was considered correct, and after a meeting of the común Don Diego Antonio López was presented with the gobernador's rod, with Don Andrés Antonio López as his alcalde. Don Juan Santos refused to comply with the transfer of power. He had taken all of the documents home, including the accounts. The municipal treasury was empty. A few months later, however, in February 1756, it was Don Diego Antonio López's turn to refuse to hold elections. Don Juan Santos had begun using the tribute for the construction of a village church, and now the opponents of the new gobernador claimed that work on the construction had stopped the previous July. They accused the López family of being out to fill their own pockets. All the same, the elections were duly held in July, resulting in the election to office of another member of the family, Don Felipe de Jesús López, while Don Andrés Antonio López was reelected as alcalde. They received their insignia of office at the beginning of August. Fresh complaints about the neglect of elections came in February 1758. This time the authorities ignored the request to intervene, as they now would have realized that July was the appropriate month.[33]

The following year, however, they could not ignore a complaint. Elections were held in July 1759 by the sitting gobernador, who was still Don

Felipe de Jesús López, after many complaints in the village, but no consensus, as four of the thirteen members of the común abstained in protest; the nine other members were all relatives of the gobernador. His opponents accused López not only of fraud in the accounts and similar malpractices, but also of squandering the village income from the pulque trade. And that was important! There were five *maguey ranchos* in Axapusco, which usually provided pulque to the Spanish retailer Don Bernardo Ximenes for 2 pesos per carga. The gobernador, however, had rented out the ranchos at a rate of 1p5 per carga, resulting in a loss of a good 20 percent, or 3 reales per carga. The 3 reales disappeared in the tenant farmer's pocket. Moreover, soon after that, the pulque was no longer supplied to Don Bernardo, which endangered the security of a retail outlet. In addition, the gobernador had not deposited the rent received from 1340 cargas, or 2180 pesos, in the village treasury. In September, the alcalde mayor of Cuautitlán was asked to investigate the case, because the alcalde mayor of Otumba was not considered to be impartial. This investigatory judge found the complaint justified, took away the gobernador's rod of office, and banished him from the village for a time to prevent him from being given the opportunity of intimidating the witnesses. After detailed consultations, it was decided to transfer the rod of office to Don Esteban de Santiago, an influential cacique in the village, both as interim gobernador and as gobernador for the following year as well, since the elections were due. The contract to rent out the ranchos was declared null and void and the former situation was restored. But that was not the end of the story: the López family settled in the neighboring cabecera of Otumba and assumed power there in the 1780s, together with their allies, the Vázquez family.[34]

These problems were confined to the cabecera, but most of the complaints about the policy of the gobernadores came from the pueblos sujetos. An example from the province of Yahualica in the northeastern faldas indicates how many obligations they had to meet. The townships of Pachiquitla and Istaesoquico complained in 1790 that they both had to pay extra duties to the gobernador of Yahualica in excess of the accepted fixed sum of 162 pesos. The standard tribute here consisted of 60p to the crown, first *tercio* in April; 5p to the crown, ½ real de ministros, in April; 60p to the crown, second tercio in August; 5p to the crown, ½ *real de hospital*, in August; 20p *tequitzontli*, traditional right to the gobernador in December; 12p *solteros* to the crown and *tequiz* to the gobernador. The barrios of the pueblos paid 90, 90, and 50 pesos respectively, in three tercios. In addition, the gobernador received one further real per tributario for the tribute census, including tributarios who had died; the money that the village paid for them disappeared in the gobernador's pocket. The gobernador ordered very many faenas in the cabecera, which seemed pointless to the sujetos and barrios. He also demanded two *indios leñeros* (they were topiles) each week to gather charcoal, two *indias molenderas* for the meals in the gobernador's kitchen, and two pesos' worth of maize, usually two fanegas. Each new gobernador who assumed office had to be welcomed with a feast, paid for by the tributarios, and during his year in office he paid visits to each of the pueblos, which also had to be paid for by the tributarios. These were heavy burdens on the barrios and sujetos of a cabecera and pro-voked irritation, above all, because the caciques lived well from the proceeds and hardly showed their faces to the sujetos at all.[35]

There were similar protests by sujetos in other provinces as well. Up to 1755, the tributarios of San Mateo Mexicaltzingo had been accustomed to give the gobernador twenty-six pesos and fourteen turkeys on his assumption of office, and they considered that to be plenty. This was followed by a trans-fer of three pesos and no further donation in kind for three years in succes-sion. The new gobernador asked for the traditional donation, which was prohibited. In 1758, the cacique Don Pedro de Santiago had been governing Los Reyes Zapotitlán (Tehuacán) for five years without taking any notice of the cabildo. Thus the cabildo had no elected gobernador. A protest against this state of affairs was made by the current alcalde, Don Eugenio Ventura; two former alcaldes who had also served as fiscales; an ex-regidor mayor; a former teniente de fiscal; an ex-regidor; and an ex-alcalde of a barrio; as well as an ex-teniente de fiscal and two ex-regidores from the same barrio. The protest was joined by a former *mandón*, a low-ranking officer, and the former mayordomo of a local rural confraternity. Zapotitlán had seceded in 1753 and so had the right to a cabildo and a gobernador of its own. This secession was followed by problems with another cacique in San Martín Zapotitlán (1753). The village population there had also joined the protest by electing a shadow cabildo in secret, in the house of a third cacique who subsequently tried to obtain legitimacy from the alcalde mayor in Tehuacán.[36]

Confusion arose as soon as the question of juridical competence became unclear. Exemplary was the argument between the alcalde mayor of Zempoala and the gobernador of Otumba concerning the jurisdiction in the pueblo sujeto of Santiago Tepeyahualco. Tepeyahualco was in the province of Otumba, and therefore the preserve of the alcalde mayor of that province and of the Indian gobernador of Otumba as a pueblo sujeto for administrative purposes. How-ever, as far as the religious administration was concerned, the villagers be-longed to the parish (*doctrina*) of neighboring Zempoala, which was also a separate province. Of course, the gobernador stated that he had the right to appoint an alcalde for Tepeyahualco; the alcalde was never elected. He only visited the sujeto in person to collect tribute and to get drunk at the annual feast. On 25 July 1731, the day of the Tepeyahualco village festival, Don Diego Antonio, the gobernador of Otumba, therefore hastened to his subordinate in Tepeyahualco, Don Pascual de la Cruz, the alcalde. After he had arrived, he first asked the alcalde to arrest a muleteer who had fled to the mountains behind the village. The reports of what happened next are contradictory. The gobernador's story is that the alcalde mayor of Zempoala turned up at that moment and remarked that Don Diego Antonio did not have the right to issue such an order. The Spanish officer then swore at him, hit him with a stick, and finally clapped him in irons and sent him to Zempoala to let him cool off in a cell there. The alcalde mayor's version was that he found Don

Diego Antonio dead drunk when he arrived. Don Diego came up to him and shouted at him to disappear, because the village did not belong to the jurisdiction of Zempoala. Since he was waving about dangerously with his rod of office (his vara), the alcalde mayor thought it best to confine the gobernador to a cell for the night. This was no sooner said than done, and the gobernador was allowed to return the next day after he had slept off his hangover. The alcalde mayor explained that he had come to Tepeyahualco because of his concern about the scanty observance of law and order during village festivities. Instead of preventing excessive drinking, the alcaldes and gobernadores simply joined in. He had come to Tepeyahualco to put a stop to all that. The alcalde mayor considered himself justified in taking this measure, because the village belonged to the doctrina of Zempoala and he saw no difference between church and state. The Audiencia did see a difference, however, and reprimanded the alcalde mayor: drunk or not, the gobernador was within his rights.[37]

Another interesting example was that of Atlacomulco (Metepec-Ixtlahuaca), where gobernadoryotl and cacicazgo more or less collided literally with one another. In the last decennia of the seventeenth century, they coincided in the persons of the Los Angeles caciques, who held the gobernadoryotl for three generations. The last cacique and gobernador of this dynasty was Don Nicolás de los Angeles, who died in 1698 without a son or male heir. In addition to the común of Atlacomulco, he also controlled a few ranchos (often a sign that cacicazgo land was at stake) and the Hacienda Santo Domingo Xomejé. This hacienda was probably not a part of the cacicazgo, because the land was worked by gañanes, while groups of terrazgueros lived on the ranchos. Like the gañanes,[38] the terrazgueros worked a maximum of three days a week on the land of their *dueño*. The legal heir to this property was the daughter of the cacique, Doña Leonor de los Angeles, but she had forfeited the property through her recent marriage to Don Gaspar de Ona y Osores, who was regarded by everyone as a Spaniard. Neither he nor his children could therefore claim the cacicazgo, but his wife's terrazgueros recognized him as their *dueño,* and the ranchos remained under his control.[39]

However, he ran up against opposition from Atlacomulco. After the death of Don Nicolás de los Angeles, the alcalde mayor had appointed his opponent, Don Alonso de Aranda, as interim gobernador. In doing so, he was exceeding his jurisdiction, but this did not have any direct repercussions. More important, Don Alonso claimed to represent the pueblo in demanding the ranchos from Don Gaspar. He argued that the ranchos were nothing but pueblos sujetos and therefore came under the gobernadoryotl of himself, Don Alonso, as they had been his predecessor's, the late Don Nicolás. This demand created confusion about what belonged to the cacicazgo and what belonged to the común, and eventually even about whether the cacicazgo existed at all. No one had documents to prove ownership of the lands, so the final verdict lay in the statements of the terrazgueros. On such occasions first the use right was paramount and second the jurisdictional power: who actually worked the land

and to whom was the tribute paid? There were only difficulties for one of the ranchos. During an investigatory visit (*vista de ojos*) in 1700 by all the parties concerned in the land dispute, the procession was met on the rancho by a group of Indians ringing an old church bell and carrying a religious icon. They stated that they stood six hundred varas from their old church—some ruins were to be seen in the background—and they lived now in a neighboring barrio of Atlacomulco. After an epidemic, the ancestors of these Indians had left the spot to start a new life in the barrio, and they had taken their church bell and icon with them, so that the village still survived at a symbolic level. Now their descendants demanded the restoration of their traditional village rights.

This was a thorny problem because many villages had been abandoned like this during the epidemics in the sixteenth and seventeenth centuries, followed by a plowing, appropriation, rental or purchase of the land by caciques, hacendados, or other pueblos. Were the former residents still entitled to their rights? The Audiencia was not convinced, and ruled in favor of Don Gaspar in this case. Later, when Don Alonso was deposed in 1701 by a group of rival caciques, it turned out that he had organized this action with the church bell and religious icon to get his own way. The people from the barrio had proved willing to cooperate, to the great annoyance of the actual residents of the rancho concerned. After the demise of Don Alonso, the cat was let out of the bag: it was not land that was at dispute, but the tribute rights of the terrazgueros. Don Alonso sent the Indians under his authority to the silver mines in El Oro to pay their tribute obligation in labor. The terrazgueros from the ranchos belonging to the Los Angeles family came in handy for his gobernadoryotl, but they refused to cooperate. They knew that Don Gaspar would spare them this labor obligation and had therefore recognized him as their dueño, even though he was a Spaniard. The situation was confirmed by the Audiencia. I suspect that the terrazgueros considered as servants in the service of Don Gaspar, who advanced their tribute, were later registered as gañanes. After all, the cacicazgo belonging to Gaspar's wife had now become ordinary property, belonging to the Spanish order, and would undoubtedly be registered as such during the composiciones of the 1710s. Don Alonso de Aranda had lost his powerful position by now, although he threatened to hold on to the gobernadoryotl, with the assistance of the alcalde mayor, until 1706; but he made his threat in vain.

In a few places, the caciques of real or supposed mestizo background were able to maintain their position only by terror, particularly if the caciques had lost control over their pueblo's government. Naturally enough, terrorism of this kind led to a miserable situation and brought them in conflict not only with the gobernadores, but with the local macehuales as well. An example is provided by Tecomate, an Otomi village in the province of Tetepango. Tomasa Gertrudis López, a "mestiza" from Tecomate, applied in desperation to the alcalde mayor of Tetepango on 17 July 1778. At the time, the alcalde mayor could not have had any inkling of what a courageous step this was. Her charges against Marcelo Serón, his wife Petrona Bravo, and his mother Augustina Cervantes revealed an unprecedented tyranny. After a thorough investigation had been conducted, it transpired that a cacique family had exercised a reign of terror for years over one of the villages in the province of Tetepango, the arid area northwest of Mexico City.[40] The reaction in the village was encouraging. The villagers must have been struck by the novelty of a complaint against one of the Seróns. The action created quite a stir in the village. The first to help Tomasa was the village gobernador. He decided to support her charges by preferring charges himself against Pedro Serón, Marcelo's father, and against his sons—Marcelo, José, Pablo, Gabriel, and Antonio—of disturbing the peace in the village. To present them in an even more unfavorable light he referred to them as "Spaniards." The Seróns still worked part of the village land without paying tribute or exercising an office. The gobernador would have liked to take it away from them, on the grounds that they should relinquish their land if they did not want Indian status. The alcalde mayor compounded these charges with those brought by Tomasa and sent both dossiers, written on sealed and bound government paper, to his deputy in the village of Mixquiahuala.

Most of the villagers now followed the lead of the gobernador and deposited charges. They all stated that they were so afraid of the Seróns that they had not dared to undertake any action before. They had let the Seróns do as they pleased from fear of being beaten up. The gobernador said that the family worked land belonging to the village without paying tribute. The failure to pay tribute meant that the Seróns were no longer Indians, even though his wife enjoyed cacique rights, and should therefore be obliged to give up their land. The series of complainants listed a number of grievances. Don Marcelino de la Cruz, for example, had been beaten up by Pablo Serón two years earlier in 1776, when he was gobernador of Tecomate. He was working in his cactus field, not far from the Serón farm. Pablo first called out, rather exuberantly: "A Dios, hombre!" Taken aback, Marcelino replied in the same way. Then, Pablo Serón came up to him and said: "Aren't you the one who doesn't want to be called *hombre*? Well, just see what we do to people like that, you son of a bitch." Pablo then seized a piece of wood and beat Marcelino about the head and chest. Twelve days after the first complaints, Pedro Augustin, another Indian of the village, stated how he had been beaten up only a month earlier. He showed the investigating magistrate his scars and managed to hand over a knife, a belt—with which he had been beaten—and a handkerchief belonging to Pablo Serón as evidence. Pablo had left these belongings behind after his savage attack. The motive for the assault this time was the warm way in which Pedro Augustin had taken leave of a boy in Pablo's company. Pablo had exclaimed in rage: "What kind of a leavetaking is that, as if he were a woman?" During the fight Pablo had pulled his knife, but it had been taken away from him by the rest of the bystanders. After Pablo had dealt his opponent a blow in the head with a stone, he was shocked at the blood, got up, and ran off.

These were serious charges and required thorough investigation. It was an unusual occurrence. The Audiencia would have to be informed. At any rate, Pedro Serón was arrested and detained for a long period. In any event, he was not to be released before the trial. The deputy and the alcalde mayor himself were unable to arrest his sons or his wife, the real caciques in the village, who apparently had realized what was coming and fled. Pedro denied all the charges. The alcalde mayor decided to confiscate Pedro's sons' property to induce them to give themselves up, but when he reached the family house he came across Petrona Bravo, Marcelo's wife, acting as babysitter. He left what the women needed out of pity for the young children, but he confiscated the remaining articles and the livestock. Then the Juzgado de Indios was called in, where a clerk compiled a summary of the case. However, a Juzgado official soon noticed that the court was already dealing with the case between the Seróns and the gobernador on the question of the use of the village land. The charges against the Seróns cast new light on this matter, and the Juzgado judges asked the viceroy to allow them to deal with the case. The alcalde mayor of Tetepango was instructed to send the dossier to the Juzgado within six days, and he promptly complied with the request. That is the end of the dossier. No doubt the alcalde mayor sent the dossier, and the magistrates of the Juzgado de Indios proceeded to deal with this dossier at the same time as the other matter already under investigation. In view of the position adopted by the magistrates in other cases, there can be no doubt that the Serón family would be severely punished and deprived of its powerful position in the village. In such cases, the magistrates usually decided to enforce banishment.

The example of another political game with the Spanish authorities in the province of Huayacocotla (north of the valley of Puebla), which involved the election of Miguel Mérida as gobernador, was introduced in the preface of this book. We have also come across the revolt of the Chocho pueblo Toxtepec against the caciques of the Nahua cabecera of Santiago Tecali. Toxtepec's desire to manage its own affairs had already been voiced in the sixteenth century. With that aim in mind, the Chochos requested a merced, in 1545, to obtain land in ownership. That was a very unusual step to take at the time, making them one of the first sujetos to dispute the right of the caciques to the land. The caciques' response to the claims of the Chochos from Toxtepec was one of brutal violence in 1547, 1560, 1562, and 1567. In 1562 they even pastured their livestock in the milpas of the sujetos.[41] The violent conflict of 1734 indicates that the aggravation did not stop in those days and had even escalated. And to conclude, the Huasca case was also introduced in the preface. Every investigator is intrigued by a case that does not comply with the general picture. Of course, such cases also raise doubts in the mind of the researcher and force him to check the evidence once more and to scrutinize the arguments against the documentation. It often happens that such cases turn out to be the exceptions that prove the rule. The Huasca case was such a case, in which the request by the newly elected gobernador of Huasca Zaloya, the young Lazaro Antonio Huerta, was discussed. The striking fact was that he asked *not* to be obliged to assume office! In the end, a new candidate, Don

Luis Paulino Pérez del Castillo, did accept the *cargo* on the explicit condition that he would be held exclusively accountable for the Indians on the new list, and not for the others who owned a house in Huasca, but were never there or were exempt.

The Común Repartimiento

It is clear from a number of examples presented so far that the distribution of the municipal plots could affect the legitimacy of the gobernador. In this task and duty, he was more or less a replica of the traditional tlahtoani because he used the pueblo as a means of gaining access to land use for his kinship group. The tlahtoani gave his subjects—who were divided into calpollis and tlaxilacalli—the use right to land in return for tribute; the gobernador did the same to the tributarios in the pueblo. The land available for redistribution in this way was referred to as *tierras de común repartimiento* until late in the eighteenth century.

The land of the común was intended for distribution among the residents of a pueblo, but that was not necessarily the only land under Indian plows. Some common Indians also had land that did not belong to the común, including ranchos and other private plots of land. The town of Tlatelolco on the margin of Mexico City even owned a hacienda, the Hacienda Santa Ana Aragón. Some land outside the fundo legal was earmarked for collective, municipal tribute payment and filling the municipal treasury. The Spaniards referred to such land as propios, and assumed, by analogy with the situation in Spain, that they were rented. A number of Indian pueblos worked the extra land themselves, under the direction of a gobernador or even a Spanish alcalde mayor. Each cabecera in New Spain was expected to control such propios, but this was not the case in the highlands of Anáhuac, with the exception of the cities and a number of cabeceras, above all in the semiarid provinces. However, there were situations in which plots of the fundo legal or composiciones had been rented to outsiders, although this practice was illegal. When the Indian pueblos wanted to regain these plots of land in the eighteenth century, they had no difficulty in gaining the support of the legal authorities.[42]

All the same, for most of the tributarios the land within the fundo legal was of primary importance. The allocation was taken care of by the gobernadores. Because it led to a good many problems, a large number of cases are documented. No research has yet been conducted on the allocation procedure; research of that kind is extremely labor-intensive and complex, which probably explains why it has scared scholars away so far. The main point at issue in these cases is that of deciding whether the land belonged to the común or not; only in the first case did the gobernador have control of it. My preliminary sallies in the documentation indicate that the procedure for the allocation of land in the villages was a source of continual tension between peasants and gobernadores, as well as between rival caciques and their clients. Nevertheless, the basic rule was clear enough: every head of family who paid tribute had the right to a plot of land from the común. By law the fields were supposed to be divided into plots of equal size, but in practice the quality of the soil had to be taken into account, so that fields with good soil were smaller than those with poor soil. The incumbent gobernadores were allowed to work an extra field as compensation for their activities on behalf of the community—a vestige of the labor services from the time of the tlahtoanate.[43]

Allocation of village plots was usually carried out in the spring, after the maize harvest had been completed. The plots of land were then used as stubble fields for the livestock for a short period, but once the time came to sow the following crop, each peasant went off to work on the plot allocated to him. It was possible, however, to refuse plots. In Calimaya and Tepamaxalco (Tenango del Valle), a común repartimiento was held in each neighborhood (calpolli/ tlaxilacalli?). Tradition was respected in the townships: certain families worked the same plots of land for generations. The division was not egalitarian: the gobernador favored his relatives and friends by allocating to them the best or even most of the fields. In 1773, the tributarios of Metztitlán complained about an unfair division by which a few families were allocated an average of sixteen hectares of the común, while the poorest peasants had to make do with an average of less than a half-hectare of sowing ground.[44]

It was not universal practice to reallocate the land each year. An annual redistribution was called for in those villages whose surface area varied from year to year, municipalities like Metztitlán where agriculture depended on an overflowing river or lake (a form of Nilotic cultivation). The size of the land irrigated in this way determined the size of the común. In Indian pueblos dependent on rain (*temporal*) or with reservoirs to irrigate the soil, annual redistribution of the land had gone out of fashion. As plots of land were worked by the same peasants over a period of time, they came to be regarded as their own property, and fields belonging to the común were included in these peasants' wills. Whether the same plots of land were worked by the same peasants for long periods—or even for more than one generation—depended on the factors of population density and demographic development. A certain family in a village could cultivate the same plot of land generation after generation if no epidemics struck, while fields worked by families often afflicted by epidemics changed hands more often. It was not uncommon for the distribution of the común repartimiento to be taken into account at each tribute assessment. Some alcaldes mayores even assumed personal supervision of the matter themselves.

The verdict recorded by the Juzgado de Indios in a case involving a conflict in Acolman (Texcoco) in 1766–67 indicates the existence of clear rights of inheritance. Two brothers disputed a milpa worked by their aunt (and foster mother). The two brothers had lost their father during the great matlazahuatl epidemic in the early 1740s and were allocated the disputed land by the gobernador in office at the time. This allocation was carried out in accordance with a will their father had drawn up on his deathbed by the *escribano de pública*. At the time they were too young to work the land, but they were given a document by the gobernador stating that they would be given the use right to the land through the común repartimiento once they came of age. A good twenty years later, in 1766, when they had reached adulthood, they handed that note over to the local Spanish judge to claim their right. However, their aunt was also able to produce a will of the deceased by which the disputed milpas, each one barely a single hectare in size, had been inherited from her parents and were divided between herself and her brother. The judge declared that the latter will was authentic, and ruled that those who worked the milpas should retain their use right. The two brothers should have come earlier, he found. They were to report to their común with a request for more free land.[45]

A few statistics on the province of Chalco provide a good impression of the scope of the practice of común repartimiento among the villages in the province and the size of the plots involved. Future research will no doubt show that this situation in Chalco is representative of the general situation in the villages in Anáhuac. There were fifty-five pueblos in the province in 1769–70, most of which were pueblos sujetos. Twelve of these (22 percent of the villages) had exclusive rights to the use of land in a fundo legal. Sixteen other villages (29 percent) lived from fishing in Lake Chalco and had no fundo legal. The remaining 27 townships (49 percent) had both the fundo legal and land in the province to supplement the income derived from the fundo legal. These plots of land were worked by the residents of the municipalities themselves; they were used to growing magueys for the production of pulque, or they were rented to villagers or outsiders (hacendados). The rule was that each tributario worked a plot of land measuring 20 x 20 *brazas* for the gobernador, plus a plot of land measuring 80 x 20 brazas for himself (one *braza* was two varas: 0.113 has.). In Acolman (1766), a certain Ignacio Flores worked a plot of 42 x 42 varas or 0.72 hectares; and Pedro Marcos worked a plot of 25 x 25 varas or 0.04 hectares. Comparable statistics are scarce and extremely difficult to unearth. The only material I have seen is from the Totonac settlement Santa María Tlaslán in Zacatlán, on the border with Huauchinango. This village was not recognized, and thus the residents were unable to claim their rights from the Juzgado de Indios. All the same, there was a cabildo in 1786, and a común repartimiento was carried out on the mountain slopes. There were 135 tributarios in the cabecera. The sowing land was distributed as follows: 56 sowed approx. 1/3 ha., 54 sowed approx. 2/3 ha., 10 sowed approx 1 ha., 9 sowed approx. 1 1/3 has.; and one peasant had 1.75 ha. In addition there were 4 with milpas of 2 1/3 has. in size, and one peasant, Juan José, had a milpa of 3½ has. The proportions were similar in what were known locally as the pueblos sujetos (though they were not recognized as such): Cuauzoticpan had 1 households, with one possessing 2.5 has., with the rest less than 1 ha. Oquimotoquiliqua had 6 households, all with less than 1 ha., and so on. Since these were relatively small units in an atypical landscape, the green faldas of northeastern Anáhuac, I shall not draw any conclusions from them.[46]

Problems arose if the plots became too small as a result of overpopulatio and period redistributions. In Tlalmanalco (Chalco), the example discussed above, this problem was solved by allowing the tributarios to share in the proceeds of the municipal ranchos. Each resident was obliged to work a specific area of this field. A good 540 has. (151 fanegas) could be sown with maize on the ranchos. In addition, each of the tributarios worked an average of 8 fanegas (some 29 has.) for his own use. Later in the eighteenth century, however, even this extra was insufficient, and the younger members of the community were forced to relinquish their village rights. They could either leave the village, or choose to work as skippers on the canoes, as arrieros, or as wage laborers on haciendas. Others rented a plot of land from the caciques or the hacendados outside the fundo legal of the village.

Naturally, the extent to which the gobernadores could favor their supporters depended on their position in the village. As explained in Chapter One, a major factor was the population pressure in the townships. High population pressure made the peasants more dependent than low pressure, since a larger number of peasants competed for a share in the común. This factor in itself was already enough to account for the dramatic increase in power wielded by the gobernadores in the course of the eighteenth century. Nevertheless, the tributarios had a powerful ally on their side: their Juzgado de Indios. The large number of dossiers with complaints from peasants in the Indian pueblos concerning the procedure of the común repartimiento in their villages, preserved in the Ramo de Tierras of the national Mexican archive, proves they often resorted to their ally for a pronouncement. The ecological ethic also played an important part: a decision taken by a gobernador was contested more rapidly if he had a reputation for "doing little for the municipality." Clever gobernadores could build up a good reputation by conferring a part of their capital on the community and taking an active part in the defense of the municipal privileges, especially the boundary of the fundo legal, water rights, and the postponement of tribute payment after harvest failures or epidemics, while at the same time devoting an equal amount of energy to furthering the accumulation of their own property, use of land, and family capital.

Tributarios who felt that their rights were not being respected could usually resort to the appropriate legal channels: first the gobernador, then the alcalde mayor or subdelegado, and finally the Juzgado itself. This procedure was followed by the common Indian Pablo Marcial from San Martín Obispo, at the foot of the famous pyramids of Teotihuacán (which were covered by the milpas at the time). In the summer of 1788, Pablo Marcial had married, claiming that this entitled him to two plots of land from the común, one for himself and one for his wife. His claim was turned down because the gobernador considered that he had a sufficient amount of land. Pablo Marcial then turned to the alcalde mayor of the province. In the meantime he rented two fields from another common Indian, Martín Diego, for eight pesos a year (five reales a month), even though the rent had been reduced to five pesos in the famine year of 1786. The two fields were close to one another, separated by a road, and amounted to a total of approximately 10 has. (enormous holdings compared with the earlier examples). Since Martín Diego had a total of five such fields but only sowed one himself (two others were rented out to Don Juan Garido, the local tithe farmer), Pablo Marcial asked to be granted the milpas he rented. Despite protests on Martín Diego's part, who only rented the land because his children were not yet grown, Pablo Marcial was assigned both fields: renting land belonging to the común repartimiento was expressly prohibited since a decree of the Juzgado de Indios of 1781, so the land must be confiscated. Besides, Martín Diego lived in Mexico City![47]

Another case brings us back to the poor village of Huasca Zaloya in the province of Tulancingo, where the gobernadores went bankrupt because no tribute money was collected. Long before the problems became acute, gobernador Don Vicente López tried to increase the number of tribute-paying tributarios by allocating land from the común to outsiders. One of these outsiders was Juan Antonio Gutierrez, who started paying tribute in the early 1780s, though he actually lived as a tenant on the Hacienda Zoquital. When a villager died without an heir, the gobernador was able to give him land in a maguey field in 1782. The magueys were purchased by the former gobernador Don Salvador Policarpo, but the intervening land—there was often a strip ten or so meters wide between the rows of magueys—was fertile and Juan Antonio was prepared to turn it to good use. However, he ran into difficulties with Don Salvador Policarpo, who not only planted more magueys, but also plowed the uncultivated land between the magueys for barley. This was bound to lead to an argument, and Juan Antonio was assaulted one morning by Don Salvador Policarpo and his wife and children. The gobernador refused to allow his policy of trying to gain more genuine tributarios in the village to be thwarted by his predecessor, and he instigated proceedings. Don Salvador Policarpo was even detained for a while, but since the other villagers were not keen on the newcomer either, the Juzgado de Indios decided to oppose the allocation to Juan Antonio Gutiérrez. Other newcomers who had already begun cultivating común land without running up against such problems were left unharmed.[48]

There was nothing peculiar about the approach of the gobernador of Huasca Zaloya. Non-Indians could certainly make claims on a share in the común with success. Every newcomer—"indio," "casta," or "español"—who was prepared to pay the tribute could be considered as a candidate for the right to work a plot of land. The extent to which this happened varied from place to place, depending on such factors as the proximity of roads (in connection with migration) and the relation of the newcomer to the leading families in the village. This can be illustrated by the example of Santa Clara Coatitlán (Ecatepec), where the *indio principal*, Don Antonio Ayala (a cacique, who was also referred to as such), had refused since 1797 to grant a field from the común land to the mestizo Gregorio Antonio, a muleteer.[49] At the beginning of 1800, Ayala appealed to the Audiencia. He was a former gobernador of Coatitlán and was afraid that the power of the incumbent gobernador, Don Sebastián Soberanis, would increase in the village if outsiders were incorporated. Ayala submitted a counterclaim to back up his complaint; because he spent a lot of money on the decoration of the village church and performed the duties of fiscal in the parish, he had the right to an extra field from the común. All the same, Soberanis was more influential than Ayala. He summoned a larger number of witnesses (all intimidated by Soberanis, according to Ayala), and they had convincing arguments in the eyes of the Spanish magistrate for allocating Gregorio Antonio a plot of land. The mestizo was a respectable young man (as his calidad already showed), who had just started a family, had already lived in the village for a number of years, and paid tribute without having a share in the común. The Juzgado de Indios was given the impression that the mestizo could be expected to work his plot of land conscientiously, so that the gobernador would have no reason for confiscating the fields from him on grounds of negligence. Moreover, it proved to be the case that Ayala already had nine fields under cultivation, six of them as property outside the fundo legal and three of them within it (totaling 0.3 ha. of land). He also grew magueys on three plots of land on the slopes of a volcano. Ayala eventually gave in bitterly, in 1803. He was no longer prepared to take action on behalf of the pueblo whose control was now in Soberanis's hands instead of his own.

Many tributarios, especially those who lived above the subsistence level, had land outside the fundo legal. Further research is required to show how many tributarios—who were not caciques!—had a home in the fundo legal as well as a field of their own a few hundred meters away. An example of one of the many inheritance disputes that I came across may throw some light on the matter.[50] A tributario from Santa María Tlalmimilalpa (Tenango del Valle), Lorenzo Martín, left various fields to his family in 1722. The most important plot of land was left to his eldest son. The plot belonged to the village común and was the spot where the farmhouse stood. It was a fertile piece of land. Lorenzo Martín therefore decided that his wife and his two other sons should share the yield. He left a small field, which was also part of the común, to the confraternity to which he belonged, where candles would be burned and masses held in the village church each week for the good of his soul. The confraternity received the use rights to a few fields on the edge of the village for the same purpose. The two younger sons received other land outside the village as their own property, and the youngest was even encouraged to build his home and to settle on one of these plots. The population pressure was already making its presence felt in this village a decennium before the great matlazahuatl epidemic. Lorenzo Martín's will gives the impression that the youngest son received the best milpas in return for being prepared to leave the village.

In San Andrés Timilpan, near Huichapan in the province of Xilotepec, the Indian Gabriel Martín left ten milpas and a few fields of maguey to his children. He had inherited this property from his mother, Pascuala María, who died in the matlazahuatl epidemic in 1737. I do not know whether this land belonged to the común, but I have the impression that this was not the case. Gabriel Martín's will, which is extant in a version translated by the pueblo's *escribano de república,* determined that he was to be buried in the village church.

He left his domestic altar to his two sons, José Martín and Antonio Calixto, as well as leaving two milpas for each of them, comprising one large and one small field. The sons were also required to work two milpas and to use the yield to maintain the domestic altar. The surplus was to be donated to the village confraternity. Two others sons, Miguel Martín and Tomás Martín, each received a milpa as well, and so did his daughter and a sister. It is striking that a cousin included in the household, Bernabel Martín, shared in the inheritance with a milpa. This division of Gabriel Martín's ten milpas did not cause any problems, until nine years later José Martín and Antonio Calixto wanted to dispossess their cousin Bernabel and applied to the alcalde mayor in Xilotepec. Was there a family quarrel going on? Did Gabriel Martín's two sons want the land for their children? Didn't their own milpas yield enough? Bernabel, however, had kept a copy of his uncle's will, and since it was legally binding, the plan of José Martín and Antonio Calixto was thwarted; in fact, Bernabel's "right of possession" was confirmed.[51]

All of the examples cited in this section betray a mixed pre-Hispanic and Spanish origin, which was characteristic of all the Indian pueblos in Anáhuac. The use right of the land was allocated to villagers who paid taxes. There were also tenants and landowners who lived in the village without sharing in the común repartimiento. It is unclear whether they paid tribute, though most of them probably did. In general, it was the obligation to pay tribute and the común repartimiento, which bound the tributarios to the pueblo. They were thereby subjects of the caciques, who controlled the gobernadoryotl. The gobernadores favored themselves and their supporters during their period in office, resulting in an accumulation of property and, in particular, a monopoly of land as a means of production. It is likely that a similar process was already taking place in the pre-Hispanic era. And it was different from modern Spain, for the work of Vassberg, Cruz Villalón, García Sanz, Anes, Casado, Pulido Bueno, and others creates the impression that a larger proportion of the population was plowing village land there in the sixteenth, seventeenth, and eighteenth centuries.[52]

Epilogue: A New System?

What evidence do we have now at our disposal? Did more land come under Indian plows? I am reluctant to answer these questions, for the evidence might be too thin and I am therefore compelled to fall back on the context, the hypothesis, to fill in the gaps in the historical evidence. All the same, I am convinced of the following: the gobernadores, all members of the Indian order, behaved increasingly like the heirs of the Aztec tlahtoanate in the late eighteenth century, but inside the Spanish system because of the fundo legal legislation. I am confirmed in my belief that the growth in the number of court cases involving land is not to be explained exclusively in terms of poverty or a shortage of land, but also by an attempt on the part of the gobernadores to enhance their influence in the villages in order not only to increase their material profits but, most of all, to "reconstruct" the cacique heritage according to the new rules of the game. Whether they held office as gobernadores or not, in many cases the caciques instigated legal proceedings against a village or hacienda with this in mind. I was struck by the proto-*indigenista* language used by the gobernadores and caciques: the "Spaniards" were characterized as the unlawful owners of the soil of America. The caciques, many of whom were characterized by the Spaniards as mestizos and who enjoyed the benefits of an elite education ("Spanish style"), presented themselves in public as the defenders of a pre-Hispanic heritage.

Nevertheless, in this concluding section I shall attempt to strengthen the evidential side of my argument, hopefully at the expense of its hypothetical side. The question of how many active gobernadores and caciques there were in Anáhuac around 1800 has still not been answered. This leads us back to the 1800–1805 tribute census, which has already been discussed. This *matrícula* lists the caciques and the gobernadores in parallel columns. Most of the statistics in the source are extremely reliable, but why were there so many gobernadores and so few caciques? Particularly striking, and mentioned before, is the fact that the number of gobernadores far exceeds the number of Indian headtowns. A census is based on perception, and that perception has a large subjective, contemporary component. Censuses never reflect society with the objectivity of a mirror. They are not only subject to human error, writes the cultural historian Peter Burke, but the information they contain is also filtered through a specific system of classification. This system of classification bears witness to the way in which a society sees itself, or how one particular group sees the rest.[53] This point has already been made in the article on the tributarios and the *calidades*, or ethnic terminology.[54] It is my belief that the matrícula of 1800–1805, which is regarded as reliable, was also reliable as far as the numbers of gobernadores and caciques were concerned. There are so many gobernadores in the census, not because a vast quantity of them suddenly appeared, but because the traditional cacicazgo had by now almost entirely given way to the gobernadoryotl. By then, there was more status to be called "gobernador," "gobernador pasado," or "pasado" than merely "cacique."

The tribute register of around 1800 should be regarded, then, as a reflection of the new relations in the Indian order, in which the cacique as lord of an Indian demesne has had to make way for the cacique as gobernador, a transition that once again runs parallel to the transformation from Personenverband to Territorialverband. The gobernadores in this tribute register are the caciques who have merged with the new gobernadoryotl. The caciques column refers to the old-style caciques, linked with the old-style cacicazgos; the gobernadores column will then refer to the new-style caciques, who were linked with the gobernadoryotl. The transformation of the Territorialverband, which can be seen here, in the wake of the penetration of the proprietorship principle was not complete; that took place later with the privatization of landownership in the nineteenth and twentieth centuries (the *desamortización* of the Ley Lerdo). Personenverband and Territorialverband existed side by side and in one another, an indigenous hermaphrodite.

This is certainly sticking one's neck out. Am I fooling myself? Is this perhaps only one side of the story? Recent research has shown that the number
of gobernadores could have grown in practice. After all, Dehouve, García
Martínez, and Wood indicated a "process of secessions" that began with the
formation of the pueblos, but which became a large-scale phenomenon in the
late eighteenth century. Bitter at the many obligations the sujetos had to fulfill for the cabeceras, at the profits the caciques in the cabeceras pocketed
(think of the repartimiento trade!), and at the unsubtle abuse of power, the
nobility and their subjects in the sujetos were eager to secede from the
headtown. If they wanted to have a pueblo at their disposal, they had to build
a church where masses would be held, have a communal landbase for at least
eighty households, and form an independent village council. A church could
be built quickly enough—every modern traveler is impressed by the number
of late eighteenth-century churches in Anáhuac—the landbase could be re-
solved by means of the fundo legal, and eighty households were not a problem in the period of overpopulation of 1780–1800. And they had an
independent sujeto-village council, for the presence of alcaldes and regidores
was regarded as legitimate by the crown. If recognized as "pueblos-por-sí,"
pueblos sujetos became legal, full-fledged Indian pueblos, and the local alcaldes
became their gobernadores.[55]

The theoretical obstacle might be the fact that new "pueblos-por-sí" might
have been founded which did not come to acquire cabecera status. This implies the possibility that a "pueblo-por-sí" could not be a cabecera. According
to the matrícula there were 226 caciques and 3,056 gobernadores in the
intendancy of Mexico around 1800, connected with 778 cabeceras; in the
intendancy of Puebla there were 437 caciques, including the 241 from Tlaxcala,
where no gobernadores were included in the figures, and 1615 gobernadores,
connected with 321 cabeceras. In other words, there would have been 4
gobernadores per cabecera in Mexico and 6 in Puebla, implying an average of
4 "pueblos-por-sí" per cabecera in the intendancy of Mexico and 6 in Puebla.
This seems implausible to me, and I have not been able to find any support for
such figures in the development of local government. The documentation in
the Ramo de Indios indicates that any village which wanted to become a
"pueblo-por-sí" assumed that it would be granted the status of cabecera;
cabecera and "pueblo-por-sí" were synonyms. It was the ultimate conquest of
Spanish policy: from tlahtoanate to every settlement for itself.

The ratio of gobernador:cabecera appears in a different light if we recall
that the secessions led to an increase in the number of cabeceras. Very little
research has been conducted out on this aspect, either in institutional terms
(what is the precise meaning of terms like cabecera, barrio and sujeto?[56]), or in
chronological terms (how did the number of cabeceras develop?). In fact, no
history of the juridical development of New Spain has been written yet. If we
follow the terminology, it is possible to trace the ratio for a few provinces in
the period between the early eighteenth century and the ensuing period. For
example, according to the terminology of the time, there was one cabecera

with ten pueblos sujetos and a larger number of barrios in Teotihuacán in 1743. Around 1800 there were seven cabeceras, although this source does not state the number of sujetos or barrios. In 1743, there was one cabecera in Chalco, San Luis Obispo Tlalmanalco, and fifteen *sujetos al indio gobernador* of Tlalmanalco. The pueblo Amecameca was a pueblo sujeto of Tlalmanalco, and had twenty-nine *sub-sujetos* that year. A source from 1769–79, which already has been mentioned above, refers to the figure of fifty-five pueblos sujetos. In 1800, all of these units were simply referred to as forty cabeceras. In 1743, there was one cabecera as well as eight sujetos in the province of Mexicaltzingo, each with a number of barrios; in 1800, the province included fourteen cabeceras. In 1743, the province of Toluca had one cabecera and nineteen sujetos; in 1800, the figure was twenty-one cabeceras. In 1743, there was one cabecera and fourteen sujetos in Malinalco, each with a number of barrios; in 1800, there were eighteen cabeceras. In 1743, Tochimilco (valley of Puebla) consisted of one cabecera and eight subordinate units; in 1800, the province had five cabeceras.[57]

These scanty data suggest that the secessions really did take place all over Anáhuac, and that each of the new pueblos henceforth was led by gobernadores. However, the fact that the number of gobernadores exceeded the number of cabeceras in 1800 was the result of the increased importance of the gobernadoryotl, that is, the cacicazgo inside pueblo boundaries. If this hypothesis is correct, the following matters become clear:

1. the caciques had appropriated the gobernadoryotl in such a way that the terms *gobernador* and *cacique* were becoming synonyms; a cacique without traditional land rights was expected to take part in the village administration in order to give his kinship group access to land;
2. as a result of the gobernadoryotl, the pueblos can only be understood as units within the Herrschaft of the new-style caciques; the Indians were bound to serve the pueblo in manorial style, no matter who led this "manor" (this could rotate between various lords, as, in fact, manors generally did—and also haciendas!—and rival cacique factions competed for this position); and
3. despite the Spanish juridical and administrative system, the pueblos therefore are not to be seen as corporations of socially equal peasants, but as *clientelas* of caciques; the pueblos must therefore not be analyzed in terms of the theories of corporations, not even in terms of municipalities, perhaps, but in terms of manorial traditions.

As in Germanic and Celtic Europe, the lords preceded the villages in Mexico, which means that the villages had their roots in manorial rule. A village without a lord was inconceivable, both in the pre-Hispanic era and in colonial times. There probably has been little change in this situation up to the present century. The common Indians had allied themselves in a discourse on land

and water *with* their gobernadores and *against* outsiders like hacendados, caciques, or other pueblos, or, in some cases, precisely against their lords. In
fact, they seemed to have had no mutual link apart from this, although they
would have constructed family networks in order to be less economically dependent on the gobernadoryotl structure.

To conclude, my exploration of the land problem in Anáhuac, provisional
as it is in a field barely researched, has resulted in a confirmation of the thesis
that a process of impoverishment must have set in after around 1770 among
the lower classes of the population of the region. Although many peasants
owned small plots of land outside the común, the majority of the Indians in
the townships would have depended on the allocation of a field from the
común. Internally, as a result of the population growth, a virtually universal
land shortage made its presence felt in the Indian pueblos. The común was no
longer sufficient. It therefore seems very likely that the *indigenista* stance of
the caciques was a necessity, or even an innovation, in order to reinforce the
legitimacy of their position in the "community of tributarios," or perhaps
even to constitute the legitimacy of the "community" as an Indian unit. It
was an opportunistic response both to the impoverishment in the Indian order and to the movement that drove many common Indians elsewhere. For a
large number of the Indian mud farmers in the late eighteenth century, the
común repartimiento was becoming a social service from which they were
excluded. This endangered the position of the caciques/gobernadores, which
could be secured by warding off outsiders.[58]

Internally, within the village boundaries, and often as households, the
common Indians were usually implicated in a discourse against their
gobernadores, because the latter regarded them as dependents, who could
obtain land in return for protection, labor services, and tribute. The term
gobernadoryotl is an excellent term to describe this relationship, indicating as
it does the extent to which a Spanish administrative measure was not only
combined with a traditional Indian system, but completely integrated in it as
the Indian response to the Territorialverband, which the crown wanted to
enforce in New Spain. The situation outlined in the present chapter is the
germ of the *revolutionary cacicazgo* as described by Buve, Schryer, Thomson,
Pansters, and Jacobs for the period of the Mexican Revolution and later decades, as well as that described by Cancian, Vogt, and Köhler for the mountain villages in Chiapas, in the south of modern Mexico.[59]

6

Second Implication: Toward Proto-Industrialization

Introduction: High-pressure Solutions

In preceding chapters I have repeatedly suggested that the late eighteenth century in Anáhuac could be interpreted as "proto-industrial." In this chapter, I will explore this suggestion theoretically, and I would like to discuss some new data as well. For the peasants, appealing to their lords was one type of option to alleviate the crisis in Anáhuac, but a very traditional one. In that sense, it made little difference for the common Indians if they were registered as indios de pueblo, terrazguerros or gañanes. They all had more or less the same relationship with their lords (gobernadores, caciques, or indeed, hacendados): a piece of land for self-sufficient farming and socioeconomic and political protection—including charity—in exchange for tribute (in kind, cash, or labor). But such solutions were short-lived, of course; they were small leaps, that is, low-pressure solutions, following directly upon a harvest failure, for example. Out-migration could be a drastic measure for the migrants themselves, but those who stayed remained in the same economic situation as before. After all, the only change was the disappearance of increasing pressure on resources, while the original pressure often still remained. Extra landownership resulting from the secessions of the pueblos sujetos also had a low-pressure character since the land had already been divided. Most of the new pueblos in the late eighteenth century owned little more than their fundo legal, which was only sufficient for eighty or so families. And although the gobernadores were able to increase their power and prestige, this would logically not mean any structural change in the economy of the pueblo.

And such a structural change must have occurred, because of the population increase of the 1790s in a period of persistent droughts. With so many more mouths to be fed intensifying the danger of a year of hunger again in the early 1810s, a Malthusian situation could have been rapidly developing and low-pressure solutions would have been insufficient. However, despite the shadows that fell over Anáhuac, the rapid increase of the 1790s does suggest that the region did not fail to sustain its population at the time. Obviously, the barrier was overcome by some drastic high-pressure solutions. For small peasants, this meant switching to manufacture, a transition known among historians as *proto-industrialization* and among social scientists as *commoditization*. In fact, the question is interesting from another point of view as well. Knowing that population increase was one of the *consequences* of proto-industry in Europe, because family incomes grew and there was more opportunity for earlier marriages and larger families, the proto-industrial transformation could explain the rapid population growth in Anáhuac in the 1790s. Consequently, the next options for the peasants of Anáhuac were steps toward the modern economy.

In such circumstances, it *did* make a difference for the common Indians in how they were registered. Most of the gañanes and terrazguerros would change little, while the indios de pueblo would enter the commercial world, thereby leaving the agrarian world bit-by-bit. However, it is no simple task to pinpoint the transition, for there never was a purely agrarian world to begin with. Many social scientists nowadays realize that practically all of the "peasants" they study deliberately engaged in the commercial production of manufactures or agrarian products for the weekly markets. They lived off the proceeds. Since scholars seemed to assume that the peasants produced exclusively for subsistence before then (without historical study, incidentally), they often noted a transition to small manufacture the moment their study began. However, the small peasants who produced *exclusively* for subsistence have never been found in large numbers by historians. A few decades ago, historians did assume that peasants of this kind may have lived on the early medieval manors, but it is now known that there was production for the market combined with subsistence production; the unit of production was the household, the coresidential domestic group, not a corporate unit. All in all, this means that we are entitled to state that peasants and farmers were constantly active on the manufacturing market.

What, then, changed during proto-industrialization/commoditization? According to Marxist historian Levine, we are dealing with a stage in the transition from feudalism to capitalism, which he called "a halfway house." Bernstein argued that commoditization is a process of deepening commodity relations within the cycle of reproduction.[1] The word *reproduction* here refers to the renewal, from one round of production to another, of the social and technical elements of production and of the relations among them, usually occurring from one agricultural cycle to the next. Of course, in household production renewal of the means of production is contained within the household and involves no distribution of the product between different social groups. During the commoditization transformation, each household will be severed more and more from direct reciprocal ties for renewal of means of production and, therefore, comes to depend on commodity relations for reproduction. The reproduction cycle will be guided by the forces of the market in increasing terms. In fact, according to Bernstein, following Marx, the cycle of simple commodity production and reproduction can be summarized as $C - M - C$ (commodities-money-commodities).[2] The newly created commodity-producing households may own the most important of their means of production—for example, labor within the household and land in a corporate manner—and require for their reproduction the mobility of factors of production existing only within a capitalist economy; these relations apply to them no less than to capitalist farmers.

Thus, in periods of demographic expansion an increasing percentage of rural households are unable to meet their basic requirements without recourse to commodity exchange, that is, without marketing agricultural or other commodities or without selling their own labor either within or outside agriculture. In areas of growing rural commercialization, production inputs come to depend upon the availability of capital or credit, which tend to exercise a substantial influence over the internal operations of the farm and household. The rural households acquire a degree of independence from larger social groupings, like the local communities, but become more dependent upon external market forces, which leave little room for maneuver on the part of "those being commoditized." Some authors argue that capital penetration eventually leads to increased socioeconomic differentiation among agrarian populations, that is, they note the emergence of new class structures. Others, like Long and Smith, have stressed that even commoditized rural households still obtain many important factors of production such as land, labor, or farming knowledge through noncommoditized relationships. Indeed, some forms of nonwage work like domestic labor or unpaid inter-household reciprocal exchange are an integral part of the commoditization process. Nevertheless, in a study of a remote region of the Peruvian rain forest, Chevalier suggests that the items directly appropriated by the workers, such as land, labor, and subsistence goods, that do not pass through the market, should be seen as "commoditized," since these realize an exchange-value which is transferred to other products sold on the market. Long further argues that one needs to look at the responses of peasants from an active rather than a passive point of view: the features of the commoditization transformation are processed by the peasants themselves, integrated into their own farming strategies. Long concludes that local structures are sometimes so resilient that they shape significantly the ways in which capitalist penetration evolves. Although Bernstein emphasized the role of the state in promoting commoditization through introducing currencies or standardized forms of exchange value, powerful external forces like these are, in effect, mediated by local structures, because certain individuals like peasants must themselves come to terms with new elements in their life-worlds, and they naturally do this on the basis of their existing "worldviews" and institutional forms.[3]

Although in a lecture at the Agricultural University in Wageningen (the Netherlands), Bernstein argued that Latin America became integrated into commodity markets through Spanish and Portuguese colonial rule, dating from the sixteenth century onward, most authors would note the real commoditization process in Africa, Asia, and Latin America occurring only in the twentieth century. It is well-known that in Europe the transformation occurred at an earlier date, but that historians prefer to call it "proto-industrialization," which, according to the English historian Wall,[4] "betokens home or small workshop based manufacture of goods for a non-local market." The rise of eighteenth-century large-scale cottage industry was given this name instead of recognized as simply rural industry because manufacture was market oriented, in the first place, and second, it was for a nonlocal market; the producer and consumer did not know one another. Moreover, it was accompanied by changes in the spatial organization of the economy. Work was put out into the countryside by merchants, or early entrepreneurs, who reclaimed the completed articles for finishing and sale. Unlike small-scale cottage industries, proto-industries dominated local labor markets, employing large numbers of rural residents rather than just a handful of families. The rural workers worked for piece rates: the men in periods of little agricultural work, but the women almost on a daily basis, initiating a sexual division of labor because more women than before entered the production process. The manufacturing system in the countryside became less and less personal, and the income and economic well-being of large numbers of people became more and more tied to the vagaries and fluctuations of national and international markets, long before most workers lived in cities and worked in factories. Proto-industries were commonly found in areas of subsistence farming with large populations accessible to urban cloth merchants.[5]

To be clear: the putting-out system practiced alongside agriculture cannot in itself be called proto-industry, but the *expansion* of such cottage-industrial activity can. This expansion took place in different parts of Europe without adopting advanced technology or centralizing workers into factories. After more than a decade of intensive research, historians seem to agree on two points: first, proto-industry was central to the economy of early modern Europe; and second, it had considerable impact on demographic behavior. On all other items no agreement has been reached. Some would state that proto-industry led to population growth, which, in turn, caused proto-industry to expand further; a kind of *PI - D - PI* situation. In the end, it was thought, it led to *factory* industrialization and full-grown capitalism. Others, however, disputed this and pointed to the theories' failure to explain industrialization in specific cases. In fact, in some cases proto-industry even *hindered* the coming of factory industrialization. Then, there were cases in which proto-industry did occur, but without population growth; or population growth without proto-industry. And proto-industry might have strengthened traditional social obstacles to industrial capitalism instead of removing them.[6]

Recent students of the expansion of cottage industry had no choice but to stress the variation in proto-industrialization across different societies, all over the world. Some general ideas of the occurrence of proto-industries in areas with problems of industrial development seem to grow: proto-industry might have hindered industrial development in nineteenth-century Germany, Austria, Italy, and the Netherlands or in modern-day India and Africa. Besides, demographic fertility, which is determined by a complex matrix of economic, social, and institutional constraints, does not seem necessarily to favor development of the economy, but some relationship, still to be defined, must be recognized. Perhaps that connection does exist for a few regions, but in many cases the proto-industry developed through internal factors as a reaction to relative overpopulation. Third, recent research indicates that economic and social change can only be understood by investigating the institutional constraints thoroughly, for these constraints seem to "cause" all such regional difference. The choice of proto-industry does not necessarily have to be made exclusively by merchants or entrepreneurs, since the literature indicates that the peasants themselves can also take the initiative in choosing a retail market and then seeking contact with a merchant, for example. Too often, I believe, theorists lean too heavily on a kind of linear view of change. This permitted Levine, for instance, to call the proto-industrial stage just "a halfway house." Modern research reveals that it was definitely a separate stage in economic development, which nevertheless could continue in mechanized industrialization. Proto-industry, then, developed upon a fixed road, but that road was fixed by the institutions in a certain area and within a certain period of time.[7] I therefore retain the terminology of proto-industry, as a uniform theoretical and methodological tool, but I keep in mind that proto-industry did not necessarily usher in a process of mechanized industrialization.

It brings us to the microeconomic aspect of the peasants' operations within the framework of the pueblos. It is not easy to investigate this aspect, because the indios did not keep accounts, for example, and in all other aspects very little research exists. To this point the ground has been fairly solid, but the footing now becomes less certain. I admit to proceeding with a Fogelian "would-be" argument, without the inevitable mass of data to support it. Therefore, theory could overwhelm the data. However, the abductive claim of my approach must be remembered throughout: there is no deduction carried out here. All the same, I wish to draw a conclusion on the proto-economic position occupied by the Indians in the economy of Anáhuac in the eighteenth century. The best way of arriving at this conclusion is to start with agricultural farming itself. We shall then move on to the weekly markets and conclude with the interregional markets. At this point, we can see how important transport (arriería) must have been for the small peasant household. This chapter ends with an attempt to incorporate these elements in a dynamic model of the peasant household. I would like to begin by looking at a few assumptions, such as the character of the family household—the primary organizational form in which the peasants and farmers associated—and communal agriculture. I have encountered a lack of research on all of these points, and I am therefore compelled to argue very tentatively.

The Household Economy

The Peasant Household

The sources tend to refer to the Indian peasants as *pegujaleros*, a term that refers to workers on a small piece of sowing land. I shall follow this practice throughout the present chapter. The term *pegujaleros* also refers to small households, as distinct from the caciques who had larger tracts of sowing land at their disposal. In the cabecera of Santiago Tecali (Puebla), for example, there were around 400 small farms and 80 large ones in 1743; 399 *familias de indios* (pegujaleros) and 80 *familias de caciques* lived there. A similar ratio can be found in the pueblo of Chiazumba (near Tehuacán) for 1778, where the geographical account also mentions that the pegujaleros in the small houses wore the local dress, while the caciques dressed like the Spanish (the elite); the two-story houses in which they accommodated their servants also had a "Spanish" look about them.[8] Information of this kind is important in connection with my more general arguments. According to a good deal of research on peasants, whether by "peasant"-oriented or "petty commodity"-oriented scholars, this sort of extended family, in which a farm was shared by more than one family, was the rule for peasant households, including those in closed corporate communities.[9] The history of Europe, on the other hand, was dominated by small households. However, it appears that the variation in peasant households was much greater than the lowest common denominator, assumed by such generalizations, would allow.

There is probably no reason to characterize the peasant household in New Spain any differently. It is worth looking at this point in more detail, because a brief survey of some of the European research in this field might throw some light on the analysis of the peasant household in Anáhuac. In his large-scale investigation of the Dutch province of Overijssel, Slicher van Bath was struck by the fact that most of the families there in 1748 consisted of only one man, one woman, and their children—that is, nuclear families. Some of them had a few servants or boarders under their roof, and there were a few that deserved the title of extended families, but they formed a minority. These findings display a remarkable number of similarities to the findings of Berkner in the Austrian district of Heidenreichstein, of Shaffer on the peasantry in the French Morvan, of Sabean's West German village of Neckarhausen, of Collomp's Saint André in the Haute-Province, or of the villages investigated by Segalen in Brittany. There are also clear affinities with the peasant household in England.[10]

Extended families are certainly to be found, but only as part of what Berkner called the family cycle (in an article that has become a classic).[11] The extended family must have formed part of a cycle of three stages, which succeeded one another in every human life: a couple with children; followed by a couple with children who left home when they grew up except for one, who married and inherited the paternal farm; and followed then by the elderly couple spending their last years on the farm in the company of the family of this son (or daughter). The cycle recommenced after the death of the parents. Thus the extended family was not a static phenomenon. Berkner prefers the term *stem family* for the family in which the parents shared the farm with the family of only one of their children; the families of the other children had their own households on their own farms as nuclear families. Berkner predicts that each census of a society marked by a cycle of this kind will reveal a majority of

nuclear families—the children who left the parental home earlier—and a minority of stem families. Prosperous peasant households will also have had
boarders in service, often children of relatives living elsewhere, as Wall has
also indicated.[12]

Later research has confirmed Berkner's prognosis for Europe; it has also
demonstrated that the peasant household was not characterized by the extended family, but by a network of kinship relations (including ritual kin)
between nuclear families. This network was not confined to a particular village. Collomp suggests that the existence of this network made the village
where the small peasant lived of no more than secondary importance. The
village was less relevant for a peasant in search of social and economic security. The village was only the community that could negotiate access to land
with the government. Berkner and others denied Chayanof's "self-exploita-
tion" thesis, though they established that his ideas on taking boarders into
service (including resident servants) during the period that the children were
too young to help on the farm were undoubtedly correct. Collomp and Reher
also disputed one of Chayanof's central points: the peasant household could
not be distinguished from small commercial family enterprises in the provincial towns. These families were incorporated on an equal footing in the network which stretched throughout the countryside.[13]

Scholars also concluded that some of the intensive migration that took
place in the countryside served to maintain the network: adolescents of both
sexes migrated as boarders to the relatives who needed them, and in many
cases this migration ended in marriage. The well-known politics of marriage
of medieval and modern royal families, which was intended to reinforce or
extend the realm, can also be found among the small peasant households.
Suitable marriage partners were carefully selected to ensure that the family
household was as widely based as possible. The historians mentioned above
distinguish between landowning peasant households and those who rented
or borrowed the land they worked. The former group occupied an extremely
active position in the politics of marriage, while the latter group had a more
egalitarian right of inheritance. Segalen reminds us that this distinction should
not be allowed to divert our attention from the extreme extended system of
marriage politics among the small peasant households.[14] The small peasants,
including the family enterprises in the provincial towns, thus formed the points
of intersection in the network of households in rural Europe.

It is frustrating to try to analyze household development, when data seem
to abound in the archives, but research and research time are lacking, thus
hindering comment upon them. However, anthropologists have come across
similar networks of ("related") households in contemporary Mexico.[15] With a
dose of goodwill and realizing that we cannot employ the anecdotal technique of dredging up an example or two as if that constituted proof, traces of
them can be found in New Spain. A key point is Berkner's hypothesis on the
distribution of stem families, nuclear families, and extended families in the
villages in the countryside. The research findings of the historical demogra-

phers Cook and Borah appear to match the European material. The reliability of the census in New Spain does not appear to be at issue in this respect. The house-by-house record of the numbers of tributarios resulted in a picture of small families; in most cases, each owned a farm of its own. According to Cook and Borah, there seems to have been a tendency toward small families in the eighteenth century, with only two children living with their parents.[16] That suggests less corporate collaboration: the household falls back on its own resources in a society undergoing commoditization.

My own exploration of this aspect, dealing with the situation before the large-scale post-1780 population explosion, corresponds to these findings. The censuses for Otumba (1702), Aculco (1721), Ixmiquilpan (1743), and Teopantla (1780) refer to households of three to four persons. The quality of this material is not sufficient to present the data in a table or diagram, but a few characteristic examples can be mentioned. Approximately 120 couples with children and 17 one-parent families lived in the barrio Santa Lucía in the pueblo of Teopantla (Izúcar) in 1780; there were 62 childless couples and 26 one-person households. Taken as a whole, the Teopantla census suggests that a large number of the childless couples must have had close connections with those couples with children who were visited by the census official shortly before or soon afterward. The majority of the childless couples were tributarios who were exempt on the grounds of their seniority. The census official apparently visited them before going to the stem family to which they belonged, since the head of the family in the next house is referred to as "son of the previous person" (*hijo del anterior*). This gives the impression that the more elderly couples formed a household with one of their sons and his family, sharing the same farm but living by themselves. Berkner regards this as a major characteristic of the stem family. The rest of the childless couples were young and had only left their parental home shortly before. The census also records that a number of families included an adopted child, a nephew, or a niece. These boarders were aged between ten and fourteen years. It is striking that a significant number of people living by themselves and every couple that was elderly, ill, lame, or blind had a grandchild (*nieto, nieta*) in the house to take care of them. Thus the less well-off thus lived by themselves too. The census material from the other pueblos I was able to examine reveals the same structure. Of course, these data do not tell us anything about farms shared by more than one household in different houses. We must therefore recall, in the first place, that the theorists of the extended families assume that the extended families formed a single household, and, in the second place, that the Spanish officials used the word *casa* to refer to a house in the social sense, that is, a household, rather than to a building. It would therefore not be surprising if future research were to lead to an unproblematical comparison of the small family concerns in New Spain during the majority of the eighteenth century with those of Europe during the same period.[17] But more research is desperately needed.

As the reader may know, I am not at all immune from current number fetishism,[18] but I do not begin to claim quantitative proof where the evidence does not warrant it. Nevertheless, patterns and modes of behavior are at the heart of any historical inquiry nowadays, so it would be helpful to bring up more figures. And, in fact, there are more examples of this kind of small household in the countryside. In 1743, the town of Cholula, for example, contained 181 españoles (3.6 persons per family), 468 castas (5.4 persons per family), and 606 indios (2.9 persons per family). According to the record, the castas were manufacturers with servants who lived in, which explains the size of these households. In general, the haciendas and ranchos in this province were inhabited by the higher, specialized personnel: the craftsmen and foremen. The rural laborers who worked on these haciendas, 115 in number, lived in their villages. These servants barely accounted for 1½ percent of the 8,730 indios in the province. It is striking that the 606 indios in the town of Cholula formed the largest concentration of indios in the province. Every other cabecera in the province was smaller. Cuautlanzingo had 764 families, with a total of 2,499 residents in the cabecera and 14 (!) pueblos sujetos, yielding an average of 3.3 per family. The cabecera of Santa María Coronango, with 9 sujetos, was smaller: its 1,562 inhabitants were distributed among 552 families, averaging 2.8 per family. Finally, the cabecera of Santa Isabel with its 9 sujetos, had 1,526 persons distributed among 525 families, averaging 2.9 per family.[19] In 1743, the nearby province of Tochimilco had 2,010 tributarios living in the pueblos (which were all Nahuatl-speaking). This group consisted of 1,154 couples, 393 children, 370 people living alone, and 93 widow(er)s. They formed 527 families, averaging 4 persons per family.[20] According to the census officials, these families generally lived in separate houses. The contrast with the situation at the turn of the century cannot be greater. The 1805 tribute registers give an average family size for the fifty-one provinces of Anáhuac that is above 4 persons, including more than 1 family per *casa*. In twenty-six provinces the average family size even exceeds 4½ persons. The latter provinces were mainly situated in the faldas and in the semiarid tracts of the highlands: the in-migration areas.

Such small households—if they indeed dominated in Anáhuac—are currently often interpreted with the assistance of Hajnal's theory of the pattern of reproduction.[21] This theory describes a demographic structure characterized by (1) a high marriage age, especially for the woman, so that few children are born; and (2) a relatively large number of permanently unmarried people. The background is that marriage only takes place once a more or less stable means of subsistence has been built up—for example, if the bridegroom can take over a farm or has obtained a position as a craftsman or servant. In the ideal type of proto-industry, the worker-peasant and his entire family form a small agricultural company providing wage labor for an entrepreneur. The more productive labor the household can contribute as an input, the more money there is to be made. This encourages large families. Also, the children can rapidly establish themselves as proto-proletarians at an early age, so that relatively less agricultural land is required for their subsistence. This would mean a drop in the age of marriage. The existence of small households and the sharp rise in population around 1800 lead one to suspect that this pattern of reproduction is applicable to Anáhuac. However, I am unable to test this theory adequately because of the lack of demographic research in precisely those areas where the repartimiento flourished, particularly in the pueblos in the valleys of Toluca and Mexico.

In short, although the statistics discussed above are anything but definitive, I propose to consider the small peasant households as the most typical of eighteenth-century Anáhuac. The risks of a small household could be spread by associating with various relatives, both within and outside one's own community, and this consideration was probably put into effect. Thus there is no theoretical ground to suppose large involvement in any corporate village economy as such, such as collective agriculture, in the Anáhuac region. This is important for understanding the following sections.

Corporate Agriculture?

The peasant households are traditionally said to have been primarily concerned with subsistence agriculture. But it will be remembered that large parts, perhaps the bulk, of their production was destined for the market. Does this makes them "entrepreneurial"? In our contemporary thought, the "entrepreneur" is an impeccably neoclassical creature. He takes risks and seeks to maximize returns on capital, while most "peasants" actively sought to avoid risk and were primarily concerned with obtaining a living. Whether producing for direct consumption or for market exchange—important though this might have been—the peasants' main interest was subsistence. The interesting point to make, as introduced earlier in this book, is the fact that peasant household producers had different values from the capitalist entrepreneurs. Market orientation is generally viewed as opposed to self-sufficiency, taken as indices of "modernity" and "traditional society." But research has indicated that this simple distinction fails to do justice to the varying strategies of production and exchange followed by agrarian household producers, who were preoccupied with the interest of their family rather than the return on invested capital. In order to provide all of the goods and services needed by even the poorest families, some division of labor between households was necessary. Producers who were not market oriented generally would have needed to have been nonspecialized, while others, some of them included in their family network, were engaged in a variety of productive and service undertakings.[22]

In Anáhuac and other Latin American regions, colonial research has not been directed to such networks, but, as indicated, has concentrated on the "community" as the expression par excellence of peasant cooperation. First of all, I shall move on from the character of the household to an exploration of the possibilities of corporate agriculture in the Indian pueblos of Anáhuac in the eighteenth century. In view of the individual practice of the común repartimiento, this can only have taken place on the propios. This is very specific land, connected with the village treasury (caja de comunidad), which

eans that only cabeceras could manage such propios, since sujetos did not
)ld a caja. This is the first restriction.

The link between caja and propios had been irrevocable since 1554, when
.e crown had ordered the establishment of the cajas. The propios served as
.e financial base for the administration of the pueblo, and the proprietor
as the council as a juridical person. That is why the land was usually man-
;ed by the gobernador. Such propios were granted to the cabeceras by the
.own through mercedes in the sixteenth century. However, it was also pos-
)le for municipalities to buy land and manage it as propios, or for caciques
 donate land to some pueblos for this purpose. The gobernador could count
1 administrative assistance from the village tributarios, who worked the plots
 land in the form of faenas (unpaid collective labor). They were affected by
.e produce of the soil, which could absolve them of tribute payment and
iurch tithes on an individual basis. The obligation of the tributarios in pueb-
s to work part of the propios (from preliminary plowing to harvesting) gen-
ally applied to 10 brazas, 280 square meters per person. This too was a legacy
 the pre-Hispanic *coatequitl*, which was the privilege of the cacique. Since
.e obligation to work was not universally of this kind, it could also happen
at the gobernadores took on agricultural laborers in the village itself for a
age of 1½ real per day (sunrise to sunset); a wage also paid on the haciendas.
 the propios were run by an alcalde mayor, which was only possible in big
wns, there was exclusively wage labor. A good example is provided by the
acienda Santa Ana Aragón, which belonged to the propios of the Indian
ieblo of Santiago Tlatelolco on the edge of Mexico City. The workers on this
icienda, who were the proprietors of the hacienda as tributarios of this pueblo
: indios, were recruited as wage laborers by a manager.[23]

The village treasury was not only intended for the state tribute (this de-
:nded on tradition, but was officially and therefore usually paid three times
 year, in April, August, and December). The funds were also intended to fi-
ince some church services (the sacraments, various forms of assistance pro-
ded by the priest, and more generally, a sort of religious tribute, the
iopantequitl), and the gobernadores, despite the fact that some pueblos had
parish treasury in addition to the village treasury to pay for the masses and
 cover similar expenses.[24] Nevertheless, the wages of the other members of
ie cabildo had to be paid from the caja de comunidad as well, besides the
:penses involved in the elections and *visitas* performed by the alcaldes mayores
 subdelegados. Of course, the expenses of litigation in Mexico City or the
irchase of maize in crisis situations were met from the treasury. In special
ises, the treasury fund could be used to build churches, a widespread prac-
:e during the period of the "secession" in the late eighteenth century. It is
irdly surprising, then, that most of the village churches in the central high-
nds date from this period. This not only provided the new pueblo with a
)od church, as was officially required in order to obtain pueblo status, but
so enhanced the glory of the gobernador who had brought about the "seces-
on"—as it is actually stated, for example, in an inscription on the church

tower in Papalotla, near Texcoco. In theory, if there were any money left
the village treasury after all these deductions, it was divided. However, in mc
cases the money was spent on pueblo festivities, and to such an extent th
the cost of these festivities formed the main expense item in the account
especially the New Year festivities, which also marked the start of the ne
period of office in the pueblo. Later, after the introduction of the Bourbc
Reforms, the money reverted to the Real Hacienda, and official permissic
was required before the money could be spent.

This is probably a confusing point, because the village festivities we
usually directly connected with religious festivals. The festivities were ce
tainly organized and largely financed by Indian rural confraternities; usual
known as cofradías. These rural confraternities also had a treasury to fur
their activities. They owned land and rented mules to arrieros in the pueblc
and in particular, they owned enormous numbers of livestock, as could I
shown by Asunción Lavrin, who has written two important articles on tl
commercial activities of the rural confraternities in central Anáhuac ar
Oaxaca. However, many confraternities lived from the contributions of the
members, the villagers. It is striking that the rural confraternities were led I
cofrades (also known as *mayordomos*) who were elected in rotation, general
from the group of the local caciques, so that this office can be compared wit
that of gobernador at the political level. There were also unofficial confrate
nities (*hermandades*), which had not received the approval of a bishop. Mor
over, there were *devociones* and *cuadrillas*, consisting of small groups of village
who were occasionally entrusted with the responsibility of organizing a re.
gious festival. Their funds consisted entirely of donations. By the late eig]
teenth century, however, the cofradías in the pueblos were in a sorry stat
The archbishop of Mexico, Don Alonso Núñez de Haro (bishop from 1771
1800), was appalled to see their decline. Eventually he intervened by prohi
iting nonviable hermandades, dissolving poor cofradías, and merging ric
hermandades with rich cofradías. This rescue operation was reasonably su
cessful, although his efforts were not appreciated by all the villagers.[25]

At this point, I would like to add a few reflections that cannot be substa
tiated at present and which cannot be elaborated in more detail without ove
stepping the limits of the present book, since they concern the question
Indian identity. It is important not to overstate the difference between a puebl
led by gobernadores, and the cofradía or hermandad, led by cofrades
mayordomos. Of course, pueblo and cofradía were juridically distinct entiti
without any formal relation to each other. Indeed, it was possible in practic
and it was even customary in a number of provinces, for the members of tl
cofradía to belong to more than one pueblo, and even to include Spaniard
and there were confraternities in which a plurality of calidades were con
bined. All the same, the two entities may be seen as the political and religiou
sides of the same coin, which can also be labeled as pueblo, with its roots i
the altepetl. It is therefore not surprising that the caciques administered bot
entities as if they were the same proverbial coin. Capital, labor power, ar

dership crossed from one side of the coin to the other. In fact, where out-
lers wanted to influence the development or the income of one of these
tities, the villagers' defensive reaction was to transfer authority or capital to
e other entity. The establishment of the confraternities in the early colonial
riod could even be seen as a reaction to the government intervention to
propriate the tribute of the caja de comunidad. The confraternities, which
ere mainly outside Spanish control, enabled the civic pueblo leaders—the
bernadores—to keep their property in their own hands. Where an orderly
stem is introduced, people start to develop an orderly consciousness. Indian
dentity" here means "order-identity."

In order to sidestep this interference with the pueblo funds and to avoid
tting the surplus from the caja de comunidad disappear into the Royal Trea-
ry, the pueblos funded the municipal festivities from the municipal trea-
ry; not only the New Year festivities—for the new gobernador—but also the
ligious festivals. Besides, this provided a means of taking the pressure off the
nfraternities that had got into financial difficulties. This annoyed the po-
ical wing of the Spanish administration in New Spain, because the civil
rvants noted that the financial situation of the municipal treasuries was in a
ry poor state; and this was happening in the same period in which Núñez
: Haro introduced his reforms. One gains the impression that the govern-
ent officials, who were familiar with the propios from Spain, were extremely
rprised to see that not every village in the overseas territories had its own
opios. They were struck by this discrepancy when they were confronted
th the growing volume of legal cases involving landownership in the late
ghteenth century. It was all the more serious with regard to the success of
e Bourbon Reforms, which contained a few regulations on the financing of
bute, church tithes and the municipal school from the municipal treasury.
ne objection was not just an economic one: it was the task of the village
hool to teach the principles of Spanish civilization, particularly language
d religion, to the Indians, who were still considered as childlike *gente sin
zón*. When it was decided to give this priority, the plans were postponed
cause of the wars in Europe; they were eventually abandoned because the
panish administration was forced to withdraw in 1821.[26]

A high-ranking civil servant in Mexico City had already informed the
overnment in Madrid, in 1780, about the precarious chances of success of
overnment policy in this respect. He explicitly requested his superiors to
aw up a sound arrangement for the propios and the municipal treasury to
place the old one. As a result of the confusion on the interpretation of the
d regulations, no one knew exactly what the propios were, he claimed, and
e pueblos did not have the funds for a municipal treasury. He argued for the
rict application of the Spanish legislation on this point, by which each pueblo
ould be obliged to donate propios, including, of course, the former pueblos
jetos which received recognition as pueblos-por-sí in the late eighteenth
ntury. He also urged rigorous supervision to ensure compliance with these
ws. Furthermore, he wondered where the municipal treasury should be situ-

ated. It had been learned from experience that the site of the chest led to the wielding of actual power on the basis of social prestige. The municipal treasury was a chest with three locks, and the three keys should be, at any rate, in the hands of a gobernador, the alcalde mayor, and the priest. Since these three individuals often had conflicting interests, this would be a way of avoiding abuse. The gobernadores were already so powerful in the pueblos that it would be better for the chest to be lodged with one of the other figures who had a key. This civil servant was also opposed to the need to move the chest each time a new gobernador was appointed. The chest should be kept in a permanent place. The most suitable site was the Casa Real, the official premises of the alcalde mayor or subdelegado, but the chest should not be placed in the living quarters.[27]

These recommendations were ignored. It had now become customary for the municipalities with propios to place them under the control of a gobernador. In most cases, the others who had a key to the municipal treasury were the *regidor mayor*—often a family member of the gobernador!—and the priest or the alcalde mayor or subdelegado. Since the cabildo was also controlled by the dominant caciques in a village, the municipal treasury was usually run by the most powerful individuals in the pueblo. This might be the reason why most pueblos started to finance pueblo festivities with caja money in the late eighteenth century: the power in the pueblos was increasingly concentrated in the hands of the gobernadores. If the alcalde mayor or the priest had been able to break the power of the Indian nobles, the chest was kept in their house. Some pueblos had more than one municipal treasury; in Izúcar, a large Indian pueblo, each of the fourteen barrios had its own municipal treasury![28] All the same, the power to make decisions independently had been reduced again around 1800, because in spite of the powerful position of the gobernadores, the Spanish state intensified its supervision of the accounts of the municipal treasury and the propios. The gobernadores had to account in detail for every payment made during their period in office, from the cost of the candles carried in a procession to the whitewashing of the town hall. The surplus, after the costs of the village festivities had been deducted, went into the state treasury. Some municipalities were invited to use this surplus to buy shares in the Banco de San Carlos, the national bank of the viceroyalty, which was founded in the late eighteenth century. The pueblos that did so were mainly located in the regions of Oaxaca and Michoacán. As for the pueblos in Anáhuac, only a few of them in falda provinces, such as Acatlán, Tepejí de la Seda, and Zacatalán de las Manzanas, opted for this investment. Most of the shares, however, were purchased by the two Indian municipalities that belonged to the district of Mexico City. They held two hundred (15 percent) of the total of thirteen hundred shares sold to pueblos.[29]

Most of the pueblos with propios were situated in the faldas or in the sparsely populated, semiarid highland tracts. One example is the pueblo of Santa Cruz Tecama (Ecatepec).[30] The propios of Tecama in 1763 are indicated in Map 17. It is evident that the holdings in propios could be many times the

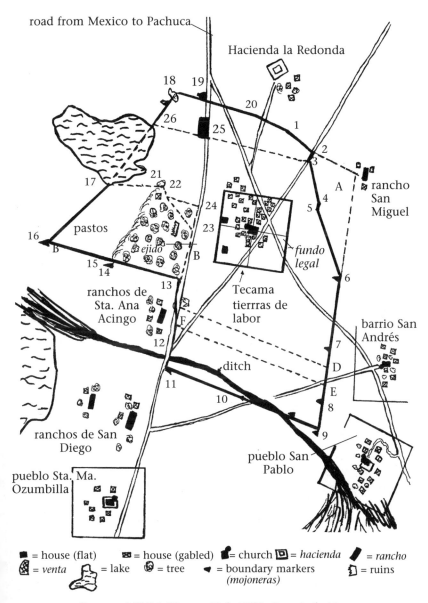

road from Mexico to Pachuca

Hacienda la Redonda

18 19

20

26

25

1

2

3

17

21 22

24

23

A rancho San Miguel

4

5

16

pastos

ejido

B

B

fundo legal

6

15

14

13

ranchos de Sta. Ana Acingo

F

Tecama tierrras de labor

barrio San Andrés

12

7

D

ditch

E

11

10

8

9

ranchos de San Diego

pueblo San Pablo

pueblo Sta. Ma. Ozumbilla

■ = house (flat)   ✖ = house (gabled)   ⛪= church 🏠 = *hacienda*   ◣ = *rancho*
▣ = *venta*   🏞 = lake   🌳 = tree   ◀ = boundary markers   🏚 = ruins
(*mojoneras*)

Source: AGNM, Tierras, Vol. 1580, Exp. 1, f. 45

ap 17 The propios of Santa Cruz Tecama (Ecatepec), 1763

size of the village's fundo legal. As usual, the land of Tecama was carefully marked off with boundary stones (*mojoneras*). A part of its propios was cultivated by the agricultural company of the San Gregorio Jesuit college in Mexico City (letter A on the map, between the boundary stones 2, 3, 4, 5, 6 and the San Miguel rancho). Another plot was once cultivated by the La Redonda hacienda, but it was reclaimed by Tecama (the area between the boundary stones 2, 3, 25, 26, 18, 19, and 20). This plot was a good 150 hectares, and included a stopping place (venta). The ownership of this plot of land was disputed by the neighboring Acingo rancho, but up to boundary stone 24 instead of 23. The rest of the land was almost 900 hectares. The description accompanying the map states that the land west of the road from Mexico City to Pachuca was used to pasture large livestock, while the land east of this road was cultivated for crops, although it was hardly sown. The thirty-three families in the village were content with their fundo legal, even though there were four farms outside the fundo legal. Most of the pegujaleros lived in the northwestern portion of the fundo legal on land described as being "as hard as stone." Each of the farms was surrounded by opuntia cacti (*nopales*) and magueys. The eastern half of the fundo legal was sown with maize, beans and barley. This was where the milpas of the común repartimiento were situated. The southwestern plot could also be sown, but a large part of it lay fallow. Magueys had been collectively planted for pulque production on the agricultural land south of the village. The ownership of part of this land was disputed by the neighboring pueblo of San Pablo (between the boundary stones 8, 9, 10, 11, and 12).

Considerable data on four other municipalities in the semiarid region have been preserved: Otumba, Ostoticpac, Cuauhtlacingo, and Axapusco. They have been published by Chávez Orozco, and recently analyzed by Tutino and Charlton.[31] These pueblos rented lands out to non-Indians and caciques to fill their municipal treasury. Some of the lands were worked collectively and the harvest sold. Pulque was the best product in this semiarid region. The propios of these pueblos were therefore divided into a number of ranchos that could be rented out to various individuals. This was not the best land, and a large part of it was heavily eroded. Many tenants therefore used the ranchos for livestock, including many pigs who grubbed for food among the magueys. It was also possible to cultivate maize there; in fact, half of the income of Otumba and Ostoticpac in 1794 was from maize cultivation on their propios. Despite what the poor quality of the soil might lead one to expect, the yields of this production were no lower than their present levels of 80:1 to 100:1.

The cases of Tecama and the pueblos near Otumba focus attention on the management of the propios. It will be obvious that the community could use municipal properties to engage in commercial trading, since Tecama used the propios for the collective production of their trato: pulque. A trato was the collectively traded product of one or more pueblos, in general traded through the repartimiento mechanism. The extant documentation contains some data that give an impression of the extent to which this actually took place.

degree of caution is required, however, because this material is fragmentary and certainly does not provide insight into a form of village accountancy. These data are exclusively of a general kind relating to the management of the pueblo's agricultural land, and since they had to be conveyed to the Spanish administration, these books were highly susceptible to being cooked. For instance, most of the extremely significant trade through the repartimiento trade, or the income from migrant labor—involving very large sums—did not appear in the municipal treasury accounts, although the money passed through the hands of the gobernadores. By the way, it should be recalled that we are here exclusively concerned with old pueblos and not with former pueblos sujetos, which "seceded" later on; anyway, they did not have any propios.

As a general rule, the municipal treasury was filled with tribute contributions. Officially, this was 1½ real per tributario, although this was not the total burden of tribute borne by the Indians in the pueblos, as Gibson and Tutino have shown. Although the contribution was sometimes collected on a house-to-house basis, the treasury was usually filled from the yield of the propios. It is clear from the accounts that most of the money was earmarked for festivities. Payment was reluctantly made to the village schoolmaster, because he was considered as a Spanish official and an unwelcome Peeping Tom, who represented the "Spanish order" anyway. In 1791, the tributarios in the pueblos of Soyatlán, Tlatelcingo, Ocuapan, and Ocotequilla in the province of Tlapa hoped to be able to divert the teacher's monthly item of six pesos and one fanega of maize to another purpose. They regarded such a large sum for a teacher as an enormous waste. However, the crown refused to see things their way, because the program of acculturation had to continue, and no teacher was prepared to work in the pueblos for less than this sum.[32]

The way in which the propios were run resembles that of a commercial agricultural company like a hacienda. A few examples can give an impression of the yield range. In 1709, the pueblo of Atzcapotzalco (Tacuba) had a rancho of four fanegas of land for maize cultivation (a good 14 has.), plus a few maguey fields. The pueblo of San Andrés (Temascaltepec) had a plot of almost 180 hectares, which was good for 50 cargas of wheat, but between 1774 and 1785 it was involved in a bitter quarrel with the neighboring pueblo of San Pedro Almoloya about obtaining sufficient water to irrigate the land. It was claimed that if the land was cultivated properly, it could yield between 500 and 1,000 cargas (that is, a yield of between 10:1 and 20:1). The inhabitants of Ajalpan (Tehuacán) acquired a few plots from a gobernador in 1720 in payment of a debt. The water required to irrigate what amounted to almost 800 hectares was rented from the "Spanish" neighbor, a hacendado. Two other villages in the province of Tehuacán bought a hacienda with 240 hectares of good agricultural land in installments in 1765. The cabecera of Tlalmanalco (Chalco) had three ranchos with a total of 540 hectares of agricultural land, but only a fraction of it was sown—5 has. maize and 14 has. wheat—while the rest lay fallow. Cultivation was by alternate rotation (año-y-vez). The maize yield in

1757 was 133:1 and in 1765 it was 52:1; the wheat yield in 1765 was almost 6:1. The villagers plowed, sowed and harvested in accordance with a prearranged schedule involving practically everyone in the pueblo. The harvest was stored in the town hall in Tlalmanalco until it could be sold to merchants from Mexico City.[33] The pueblos in the vicinity of the cabecera of Acatzingo (Tepeaca) cultivated chili peppers on the municipal fields. This labor-intensive crop yielded a very good harvest in 1778. The harvest of 1,000 cargas of wheat in the pueblos of Tochimilco in 1789 was astonishing. In 1787, a pueblo in the province of Texcoco harvested 30 fanegas of maize from the municipal fields, which was only 1 fanega (3½ has.) in size (that is, 30:1). Including the sale of the maize stalks (*tlazole*), and prior to deduction for the tithe and selected sowing seed, this brought in 34p4½ for the municipal treasury.[34]

Some of these yields do indeed resemble those of the haciendas. The same is true of the style of management carried out in the pueblo of Santa María Tepexpan (Teotihuacán), for example, and in the pueblos in Metztitlán.[35] The gobernadores of Tepexpan kept a close record of all income and expenditure relating to the management of the municipal land, despite the small harvest (2 to 3 cargas of wheat in the 1760s and 8 to 12 cargas in the 1770s). For the threshing they hired a team of threshing horses from a neighboring hacienda for seven pesos. The gobernadores compared the prices for this team of the various haciendas in the neighborhood with one another in order to secure the most favorable terms. A tithe collector came regularly to collect his dues, and the straw was sold to passing mule teams. The alcalde mayor of Metztitlán, who was in control of a municipal plot of land on which maize and beans were grown, took on between ten and twenty-four hands a day to harvest the beans in the months of July and August, and between sixty and eighty-six hands a day to harvest the maize in October. The milpas were guarded by a *milpero* for 3½ months (for 1 real a week, plus maize rations), and hands were needed to husk the maize and to thresh the beans; many haciendas employed women to do this work. The harvest was transported to the town hall of Metztitlán by 18 arrieros with a total of 139 mules, who made fifty-eight trips. The maize and beans were sold to sixty-one different customers from the village and elsewhere.

Now, despite my own strictures about the statistical value of all these examples, I think one may conclude from reading the records from later in the eighteenth century that they indicate a deterioration. The accounts of various gobernadores of pueblos in the province of Texcoco between 1787 and 1808 reveal low profits as well as losses. The full tribute was not always paid to the state treasury because the tribute had to cover the expenses of the municipal treasury. This was the case in Texcoco in 1808; it was not yet practiced in 1787, resulting in a deficit. The income from the propios was only exceptionally sufficient to balance the accounts, as in the case of the gobernador of Cuauhtlanzingo (Otumba). He received 31p6 in 1792 from the sale of maize, tlazole, barley, and straw. This was a poor performance because of the bad harvest that year. His expenses on paper (for the accounts), masses, festivities and the schoolmaster were so high that he added 6p4 from his own pocket. The situation the following year was slightly improved. He had rented four milpas for a total of 16 pesos and had sold pulque on the local weekly markets for 50p6, yielding a profit of 16 pesos. But the final surpluses of the following years rose extraordinarily. In 1793–94, the new gobernador sold maize, tlazole, barley, straw, and pulque for 241p5½, and there was also income from the rental of the four milpas and the sale of pulse. The expenses on festivities, masses, and miscellaneous items, including the transport of the maize and the purchase of packaging material, totaled 127 pesos, yielding a profit of 114p5½ to be paid to the state treasury. This profit was primarily the result of the high prices of agricultural products at the time.[36] Receipts were good if the harvest from pueblo land could be sold for a good price, but it was more common for the harvests to fail and for large losses to be incurred. One way of covering them, as in Texcoco, was not to pay the full tribute, a measure which, though not illegal, was not customary.

The losses, however, were primarily due to the expenses. The pueblos bought impressive quantities of wax for the manufacture of figures and candles to be used in church or in the processions. They bought vast quantities of fireworks. The village priests received large amounts of money for administering the sacraments and reading mass. There were certainly many festivals. The major ones were New Year, Easter, Corpus Christi, Christmas, and the anniversary of the patron saint of the pueblo (*fiesta titular*). The confraternities were responsible for organizing most of these festivals, but, it will be remembered, the gobernadores increasingly funded them, and not just for the electoral festivities during or shortly after the New Year celebrations.

There is probably a fraud factor at work here, although its nature and scope are still unclear to me. In 1807, the gobernadores of Otumba were accused of having deliberately brought about the losses of the municipal treasury by overpaying the priests. The gobernadores, in turn, accused the priests of asking for excessively high payments. It was certainly true at that time that the priests compensated the loss of salary imposed on them by the Spanish state by stepping up the payments that the parish had to make for their services. All the same, the government officials from Mexico City correctly pointed out that this was only half the story, because the high expenses for candles, wax, and fireworks could not be blamed on the priests. In one case seventy-five pesos had been spent on candles, while the priest—who traded in candles—had only received twenty-five pesos. Where were the other fifty pesos which the gobernador had taken from the municipal treasury? One of the gobernadores asked the crown to recall the officials who had been sent to investigate the matter because "the Indians in the village were very religious and did not complain about the large sums which they had to pay for their festivals." This argument should not be underestimated. My impression is that the festivals increased in scale during the last decennia of the eighteenth century.[37] The case of Miguel Merida and the elections in Huayacocotla discussed in the preface indicates that the legitimacy of an official could be bought with festivities. This hypothesis should be examined further in connection with the earlier conclusion on the development of the gobernadoryotl and the defense of the boundaries of the fundo legal.

This brings us back to the attempt of the gobernadores/caciques to maintain or increase their legitimacy in the pueblos. In the course of the late eighteenth century the Indians appear to have turned their backs on communal labor on the municipal fields. Once again, this fits in with the theory of commoditization. Various observations by priests of the period indicate that the peasants obliged to work on the land had failed to meet their obligations en masse and had rented agricultural land elsewhere. This dereliction of duty led the gobernador to respond by denying them a milpa on the común. Elsewhere, the peasants acted with more acumen: in the province of Tehuacán they took the collectively produced maize harvest from the municipal lands home with them for their own consumption. The gobernadores must have been powerless to do anything, since they gave up working the land through faenas before but started recruiting wage laborers. It is debatable whether this movement is exclusively due to overpopulation. The gobernadores never stopped favoring their relatives. They also ensured that the small peasants were dependent on them through debt. Many caciques owned shops or liquor stores where purchases could be made on credit, allowing the debts to run up until the moment of repayment arrived. This moment was determined by the caciques themselves. They also advanced the tribute payment on behalf of many of the villagers, with the same result. It is likely that, confronted as they were with a falling standard of living, the young sons in the villages did their best to break out of this vicious circle.[38]

In the light of these cases, it is hard to avoid the conclusion that the management of the municipal and confraternity treasuries was more beneficial to the gobernadores/caciques than to the tributarios and members of the rural confraternities. It is thus not only a sign of commoditization, but it is also the opposite of a leveling mechanism, which played such an important role in the theory of the closed corporate peasant community. In fact, I have even seen a request addressed to the Audiencia by a gobernador in which he called for legislation to determine a maximum amount for the increasing costs of the village festival, depending on the number of tributarios. The gobernador of Zacatlán, Don Juan Carlos Sánchez, stated in October 1769 that those under his rule wanted more and more fireworks and were buying increasing quantities of wax. The four main festivals in the pueblo had cost five hundred pesos, thereby emptying the municipal treasury, so there was no money to pay tribute either. The gobernador would therefore have to pay it out of his own pocket. He considered this unfair, and was supported in his position by Mexico City. As a result, the Indians in Zacatlán were forbidden to spend more than three hundred pesos on their festivities in December 1759. The gobernadores did not want to have to cover the expenses; on the contrary, they hoped to make a profit from their *cargos*. This conclusion is in accordance with remarks on the cargo system by such anthropologists as Wasserstrom and Schryer.[39]

Unfortunately, very little research has been conducted in this area, and case studies of the pueblos in Anáhuac during the colonial period still must be carried out. The scanty documentation on which I drew for the present chapter suggests a general pauperization in the Indian municipalities around 1800. The central religious and secular authorities seem to have been already aware of this situation in the 1780s. Attempts were made to reorganize the cofradías to ensure the survival of the fittest and to support the existence of their members; the cofradías and hermandades were responsible for allowances for widows, orphans, the sick, invalids, and the aged. Attempts were made to set up propios and people hoped that the gobernadores could be encouraged to run the municipal treasury properly.[40] The result was considered disappointing.

Household Agriculture

In the main, the family households of the small peasants in Anáhuac had to find a way out of impoverishment by themselves, and with the assistance of relatives and ritual kin, if at all. This brings us to ask to what extent these households were able to make a Great Leap Forward. This section is concerned with the agrarian aspect of this question. In structural terms, however, it was hardly possible to intensify the agricultural system in Anáhuac. According to the agronomist Wilken, who is theoretically and practically familiar with the agricultural methods used in central Mexico, the methods of cultivation used in the region can barely be improved without extremely modern resources like tractors, artificial fertilizer, and mechanical sowers. The traditional cultivation of the milpas in Mexico and Guatemala is, in fact, one of the most intensive techniques that can be utilized in a relatively dry and cold climate and on a shallow soil.[41] Few who are familiar with these methods of cultivation will be prepared to contradict him. However, one disadvantage of the method is the high intensity of labor. Because of the high labor costs, the milpa was very expensive for the larger agriculturalists when the price of maize was low.[42] Mechanization is difficult because of the varying cycles of the plants, and the yields are slightly lower than in the case of large-scale monoculture. The milpa is practical for a household without high labor costs. The method is therefore less suitable as a means of feeding large families, and is quite unsuitable for concentrations of population on the scale of Mexico City in the eighteenth century.

Two other agronomists, Enge and Whiteford, dispute the often-heard "myth of the stupid peasant" who has to be told by outsiders how to increase the yield of his land.[43] Like Wilken, they claim that the Indians have little to learn from European or North American specialists, because the milpa cultivation is still the most efficient method of cultivation that can be applied in the Mexican highlands. Indian farmers not only know more about strategically relevant local resources than outside experts; they also possess a diverse and sophisticated set of resource-management tactics, have a truly vast array of methods for managing crops, and generally strive to employ the most suitable techniques for the local ecological and economic context. In their critique of Wolf and Palerm, they add that the Indians' mastery of irrigation in the pre-Hispanic era was such that everyone received his share without any need for further state intervention. It is striking that they see a continuity between the present and the pre-Hispanic past, adding that the Indians probably fared less well in the colonial period. However, these authors only had very outdated literature at their disposal for the colonial period, based on the perspective of the Black Legend. Recent historical research, summarized below, contains only scanty information on this topic, but it is nevertheless enough to conclude that the Indians were "technologically wise" and "institutionally creative" in the colonial period as well.

The secret of the traditional milpa lies in the use of space. The method produced highly nutritional foods in a way that made optimal use of the horizontal and vertical space. Sowing and planting different crops in the same field reduced the danger of plagues and erosion. Maize was grown in rows on a small surface area. Straight and curved drills were made, depending on the slope of the fields, since the milpas were usually on an incline or at the foot of a hill, and the seeds were then sown in these drills, in small holes close to one another. Only four or five seeds were used in each one. The maize grew to a height of two or three meters. During the process of growth the earth was piled up around the stalks, which came to stand on a raised mound. This reduced the impact of the wind on the plants, while rainwater could drain in the newly formed gullies between the drills. In the meantime pulse was sown at the foot of the maize stalks; the most popular was the red bean (*frijol*). During the process of growth, these beans could use the maize stalks and benefit from the piling up of earth and from the weeding. The beans grew half the height of the maize. Beans and maize complement one another in the field, since the beans provide the ground with nitrogen and thus speed up the growth process of the maize. This dispensed with the need for a rotation of nitrogen producers and nitrogen consumers on the milpas, which was one of the secrets of the so-called Agricultural Revolution, or rather New Husbandry, in early modern England. The peasants grew gourds on the ground between the drills, where the soil was well irrigated.[44]

The tools the peasants used were the most appropriate ones. Complex agricultural techniques like these call for small instruments, such as the digging-stick (*coa*): this tool does not disturb much soil, and its intensive use in sowing is economical on seed. Plows require much more room, if only because of the traction by oxen or mules, especially in the period of building up the soil so that the animals can walk between the plants (three or four times after sowing). The labor-saving aspect of the plow demands so much space that it would be a drawback in densely populated areas. Wilken and Cook are right in stating that the use of the plow could be a retrograde step in terms of agricultural technology: it becomes more difficult to cultivate a variety of crops in the same field. In this case, maize cultivation could literally gain ground, but at the expense of the simultaneous milpa of beans, gourds, and herbs.[45] Since it is precisely this step that is often made necessary by population pressure, it is only natural to concentrate in this section on the shift which took place in Mexico from milpa cultivation in the hills to field cultivation on the open land.

The historical geographer Trautmann also considers that the agricultural technique practiced by the pegujaleros in Anáhuac could hardly be improved upon. He sees the main advantage of the milpas outside the hilly land in the various forms of irrigation and semi-irrigation. The chinampa technique is the most familiar and has received the most attention. It involves the cultivation of a number of different crops (including maize) on woven straw mats on the banks of shallow lakes, with mud from the bottom of the lake constantly fertilizing the fields. This technique was used mainly on the lakes in the environs of Mexico City. Further inland, rivers and ponds, small dams, locks, and mountain streams tapped in the rainy season could provide sufficient water for a method that closely resembled the chinampa, involving the artificial inundation of several fields. An intermediate form of these techniques utilized land that was under water during the rainy season.[46] However, milpas on slopes of hills and mountains (where the most rainwater could be collected) or on the shores of lakes are extremely vulnerable in periods of drought. It was here that the danger lay in the last decennia of the eighteenth century, when the spring rains failed to materialize, for each milpa cycle runs its course with the rainy season. Alzate noted around 1800 that many hectares of chinampas near Mexico City had completely dried up for a number of years. His impressive survey of the places that once had been the sites of chinampa cultivation but now were reduced to dust gives an impression of ecological disruption.[47]

The material consulted for the present investigation supports the conclusion that there was a general distribution of the highly intensive agriculture on small milpas at the feet of the hills and on the banks of rivers and lakes. The water that ran down the hills was essential input for the village irrigation systems in addition to the ordinary rain that fell. The practice of constructing large and very expensive water reservoirs (jagüeyes) was mainly used on the haciendas; the Indian peasants irrigated the land directly and hardly stored any water, although this did occur in some cases. Terraces were constructed to stop the water from draining away too rapidly, but it was important that not too much water was left behind; otherwise, the plants would be ruined. This all entailed a great deal of activity in the spring to prepare the cycle.[48]

It was barely possible to obtain more than one harvest in the highlands. The agricultural calendar on the Mesa de Anáhuac was confined to the months between the last night frost of spring and the first night frost of autumn. The only way to extend or alter this calendar was through irrigation. Peasants could try sowing flowers on a few damp plots after the harvest, which provided a good cash crop in connection with all of the New Year festivities. Since the milpas did not have large water reserves, cultivation was mainly tied to the cultivo de temporal, the regular agricultural pattern that was dependent on the rainy season. As soon as the harvest of maize stalks (tlazole, used as

fodder) was over, December and January saw the commencement of prepara-
tory activities for the following year: digging or plowing the fields. Many
pegujaleros owned teams of oxen in the eighteenth century, either individually or on a joint basis. Some pueblos had so many that the haciendas came to
hire them. Maize sowing, using the coa, was done in March and April, but
sometimes postponed until the beginning of May if the rainy season was late.
Heaping up the soil on the milpas was done in the summer months at the
same time as weeding. The beans were sowed in June and harvested in October or November, shortly before the harvest of the maize ears (*elotes*) in November and December. A good harvest was sufficient for an entire year, and a
run of good harvests made it possible to lay in stores. This system broke down
after 1770, when many harvests were only sufficient to last until the summer
of the following year. When the stores ran out after a few successive harvest
failures (1784–85!), the peasants were forced to resort to the market in the
early autumn.[49]

The data relating to the distribution of the común repartimiento in the
mid-eighteenth century indicate the existence of small farms surrounded by
small milpas. Travel accounts, wills, and other documents from a half century
later, however, give the impression that the most important fields of the
pegujaleros were situated further away by then: on the edge of the village, and
usually outside the fundo legal. The documentation also suggests that work
on the land was a male occupation, with women and children only lending a
helping hand when haste was called for (for example, if the harvest was in
danger because of heavy rains). The travelers who visited New Spain in the
late eighteenth century were struck by the quiet in the pueblos if the men
were at work on the land and the children were roaming the hills with the
livestock. Although little is known about land use, this suggests that the farmyard within the fundo legal occupied a less important role around 1800.[50]

An example of milpas on the edge of the pueblo can be seen in Map 18
(the pueblo of Malinaltenango in Zacualpan in 1771).[51] The pueblo was
hemmed in between two gulleys (*barrancas*) that provided water to irrigate
the fields in the summer. The gobernador wanted a fundo legal excluding the
living quarters of the pegujaleros, and he had submitted a request to the
Audiencia to that end. The larger milpas were north of the center of the pueblo,
bordering on a meadow where the peasants grazed their livestock. This bears
some resemblance to the open-field system practiced in England at the time,
or to that practiced in the northeastern Netherlands. The milpas were probably still too small, because the villagers asked the state for the property rights
to a plot of land to the left of the road leading to the pueblo.

The pattern of settlement of scattered houses, each with its own farmyard, meant that neighbors were separated from one another. Travellers saw
in this an obstacle to lively discussions among the women. Their household
chores did not leave the women much time to spare. A woman's day was
dominated by the preparation of meals. After breakfast (atole, a maize porridge with honey), the men set off to work and the women started grinding

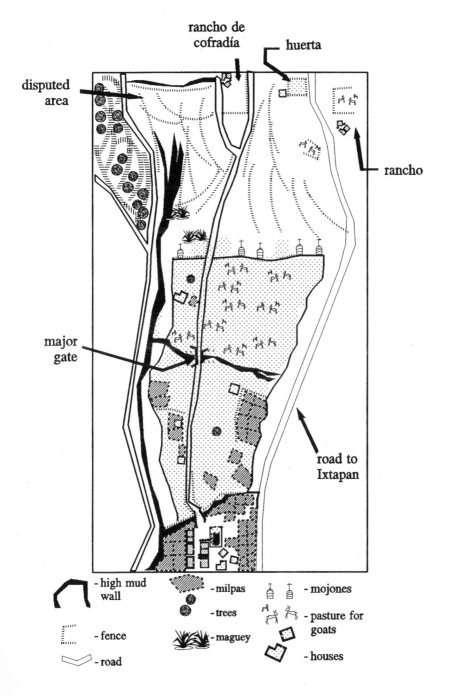

rancho de
cofradía

huerta

disputed
area

rancho

major
gate

road to
Ixtapan

- high mud
  wall

- milpas

- mojones

- trees

- pasture for
  goats

- fence

- maguey

- houses

- road

Map 18 The agricultural land of Malinaltenango (Zacualpan), 1771

cooking, kneading, and roasting the maize dough.[52] Tortillas soon dry out and lose a substantial part of their nutritional value, which is why they need to be made daily. After the midday meal, the women left for the hills to collect firewood (*leña*), or they engaged in weaving and needlework, making pots or other handicrafts. If there was not much to do on the land, the men stayed at home with their wives after the midday meal and helped them with their handicrafts. The pueblos were livelier during times like these. The women regularly set off together for the nearest river, lake, or irrigation channel to do the washing. There was also social contact once a week in the market and in church on Sunday, of course.

The farmhouses themselves were little more than simple constructions of adobe, wood, and brick. They had a gabled or a flat roof, depending on the customs and situation of the pueblo (a gabled roof was necessary in the areas near the volcanoes, which were subjected to heavy rainfall). The roof was made of beams and planks. Flat roofs were covered with a layer of boulder clay (*tepetate*); gabled roofs were tiled. In the warmer regions, the farmhouses consisted entirely of straw. As a general rule, the farmhouse only had one, sparsely furnished living room. There was a woven palm-leaf mat on the floor (*petate*) and a kitchen area where the hearth fire smoldered. At night the peasants slept on the mat by the fireside, wrapped in a blanket. The blanket was to ward off the direct danger of insect and scorpion bites and to offer protection against the cold, which could be severe at times. Tools and baskets full of dried meat and fish, herbs, beans, dried and fresh chili peppers, and the maize due to be ground hung from the walls. Each house had one or two domestic altars. Turkeys, chickens, pigs, sheep, goats, and dogs ran loose in the farmyard, where the mules or donkeys used for transport were tethered (most pegujaleros were arrieros, of course). The cattle were sometimes kept in small fenced areas, but usually they roamed loose. Each farmyard also had its characteristic maize shed. The maize was kept in *cuescomates* or *zencales*,[53] depending on local practice. When it was brought in from the field, it was still damp and had to be dried in the sun. This was done on the flat farmhouse roofs or on a part of the farmyard set aside for this purpose. Good dry maize in the cob (*mazorcas*) could be kept for two or three years; loose seeds were likely to go moldy at the point where they had been detached from the ear. This was one reason why the maize seeds were husked (*desgranado*) and ground each day.[54]

It is impossible to say how much the pegujaleros in Anáhuac produced on their holdings. The source material is not even sufficient to support simple estimates. All one can do is guess about the harvests. It is striking that the data on maize cultivation on the individual plots (*trechos*) or común repartimiento plots indicate that the pueblos hardly used the propios for their own subsistence, if at all. Axapusco and Otumba, the two villages in the semiarid area in the province of Otumba, claimed that each tributary received a field as usual; two other pueblos in this area, Ostoticpac and Cuauhtlacingo, stated both the number of fields and the approximate number of fanegas planted in each.[55] I have not seen statistics like these for any other pueblo, and they are undoubt-

edly the result of the investigation of the factional quarrel in Otumba between different Indian nobles. The yields of these plots varied in 1794 between 24:1 and 103:1, depending on the nature of the soil. These are normal
figures, so that bigger harvests must surely have been a possibility in better
years, for the early 1790s were drought years. Tutino estimated that the 197
households in Ostoticpac worked 197 milpas. Each milpa had a surface area
of between 6 and 8 cuartillos of sowing land (about half a hectare). With a
yield factor of 450:1 per peasant, the harvest in a good year was around 10
fanegas. This corresponds to the high figures Osborn gives for Metztitlán (see
chapter three). However, not all the land of the común repartimiento was
divided. The pueblo of Ostoticpac controlled at least 100 has. of floodwater-
irrigated lands—the size of the fundo legal!—but in 1794 the municipal leaders assigned only some 74 hectares to the 197 households; sometimes it was
less, and the tributarios worked between 49 and 74 hectares. Nearby
Cuauhtlacingo possessed about 112 hectares of floodwater-irrigated lands, in
addition to 88 hectares of temporal lands, and assigned no more than 30 hectares to the 80 tributarios (household heads). These Indians obviously did not
need more than their fundo legal for subsistence; in principle, the común
repartimiento could provide enough maize annually, and their municipal treasury had a good income from the propios.

To sum up, we can draw two conclusions:

1. the agriculture of the pegujaleros in the pueblos in Anáhuac was
   already extremely intensive; the work, mainly carried out by men,
   could hardly be improved within the constraints of traditional
   agriculture; and
2. it is likely that a shift took place in the second half of the eighteenth century from agriculture in the center of the fundo legal to
   cultivation on the edge of the village, or even outside it; in many
   cases this was a shift from the hills to the valley, combined with a
   certain increase of scale because of the use of the plow.

However, as long as we lack more details for a large sample of pueblos over a
long period of time, these conclusions remain extremely tenuous.

Production for the Tianguiz

In an earlier chapter, the repartimiento trade was adduced as an important
nonagricultural source of income for the inhabitants of the pueblos de indios.
In fact, the repartimiento was the main instrument of commoditization. The
Indians could make good the deficits that had arisen through the agricultural
shortfall by producing for the interregional trade. Contracts for this purpose
were concluded between representatives of the pueblos (the gobernadores)
and the alcaldes mayores. This is why the sources refer to the manufactures
and specific agricultural products, which the villagers produced in this connection, under the general term of contract products (*tratos*). The pueblos can

certainly be regarded as proto-industrial entities in view of their repartimiento retail. It is worth stressing this point here because it is natural to suppose that the pegujaleros did not stop producing artesanía once the terms of a repartimiento contract had been fulfilled. The local retail trade, including the division of labor that it encouraged, was equally important. The trato goods were sold in Anáhuac's weekly markets (tianguiz). The repartimiento, intralocal as it was, may therefore also be regarded as a catalytic agent for the development of the local economy. For our present purposes, these are the two retail markets for the peasants of Anáhuac. Starting with the local market, this section is an attempt to determine whether a growth can be detected in the retail on the weekly markets—a very important point for the question of commoditization.

We cannot tackle an economic question of this kind without examining the structural functioning of the system of weekly markets in Anáhuac. The tianguiz also formed a network by which the "pegujaleros" could guarantee their livelihood. As Greenow and others have shown, the contacts between the families from different pueblos were made at the weekly and annual markets in the eighteenth century.[56] The scope of the local markets depended to a large extent on the density of population of the municipalities, the level of transport costs, the accessibility of the markets, the differences in prices between the markets, and the extent to which nonagrarian producers appeared on the markets in the role of consumers. These factors were not all to be found at the same time, nor to an equal extent. Moreover, besides the nonagrarian producers who came to the markets as consumers at regular intervals, there were the agrarian producers whose own stocks had run out. This is why factors like population growth and bad harvests played a role. In view of these considerations, it will not be easy to provide an adequate typology of the local market economy.[57]

Nevertheless, economic geographers and economic anthropologists have tried to devise a theory of the local market system. The result of their work is a diversity of models, all displaying one major weakness: they are static. The various factors, listed above, that can influence the scope and functioning of the local markets lead one to expect dynamic models. Despite differences of opinion, the geographers and anthropologists were agreed that there was a hierarchy of local markets, formed by a central market and a small number of satellite markets. The central market is the core of a local system of exchange, but at the same time it is the link with a similar neighboring system. In this way, various areas are economically linked with one another. Within the system, each place of local importance has a big outdoor market each week and on a fixed day, at which not only goods and crops from the area, but also products from elsewhere are put on sale.[58]

The seven-day weekly market cycle existed in New Spain from the seventeenth century on. Hassig describes the difficulty with which this cycle was developed. The days in the cycle were fixed in such a way that each market could attract the maximum number of customers. The distribution of the market days gave the traders the opportunity to offer something each day to as wide a circle of customers as possible. It was only in a few very large centers of population, like the big cities, that there was a daily market. As the density of the population increased, means of transport were improved, and certain markets grew in popularity, the system could be adjusted. The pueblo of Chiconcuac, near the city of Texcoco, for example, had a market day on Tuesday in the colonial period, but the pueblo specialty—woolen jumpers and cardigans—became so popular among the inhabitants of Mexico City that market days were introduced on Saturday and Sunday in the course of the nineteenth and twentieth centuries.[59] The places where central markets were held in the region of Guadalajara in the eighteenth century were, without exception, cabeceras; the smaller markets were held in the pueblos sujetos. Since, in general, the same kinds of goods were traded on the markets in the sujetos, they had little contact with one another, although each of them maintained extremely good contact with the cabecera.[60]

A market system bearing a close resemblance to this is the so-called star system, in which the large markets were surrounded by the smaller ones. According to Gormsen, in 1964 the cabecera markets in the federal state of Puebla were also organized in a star system of large-scale and small-scale central markets. The majority of the markets were held on Sunday. They were of importance for the cabecera and its immediate surroundings, but their commercial importance was overshadowed by the large-scale weekly markets, which combined a number of these small-scale weekly markets. The large-scale weekly markets therefore were almost never held on a Sunday. The documents I have consulted indicate a very similar structure for the diocese of Puebla in the eighteenth century. The same is true of the weekly markets in what is now the federal state of Mexico and the source material on the eighteenth-century diocese of Mexico. It is possible to draw up a tentative tianguiz map on the basis of this material to illustrate how cabecera markets are linked to one another through star systems. (See Map 19; the specific accuracy is less important in this case because the quantity of data is insufficient, and I do not want to give the impression of accuracy where there is hardly any.) Incidentally, this also indicates that there was a relatively limited number of weekly markets. Not every pueblo sujeto had a weekly market; it can hardly have been commercially viable. The question arises as to whether it was the population density and the religious structure (which were interconnected) that determined the pattern of the market days, instead of the economic structure, as the economic geographers and anthropologists suspected.[61]

There are more data available on the internal functioning of the weekly markets than on their hierarchical relations with one another. Drawings, paintings, and travel accounts from the late seventeenth, eighteenth, and early nineteenth centuries indicate that each weekly market consisted of two parts. One part was composed of wooden stalls, each with a piece of canvas to provide shadow. This was where the large-scale traders, hacendados, and peddlers sold their wares. In the other part, the small-scale traders, including many

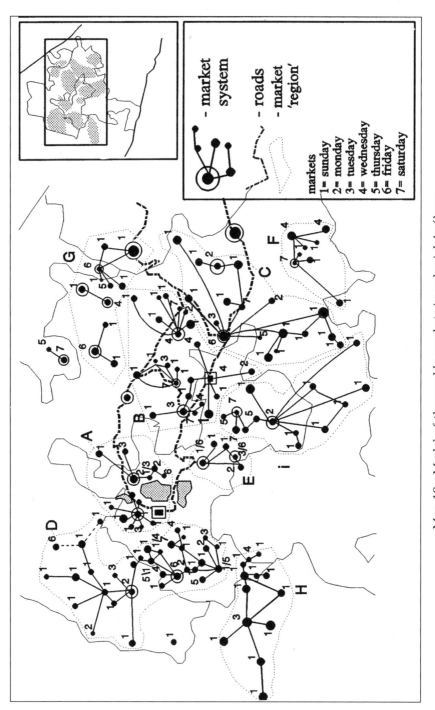

Map 19   Model of the weekly markets in colonial Anáhuac

women, spread their wares on mats on the ground. Here, too, there were screens and large sheets stretched between poles to protect the articles against the sun. The term *tianguiz* referred primarily to this section of the market, while the area with the stalls was often referred to as the *plaza*. There were places to eat and drink all over the market, thus emphasizing the social function of the markets. They had a reputation for the drinking that went on in the afternoons after the market had closed and the peasants had spent some of their earnings on alcohol. Most of the alcohol served on the markets in Anáhuac was pulque or aguardiente. The pulque was sold by women from the pulque districts of Anáhuac and Oaxaca. Drunkenness was a genuine plague of the weekly markets. Sunday, in particular, was regarded as the day to get drunk. The resultant combination of Sunday mass, market day, and inebriation was frequently observed by priests at the time, as well as by anthropologists in contemporary villages in Mexico and Guatemala.[62]

The big traders did not set up their stalls on the smaller markets. These markets did not have sufficient retail outlets to attract them, because there was less demand for the luxury goods they sold. The high costs of transporting these goods could only be recovered if sales were high. The same applied generally to the maize that the haciendas had produced with the assistance of farmhands. The smaller markets were thus only profitable for peasants from the neighborhood and for peddlers. The latter were very important for the range of articles offered on the smaller markets. As they traveled from one market to another, the peddlers bought maize, beans, lard, foodstuffs, household items, and manufactures from hacendados or on the weekly markets. They often had a permanent network of suppliers. In 1771, a merchant in Chalco wrote that the peasants in the remote areas would suffer from shortages if it were not for the peddlers. The central market in the province of Chalco was held in the cabecera of Chalco on Friday. The merchant described how men, women, and even whole families came from the neighboring pueblos to this central market to replenish their weekly supply. The rest of the week, however, there was hardly anything to be had in the province, and the only people who could offer anything on those days were the peddlers. He added that the hacendados in the province welcomed the arrival of the peddlers, because these middlemen helped them to dispose of a large part of their surplus.[63]

Although it was not officially allowed, a levy was charged for a market stall in some provinces. In such cases, each trader was asked to pay a small sum in cash, depending on the area that he occupied on the tianguiz. Officials from the capital, who were obliged by the laws in force at the time to prevent unnecessary increases in food prices, raised strong objections to this market tax, since it was passed on in the prices. Nevertheless, the market levy was so customary in the provinces that the taxes are even sometimes traceable in the official government accounts. A case from the province of Chalco, west of the volcano of Ixtaccihuatl, covering the years 1764–68, suggests that the revenue from the market levy accounted for between one-quarter and one-third of the

Table 10   Market revenue as a component
of the alcabala in the province
of Chalco, 1764–68

| | State revenue from: | | | |
| | market | | alcabala totals | |
Year	(absolute)	%	(absolute)	%
1764	1,234	28	4,468	100
1765	1,683	31	5,374	100
1766	1,655	28	5,874	100
1767	1,374	26	5,209	100
1768	1,245	23	5,288	100

Source: AGI, Audiencia México, Leg. 2096

annual revenue from the tax on trading (*alcabala*); see Table 10. This tax was also levied on the weekly market in Tochimilco, on the eastern side of the volcano. It would be rash, however, to assume that this was the practice throughout the region. More research is required on sources of this kind, because they can provide an indication of the development of the economy in the countryside. With reference to England, the historian Hilton claims that the increase in sales of retail items on the local markets is an indication of a step toward proto-industrialization.[64]

The tianguiz are important in this connection because they were a means of redistribution of local specialties, particularly during periods of high population density. Though they included primary foodstuffs, the main items were the more expensive crops (pulse, vegetables), fruit, cash crops, and manufactures. The weekly markets served the local trade, not the interlocal trade, although the products traded on an exclusively local scale in the late seventeenth century found their way to the farthest corners of the Spanish empire in Mexico and Central America in the late eighteenth century. There was a wide variety of products. Textile manufactures, eggs, and lacquered articles have already been mentioned. McMillen's thesis mentions various pueblos in the valley of Toluca that increasingly specialized in the production of a particular kind of pottery in the eighteenth century. Village production was specifically geared to the taste and requirements of the urban customers: a variety of kinds of pans, dishes, flower pots, and wall tiles (*azulejos*) were made in Spanish shapes and decorated with Spanish motifs. This pottery reached cities like Toluca and Mexico City by way of the repartimiento trade and the tianguiz trade.[65] The provinces in the highland faldas were well-known manufacturing areas at the time. The tropical fruits and goods that could only be produced there because of the absence of tropical raw materials in the highlands—such as hats and mats (*petates*) woven from palm leaves—were sold on a large scale in the highlands. These Indian municipalities also had a near-monopoly of the manufacture of packing material. Another well-known specialty was salt production. Almost every village on a lake had a number of salt producers among its residents. These pueblos were also specialists in the fresh and dried fish trade. The pueblos in the Llanos de Apan, northwest of Mexico City, produced pulque on a large scale, but they were not the only ones to do so. A good example is provided by the career of Doña Micaela Angela Carrillo in the pueblo of Amozoc (Puebla), which has been described by Couturier. The wealth of this widow of a cacique was derived from a number of maguey fields. Less well-off villagers who were in her debt regularly had to concede their maguey fields to her. The rest of her family ran the production of decorative wrought-iron work, the pueblo specialty. In addition to these telling examples, we must mention the wide variety of vegetables and fruit that the "pegujaleros" in each pueblo cultivated and brought to the market. According to Gibson, the supply of vegetables and fruit in Mexico City was so large that certain vegetables had to be written off after two days and sold to livestock traders. The municipalities in the provinces of Xochimilco, Coyoacán, and Chalco and those in the south of the province of Tlaxcala enjoyed a special reputation as market gardens.[66]

The pueblos that did not have a specialty of this kind had a large variety of products which could be produced for the market. A good example is provided by the priest of Capulhuac (Tenango del Valle) in his reply to the 1776 survey. His cabecera contained 108 families with a non-Indian calidad (678 persons, including 237 servants with the *calidad mulato* and some 200 artesans with a *calidad mestizo*). The community also included 489 Nahuatl-speaking indios. Each of the households in the cabecera grew maize, broad beans and other pulse in the fields. These varieties of pulse, as well as barley, wooden beams and planks, were the specialty of the pueblos in this province. However, each peasant had a handicraft too. They made wooden spindles and spools (*malacates*) to spin cotton and wool. Other peasants in the cabecera concentrated on weaving hats, for which they imported palm leaves from the tierra caliente. There were also many peddlers from this pueblo who bought up all kinds of manufactures from the region and resold them in the tianguiz in the highlands. A few mestizos from the village working as arrieros bought sugar loaves in the province of Cuernavaca and sold them in the village. Others produced honey, a popular product because of the custom of using it to sweeten atole. Two of the three pueblos sujetos of Capulhuac produced plows and yokes that were sold to the hacendados in the neighborhood, besides performing the usual agricultural work in the fields of the común. A third sujeto was by a lake and made a living from fishing; the women specialized in breeding turkeys, which they sold in the tianguiz. The fourth sujeto, containing 277 families, owned a lot of woodland (*monte*), thus competing with the wood production in the cabecera. A few of the villagers had become genuine artists in wood.[67]

Most of the reports on the scope of specialization of this kind date from the late eighteenth century. This is an interesting point. Although the specialization in Anáhuac already must have been a feature of the pre-Hispanic period, when the region was exceptionally densely populated, an increase in activity can be detected in the eighteenth century. Almost all of the sources on the late eighteenth century used in this section refer to "more business than before" in the tianguiz or to "an increase in trade between the villages." Unfortunately, it is impossible to quantify this development, and we are forced to fall back on the scanty data found in the archives. At first sight, the main sources are the geographical accounts from 1742–43, 1777–78, 1794, and 1804, but there is only material covering the whole century from a few provinces. Most of the data come from the valley of Puebla. The pueblos in the province of Tepeaca, for example, already had a reputation as textile producers in 1743, although most of it was wool. The products were sold through the repartimiento trade to the alcaldes mayores and on the central Friday market in the town of Tepeaca. Not all of the pueblos in the province produced this trato. San Agustín de Palmar and Quechula, for example, where each family owned four or five mules, lived exclusively from the arriería. Chalchicomula, at the foot of the volcano Citlaltepetl, was a lumberjack village in 1743, while the villagers in Acatzingo were fruit growers and cotton weavers. The inhabitants of San Hipolito supplemented the yield of their milpas with sheep shearing on the neighboring livestock haciendas. It was only the residents of a couple of villages, such as Tecamachalco, Nopalucan, and the suburbs of Tepeaca, who went to work on the land of the hacendados at that time. The situation was more or less the same in 1804, with one clear difference: the general spread of cotton weaving. This must have created problems for the hacendados, because the governors of the few pueblos that traditionally provided them with migrant labor were now less inclined to look for work on the haciendas for their subordinates; Thomson reports aggressive behavior by the hacendados when it was a question of hanging on to the hands.[68]

This conclusion is confirmed by other examples. In 1743, the main products of the nine pueblos in the province of Tochimilco on the eastern slopes of a volcano were wood and coal to supplement the yield of the común. Two pueblos still grew cochineal—the main specialty there until the seventeenth century—and another pueblo concentrated on fruit. Hardly any of the villagers worked as migrant laborers on the haciendas in the valley. The geographical accounts from 1770 and 1789 (two very different years in this respect!) refer to the same tratos. In 1789, the priest added that the villages could make a good living from their agricultural activities and the retail of the trato products on the weekly markets, without having to look for extra earnings from the haciendas. Every year, the peasants bought 150 bulls, 100 sheep, and 175 pigs from the alcalde mayor through the repartimiento trade. In 1804, however, the situation had changed. Many villagers now worked as migrant laborers in the valley, sometimes staying away from home for months. Cotton weaving had been introduced, and the arriería had increased considerably, while cochineal had disappeared. This is a shift typical of other villages in the valley of Puebla.[69]

We have a more detailed account of Malinalco, a province in the valley of Toluca. In 1743, the alcalde mayor responded to a request from the crown to send a geographical account of his province to the capital of New Spain. He sent a diary of a tour on horseback from village to village and covering all of the haciendas, lasting a number of days. All of the villages in the province compensated the agricultural risks by means of their trato. This was apparently sufficient, since he claimed that there was too much time left over for the consumption of the stocks of pulque and aguardiente accumulated by the villagers. It would be better for them to spend their time working on the haciendas, he stated, because they were always in need of hands. In the vicinity of the pueblo of Tenancingo, however, the alcalde mayor came across pueblos dependent on furnishing migrant labor to the haciendas and to the silver mines in Taxco, Zacualpan, and Sultepec. Near the pueblo of San Lucas was a pueblo sujeto consisting of seven families living entirely from wheat production on a few large plots of land. In a certain sense, the alcalde mayor's wishes were already fulfilled in 1777, for in that year the priest of Malinalco sent a description of the province to Madrid that made mention of migrant labor to the haciendas. All the same, most of the peasants could still survive on their tratos. The weekly markets in Tenancingo (Tuesday and Sunday), Tianguiztengo (Wednesday), and Santa Cruz (Sunday) were larger than ever. Many "pegujaleros" went to the markets in Taxco, Zacualpan, and Tetecala (Cuernavaca) to sell their wares. They invested in mules, oxen, and small livestock, which they purchased through the intermediary of the alcalde mayor, on a larger scale than before. The tratos of these villages displayed an enormous variety: chili peppers, bananas, citrus fruit, tropical fruit, broad beans, lentils, barley, and woolen ponchos (*gabanes*) with black and gray-white decoration. The Tenancingo district had developed a flourishing industry in fine cotton and silk embroidery, in addition to the well-known wrought-iron decorations produced by the men. After 1800, however, there are few reports of large-scale migrant labor and problems in the retail of the tratos.[70]

The scale of the production of local agrarian and handicraft specialties and their apparent growth in the middle decennia of the eighteenth century suggest that the small peasants were not defenseless in the face of change in economic activity, as has often been suggested in the peasant debate. The small peasant households in Anáhuac certainly experienced great difficulties in selling their products, which is why they might have been—in theory that is—reluctant to devote a large share of their factors of production to the production of cash crops and artesanía. However, since the repartimiento trade helped to guarantee their livelihood, the room was created for local retail, resulting in an increased local division of labor. The threshold of an expansion of scale of the small peasant household was lowered in eighteenth-century Anáhuac. This was a "step by step substitution of subsistence economy by commodity consumption and production," a process that has also been perceived in Europe. Burke even argues that this process led to a brief heyday of popular culture in Europe.[71] The conditions might not have been very different in Anáhuac.

Crown Interference

Employment, Transport, and the Urban Market

This brings us a rung higher. Nowhere was proto-industry as evident as in interlocal trade, which linked the Indian pueblos with the urban economy. Production for the repartimiento is familiar enough by now. These data place the role of the cities in New Spain in a different light from the way in which development sociologists saw them. The traditional thesis of these thinkers is that the cities only functioned as administrative centers of the colonial power and as a domicile for the Spanish elite.[72] The attraction of the cities was naturally due to the employment opportunities they offered. In contrast to much of the literature of development theory, modern historical literature documents a growth of activity in the cities of New Spain as a result of in-migration. However, Anáhuac only had two large cities. The population of Mexico City in 1790 was approximately 110,000 and that of Puebla de los Angeles was around 60,000. These statistics indicate that the Mexican cities were relatively small compared with other urban centers of the period. Approximate figures for some European cities around 1800 are: London 900,000, Paris 550,000, and Naples 500,000. Even cities like St. Petersburg (218,000 in 1789), Amsterdam (217,000 in 1795) or Madrid (148,000 on 1793) were larger than Mexico City. Nevertheless, the level of urbanization in New Spain seems to have been remarkably high. A good 13 percent of the population of Anáhuac (170,000/1,300,000) lived in Mexico City around 1800, while less than 5 percent of the population of eighteenth-century Castilia lived in Madrid. Moreover, half of the population of New Spain lived in the Anáhuac region at the time. Statistics like these emphasize the great importance of the Mexican capital for the economy of New Spain.[73]

The biggest employer in the capital was the tobacco factory. By the end of the eighteenth century, a few decennia after its foundation, this factory employed some eight thousand hands. Day laborers were 95 percent of these employees, and women were 50 percent. Their daily wage was much higher than what they could earn in the countryside. There were also tobacco factories in Guadalajara (fifteen hundred employees), Querétaro (fourteen hundred employees), Puebla (at least one thousand employees), Oaxaca (six hundred employees) and in Orizaba (four hundred employees). The tobacco for Anáhuac was grown by peasants in the eastern falda provinces of Orizaba, Xalapa, and Córdoba. The trade was a state monopoly, and a good source of revenue for the treasury. By the end of the eighteenth century every street corner in the cities of New Spain had a tobacconist's shop, which was strictly controlled by the state. The private production and retailing of cigarettes was prohibited. It is evident that smoking was one of the great vices of the population of New Spain. The Spaniard Ajofrín, who was not accustomed to these practices, was very perturbed by them. His diary is an incessant complaint about the fact that it was impossible to go into a house without the room being full of smoke and that every conversation was disrupted by the search for cigarettes. There were no smoke-free areas; people even smoked in coaches and in church. In 1823, the Englishman Bullock was surprised to see many women smokers. Someone played the piano with a cigarette stuck between her lips, and "exhaled the smoke without even interrupting the sonata." A compatriot, the lady's man Beaufoy, was amused and wrote in 1825:

> If a Señorita wishes to show you particular attention, she puts her hand into her bosom, pulls out a number of cigarritos, and entreats your acceptance of one. Even I, who detest tobacco, have been thus forced to make myself sick more than once; for who could reject a cigar from such a place?[74]

But it was more usual for the cigarettes to appear from a cigarette box.

All the same, only a small percentage of the arrieros can have been involved in the transport of tobacco leaves. At first, the most work for them was provided by small manufacturers, organized in guilds, who carried out their work in small workshops. This manufacture was organized hierarchically in terms of social prestige, calidad, the value of the company and the income of the proprietor. According to Alzate, there were almost nineteen thousand guild craftsmen in Mexico City in 1790. Manufacture provided employment for between one-third and one-half of the population of the capital (excluding the tobacco workers). Most of them worked in construction or textile production. We do not know how many nonregistered hands there were, but it is obvious that the supply of labor power increased dramatically as a result of immigration. Thus the situation in the late eighteenth century changed drastically. The large-scale traders seized the opportunity to profit from the population growth. With the assistance of dependent weavers, spinners, and dyers they built up a textile industry outside the guild organization. This sector (which has been extensively discussed by Miño) was the first to enlist cottage industry on a large scale. While the merchants had previously confined their activities to trading, now they actively interfered in production itself. As demonstrated in an earlier chapter, the cottage industry involved not only many weavers who worked in their homes in the city, but also Indian villagers from the countryside, combined with the processing of the materials in factories in Mexico City.[75]

The real background to the revival of the repartimiento trade in the 1790s now comes to light. The basic processing of textiles (spinning, dying, and weaving) was a rural occupation from the middle of the eighteenth century. The growth in the number of weavers is expressed by the impressive increase in the number of hip-looms; at least as far as the Spanish government could estimate it, for it is still uncertain exactly how many there were around 1790. It was difficult to register hip-looms, because only four sticks of wood were necessary; the loom was tied to a support or a tree, and the weaver squatted at the other end. Every observer notes that weaving in the countryside was no more than a way for men to earn money on the side—and women, too, for many women naturally took part in cottage industries—because wages were lower there than in the towns. For example, in the pueblos of Atlixco, Ixmiquilpan, and Zacatalán, the most a weaver could get for a cotton cloth (a manta) was four reales, while the maximum in the densely populated provinces of Tlaxcala and Tepeaca was three reales. It usually took two days to weave one piece of cloth, so this was the equivalent to the maximum daily wage of two reales which a seasonal laborer could earn on a hacienda.[76]

It is the merit of the historian Miño Grijalva to have charted the real extent of this domestic production.[77] He gives many examples of merchants who set up rural manufacture at the expense of the industrial weaving mills like the *obrajes,* operating near the big cities of Puebla and Mexico City and in a few falda provinces and implicating the gobernadores in the pueblos. The merchants bought raw cotton in the faldas, selling it through the repartimiento and the gobernadores to weavers in the villagers, or offering it in village stores without any official repartimiento. In the light of the marginal profit produced by this trade, the weaver operated as a paid hand. This resulted in a flourishing textile industry in the countryside, above all in the 1790s, after the embargo on the repartimientos had been lifted. The province of Texcoco, for example, had a turnover of 2,237 cargas in 1791. There was no textile manufacture in Ixmiquilpan before 1790, but it would be found in every pueblo afterward. The growth rate in Chalco in the second half of the 1790s was more than 100 percent, especially in the pueblos of Tláhuac, Ozumba, and Amecameca; 1,749 of the 1,951 *familias* in Chilapa, half of whom were Indian, worked as *operarias* for Spanish textile barons in the 1790s. The women, in particular, had obtained more work in all of the provinces, marking a new sexual division of labor. Miño's extensive review of the distribution of cottage industry in Anáhuac convincingly demonstrates that the earlier estimates by Thomson and Salvucci were much too low.[78] These writers attached too much importance to the official 1793 statistics, which are incomplete, because a lot of people avoided registration in connection with the tax laws. They did their weaving in the patios of their tiny farmyards, a spot not usually visited by the Spanish civil servants.

The finishing of articles of clothing and wraps (*rebozos*) took place in the cities in *fábricas de indianillas*, which assumed responsibility for the finishing of materials supplied by the pueblos and from the Philippines. These urban textile factories were a new phenomenon in the late eighteenth century. Don Francisco de Belén's factory in Mexico City, for example, employed around five hundred workers in the period around 1790, rising to two thousand two decennia later. In addition, the factory had many employees who did their work at home in the suburbs. They earned around 1½ real a day, a normal wage for the time. The weavers recruited in the towns or in the countryside by the textile entrepreneurs were no longer regarded as independent craftsmen (guild masters!), but as piece workers in the factory's employ.[79]

Thus the term *proto-industry* is really applicable here: manufacture was primarily market oriented, it was aimed at retail outside the neighborhood, and the producer had hardly any contact with the consumer. Moreover, it was accompanied by changes in the spatial organization of the economy, and perhaps in the sexual division of labor. There are a few extra points that should be added. Consumers already showed a preference at this time for hand-woven products rather than the "mass-produced" goods from the big factories in the cities. For instance, middlemen were aware of the general popularity of handwoven rebozos from Sultepec and Temascaltapec in the faldas southwest of Toluca. They visited the villages in the area to buy the rebozos. After the decline of silver production in the provinces, textile manufacture had become the main means of earning a living for the peasants in these provinces. There were good retail openings for the producers in the neighboring provinces in the region of Michoacán (Querétaro, Guanajuato). Their products had a reputation for being of better quality than the factory products, which were supposed to be full of flaws. Sometimes the trade was in the hands of one of the weavers, who sold the products and shared the profits with the others when he returned to their pueblo. It was only a small step from this situation to a putting-out system, in which the merchants advanced credit or raw cotton to the weavers. This took place on a large scale in the late eighteenth century. The weavers received sixty to six hundred pesos for a dozen rebozos, a price which was between four and ten times as high as that of the textile factories in Puebla. This made cottage industry a profitable alternative for the poor peasant population.[80]

A large number of the arrieros were attracted to Puebla as a manufacturing center. In the late 1760s, Ajofrín compared Puebla to Barcelona because of the large number of craftsmen who worked in the textile sector. Thirty years later, in 1794, Puebla had 2 cloth factories, 9 coarse yarn workshops (where wool was processed), 1,177 smaller tailors (which made wraps and head-scarves (rebozos), 30 potteries, and 13 hatters. In 1802, there were 1,200 registered cotton looms in the city, whose operations were managed by 28 trading companies. This cotton was supplied by between 17,000 and 20,000 spinners from the surrounding countryside. The articles of clothing were sold to the non-Indian groups in the towns and pueblos of Anáhuac, or exported to the mining enclaves in the west and north of the viceroyalty. The countryside benefited as well. Thomson singles out the brief period between 1795 and 1801 as an "exceptional interlude of prosperity."[81] After the prohibition of the repartimiento, the merchants had switched immediately to rural cotton production, so that finally a handful of wholesalers enjoyed a veritable cotton monopoly in the area around Puebla de los Angeles; in 1789, eight wholesalers accounted for 60 percent of the cotton supplied in this area. In the end, the guilds no longer had any say in this production. There were still fifty guilds in Puebla in the middle of the eighteenth century, which still enjoyed considerable political power, but by the beginning of the nineteenth century their number had dwindled to thirteen, and they were no longer politically significant. The bishop of Puebla regarded this development as a major threat to the traditional order. The guilds had lost all of their influence on textile production, and the government, which had always chosen the side of the guilds, did nothing to interrupt the process. The government officials realized that tough intervention could endanger the jobs of almost 100,000 small peasants and urban poor.[82]

Perhaps the bishop was right, because industry in the city itself was in a major crisis in the late eighteenth century. The exceptional interlude of prosperity, according to Thomson, was "disguising an underlying secular decline in Puebla's competitive position *vis-à-vis* other Mexican regions and . . . with an industrializing Europe." The latter point refers to the opening of the borders for more European imports. Moreover, the competition from the Guadalajara region drove the Pueblan merchants out of the market around 1800. Production stagnated too. The inevitable modernization had not yet been introduced to the city because of the success of rural production. As we have seen, a large part of the urban population left for Mexico City. The migrants must have included many artesanos. Thomson's book on Puebla is even explicitly based on the post-1800 depression thesis. He therefore advises against use of the term *proto-industrialization,* because that "would be to overestimate the importance of a sector which . . . would not be instrumental in transforming Mexico from being a predominantly rural and agricultural society until beyond the middle of the twentieth century."[83] This point of view is correct if the term *proto-industry* is used to indicate a first stage of industrialization, but that is thus no longer on the agenda for the time being. It has been purified of the element of transition. Thus the textile industry in the valley of Puebla depicted by Thomson certainly does correspond to the more modest definition introduced earlier in this chapter.

Pottery production was as profitable an activity as textile production, especially for the small peasants in the pueblos near Toluca.[84] For a long time, commercial pottery, tile production, and brick manufacture had been a protected monopoly of the Spanish guilds, who controlled the primarily urban market. The producers from the pueblos did not have access to this market because they were not in possession of the required guild documents. However, in the course of the eighteenth century, during the growth of the demand in the cities, a growing number of unqualified potters were incorporated in the commercial circuit, including many migrants from pueblos. In the end, the urban ateliers switched to the processing of pottery especially ordered from the countryside for that purpose. This was followed by a tremendous increase in the number of illegal potteries in the towns and pueblos. The potters and tile producers from the pueblos in the countryside supplied the urban buyers with typically Spanish colors and motifs: by 1800 the guilds had lost their monopoly in this sector as well.

In the end, the guilds got the worst of it in all of the towns in New Spain. They had directly controlled the running of the labor market in the cities and barred outsiders from legal manufacture until late in the eighteenth century. They also guaranteed a labor distribution system—which was regarded positively at the time since it contributed to social order and belonged to the charity system—and the promotion of skills and good behavior of the craftsmen, because they combated undercutting and other forms of detrimental behavior among fellow workers. Later in the eighteenth century, however, after the prohibition on the repartimiento trade had been lifted, a new generation of large-scale traders displayed a strong distaste for the guilds' regulatory functions and supported a movement to abolish them. The traditional government had lost their confidence because it had hit their purses. Brading argues that a whole generation of merchants had withdrawn from trading after the prohibition.[85] The younger generation of merchants therefore wanted to do business outside the traditional institutions, and with success. The guilds proved unable to find an answer to the rapid growth of the number of illegal workshops that belonged to immigrants. The fact that the big merchants now shared the same interests as the poor in-migrants, the peasants, and the small craftsmen was of decisive importance. They employed or traded with nonguild members on a large scale. The collapse of the privileged position that the guilds had enjoyed until then can be observed all over New Spain around 1800. The Bourbon Reforms were a catalyst; as a result of the growth of the labor reserve army in the towns and pueblos, many employers could produce more cheaply and efficiently outside the guilds.[86] A similar process took place in Europe at the same time.

This brings us to a closely related aspect of employment—transport. The geographical situation was favorable to the Indians. The transport of commodities posed great problems for the entrepreneurs. It was precisely these difficulties which led many merchants to decide to farm out the transport risk to a middleman or to independent transporters. An important advantage of this farming out was the relatively low cost price. Moreover, the same entrepreneurs who wanted to use the cheap transport sector were also the suppliers of the beasts of burden used in the same sector. The repartimiento trade, involving the trade in commodities like eggs, enameled goods, and textiles, on the one hand, and a flourishing trade in beasts of burden, on the other hand, provided the center of New Spain with its unique structure. In Europe, the growth of internal trade was accompanied by the digging of canals and the improvement of the roads. Both the construction of infrastructural improvements and the growth of the transport sector itself provided jobs. The lack of similar means of transport in New Spain has already been mentioned. The roads were too bad for transport by cart or wagon. In the late eighteenth century, the state encouraged the improvement of the roads, but little came of it. Practically every relevant document that I have examined—nearly every travel account of the period on the topic—includes a complaint about the poor execution of the plans. A few bridges were constructed over ravines, but the roads were still almost impassable for carts. It was not until very late in the eighteenth century that convoys of at least eight carts left for the regions of Michoacán and Guadalajara or the north of New Spain, and they were so rare that whole pueblos turned out to see this curiosity pass by.[87]

An important reason for the mediocre success of the road construction program lies in the nature of the landscape and climate: large differences in altitudes, ground difficult to level, and torrential rains. The road network in modern Mexico is still heavily damaged in the rainy season, and it is not unusual for it to have to be resurfaced in October and November. There is another factor that explains the stagnation in this connection: the activities of the House of Bourbon were more concerned with devising plans in this respect than with putting them into practice. This conclusion can also be drawn from the policy followed in Europe. One of the main wheat regions in eighteenth-century Europe, for example, was Sicily, which belonged to the Spanish empire and is comparable to New Spain for the purposes of the present argument. All of the wheat was transported by mule to the coast, which entailed an extremely high cost price. The German writer Goethe, who traveled through the island in 1787, remarked that the landscape was quite suitable for improving the roads. However, there were not even bridges over the rivers, and he often had to get the peasants to carry him to the other side. The situation was the same in Spain. The crown devised the scheme of connecting the Manzanares and Tajo rivers by a canal to make it much cheaper to bring supplies to Madrid, which was expanding rapidly, but the execution of the plan was left up to the recommendations of a council of theologians. And this council concluded that if God had intended the rivers to be connected, He would have made them so.[88]

Not many people in New Spain endeavored to improve the situation for transport by cart, so they remained dependent on mules. Carts and wagons could only be used for short distances, such as on haciendas or in towns. It seems that the carriages were of poor quality, for writers like Gemelli, Ajofrín, and Bullock take a perverse pleasure in recounting serious shortcomings like broken wheels and the overturning of a coach at the slightest disturbance in the surface of the road. A lot of transport was paralyzed during the rainy season. There are reports of hundreds of carts stuck in the mud in the towns and of mules collapsing under the loads they had to pull out. In 1806, an attempt was made on the Hacienda Tulancalco to construct wagons to transport the barley from the fields to the barns more cheaply and quickly, but the wagons were so heavy that they could not be moved. Such examples indicate that there was no alternative to mule transport. The Spanish historian Ramón Serrera therefore rightly calls the mule routes the vertebrae of communication in New Spain.

Certain aspects of the arriería help to throw light on the problems of the development of the transport system in the late eighteenth century. The advantage of mules over horses lay in the following aspects: they were more economical in their consumption of fodder; they were sturdier; and they were more able to resist illnesses and parasites. All the same, European visitors were surprised and shocked at the treatment of the animals. The fodder was inadequate. The idea was to rent pastures beforehand and to get the animals to graze there on the journey, or to carry their own barley and maize stalks (zacate). In both cases, the measures were inadequate because they increased the cost price. Moreover, the animals were too heavily loaded and on the point of exhaustion because they were not given enough time to recover. If the Englishman Beaufoy is to be trusted, the attitude about caring for the animals was laconic. When he pointed out that his mules were overladen to an arriero during a trip in Anáhuac, the latter replied: "I'm not afraid of anything. They go with God and Christ and that is why they are content. The padre told me that when he blessed them." It is therefore hardly surprising that dead horses and mules were to be seen on all of the roads. There were various causes of death: exhaustion, falling into a ravine, breaking a leg and being shot, or drowning in the mud during the rainy season and serving as prey for the wolves, dogs, and vultures (*zapilotes*). The loss of animals that died en route was included in the transport price. This factor in pushing up the cost price probably played a large part in the late eighteenth century, when there was an exceptionally high mortality of livestock because of the recurrent droughts. Humboldt noted that the introduction of camels in New Spain would have been a move in the right direction: these animals could carry heavier loads than mules and were more able to stand up to the drought that proved fatal to so many mules.[89]

Transport was in caravans or on a small scale with arrieros, with between five and eight mules. The big caravans were the property of the merchants and employed many drivers. In the decennia after 1760, the main road from Anáhuac to the mining areas was particularly important. The entrepreneur Don Pedro Romero de Toreros made a fortune by transporting wheat from the Bajío to the mining regions, cotton cloths from Oaxaca to the north, and silver to Mexico City. He invested this fortune in a silver mine in Pachuca (Real del Monte), which he managed to turn into a success. At his death, he was one of the richest entrepreneurs of his day, and had been given the aristocratic title of Conde de Regla during his lifetime. His fortune was eventually so large that he was the only person who could buy up the property that the crown took over from the Jesuits. After years of negotiations with the state, he bought up twenty-one former Jesuit haciendas.[90]

The independent arrieros were employed in large numbers for the strongly developing interregional trade. Each of the mule drivers had around five animals. Most of them came from the pueblos or from ranchos near the main trade routes. For instance, the pueblos of Ixtenco and Nativitas in the province of Tlaxcala had six arrieros with a total of forty-eight animals (varying from four to twelve per arriero), and eleven arrieros with a total of ninety-six animals (varying from four to twenty-four animals per driver). The village of Tepetlaoztoc near Mexico City had 150 families in the late eighteenth century; 45 of them were involved in the arriería. Not all arrieros had their own animals or sufficient numbers of them, so they hired animals from haciendas or traders. Others used donkeys. The arrieros were serious rivals to rich transport entrepreneurs like Romero de Torres. There was a constant traffic of between fifty thousand and seventy thousand mules on the road to Veracruz at his time, providing employment for at least eight thousand people. It was less expensive for the large-scale merchants to use the small transporters than to take on permanent transporters because the former were satisfied to receive lower wages; transport was a secondary source of income beside agriculture for the arrieros. And since the quota of the alcabala was adjusted to take into account small consignments and the calidad of the transporter—Indians were not required to pay tax on all products—this gave the merchants an extra reason to prefer the small-scale, independent arrieros. A disadvantage lay in the fact that the small-scale transports were only available at certain periods, when they did not have to work on their own land in the pueblos or on the ranchos. Ringrose notes that this phenomenon of small-scale, free-lance transporters also occurred in Europe at this time, and that it was responsible for keeping transport costs within manageable proportions.[91]

The danger of being attacked by bandits and robbers posed a great threat to interregional trade in Anáhuac. They operated mainly on the roads leading to places where weekly markets or annual markets were held, and on the main roads (caminos reales) to the big cities. The forests and mountains, in particular, provided the bandits with good hiding places. The mountainous areas in the falda provinces were notorious, forming a barrier to the routes to Michoacán, Acapulco, and Veracruz. Another spot of ill-repute was the slope of the Ixtaccihuatl volcano, between the valleys of Puebla and Mexico; many attacks took place there in the provinces of Cholula, Coatepec, and Huejotzingo. The eighteenth-century writer de Lizardi notes that these were bandits from the capital, who went "on missions" to the countryside. The Tribunal de Acordada found an excellent way of combating banditry in the years after 1790. Tribunal patrols regularly returned to Mexico City carrying the heads of notorious bandits on pikes, which they bore to warn the common people in the city not "to go out on missions." A total of 181 gangs were unmasked by the tribunal between 1791 and 1803, consisting of 1,162 bandits (around 6 per gang).[92] Remarkably enough, this seems to indicate that interregional trade was on the increase again.

A new insight into the organization of banditry in New Spain around 1810 has recently been acquired. Archer, Van Young, Tutino, and Hamnett point to the intimate relation that must have existed between arriería and banditry. On the indios in the pueblo of Huichapan (Xilotepec), Hamnett writes, that "the menfolk of Huichapan worked as muledrivers in good times, but applied their intimate knowledge of the countryside to banditry in hard times."[93] The contractors and the state were thus confronted by the insoluble problem of irregular thefts carried out by the arrieros themselves, who sold the commodities to fences on the way to their destination. When they eventually arrived, all they had to do was report that they had been professionally robbed by one of the well-known bandits. However, this excuse was not always used. The priest of Zempoala was faced with an exceptional case in the crisis year of 1786. He wrote a letter to the government accusing the local arrieros of speculating with food stocks (regatonería) during a shortage. He claimed that it was customary for the arrieros from the Indian pueblos to leave en masse if a maize shortage were expected. They bought food elsewhere and marketed it at a high price. He himself had sent a number of them out to add to the maize stocks of his parish with an advance from the church treasury, but on the way back the arrieros had sold the maize at an enormous profit and repaid his advance to the priest when they returned. As a result, the parish did not have any maize.[94]

There were regular stopping places to alleviate the dangers in transporting by night. They were usually places where goods could be transferred, which encouraged their distribution. A good example is provided by the small town of Lerma in the valley of Toluca. Practically every transport from the region of Michoacán or Guadalajara, or from the valley itself, passed through Lerma on the way to the capital of the viceroyalty. The main items transferred or traded in Lerma were livestock from Guadalajara, silver from Zacualpan and Temascaltepec, and maize and pulse from the provinces in the valley. The townspeople had organized their lives around the transfer of goods, the provision of accommodation, and care of the beasts of burden. A similar process took place on a smaller scale in the pueblos and towns through which the main trade routes passed. A key role was played by the inns, which also had storage room and fodder at their disposal. These facilities were by no means luxurious. Generally speaking, the hygiene in these inns was poor, the rates relatively high, and the sleeping quarters anything but agreeable. The Italian traveler Gemelli, who was robbed in these inns on more than one occasion, used to put his boots on the bed "to prevent the mice running off with them." He referred to nearly every innkeeper he encountered as a typical bandit. The impoverished figure who ran the inn in Río Frío, located on the road from Mexico City to Puebla de los Angeles, and right under the ice-cap of the Ixtaccihuatl volcano, charged one real a night, which was almost a daily wage for a rural laborer. The Spaniard Ajofrín, who visited the country half a century later, had the same experience. He advised everyone to copy the local travelers' customs and take their own bed linen, mats, and tent canvas to camp in the pueblos. This was a cheap and safe alternative. Both Gemelli and Ajofrín were amazed at the special assistance received by the traveler in the south of the province of Cuernavaca, where someone paid by the pueblo bought everything the traveler needed, found a good bed for him, made it in his presence, and found a good stall for the beasts of burden and mounts.[95] It was a traveler's paradise!

An alternative to the inns was the venta, a hacienda that functioned as a stopping place, where a lot of activity in the transfer of goods, intermediate trade, and the purchase of stolen goods went on. A striking feature of these ventas is that they were often owned by the church, as though the biblical commandment to provide shelter for tired travelers served as the pretext to set up a commercial business. The Hacienda Piedras Negras in the province of Tlaxcala, which was owned by Bethlehemites, was one of the major stopping places on the trade route from Mexico City to Veracruz. The hacienda grew barley, which was sold to the passing arrieros at a cheap price. There were also fifty-two thousand magueys in 1793, used to make the pulque the customers drank. The hacienda also incorporated its own herds of sheep in the meals it provided; the local specialty (*mixote*) knocked the rest into a cocked hat. There were twenty-three rooms and a larger number of beds in the main premises, as well as storage areas and stalls. There was good pasture for the beasts of burden in the summer and the autumn. The Jesuits in Puebla had organized the Hacienda San Pablo on the main road to Veracruz in a similar way. It is not clear whether the ventas were a good source of income for those who ran them. According to a report from 1743, the well-known Mesón de Pasajeros venta, connected with the Hacienda Santa María Texomulco near the pueblo of Texmelucan in the province of Huejotzingo, had been under government control for more than twenty years because the creditors could not agree on how the debts were to be paid. The German historical geographer Trautmann doubts whether these ventas were a stable factor in the economic system of the time. He was struck by the fact that most of the ventas did not last long.[96]

To sum up, proto-industrial artesanía production and the arriería were two ways in which the small peasant households in the Indian pueblos in Anáhuac were incorporated into the broader economy of New Spain. The reverse is also true: the economy of New Spain would hardly have been able to function without the peasant households in the pueblos, at least as far as Anáhuac is concerned. The repartimiento for the interlocal and interregional markets and the tianguiz for the local market formed a proto-industrial solution to the threat of poverty after bad harvests and during a period of relative overpopulation. The prohibition of the repartimiento trade in the late 1780s had increased a crisis that was probably overcome in the 1790s. Thomson even detects a brief period of prosperity in the late 1790s, a suggestion which finds support in other data. This may well explain the rapid growth of the population during this period, since jobs were created for a larger body of people. In that case, no Malthusian crisis had ever been close to Anáhuac's population. At first, the role of the viceregal government was a negative one, but after a *obedezco pero no cumplo* (the legalization of the repartimiento), it assumed a promotional role later on. This was not merely confined to the toleration of the repartimiento, because the government officials even tried to encourage the growing production of manufactures from above. However, remarkably enough, the motive for this might not have been an economic one.

Encouragement of Demand

The development that naturally led to a new relation of exchange in both economic and sociopolitical terms—important was the increasing dependence of the peasants on the elite—led members of the elite and government representatives to make demands on their life-style. This was when the so-called civilizing offensive—which is assumed to have affected the European countryside in the seventeenth and eighteenth centuries, according to scholars like Elias, Burke, Hoffman, and Muchembled[97]—got under way in Spain. As important innovation took place in the field of dress. It was now possible to put an end to the sinful nakedness of the girls and women in the Indian villages. To the concern of the religious and secular authorities, most of the women in Anáhuac still wore hardly any clothing on the upper part of their body, dressing mainly in a wrap or a transparent piece of cotton. In some villages, the priests set up textile workshops to get the girls to abandon their traditional style of dress. The employees in the textile factories in the cities were offered clothes at reduced prices. In this way, the moral outlook provided more jobs, both in the urban textile industry and in the rural transport sector.

The most important expression of the new moral outlook was that all those employed by the government were required to conform to the new clothing regulations issued by the viceroyalty: a shirt, jacket or apron, smock or jerkin, trousers or skirt and stockings. They were also obliged to have footwear. Workers who did not observe the regulation on the "five articles of clothing" were threatened with a reduction in wages. The guards in the towns were instructed to bring their shabby apparel to the attention of the poor in the streets. The priests continually mentioned the sinful aspects of the native popular dress, which left the upper part of the body bare. The members of the rural confraternities were instructed to dress according to the regulations at every festival and procession. Those engaged in manufacture were apparently supposed to set an example, for observers reported that the government measure had a particularly noticeable effect in the towns. Provincial government officials also noted the gradual disappearance of the immoral peasant dress. The last decennia of the eighteenth century saw a growing conformity in the norms imposed by the church and the state in the towns and provinces. The "five articles of clothing" were gradually incorporated in pueblo tradition: each pueblo had its own design, color, and decoration. These were the articles of clothing produced in large numbers in the textile boom of the late eighteenth century. They were usually made in the colors of the areas where they were to be sold.[98]

It is worth looking a little more closely at the popularity of traditional costume in the Indian villages. After all, in our own times, nothing appears more ancient and linked to the pre-Hispanic past than the sight of Indian villagers wearing elaborately woven or embroidered clothing in their everyday lives. Many writers assume that modern Mexican costume goes back a long way. The British anthropologist Sayer wrote:

> In ancient Mexico costume differences not only set the rich and
> powerful apart from the poor; they also indicated the wearer's
> cultural group and place of origin. Today there are still over fifty
> different Indian peoples living in Mexico, many of whom have kept
> to a particular style of dress, with variations to distinguish each
> village within a community.[99]

This is also assumed to have been the case in the colonial era as a link between these two periods. However, it is evident from many sources that the commoners in the Indian pueblos were scantily clad.[100] Little is known about the

caciques in general in this respect, but we do have information about the
dress of the caciques in the province of Chalco in 1722, when all the members
of the village councils in the provinces came to testify in the case of Don
Phelipe Díez de Palacios. Naturally enough, they had put on their best clothes
to make as good an impression as they could, or they considered this an occasion for wearing their official dress. A number of them, mainly the caciques,
wore simple Spanish dress, with shoes, knee-length trousers, a cape, and the
typical headscarf we know from the priest Morelos and from figures on Spanish paintings of the period. The other Indian cabildo members, however, wore
typical blue-white smocks, woolen *tilmas,* without any blouses or other clothes
worn directly over the upper part of the body. These blue-white smocks, which
resembled sleeved *ponchos,* are also to be seen on depictions of Indians on
Mexican paintings. In the first place, these are the paintings of the mestizaje,[101]
but, above all, paintings that hung in churches, like those which can still be
seen in Ocotlán and Zacatelco (Tlaxcala). Presumably, the paintings in the
churches had an educational function: that was how one was supposed to
dress. Both caciques and noncaciques wore long plaits in front of their ears, a
kind of sideburns called *balcarrotas* (like the plaits worn by orthodox Jews).
Apart from that, the Indians wore their hair short.[102] To sum up, there is little
evidence to support Sayer's generalization, despite its general acceptance by
anthropologists. The wide diffusion of Indian costume has a colonial origin.

Judging from the reports on the clothing program, the new costume had
gained ground by about 1800. This was a case of what Hobsbawm calls *invention of tradition*:

> "Invented tradition" is taken to mean a set of practices, normally
> governed by overtly or tacitly accepted rules and of a ritual or
> symbolic nature, which seek to inculcate certain values and norms of
> behavior by repetition, which automatically implies continuity with
> the past.[103]

The wearing of costume during festivals, as the priests prescribed in Anáhuac,
was a part of this process. The object of the priests and the government was
moral, not cultural, aimed at combating immoral nudity. At a time of secession and atomization, however, the Indians probably saw the new legislation
as a suitable way of marking themselves off more distinctively from the old
cabeceras. It would be worth investigating this hypothesis in more detail, but
for now, the discussion falls outside the confines of the present work.

Be that as it may, the government was even prepared to put its money
where its mouth was. Priests and entrepreneurs thronged the entrance to the
Audiencia with requests to subsidize employment programs that would bring
the dress of the poor strata of the population in line with the dominant moral
norms. One example is the proprietor of the Molino Santa Monica (Tacuba)
who wanted to expand his company with an "open" *obraje* in 1786. In most
cases, an obraje was a semiclosed work camp where, alongside the contracted
laborers (usually gañanes), criminals, vagrants, and orphans were confined

and underwent a sort of work therapy based on the production of woolen blankets.[104] However, not every obraje was semiclosed, some had an open character. The proposal by the owner of the Santa Monica mill, a member of the elite, envisaged a variant of this open kind of textile factory. The workers would be recruited on a voluntary basis in the pueblos in the province of Tacuba, where overpopulation had caused extreme poverty. Since the men were on the road with their mules or were working on the land, it was mainly the women and girls who were to be provided with jobs to prevent "public health from deteriorating." This was a reference to the social tensions, increased migration or even rebellion. On the one hand, this would enable Indian peasant families to have enough money at their disposal to buy the mules and oxen they needed to run their peasant households. On the other hand, it would enable them to obtain the clothing needed to put an end to their near-nudism. The owner of the mill hoped that the government would make a contribution to the company expenses.[105]

The same hopes were shared by Fray Ildefonso Trujillo, a priest who wanted to begin a similar textile manufacture project in 1785. His idea was to use mallow roots instead of wool. The process of spinning thread and weaving cloth from this material was an extremely labor-intensive one, but the great advantage stressed by the priest was the fact that the plant grew wild in the hills, so that the roots could be picked there. The bundles of thread then had to be heated before they could be spun. This work could be done by Indian girls in the pueblos. The lower civil servant who had to assess the request was positive. He was particularly delighted with the idea that the girls from the pueblos would be encouraging the clothing industry in this way. "It hurts your eyes to see the naked women in the villages," he wrote. Fray Ildefonso could help to implement the new clothing regulation in practice, precisely because the textiles made from mallow were cheaper than woolen or cotton clothes. The lower government official added a Ciceronian ring to his assessment in stating that violence, if necessary, should be used to get the indios to abandon their nakedness: why not throw naked women or men in jail or beat them? The Audiencia was not prepared to go to such lengths, but it did grant Fray Ildefonso a starting capital of two hundred pesos.[106] It is not known whether the experiment was a success or not.

The arguments put forward by the priests and the mill owner recur in broad outline in many Mexican texts of the period. The "civilizing offensive" in Europe also coincided with a process aimed at restoring the equilibrium of the system that had been disrupted by population growth and poor harvests. The key to this restoration was in the hands of the elite and the authorities, because they had the power of decision regarding— and access to—the means of production. They were the ones who took decisions on employment. Increasing employment inevitably entailed increasing the demand for textiles and manufactures. Of course, the government clothing regulations only go part of the way toward explaining the growth of textile production in New Spain. They were successful in the pueblos, but they failed (as yet) to revolutionize the dress of the peasants. All the same, there was an increase in the number of individuals who dressed in accordance with the new norms, even if they only did so at work.[107]

To conclude, government policy seems to have been an important factor in the development of the textile industry in Anáhuac. It is uncertain, however, to what extent this was the main demand factor, for the literature reveals the extent to which the market had grown in the meantime. Salvucci claims that at least 40 percent of the population of New Spain was dependent on the market for clothing. It has been shown that the repartimiento brought a lot of textiles to the northern and western mining enclaves; they were mainly produced in the factories in Querétaro and Michoacán, and by the weavers in Oaxaca. The customers for textiles in Anáhuac itself were primarily the nonagrarian population living on the haciendas and in the pueblos and towns.[108] Many of those who lived in the pueblos adapted their mode of dress. On the basis of moral considerations and changed political relations between state and subject as a result of the relative increase in population, the government and the elite had created a demand that encouraged the economic development of Anáhuac.

Epilogue: A Model for the Small Peasant in Anáhuac

This brings us back to the farms in the pueblos de indios, where the women worked hard to prepare the daily meals, collect wood, produce pottery and especially textiles—in order to dress "better" perhaps—and the men worked on the milpas, supplementing their work on the land by looking for work with their mules in the interlocal and interregional trade. Although, to a large extent, the small peasant households were integrated in the economy of the region of Anáhuac, they probably could count only on the support of relatives; the municipal facilities, including the propios, either were used exclusively to finance the festivals or were often abused by the gobernadores to increase their own prosperity. There was only collective property in land and the corporate "social insurance" provided by the confraternities.

Households had to be kept small if they were to survive. The intensification of the economic activities of the small peasant households, the main high-pressure solution in a period of relative overpopulation, ran up against great difficulties. It was hardly possible to improve agriculture any further without the modern aids of the twentieth century because it was already intensive. All the same, there were modest signs of an economic development in this sector. Proto-industrialization was ready to go in the middle of the eighteenth century at the earliest, and particularly so toward the end of the century. This had its results, perhaps for the very reason that households were small. The successes may have encouraged a new population growth—an expansion that must have been one step too far and led to further impoverishment in the countryside around 1800. Or it led to frustrated expectations after a decade of proto-industrial growth. I have not investigated this point; indeed, it is difficult to examine it because the post-1810 documentation is dominated by the rebellion of Hidalgo and Morelos. It seems that the proto-industrialization of the late eighteenth century was inadequate to deal with the problems raised by bad harvests and relative overpopulation. At any rate, that is the way contemporaries saw it. I could borrow the metaphor of the seed that has not fully ripened (*quedó pachacate*)—a metaphor used by many writers at the time to describe the poverty in the pueblos around 1800—for my analysis of the village economy. This would stress the "frustrated expectations" argument.

If these indications are reliable, it may be assumed that the small peasant household in Anáhuac in the late eighteenth century, that is, before the post-1800 collapse, spent more time on cottage industry and migrant labor on the haciendas than earlier in the century. This was at the expense of work on the land, including the municipal plots. The annual work cycle of the "pegujaleros" was fixed, to a large extent: in running their own agricultural holdings and engaging in migrant labor to haciendas. The pegujaleros' own agricultural holdings demanded the most time in March and April (sowing the milpas) and during the period from November to February (the bean harvest, followed by the maize harvest and the maize-stalk harvest). The remaining months could be devoted to household crafts, sometimes interrupted by work on a hacienda and work on the milpas (piling up the soil and weeding). This migrant labor was primarily concerned with seasonal labor on the haciendas in the months of May and June, sometimes extending until late in July.[109] These were the so-called "wheat-maize haciendas," which required harvesters for the wheat (the maize was harvested by hands, gañanes, who lived on the haciendas). Only small haciendas, like those in Cholula, required laborers from the pueblos all year round because they could not support gañanes.

We can thus follow the Dutch historian Jan Lucassen in illustrating the employment cycle with a diagram.[110] The income of a peasant household can be represented as a circle in which the segments of the circle correspond to the months of the year. This circle demonstrates the way in which income was tied to specific seasons. Lucassen set the activities on their own holdings in an inner circle, separated from the outer circle by broken and continuous lines. This position symbolizes the fact that this is the key source of income and supplementary income. Migrant labor and cottage industry are assigned a larger surface area by being set in the outer circle. This is justified by the relatively large sums of money these activities brought in. The combination of the two circles and the time flow over a twelve-month period indicates the distribution of the different kinds of work in the labor cycle. This makes it possible to construct a model for eighteenth-century Anáhuac in which the importance of the outer circle can be shown (see Figure 5). The model consists of two circles. The left-hand circle illustrates the situation in the middle of the eighteenth century; the right-hand circle illustrates the situation around 1800. It indicates that less attention was paid to the peasants' own holdings around 1800.

This model does not apply equally to each household, nor is it impervi-

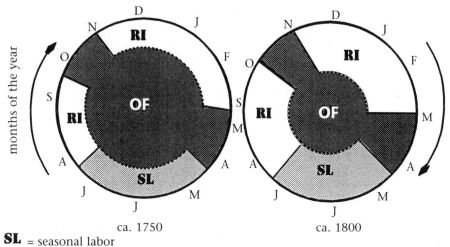

OF = own farm

RI = rural industry

SL = seasonal labor

Figure 5 Diagram of the employment cycle of small peasant households in Anáhuac, ca. 1750 and ca. 1800

ous to changes in the development of the household itself (the life cycle of the household from nuclear to stem to nuclear). The sources of income in Anáhuac in the eighteenth century, and thus the distribution of the labor cycle among the three main components—agricultural holdings, cottage industry, and migrant labor/arriería—varied for each household at different places and in different times. Lucassen rightly points out—for northwestern Europe, that is—that the more a household derived its income from a single one of these three main components, the less the other possibilities could be considered as alternatives. The priorities were as follows: their own landholdings, then cottage industry, then migrant labor. Some small peasant households in Anáhuac were dependent on migrant labor, but the majority had concentrated on cottage industry, which was the main component in their case. This trend grew more pronounced as the eighteenth century progressed, as can be seen in Figure 5. This indicates the lack of importance of work on the haciendas for the "pegujaleros" in the densely populated highlands of Anáhuac. The small peasant households had their own network of social and economic relations, integrated in the macroeconomic system of New Spain in the broad sense, which minimalized the need to depend on migrant labor.

An extremely important role is played in all this by the subsistence line,

discussed in Chapter One. In the long run, those who were the most dependent on the municipal institutions were the peasants below the subsistence
line. In the late eighteenth century, this group was on the increase as a result
of the fragmentation of the común. They were prepared to follow the
gobernadores/caciques in their attempt to modify or possibly even expand
the village holdings. This gave the gobernadores/caciques the image of doing
something for the poorest sectors in return for the social prestige they enjoyed in the pueblos and for the economic advantages they gained from the
offices of gobernador or mayordomo. The moral foundation of this reciprocal
relationship could be underlined during village festivities. It is precisely this
aspect of the ecological ethic that creates inequality, as Scott correctly points
out:

> Village redistribution worked unevenly and, even at its best,
> produced no egalitarian utopia. We may suppose that there was
> always some tension in the village between the better-off who hoped
> to minimize their obligations and the poor who had most to gain
> from communal social guarantees. . . . What moral solidarity the
> village possessed as a village was in fact based ultimately on its
> capacity to protect and feed its inhabitants. So long as village
> membership was valuable in a pinch, the "little tradition" of village
> norms and customs would command a broad acceptance.[111]

The gobernadores and mayordomos were expected to guarantee the subsistence of the villagers. However, these authorities also knew that a reduction of
the poverty of the "pegujaleros" would threaten their influence in the community. The pueblos of Anáhuac were caught between these two extremes.

The time seems to have come for a closer investigation of the small peasantry of colonial Mexico from this perspective. This will not only encourage
the peasant debate, but also contribute to our knowledge of the character of
the Spanish system in America. Much can be learned from the European research, referred to in this chapter, on the functioning of the domestic economy
in the past. My tentative exploration of the Mexican material might have
revealed a number of correspondences: a family network of small families, the
view of the community as a link between peasants and government, and the
phenomenon of proto-industrialization. The demographic factor constantly
recurs in a different guise. These problems must be considered in the light of
the bad harvests, increased migration in the countryside, and the prohibition
on the repartimiento trade. The definitive solution had still not been found.
The road along which a new Great Leap Forward was set in motion in pre-
1800 Anáhuac was full of obstacles.

Epilogue:
Rethinking Indian
Economic Participation

The Indian Inside Us

If the foregoing discussion leads us anywhere, it is, I think, to a critique of conceptualization. The reader will have noted that one key question injected in my argument is how we can best know the past—an ancient question. I have chosen an ecological approach to the heuristics of historical research. The conceptual difficulty involved in the present work is still not completely clear. Because of its complexity I wish to introduce this with a dialogue translated from the Italian:

> Of witches I do not know if there are any; and of *benandanti* I do not know of any others besides myself.
>
> Questioned: what does this word *benandante* mean? he replied:
>
> *Benandanti* I call those who pay me well, I go willingly. . . . I cannot speak about the others because I do not want to go against divine will. . . . I am a *benandante* because I go with the others to fight four times a year, that is during the Ember Days, at night; I go invisibly in spirit and the body remains behind; we go forth in the service of Christ, and the witches of the devil; we fight each other, we with bundles of fennel and they with sorghum stalks. And if we are the victors that year there is abundance, but if we lose there is famine.
>
> Questioned: how long have you been involved in this and are you now? he replied:
>
> All those who have been born with the caul belong to it, and when they reach the age of twenty they are summoned by means of a drum the same as soldiers, and they are obliged to respond. . . . We are a great multitude, and at times we are five-thousand and more. . . . In the fighting that we do, one time we fight over the wheat and all the other grains, another time over the livestock, and other times over the vineyards. And so, on four occasions we fight over all the fruits of the earth and for those things won by the benandanti that year there is abundance. . . . I cannot say the names of my companions because I would be beaten by the entire company.[1]

"Can I make sense of this?" each of the priests of the Italian Inquisition must have wondered. "Can I make sense of this?" the historian Carlo Ginzburg must have asked himself when he read the records of the inquisition in Friuli, Italy. The audience was bewildered, and still is.

This example reveals a peasant mentality that had room for the organization of the strange forms of witchcraft and fertility rites. And yet these natives of the Italian countryside saw themselves as model Catholics. They were just as puzzled by the interrogation as their inquisitors were. Were they being viewed as heretics, pagans, or superstitious fools? What a stupid mistake! After all, they gave the witches a good bashing! And they did so in the name of Christ; surely the judges could not object to that? The inquisitors of the church did not know what to make of it and tried to fit the confessions into their own mental framework, which was projected onto the actual experience of the peasants. Ginzburg's work is full of inquisitors who try to force the confessions of peasants and other inhabitants of the countryside—his account of the case of the miller Menocchio is well known[2]—into their own ideological and dogmatic construction. Ginzburg was well aware of the fact himself. He faced the same problem as the inquisitors and must have thought: what am I to make of this? Therefore, he immediately added another question: how can I escape from the trap that the schemes of the twentieth century have put into my head?

Every historian, of course, has to confront these same questions. Historical training usually includes the exercise of historical criticism. We know that material from the past is fragmentary: it is incomplete, biased, and falsified. The critical historical method helps the historian achieve a maximum degree of accuracy and reliability in using the source material from the past. All the same, if this fragmentary material is to result in a historical representation, the historian must recognize the force of imagination in the highly individual nature of his contribution and the explanation of the results of the investigation. Thus the historian is caught between criticism and illusion.[3] The researcher hopes that the recreation of the world of the past is, indeed, a reconstruction, not an invention. Illusion is the certainty of doubt, an attempt to find an appropriate image of the past with the possibility of providing explanations. It is patently obvious that the balance of criticism and illusion, the search for historical explanations, is made more difficult by the barriers thrown up by chronology—the historian is the survivor among the dead—and culture. A historical reality is a contradiction in terms, precisely because the past is imaginary.

And yet my argument compels me to "conclude." Like any researcher, the historian interprets and judges the source material in terms of his prior knowledge and his own set of biases. Nowadays, the original confidence in objectivity, an attitude reflected in the omniscience of the narrator, has given way to the insight that every point of view can be replaced by a different one. If my reading of the literature is correct, I think it is theory that directs much historical research on Latin America and introduces bias. Indeed, it is striking that, despite this inductive tendency, which comes naturally to the science of history, historians keep running up against myths. The English historian Peter Laslett has reminded us, in a popular BBC radio series, that "the world we have lost" is so irretrievably lost that people have invented a myth to fill the gap in their memory.[4] This makes "theory" synonymous with "myth." The recognition of the personal point of view not only means that researchers are engaged in introspection in order to decipher such myths, but, in fact, are struggling constantly with the myths repeatedly told by the nonhistorical community. No matter whether historical interpretation is carried out by historians, sociologists, anthropologists, or economists, myths arise where there is a lack or loss of empirical investigation and data, in situations or periods with a strong urge to explain the present in terms of the past.[5]

This was the case some twenty-five years ago, when development economist André G. Frank, one of the leading protagonists of the *dependencia* theory, wrote that poverty and development in Latin America can only be understood by looking at a global context. He invited the reader to solve a puzzle that was supposed to be an accurate depiction of the continent's *problématique*. The riddle was to connect nine points with a single line. There was one condition: the line may consist of a maximum of four square segments, and may on no account consist of five. This puzzle is insoluble as long as one remains within the framework of the nine points. Its solution requires one to move out of the square. According to Frank, the square imposes this solution on the reader:

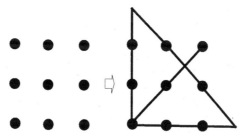

Figure 6   Frank's development puzzle

Frank explains the connection of this puzzle with the analysis of Latin American society, as follows:

> Similarly, if we are to understand the Latin American problématique we must begin with the world system that creates it and go outside the self-imposed optical and mental illusion of the Ibero-American or national frame.[6]

The historian's discipline leads him to raise objections to the deductive prior condition laid down by Frank: Why is a line with five segments not allowed? Is it not more interesting to see whether the solution cannot be found within the nine points? Can Frank's model exist without his prior condition? If the prior condition is ignored, it is indeed possible to devise more than one way of linking the points, but it is impossible to follow his restriction to four segments. Frank's prior condition thus stands in the way of an examination of the internally closed system.

That has been the problem, I think, with colonial historiography for a long time, dominated as it was by the Black Legend. It encompassed a "scientific" theory that emphasized the never-ending conflict between Spaniards and Indians. This conflict resulted in displacement and Indian survival only in isolated fringe areas. Sometimes the Indians rebelled; most of the time, however, they were a passive labor force for Spanish exploitation. The Indians were seen as noodles, not capable of acting their own way out of the Spanish invasion. The picture is still very popular. Eric Wolf's seminal *Europe and the People Without History*, for example, which is widely used in the social sciences, also depicts the indios of Mexico as the docile victims of brutal Spanish violence; three hundred years of Spanish rule are reduced to fifty years of conquest. Wolf argued that the Indians were no more than creatures who provided labor power for the Spanish export industry (the silver mines and their supply industries):

> Towns and mines came to be ringed about by haciendas; the haciendas were in turn surrounded by settlements of the surviving native populations. This settlement pattern was oriented toward the mines; yet it was not merely geographic or ecological. It was organized by the political economy it embodied, in which each lower level yielded surplus to the level above it. Miners sold to merchants, who extracted high prices for European manufactured goods. Mine owners then pressed upon hacienda owners or managers to supply them with foodstuffs and raw materials at low prices. Hacienda owners and managers pressed upon the native communities, drawing their members either into dependent serftenancy on the estates or into seasonal employment at low wages. Within this hierarchy, the emerging Indian communities came to occupy the lowest rung.[7]

This is the full-blown *latifundium/minifundium model*, which echoes Frank's assumption that the Spanish and Indian elements in Latin America have to be understood in terms of the background of general European expansion.

The Black Legend does have European roots, but not in the way that Wolf and Frank guessed. In fact, the legend should be judged as "Eurocentric." Critics have noted that communities like those of the Mexican Indians hold a great attraction for Europeans and North Americans because they evoke the ideal picture of the uncomplicated, stable, and socially harmonious communities that are no longer to be found in Europe. They bear a close resemblance to the traditional medieval communities described by Laslett as *The World We Have Lost*.[8] According to Laslett, Westerners who have grown accustomed to the mobile, urbanized society apparently yearn for the peaceful idyll that these communities promise. Ever since the first industrial development, anthropologists have spread over the still uncultivated tracts of Africa, Asia, and Latin America. Painters like Emile Bernard and Paul Gauguin sought these communities in Brittany; Gauguin later left for the island of Tahiti in the Pacific. In the 1960s, young North American tourists, the hippies, were to be found on the peaks of Nepal, among the ruins of Macchu Picchu in Peru, and on the Isla de las Mujeres off the coast of Yucatán. Nowadays, thousands of tourists travel in groups to China, Thailand, Kenya, or Mexico in search of an identical, unspoiled society and the "noble savage."

The fact that the ideas entertained by these visitors about life there do not usually bear much resemblance to the actual situation of the local population can be seen in the reaction of literate islanders in Samoa and New Guinea, who bluntly denied the anthropologist Margaret Mead access to the island; otherwise, she would be beaten up and thrown into the sea because she had presented an incorrect version of life on the islands and had made public all kinds of matters that should have remained private. The anthropologist's ethnographic reality proved to be painfully out of key with the islanders' own experiences. The latter indicated that the description of the Mundugumor, who shared their bed with their children, killed new-born babies, and ate one another, was complete nonsense. In her description of the Samoans as peaceful individuals who lived in blissful harmony with one another and with their surroundings, Mead had unconsciously wanted no more than to hold up a mirror to her own society.[9]

Mead was not the first to leave the Western world with a mirror in her hand. The idealization of the way of life of people in what has been known for a long time as the Third World, and more recently as the South, is not an isolated phenomenon. Europeans always seem to have been searching for the people who live in a natural state, the idyllic community, and the Golden Age. There was a simple term for this in the Middle Ages: Paradise. The idea was that if Adam and Eve had been expelled from Paradise, it must still be somewhere to be found. At first it was sought in the East and in the Southeast. The famous empire of the Christians in Ethiopia might well border on Paradise; or perhaps it was Paradise itself! When Paradise proved impossible to find in the South or in the East, attention shifted around 1450 to the West. Was that where the lost continent of Atlantis was to be found? Plato imagined it in the West, which was where the Islands of the Blessed and Arcadia were situated. The Spanish Christians who had fled from the Moors in the early Middle Ages were supposed to have settled beyond the Canary Islands, on what was known as the archipelago of Antilia. Saint Brendan found a sort of paradise in the Southwest of the ocean; the legend of his travels became immensely popular at the time, told over and over again.

In his *De Indiaan in ons bewustzijn* (*The Indian in our Consciousness*), the Dutch philosopher Ton Lemaire correctly points out that the discovery of America was not really due to chance.[10] The discovery had already been in preparation for a long time, and in fact, was one of the expectations in the geographical conceptions of the Old World—note the popularity of Saint Brendan in the Middle Ages—in which scientifically acquired empirical geographical knowledge was sometimes inextricably intertwined with ancient theological and mythical components. There was excitement over the discovery within the limited circle of the powers that be and the intelligentsia. The humanist Thomas More incorporated the reports of the paradise that had been found in Latin America, the state of nature of the Indians, in his blueprint for his *Utopia*, situated in the new Western world. He wrote his book within fifteen years after Columbus's arrival, before Latin America had been included on all the maps of the world or on navigational charts. This was remarkable enough, because between 1480 and 1609 the literature on the Turks and on Asia was four times as voluminous as that on America. All the same, the recollection of the people living in a natural state and their mighty rulers continued to appeal to the imagination for centuries. Even Louis XIV followed the example of the ruler of the Incas in adopting the name of the Sun King.

The Spaniards arrived on the American continent in search of the same kind of paradise. When they asked the way, they usually mentioned the word *gold*. The conquistadores are always described as being driven by an unprecedented hunger for gold. Cortés is supposed to have said to the Aztec ruler: "The Spaniards are plagued by an illness of the heart which can only be cured with gold." No doubt, this was the manifestation of a passion with which we are familiar: the thirst for riches. The hunger for gold is seen as the expression of emergent capitalism in the early sixteenth century. Although this view contains a core of truth, and I do not wish to dispute the traditional view on Cortés in particular, in general it might be too one-sided. Historians who have investigated the mental world of the Spaniards at the time emphasize the medieval elements that inspired their activities. To recall Las Casas's vision of God's State on Earth, gold was one of its components. Gold had a mythical dimension at the time, because of the shared conviction that it was to be found in the rivers of paradise. Life in paradise is described as the Golden Age, El Dorado, the happiest time of mankind. The search for gold and the desire to rediscover the lost paradise are so closely connected with one another that it is hardly possible to refer to them as separate goals.[11]

Our views of the Golden Age are inherited from our culture's Greco-Roman roots, the collective memory of the West. According to ancient tradition, mankind once lived in complete harmony. Arcadia had no laws to fetter human behavior. They were redundant since there was no knowledge of injustice, crime, or war. In Christian teachings, this idea of the origin of mankind can be found in the Biblical text on paradise. When the ancient Greek and Roman authors were read again in the fifteenth and sixteenth centuries—and indeed, could be read again, for knowledge of the classical languages had been the preserve of the monasteries for a long period—the image of the Golden Age found explicit expression once more in the arts of the Renaissance. We have not lost it since, and once they arrive in America, the Europeans seem to see the proof of their ideal. Columbus, who heard the song of the nightingale in America—where the bird is not to be found; he wrote about it because the nightingale belongs in paradise—and Malcolm Lowry, who recognizes paradise and eventually the Last Judgment in a garden in Mexican Cuernavaca, are not so far apart.[12] Las Casas also used the key to the collective memory of the West. It fits in better with our present-day views of the ideal society than the work of his opponents, who laid more stress on the division between civilization and barbarism.

In short, we, Europeans and North Americans, have used the "primitive world" to hold up a moral mirror to ourselves. The utopian society of people in a state of nature has been an instrument for the critique of our own society for centuries. More's *Utopia,* the sublunar artificial paradise, was an American export. It was reimported by the Spaniards, the European travelers, and the development theorist to be implemented there. Mexico occupies a special position in this process. Mexican history is not only the history of oppression, but also the history of salvation and hope. A small world—whether it is called European, Western, or urban—has been projecting its own lost idyll, Western nostalgia, ideology, and cultural critique on the Indians of Latin America for five hundred years. This has a decisive impact on the vision of Latin America itself: "I hated being a European," Lemaire said to his interviewers after the publication of his book *The Indian in Our Consciousness.* After all, was it not the Europeans who had destroyed that paradise?

The only response to a guilt complex of this kind is politically correct solidarity with the oppressed Indians. From scratch, most texts about Latin American history were formulated from this discursive ideology. Recognition of this background to our view of the history of Latin America is bound to lead us to forget Europe and to turn to Mexico. This seems a fairly obvious step to take. Indeed, it has already been taken, many a critic will mutter; consider Wachtel's work on Peru, for instance. It is interesting to see how the well-known book *La vision des vaincus* (1971) by this French author still stressed the "trauma" that the conquest was assumed to have brought about among the Indian population, although ten years later his contribution to the *Cambridge History of Latin America* devotes much more space to the resistance and resilience of Indian society. Indeed, the Indian as victim makes way for the Indian as agent, who has played a hand in determining the course of history. The same tendency can be seen in the historiography of Mexico and Guatemala, of Mesoamerica. For example, Nancy Farriss asserts that Mesoamerican Indians should not be viewed as anachronistic vestiges of a pre-Hispanic past, nor as passive objects of colonial or neocolonial rule, but as independent subjects, making or reshaping the social conditions of their existence.[13]

When considered properly and in more detail, however, I see this as no more than a shift in emphasis. As I have attempted to show in the previous chapters, the Indian is still a creation of our Western preconceptions as long as he remains the prisoner of the Black Legend heritage. Indians are described as active subjects, but living in "refuge areas," removed from the center of their old world, victims of the conquest, as Wolf argued. In a recent article in the *Latin American Research Review*, W. George Lovell still tries to convince the reader of the conquest "not as a remote, historical experience but as a visible, present condition." Although both Farriss and Lovell are referring to cultural factors ("strategic acculturation in order to preserve essentials," is Farriss's topic), there is no doubt that they would extend their argument to the socioeconomic sphere; they both approvingly cite Gibson's *Aztecs under Spanish Rule*, thus recognizing, as Lovell actually states, that "closed and corporate or open and heterogeneous, native life . . . was founded (to reiterate Wolf's telling phrase) on the 'dualization of society,' which means that Indians existed in varying degrees of servitude to Spaniards."[14]

The revision is thus only apparent. The traditional version lives on, the Indian is still the prisoner of a Western construct, which—ironically—achieved its actual popularity in Latin America itself in the so-called dependencia theory. This theory is always presented as a Latin American response to European Marxist theories. Constructed on Frank's ideas, among others, it is—like the myth of the Indian—less "native" than it is supposed to be.[15] This foundation of modern development theory has been transmitted from generation to generation as a cultural imperative. It is well known that culture is a system of learned attitudes, values, and knowledge widely shared within a society, though varying from one society to another, and indeed, transmitted from generation to generation. From a personal point of view, we could repeat a well-known observation, made by Kuhn, that the more central and early-learned aspects of culture are resistant to change, both because a massive effort is required to change central elements of an adult's cognitive organization, and because one's most central values become ends in themselves, whose abandonment would produce deep uncertainty and anxiety.[16] Only in the face of major and enduring shifts in societal conditions may central parts of a culture be transformed. Usually, however, it is change through intergenerational population replacement and not by the conversion of already socialized adults. Thus Kuhn's account of paradigm change in scientific revolutions provides an interesting analogy:[17] replace "adult" with "scientist" and "culture' with "paradigm" or "scientific knowledge" and one would agree that only enduring shifts in scientific insight and knowledge or "intergenerational replacement" at the universities would change the central elements of the Latin Americanists' cognitive organization.

Of course, the views of Gunder Frank and Wolf are not without their value. The influence of external circumstances on the economic system of Latin America was an important factor in the development of the continent. But historians have demonstrated that it is possible to investigate the development of the continent from within and without heading straight for the oceans. For example, they have shown how important production for the internal market was in colonial Spanish America, a domestic market that had little or no connection with mining in most areas. In his survey of the late eighteenth century—a century generally viewed as a period of considerable export development in Spanish America—Brading noted that the export production of the continent of Spanish America in 1789, employing 14½ million workers, was the same as that of the French colony Saint-Domingue, which had a population of 450,000 at the time. He concluded:

> Clearly, if the export earnings of the 14½ million inhabitants of Spanish America barely exceeded the output value of a single island in the Caribbean, it was because the bulk of its population found occupation and sustenance in the domestic economy.[18]

At first sight, inductive research comes up with the same result as deductive research in the related disciplines of sociology and anthropology, according to the theoretical models of the late twentieth century, namely, deconstruction. My criticism of the remnants of the Black Legend philosophy is supported by the Zeitgeist; perhaps it is one of its products. At the time of writing, there is not much left intact of the claims of the traditional social sciences and, in particular, of development studies. The desire for a new world and a new humanity, attested by Wolf, Gunder Frank, and others, has been left stranded in the totalitarian débâcle to which the artistic and social scientific avant-garde has unfortunately contributed. It goes some way toward explaining the current hesitation to see the practice of the social sciences as an important force in social change. If that was ever the case, it certainly is not so now.[19] Nevertheless, this field seems to be nothing more than the last convulsion heralding the onset of rigor mortis. What started as resistance and a desire for change and revolution—in the Mexican case one might think of Andrés Molina Enríquez, José Vasconcelos, Enrique Florescano, or Charles Gibson— has ended up as a large-scale process of sobering up, which can be conveniently summed up in the term *postmodernism*. For at least for the time being, it seems that the massive spiritual and social aspirations of the arts and sciences, which began in the seventeenth century, have run their course.[20]

This ought to give historians cause for alarm over a diminishing historical awareness in modern society. In Europe, and probably in the United States as well, people have believed for some time that the main era of historical remembrance has come to an end, along with the weakening of the national framework and the disappearance of the major liberation movements. This partly explains the general popularity of the European Community. It seems that this affects historical engagement adversely, because the link with the previous generations is broken. After all, in the European historiographical tradition the historian has a cultural and a moral function. Within this perspective, the historian's activity is not an arbitrary one, but it entails a special obligation: to chronicle, remember, and recall the past in the conviction that no society or individual can survive without an awareness of the continuity between past and future. Rationality and utopia accompanied this process hand in hand, and the search for Paradise in the West was a part of it all.

Deconstruction and postmodernist discourse or not, the romantic modernists' embers still glow. Latin American studies seem to escape from the clutches of the Zeitgeist. Two explanations can be offered for this:

1. the shift in the social sciences came all of a sudden, at a time when the historiography of Latin America was trying to establish contact with anthropology more than ever before; as a result, historians have been "catching up" on the entire history of anthropology and thus have not yet reached the deconstructive phase;
2. we write the history of the Indians, and thereby come into contact with the persistent mythology of the destruction of the "Indian paradise."

And there was certainly no mention of "deconstruction" in this field when I began my research in 1980. In all, the profound revision of the 1970s and 1980s has not yet led to the formulation of a new epistemological interpretative model. On the contrary, most historians have endeavored to fit their findings into the traditional one.[21] The symbiosis model, as defined by Gibson, only deviates on points of detail from Wolf's 1959 definition of the conflict model.[22]

Historians have not gone far enough in their critique because the myth of the Indian has performed an important conservative function *as an authoritative text*. Although this myth has been losing ground gradually in the historical and anthropological sciences, it still holds researchers in its thrall because the entire field of Latin American studies seems saturated by it. Therefore, it is clear enough what still sustains the myth in our era determining our attitude toward the Indians in a certain sense: the indigenista novels. It is in our time that literary sources have the image of revealing a truth that could never be portrayed by legal actions, documents, or photographs. In the twentieth century the novel has taken the place of the moralizing works with a philosophical coloring of the past (Plato, Augustine, Nietzsche, Marx).[23]

Various examples could be cited in connection with the history of Latin America, but I will limit my remarks for reasons of space. The historian Robert Keith published a collection entitled *Haciendas and Plantations in Latin American History* in 1977, containing an introduction by Keith and a selection from the available literature. The year 1977 arrived shortly after the breakthrough of modern historiography in the early 1970s, so Keith had included some of the good historical material that was then available.[24] This accounts for five of the eighteen texts. Another seven are in the studies of social sciences. Where there was no research available, he opted for literature—political or literary essays, or even novels. These texts from works by Antonil, Ciro Alegría, Ramiro Guerra y Sánchez, Jorge Icaza, José García de Arboleya, Euclides da Cunha, and Domingo Sarmiento accounted for another seven chapters, thereby claiming a larger share of "historical truth" than that allocated to the academic historians!

The work of the Peruvian José María Arguedas also seems to play an important role. He is widely read by my colleagues, as their bibliographies indicate. Arguedas's credibility with his audience is an important factor. He was brought up by Indians, spoke only Quechua up to the age of eight, and campaigned for equal rights for Indians as an "anthropologist" and novelist. His novel *Los ríos profundos* combines class and culture in a manner typical of the indigenista movement.[25] The main character, Arguedas's own alter ego, sees Indian reality as a harmonious community of humans, nature, and animals confronted by the conflict-ridden reality of the clash between "white" and "Indian." Arguedas later opted for the creation of the "new" Indian, the product of a cultural merger combining Western technology with the retention of Indian collective property, mutual solidarity, and respect for nature.

Others read the work of the Guatemalan writer Miguel Angel Asturias. In particular, his *Hombres del maíz* is supposed to contain a "view from inside" of Quiché-Maya Indian life. Asturias's use of exotic words and striking symbols creates a world that comes over as authentically Maya. In fact, however, according to the literary critic Lienhard, this is a completely mythical presentation demonstrably based on anthropological texts—which, as we know by now, were also entangled in problems of representation—and Aztec (!) texts, rather than on participation in village life in the Guatemalan countryside itself.[26] When fragments of the book were read in translation to a couple of Mayan Quiché-speaking peasants, they burst out laughing, but later the same day they vented their anger at this "man from the city" who claimed to know what they thought and did better than they did themselves. Although more extreme cases could be quoted—such as the novel *El Indio* (1935) by the Mexican writer Gregorio López y Fuentes, in which the Indian is portrayed as a kind of anonymous animal in the jungle—it is evident that Asturias has been influenced by suppositions derived from urban academic circles.

If Latin American authors of novels, poems, plays, or film scripts share the ideas of an Arguedas or an Asturias, and if local peasant leaders—many after receiving training in the national universities—Latin American agrarian sociologists, anthropologists, and historians, or foreign researchers, development workers, or volunteers follow them in their beliefs, then it is obvious that the Black Legend is a modern reality and not just a scholarly ideology.[27] In his book on the relation between ethnicity and class, anthropologist Frans J. Schryer writes that historians and social scientists cannot just point out that certain theories or principles do not "fit the facts."[28] Precisely because the "misguided opinions"—as seen by the academically trained outsider—are an essential part of the present-day reality of the Latin American countryside because of the local education of peasant leaders, politicians, or development workers, they have to be taken into account in questions of policy. The same goes for those who *collect* material for field reports, dissertations, or academic publications as students or researchers of the small peasantry, including the Indians. But what about the *interpretation* of our data? Is it not time to think about *Indians* in a less romantic fashion and to open our eyes to the possibility of a more realistic historical object? Besides, this historical reality has the advantage of presenting a peasantry able to defend itself effectively and independently, rather than the black image of a bunch of innocents who get butchered by a handful of Spaniards in just a few years.

The Ecological Approach

But the Indians did have their own economic history. In encountering this fact, I found a way to provide a counterbalance to the voice of the Indian inside us. It involved letting the European peasant also have a say, someone who lived in the same period and in more or less the same agrarian and eco-logical circumstances, returning to the *World We Have Lost*. Thus in acknowl-edging the existence of these twentieth-century discursive traps, I have tried to do so on the assumption that the life of a peasant in Anáhuac was not so very different from that a peasant in Languedoc, Overijssel, the Ardennes, Kent, Southern Germany, or any other European region mentioned in my text. The image, then, becomes differentiated. We see that the relations be-tween the hacendados and merchants, the residents of the pueblos de indios, the priests, and the civil servants in Anáhuac were determined by the presence of a multilateral interdependency, which in the eighteenth century had little connection with the direct and traceable consequences of the "trauma" of con-quest. This stance makes it possible to present a different interpretation, based on the ecological approach familiar from European historiography.

The main assumption of the ecological approach—and the only serious one, I hope—is the premise of demographic pressure. This assumption was absent from the old utopian theories. A growing population has to be fed, clothed, and housed, and in a specific region this can only be achieved be-neath a critical level that can be scientifically determined. Once this level has been reached, drastic measures are called for, which usually tend toward in-tensification, trade with other regions, industrialization, and increase in scale. According to Lester Brown, the world has now reached the limits of this ex-pansion.[29] It remains to be seen whether he is right, but that there is a crisis is obvious to all. People are talking about it more than ever before. The English pathologist Maurice King, for example, stated that several developing coun-tries should opt for the China-model—one child per family—or starve. But even then, Indonesia, a country with satisfactory family planning, has a popu-lation of about 180 million and an expected growth of another 100 million. Most of these people must live on Java, an island where every square kilome-ter is in use for food and industrial production: there *is* no land for the Indo-nesians anymore. Or consider the Egyptian president Mubarak, another example, who warned the Egyptians on the first of May 1989, the Day of Labor, that in his country production must be stepped up on all fronts apart from the production of children. The state was able to provide an artificial solution for the situation that had arisen, but it could not continue to do so indefinitely: "In the public sector we now have fifteen people working where two are required," the president stated. "Is their number to swell to fifty or a hundred?"[30] All the achievements of economic progress, he claimed, were immediately counteracted by rapid population growth. This might well be the key to the crisis in Anáhuac after 1800.

Although Amartya Sen is right in focusing on ownership and exchange—

on relations of power—rather than on food supply in analyzing famines, he neglects the enormous consequences of population growth in small areas. Changing the relations of power in a country or region might not be sufficient: the dilemma of "less children or starve" is typical for the South nowadays. This dilemma was experienced earlier by several regions of Europe and the South, especially when a Great Leap could be taken to feed a growing population, but not the expected increase launched by the Great Leap itself. And that is precisely the root of the dilemma: one Great Leap, a solution to the problems of past demographic growth, stimulates in itself population increase again. And with every stage, every new Great Leap—expansion of the acreage, intensification of agricultural methods and of labor, proto-industrialization or even industrialization—regions with a limited agricultural surface and relatively big difficulties in transport to overcome (think of the very poor surfaces of roads or even mountains to be crossed by mules, horses, or wagons) were the first to experience poverty, famines, and deprivation. Java or Egypt might experience such a problem in the near future, Anáhuac was a candidate around 1800, after the obvious successful initial stage of proto-industry in earlier decades of the eighteenth century.[31]

This demographic factor, therefore, is at the heart of the ecological approach to economic development in Anáhuac. The word *ecological* then does not refer to "Green History," or to the "New Ecological History," with its objective of describing environmental degradation. My ecological approach is economic history, the history of man in its natural habitat. It consists of four elements:

1. A geographical element: the preconditions formed by the landscape and climate would have had considerable influence on the degree of access to the means of production.
2. A demographic element: beyond a certain level, population growth in a particular region or habitat would have exceeded the agricultural sustaining power of the region; the number of people living below subsistence level increased, and social stratification would have extended.
3. An economic element: in general a population in danger of running out of adequate means of subsistence will step up its economic activity, and if the two primary ecological elements check the extension of the surface under cultivation, proto-industrialization takes place; this is what might be called the Great Leap Forward.
4. A cultural element: the ecological set of values brings about the consensus required for the Great Leap Forward. This set of values determines the claim to the right of self-sufficiency in cultural terms to make up for the loss of the economic claims. In the case of bad harvests, the set of values gave the peasants access to the food produced in the region.

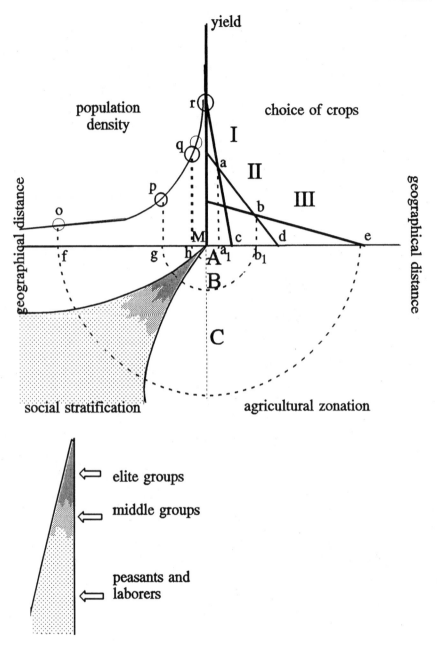

Figure 7 Population density, economic differentiation, choice of crops and social stratification in terms of yield and geographical distance

I have tried to sum up the main elements in a simple model. Figure 7 consists of the following components, each with a centripetal tendency toward point M: first, following von Thünen, a model of the crop choice; second, the system of agricultural zones that can be derived from it; and, third, a representation of population density. The first component is derived from an interpretation of von Thünen's work by the economists Lösch and Dunn.[32] The following formula is used:

$$R = E(p - a) - EfK$$

where R is the rent per unit of land, E is the yield per unit of land, K is distance in kilometers, p is the market price per unit of commodity, a is the production cost per unit of commodity and f is the transport rate per unit of distance for each commodity. The crops with the highest R are produced closest to the market. This is crop I in the model in Figure 7; crops II and III have a lower yield in money terms for the producer. The transport costs involved in bringing crop I to the market M are much higher and therefore more unfavorable than those for the two other crops. As a result of the high transport costs, the economic rent R of crop I drops to zero at point c in Figure 7. Crop II yields a lower R, but as a result of the lower transport costs it takes longer for its R to drop to zero (point d). This crop can thus be produced at a greater distance (in kilometers) from the market. The producer can maintain the commercial production of crop III until point e is reached. In terms of maximizing profits, the producer will cultivate crop I until point a is reached; geographically seen from the market this is point a_1. At that point he switches to crop II until point b (b_1 as seen from the market) is reached, after which crop III will give him the best yield.

The circles of the agricultural zones can be derived from the points a_1, b_1, and e. As can be easily understood, the costs of labor also have an influence on the choice of crops. It often has been shown that the most profitable crops were also the most labor-intensive. According to von Thünen, vegetable and fruit cultivation was closest to the market, but timber production could not be located very far away either. The food crops were produced a little further away from the market. This is in agreement with the research results of Van Oss and Slicher, in which the agricultural zones can also be regarded generally as zones of labor intensity. In this model of the "isolated state," zone A is that of the many-sided economy, zone B that of the supportive economy, and zone C tends toward the peripheral economy. Of course, these definitions are relative: zone A and B, taken together, may form the many-sided economy while zone C forms the supportive economy. The third component is illustrated by the left-upper part of the figure. As has been stated, the Slicher model is characterized by the directly visible connection between the degree of economic differentiation and the population density. I have tried to illustrate this with the curve passing through the points fo, gp, hq, and mr. Population density is correlated to proximity to the point M. The higher the density the closer the region scores to this point.

The component of social power is much more difficult to introduce in the figure, and with some imagination I hope the reader will recognize this in a stratification pyramid. The highly differentiated social stratification in a region like Anáhuac has already been discussed. The pyramid is divided into three analytical categories: elite, intermediate group—including the caciques—and the mass of peasants and agricultural workers. Intensive social mobility between the various strata was an important feature of this model. In this respect, the mass of peasants and laborers was tied to a very limited differentiation. The stratification pyramid in Figure 7 is on its side because I wished to adapt it to the geographical model outlined there: the elite had its headquarters in the center of the economic system (M), usually the capital of a state or kingdom; in New Spain this was Mexico City. The mass of peasants was situated in the countryside, but it should be recalled that this countryside began immediately outside the city limits. The caciques lived in the countryside, but had their eyes directed toward the capital as well. If the stratification pyramid is connected with the population density curve, the link with the economic positions of power should be striking. The elite that developed its activities in the center M could work there with a large labor force. Because it was able to select, the elite dictated the terms of the labor contract. High population density meant a weakening of the position of the workers and peasants on this very point. The position of the elite was much weaker in the more sparsely populated areas, which explains the better bargaining position of the rural mass. Increased population density was in the interest of the elite.

The effect of a general population growth in the area under review can be imagined from Figure 7. The first possibility is a total expansion of the model. In geographical terms, the economic area expands; zone A extends into B, and B into C. Since C in turn extends into uncultivated territory, there is in theory little change. In absolute terms more people are involved in the production of labor-intensive goods. The elite status can be shared by more people, while the former elite itself becomes richer, can develop more activities, and so on. Since productive activity also increases, this might mark a gradual process of industrialization. There is a change at the level of the scope of activity, but nothing changes in depth. It is only a Small Leap Forward.

The situation is completely different if zone C is unable to expand. This leads to a fragmentation of the fields, usually resulting in plots that are too small, so that the peasantry gets into difficulties. This increases their dependence on the members of the elite, so that the relation of exchange between peasants and elite undergoes a change which is unfavorable to the former. In the end, the peasants who have become landless now decide to work in the companies of the elite, which might be a step in the direction of industrialization. The elite is able to defend itself against loss of status and political power. The social groups who profit from the extension of A into B and B into C form intermediate strata in the stratification; consequently the social ladder is "extended" because it consists of more strata. If a new ecological equilibrium can be found and everyone's existence can be guaranteed again, the new society is a radically different one. I have already labeled this development as a Great

Leap Forward, a general differentiation and intensification of economic activity, but it is clear that it is achieved out of sheer necessity.

The geographical element of this model throws light on the specific situation of the region of Anáhuac, the most densely populated region of New Spain in the eighteenth century. In Anáhuac, it is generally the case that altitude determines the temperature and precipitation determines the degree of moisture required by the germinating seed. Night frost in the spring and autumn and drought in the months of May and June were the main threat to agriculture carried on at the altitude of the central area of the region (consisting of the valleys of Toluca, Mexico, and Puebla). It was not possible to secure more than one maize harvest and one wheat harvest each year. The fact that the region was at a higher altitude than the neighboring regions of Michoacán, Oaxaca, or Guadalajara was also a source of major transport problems in the eighteenth century. The rugged faldas of the central highlands of Anáhuac formed a mountain landscape difficult to cross. This obstacle reduced the possibilities of crop substitution on the highlands. Besides this, the relatively high transport charges made maize and wheat imports too expensive for the majority of the population.

The problems encountered by agriculture seem to have been much greater than has been supposed in the literature to date. Every agriculturalist was tied to a very brief rainy season, and Anáhuac was an extremely dry region in the late eighteenth century. I believe that there is sufficient evidence to suppose that in fifteen out of the last forty years prior to Hidalgo's revolt, there were no sufficient spring rains in Anáhuac: in these years, the rain fell later. Therefore, the inhabitants of the pueblos faced a series of bad harvests in the last period of Spanish rule. The poorer members of these municipalities became dependent on the production of the large-scale agriculturalists (hacendados, but also caciques), who had irrigation systems and enough land to cultivate reasonable quantities of irrigated—and non-irrigated—maize. The large number of bad harvests increased the group of those living below subsistence level and created a situation of relative overpopulation.

The situation in the last forty years preceding Hidalgo's revolt was not equally bad everywhere. The provinces in the valleys of Toluca and Mexico benefited from the attraction exerted on rain clouds by the volcanoes. There was a relative abundance of rain there, even during the previously mentioned forty years of drought. Both valleys did have a disadvantage, however: their high altitude meant that they were plagued by heavy night frosts. There was also extremely poor drainage, so that the abundance of rainwater encouraged the formation of marshes. The valley of Puebla, which was not as high as the others and thus less affected by night frosts, also received less rainwater as a rule. This caused serious problems in the pueblos, especially after 1770. Despite these imbalances in precipitation, however, the portrait remains of a general reduction in rainfall during this period. As shown earlier, people nostalgically recalled the time before the droughts. The eighteenth-century writer Alzate remembered a genuine Octavian peace, forever lost.

The cause of the drought is unclear. Some historians speculate on the

Small Ice Age, which is supposed to have affected the world at this time. It is certainly true that the weather was out of sorts in Europe and Asia at the time. A more obvious explanation for a worldwide disruption of the climate may be sought in the series of volcanic eruptions in Iceland and Asia, which must have introduced a thick layer of dust and ash into the stratosphere. This layer prevented the sun's rays from reaching the earth, so that the balance between the high- and low-air-pressure poles was disturbed. This meant that rain fell where drought was expected, and vice versa. Such climatological deviations can often be connected with a deviation in the pattern of the ocean currents. In this connection, I have referred to the warm gulf stream El Niño, which is accompanied by a high-air-pressure system above Mexico, Central America, and Peru in the summer, bringing drought. Although El Niño has occurred without volcanic eruptions—thereby depriving the scientists of an explanation for this recurrent phenomenon—interested historians should closely follow the meteorologists in their publications on the effects of volcanic eruptions and El Niño.

The relative overpopulation, indicating a growth above the level that the agricultural power of the region could sustain, is the second ecological element in my investigation, but the main one. As has been stated, the drought must have been relatively favorable for those producers who had irrigation systems at their disposal, because new markets were opened up to them which had been closed before. Moreover, access to the means of production per head of family was reduced for the majority of Indians as a result of the new relations of exchange that arose after the high population growth. In such a situation, there is a direct relation between the existing division of prosperity and the existing relations of exchange in the economic system; the rich grew richer where the poor grew poorer.[33]

Population growth in colonial Mexico is a variable that is not easy to investigate, because the only detailed statistics available are those of the tributarios. In its rule over the viceroyalty, the Spanish government maintained a juridical distinction between Indians and non-Indians. The majority of the tributarios lived in the pueblos de indios and were therefore labeled as Indians. Most of the Indians who left for the cities that were no longer featured on tribute lists were no longer counted as tributarios and came to be grouped with the non-Indians. The consequences of the matlazahuatl epidemics and migration of the tributarios to the cities, to villages in the western part of Anáhuac, and to villages situated in the faldas led to a stagnation in the number of tributarios in the pueblos roughly between 1736 and 1786. The number of non-Indians increased especially after 1786, and there seems to be an obvious connection between this phenomenon and the large number of bad harvests: in this period, the number of non-Indians seems to have increased strikingly. The increase of these population groups—often classified as "urban residents"—has been investigated in light of the transformations that took place in social stratification.

This migration pattern must have "Hispanicized" the economy, introducing an increase of scale in economic activity—an increase of scale resulting in an extension of the social ladder. Thus it may be supposed that it was not only push factors which were operative here, but that pull factors must also, if not primarily, be taken into account: the possibilities for employment attracted people to industry. It is no surprise that despite the bad harvests and the population growth in this period, a flourishing urban economy was manifest in Anáhuac. Mexico City and Puebla de los Angeles, in particular, acquired active industrial sectors dominated by textiles, pottery, and the production of cigars and cigarettes. Besides, small-scale traditional craft centers sprang up like mushrooms in the course of the eighteenth century in both the cities and the provincial parishes. This development appears to have started in the period of the restoration of population growth in the pueblos around 1740. Despite the migration to the townships, the number of tributarios had risen dramatically by about 1800 to a level far above that of 1736. There is only one plausible explanation for this phenomenon: the rural economy of Anáhuac must have entered a phase of proto-industrialization.

After the harvest failures, population growth, and the prohibition of the repartimiento de comercios a special situation occurred: relative overpopulation led to an "extended" social ladder—in the Mexican case, the increase in the number of castas—reflecting what I called a Great Leap Forward in economic development. This would mean intensification of economic activity, probably resulting in proto-industrialization. This conforms to the rule that in a situation of population growth, the number of persons above the *subsistence line* increases at a slower rate than that of the number of persons below it. The relation between patriciate and plebs will be transformed, and what emerges would be a virtually landless proletariat of day laborers, impoverished dirt farmers, weavers, and the like. The group below the subsistence line will come into acute difficulties unless a way out is found in the intensification of economic activity. An intensification of this kind did, in fact, take place in such various areas as the Eastern Netherlands, the Ardennes, Flanders, Switzerland, Burgundy, Languedoc, Saxony, and parts of Sweden and Germany. The Mexican region of Anáhuac, I strongly believe, was no exception to this rule.

The countryside became intensely involved in the growth of the cities. In the eastern and southern falda provinces, the Indians began to produce cotton and tobacco, which were sold to merchants from Puebla and Mexico City by means of the repartimiento trade. The merchants passed on the unspun cotton to Indians in the highlands, who turned it into cotton sheets. The development led to an adaptation of the agrarian structure that makes it no longer possible to refer exclusively to haciendas and villages—Frank's and Wolf's *latifundio* and *minifundio*—as the supports of the Central Mexican economic system. It was the urban economy that mainly guaranteed the cohesion of the system. The transformation of the agricultural enterprises, from peasant to hacienda, meant that every peasant became a part of the large network of the urban economy. It is therefore legitimate to seek a theoretical framework in the findings of European research on the characteristics of proto-industrialization.

The relatively favorable *entitlement* position of the laboring poor also played a part in lifting the ban on the repartimiento. The Audiencia risked and ignored a conflict with this open "obedezco, pero no cumplo." Of course, the merchants also stood to gain commercially from this policy, but as Brading has shown, they had quickly pulled out of repartimiento trade after the prohibition. The merchants did not throw themselves into the trade in manufactures and livestock again until after the decree of the Audiencia, which meant that these merchants belonged to a new generation. They then proceeded to open the road to commercialization for themselves, so that the traditional guilds, which were also a part of the moral system, broke down. While the moral system was an obstacle to a genuinely commercial development in the food market, the opportunities for profit in the manufacturing sector were so large that the charity system was adjusted in that area. Paradoxically, the entitlement to command commodity bundles on the food market was linked to the rules of the ecological ethic, but in the manufacturing sector it gave the new commercial mentality a free hand. To put it more starkly: in order to make profits where it could—in the manufacturing sector—the elite convincingly observed the rules of the ecological ethic elsewhere, on the food market.

The decisive factor was the deterioration in the bargaining position of the poor after so many years of population growth. Theoretically, this development opened up the possibility of an impressive social mobility. For instance, in his research on the history of the province of Overijssel in the eastern Netherlands, Slicher van Bath noted that the upper limit that had previously prevented any further climbing was removed in such a situation, making it possible to reach a higher rung. Burke speaks in this connection of a "commercial revolution," a revolution in the pattern of consumption. He refers to the seventeenth-century custom of English peasants of sleeping on mats, while beds were used after commercialization. The most striking feature of this revolution was probably the fact that in large areas of the English countryside, farms were rebuilt and refurnished with manufactured products from the locality, the town, or outside the area in the sixteenth and seventeenth centuries. Although England was exceptional at this time—travelers from the European continent condemned the luxury in which the peasants lived there—Burke brings an important variable to the fore: the increased spending power of the rural population.[34] This flexibility did not exist in Anáhuac; the price of maize rose. All the same, there was an increase in trade, particularly among textiles. The repartimiento enters the discussion again at this point, in fact, this economic development remained at the level of barter. I have shown that the sale of repartimiento goods was concentrated in the countryside of Anáhuac, in its villages and haciendas, but also in the mines surrounding the highlands (or elsewhere in the viceroyalty). Where there was a shortage of coin, people resorted to barter, which was where the repartimiento came in handy.

Although there has not been much in-depth investigation of the transition to proto-industrialization in Anáhuac in the eighteenth century, there are numerous indications that the role of the merchant as "organizer" of the process of production in the region was a new phenomenon. In the cities the guilds began to lose their influence, there was a reduction in the influence of the alhóndiga on the maize market, and the prices of maize and wheat were adjusted to the high increase in demand. Formerly exclusively agrarian households abandoned their farming traditions and became artisanal households. The market economy came to acquire increased importance, and so did dependence from middlemen, wholesale buyers, traveling vendors, and merchants. Observations from the late eighteenth century suggest that the weavers in the villages should really be considered as wage laborers. The traditional system in the countryside was in a state of dislocation.

The signs of a Great Leap Forward in Anáhuac that are to be found in the documents are not just qualitative. Quantitative records, however, do not offer only a positive picture; time and again, impoverishment can be detected for the period around 1800. Because the statistical data are extremely uneven, it was no easy task to determine the period in which the Great Leap Forward was taken, or the period in which the Great Leap began to stumble. The chronological picture that emerges is one of a moderate expansion of the economy in the middle of the eighteenth century and a rapid one during the 1790s. Garner recently argued that the economy of New Spain did not suffer from a Malthusian check; I would take his argument even further: there might have been much truth in Humboldt's conclusion of economic development, but this obviously did not mean wealth for everyone. One could spend much time in unpacking the implications of Humboldt's conclusion, and it certainly has been done, but it is undisputed that the German scientist was restricted by the elitist point of view, noting only the bright side of the "chiaroscuro century."

How long did the revival last? Textile production was probably the only branch to be sufficiently profitmaking to remain intact after 1800. Humboldt observed a crisis in 1803. Contemporary scholars have confirmed this perception. Apparently the great leap was a failure after 1800. Despite the aims of the Bourbon reforms to clothe the Indians, encourage domestic trade, and increase exports, they had a negative effect on the possibility of making a second Great Leap: further industrialization. This second leap was necessary because the first, as was to be expected, had resulted in population growth once more. The negative role of the crown was expressed in the effects of the reform program that had been initiated in the course of the eighteenth century. The tax reforms certainly brought increased revenue for the treasury, but it proved impossible to ascertain to what extent the enlarged quota and the tightening up of collection were felt in the merchants' pockets. However, the literature is clear on the effect of the *Consolidación de Vales Reales,* which drained considerable capital from the economy of New Spain after 1804.[35] The success of the repartimiento—and thereby of employment in both the manufacturing and the transport sectors—was thus confined to a very limited period indeed. The negative role of the crown was the result of both the notion that the colony of New Spain was intended to enrich the economy of the mother country—colonialism!—and to fill the treasury quickly to finance the wars that had broken out in Europe after the French Revolution. The external factor of the role of the House of Bourbon should not be allowed to deflect attention from the internal problems facing the economy of Anáhuac. The Mexicans were not brought down economically; they brought about their own downfall.

Indian Strategies

The region of Anáhuac became most clearly an arena of political and cultural contention at the end of November 1810, when an army of eighty thousand rebels, led by the priest Miguel Hidalgo, marched into the valley of Toluca to bring down the Spanish regime in Mexico City. Hidalgo naturally had expected massive support in the impoverished highlands. His army set up camp near a few pueblos that had been involved in a land conflict with the count of Santiago, a member of the primary elite, for more than twenty years. The conflict had escalated to a violent phase after the court case had been decided in favor of the count; there were many wounded and a few killed during the invasions. All the same, this was no breeding ground for support for Hidalgo. The rebels from Michoacán and Guadalajara could barely count on food supplies from the villages, and they even experienced a degree of hostility on the part of the pueblos during their stay in the valley of Toluca.[36]

Tutino claims that the Indian peasants of Anáhuac reacted as inhabitants of the Indian communities rather than as individuals. In other words, the reaction of the small peasants to their potential companions in adversity who had joined Hidalgo must have been articulated by the gobernadores. The gobernadores reacted as any civil servant or mayor would do: they expressed loyalty to the Spanish king. They did so by placing declarations in this tone in the Mexican daily *El Gazeta de México*. However, elsewhere, in Amecameca (Chalco), the caciques threatened to join Hidalgo if a current court case involving landownership was not rapidly decided in their favor; this led the Audiencia to deliver a positive verdict in favor of the pueblo involved without delay.[37]

All the same, two major preconditions for a peasant revolt do seem to have been present in Anáhuac. First, the impoverishment of the late eighteenth century had brought a larger proportion of the population of the region below the subsistence line. These people became increasingly dependent on the owners of the means of production, namely, the members of the elite. A growing number among this impoverished population had no alternative to offering themselves as workers in the towns, usually for small-scale craftsmen. Second, new social relations had arisen in the countryside as a result of the arrival of a putting-out system. Although there were strong complaints about the *regatones* who controlled the market, and bandits operating in a few provinces could count on some support from the pueblos (around 1810, the cacique Osorno controlled the northern faldas from Apan to Zacatlán for a short time), the power of the *gachupines* from the mother country in Anáhuac was not questioned in principle. Apparently, the fear of the loss of subsistence had not increased.

There were three strategies that the inhabitants of the pueblos *simultaneously* developed to guarantee their subsistence. First of all, there was the strategy of family bonds, a network of blood kin and ritual kin. In order to extend the circle of direct relatives in their own villages, the Indians probably showed a preference for relations with Indians in other villages. The second strategy was to participate in vertical relations in the pueblos to which they belonged. The caciques and other Indian elite members who dispensed the administrative and religious positions in their villages through gobernadoryotl, patronage, and nepotism also arranged the contracts for seasonal work and the repartimiento trade as well as determining how the regular redistribution of the agricultural territory in the villages (común repartimiento) would be carried out. Their mediatory function gave them economic and social privileges. When the population pressure rose in the villages, they made the necessary juridical efforts to expand the area of land available to the villagers. The Audiencia in Mexico City was flooded with requests from the pueblos right up to the 1790s, written by the gobernadores. The population pressure constituted a threat to the economic and social privileges, since more and more peasants found themselves outside the borders of the fundo legal. Therefore a third strategy could be adopted: an appeal to charity. This appeal could be made to the caciques, but it was usually addressed to hacendados, priests, and alcaldes mayores/subdelegados. The requests were for favorable terms of lease, the opening of field kitchens in times of extreme scarcity, the reduction of food prices after bad harvests, and so on. This strategy assumed a violent character if the person to whom the appeal was addressed refused to cooperate.

Anáhuac was probably a special case because around 1800 these three strategies were combined, resulting in relative tranquillity in the countryside on the highlands, while other regions, especially Michoacán and Guadalajara, and some falda or semiarid provinces around the highlands of Anáhuac (Tetepango, Actopan, and Metztitlán, and the Cuernavaca-valley) saw a lot of violence. Of course, the attitude of the church and government must have had a calming effect, especially that of the lower-ranking government officials and priests. Many priests, bishops, and government officials were often prepared to make efforts to mitigate the immediate needs of the poor at a relatively high cost. Consequently, the farming population of Anáhuac was assured of its right to subsistence. In the first instance, the attitude of the caciques within gobernadoryotl must have played a part in this. Their proto-indigenista rhetoric, their unflagging efforts to get the "municipal issue" discussed in court, and their readiness to lead violent action if necessary must have created the impression that the way out of the crisis was close at hand. Their prosperous position and the legitimacy of their authority depended on the maintenance of this image, which was in no way hindered by the increased income that they derived from their manipulations in the villages. I do not get the impression that their image was tarnished by the fact that the end of the prohibition on the repartimiento, which had also threatened their prosperity, was in their own interests. Second, the attitude of the hacendados must have been important. Their charitable image was maintained intact, despite the fact that in the late eighteenth century (when maize prices had become so high) this was an economically advantageous way for them to evade the high costs attached to the facilities of the hacienda. Moreover, many hacendados were prepared to open field kitchens in bad years or to sell their maize for lower prices at the door of the hacienda.

We thus find an interdependence between gobernadores/caciques and hacendados, on the one hand, and Indians, on the other, which confirmed the conviction that the old, consensus-based order should not be disturbed. New Spain was a highly religious and "traditional" colony. The ecological system of values, backed up by church regulations, guaranteed the continuing existence of the economic system of Anáhuac. Although the bargaining power of the poorest sectors involved in the economic process had deteriorated by 1800, what Sen calls the "entitlement to subsistence" had not. The claims to self-sufficiency were commanded, to some extent, by the poorest sectors. The active integration of the Indian municipalities in the economic functioning of this central Mexican region (agricultural labor, industry, transport) meant that the entrepreneurs could not abandon the Indians without losing pocket. Second, a fear of the peasant revolt, a "miedo a la revolución," encouraged the elite to maintain their charitable activities.

All the same, the claims were also an ethical issue. The moral values of charity dominated the ideas of most of the residents of Anáhuac throughout the eighteenth century. According to Dealy, these moral values were the foundation of the independence of Mexico in 1821: an attempt to put an end to the enlightened, "French" regime of the monarch in Madrid. The post-1789 "French" regime was regarded as the government of the Antichrist; Napoleon, in particular, was seen as the Antichrist by many people. The restoration of Ferdinand VII in Spain after the fall of Napoleon was seen as an extension of that government because people no longer felt that an attempt was being made to abide by the consensus. The elite that seized the government from the Spanish king in Mexico City in 1821 tried to restore the consensus, which meant giving in to the demands of the ecological ethic.[38]

This situation is perhaps determinant for historical discourse inspired by the ecological approach. People are dependent on one another in the fields of biological characteristics, socioeconomic organization, and the administration of local government. These interdependent sectors keep up an internal strength that is nourished by the moral values of the participants.[39] A Great Leap Forward in the economic system entails exceptionally heavy social tensions and thus must be adopted without resistance and in consensus. The new ecological equilibrium brings the rich material and social benefits, but the guarantee of economic security for the poorer strata lies in their dependence. The "chiaroscuro century" provoked inequality and security at the same time

A Final Thought

The picture of the development of the Mexican countryside presented in this book diverges from the account to be found in the traditional literature. Traditional scholarship contains a mythification of the past in many cases. In Mexico itself, mural painters like Rivera and Siqueiros identified completely with the mythification of the history of their country and presented this view of Mexican history commissioned by Vasconcelos as the national heritage. The Mexican landscape was viewed as the land of the oppressed, a vision that has been followed by contemporary writers.[40] At the same time, these writers and thinkers accept the discriminating image outlined during the mythification of the Indian as a stupid or naive figure—like a doe-eyed child—who does not know what has happened to him. Politicians mentioned in these pages like Vasconcelos, and their recent successors like Wolf, Florescano, or Frank, defend a view that does not do full justice to the strength and independence demonstrated by the Indians in Mexican history. Modern historical research must make it possible not only to expose the myths, but eventually to ignore them and to attempt to define the variables that allow us to come closer to the true history of the Mexican Indians. This is virtually bound to lead to what might be called a *rehabilitation* of the Indians in Mexican historiography.

As a contribution to the research that this endeavor requires, I have chosen an ecological approach to the economic development of Mexico during the late colonial period. This approach enabled me to acquire some antithetical insights into the position of the Indians in Anáhuac and their economic activities. I did not find a history of ruthless exploitation. On the contrary, I was able to join forces with the reinterpretation of the role of the Indians in the historical process that is being stressed in some recently published Latin American historiography. Indians in the Mexican countryside fought for survival against the obstacles in their path raised by the geographical environment. This struggle was fought in the colonial period, with the assistance of the Spanish state and often with the cooperation of the hacendados. The poverty into which the Indians eventually could have fallen after the 1770s, and especially around the 1800s, was due to the sharp increase in their numbers, as the population swelled to a level that the agriculture could no longer support. This development enabled the members of the elite, aided by industry and commerce, to turn the socioeconomic system more to their own advantage. The urban element grew in importance, and to a certain extent there was scope for the creation of new employment possibilities. This was the result of an internal dynamic, a general mechanism whose characteristics historians have only recently started to define. The history of a region like Anáhuac is, in this respect, not different from that of a good many parts of Europe. It is an experience that the Indians of Mexico shared with peasants from many parts of the European continent.

Notes

Prologue

1. AGI, Audiencia México, Leg. 1411, Exp. 836.
2. AGNM, Tierras, Vol. 1351, Exp. 10.
3. Ladd, *Making of a Strike.*
4. Randall, *Real del Monte,* p. 15.
5. Wilkinson, *Poverty and Progress;* Skipp, *Crisis and Development.*
6. Wilken, *Good Farmers,* p. 2. Also, Enge and Whiteford, *Keepers of Water and Earth.*
7. Berkowitz, *Survey of Social Psychology,* p. 495.
8. See Martínez-Alier, "Ecology and the Poor," and Goodman and Redclift, *Environment and Development.* These works analyze environmental degradation through the eyes of the *latifundium/minifundium complex,* as if no criticism at all has been developed in the past decades.
9. Chase, "Can History be Green?"
10. Sheail, "Green History."
11. On sustainability, see WCED, *Our Common Future,* also referred to as the "Brundtland Report."
12. And, until recently, unchanged by the forces of political economy. The literature mentioned in this paragraph include, Martínez-Alier, "Ecology"; Redclift, *Sustainable Development*; Crosby, *Ecological Imperialism*; Harrison, *Third Revolution*; Thorpe and Bertram, *Peru 1890–1977*; Bunker, *Underdeveloping the Amazon*; Sunkel and Gligo, eds., *Estilos*; Díaz Palacios, El Perú; Pfister and Brimblecombe, *Silent Countdown*; Moore, *Changing Environment*; Baumol and Oates, *Economics*; Tansley, "Use and Abuse."
13. Humboldt, *Ensayo político,* pp. 5, 19, 23, 35, 155, 194, 343, 463, 511.
14. Van Young, "The Age of Paradox," quote from pp. 64–65. See also this text for a discussion of the problematic. I borrowed the image earlier for the introduction of the collection of essays *Empresarios, indios y estado,* pp. 1–14; that volume also contains a conclusion of Van Young, "A modo de conclusión," pp. 206–31, in which he further developed the paradox of rich and poor in late eighteenth-century Mexico. See also the essays in Van Young, *Crisis del orden colonial.*
15. Hamnett, *Roots of Insurgency*; Tutino, *From Insurrection to Revolution.*
16. Garner, *Economic Growth*—for the data see p. 47; I felt much of his argument as a response to, among others, my essay, written with Catrien Bijleveld, "Economic Cycle in Bourbon Central Mexico," in which price-inflationary movements for the late eighteenth century were observed (though no precise calculation of these were given).

17. TePaske, "Economic Cycles in New Spain," p. 126; Van Young, "Rich Get Richer," p. 38, also in idem, *Crisis del orden colonial*, p. 99.

18. Florescano, *Precios del maíz.*

19. Van Young, "Rich Get Richer," Appendix A.

20. See Ouweneel, "Growth, Stagnation, and Migration."

21. Why the faldas? Was there more space there? The documentation that I have seen contains complaints about the rapid growth of the villages in the faldas. Around 1800 these were sometimes assumed to have become larger than those in the high-lands, no doubt as a result of the arrival of the migrants. The situation was compared with that of a half-century earlier around 1750, when the provinces there were more sparsely populated than those in the highlands. The faldas were in demand because in most provinces they were not faced with the problem of drought. One disadvantage lay in their ruggedness, the difficult communication routes, and the presence of very steep inclines that hampered cultivation. The provinces in the highlands were smaller than those in the faldas, and they had relatively more villages as well. Separate calculations have been made to ascertain whether the townships in the faldas at the end of the eighteenth century really were relatively larger than those in the highlands. I have used a published source from 1794, which gives the number of villages per province and the number of residents in each village (Urrutia, who originally collected these statistics, refers to "souls"); see Urrutia in Florescano and Gil, eds., *Descripciones económicas regionales*, pp. 68–127.

As the source indicates, a classification has been made in terms of the number of residents per village and the number of villages per province. The highest number of residents per village was 4,385, the lowest was 283. The range of 4,102 (4,385–293) yields five categories of 820 residents each. It was decided to adopt this figure for the classification of the villages. The statistics are rather arbitrary, but they do not deviate appreciably from contemporary statistics from England, for example. The average num-ber of residents in an English village around 1700 was 300, but there were small villages with a mere 160 residents, as well as a few larger ones with around 500 residents. Simi-lar low figures for the number of residents in the villages can be culled from the Dutch province of Overijssel, the South German Hohenlohe region, the Auffay district in Western France, or the Spanish parish of Segovia. See Laslett, *World We Have Lost*, pp. 54–55; Slicher van Bath, *Samenleving onder spanning*, pp. 51–80; Sabean, *Power in the Blood*, passim; Robisheaux, *Rural Society*, pp. 74–91; García Sanz, *Desarrollo*, pp. 46–49; Gullickson, *Spinners*, passim. Perhaps the Mexican villages were somewhat on the large side. The majority of the villages in Anáhuac belonged to the first two categories (cat-egory A = 0–820, category B = 821–1,640). I have therefore combined the remaining categories in category C (1,641 residents and more). The number of villages per prov-ince was also grouped for illustrative purposes; this procedure resulted in three catego-ries, with categories of 26 townships. Half of the number of provinces had a small number of villages (27 in category X: less than 26). The majority of the other half included between 26 and 52 villages (16 villages in category Y); the rest included a very large number of villages (9 provinces with more than 52 villages; category Z). According to my hypothesis, the X category provinces should have been the sparsely populated prov-inces in the faldas. That is where many of the B and C category villages must have been situated.

Number of villages per province in relation
to number of residents per village
Anáhuac, 1794

			residents per village			
			A	B	C	
	number		under 820	820–1,640	above 1,640	total
villages	X	0–26	11	13	3	27
per	Y	27–52	11	5	–	16
province	Z	52 <	8	1	–	9
	total		30	19	3	52

The table above shows the inclusion of both classifications in a matrix designed to trace the pattern that we are looking for. The matrix indicates that the villages were small on the whole; thirty of the fifty-two villages had fewer than 820 residents. These were situated in provinces with a low or medium number of villages, usually in the highlands or on the faldas— the combinations AX and AY in the matrix. These were the highland provinces of Tula, Cuautitlán, Ecatepec, Coatepec, Mexicalcingo, Tochimilco, Lerma, Toluca, Tecali, Tacuba, Metepec, Atlixco, Huejotzingo and the falda provinces of Acatlán, Chiautla, Tepejí, Izúcar, Chilapa, and Temascaltepec. The remaining small villages were situated in the larger provinces in the highlands— combination AZ, such as Tepeaca. These were villages whose residents consisted almost exclusively of tributarios. An exception was formed by the villages in the valley of Puebla, where the percentage of tributarios was lower—in fact, around 70 percent. Another category was the larger townships (820 to 1,640 residents) in the less fertile areas with less favorable economic prospects. These were the provinces in the semi-arid region, such as Actopan, Tetepango, Ixmiquilpan, Cempoala, and Zumpango. In general these villages were only viable on the banks of a narrow river. However, they were also to be found in the mining areas, such as Zimapan, Pachuca, Taxco, Cuautla Amilpas, Chietla, and Tetela de Xonotla. These villages were absent in the heart of Anáhuac, with the exception of the provinces of Malinalco and Coyoacán. Malinalco is enclosed in a small valley on the southern border of the central highlands, while Coyoacán was already a sort of "suburb" of Mexico City at the time. The large townships in the larger provinces were situated in the faldas. The villages were all large (combination BY) in five provinces: Sochicoatlan, Huayacocotla, Zacatlán, Tehuacán, and Zacualpan. These were provinces in the faldas, to which they owed their origin. Finally, there were three provinces where the "large villages" can in fact be regarded as small towns: Texcoco, Apan, and San Juan de los Llanos (combination CX).

This picture would gain relief if statistics from an earlier period were set beside it, but they hardly exist. However, a 1770 survey may well provide some points of contact; source: BNMa, Ms. 18714, no. 30. It is striking that the increase between 1770 and 1794 in most of the villages in the highlands was less than 50 percent: 39 percent in Huejotzingo (from 383 to 628 households); 30 percent in San Cristóbal Ecatepec (from 443 to 636); 16.5 percent in Chalco (from 567 to 679); 11 percent in Tacuba (from 639 to 720)—these are the provinces with the "better" harvests so far!—36 percent in Zacatlán (from 649 to 1,013); 32 percent in Tulancingo (from 460 to 681), which has just been mentioned as an immigration area; 31 percent in San Juan de los Llanos (from 1,250 to 1,823), which is partly a falda province; 28 percent in semi-arid Zempoala (from 395 to 546); 11 percent in Tepeaca (from 1,220 to 1,367); 10 percent in semi-arid Tula (from 423 to 469). There were also villages with a sharper increase, such as the 62.5 growth in semi-arid Apan (from 793 to 2,116 households per village, even though there were three villages in 1770 and four in 1794). It is hardly surprising to note the drop in the number of households in a few of the highland provinces: 27 percent in overpopulated Cholula (from 678 to 534); 38 percent in overpopulated Izúcar (from 805 to 583); 39 percent in conflict-ridden Tecali (from 791 to 568)—I shall return to this later on; 24 percent in semi-arid Tehuacán (from 1,262 to 1,016); 29.5 percent in densely populated Tetepango (from 1,186 to 916); 20 percent in dry Zempoala (from 395 to 546). There was a very sharp drop in the equally dry province of Otumba, where the figure fell by almost 72 percent (from 1,957 to 1,140). The documentation on which these figures are based does not contain much usable material on the falda provinces, but what there is indicates an increase of a mere 3 percent in relatively densely populated Acatlán; 46 percent in the Chiautla mining area (from 271 to 490); 42 percent in Temascaltepec (from 400 to 686); and a small increase of 8 percent in Huauchinango (from 341 to 369). The pattern that emerges from the data from 1770 and 1794 and in those discussed earlier enables us to conclude that the villages in the densely populated highlands were relatively small in most cases, while those in the dry regions and in the faldas around 1790 were larger. In other words, it is reasonable to suppose that the villages in the faldas really did increase in size as a result of the migration.

22. See *Migration in Colonial Spanish America*, edited by Robinson; for Michoacán, among others, Yacher, *Marriage*; for northern Mexico, Swann, *Tierra Adentro* and *Migrants in the Mexican North*. The best methodology has been demonstrated by Robinson and McGovern, "Migración regional yucateca"; Robinson, "Migration in Eighteenth-Century Mexico"; and Swann, "Spatial Dimensions."

23. Ouweneel, "Growth, Stagnation, and Migration," pp. 553–69.

24. See ibid. p. 555.

25. Compare the figures of independent church counting in 110 parishes of the archbishopric of Mexico in my "Growth, Stagnation, and Migration," p. 559, figure 3.

26. AGNM, Tributos, Vol. 47, Exp. 10.

27. AGNM, Tributos, Vol. 47, Exp. 16.

28. AGNM, Tributos, Vol. 44, Exp. 8; and AGNM, Tributos, Vol. 52, Exps. 1–7.

29. Among others: Cooper, *Epidemic Disease*, pp. 70–84; Florescano, *Precios del maíz*, pp. 148–72; Van Young, "Modo de conclusión," based on his "Age of Paradox"; Hamnett, *Roots of Insurgency*; Tutino, *From Insurrection*.

30. Compare the patterns described here with a map published by McGovern-Bowen and the figures provided by Spillman, who documented a 200 to 300 percent increase in the number of burials between 1784 and 1786 in many parishes there. In general, the overall intensity of mortality during the crisis decreased with distance from the central core of Guanajuato, San Miguel de Allende, León, and Celaya. The disaster would have caused migration to Anáhuac, where the problems were not as great, leaving the mortality rate below 50 percent! See, McGovern-Bowen, *Mortality and Crisis Mortality*; Spillman, "Disaster Complex"; Morin, *Michoacán*, pp. 56–58.

31. Some measures could have contributed to an increase in the 1800 figures. But it proved extremely difficult to register, for example, all males from eighteen to fifty years as full tributarios. Where it was enforced, one might have found higher numbers of tributarios, but such provinces would have been exceptions. Gibson published a short

list of test areas, some provinces in the valley of Mexico, where the new form was introduced as an experiment. The Spanish state wanted to determine the increase in the number of tributarios under a new definition. The results were inconclusive, for the "Indians" who were to be included in the counts moved to nontest areas, where the traditional system was still operating. Nevertheless, the counts of the "new system" of 1797–1804 resulted in a statistical increase by about 17 percent compared to counts according to the "old system" in the same provinces. See Gibson, *Aztecs Under Spanish Rule*, p. 208. Official reports state that the measure was certainly not in effect during the 1790s in most provinces. In fact, the proposed modernization would have influenced the sums of money collected, but not the number of tributarios, for the adult sons had been included in the counts from the seventeenth-century reforms onward. In the 1740s and the 1750s women had been exempted from payments, although villagers continued to hold women using corporate lands for payment. After 1798 the free mulatos were included among the tributarios anyway, since the majority of them had become residents of the pueblos de indios by now and it was virtually impossible for the government to distinguish them from the other residents. This measure led to a minor increase in the number of tributarios during the following census around 1800. See my "Growth, Stagnation, and Migration," p. 541, note 17.

32. See, for example, Salvucci, *Textiles*, pp. 111–22; and Miño, *Obrajes y tejedores*.

33. Taylor, "Indian Pueblos," quote from p. 162.

34. Bartlett, *Making of Europe*, p. 197.

35. Taylor, "Indian Pueblos"; García Martínez, *Pueblos de la Sierra*, and, above all, "*Pueblos de Indios*."

36. On the orders see as well Knowles, *Evolution*, pp. 255–68; Duby, *Trois ordres*.

37. Cope, "Limits," pp. 58–59.

38. The problem of ethnicity in colonial New Spain is discussed by Chance and Taylor, "Estate and Class in a Colonial City." Reactions followed by Valdes, "Decline"; Chance, *Race and Class*, and "Ecology"; later supported by Seed and Rust, "Estate and Class"; Seed, "Social Dimensions"; Wu, "Population"; McCaa, Schwartz, and Grubessich, "Race and Class," replied by Chance and Taylor, "Estate and Class, A Reply." McCaa added later a new dimension to the debate with his "*Calidad*," introducing the *calidad*. This research has been synthesized by Bronner, "Urban Society," pp. 30–31. See also, Mörner, "Economic Factors"; Greenow, "Marriage Patterns"; Swann, *Tierra Adentro*, pp. 150–52 and 177–80; Osborn, "Community Study," pp. 11–16; McCaa and Swann, *Social Theory*; Cope, "Limits."

39. Humboldt, cited by Marshall, in his "Birth," quote on p. 184; for Vicente García, see AGNM, Civil, Vol. 1646, Exp. 18.

40. Seed, "Social Dimensions," passim.

41. Cited by Chance, *Race and Class*, pp. 178–79.

42. Cope, "Limits," p. 59.

43. Ibid., p. 328.

44. Chance, *Race and Class*, p. 177.

45. Skipp, *Crisis and Development*, p. 10.

46. See Muir, "Introduction," p. xviii; as well as the texts on philosopher Charles Peirce in Eco and Sebeok, eds., *Sign of Three*.

47. Corbin, *Le territoire du vide;* I used the translation *Het verlangen naar de kust*.

48. Roessingh, "Veluwe"; this essay contains only a description, no interpretation. The figures are 1650–1749 an annual increase of 0.29 percent; 1815–29 an annual increase of 1.66 percent; and, in rural areas 0.39 percent per annum.

49. Wilkinson, *Poverty and Progress*, pp. 103–5, diagram on p. 104.

50. Levine, *Family Formation*, pp. 5 and 11. Although more titles on proto-industrialization will follow in chapter 8, mentioned here are: Mendels, "Proto-Industrialization"; Fischer, "Rural Industrialization"; Medick, "Proto-Industrial Family Economy"; Gutmann, *Toward the Modern Economy*. Also see Ingham, *Mary, Michael and Lucifer*, pp. 56–77.

Chapter 1

1. Fischer, *Historians' Fallacies*, p. 243.

2. See, among many others, Momigliano, *Classical Foundations*.

3. Ankersmit, *Narrative Logic*; see also a collection of his essays, *Navel van de geschiedenis*.

4. Schama, *Dead Certainties*.

5. On the postmodernists, see Norris, *What's Wrong with Postmodernism*.

6. Fischer, *Historians' Fallacies*, p. 259.

7. See also Cohen, *Whalsay*, pp. 203–12.

8. See, among others, Carmagnani, *Regreso de los dioses*.

9. Hochstadt, "Migration," pp. 195–96.

10. In the Mexican case, as expressed in the 1991 article, this meant the increase in the number of non-Indians; see Ouweneel, "Growth, Stagnation, and Migration," pp. 562–68. While the urban Spanish república grew in numbers as a result of migration and individual adjustment by the calidad (*mestizaje*), the growth in the number of members belonging to the Indian república in the countryside was reduced by emigration, particularly after the great matlazahuatl epidemic of 1736–39.

11. See, among others, the essays in Walter and Schofield, eds., *Famine*.

12. Slicher van Bath, "Twee sociale stratificaties." This is summarized in his chapter "Agriculture in the Vital Revolution," pp. 123–25. Also see Mörner, "Economic Factors," pp. 343–44, and Table I.

13. On the rancheros, see Brading, *Haciendas and Ranchos*.

14. Slicher van Bath, *Agrarische geschiedenis*, pp. 340–42; in the English edition, pp. 310ff.

15. Mauzi, *Idée du bonheur*, p. 156.

16. There is an excellent discussion of this material in the two books by David Grigg to which I have already drawn attention, *Population Growth*, and *Dynamics*. See also Malthus, *Essay*; Boserup, *Conditions*, later also in her *Population and Technology*.

17. See Morineau, *Faux-semblants*, pp. 7–96, 289–338; Lis and Soly, *Poverty and Capitalism*; Weir, "Life under Pressure," and earlier in "Fertility Transition"; and the literature reviewed by Goldsmith, "Agrarian History." Defending the French method is Foster, "Obstacles," and, above all, in his article "Achievements." It is evident that the French School referred to here is the so-called Annales School associated with the journal *Annales*. The static views of these historians have come under heavy attack since the 1980s.

18. Titow, "Evidence of Weather." On *pulque*-drinking, see Hernández Palomo, *Renta del pulque*.

19. James C. Riley, "Insects," see his remarks on the transmission of the bacillu Shigella Dysenteriae by flies on p. 845; Slicher van Bath, "Problèmes fondamentaux," p 35. Also, Van den Eerenbeemt, "'Rode Dood'"; Mentink, "Rode loop in Gelderland, two parts. See also Delort, *Animaux ont une histoire*.

20. AGNM, Alhóndigas, Vol. 15, Exps. 7 and 9.

21. Larson, "Rural Rhythms," pp. 416–19; Appleby, "Grain Prices," pp. 867–68; Cipolla, *Before the Industrial Revolution*, p. 33; De Vries, *Economy of Europe*, pp. 182–83; Dirks, "Social Responses." Post claims that mortality was lower in regions with an efficient government organization: Post, "Climatic Variability." Interesting in this respect is Loewenberg, "Psychohistorical Origins of the Nazi Youth Cohort."

22. Dirks, "Social Responses."

23. The *moral economy* is discussed by Thompson in his *Making*, pp. 68–73, and "Moral Economy." Thompson got the idea for the existence of a latent "moral economic ethic" after reading Tawney's *Agrarian Problem*. See also Rudé, *Crowd in History*, and *Ideology*. For a long time the moral economy was only studied in the context of riots and rebellions. This applies to Tutino, *From Insurrection*; Phelan, *People and the King*; McFarlane, "Civil Disorders"; Larson, *Colonialism*; Langer, "Labor Strikes"; Stavig, "Ethnic Conflict"; Schryer, "Peasant Quiescence"; Vanderwood, "Comparing Mexican Independence." However, following Thompson, the "latent moral economy ethic" has come in for more attention recently. See, for instance, Levi, *Inheriting Power*, and Appleby, *Economic Thought*. This is the direction I am following. It will be clear that the moral economic ethic cannot be studied in isolation, but it has to be set against the context of socioeconomic struggle—what Thompson refers to as "class struggle"; see my "Don Claudio Pesero," pp. 166, 171–74, 180–81. On the other hand, the anthropologist James Scott linked the concept, incorrectly I think, with one similar to the historically static "closed corporate peasant community," in an interpretation of peasant unrest in Southeast Asia. Scott presents Thompson's "moral economy thesis" as simply another—though the most important—theory of relative deprivation; Scott, *Moral Economy*, *Weapons of the Weak*, and "Exploitation."

24. The theoretical concepts of *Personenverband* and *territorialverband* were developed to interpret medieval social and political relationships. The concepts, of course, form a dichotomy designed for analytical reasons and consequently oversimplify historical reality. In fact, in Europe they coexisted under the dominance of *Personenverband* until the thirteenth century and under the dominance of *Territorialverband* since the sixteenth century. The dichotomy was elaborated by Mitteis, *Staat des hohen Mittelalters*. Also see Southern, *Making of the Middle Ages*, pp. 73–114. Wunder, *Bäuerliche Gemeinde*, discusses the same dichotomy, but as seen from the ruler or state.

25. Wilkinson, *Poverty and Progress*, p. 8, see also pp. 4 and 54.

26. Slicher van Bath, "Economische toestand," quote from pp. 368–69.

27. Wilkinson, *Poverty and Progess*, p. 48.

28. Mann, *Sources*, pp. 38–40, 105–27. The extension of the social ladder, the process of stratification referred to by Mann, is familiar from European history, but Wilkinson did not include it in his model.

29. See, for instance, Wykstra, *Introductory Economics*, pp. 21–22.

30. See the excellent discussion in Appleby, *Economic Thought*, pp. 52–72.

31. Thompson, "Moral Economy," pp. 78–79, also for a political statement. Also see Rudé, *Ideology*, p. 28. In this connection the modern industrial sector is regarded as the *political economy of entrepreneurship and state policy*. This is the kind of economy studied by classical and neoclassical economists. The term *political economy* can therefore be regarded as a synonym for the *capitalist economy*.

32. Darnton, *Great Cat Massacre*, pp. 31–32. The same point was brought forward by Laslett, *World We Have Lost*; Thomas, *Religion*.

33. For some generalizations, see Lindzey, Hall, and Thompson, *Psychology*; or Hilgard, Atkinson, and Atkinson, *Introduction to Psychology*.

34. See, for instance, Levi, *Inheriting Power*, pp. 66–99; Reher, "Old Issues." Also see the essays edited by Medick and Sabean, *Interest and Emotion*.

35. O'Neill, *Social Inequality*, pp. 154–59, 171–74, 10, 316, quote from p. 171; Orlove, "Inequality Among Peasants."

36. Levi, *Inheriting Power*, pp. 66–99. This is in contrast to Sahlins, *Stone Age Economics*; and Macfarlane, *Origins of English Individualism*, sharply criticized by Levi. See also Razi, "Family"; Howell, *Land, Family and Inheritance*; Geertz, *Peddlers and Princes*; Wilson, *Feuding, Conflict and Banditry*, esp. chapter 3, pp. 61–90.

37. Mann, *Sources*, pp. 51–55.

38. Sabean, *Power in the Blood*, pp. 23–26, 37–93, quote from p. 25. See also Robisheaux, *Rural Society*, esp. pp. 6–9. I have used the ideas expressed in these studies for my *"Altepeme* and *Pueblos de Indios."* A further elaboration can be found in Rik Hoekstra's book on the changing relationships between Indian lords and Indian commoners in the valley of Puebla, during the sixteenth and early seventeenth centuries, *Two Worlds Merging*.

39. Mewett, "Boundaries and Discourse."

40. Mewett, "Boundaries and Discourse," pp. 84–85; Suttles, *Social Construction*; Gusfield, *Community*; Cohen, *Symbolic Construction*.

41. Spalding, "Colonial Indian," p. 58; Schryer, "Ethnicity and Politics," p. 103, and "Class Conflict," pp. 99–104, 115–16; Georgescu-Roegen, "Institutional Aspects," pp. 61–65.

42. About "petty commodity producers," see Friedmann, "Household Production"; Ennew, Hirst, and Tribe, "'Peasantry.'"

43. Wolf, *Peasants*, pp. 14–15; Hewitt, "Boundaries," pp. 95–96; Grigg, *Dynamics*, pp. 93–94; Schejtman, "Elementos," pp. 491–497; Foster, "Peasant Society," p. 307; but most important on Chayanov, see Sabean, *Property*, pp. 88–101, a chapter entitled "The Ideology of the House"; see also, O'Neill, *Family and Farm*, 5–21, quotes from pp. 5, 6, and 7; Kochanowicz, "Peasant Family"; and Smith, "Families," pp. 6–21, as well as "Some Reflections."

44. For a short discussion, see also Schryer, *Ethnicity*, pp. 27–49.

45. Wolf, "Vicissitudes."

46. Schryer, "Ethnicity and Politics," pp. 104–5; Wasserstrom, *Class and Society*; Chamoux, *Nahuas*; Van Young, "Conflict," pp. 56–57; see also the essays in Ouweneel and Miller, eds., *Indian Community*; LeRoy Ladurie, *Montaillou*.

47. Friedmann, "Household Production," p. 163; Bernstein, "Concepts".

48. Hanawalt, *Ties that Bound*, p. 5, quoting Hilton, *English Peasantry*, p. 13.

49. Macfarlane et al., *Reconstructing*, p. 1. He refers to F. Tönnies, *Community and Association*, published in 1887, translated into English in 1955. See also Macfarlane's *Culture of Capitalism*, pp. 1–24 ("Peasants: The Peasantry in England before the Industrial Revolution—A Mythical Model").

50. O'Neill, *Social Inequality*, p. 2.

51. Jones, *Politics and Rural Society*, pp. 107–8.

52. Laslett, *World We Have Lost*, pp. 54–79, quote from p. 79. Also Jones, *Politics*, pp. 112, 118, 144; Butlin, *Transformation*, pp. 32–33; Shaffer, *Family and Farm*; Spufford, *Contrasting Communities*; Kamen, *European Society*, p. 17; Rebel, *Peasant Classes*; Manning, *Village Revolts*; Briggs, *Early Modern France*, pp. 47–54; Borrero Fernández, *Mundo rural sevillano*, pp. pp. 199–211, 310–14; Casado, *Señores*, pp. 49–83, 511–48.

53. Black, "Tyranny," quote from p. 614.

54. It has been customarily assumed that classes have "interests," which result

from the overall structure of class relations, and which function, a priori, as the necessary basis for the mobilization of actors, divorced from any analysis of the varied constitution of the social subject or the dynamic of collective wills. In fact, some authors state that the failure of "classes" to become conscious of their "interests" gives rise to the notion of "false consciousness." In Marxism, classes are viewed as "unconscious agents" of the historical process. Such an analysis of classes in fact has been granted theoretical primacy in Robert Brenner's well-known and hotly debated interpretation of economic development in preindustrial Europe. See, Brenner, "Agrarian Class Structure." See also the criticism by Postan and Hatcher, "Population"; Croot and Parker, "Agrarian Class Structure"; and Wunder, "Peasant Organization"; see also LeRoy Ladurie, "Reply"; Bois, "Against"; Hilton, "Crisis"; and, Cooper, "In Search." Brenner's answer was published a few years later, "Agrarian Class: Structure Agrarian Roots." However, the debate does not seem to end there; see, Searle, "Custom"; or Seccombe, "Marxism." However, recent criticism brought not only their heterogeneity to the attention of theorists, but above all the complex constitution of individual identities. The political scientist James Scott made the same step:

Class, after all, does not exhaust the total explanatory space of social actions. Nowhere is this more true than within the peasant village, where class may compete with kinship, neighborhood, faction, and ritual links as foci of human identity and solidarity. Beyond the village level, it may also compete with ethnicity, language groups, religion, and region as a focus of loyalty. . . . Those who are tempted to dismiss all principles of human action that contend with class identity as "false consciousness" and wait for Althusser's "determination in the last instance" are likely to wait in vain.

Scott, *Weapons*, p. 43. For a similar critique, see the field of the so-called New Social Movements. For a general picture of this field, see Slater, ed., *New Social Movements*; Foss and Larkin, *Beyond Revolution*; or Assies, Burgwal, and Salman, *Structures of Power*. Also see Slater, "Power and Social Movements." On classes as unconscious agents, see Castoriadis, *Imaginary Institution*, esp. p. 29. Also see Giddens, *Constitution of Society*.

55. Mouffe, quoted by Slater, "Power and Social Movements," p. 6.

56. Robisheaux, *Rural Society*, p. 9. For an extended discussion of *Herrschaft* see also Brunner, Conze, and Kosseleck, eds., *Geschichtliche Grundbegriffe*, 3, pp. 1–102. Hoekstra convincingly argues that *Schutz und Schirm* was present in Aztec society before the coming of the Spaniards; this is expressed by the Nahuatl terms *teucyotl* and *tlatocayotl*—see *Two Worlds Merging*.

57. But most often it would originate from struggle with outside elites, landlords, merchants, or church and state officials. See Sabean, *Power*, p. 29:

The issue is . . . in what way a collectivity such as a village or a neighborhood is bound together through mediated relationships involving aid, conflict, aggression, and sharing. In the way that we confront the reality of village life, we see that community was not something "pre-modern," unchanging, structural, but *was constructed*, changed with time, and can only be grasped as historical process because those elements through which relations were constructed, whether "real" or symbolic resources, were constantly in movement.

58. Tajfel, "Instrumentality," esp. p. 485. Cohen, *Whalsay*.

59. This paragraph is based on Muchembled's important book, *Culture populaire*. However, see also Hoffman's study, *Church and Community*. The German Peasant Revolt of 1525 is a good example. At its peak, in April 1525, it extended from the Vosges area in what is now eastern France to Salzburg in present-day Austria. Sabean and Blickle trace the causes of this revolt in the demographic developments of the seventy-five

years that preceded it. Population growth meant that the demand for land increased at a faster rate than the supply. As a result, the lords were prepared to make fewer concessions or none at all to the small peasants and tenant farmers during the "negotiations." In fact, the lords felt confident enough to implement all kinds of changes in the economic system. The peasants considered these changes as a direct threat to their existence. This way of going about things was in conflict with the old normative economy and led to the emergence of a new one. It is striking that in the areas where the fighting was the heaviest, the price increases for agricultural products had removed many of the disadvantages of the ecological pressure. The fact that it was precisely there that the war was the most severe is due to the changes that the lords wanted to implement in their own interests. The records of the complaints by peasants about the attack on their rights contain phrases like "it wasn't like this in the past" and "everything should be kept as it was" as crucial points in the argument. Although population growth in Bavaria was no less than in the neighboring regions, it kept out of the fighting: the elite did not want to introduce changes in the economic system. This must be due to the fact that the changes in question had already been implemented there earlier on, so that the Bavarian peasants did not notice any new disruption of the system. According to Sabean and Blickle, population growth and an assault on the traditional rights of the peasants within a short timespan were the clearest cause of the violent revolt of the peasants against the lords, the elite, and state in 1525. See, Sabean, *Landbesitz und Gesellschaft*; Scribner and Benecke, *German Peasant War*; Abel, *Massenarmut und Hungerkrisen im vorindustriellen Europa*; Robisheaux, *Rural Society*; Blickle, *Deutsche Untertanen*; Wunder, *Bäuerliche Gemeinde*; Press, "Herrschaft."

60. Sabean, *Power*, pp. 20–27.

61. Foucault, *History*, pp. 100–01.

62. Wilkinson, *Poverty and Progress*, p. 11.

63. Robisheaux, *Rural Society*, pp. 147–74.

64. See also Scott, "Exploitation," p. 494. The formula seems to be rather misunderstood by Margarita Menegus Bornemann in *HMex*, 42:1 (1992/165), p. 139.

65. Mann, *Sources*, p. 24.

66. Thompson, "Moral Economy," p. 78; Sabean, *Power in the Blood*, p. 13; Appleby, *Economic Thought*, pp. 242–79; Macfarlane, *Culture of Capitalism*, pp. 223–27; Braudel, *Structures*, pp. 23–24.

67. Adorno, Frenkel-Brunswik, Levinson, and Sanford, *Authoritarian Personality*.

68. Moore, *Social Origins*, esp. pp. 468–70 and 497–98.

69. Mitzman, "Sociability," p. 102; Frijhoff, "Cultuur en mentaliteit"; Burke, *Popular Culture*. See also the review essay by Hutton, "History of Mentalities."

70. Dumont, *Religion*, p. 85; Derrida, *The Post Card*, or his *Margins of Philosophy*.

Chapter 2

1. See Mitzman, "Sociability," p. 110.

2. Patch, "Agrarian Change," p. 47. Also, see Van Young, "Mexican Rural History," p. 25.

3. Reyes, *Visión de Anáhuac*, pp. 11–12.

4. Wilkinson, *Poverty and Progress*, p. 218.

5. Humboldt, *Ensayo político*. The texts by Alzate are published by Sonia Lombardo de Ruíz, *Antología de textos*.

6. Trautmann, *Transformaciones*.

Notes to Pages 62–5 343

7. The characteristics of the regions of New Spain are defined by Van Oss, "Architectural Activity"; and, Slicher van Bath, *Bevolking en economie*, as well as a summary of his research in "Dos modelos," pp. 26–33.

8. On Oaxaca: Taylor, *Landlord and Peasant*; Chance, *Conquest of the Sierra*; Carmagnani, *Regreso de los dioses*; Pastor, *Campesinos y reformas*; Romero Frizzi, *Economía y vida*; Hamnett, *Politics and Trade*. On Guadalajara: Van Young, *Hacienda and Market*; Serrera Contreras, *Guadalajara ganadera*; Lindley, *Haciendas*. On Michoacán: Brading, *Haciendas and Ranchos*; Morin, *Michoacán*; Tutino, *From Insurrection to Revolution*; Rabell Romero, "San Luis de la Paz"; Super, *Vida en Querétaro*. On Anáhuac: García Martínez, *Pueblos de la sierra*; Gibson, *Aztecs under Spanish Rule*; Jarquín, *Formación y desarrollo*; Kicza, *Colonial Entrepeneurs*; Martin, *Rural Society*; Nickel, *Soziale Morphologie*; Trautmann, *Transformaciones*; Tutino, "Creole Mexico"; Von Wobeser, *San Carlos Borromeo* and *Formación de la hacienda*; Haskett, "Social History"; Konrad, *Jesuit Hacienda*; Liehr, *Stadtrat*; Osborn, "Community Study"; Riley, *Hacendados jesuitas*; Taylor, *Drinking*; Thomson, *Puebla de los Angeles*; Wood, "Corporate Adjustment."

9. Brading, "Comments," correctly stressed this point.

10. Ibid., p. 532.

11. Slicher van Bath, "Dos modelos," diagram 1, p. 27.

12. Wolf, *Europe*, p. 145.

13. Slicher's statistics are limited to some extent. They are derived from a summary of an inquiry conducted in 1742–43 and published by Villaseñor y Sánchez. Is the model constructed on the basis of this material also applicable to the late eighteenth century? The original documents drawn up by the provincial administration indicate that the economy of the time was still seriously handicapped by the effects of the epidemic that had swept through the viceroyalty between 1736 and 1739. Many economic activities were no longer carried out because a significant percentage of the population had died or left. Some of these economic activities are mentioned in his book by Villaseñor, but not all of them. For the original documents, see AGI, Indiferente General, Legs. 107 and 108. The present inquiry calls for a comparison of the 1743 data with data from a later period. We know that a survey was held in 1776–77, but only a few replies have been traced in the archives thus far. See BNMa, Mss. 2449 and 2450; AGNM, Historia, Vol. 578. A serviceable document, however, has been found for the years 1782–83. Like the one used by Villaseñor, this document gives the main item of trade, interestingly referred to as the *trato*, for each province. The document of 1782–83 is published by Florescano and Gil, *Descripciones económicas generales*, pp. 11–33. The *trato* was usually traded through the *repartimiento de comercios*, which will be discussed later on. It gives an indication of the regional division of labor.

The economic activities mentioned in this document are listed in fourteen categories: fishing, in the sea, rivers, and lakes; maize and wheat (listed separately); seed (*semillas*, a term covering beans, broad beans, chick peas, and other types of pulse); small livestock farming (sheep and goats); pig keeping and chicken farming; large livestock farming; forestry; textile industry; the cultivation and processing of cotton; vegetable and fruit cultivation; handicrafts excluding textiles (leather, wood and metal working, as well as the production of laxatives, starch and wax, hats, and mats); plantation products and cash crops (especially sugar); and finally, mining. It should be noted that, in many cases, these tratos were not produced by entrepreneurs from the towns or hacendados, but by producers from the Indian townships. Textile industry is a case in point. The anonymous author of the document distinguishes within the category of textiles between the production of clothing, which was seen as an industry, and the cultivation of cotton, immediately followed by its processing, including weaving. Although in more recent history, cotton cultivation was in the hands of the large plantation owners, at that time it was carried out by small farmers and peasants. They also supplied the clothing industry in the large cities with ready-made mantles. It was only in the villages of Oaxaca that the cultivation and processing of cotton and the manufacture of mantles all took place.

There is no reason to distrust Villaseñor's 1743 statistics: these data confirm the results of Slicher's investigations. It is obvious that handicrafts were performed in the centers of the four regional economic units and *semillas*, maize, wheat, and timber were produced. The more peripheral areas outside these centers were the site of large livestock breeding, and sugar and cotton production. There are also variations from one region to another. Wheat was a characteristic product of Anáhuac and the northern part of Michoacán. Nontextile handicrafts were concentrated in Anáhuac. The Oaxaca region is a specifically artisanal region, specializing in cotton, "textiles," and particularly cochineal. These typically *indígena* village activities are not indicated for the Michoacán or Guadalajara regions. Large livestock breeding took place mainly in the Michoacán region. The silver mines were generally situated outside the regions, on the periphery, but the concentration of mines in or on the boundary of Michoacán should not be ignored.

14. On von Thünen, see Peet, "Von Thünen-Theory"; Chisholm, *Rural Settlement*, pp. 38–40; Grigg, *Population Growth* and, especially, *Dynamics*, pp. 135–50.

15. Humboldt, *Ensayo política*, pp. 22–23.

16. Wolf, *Sons*, p. 7.

17. BNMa, Ms. 19503.

18. Humboldt, *Ensayo político*, p. 26.

19. Werner, "Consecuencias"; Cook, *Historical Demography*.

20. Yield ratio = sowing seed in units/harvest result in units. See Slicher van Bath, "Yield Ratios"; Loomis, "Agricultural Systems," p. 102.

21. See Tutino, "Creole Mexico," p. 55. Also, note some details in Bataillon, *Ciudad*, pp. 32–38.

22. Alzate in Lombardo, *Antología*, p. 223.

23. Ewald, *Mexican Salt Industry*, esp. pp. 17–25, 39–55.

24. Alzate, in Lombardo, *Antología*, pp. 206–7. On the lakes, see *Diario del viaje*, 1, pp. 52–53, 72–76; Beaufoy, *Mexican Illustrations*, p. 176; Urrutia, in Florescano and Gil, *Descripción*, pp. 103 and 112; Bullock, *Seis meses*; Pedro O'Crouley in BNMA, Ms. 4532; Gibson, *Aztecs under Spanish Rule*, pp. 236–42, 305.

25. Cook, *Historical Demography*, pp. 57–58.

26. Ouweneel, "Growth, Stagnation, and Migration."

27. Ajofrín, *Diario*, 1, pp. 72–73; Beaufoy, *Mexican Illustrations*, pp. 179–80; Gemelli Careri, *Viaje a la Nueva España*, p. 147. See Bassols Batalla, *Recursos naturales*, pp. 113ff. See Gabriel García Márquez's short story "Monologue of Isabel Watching It Rain in Macondo," published in *Latin American Literature Today*, trans. Anne Fremantle. See also Rulfo, *El llano en llamas*.

28. Bassols Batalla, *Recursos naturales*, pp. 114–16, 134–35; Schmidt, *Mexiko*, pp. 24–25, containing data from the weather station of Tacubaya, 1900–16; Alzate, in Lombardo, *Antología*, pp. 243–51; Humboldt, *Ensayo político*, pp. 27–29; Lauer, "Altitudinal Belts," pp. 107–11, Figures 10 and 12; Lauer and Klaus, "Thermal Circulation."

29. AGI, Indiferente General, Legs. 1560 and 108 (Chalco).

30. Lauer and Klaus, "Thermal Circulation," pp. 344–47.

31. AGI, Indiferente General, Leg. 108.

32. I have been able to consult one book from this series of observations: BNMa, 13244 ("Efermérides astronómicas arregladas al meridiano de México, 1775–1785"). If the rest can be traced in the archives, it will provide an invaluable source for agrarian history. All the data in this section are based on this source. Another volume, a day-by-day record from 1763 to 1773 (that is, the preceding one) has been found by Gibson in the Sutro Library, San Francisco; see Gibson, *Aztecs under Spanish Rule*, p. 550, note 12, and, Appendix 5, pp. 456–59.

33. The reports by this manager have been edited and discussed by Swan, "Climate," pp. 62–67, Table 1.

34. AGI, Indiferente General, Leg. 1560; also AGI, México, Leg. 1421, Exp. 80; AGNM, Intendentes, Vol. 73, Exp. 9.

35. UIA, Ac 2.1.16, 17 and 18; FMMN, Serie Tlaxcala, Rollo 10, no. 425; Trautmann, *Transformaciones*, p. 209.

36. AGI, Indiferente General, Leg 107; BNMa, Ms. 2449, Exp. 18.

37. Florescano, *Precios del maíz*, pp. 150–52, 201–27; Florescano and San Vicente, *Fuentes para la historia de la crisis agrícola (1809–1811)*. On 1810, see Archer, *Army*, pp. 293–94; Hamnett, *Roots of Insurgency*, pp. 116–23; Van Young, "Raw and the Cooked."

38. AGI, Indiferente General, Leg. 1560.

39. Swan, "Climate"; also, see Gibson, *Aztecs under Spanish Rule*, Appendix 5, pp. 456–59.

40. Von Wobeser, *Formación*; Licate, *Creation*; Lipsett, "Water"; Trautmann, *Transformaciones*, pp. 221–31; Gibson, *Aztecs Under Spanish Rule*, pp. 214, 279–80; Martin, *Rural Society*, pp. 113-120. Also, among many, see AGNM, Tierras, Vol. 1509, Exp. 7; AGNM, Tierras, Vol. 2, Exp. 15; AGNM, Tierras, Vol. 901, Exp. 1; AGNM, Tierras, Vol. 3618, Exp. 1; AGNM, Tierras, Vol. 222, 2a parte, Exp. 2; AGNM, Tierras, Vol. 1170, Exp. 1; AGNM, Tierras, Vol. 565, 2a parte, Exp. 1; AGNM, Tierras, Vol. 1110, Exp. 6; AGNM, Tierras, Vol. 2055, Exp. 1; and, AGNM, Tierras, Vol. 3539, Exp. 11.

41. Martin, *Rural Society*, pp. 110–11.

42. AGNM, Tierras, Vol. 485, 2a parte, Exp. 1; AGNM, Tierras, Vol. 632, Exp. 1; AGNM, Tierras, Vol. 1001, Exp. 4; AGNM, Tierras, Vol. 940, Exps. 4 and 5; AGNM, Tierras, Vol. 635, Exp. 1; AGNM, Tierras, Vol. 222, 2a parte, Exp. 2; AGNM, Tierras, Vol. 565, 2a parte, Exp. 2; AGNM, Tierras, Vol. 273, Exp. 4; AGNM, Indios, Vol. 38, Exp. 51; AGNM, Indios, Vol. 40, Exp. 10. On Ajalpan see AGNM, Tierras, Vol. 901, Exp. 1; AGNM, Tierras, Vol. 902, Exp. 2; AGNM, Tierras, Vol. 1058, Exp. 2. On Izucar I have consulted AGNM, Tierras, Vol. 273, Exp. 4; AGNM, Tierras, Vol. 391, Exp. 1; AGNM, Tierras, Vol. 395, Exp. 5; AGNM, Tierras, Vol. 1139, Exp. 7; AGNM, Tierras, Vol. 1140, Exp. 3; AGNM, Tierras, Vol. 1141, Exp. 1; AGNM, Tierras, Vol. 1284, Exp. 1; AGNM, Tierras, Vol. 1313, Exp. 16; AGNM, Tierras, Vol. 441, Exp. 1; AGNM, Tierras, Vol. 621, Exp. 6; AGNM, Tierras, Vol. 710, Exp. 3; AGNM, Tierras, Vol. 739, Exp. 3; AGNM, Tierras, Vol. 838, Exp. 7; AGNM, Tierras, Vol. 839, Exp. 1; AGNM, Tierras, Vol. 1034, Exp. 1; AGNM, Tierras, Vol. 1045, Exp. 1; AGNM, Tierras, Vol. 1064, Exp. 6; AGNM, Tierras, Vol. 1123, Exp. 1; AGNM, Tierras, Vol. 1097, Exp. 1; AGNM, Tierras, Vol. 1179, Exp. 2; AGNM, Tierras, Vol. 1222, Exp. 9; AGNM, Tierras, Vol. 1320, Exp. 9; AGNM, Tierras, Vol. 2161, Exp. 2; AGNM, Tierras, Vol. 2672, Exp. 31; and Biblioteca Nacional, Mexico City, Tenencia de la Tierra, Puebla Leg. 7 (1788). See also Greenleaf, "Land and Water"; Taylor, "Land and Water"; Lippsett, "Water and Social Conflict"; and Murphy, *Irrigation*.

43. Martin, *Rural Society*, pp. 110–20.

44. Swan, "Climate," pp. 57–59; Alzate, in Lombardo, *Antología*, pp. 263–64.

45. Grigg, *Dynamics*, pp. 68–80; Slicher van Bath, "Agriculture in the Vital Revolution"; Kuperus, "Honderd jaar bedrijfsresultaten," p. 189.

46. Alzate, in Lombardo, *Antología*, p. 260, n. 1.

47. Eddy, "Climate"; Bryson and Padoch, "On the Climates of History"; Lamb, *Climate*, pp. 201–30, but also pp. 231–51; Matthews, "What's Happening to Our Climate?" It is important for historians to follow popular scientific publications on the disruption of the climate, as I will try to demonstrate below.

A simple calculation of correlations shows that the pattern of the Mexican maize prices is not analogous to that of the European wheat prices, as I shall now proceed to demonstrate. The main European grain market was in Amsterdam. My calculations show that there was a clear connection between wheat prices in Amsterdam, Barcelona, and Madrid (R^2 x 100 of 88% to 94%). It is also possible to include the Parisian prices here, though in an indirect way: Le Roy Ladurie and Baulant detected a connection between the starting date of the French grape-plucking and wheat prices in Paris, resulting from the same problems of the volume of rainfall (R^2 of 75%). This series reveals a correspondence with the Amsterdam series and the two Spanish series of prices, of R between -.74 and -.83. This can be interpreted as an illustration of the unity of the European wheat market, led by the central market in Amsterdam. Grain imported from eastern Europe was traded in Amsterdam, involving large parts of Western Europe. The correlation of all of these European series with that for the maize prices in Mexico City is low. The correlations vary from R +.50 to R -.64 (R^2 x 100 between 24% and 41%), which is far under what is required for a demonstrable connection. The factor of cohesion linking the other series is absent in this case.

The correlations are calculated on the basis of the figures shown in the table on next page.

48. Baars, *Geschiedenis van de landbouw*, pp. 152–53. See also Post, *Last Great Subsistence Crisis*; Pfister, *Agrarkonjunktur*. Bibliography in: Post, "Climatic Variability."

49. Global: Lamb, *Climate*, pp. 15, 17, 25, 50–51, 64–65, 86, 186, 202–3, 228. Central Mexico: Lauer, "Medio ambiente." North America: Gunn and Adams, "Climatic Change." Mesoamerica: Messenger, "Ancient Winds."

50. Messenger, "Ancient Winds."

51. Lamb, *Climate History*, pp. 235–38, 314–16. Lamb's findings were recently confirmed by Kingston, *Weather of the 1780s*. The synoptic weather charts in this book are the oldest based on quantitative instrumental data in the history of meteorology. They give the distribution of air pressure above Europe day by day for 1781–86, and in many cases the position of the warm and cold fronts is indicated too. It is obvious that the temperature must have been influenced by an increase in volcanic activity, which continually blew large quantities of dust into the upper regions of the atmosphere.

52. Alzate, in Lombardo, *Antología*, pp. 259–60.

53. AGI, Indiferente General, Leg. 108.

54. Don Felipe in BNMa, Ms. 13244. Other information can be found in Juan Francisco Sahagún de Arevalo, *Gaceta de México, 1728-1742* (several vols., Mexico City, 1949–50); José Manuel de Castro Santa-Anna, "Diario de sucesos notables escrito por . . . ," in *Documentos para la historia de México* (Mexico City, 1854), esp. vols. 4, pp. 89, 130–31, 5, pp 29, 31–32, 60, and 6; Moreno, *Joaquín Velázquez de León*, p. 273. Besides these, see *Gazeta de México*, edited by Don Manuel Antonio Valdés and published by Don Felipe Zuñiga y Ontiveros (Mexico City, 1784–1810), see vols. 2, n. 45 p. 448; 3, n. 35 p. 342; 4, n. 74 p. 714; and AGNM, Correspondencia de Virreyes, Vol. 12 2a parte, Exp. 410; AGNM, Correspondencia de Virreyes, Vol. 41, 1a serie, Exp. 1075; AGNM,

	Mexico	Amsterdam	France	Barcelona	Castille
	A	B	C	D	E
period	maize	wheat	grape-picking	wheat	wheat
1721–30	91	90	114	96	81
1731–40	104	80	95	103	109
1741–50	125	120	100	107	115
1751–60	94	102	98	118	129
1761–70	81	120	101	151	165
1771–80	105	134	99	165	185
1781–90	178	140	89	190	224
1791–99	132	178	83	272	267
(cont.)	D	-	-	-	0.97
	C	-	-	-0.78	-0.83
	B	-	-0.74	0.95	0.94
	A	0.55	-0.64	0.50	0.59

These are indices: 1721–1745 = 100
[Correlations R^2 x 100 > 50% are underlined.]
Sources: A and B: Slicher van Bath, "Feudalismo," Tabla 1; C: LeRoy Ladurie and Baulant, "Grape Harvests," pp. 841–43; D and E: Vilar, *Catalogne*.

Correspondencia de Virreyes, Vol. 78, Exp. 2229; AGNM, Correspondencia de Virreyes, Vol. 141 1a serie, Exp. 253; ANM, Correspondencia de Virreyes, Vol. 199, Exp. 831.

55. Informative are Canby, "The Year the Weather Went Wild" and "El Niño's Ill Wind."

56. In fact, it is interesting to note that the droughts of 1808–10 in Anáhuac were complemented by excessive rainfall in Europe, precisely according to modern El Niño theory. A sad witness of this phenomenon were the dead in the tiny Dutch town of Zaltbommel who died in the enormous floods of 1809, caused by heavy rainfall in the Swiss and German hinterlands of the River Rhine; see the pictures and drawings in its city museum.

57. See the publication by H. R. Shaw and J. C. Moore, staff officers of the United States Geological Survey, Menlo Park, California, in *EOS*, 8 November 1988. The two authors make a connection between the endogenous play of forces of the earth, driven by natural radioactive processes of decay, resulting in the volcanic activity referred to here, and the exogenous forces outside the earth where the sun operates as a motor and which drive on or hold back *El Niño*.

Chapter 3

1. Behrens, *Ancien Régime*, pp. 87–88; for comparison, see the work of Sahagún on the "good lord" and on the "good father," *Florentine Codex*, Book 6, Chapter 15, p. 79. See also Hoekstra, *Two Worlds Merging*, pp. 40–47.

2. Humboldt, *Ensayo político*, pp. 39–41, 47–48, 69–70.

3. De Swaan, *Zorg en de staat*, translation of *In Care of the State*.

4. Wood, "*Fundo Legal*," p. 117.

5. De Swaan, *Zorg en de staat*, p. 35.

6. Sen, *Poverty*, p. 45.

7. For a survey of the policy of the state during this period in Europe and the United States, including the theoretical background, see also De Swaan, *Zorg en de staat/ In Care of the State*.

8. A sign of the operation of a system of charity in New Spain cannot be detected from the collection of taxes, which was tightened up with the arrival of the subdelegados, resulting in higher state revenues. In an earlier publication I called this the "bureaucratic component" of the Real Caja figures; see Ouweneel and Bijleveld, "Economic Cycle in Bourbon Central Mexico," pp. 494–96, and, 500–04. In the light of this, there is no point in discussing a mass of statistics in order to compare the situation in the 1780s and 1790s with earlier periods. However, the bureaucratic component lies not only in the improved collection of state taxes. No matter how up to date the state hoped to be, it was still tied to the informal *pacto de reciprocidad* of the moral economy of provision. This means that the food market and the grain prices, in particular, were subject to stringent governmental control. With the assistance of decrees and the enforcement of an active retail policy through the corn exchanges, it was possible to keep excessively steep price increases at bay as well as to prevent the prices from falling too dramatically. Both grain and flour prices reflected the normative economics of trade on the exchanges in Mexico City, not the positive economics. And this was not the case in the city, and less so in the entire region, for it is debatable whether these data can be said to apply to the whole of Anáhuac in view of their urban character.

9. Thompson, "Moral Economy," pp. 82–136.

10. Quote in Hilton, "Medieval Market Towns," p. 22.

11. Le Goff, *Woekeraar*, pp. 35, 43, 45–48, 50–51; also, Burke, *Popular Culture*; Tribe, *Land*; Hoffman, *Church and Society*; Muchembled, *Culture populaire*; Brading, "Tridentine Catholicism," p. 5. Le Goff is right in pointing out that the abhorrence of this "theft of time" was incorporated in the collective unconscious of the Christians.

12. I follow Burke, *Popular Culture*; Flynn, *Sacred Charity*; and, Hoffman, *Church and Community* in labeling this orthodox Catholicism simply as the Counter-Reformation in the cultural-philosophical sense of the term. The ordinances of the Council of Trent took two centuries to take root in Europe. The situation in Latin America will have been the same. See also Brading, *First America*.

13. Van Oss, "Printed Culture," p. 107; Brading, "Tridentine Catholicism"; Mecham, *Church and State*; Burke, *Popular Culture*, pp. 213, 232, and 243.

14. AGNM, Civil, Vol. 1646, Exp. 16.

15. Córdova's text can be found in AGNM, Pósito y Alhóndiga, Leg. 2, Exp. 91.

16. See also AGI, Audiencia México, Vol. 1421; Van Young, "Urban Market," p. 602.

17. The meaning of the word *labrador* was comparable with English *husband*; see Tribe, *Land*.

18. AGNM, Alhóndigas, Vol. 15, Exp. 6; AGNM, Civil, Vol. 1435, Exp. 14; Swan, "Climate," pp. 259–60 note 6.

19. Tribe, *Land*; Thompson, "Moral Economy," pp. 90–99.

20. AGNM, Civil, Vol. 1418, Exp. 7.

21. *Gazeta de México*, 2:19 (1786), p. 211.

22. AGNM, Civil, Vol. 1646, Exps. 7 and 18.

23. *Gazeta de México*, Vol. 2:8 (1786), p. 101, 2:10 (1786), pp. 124–25, and 2:4 (1786), p. 52. For a European comparison, see Abel, *Massenarmut*.

24. In fact, this was the reason for publishing Ouweneel and Bijleveld, "Economic Cycle." See also Florescano, *Precios del maíz*; Suárez Argüello, *Política cerealera*; García Acosta, "Oscilación de los precios"; and Florescano and Gil, *Descripciones económicas regionales*, pp. 158–81.

25. AGNM, Intendentes, Vol. 73, Exp. 4; AGNM, Alhóndigas, Vol. 15, Exp. 6; also Hamnett, *Roots of Insurgency*, pp. 103–4; Tutino, "Creole Mexico," p. 125, Table 3.4.

26. Slicher van Bath, "Yield Ratios."

27. The figures given are averages. Documentation in AGNM, Tierras, Vols. 1891, Exp. 1; AGNM, Tierras, Vol. 1429, Exp. 1; AGNM, Tierras, Vol. 1931, Exp. 1; AGNM, Colegios, Vols. 12, 30, 31, 33; AGET, 1761, Leg. 2, Exp. 6; Ewald, "San Francisco Xavier," pp. 52 and 57, and *Estudios*, pp. 54–68, Tablas 18 and 21; Rodríguez, *Comunidades*, p. 71; Trautmann, *Transformaciones*, pp. 182–83; Ouweneel, "Eighteenth-Century Tlaxcalan Agriculture"; Florescano and Gil, *Descripciones económicas regionales*, pp. 162–80; Gibson, *Aztecs under Spanish Rule*, p. 329; Morin, *Michoacán*, pp. 238–40; Brading, *Haciendas and Ranchos*, pp. 73, 79–84, 89; Maya Ambia, "Tres ensayos," pp. 132–33; Romero and Villamar, "Acolman," p. 160; Humboldt, *Ensayo político*, p. 257; Ortíz de la Tabla, *Comercio exterior*, pp. 99–115.

28. See Ouweneel, "Schedules."

29. AGNM, Civil, Vol. 1646, Exp. 12.

30. Ouweneel, "Schedules," pp. 76–78, and, "Claudio Pesero"; AGNM, Tributos, Vols. 3, 17, 19; AGNM, Tierras, Vols. 1429, exp. 1; AGNM, Tierras, Vol. 1931, Exp. 1; AGNM, Tierras, Vol. 1891, Exp. 1; AGNM, Tierras, Vol. 2545, Exp. 1; Ewald, "San Francisco Xavier," p. 57; Leal and Huacuja, *Economía*, p. 47.

31. AGI, Audiencia México, Leg. 2096, fs. 11v, 33v–34r; Sarrablo Aguareles, *Conde de Fuenclara*, pp. 583-584; Van Young, "Rural Life," pp. 146, 602, 632–33; Florescano, *Precios del maíz*, p. 86; Gibson, *Aztecs Under Spanish Rule*, pp. 324–27; Morin, *Michoacán*; Martin, "Haciendas," p. 413. For Spain see, for example, Anes, *Economía*. Liehr, *Stadtrat*, pp. 118–20; Suárez Argüello, *Política cerealera*.

32. AGI, Audiencia México, Leg. 781; AGNM, Colegios, Vols. 14, 23, 24, 31, 33; Florescano, *Precios del maíz*; Liehr, *Stadtrat*, pp. 124–26.

33. AGI, Indiferente General, Leg. 108; AGNM, Civil, Vol. 1435, Exp. 14; AGNM, Tierras, Vol. 2545, Exp. 1; Florescano, *Precios del maíz*, pp. 69-70, 96 n.9; Semo and Pedrero, "Vida," pp. 280–81; Gibson, *Aztecs under Spanish Rule*, pp. 308, 328–29, 364–65; Hassig, *Trade*, pp. 64, 193–94.

34. Thomson, *Puebla de los Angeles*, pp. 114–30.

35. AGNM, Alhóndigas, 1761-1810, 7; AGNM, Consulados, Vol. 200; AGNM, Tributos, Vol. 2, Exp. 8; AHNE, Consejos, Leg. 20.723, Exp. 6; Florescano, *Precios del maíz*, p. 95 note 6; Gibson, *Aztecs Under Spanish Rule*, p. 311; Hassig, *Trade*, p. 20; Tutino, "Creole Mexico," pp. 301–2 note 113; Cook and Borah, *Essays*, 3, pp. 141–67.

36. Florescano, *Precios del maíz*, pp. 59–60, 89–91, and p. 231, Apéndice III.

37. Florescano, *Precios del maíz*; Van Young, "Urban Market," pp. 627–728; Rabell Romero, "San Luis de la Paz," p. 314.

38. AGNM, Correspondencia Virreyes, Vol. 138, 1a parte; AGI, Audiencia México, Leg. 2096; Tutino, "Creole Mexico," pp. 129–32; Van Young, "Rural Life," p. 146 Fig. 5-2, and, "Urban Market," pp. 632–33; Morin, *Michoacán*, Graf. IV.2; Gibson, *Aztecs under Spanish Rule*, pp. 324–27. Brading, in his *Haciendas and Ranchos*, p. 35, Table 5; p. 100, Table 26; p. 342 gives an example of hoarding policy for the haciendas in the Bajío of Michoacán. During the period 1811–18 the hacienda in this example sold annually between 50 and 80 percent of the maize that it had in store on the neighboring market

of the town Silao. This yields a correlation between the sales of this hacienda and the maize price in Silao of $R = 0.737$. Similar calculations can be made for the statistics of other haciendas in the area published by Brading: the Juchitán and Los Panales haciendas, for instance, followed the maize prices of neighboring Dolores; a correlation of $R = 0.792$. Similar examples can be found all over agrarian Mexico, although the calculation of the coefficient is difficult if an *encomendero* was involved in the transaction, as in Anáhuac, because his intervention affected the price.

It is also worth considering the Jesuits in view of the character of their business activities. The traditional literature assumes that the Jesuit order possessed an unparalleled wealth, conferring an enormous economic power on the order. However, in addition to the gifts of private individuals, the order was primarily dependent for its income on the revenue from the agricultural companies. They did not dare to risk other investments beside agricultural ones, because their yield was too low. It is striking that the majority of the numerous houses given to the order by people in their wills were rapidly sold. The ownership of real estate did not bring in much of an income because of the low rents and the high maintenance costs due to the risks of earthquakes and floods. The documentation that I consulted for the present investigation contained very few traces of hoarding policies by small hacendados from the second stratum of the elite; the very category that formed the majority of the hacendados in numerical terms. Neither these members of the elite nor the Jesuits had sufficient capital to become involved intensively in wholesale activities. This might explain the fact that the Jesuits hardly engaged in hoarding policies and that their maize was offered on the market remarkably early. The managers of their companies were probably instructed to implement a policy of hoarding if the opportunity was forthcoming, because when one of them managed to do so in 1735, he was congratulated on all sides. A more suitable price policy consisted of profiting from the price difference between the local markets and the alhóndigas.

39. Van der Meer, "Suikerrietcultures," pp. 41, 50–51; Riley, *Hacendados jesuitas*, pp. 101–3.

40. AGNM, Civil, Vol. 1827, Exp. 9; Florescano, *Precios del maíz*, pp. 56–60, 83–185.

41. AGNM, Alhóndigas, Vol. 15, Exp. 6; Liehr, *Stadtrat*, pp. 126–28.

42. On the wheat market, see Garner, *Economic Growth*, pp. 97–107.

43. Thomson, *Puebla de los Angeles*, pp. 135–40. The haciendas in the valley of Mexico produced 60 percent of the wheat for the capital. The wheat for Puebla de los Angeles was produced by haciendas in the provinces of Atlixco, Huejotzingo, Tepeaca, Tecali, and Tlaxcala. The mills in Mexico City also milled wheat from the Bajío de Michoacán when the wheat prices were high, which was some twenty reales per carga more expensive than wheat from Anáhuac because of the higher transport costs. There were times when this wheat from the Bajío could account for around 30 percent of the flour sold in the city. When prices were low the *molineros* confined themselves to wheat from the neighboring haciendas, and the Bajío only provided a maximum of 15 percent of the flour sold in the city at such times. The imports from the Bajío took place particularly in the late eighteenth century, when it was no longer possible to import wheat from the southern falda province of Cuernavaca because the haciendas there had switched back to sugar with the recovery of the price of sugar. The Bajío haciendas also produced for the *tierra adentro*, the mining provinces in the west and northwest of the viceroyalty. See: Hamnett, *Roots of Insurgency*, p. 33; Super, "Bread," pp. 181—82; García Acosta, "Manufactura," pp. 159–61; Artís Espríu, "Economía administrada," pp. 28–35 cuadro 1; Swan, "Climate," pp. 185–88 Table 6; Suárez Argüello, *Política cerealera*, pp.

71–82; Martin, *Rural Society*, pp. 99–105; Tutino, "Creole Mexico," p. 131. Morin, in his *Michoacán*, p. 142, claims that 75 percent of the flour in Mexico City must have come from Bajío. This is not confirmed by any of the sources I have seen. At any rate, the transport costs must have been too high for such an enormous import. It was only feasible if prices in Mexico City were extremely high, which was hardly the case.

Relatively little wheat came from the valley of Toluca because it was of the same poor quality as Tolucan maize and was only used for the cheapest kinds of bread (though often mixed with good quality Bajío flour). However, there are some signs of wheat expansion in the northern parts of the province of Ixtlahuaca, but this would have been meager. There was no wheat cultivation in most of the provinces on the flanks of the highlands and in the tierra caliente, because it was too damp there. The towns and villages in the tierra caliente thus had to depend on imports from the highlands. However, the volume of this trade was small because of the small number of Spaniards and castas in the area; there was thus insufficient demand to be able to offer a solution to the overproduction of wheat in the highlands, and certainly not when this market was taken over by producers from Michoacán and Guadalajara. It is evident that in these circumstances the hacendados did not want to extend the area of land used for wheat cultivation.

44. AGNM, Tierras, Vol. 1764, Exp. 1; AGNM, Tierras, Vol. 2131, Exps. 2 and 3; AGNM, Tierras, Vol. 2143, Exps. 1 and 2; AGNM, Tierras, Vol. 2144, Exp. 1; García Acosta, "Manufactura," pp. 42, 47–48, 52–56, 224–25, and, "Oscilación," Cuadro 1; Liehr, *Stadtrat*, p. 12; Super, "Bread," pp. 166–68, and, "Pan," p. 259.

45. Slicher van Bath, *Samenleving*, pp. 391, 654.

46. Slicher van Bath, *Agrarische geschiedenis*, pp. 340–42; Butlin, *Transformation*, pp. 32–33; Vassberg, *Tierra y sociedad*, pp. 16–18, 25–32.

47. Slicher van Bath, *Agrarische geschiedenis*, p. 44; Vassberg, *Tierra y sociedad*, pp. 51–54, 69–76; Wunder, *Bäuerliche Gemeinde*, pp. 58–61. For Spain see Casado, *Señores*; also the essays in García de Cortázar, *et al.*, *Organización del espacio*; García de Cortázar, *Sociedad rural*; Herrera García, *Aljarafe sevillano*, pp. 356–74, containing a description of *cargos oficiales* in Spanish villages; Ortega, *Lucha por la tierra*; Sánchez Salazar, "Repartos"; Pulido Bueno, *Tierra de Huelva*.

48. Borah, *Justice by Insurance*, p. 38.

49. A typical example of this is Carmagnani's, *Regreso de los dioses*, in which chapters 1 and 2 are based on archaeological and anthropological assumptions. Pre-Hispanic and contemporary characteristics of the Oaxacan Indian community abound. Chapters 3 and 4 are designed to bridge the "colonial" gap between the two.

50. See my "*Altepeme* and *Pueblos de Indios*," as well as an essay written with Rik Hoekstra, "Tierras concejiles."

51. Derrida, *Margins of Philosophy*.

52. See the glossary on pp. 291 and 293 of Lockhart, *Nahuas and Spaniards*. See also his essay "Postconquest Nahua Society," in that book, esp. pp. 9–10.

53. Van Young, "Mexican Rural History," pp. 27–28.

54. Dyer, "Past," pp. 38–42.

55. Kay, *Sistema señorial*, pp. 25–57; see also his essay "Development."

56. Dyer, "Past," p. 39; but for comments, see Gregson, "Multiple Estate Model."

57. McIntosh, *Autonomy and Community*.

58. Harvey, "Aspects."

59. This is shortly discussed in Ouweneel and Hoekstra, "Tierras concejiles"; and Hoekstra, *Two Worlds Merging*, see also Chapter 7. Hoyt and Chodorow, *Europe in the*

Middle Ages, pp. 212–17; McKitterick, *Frankish Kingdoms*; Reynolds, *Kingdoms*; and Duby, *Trois ordres*.

60. The theoretical concepts of Personenverband and Territorialverband, to repeat, were developed to interpret medieval social and political relationships. The concepts, of course, form a dichotomy designed for analytical reasons and consequently oversimplify historical reality. In fact, in Europe they coexisted under the dominance of Personenverband until the thirteenth century and under the dominance of Territorialverband since the sixteenth century. The dichotomy was elaborated by Mitteis, *Staat des hohen Mittelalters*. Also see Southern, *Making of the Middle Ages*, pp. 73–114. Wunder, *Bäuerliche Gemeinde*, speaks of "governing with the peasants" and "governing over the peasants," which is the same dichotomy, but seen from the viewpoint of the ruler or the state.

61. The *relaciones geográficas*: Acuña, *Relaciones geográficas*, 9 vols. The image of Aztec society is a personal interpretation of the data published by: Aguirre Beltrán, *Congregación*; Aguirre Beltrán, *Señorío de Cuautochco*; Cline, *Colonial Culhuacan*; Dehouve, *Quand les banquiers*; Dyckerhof, "Colonial Indian Corporate Landholding"; García Martínez, *Pueblos de la Sierra*, and "Jurisdicción y propiedad"; Gibson, *Tlaxcala*, and, *Aztecs under Spanish Rule*, above all, pp. 34 and 152; Haskett, *Indigenous Rulers*; Hassig, *Trade*; Hoekstra, *Two Worlds Merging*; Kirchhoff, "Land Tenure"; Lewis, "In Mexico City's Shadow"; Lockhart, *Nahuas and Spaniards*; Munch, *Cacicazgo*; Olivera, *Pillis y macehuales*; Prem, *Milpa y hacienda*; Schroeder, *Chimalpahin*; Taylor, "Conflict"; Williams, "Lands"; and the essays in Carrasco and Broda, eds., *Estratificación social*, and *Economía política e ideología*.

Many different interpretations of the character of the calpolli have been advanced. It has been described as a clan, a ward, a neighbourhood, or a parish. The calpolli should probably be viewed as an expression of horizontal social relations. After all, we are considering an agrarian society, in which personal relations are characterized by the horizontal variant between persons of the same status and the vertical variant of hierarchical subordination. The altepetl was the expression of a pyramid of hierarchically structured lords. Although everyone belonged to a calpolli, most calpolli consisted of macehualtin (macehualtin in the sense of "commoners"); the nobles were united in a so-called tecpancalli. The calpolli had probably been a clanlike organization in the past based on ties of kinship, but in the late Aztec period membership of the organization was open to all, irrespective of ethnic origin or linguistic affinity. By this time the calpolli had become nothing more than an instrument within the native organization for the receipt of tribute, the management of services to the lord, and the performance of a military task. For these reasons the calpolli consisted of a specific number of smaller households; usually five, twenty, or one hundred. The calpolli in the Aztec capital Tenochtitlán were also obliged to perform temple duties.

Surveying literature and sources, I hardly find differences between a calpolli and a tlaxilacalli in this respect. According to Gibson, both were group units in which a number of Indian families were associated; according to Hoekstra, they were tribute units belonging to a noble's house, cultivating land in use right. Their land had some known spatial boundaries, mostly dependent upon the number of households. According to Schroeder the term tlaxilacalli was used by the seventeenth-century Nahua chronicler Chimalpahin only in reference to the post-conquest period, and apparently as a term synonymous with *calpolli* in connection with the preconquest period. According to Williams, some differences might be that settlement sizes within a tlaxilacalli were *not* dictated by specific numbers of households as they were in the calpolli, and that the tlaxilacalli obviously required no elaborate public architecture like pyramids. She suggests that "a prevalence of tlaxilacalli organization might explain the lack of regularly spaced civic-ceremonial architecture in the archaeological record of the Texcocan countryside." Rights of usufruct, of course, does not indicate *ownership* of land in the Roman sense.

62. García Martínez, *Pueblos de la sierra*, p. 77. On the bureaucratization of local households, see Rebel, *Peasant Classes*, for the Habsburg equivalent in Eastern Central Europe.

63. Haskett, "Indian Community Land," p. 134.

64. Bartlett, *Making of Europe*, pp. 197, 204–19. I have found an analogy in the Carolingian empire. Reading Davies's study on the village community in early medieval Brittany one finds striking similarities between the altepetl and the *plou* (or *plebs*, in Latin), and the tlahtoani, or lord, and the *machtiern*. See Davies, *Small Worlds*; Reynolds, *Kingdoms*, pp. 138–48; Mckitterick, *Frankish Kingdoms*, pp. 77–105.

65. Among others, AGNM, Civil, Vol. 1690, Exps. 1, 2, and 3.

66. García Martínez, *Pueblos de la sierra*, p. 73; Haskett, "Indian Town Government"; Harvey, "Aspects."

67. It is important to repeat that there is considerable controversy over the character of the calpolli. The calpolli or tlaxilacalli are not seen by all researchers as nothing more than an instrument of tribute collection. Some authors believe the word referred to a certain local shrine, others maintain that the traditional translation of *barrio*, or district, must be the proper one. The traditional view is expressed most clearly by Lockhart in stating that the calpolli was a community, barrio, in its own right and with its own territorial dimensions. Nevertheless, people belonging to calpollis can be identified by it. It is well known that in contemporary Nahua townships a separate set of names, toponyms, is used to refer simultaneously to a person and the calpolli he or she belongs to. Such Nahua names are kept on accurate lists of all those who were expected to perform obligatory communal work or of those who owe money or tributes to their community. Eighteenth-century hacienda records, maintained for payment of migrant workers from the nearby pueblos, reveal the existence of similar lists. To me, collective landownership was not the unifying element: rather, tribute was, and, therefore, the Personenverband with the lords. The households forming part of a calpolli had use rights to land that belonged to the nobles in exchange for tribute paid to them. See Lockhart, "Capital and Province"; Dyckerhof, "Colonial Indian Corporate Landholding"; Hoekstra, "Different Way of Thinking"; also García Martínez, *Pueblos de la sierra*; Reyes García, *Cuauhtinchan*; Cline *Colonial Culhuacán*, p. 54; Olivera, *Pillis*; Prem, *Milpa*; Schryer, *Ethnicity*, pp. 62–66; Chamoux, *Nahuas de Huauchinango*, pp. 79–94.

68. Gruzinski, "Mère dévorante," esp. pp. 22–26.

69. Hoekstra, *Two Worlds Merging*. See also the documentation in Aguirre Beltrán, *Congregación*; Gibson, *Aztecs Under Spanish Rule*, pp. 220–28.

70. Hoekstra, *Two Worlds Merging*.

71. Hoekstra, "Different Way of Thinking"; García Martínez, *Pueblos de la sierra*, and "Jurisdicción."

72. Dyckerhoff, "Colonial Indian Corporate Landholding"; Hoekstra, "Different Way of Thinking" and *Two Worlds Merging*; Williams, "Lands," p. 199 Table 8.4; Menegus, "Parcela," quote on p. 128; Katz, "Rural Uprisings," p. 79.

73. García Martínez, "*Pueblos de Indios*"; Hoekstra, "Different Way of Thinking"; Torales Pacheco, "Note on the *Composiciones de Tierra*"; Osborn, "Indian Land Retention"; Wood, "Corporate Adjustments," pp. 110–53.

74. BNM-P 13/420; BNM-P 13/423; BNM-P 14/451; BNM-P 25/619; BNM-P 25/635;

BNM-P 25/641; BNM-P 31/815; BNM-P 38/1047; BNM-P 37/1024; AGNM, Tierras, Vol. 2700, Exp. 5; AGNM, Tierras, Vol. 2703, Exp. 15; AGNM, Tierras, Vol. 2085, Exp. 9; AGNM, Tierras, Vol. 1873, Exp. 2. See also Osborn, "Indian Land Retention," for data of the Metztitlán area. On the Puebla data, see Vigil B., *Catálogo*.

75. AGI, Audiencia México, Legs. 664 and 665; and Indiferente General, Leg. 1661.

76. Wood, "Corporate Adjustments," pp. 110–53.

77. See, Gruzinski, *Colonización*, pp 104–48. Also, Lockhart, "Views"; Wood, "Corporate Adjustments," pp. 300–62; Haskett, "Indian Community Lands"; Borah, "Yet Another Look."

78. Wood, "Lands *Por Razón de Pueblo*," pp. 119–25.

79. AGNM, Tierras, Vol. 552, Exp. 2; AGNM, Tierras, Vol. 565, part 1, Exp. 2; AGNM, Tierras, Vol. 1704, Exp. 1; AGNM, Tierras, Vol. 1535, Exp. 1; AGNM, Tierras, Vol. 2091, Exp. 2; AGNM, Tierras, Vol. 1605, Exp. 9; E. Barrett, "Indian Community Lands," p. 98; Taylor, *Drinking*, pp. 24–25; Trautmann, *Transformaciones*, pp. 107–11; Gibson, *Aztecs under Spanish Rule*, pp. 267–70; Wood, "Lands *Por Razón de Pueblo*," p. 119; Dyckerhoff, "Colonial Indian Corporate Landholding," pp. 47–48.

80. For literature and correlations see Ouweneel and Bijleveld, "Economic Cycle," discussion on pp. 504–8, Figures 6 and 7, n.35, and source on p. 491, n.16.

81. AGNM, Tierras, Vol. 1599, Exp. 2; AGNM, Tierras, Vol. 1535, Exp. 1; AGNM, Tierras, Vol. 1600, Exp. 13; AGNM, Tierras, Vol. 1834, Exp. 2; AGNM, Tierras, Vol. 1508, Exp. 6; AGNM, Tierras, Vol. 354, Exp. 4; AGNM, Tierras, Vol. 1598, Exp. 1; AGNM, Tierras, Vol. 1581, Exp. 2; AGNM, Tierras, Vol. 1542, Exp. 2; AGNM, Tierras, Vol. 1513, Exp. 9; AGNM, Tierras, Vol. 1637, Exp. 6; AGNM, Tierras, Vol. 1465, Exp. 4; AGNM, Tierras, Vol. 1510, Exp. 4; AGNM, Tierras, Vol. 1612, Exp. 5; AGNM, Tierras, Vol. 1602, Exp. 8; AGNM, Tierras, Vol. 1097, Exp. 3; AGNM, Tierras, Vol. 1666, Exps. 3, 8, 9, and 14; AGNM, Tierras, Vol. 1549, Exp. 5; AGNM, Tierras, Vol. 1518, Exp. 5; AGNM, Tierras, Vol. 2683, Exp. 8; AGNM, Tierras, Vol. 1475, Exp. 4; AGNM, Tierras, Vol. 1680, Exp. 4; AGNM, Tierras, Vol. 1548, Exp. 1; AGNM, Tierras, Vol. 1600, Exp. 6; AGNM, Tierras, Vol. 1482, Exp. 6; AGNM, Tierras, Vol. 1517, Exp. 2; AGNM, Tierras, Vol. 1531, Exp. 8.

82. AGNM, Tierras, Vol. 387, Exp. 6; AGNM, Tierras, Vol. 1457, Exp. 6; AGNM, Tierras, Vol. 487, Exp. 1; AGNM, Tierras, Vol. 552, Exp. 4; AGNM, Tierras, Vol. 527, Exp. 9; AGNM, Tierras, Vol. 1443, Exp. 2; AGNM, Tierras, Vol. 958, Exp. 2; AGNM, Tierras, Vol. 1056, Exp. 7; AGNM, Tierras, Vol. 1366, Exp. 3; AGNM, Tierras, Vol. 2732, Exp. 5; AGNM, Tierras, Vol. 180, Exp. 5; AGNM, Tierras, Vol. 2694, Exp. 8; AGNM, Tierras, Vol. 2725, Exp. 24; AGNM, Tierras, Vol. 1296, Exp. 6; AGNM, Tierras, Vol. 1320, Exp. 7; AGNM, Tierras, Vol. 1354, Exp. 4; AGNM, Tierras, Vol. 1384, Exp. 4; AGNM, Tierras, Vol. 1404, Exp. 12; AGNM, Tierras, Vol. 1411, Exp. 6; AGNM, Tierras, Vol. 2709, Exps. 2 and 3; AGNM, Tierras, Vol. 1175, Exp. 3; AGNM, Tierras, Vol. 1216, Exp. 3; AGNM, Tierras, Vol. 2710, Exp. 2; AGNM, Tierras, Vol. 1263, Exp. 1; AGNM, Tierras, Vol. 1276, Exp. 10; AGNM, Tierras, Vol. 2772, Exp. 13.

83. AGNM, Tierras, Vol. 2200, Exp. 1; AGNM, Tierras, Vol. 1839, Exp. 3; AGNM, Tierras, Vol. 1854, Exp. 8; AGNM, Tierras, Vol. 2205, Exp. 1; AGNM, Tierras, Vol. 1512, Exp. 5; AGNM, Tierras, Vol. 1463, Exp. 1; AGNM, Tierras, Vol. 2207, Exp. 1; AGNM, Tierras, Vol. 1017, Exp. 6; AGNM, Tierras, Vol. 1507, Exp. 2; AGNM, Tierras, Vol. 1604, Exp. 2; AGNM, Tierras, Vol. 2209, Exp. 9; AGNM, Tierras, Vol. 1657, Exp. 2; AGNM, Tierras, Vol. 1641, Exp. 5; AGNM, Tierras, Vol. 2206, Exp. 1; AGNM, Tierras, Vol. 1240, Exp. 15; AGNM, Tierras, Vol. 2207, Exp. 2; AGNM, Tierras, Vol. 2197, Exp. 4; AGNM, Tierras, Vol. 1700, Exp. 5; AGNM, Tierras, Vol. 1510, Exp. 1; AGNM, Tierras, Vol. 309, Exp. 2; AGNM, Tierras, Vol. 1140, Exp. 3; AGNM, Tierras, Vol. 391, Exp. 1; AGNM,

Tierras, Vol. 621, Exp. 6; AGNM, Tierras, Vol. 1139, Exp. 7; AGNM, Tierras, Vol. 710, Exp. 3; AGNM, Tierras, Vol. 978, Exp. 1; AGNM, Tierras, Vol. 739, Exp. 3; AGNM, Tierras, Vol. 2161, Exp. 1; AGNM, Tierras, Vol. 965, Exp. 1; AGNM, Tierras, Vol. 799; AGNM, Tierras, Vol. 391, Exp. 1; AGNM, Tierras, Vol. 621, Exp. 6; AGNM, Tierras, Vol. 1139, Exp. 7; AGNM, Tierras, Vol. 710, Exp. 3; AGNM, Tierras, Vol. 978e1; AGNM, Tierras, Vol. 739, Exp. 3; AGNM, Tierras, Vol. 2161, Exp. 1; AGNM, Tierras, Vol. 965, Exp. 1; AGNM, Tierras, Vol. 799, Exp. 1; AGNM, Tierras, Vol. 838, Exps. 7 (two cases) and 8; AGNM, Tierras, Vol. 1123, Exp. 1; AGNM, Tierras, Vol. 1015, Exp. 1; AGNM, Tierras, Vol. 1408, Exp. 4; AGNM, Tierras, Vol. 1097, Exp. 1; AGNM, Tierras, Vol. 2730, Exp. 7; AGNM, Tierras, Vol. 2161, Exp. 5; AGNM, Tierras, Vol. 1320, Exp. 9; AGNM, Tierras, Vol. 1141, Exp. 3; AGNM, Tierras, Vol. 2676, Exp. 8; AGNM, Tierras, Vol. 1154, Exp. 4; AGNM, Tierras, Vol. 1179, Exp. 2; AGNM, Tierras, Vol. 1209, Exp. 13; AGNM, Tierras, Vol. 1222, Exp. 9; AGNM, Tierras, Vol. 2680, Exp. 4; AGNM, Tierras, Vol. 1284, Exp. 1; AGNM, Tierras, Vol. 1313, Exp. 16; AGNM, Tierras, Vol. 1335, Exp. 9; AGNM, Tierras, Vol. 1343, Exp. 10; AGNM, Tierras, Vol. 1349, Exps. 4 and 5; AGNM, Tierras, Vol. 1351, Exp. 7; AGNM, Tierras, Vol. 1363, Exp. 5; AGNM, Tierras, Vol. 1364, Exp. 12; AGNM, Tierras, Vol. 1369, Exp. 3; AGNM, Tierras, Vol. 1403, Exp. 6; AGNM, Tierras, Vol. 1403, Exp. 5; AGNM, Tierras, Vol. 1373, Exp. 9 (two cases).

84. AGNM, Tierras, Vol. 1430, Exp. 4; AGNM, Tierras, Vol. 1676, Exp. 3; AGNM, Tierras, Vol. 1502, Exp. 4; AGNM, Tierras, Vol. 1643, Exp. 1; AGNM, Tierras, Vol. 2387, Exp. 9; AGNM, Tierras, Vol. 1671, Exp. 12; AGNM, Tierras, Vol. 1687, Exp. 1; AGNM, Tierras, Vol. 1668, Exp. 5; AGNM, Tierras, Vol. 1512, Exp. 2; AGNM, Tierras, Vol. 1561, Exp. 2; AGNM, Tierras, Vol. 1612, Exp. 6; AGNM, Tierras, Vol. 2590, Exp. 1; AGNM, Tierras, Vol. 1487, Exp. 1; AGNM, Tierras, Vol. 1601, Exp. 2; AGNM, Tierras, Vol. 2255, Exp. 5; AGNM, Tierras, Vol. 1561, Exp. 1; AGNM, Tierras, Vol. 1613, Exp. 1; AGNM, Tierras, Vol. 1615, Exp. 4; AGNM, Tierras, Vol. 1584, Exp. 2; AGNM, Tierras, Vol. 1676, Exp. 1; AGNM, Tierras, Vol. 1561, Exp. 3; AGNM, Tierras, Vol. 2254, Exp. 2; AGNM, Tierras, Vol. 1680, Exp. 2; AGNM, Tierras, Vol. 1627, Exp. 2; AGNM, Tierras, Vol. 1518, Exp. 3; AGNM, Tierras, Vol. 1667, Exp. 6. Two typical "gobernadoryotl-conflicts": AGNM, Tierras, Vol. 1587, Exp. 1; and, AGNM, Tierras, Vol. 1486, Exp. 2. Also see AGNM, Civil, Vol. 241, 1756; Taylor, *Drinking, Homicide and Rebellion*, pp. 138–39. On Metztitlán: Osborn, "Community Study".

85. Hamnett, *Roots of Insurgency*, pp. 96–97; Ladd, *Making of a Strike*; Taylor, *Drinking, Homicide and Rebellion*, pp. 124–25.

86. It is difficult to estimate the number of hectares required to provide a township or town with sufficient maize. The cuartillo required to feed one person a day is the rough equivalent of 7.6 fanegas a year. Assuming the *fanega de sembradura* as the sowing unit of approx. 3.57 has. (though without taking the difference in soil quality into account), and assuming a yield ratio of 1:1, a milpa of 27.146 has. would be required. However, maize had higher yield rations; 100:1 was not exceptional. This can be expressed as:

$$\frac{P \times 27.146}{Y} = MH,$$

in which MH = *milpa* in hectares; P = population; and Y = yield ratio. Thus the total of 33,000 "indio" and casta consumers of maize in Mexico City in 1790, assuming a yield ratio of 100:1, would require:

$$\frac{33,000 \times 27.146}{100} = 8958.2 \text{ has.}$$

A yield of 140:1 means that 2,000 has. less are required; a poorer harvest, with a yield ratio of, say, 80:1, would require an additional 11,000 has. In Metztitlán, with an Indian population of around 31,500 and a yield ratio of 500:1, the surface area of agricultural land required at the time was:

$$\frac{31{,}500 \times 27.146}{500} = 1710 \text{ has.}$$

According to Osborn's statistics, the peasants in Metzitlán still had enough agricultural land in 1803.

87. Borah, *Justice by Insurance*, pp. 136–38.

88. Wood, "Lands *Por Razón de Pueblo*," p. 119.

89. Gibson, *Aztecs under Spanish Rule*. The essays of Gibson and Florescano in *The Cambridge History of Latin America* can also be found in the paperback edition edited by Leslie Bethell, *Colonial Spanish America*: Gibson, "Indian Societies"; and Florescano, "Hacienda in New Spain."

90. Did Wolf himself not state that if it could be proved that the Indian communities had enough land, the theory of the closed corporate communities could be abandoned? However, I could not follow up the question that easily, for the relationship between haciendas, landowning communities, and cacique property in Anáhuac has not been charted. All the same, in order to get an impression of the situation, I carried out an exploration of the holdings of the Archivo General de la Nación in Mexico City in 1984, tracing maps and studying the relevant documentation. I shall use a few of these maps to provide examples from the eighteenth century of the plotting of fundos legales to the advantage of the townships and to the detriment of the haciendas. Although these are certainly not exceptional cases, the picture is far from being complete. I have little information about regional variation or differences in the course of time.

91. Wood, "Lands *Por Razón de Pueblo*," p. 122; AGNM, Ramo Tierras, Vol. 1928, Exp. 2.

92. Dyckerhoff, "Colonial Indian Corporate Landholding," p. 51. And see AGNM, Tierras, Vol. 1644, Exp. 4; AGNM, Tierras, Vol. 2709, Exp. 3; AGNM, Tributos, Vol. 43.

93. AGNM, Tierras, Vol. 1644, Exp. 4; AGNM, Tierras, Vol. 2709, Exp. 3. If 36 families—162 individuals—brought in a normal harvest of 100:1, approx. 44 hectares of agricultural land would be required (twice as many with alternate rotation):

$$\frac{162 \times 27.146}{100} = 43.9 \text{ hectares,}$$

This is equivalent to one cabellería of *pan llevar* quality (good ground, assuming an even quality for the whole area). The fundo legal included more than the double, 101 hectares.

94. The assessor did his very best to include every detail of the village accurately on the map. The map and the description were signed by witnesses and deposited in the archive. The map is also published in Von Wobeser, *Formación*, pp. 136–37, Mapa 10. I used the map to be found in AGNM, Tierras, Vol. 476, Exp. 1.

95. Wood, "Lands *Por Razón de Pueblo*," p. 125; concerning the village of Santiago Tlacotepec, AGNM, Tierras, Vol. 2234, Cuadernos 3 and 4. Similar offers were made in vain in two other cases!

96. AGNM, Vinculos, Vol. 244, Exp. 1; AGI, Audiencia México, Leg. 664.

97. AGNM, Tierras, Vol. 1811, Exp. 1.

98. AGNM, Tierras, Vol. 2911, Exp. 1.

99. AGNM, Tierras, Vol. 1542, Exp. 2; on Tetepango, see Badura, "Biografía," pp. 91–93, 95–99.

100. AGNM, Tierras, Vol. 1471; GRAL, *Valle de Toluca*; García Martínez, *Marquesado*, p. 165.

101. AGNM, Tierras, Vol. 1404, Exp. 9.

102. AGNM, Tierras, Vol. 1675, Exp. 1.

103. AGNM, Tierras, Vol. 624, Part one, Exp. 1; and Part two, Exp. 2.

104. AGET, 1742, Leg. 2, Exp. 37; Ewald, "Versuche"; Osborn, "Community Study," pp. 121–24.

105. Loera, "Calimaya," p. 77; Pérez Rocha, *Tierra y hombre*, pp. 108–9. Also Wasserstrom, *Class and Society*.

106. AHNE, Consejos, Leg. 20.727; Tutino, "Hacienda," pp. 500–501.

Chapter 4

1. AGI, Audiencia México, Leg. 1675.

2. Ibid.

3. Ibid.; Brading, *First America*, p. 476.

4. R. J. Salvucci and L. K. Salvucci, "Crecimiento económico"; Garner, *Economic Growth and Change*, pp. 2, 194–99, 203; Van Young, "Age of Paradox," "Modo de Conclusión," and his essays in *Crisis del orden colonial*; or Brading, "Bourbon Spain." See also, with a negative tone, Brading, *First America*, pp. 475–77 on Mexico, and pp. 470–71 and 485–87 on Peru. The major title on Oaxaca is Hamnett, *Politics and Trade*.

5. Humboldt, *Ensayo político*, p. 68.

6. Haring, *Spanish Empire*, pp. 67-68.

7. Ibid., p. 133.

8. Ibid., p. 68, note 75.

9. Gibson, *Aztecs under Spanish Rule*, pp. 94–95. Gibson repeated this view in his chapter "Indian Societies," p. 415.

10. Ibid., pp. 95.

11. MacLeod, *Spanish Central America*, p. 316, also pp. 317, 326, 344–45; Pastor, *Campesinos y reformas*, pp. 153–57; Larson, *Colonialism*, pp. 119–28. The terminology in the literature is confusing. The term *reparto* was often used in Peru, while *repartimiento* was common in New Spain and Central America. The merchandise traded through the mechanism was referred to as *comercio(s), mercancías, efectos,* or *tratos*; all of these words meant virtually the same.

12. Brading, *Miners and Merchants*, p. 48; Hamnett, *Politics and Trade*, p. 6. See also Hamnett, *Roots of Insurgency*, for an emphasis on the role of the *merchant-investor* and a discussion of the importance of the repartimiento, pp. 26 and 78–79. Chance follows Hamnett and Brading in his book *Conquest of the Sierra*, pp. 102–8 and 146–47.

13. Brading, *Miners and Merchants*, p. 51. Also, see Stein, "Bureaucracy."

14. Pietschmann, "*Alcaldes mayores,*" "*Repartimiento-*Handel," and "Agricultura e industria"; Borah, *Justice by Insurance*, pp. 149–61; Dehouve, "Pueblo de indios" and *Quand les Banquiers*; Farriss, *Maya Society*, pp. 43–45; Wasserstom, *Class and Society*, pp. 35–36, 46–49, 60–64. Also, see MacLachlan and Rodríguez, *Forging*, pp. 111–12.

15. Pietschmann, "*Alcaldes mayores,*" p. 176.

16. MacLachlan and Rodríguez, *Forging*, pp. 111–12; Brading, *First America*, p. 476.

17. Hoekstra, *Two Worlds Merging*, Chapter 4.

18. Slicher van Bath, *Agrarische geschiedenis*, pp. 35–85.

19. Hoekstra, *Two Worlds Merging*, Chapter 4, for examples from the valley of Puebla, 1590. On Tlalmanalco: AGNM, Civil, Vol. 1690, Exps. 1, 2, and 3 (Díez de Palacios case).

20. The documentation of this case is to be found in AGNM, Indios, Vol. 50, Exps. 30, 31, 90, and 91 (1724); AGNM, Tierras, Vol. 2832, Exps. 12 and 13; AGNM, Tierras, Vol. 2774, Exp. 6 and 9; and AGNM, Tierras, Vol. 3207, Exps. 2, 3, and 16.

21. Van Oss, "Catholic Colonialism," pp. 165–66.

22. Hoekstra, *Two Worlds Merging*, Chapter 4.

23. Pietschmann, *Estado y su evolución*, p. 162. The word *Herrschaft* is used in my text *without* reference to Weber. Weber simply borrowed a much-used terminology.

24. See the statements by the Indians in all the repartimiento documentation consulted (references in preceding or following notes).

25. Riley, "Landlords," p. 237.

26. AGI, Audiencia México, Leg. 1939. See Taylor, "Conflict and Balance," pp. 277–81, for a different interpretation of the documents.

27. AGI, Audiencia México, Leg. 1939, cuaderno 7.

28. For this definition, compare Manning, *Village Revolts*, pp. 159–61.

29. The designation "revolution in government" was introduced by Brading, *Miners and Merchants*. See also Bravo Ugarte, ed., *Conde de Revilla Gigedo*, pp. 189–96; Lockhart and Schwartz, *Early Latin America*, pp. 355 and 392; Brading, "Bourbon Spain."

30. Priestley, *José de Gálvez*; Brading, "Bourbon Spain"; L. Salvucci, "Costumbres viejas," pp. 228–29, 256–57; Arnold, "Bureaucracy," pp. 90–91, 122; Lewis, "New Spain"; Mörner, *Andean Past*, pp. 95–96.

31. Most of the material on the "repartimiento de comercios" is to be found in AGI, Indiferente General, Legs. 107 and 108; and AGI, Audiencia de México, Legs. 1675, 1868, 1872. However, I have checked these data against other material.

32. But I have my doubts. The Peruvian data should be reexamined from another, more realistic and less a Black Legend, point of view.

33. AGI, Audiencia México, Leg. 1675; on the rebellion in Actopan, see Ladd, *Making of a Strike*, pp. 29–44.

34. AGNM, Tierras, Vol. 2690, Exp. 3; for Tulancingo, see AGNM, Tributos, Vol. 24, Exp. 8, fs. 145–57.

35. AGI, Audiencia México, Leg. 1939.

36. AGNM, Alhóndigas, Vol. 15, Exp. 4; AGI, Audiencia México, Leg. 1675; also Pietschmann, "Dependencia-Theorie," esp. p. 158.

37. AGNM, Alhóndigas, Vol. 15, Exp. 4.

38. AGI, Audiencia México, Legs. 1739, 1868, 1872, and 1675; Pietschmann, "*Repartimiento*-Handel," p. 245; Florescano and Gil, *Descripciones económicas generales*, pp. 158–84. Also Tutino, "Creole Mexico," p. 167.

39. AGI, Audiencia México, Leg. 1939.

40. Dehouve, "Pueblo de indios"; AGI, Indiferente General, Leg. 108.

41. AGI, Audiencia México, Leg. 1675, Exp. 1.

42. AGI, Audiencia México, Leg. 1939, Cuaderno 8.

43. For the tribute figures, see Ouweneel, "Growth, Stagnation, and Migration"; Urrutia, in Florescano and Gil, *Descripciones económicas generales*, p. 115; Flon, in ibid., p. 117.

44. I found out that Basque immigrants had an unusual interest in the repartimiento trade. This topic will be investigated more thoroughly by Cristina Torales Pacheco of the Universidad Iberoamericana, Mexico City.

45. This is the first of the inaccuracies in Gibson's analysis; as an earlier quotation

shows, he regarded Velarde and De la Torre as Indian subordinates.

46. The documentation on which my argument is based is to be found in AGNM, Civil, Vol. 1690, Exps. 1, 2, and 3.

47. For the *familias de indios*, see AGI, Indiferente General, Leg. 107, fs. 283–86; the number of tributarios in Ouweneel, "Growth, Stagnation, and Migration," Appendix, pp. 571–77. The province of Chalco had 8,626 tributarios in 1745, divided among 6,684 familias de indios. This gives an index of 77.5, taking 1745 = 100. In 1722 the number of tributarios was 7,415, and could thus have been divided among 5,746 familias de indios. The index of the difference is 85.9 (1745 = 100). This index has been used for each village to calculate the number of familias de indios.

48. Tutino, "Creole Mexico," p. 348.

49. AGNM, Tributos, Vol. 22, Exp. 2 and 3; also, for a similar case in Chalco 1749, see AGNM, Tierras, Vol. 2553, Exp. 11.

50. AGNM, Tributos, Vol. 47, Exp. 11, fs. 211–340.

51. Serrera Contreras, *Guadalajara ganadera*, pp. 76, 84, 93–96, 192–93, 200–201, 209, 258, 265–66, 270–71; Tutino, "Creole Mexico," pp. 157–58; Brading, "Population"; Van Young, "Rural Life," pp. 355–79.

52. AGI, Audiencia México, Leg. 1675; AGET, 1767, Leg. 4, Exp. 57; and AGET, 1767, Leg. 3, Exp. 38; for a similar example, see Osborn, "Community Study," p. 83.

53. AGET, 1772, Leg. 1, sueltos.

54. AGET, 1773, Leg. 3, Exp. 70.

55. AGI, Audiencia México, Leg. 1675.

56. Pietschmann, "*Repartimiento*-Handel," pp. 243 (incl. n. 10), 244, 246–47.

57. AGNM, Subdelegados, Vol. 34; AGI, Audiencia México, Leg. 1675, Exp. 1.

58. On colonial salt production, see Ewald, *Mexican Salt Industry*.

59. See AGNM, Tributos, Vol. 2, Exp. 7.

60. AGI, Audiencia México, Leg. 1675.

61. Humboldt, *Ensayo político*, p. 295.

62. AGNM, Civil, Vol. 1608, Exp. 10; and AGNM, Civil, Vol. 1659, Exp. 6. The documentation has also been consulted by Haskett, "'Our Suffering with the Taxco Tribute.'"

63. See Ewald, *Mexican Salt Industry*, pp. 20, 44, 47–50, 252–53 n. 16.

64. There was even an official 1777 list of the provinces that were "lucrative" and "nonlucrative" for them. This list, which is not confined to the repartimiento, was published by Pietschmann, but I mention it here because Gibson also referred to it; see Gibson, *Aztecs under Spanish Rule*, pp. 96–97; H. Pietschmann, "Alcaldes Mayores," esp. pp. 240–57. However, a glance at these statistics is enough to show that they are not of much use for present purposes. The data were in fact only of interest to someone who wanted to know where farming was bad. There were four categories, based on criteria of the possible level of income that the alcalde mayor could make there, "if well adminis-tered." The most lucrative provinces in Anáhuac were Chalco, Puebla, Tlaxcala, and Tepeaca in the central highlands. The combination is remarkable. These were the densely populated provinces where, strikingly enough, the main crop was maize for the corn exchanges in Mexico City and Puebla. I do not know how much the alcaldes mayores earned from this. At any rate, the repartimiento certainly was important in some of these provinces (Chalco, Tlapa), but not in others (Tepeaca, Tlaxcala, Puebla, Taxco). This category also included Tlapa, Chilapa, and Taxco in the faldas, on the road from Acapulco. The second category consisted of Metepec, Ixtlahuaca, Toluca, Tenango del Valle, Pachuca, Cuautitlán, Texcoco, Atlixco, Cholula in the highlands; and Actopan,

Zacatlán, Tulancingo, San Juan de los Llanos, Xalapa, Córdoba, Orizaba, Tepejí de la Seda, Izúcar, Acatlán, Cuernavaca, Malinalco, Zacualpan, and Temascaltepec in the faldas. These were all provinces with a supportive economy, with the exception of those in the valley of Toluca. However, it is precisely the presence of the Toluca provinces in this category that is so difficult to account for. The least interesting categories, the third and the fourth, consisted of Tetepango, Tacuba, Xochimilco, Zumpango de la Laguna, Zempoala, Ecatepec, Teotihuacán, Apan, Otumba, Coatepec, Huejotzingo, Tochimilco, and Tecali in the highlands; and Yahualica, Huayacocotla, Huauchinango, and Cuautla Amilpas in the faldas. It is obvious that both the dry provinces subject to erosion and alkali winds to the north and northeast of Mexico City, and the heavily urbanized provinces near the capital, such as Tacuba and Xochimilco, were not attractive for the alcaldes mayores. Tecali and Tochimilco also belonged to this group; why this was so will be shown elsewhere in this book.

65. Taylor, "Conflict and Balance," p. 279.

66. Hamnett, *Politics and Trade*, pp. 18–95.

67. Dehouve, "'Secession'," esp. pp. 173–78.

68. AGI, Audiencia México, Legs. 839, 840, 841, and 842; AGI, Audiencia México, Vol. 1675. There is also a summary of the events in Taylor, "Conflict and Balance," pp. 272–76.

69. AGI, Audiencia México, Leg. 1675.

70. AGNM, Civil, Vol. 1690, Exp. 2 and 3.

71. For the question of the Tenayuca rancho see also AGNM, Indios, Vol. 44, Exp. 178; AGNM, Indios, Vol. 46, Exp. 97; AGNM, Indios, Vol. 47, Exp. 81; and AGNM, Indios, Vol. 49, Exps. 19 and 46; AGNM, Tierras, Vol. 1923, Exp. 1.

72. Gibson, *Aztecs under Spanish Rule*, pp. 94–95.

73. Gibson, *Tlaxcala*.

74. Chance, *Conquest*, p. 187.

75. AGI, Audiencia México, Leg. 1675; and AGI, Indiferente General, Leg. 107; BNMa, Ms. 2450, Exp. 122; as well as in Stein, "Bureaucracy and Business"; Farriss, *Maya Society*, pp. 44–79, 83–85, 194, 266, 284, 359, 369–70.

Chapter 5

1. See Ouweneel, "*Altepeme* and *Pueblos de Indios*"; and Hoekstra, "Different Way of Thinking"; Ouweneel and Hoekstra, "Tierras concejiles"; also Hoekstra, *Two Worlds Merging*. Full references to the literature are to be found in these studies. See also the reference and analysis in Schryer, *Ethnicity and Class Conflict*; Ouweneel, "From *Tlahtocayotl* to *Gobernadoryotl*."

2. Gibson, *Aztecs under Spanish Rule*, pp. 155–64; Haskett, "Social History," p. 470; Dehouve, *Quand les banquiers*, pp. 134–41; Taylor, *Landlord and Peasant*, pp. 35–66. Taylor wrote about the terrazguero: "the term frequently used in colonial records to identify the occupants of cacicazgo lands, had a broader meaning than its modern definition a laborer who pays rent to the lord of the manor for the land that he occupies. In colonial usage terrasguerro status did not denote an exclusively financial relationship and might include obligations to cultivate a plot of land for the cacique and to perform other unspecified services" (p.41).

3. Trautmann, *Transformaciones*, pp. 110, 146.

4. Taylor, *Landlord and Peasant*, p. 35.

5. AGNM, Tributos, Vol. 43, Exp. 9.

6. Titles on which this rather tentative conclusion has been founded are given in Ouweneel, "*Altepeme* and *Pueblos de Indios*," pp. 32–37.

7. Trautmann, *Transformaciones*, p. 98, Mapa 5; AGI, Indiferente General, Legs. 107 and 108; AGI, Audiencia México, Leg. 2578, Exp. 11.

8. AGI, Indiferente General, Leg. 1662, Exp. 108.

9. AGNM, Tierras, Vol. 1874, Exp. 2; AGNM, Tierras, Vol. 1442, Exp.8; and AGNM, Tierras, Vol. 488, Exp. 3.

10. AGNM, Tierras, Vol. 500, Exp. 4; AGNM, Tierras, Vol. 609, Exp. 1; and AGNM, Tierras, Vol. 643, Exp. 3; also AGNM, Tierras, Vol. 1870, Exp. 16.

11. AGNM, Tierras, Vol. 1518, Exp. 5. I intend to describe this case in more detail in a monograph on relations of power in a "pueblo de indios."

12. See Van Young, "Millennium," p. 404.

13. See Gibson, *Aztecs under Spanish Rule*, pp. 51, 118, 157, 164–6,5 and 171, quote from p. 164; also, see Pérez-Rocha, *Tierra*, pp. 81–100, esp. 84, 87, 95–98.

14. See Munch, *Cacicazgo*, pp. 33–41, Fig. 1.

15. Chance, *Conquest*, pp. 125–32.

16. The new caciques, however, were lords who carried out their activities, sought their alliances, and wielded their influence within the boundaries of the pueblos. It was not just a political matter: Haskett concludes that despite signals of mestizaje, such as Spanish dress, use of the Spanish language, and horse-riding, "the indigenous ruling group retained a good deal of its prehispanic culture . . . and did not lose its position in local society through the adoption of the outward symbols of Iberian culture." In fact, the dress and horse-riding were a good adaptation of "aristocratic thought": the nobility—and that was what the caciques were, after all—were expected to ride horses and to set themselves apart culturally. If they had dressed exactly as their fellow Indians did, they would never have held on to their status. See, Haskett, "Social History," pp. 363, 440. Also, see Farriss, *Maya Society*, pp. 29–32.

17. See, for example, the statements by village leaders in Tlalmanalco, 1720s, AGNM, Civil, Vol. 1690, Exps. 1, 2, and 3.

18. I have consulted a large number of Spanish-language documents in the Ramo de Indios of the AGNM for the village elections. This is not the place to refer to all of these documents; I shall only do so for specific cases. Haskett's thesis is also essential for a good grasp of Indian town government. Through systematic research of Nahuatl language documents, he came to the same conclusion that I had reached on the basis of sampling, exploration, and intuition; see his "Social History." The present quotation is taken from p. 4 of that article. I was only able to consult this thesis in 1987, after my archival research in Mexico, just in time to incorporate a few conclusions and references in the Dutch version of this book. He has revised the text for publication, *Indigenous Rulers*. Also, see Chávez Orozco, *Instituciones democráticas*. Another elaboration of this discussion is published in the December 1995 *American Ethnologist*. I thank the AAA for permission to reproduce these materials here.

19. AGNM, Indios, Vol. 80; AGI, Audiencia México, Leg. 1939; AGNM, Tributos, Vol. 2, Exp. 6; Gibson, *Aztecs under Spanish Rule*, pp. 126, 167, 180, 217–19, 389; López Sarrelangue, *Villa mexicana*, p. 228; Tutino, "Provincial Spaniards," pp. 182–87; Van Young, "Conflict and Solidarity," pp. 75–79; Dehouve, "Pueblo de indios," pp. 92–93.

20. AGI, Audiencia México, Leg. 1939, Exp. 3. This source has also been utilized by Taylor, "Conflict and Balance," pp. 277–81.

21. AGI, Indiferente General, Leg. 107; Tutino, "Provincial Spaniards," p. 186; Haskett, "Social History," pp. 74–75.

22. Haskett, "Social History," p. 35; also Jarquín, *Formación y desarrollo*, pp. 39–43.
23. The text reads "el gobernador electo nombra alcaldes y demás oficiales de su república," among others in AGNM, Tierras, Vol. 1351, Exp. 10.
24. AGNM, Tierras, Vol. 1811, Exp. 1; AGNM, Civil, Vol. 1690, Exps. 1, 2, and 3.
25. AGI, Audiencia México, Leg. 1939, Exp. 3 (Zacatlán); AGNM, Indios, Vol. 55, Exp. 22 (Temoaya); AGNM, Indios, Vol. 57, Exp. 208 (Cuautinchán). The conflict in Cuautinchán is also to be found in other parts of the Ramo de Indios (*expedientes* in brackets): Vols. 2 (51, 526), 3 (597), 4 (258), 10 (a: 238, 264; b: 95, 132 135), 13 (89b), 17 (15), 18 (278, 183), 19 (265, 715), 20 (93, 270, 277), 21 (83, 298), 26 (56, 93, 66), 29 (171), and 34 (121). This documentation makes it possible to trace the conflict between the factions there back into the sixteenth century.
26. Osborn, "Community Study," pp. 56–62; Tutino, "Creole Mexico," pp. 276–81.
27. Herrera García, *Aljarafe sevillano*, pp. 356–60; Moreno Ollero, *Sanlucar de Barrameda*, pp. 49–65.
28. Luria, *Territories*, pp. 174–202.
29. AGI, Audiencia México, Leg. 1823, Exp. 6; AGI, Audiencia México, Leg. 1411, Exp. 836; Osborn, "Community Study," pp. 118–19; Van Young, "Conflict and Solidarity," p. 67; Tutino, "Provincial Spaniards," pp. 183–87; Haskett, "Social History," p. 88.
30. AGNM, Indios, Vol. 59, Exp. 63; Haskett, "Social History," pp. 134–39, 141–42, 167, and *passim*; Chance, "Indian elites," p. 11 (the other features that Chance mentions as exceptional were in fact rather common: collection of tributes, funding of lawsuits, fiestas and political ceremonies, and the receipt of household servants); Tutino, "Provincial Spaniards," pp. 182–87.
31. AGNM, Indios, Vol. 69, exps. 149, 187, 189, 193, 223.
32. See AGNM, Tributos, Vol. 18, Exps. 7, 8, and 9.
33. AGNM, Indios, Vol. 54, Exps. 203, 213, 228, 233, 262, 299, 302; AGNM, Indios, Vol. 55, Exps. 84, 103, 121, 139, 234, 368, 378, 379; AGNM, Indios, Vol. 57, Exps. 185, 190, 213, 245; and AGNM, Indios, Vol. 59, Exps. 60, 151, 152.
34. See Tutino, "Provincial Spaniards," p. 185.
35. AGNM, Tierras, Vol. 3207, Exp. 60.
36. AGNM, Indios, Vol. 57, Exp. 51; AGNM, Indios, Vol. 92, exp. 92; AGNM, Indios, Vol. 59, Exp. 71. Also, see Wood, "Corporate Adjustments," pp. 198, 203, 205.
37. AGNM, Indios, Vol. 53, Exp. 16.
38. Ouweneel, "Schedules."
39. This case is described by Anne Bos in her *doctoraalscriptie*; based *inter alia* on the following archival documents: AGNM, Tierras, Vol. 1764, Exp. 1; AGNM, Tierras, Vol. 2, Exp. 14; AGNM, Tierras, Vol. 2231, Exp. 1; AGNM, Tierras, Vol. 2409, Exp. 1; also, see AGNM, Tierras, Vol. 3672, Exp. 5; AGNM, Tierras, Vol. 3672, Exp. 5; AGNM, Tierras, Vol. 1550, Exp. 2.
40. AGNM, Criminal, Vol. 54, Exp. 11. However, I have followed Van der Valk, "Vrouwen."
41. Hoekstra, *Two Worlds Merging*.
42. AGNM, Tierras, Vol. 1518, Exp. 1; Barrett, "Indian Community Lands," pp 77–98, 100–102; Martin, "Haciendas," pp. 415–16; Tutino, "Creole Mexico," p. 276 Gibson, *Aztecs under Spanish Rule*, pp. 257–70; López Sarrelangue, *Villa mexicana*, pp 228, 230, 243; Loera, *Economía campesina indígena*, pp. 61–64; Ouweneel, "Schedules," pp. 65–68.
43. See, among others, the cases in AGNM, Tierras, Vol. 1538, Exp. 10; AGNM Tierras, Vol. 1604, Exp. 6; AGNM, Tierras, Vol. 1855, Exp. 2; AGNM, Tierras, Vol. 2028 Exp. 9; AGNM, Tierras, Vol. 2064, Exp. 7; AGNM, Tierras, Vol. 2093, Exp. 7; AGNM

Tierras, Vol. 2108, Exp. 4; AGNM, Tierras, Vol. 2225, Exp. 2; AGNM, Tierras, Vol. 2344, Exp. 4; AGNM, Tierras, Vol. 2345, Exp. 15; AGNM, Tierras, Vol. 2349, Exp. 19; AGNM, Tierras, Vol. 2361, Exp. 3; AGNM, Tierras, Vol. 2370, Exp. 4; AGNM, Tierras, Vol. 2382, Exps. 9 and 11; AGNM, Tierras, Vol. 2397, Exp. 1; AGNM, Tierras, Vol. 2450, Exp. 1; AGNM, Tierras, Vol. 2452, Exps. 3, 11 and 12; AGNM, Tierras, Vol. 2502, Exp. 9; AGNM, Tierras, Vol. 2506, Exp. 5; AGNM, Tierras, Vol. 2508, Exp. 3; AGNM, Tierras, Vol. 2510, Exps. 4 and 9; AGNM, Tierras, Vol. 2513, Exp. 10; AGNM, Tierras, Vol. 2522, Exp. 1; AGNM, Tierras, Vol. 2538, Exp. 2; AGNM, Tierras, Vol. 2551, Exp. 14; AGNM, Tierras, Vol. 2552, Exp. 20; AGNM, Tierras, Vol. 2553, Exp. 9; AGNM, Tierras, Vol. 2554, Exp. 16; AGNM, Tierras, Vol. 2575, Exp. 6; AGNM, Tierras, Vol. 2605, Exp. 9; AGNM, Tierras, Vol. 2621, Exp. 15; AGNM, Tierras, Vol. 2626, Exp. 3; AGNM, Tierras, Vol. 2690, Exp. 3; and many, many more.

44. AGNM, Tributos, Vol. 22; AGNM, Tributos, Vol. 24; AGNM, Tributos, Vol. 2; AGNM, Tributos, Vol. 35; AGNM, Tributos, Vol. 8; AGNM, Intendentes, Vol. 73; AGNM, Historia, Vol. 578; AGNM-AHH, Leg. 385; AGNM-AHH, Leg. 386; AGET, 1772, Leg. 1; AGET, 1742, sueltos; AGET, 1757, sueltos; AHNE, Consejos, Leg. 20.723; AHNE, Consejos, Leg. 21.460; AHNE, Jesuitas, Leg. 89; AGNM, Tierras, Vol. 445; AGNM, Tierras, Vol. 2771; AGNM, Tierras, Vol. 2452; AGNM, Tierras, Vol. 1508, Exp. 4; GRAL, *Valle de Toluca*, pp. 10-11, 16; Osborn, "Community Study," pp. 118–28; Tutino, "Provincial Spaniards," pp. 183-186.

45. AGNM, Tierras, Vol. 2522, Exp. 1.

46. Rodríguez, *Comunidades*, pp. 54–57; AGI, Audiencia México, Leg. 1939, Exp. 7; AGNM, Tierras, Vol. 2522, Exp. 1.

47. AGNM, Tierras, Vol. 2605, Exp. 7.

48. AGNM, Tierras, Vol. 2575, Exp. 6.

49. AGNM, Tierras, Vol. 108, Exp. 4.

50. AGNM, Tributos, Vol. 24, Exp. 26.

51. AGNM, Tierras, Vol. 2093, Exp. 7.

52. Casado, *Señores, mercaderes y campesinos*; Vassberg, *Tierra y sociedad*, p. 34; Herrera García, *Aljarafe sevillano*, pp. 356–74; García Sanz, *Desarrollo y crisis*; Pulido Bueno, *Tierra de Huelva*; Taylor, *Landlord and Peasant*, pp. 67–75.

53. Burke, *Historical Anthropology*, but I have consulted the Dutch translation *Stadscultuur*, especially the third essay, entitled "Tellen, schatten, classificeren: de volkstelling als collectieve voorstelling," pp. 43–58.

54. Ouweneel, "Growth, Stagnation, and Migration."

55. On the village separations see García Martínez, *Pueblos de la sierra*, pp. 268–88, and his *Historia de México*, pp. 79–80; Dehouve, *Quand les banquiers*, pp. 142–52, and "'Secession' of Villages"; Wood, "Corporate Adjustments," pp. 195—213; Jarquín, *Formación y desarrollo*, p. 47.

56. Recently Professor Chance of Arizona State University has been so kind in sending me a paper on precisely this topic; see his "Barrios of Colonial Tecali."

57. Source 1800: see above. Source of other data: AGI, Indiferente General, Vols. 108 and 108.

58. For comparative reasons, see Schryer, "Peasants and the Law"; Favre, "Dynamics"; and Farriss, *Maya Society under Spanish Rule*.

59. Buve, "Peasant Mobilization" and "Agricultores"; Buve and Falcón, "Tlaxcala and San Luis Potosí"; Jacobs, *Ranchero Revolt*; Schryer, *Rancheros de Pisaflores* and "*Ranchero* Elite"; Thomson, "Regional Power Groups"; Pansters, "Paradoxes of Regional Power"; Köhler, "Estructura y funcionamiento," pp. 144ff.

364 Notes to Pages 254–64

Chapter 6

1. Levine, *Family Formation*, p. 1; Bernstein, "Concepts," pp. 5–6; also, see Friedmann, "Household Production," pp. 162–64; and above all, the essays in Long, Van der Ploeg, Curtin and Box, eds., *Commoditization Debate*.

2. Bernstein, "African Peasantries," p. 425, or "Agrarian Crisis."

3. See Long, "Commoditization: Thesis and Antithesis"; Smith, "Reflections," esp. p. 101; Chevalier, *Civilization*, pp. 117–22. See also Fox, ed., *Hidden in the Household*; Redclift and Mingione, eds., *Beyond Employment*.

4. Wall, "Leaving Home," pp. 83 and 99, n. 16. Mendels, "Proto-industrialization," esp. p. 241; Gutmann, *Toward*; Gullickson, *Spinners*; Clarkson, *Proto-industrialisation*, esp. pp. 28–38.

5. See for a good discussion: Gullickson, *Spinners*, pp. 1–6.

6. Excellent is Ogilvie, "Proto-industrialization in Europe."

7. Ibid.; Gutmann, *Toward the Modern Economy*, pp. 5–6; Mokyr, *Industrialization*, pp. 10–12, 133–44; Van Zanden, *Arbeid*, pp. 112–17; Levine, *Family Formation*; Kriedte, *Peasants*, pp. 12–13.

8. AGI, Indiferente General, Leg. 108; BNMa, Ms. 249, Exp. 19.

9. See the summary in, Papousek, *Op eigen houtje*, p. 32, for example, or Nutini and Bell, *Ritual Kinship*, parts 1 and 2.

10. Slicher van Bath, *Samenleving*, pp. 109–12, 114–15; Berkner, "Inheritance," passim, and "Stem Family"; Collomp, "Alliance," "From Stem Family to Nuclear Family," pp. 77–80, and "Tensions"; Reher, "Old Issues"; Sabean, "Aspects"; Segalen, "Avoir"; Shaffer, *Family*; Spufford, *Contrasting*; Wall, "Leaving Home"; see also the other articles published in Goody, Thirsk, and Thompson, *Family and Inheritance*; and Medick and Sabean, *Interest and Emotion*.

11. Berkner, "Inheritance."

12. Berkner, "Stem Family," passim; Wall, "Leaving Home," passim.

13. Shaffer, *Family*, pp. 4–5; Segalen, "Avoir," pp. 132 and 143; Berkner, "Stem Family," pp. 414–15; Collomp, "Alliance," passim; Reher, "Old Issues," passim; also, see Chayanov, *Theory*, pp. 55–69, 110–12.

14. Segalen, "Avoir," passim.

15. See the literature discussed by Nutini and Bell, *Ritual Kinship*, 2 vols.

16. AGNM, Tributos, Vol. 43, Exp. 9; Cook and Borah, *Ensayos*, 1, pp. 143–52, 175, 196.

17. AGNM, Tributos, Vol. 8, Exp. 1; AGNM, Tributos, Vol. 11, Exps 5 and 8; AGI, Indiferente General, Leg. 107.

18. Some of the commentators of the article I wrote with Catrien Bijleveld pointed to this.

19. AGI, Indiferente General, Leg. 107.

20. BNMa, Ms. 2450, Exp. 106; AGNM, Tributos, Vol. 43.

21. Hajnal, "European Marriage Patterns."

22. On this topic, see the short discussion in Reed, "'Gnawing It Out.'"

23. Ouweneel, "Schedules," p. 65. See also Dyckerhoff, "Colonial Indian," pp. 48–50, Gibson, *Aztecs under Spanish Rule*, pp. 213–14; Haskett, "Social History," p. 208–10, Dehouve, *Quand les banquiers*, pp. 168–69.

24. Dehouve, *Quand les banquiers*, p. 169.

25. Lavrin, "Mundos en contraste," pp. 3–28, and, "Rural Confraternities"; Hoekstra, *Two Worlds Merging*; Chance and Taylor, "*Cofradías* and *Cargos*," pp. 463–64, 467; AGNM Bienes Nacionales, Vol. 585. On the *cofradía*, see also Wasserstrom, *Class and Society*, pp

23–31, 40–41, 70–77, 87–89; Dehouve, *Quand les banquiers*, pp. 170–73; and, Jarquín, *Formación*, pp. 123–39. Particularly instructive are the essays in a volume edited by Meyers and Hopkins, *Manipulating the Saints*.

26. AHH, Vol. 385, Exp. 1; AHH, Vol. 386, Exp. 4; AHNE, Consejos, Legs. 20.723, 20.727, and 21.460; AGNM, Indios, Vol. 80; AGI, Audiencia México, Leg. 1868; AGNM, Bienes Nacionales, Leg. 585; Osborn, "Community Study," pp. 127–28, 143, 189–93; Gruzinski, "Segunda aculturación," passim.

27. AGI, Audiencia México, Leg. 1868.

28. Officially there were twenty-six pueblos de indios in this province, but eighty-four *gobernadores* were recorded around 1800, fourteen of them in the village of Izúcar itself, and an average of two or three in the other villages.

29. AGI, Audiencia México, Leg. 1868; AGNM, Tributos, Vol. 43, Exp. 9; Osborn, "Community Study," pp. 189–93; Henao, *Tehuacán*, pp. 75–78; Calderón Quijano, *Banco de San Carlos*, pp. 62–72, 113–14.

30. AGNM, Tierras, Vol. 1580, Exp. 1.

31. Chávez Orozco, *Cajas de comunidades indígenas*. Tutino, "Creole Mexico," pp. 265–68, 284–88, 301, and passim; Charlton, "Land Tenure"; all including data from AGNM, Indios, Vol. 80, Exps. 3, fs 82-139, and, 6, fs. 190-217; and, AGNM, Tierras, Vol. 2607, Exp. 1.

32. See on this topic, among others, Boletín AGNM, 3a serie, 7:2 (1983/23), pp. 7–10; Sabean, *Power in the Blood*, pp. 16–17; Spufford, *Contrasting Communities*, passim; Gruzinski, "Segunda aculturación," p. 186; Köhler, "Estructura," passim, and "Ciclos de poder," passim.

33. AGNM, Civil, Vol. 1418, Exp. 3; Pérez Rocha, *Tierra*, pp. 68, 111–12; Henao, *Tehuacán*, pp. 70–71, 78–79; Gibson, *Aztecs under Spanish Rule*, p. 310; Rodríguez, *Comunidades*, pp. 54–56.

34. AHH, Leg. 385, Exp. 1; BNMa, Ms. 2449, Exp. 5; BNMa, Ms. 2450, Exp. 105; Rodríguez, *Comunidades*, pp. 71–72.

35. AGNM, Tributos, Vol. 35, Exp. 1; AGNM, Tributos, Vol. 22, Exp. 3.

36. AHH, Leg. 386, Exp. 4; AHH, Leg. 385, Exps 1 and 6; *Boletín AGNM*, 3a serie, 7:2 (1983/23), pp. 20–36.

37. *Boletín AGNM*, 3a serie, 7:2 (1983/23), pp. 11–20; Rodríguez, *Comunidades*, p. 55.

38. AGNM, Tierras, Vol. 1109, Exp. 3; AGNM, Tierras, Vol. 2774, Exp. 11; FMMN, Serie Tlaxcala, Rollo 11, no. 473; AGNM, Bienes Nacionales, Vol. 585; AHNE, Consejos, Leg. 20.723, Exp. 3; AHNE, Consejos, Leg. 20.727, Exp. 1; Henao, *Tehuacán*, pp. 79–81; Tutino, "Creole Mexico," pp. 276–87; Rodríguez, *Comunidades*, pp. 57, 103, 128; López Sarrelangue, *Villa mexicana*, pp. 229–30, 236, 239; Pérez Rocha, *Tierra*, pp. 68, 94–99, 107–9, 111–12, 150; Taylor, *Drinking*, pp. 24–25, 49–53; Van Oss, "Catholic Colonialism," pp. 333–36; Osborn, "Community Study," pp. 150–54; Karremans, *Zon*, pp. 228–33.

39. AGNM, Indios, Vol. 59, Exp. 153, fs. 156v-158r; also, see Wasserstrom, *Class and Society*, passim; Schryer, "Class Conflict," and "Peasants and the Law."

40. AHNE, Consejos, Leg. 20.723, Exp. 3; Brading, "Tridentine Catholicism," pp. 12–13.

41. Wilken, *Good Farmers*, and "Management."

42. See Ouweneel, "Schedules."

43. Enge and Whiteford, *Keepers of Water and Earth*.

44. Loomis, "Agricultural System," p. 100; Chorley, "Agricultural Revolution," passim. I was initiated into this aspect of the agrarian world by don Juan Faustino Suárez Vázquez, a retired agricultural teacher from Tlaxcala. As we walked for hours

Notes to Pages 274–83

through the *montes* and past the milpas near Tlaxcala City, he explained to me every detail of the specificities of Mexican agriculture.

45. Cook, "Historical Demography," pp. 52–53; Wilken, "Management," p. 410; Gibson, *Aztecs under Spanish Rule*, pp. 309–10.

46. AGI, Indiferente General, Leg. 107; AGNM, Tierras, Vol. 710, Exp. 1; Trautmann, *Transformaciones*, pp. 52–56.

47. Alzate in Lombardo de Ruíz, *Antología*, p. 252, n. 1, p. 253, n. 1; AGI, Indiferente General, Leg. 107.

48. Alzate, in Lombardo de Ruíz, *Antología*, pp. 215–16, 222, 224–25; also, see Murphy, "Irrigation."

49. Among others, BNMa, Ms. 2449, Exp. 5; Gibson, *Aztecs under Spanish Rule*, pp. 308–11, 320–21; Loera, *Calimaya*, p. 81; Malvido, "Abandono," pp. 528–29; Bullock, *Seis meses*, p. 163.

50. AGI, Audiencia México, Leg. 2096; see also the documentation of Chapter Five. I intend to work through this material for a special article on the común repartimiento in the near future. Also, Bullock, *Seis meses*, passim; Gibson, *Aztecs under Spanish Rule*, p. 311.

51. AGNM, Tierras, Vol. 1547, Exp. 1; also, see Harvey, "Planned Field Systems," pp. 92–94.

52. See Bauer, "Millers and Grinders."

53. The *cuescomates* were shaped like large rounded pots, with a pointed straw roof covering the opening at the top. The pots were a few meters high and at least two meters in diameter at their widest point. They were made from clay and wood, and rested on a small platform to protect them from pests. There was a small opening at the base where the daily ration could be shoveled out. The *zencal* was a rectangular wooden shed, which was also covered with a pointed roof and rested on a platform. The cuescomates were usually situated in a central position in the farmyard and near the farmhouse, while the zencales were placed on the edge of the farmyard. The cuescomates were more common in central and eastern Anáhuac, while the zencales were generally found in the west. See Seele and Tyrakowski, *Cuescomate y zencal*, also, see Careri, *Viaje*, p. 16.

54. AGI, Audiencia México, Leg. 2096; Trautmann, *Transformaciones*, p. 73; Ajofrín, *Diario*; Bullock, *Seis meses*.

55. Chávez Orozco, *Cajas de comunidades indígenas*, passim; Charlton, "Land Tenure," pp. 257–61; Tutino, "Creole Mexico," pp. 284–88; Cook, "Historical Demography," pp. 29, 35–36, 49–51; Gibson, *Aztecs under Spanish Rule*, p. 308; Loera, *Calimaya*, p. 81; Taylor, *Landlord and Peasant*, p. 77.

56. Greenow, "Marriage Patterns."

57. AGNM, Tierras, Vol. 566, Exp. 4; De Vries, *Economy*, pp. 162–63.

58. See, among others, the articles in a special issue of *Nueva Antropología*, 6 (1982/19); Smith, "Estudio Económico," pp. 29–31.

59. AGI, Audiencia México, Leg. 2096; Hassig, *Trade*, pp. 67–74, 231–33; Larson, "Rural Rhythms," pp. 411–12.

60. Greenow, "Marriage Patterns."

61. AGET, 1764, Leg. 1, Exp. 1; AGNM, Historia, Vol. 578; AGNM, Alhóndigas, Vol. 15, Exp. 6; AGI, Audiencia México, Leg. 2096; AGI, Indiferente General, Leg. 108; AHNE, Colegios, Leg. 20.178, Exp. 1; BNMa, Mss. 2449 and 2450; Smith, "Estudio económico," pp. 18–19; Gormsen, "Wochenmärkte."

62. Bullock, *Seis meses*, pp. 93–95; Ajofrín, *Diario*; Couturier, "Micaela Angela Carrillo"; Taylor, *Drinking, Homicide and Rebellion*, pp. 53, 58–60; Gibson, *Aztec unde*

Spanish Rule, p. 338; Museo de América, *Mestizaje americano,* pp. 372–73.

63. AGNM, Historia, Vol. 578; AGI, Audiencia México, Leg. 2096; Gibson, *Aztecs under Spanish Rule,* p. 328; Riley, "Santa Lucia," p. 269, and *Hacendados Jesuitas,* pp. 95–96; Trautmann, *Transformaciones,* p. 186; Tutino, "Creole Mexico," pp. 133 and 159.

64. AGNM, Historia, Vol. 578; Hilton, "Medieval Market Towns."

65. Comparison of the 1742–43 *relaciones geográficas* and those in 1776–77 ones show an increased specialization; AGI, Indiferente General, Legs. 107 and 198; BNMa, Mss. 2449 and 2450. Also McMillen, "Alfarería," pp. 63–165, esp. pp. 116, 151–56.

66. BNMa, Ms. 2450, Exp. 122: Ixtapan la Sal specialized in producing pottery for the Taxco mines. Also Couturier, "Micaela Angela Carrillo"; Taylor, *Drinking,* pp. 45–68; Trautmann, *Transformaciones,* pp. 112–13; López Sarrelangue, *Villa mexicana,* p. 18; Gibson, *Aztecs under Spanish Rule;* Ajofrín, *Diario,* pp. 52–53; Alzate, in Lombardo de Ruíz, *Antología,* p. 282, n. 1; Ewald, *Mexican Salt Industry.*

67. BNMa, Ms. 2449, Exps. 16, 18, and 19.

68. AGI, Indiferente General, Legs. 107 and 108; BNMa, Mss. 2449 and 250; Florescano and Gil, *Descripciones económicas regionales,* pp. 158–84; Thomson, "Cotton, Textile Industry."

69. AGI, Indiferente General, Leg. 108; AGNM, Historia, Vol. 578; Florescano and Gil, *Descripciones económicas regionales,* pp. 168–72.

70. AGI, Indiferente General, Leg. 107; BNMa, Ms. 2449, Exp. 54.

71. Sabean, *Power and the Blood,* p. 10; also, see Burke, *Popular Culture,* passim.

72. The literature on development theory gives the impression of a sort of palatial complex: the Spanish landlords, the religious officials and the civil servants lived in imposing constructions around a large square, surrounded by the shabby homes of their servants—Mexico City as a Spanish-American version of Versailles or Aranjuez! However, while Versailles was directly connected with the neighboring capital of Paris, the center of the economic system of northern France, and Aranjuez was built on one of the main roads to Madrid, the capital of New Spain is presented as no more than an administrative center, since the economic system of this Spanish colony is supposed to have been based on self-support and export. The development sociologist Germani, in his "Stages of Modernization," esp. p. 16, recommends taking medieval Europe as a point of comparison for colonial Latin America: "The development of the hacienda system involved a weakening of the role of the cities, and the 'decentralization of the New World society around the landed estate' in a fashion not dissimilar to post-Roman Europe."

73. Hoberman and Socolow, *Cities and Society,* p. 5; Wrigley, "Simple Model," pp. 44–45, 60–65; Romero de Solís, *Población española,* pp. 143–47; García Sanz, "Interior peninsular," p. 632; Reher, *Familia, población y sociedad,* p. 6, 25, 154; Cipolla, *Before the Industrial Revolution,* pp. 69, 81, 85 tables 2-10 and 2-13; Braudel, *Structures of Everyday Life,* pp. 483, 526, 531, 532, 538, 548; Rebel, *Peasant Classes,* pp. 43–76; Nusteling, *Welvaart,* p. 248 app. 3.2; Slicher van Bath, *Bevolking,* app. 1.

74. AGI, Audiencia México, Legs. 1406 and 1409; Beaufoy, *Mexican Illustrations,* pp. 126–27, 130; Humboldt, *Ensayo político,* p. 453; Ajofrín, *Diario,* 1, p. 79; Bullock, *seis meses,* p. 74; Ros, "Real Fábrica"; Deans-Smith, "Money Plant."

75. This is taken from a text from Alzate, in AHNE, Consejos, Leg. 20.723, Exp. 6; Kicza, *Colonial Entrepreneurs,* pp. 207–13, table 33; Miño Grijalva, *Obrajes y tejedores.*

76. Miño Grijalva, *Obrajes y tejedores,* pp. 103–17, 160–69, 177, 194–203, 231–37, 244–55.

77. Ibid.

78. Thomson, *Puebla de los Angeles,* pp. 33–59; Salvucci, *Textiles and Capitalism,* pp.

9–31. The data referred to by Miño can be compared to data from the AGET. I have consulted these data and incorporated them in the Dutch version of this book. The far more extensive and in-depth analysis contained in Miño's *Obrajes* confirms my suspicion that Thomson and Salvucci underrated the level of rural manufacture.

79. AGNM, Alcabalas, Leg. 37; AGNM, Civil, Vol. 1435, Exp. 13; BNMa, Ms. 2449, Exp. 16; AGI, Indiferente General, Leg. 108; Miño, *Obrajes*, pp. 244–55, and "Camino hacía la fábrica," p. 144; Thomson, "Cotton Textile Industry," pp. 178–83; Trautmann, *Transformaciones*, p. 102; Hamnett, *Roots of Insurgency*, pp. 34–39; Salvucci, "Entrepreneurial Culture," pp. 403–4; Liehr, *Stadtrat*, pp. 18, 120–23; Tutino, "Creole Mexico," p. 273; Bravo, *Conde de Revilla Gigedo*, p. 191; and Izard, "Metropolitanos," pp. 192–93.

80. AGNM, Alcabalas, Leg. 165; also discussed by Salvucci, *Textiles*, pp. 20–21.

81. Thomson, *Puebla de los Angeles*, p. 44.

82. AGI, Audiencia de México, Leg. 2096; Miño, "Espacio económico," p. 536; Thomson, "Cotton Textile Industry," pp. 169, 173–77; Ajofrín, *Diario*, 1, p. 45; Humboldt, *Ensayo político*, pp. 451 and 453; Florescano and Gil, *Descripciones económicas general*, pp. 43–44, 163–64; Liehr, *Stadtrat*, pp. 14–23; and, Heath Constable, *Lucha de clases*, pp. 62–63.

83. Thomson, *Puebla de los Angeles*, p. 33.

84. McMillen, "Alfarería," pp. 116–32, 146–56, 163–66.

85. Brading, *Miners and Merchants*, 2d part, chapter 1.

86. Johnson, "Artisans," pp. 227–29, 244–47; Kicza, *Colonial Entrepreneurs*, pp. 207–13; González Angulo, *Artesanado*, pp. 32–33; Tanck de Estrada, "Abolición"; also, see Nusteling, *Welvaart*, pp. 147–57.

87. BNMa, Ms. 19.266.

88. De Vries, *Economy*, pp. 168–70.

89. AGNM, Civil, Vol. 1817, Exp. 10; AGNM, Civil, Vol. 1646, Exp. 18; Beaufoy, *Mexican Illustrations*, p. 150; Bullock, *Seis meses*, pp. 148–51; Ajofrín, *Diario*, pp. 17, 87, 243; Humboldt, *Ensayo político*, p. 467; Bahena Pérez, "Transportación," pp. 135–38; Brading, *Haciendas and Ranchos*, p. 199; Kollonitz, *Eerste dagen*, p. 197; Rees, *Transportes*, pp. 85–87, 219; Hassig, *Trade*, pp. 78–79.

90. AGNM, Virreyes, Vol. 26; Serrera, *Guadalajara ganadera*, pp. 217-224, 264-268; Hamnett, *Roots of Insurgency*, pp. 25–26; Bahena Pérez, "Transportación," pp. 63–68, 106, 135; Couturier, "Hacienda of Hueyapan," pp. 72–86, and, "Pedro Romero de Terreros"; Ladd, *Making of a Strike*, pp. 30–34, 45–47, 85–97; Morin, *Michoacán*, pp. 173–74; De Vries, *Economy of Europe*, pp. 614–16; Ringrose, "Transportation," pp. 51–53.

91. AGET, 1770, Leg. 1, Exp. 2; AGNM, Padrones, Vol. 43, f. 10; AGNM, Alhóndigas, Vol. 15, Exp. 6; Humboldt, *Ensayo político*, pp. 258, 300; Bahena Pérez, "Transportación," pp. 76-77, 98, 102-103; Hassig, *Trade*, p. 193; for Europe, Ringrose, "Transportation," pp. 78-79.

92. Bahena Pérez, "Transportación," pp. 188–90. There is a nice book on the *Tribunal de Acordada* by MacLachlan, *Criminal Justice*. Also the novel by Fernández de Lizardi, *El Periquillo Sarniento*.

93. Hamnett, *Roots of Insurgency*, p. 138.

94. AGNM, Alhóndigas, Vol. 15, Exp. 6.

95. AGI, Indiferente General, Leg. 107; Ajofrín, *Diario*, 1, pp. 87, 243; Gemelli, *Viaje*, pp. 16–17; Bahena Pérez, "Transportación," pp. 182–86.

96. AGI, Indiferente General, Leg. 107; Trautmann, *Transformaciones*, pp. 204, 210–11; Parker, *San Mateo Huiscolotepec*, pp. 61–68; Ewald, *Estudios*, pp. 45–53, 69–78.

97. Among others Burke, *Popular Culture*, p. 207ff.; Hoffman, *Church and Community*, pp. 98–138; and Muchembled, *Invention*. However, I have considerable reserva-

tions with regard to Muchembled's book. Following Norbert Elias, he describes the civilization offensive in the light of Freudian theory, despite the fact that this theory rests on ideological rather than scientific foundations. I never once encountered reasonable scientific evidence by a Freudian psychologist during my years on the psychology faculty. To make matters worse, Muchembled is ill-informed about modern criticisms of the traditional anthropological community theory. He assumes the existence of closed corporate communities in medieval Europe!

98. BNMa, Ms. 2449, Exps. 4 and 19; AGET, 1761, Leg. 2, Exp. 23; Thomson, "Cotton Textile Industry," pp. 183–85; Liehr, *Stadtrat*, pp. 16–17, 27; Miño, "Camino hacía la fábrica," pp. 144–45; Izard, "Metropolitanos," pp. 190–91; Martin, "Desnudez," pp. 273–74, 281–93, and his *Vagabundos*; Gruzinski, "Segundo aculturación," pp. 198–201.

99. Sayer, *Mexican Costume*, p. 9.

100. See, for example, the documents in BNMa, Mss. 2449 and 2450.

101. Museo de América, *Mestizaje Americano*.

102. AGNM, Civil, Vol. 1690, Exps. 1, 2, and 3.

103. See the essays in Hobsbawm and Ranger, eds., *Invention;* the quote is from Hobsbawm's introductory essay, pp. 1–2.

104. Interesting is Kagan, *Penal Servitude*. For a strictly, and somewhat reductionist, economic analysis of the *obraje*, see Salvucci, *Textiles*.

105. AGI, Audiencia México, Leg. 1283, Exp. 12.

106. AGI, Audiencia México, Leg. 1872.

107. Wilkinson, *Poverty and Progress*, pp. 18–19; De Vries, *Economy*, pp. 176–82. On labor conditions, pauperization, and the relation of reciprocity with the elite, see, for instance, Coleman, "Labour"; Freudenberger, "Arbeitsjahr"; Abel, *Agrarkrisen*; Wiles, "Theory of Wages"; Lindert and Williamson, "English Workers' Living Standards"; Hilton, "Medieval Market Towns"; Sabean, *Landbesitz*; Hagen, "Working"; Woodward, "Wage Rates." Van Young, "Rich Get Richer," is an exploration of the Latin American situation.

108. Thomson, "Cotton Textile Industry," pp. 183, 196; Miño, "Camino hacía la fábrica," p. 141, and "Espacio económico," p. 540; Salvucci, *Textiles*, pp. 18–21; Kriedte, *Peasants*, p. 15.

109. Ouweneel, "Schedules."

110. Lucassen, "Naar de kusten van de Noordzee," pp. 120–23.

111. Scott, *Moral Economy*, pp. 43–44.

Epilogue

1. For this dialogue, see Ginzburg, *I Benandanti*, as well as *The Night Battles*, pp. 153–55.

2. Carlo Ginzburg's beautiful book, *Il Formaggio e i Vermi*, is available in English translation as *The Cheese and the Worms*. I have used the Dutch translation, *De kaas en de wormen*.

3. See Slicher van Bath, "Geschiedenis tussen kritiek en illusie."

4. Laslett, *World We Have Lost*.

5. See Cuello, "Mito de la hacienda colonial en el norte de México," especially the introduction.

6. Frank, *Latin America*, p. 231.

7. Wolf, *Europe*, p. 145.

8. Laslett, *World We Have Lost*. These radio broadcasts, which were made in 1960, 1962, and 1963, were published in book form in 1965, and since then, have been re-

printed eight times in large print runs.

9. See Kloos, *Door het oog van de antropoloog*.

10. The same point of view is in Lemaire, *Indiaan*, as well as in Gil, *Mitos y utopías*.

11. See Brading, *Prophecy and Myth*, pp. 7–27. Also, see Lemaire, *Indiaan*, pp. 36–38.

12. Lowry, *Under the Volcano*.

13. Wachtel, *Vision des vaincus*, and "Indian"; Farriss, "Indians," esp. pp. 2 and 19.

14. Lovell, "Surviving Conquest," quotes from pp. 25 and 36. Also, see Lovell, *Conquest and Survival*, pp. 204, n. 50, and especially 219, n. 23; Farriss, *Maya Society Under Colonial Rule*, pp. 197–98 and passim.

15. Smith, "Ideologies."

16. The wording this time can be found in Inglehart, *Culture Shift*, pp. 18–19.

17. Kuhn, *Structure*; the idea for this comparison is Inglehart's (see preceding note).

18. Brading, "Bourbon Spain," p. 426.

19. The same goes, for example, for the "new social movements," which have attracted so much attention during the past few years. As David Slater puts it, this was a field that had "held open, no matter how tenuously, the possibility of another horizon; optimism of the will, in a time of disenchantment, has been given a new dynamic." Slater, "Power and Social Movements," p. 2.

20. See Toulmin, *Cosmopolis*.

21. See, for example, Carmagnani's *Regreso de los dioses*.

22. Wolf, *Sons*, p. 230. Wolf's terminology is echoed in the work of Tutino; see *From Insurrection*, pp. 143–48, 246.

23. On this, see the philosopher Rorty, *Solidariteit of objectiviteit*, a translation of *Irony, Contingency, Solidarity*.

24. Keith, ed., *Haciendas and Plantations*.

25. Arguedas, *Los ríos profundos*.

26. Lienhard, "Legitimación indígena." For a rather uncritical analysis, see the essay "*Men of Maize*," in Dorfman's, *Some Write to the Future*, pp. 1–23, written in 1967.

27. The year 1992 saw a powerful demonstration of this.

28. Schryer, *Ethnicity and Class Conflict*, p. 323.

29. Brown et al., *State of the World 1990*.

30. I have recorded this speech from television.

31. Sen, *Poverty and Famines*; Grigg, *Dynamics*, pp. 135–50.

32. See Grigg, *Dynamics*, pp. 136–38, Figure 22; referring to Lösch, *Economics of Location*, pp. 36–59; and Dunn, *Location of Agricultural Production*, pp. 5–12.

33. Skipp, *Crisis and Development*, p. 10. The image is borrowed from Van Young, "Rich Get Richer."

34. Burke, *Popular Culture*, pp. 244–47; Slicher van Bath, *Samenleving onder spanning*, p. 417; Kriedte, *Peasants*, pp. 18–60, 101–57.

35. On the *Consolidación*, see, among others, Lavrin, "Execution"; Liehr, "Endeudamiento estatal"; and Hamnett, *Roots of Insurgency*, pp. 89–90, 121.

36. Tutino, *From Insurrection*, pp. 140–41, and "Creole Mexico," pp. 348–52.

37. Tutino, *From Insurrection*.

38. Dealy, "Prolegomena," and "Tradition of Monistic Thought." Also, see Hoberman, "Hispanic American Political Theory."

39. Peeters, *Historische gedragswetenschap*, pp. 61–63; Thompson, *Making*; Hoffman, *Church*, pp. 83–95.

40. Brading, *Prophecy and Myth*, pp. 5–6.

Weights
and Measures

Standard Weights:

carga	fanega	media	cuartilla	almud	cuartillo
1	2	4	8	24	96
	1	2	4	12	48
		1	2	6	24
			1	3	12
				1	4

During the Bourbon Reforms, the following system was introduced:

maize

carga	fanega	quintal	arroba	libra	(kilo)
1	3	3	12	300	(138.1)
	1	1	4	100	(46.0)
			1	25	(11.5)
				1	(0.5)

wheat

carga	fanega	arroba	libra	(kilo)
1	4	13	325	(149.6)
	1	3	81	(37.4)

Measures

Standard was the *vara de Burgos* of 83.73 or 83.916 centimeters. It was used to indicate the *legua*:

1 legua = 2 medias = 4 cuartos = 100 cordeles = 5,000 varas,

which is about 4,190 meters. Then there was the *braza* or *brazada* of two *varas*, thus 1.67 meters.

Agricultural surfaces were measured according to sowing units: the *fanega* (maize) or *carga* (wheat) *de sembradura*. Because of the different qualities of the soil, these units would differ from field to field. Nevertheless, there was a standard:

surface	*in: varas*	*caballerías*	*hectares*
fanega de sembradura (maize)	276 x 184	0.080	3.57
cuartilla sembradura (maize)	250 x 100	0.040	1.75
carga de sembradura (wheat)	376 x 184	0.080	3.57
caballería	1,104 x 552	1	42.79
sitio ganado mayor	5,000 x 5,000	41.023	1,755.67
sitio ganado menor	333 x 333	18.232	780.27
fundo legal	1,200 x 1,200	2.360	101.12
labor	1,000 x 1,000	1.641	70.22
suerte	552 x 276	0.250	10.69
solar (near house)	50 x 50	0.004	0.17
solar (near mill)	100 x 100	0.008	0.35

Water surfaces:

	square pulgadas	*square granos*	*square centimeters*
buey	1,296	36,864	7,022.44
surco	27	768	144.30
naranja	9	256	48.76

A *buey* would be 8,931.2 liters per minute; a *surco*, 194.4 liters.

Bibliography

Abbreviations

Full references to the literature are given only in the bibliography. References to archival documents are given by volume (Vol.), legajo (Leg.), expediente (Exp.), and folio (f. or ff.). The following abbreviations are also used:

AAG Bijdragen   Afdeling Agrarische Geschiedenis van de Landbouwhogeschool Wageningen, Bijdragen

Actas ICA   Actas del Congreso Internacional de Americanistas

AGI   Archivo General de Indias, Sevilla, España

AGNM   Archivo General de la Nación, Mexico City

AGET   Archivo General del Estado de Tlaxcala, Exconvento de San Francisco in Tlaxcala, now housed in the city itself

AgHR   Agricultural History Review

AH   Agricultural History

AHH   Archivo Histórico de Hacienda, located in AGNM

AHNE   Archivo Histórico Nacional de España, Madrid

AI   América Indígena

AJAE   American Journal of Agricultural Economics

AmHR   American Historical Review

Annales ESC   Annales Economies, Sociétés, Civilisations

Anuario CHSC   Anuario Colombiano de Historia Social y de la Cultura

Anuario dEA   Anuario de Estudios Americanos

Anuario ECA   Anuario de Estudios Centroamericanos

ArchHisp   Archivo Hispalense, 2a época

BAG   B. H. Slicher van Bath, *Bijdragen tot de agrarische geschiedenis* (Utrecht, 1978)

BLAR   Bulletin of Latin American Research

BMVG   Bijdragen en Mededelingen Vereniging Gelre

BNMA   Biblioteca Nacional, Madrid, Spain

BolAm   Boletín Americanista

Boletín   Boletín de Estudios Latinoamericanos y del Caribe (CEDLA)

Bulletin SLAS   Bulletin of the Society of Latin American Studies, United Kingdom

CaC   Continuity and Change

CAL   Cahiers des Amériques Latines

CEHE   Cambridge Economic History of Europe

CHLA   Cambridge History of Latin America

CSSH   Comparative Studies in Society and History

EcHR   Economic History Review, 2nd series

EEH	Explorations in Economic History
EHMCM	Estudios de Historia Moderna y Contemporánea de México
EHSE	Estudios de Historia Social de España
ERLACS	European Review of Latin American and Caribbean Studies (CEDLA)
ESHJ	Economisch en Sociaal-Historisch Jaarboek
FMMN	Instituto Nacional de Antropología e Historia, Mexico City, Microfilm Series
Fuentes	Enrique Florescano and Rodolfo Pastor, eds., *Fuentes para la historia de la crisis agrícola de 1785–1786* (Mexico City, 1981)
HAHR	Hispanic American Historical Review
HaT	History and Theory
HGdM	*Historia General de México* (4 vols., Mexico City, 1976)
HMAI	Handbook of Middle American Indians
HMex	Historia Mexicana
IAAnf	Ibero-Amerikanisches Archiv, neue folge
IJURR	International Journal of Urban and Regional Research
JbLA	Jahrbuch für Geschichte von Staat, Wirtschaft, und Gesellschaft Lateinamerikas
JEEH	Journal of European Economic History
JEH	Journal of Economic History
JFH	Journal of Family History
JHId	Journal of the History of Ideas
JIH	Journal of Interdisciplinary History
JLAS	Journal of Latin American Studies
JMH	Journal of Modern History
JPS	Journal of Peasant Studies
JSH	Journal of Social History
LAP	Latin American Perspectives
LARR	Latin American Research Review
MS/EM	Mexican Studies/Estudios Mexicanos
NG	National Geographic
NS	NorthSouth/NordSud/NorteSur
PaP	Past and Present
PHR	Pacific Historical Review
RdI	Revista de Indias, Madrid
RMCPS	Revista Mexicana de Ciencias Políticas y Sociales
SWJA	Southwestern Journal of Anthropology
TAm	The Americas
TvG	Tijdschrift voor Geschiedenis
TvSG	Tijdschrift voor Sociale Geschiedenis
AH-UIA	Archivo Histórico de la Universidad Iberoamericana, Mexico City
ZAA	Zeitschrift für Agrargeschichte und Agrarsoziologie

Literature Cited

Abel, W.
Agrarkrisen und Agrarkonjunktur. 2d. ed.
Hamburg, 1966.
*Massenarmut und Hungerkrisen im
vorindustriellen Europa. Versuch einer
Synopsis.* Göttingen, 1974.
*Agricultural Fluctuations in Europe. From
the Thirteenth to the Twentieth
Centuries.* trans. from the German.
London, 1980.

Acuña, R., comp.
Relaciones geográficas del siglo xvi. 9 vols.
Mexico City, 1983–1987.

Adorno, T. W., E. Frenkel-Brunswik, D. J.
Levinson, and R. N. Sanford.
The Authoritarian Personality. New York,
1950.

Aguirre Beltrán, G.
*El señorío de Cuauhtochco. Luchas agrarias
en México durante el Virreinato.* Mexico
City, 1940.

Aguirre Beltrán, H.J.
*La congregación de Tlacotepec (1604–
1606). Pueblo de indios de Tepeaca,
Puebla.* Mexico City, 1984.

Ajofrín, Fray Francisco de.
*Diario del viaje que hizo a la América en el
siglo XVIII el P. Fray Francisco de
Ajofrín, 1763–1766.* 2 vols. Mexico
City, 1964.

Alanis Boyso, J. L.
"Corregimiento de Toluca—Pueblos y
elecciones de república en el siglo
XVIII." *HMex* 25 (1976/99), pp.
455–77.

Altman, I., and J. Lockhart, eds.
*Provinces of Early Mexico. Variants of
Spanish American Regional Evolution.*
Los Angeles, 1976.

Amussen, S. D.
"Governors and Governed: Class and
Gender Relations in English Villages,
1590–1725." Ph.D. diss., Brown
University, 1982.

Anderson, R. D.
"Race and Social Stratification: A
Comparison of Working-Class
Spaniards, Indians, and Castas in
Guadalajara, Mexico in 1821." *HAHR*
68:2 (1988), pp. 209–43.

Anes, G.
*Economía e 'Ilustración' en la España del
siglo xviii.* 3d, rev. ed. Barcelona, 1981.

Anes, G., ed.
*La economía española al final del Antiguo
Régimen. Vol. I. Agricultura.* Madrid,
1982.

Ankersmit, F. R.
*Narrative Logic. A Semantic Analysis of the
Historian's Language.* The Hague, 1983.
*De navel van de geschiedenis. Over de
interpretatie, representatie en historische
realiteit.* Groningen, 1991.

Ankerson, D.
*Agrarian Warlord: Saturnino Cedillo and
the Mexican Revolution in San Luis
Potosi.* DeKalb, Ill., 1984.

375

Appleby, A.
"Grain Prices and Subsistence Crisis in
England and France, 1590–1740." *JEH*
39 (1979), pp. 865–87.
Appleby, J. O.
*Economic Thought and Ideology in
Seventeenth-Century England.* Princeton,
1978.
Archer, C. I.
The Army in Bourbon Mexico, 1760–1810.
Albuquerque, 1977.
Arguedas, J. M.
Los rios profundos. Lima, 1958.
Arnold, L. J.
"Bureaucracy and Bureaucrats in Mexico
City, 1808–1824." Ph.D. diss.,
University of Texas, Austin, 1975.
"Social, Economic, and Political Status in
the Mexico City Central Bureaucracy,
1808–1822." In Frost, Meyer and
Zoraída Vázquez, eds., *Trabajo*, pp.
281–310.
Artís Espríu, G.
"Economía administrada y estrategias de
regatones y maquileros: el mercado de
trigo en la ciudad de México (siglo
XVIII)." Tésis Lic., Universidad
Iberoamericana, Mexico City, 1984.
Assies, W., G. Burgwal, and T. Salman.
*Structures of Power, Movements of
Resistance. An Introduction to the
Theories of Urban Movements in Latin
America.* Amsterdam, 1990.
Baars, C.
*De geschiedenis van de landbouw in de
Beijerlanden.* Wageningen, 1973.
Badura, B.
"Biografía de la hacienda de San Nicolás
de Ulapa." *Ibero Americana Pragensia* 4
(1970), pp. 75–111.
Baehrel, R.
*Une croissance: la Basse-Provence rurale (fin
de XVIe–1789).* Paris, 1961.
Bahena Pérez, M.
"La transportación de carga en el
comercio de la Nueva España: la
arriería (1789–1810)." Tesis Maestría,
Universidad Iberoamericana, Mexico
City, 1985.

Barrett, E.
*Land Tenure and Settlement in the
Tepalcatepec Lowland, Mexico.* Ann
Arbor, 1970.
"Encomiendas, Mercedes and Haciendas
in the *Tierra caliente* of Michoacán."
JbLA 10 (1973), pp. 71–112.
"Indian Community Lands in the *Tierra
caliente* of Michoacán." *JbLA* 11
(1974), pp. 78–120.
Bartlett, R.
*The Making of Europe. Conquest,
Colonization and Cultural Change,
950–1350.* London, 1993.
Bassols Batalla, A.
*Recursos naturales de México. Teoría,
conocimiento y uso.* Mexico City, 1981.
Bataillon, C.
Las regiones geográficas en México. Mexico
City, 1969.
La ciudad y el campo en el México Central.
Mexico City, 1972.
Bauer, A. J.
"The Church and Spanish American
Agrarian Structures, 1765–1865." *TAm*
18 (1971), pp. 78–98.
"Rural Workers in Spanish America:
Problems of Peonage and Oppression."
HAHR 59 (1979), pp. 34–63.
"The Church in the Economy of Spanish
America: *Censos* and *Dépositos* in the
Eighteenth and Nineteenth
Centuries." *HAHR* 63 (1983), pp.
707–33.
"Jesuit Enterprise in Colonial Latin
America: A Review Essay." *AH* 57
(1983), pp. 90–104.
"Millers and Grinders: Technology and
Household Economy in Meso-
America." *AH* 64 (1990), pp. 1–17.
Baumol, W. J., and W. E. Oates.
*Economics, Environmental Policy, and the
Quality of Life.* Englewood Cliffs, 1979.
Beaufoy, M.
Mexican Illustrations, Founded Upon Facts.
London, 1828; rep. Washington, 1987.
Beckett, J. V.
"The Decline of the Small Landowner in
Eighteenth- and Nineteenth-Century

England: Some Regional
Considerations." *AgHR* 30:2 (1982),
pp. 97–111.
Behrens, C. B. A.
The Ancien Régime. London, 1975.
Beltrán, U. B.
"La hacienda de San Pedro Jorullo,
Michoacán, 1585–1795." *HMex* 26
(1977/104), pp. 540–75.
Berkner, L.
"The Stem Family and the
Developmental Cycle of the Peasant
Household: An Eighteenth-Century
Austrian Example." *AmHR* 77 (1972),
pp. 398–17.
"Inheritance, Land Tenure and Peasant
Family Structure: A German Regional
Comparison." In Goody, Thirsk,
Thompson, eds., *Family,* pp. 71–95.
Berkowitz, L.
A Survey of Social Psychology. Hinsdale,
1975.
Bernstein, H.
"African Peasantries: A Theoretical
Framework." *JPS* 6:4 (1979), pp.
421–43.
"The Agrarian Crisis and
Commoditization in Africa."
Agricultural University, Studium
Generale Paper 84, Wageningen, 1985.
Besouw, F. van, et al., eds.
*Balans en perspectief. Visies op de
geschiedwetenschap in Nederlands.*
Groningen, 1987.
Bethell, L., ed.
The Cambridge History of Latin America. 8
vols. Cambridge, 1984–1991.
Biddick, K.
"Medieval English Peasants and Market
Involvement." *JEH* 38 (1985), pp.
823–29.
Bishko, Ch. J.
"The Peninsular Background of Latin
American Cattle Ranching." *HAHR* 32
(1952), pp. 491–515.
Black, J.
"Tyranny as a Strategy for Survival in an
'Egalitarian' Society: Lurid Facts versus
an Anthropological Mystique." *Man*

7:4 (1972), pp. 614–34.
Blickle, P.
Die Revolution von 1525. 2nd ed. Munich,
1981.
Deutsche Untertanen, Ein Widerspruch.
Munich, 1981.
Bloch, M.
*Feudal Society. Volume One: The Growth of
the Ties of Dependence.* trans. from the
French, London, 1961.
*French Rural History. An Essay on Its Basic
Characteristics.* trans. from the French,
Berkeley, 1966.
Blum, J.
"The Rise of Serfdom in Eastern Europe."
AmHR 42 (1957), pp. 807–36.
The End of the Old Order in Rural Europe.
Princeton, 1978.
Bog, I., et al.
*Wirtschaftliche und soziale Strukturen im
saekularen Wandel.* Hannover, 1974.
Bois, G.
"Against the Neo-Malthusian
Orthodoxy." *PaP* 79 (1978), pp. 60–69.
Bolhuis, E. E., and J. D. van der Ploeg.
*Boerenarbeid en stijlen van
landbouwbeoefening.* Leiden, 1985.
Bonfil Batalla, G.
*Cholula. La ciudad sagrada en la era
industrial.* Mexico City, 1973.
México profundo. Una civilización negada.
Mexico City, 1987; repr., 1990.
Borah, W.
"Race and Class in Mexico." *PHR* 23
(1954), pp. 331–42.
*Justice by Insurance. The General Indian
Court of Colonial Mexico and the Legal
Aides of the Half Real.* Berkeley, 1983.
"Trends in Recent Studies of Colonial
Latin American Cities." *HAHR* 64
(1984), pp. 535–54.
"El status jurídico de los indios en Nueva
España." *AI* 45:2 (1985), pp. 257–76.
"Yet Another Look at the Techialoyan
Codices." In Harvey, ed., *Land,* pp.
209–21.
Borah, W., and S. F. Cook.
*The Population of Central Mexico in 1548.
An Analysis of the Suma de Visitas de*

Pueblo. Berkeley, 1963.
The Aboriginal Population of Central Mexico on the Eve of the Spanish Conquest. Berkeley, 1963.
Borrero Fernández, M.
"Gran propiedad y minifundismo en la 'tierra' sevillana a fines de la Edad Media: el ejemplo de Valencina del Alcor." *ArchHisp* 193/194 (1980), pp. 11–40.
El mundo rural sevillano en el siglo xv: Aljarafe y Ribera. Seville, 1983.
Bos, A.
"Don Gaspar contra Don Alonso. Conflicten in de Indiaanse gemeenschap van Atlacomulco, vallei van Toluca (1700–1713)." Doctoraalscriptie, Erasmus Universiteit Rotterdam, 1992.
Bosserup, E.
The Conditions of Agricultural Growth: The Economics of Agrarian Change Under Population Pressure. London, 1965.
Population and Technology. Oxford, 1981.
Brading, D. A.
Miners and Merchants in Bourbon Mexico, 1763–1810. Cambridge, 1971.
"Los españoles en México hacia 1792." *HMex* 23 (1973/89), pp. 126–44.
Los orígenes del nacionalismo mexicano. Mexico City, 1973.
"Estructura de la producción agrícola en El Bajío, 1700 a 1850." In Florescano, ed., *Haciendas,* pp. 105–31.
"The Capital Structure of Mexican Haciendas León, 1700–1850." *IAAnf* 1:2 (1975), pp. 151–83.
"The Historical Demography of Eighteenth-Century Mexico. A Review." *Bulletin SLAS* 25 (1976), pp. 3–17.
"Hacienda Profits and Tenant Farming in the Mexican Bajío, 1700–1860." In Duncan and Rutledge, eds., *Land,* pp. 23–58.
Haciendas and Ranchos in the Mexican Bajío. León 1700–1860. Cambridge, 1978.
"Population and Agriculture in Colonial Mexico." *JLAS* 13 (1981), pp. 404–5.

"Tridentine Catholicism and Enlightened Despotism in Bourbon Mexico." *JLAS* 15 (1983), pp. 1–22.
"Bourbon Spain and its American Empire." *CHLA* (1984), 1, pp. 389–439.
Prophecy and Myth in Mexican History. Cambridge, 1984.
"Facts and Figments in Bourbon Mexico." *BLAR* 4:1 (1985), pp. 61–64.
The Origins of Mexican Nationalism. Cambridge, 1985.
The First America. The Spanish Monarchy, Creole Patriots, and the Liberal State 1492–1867. Cambridge, 1991.
Brading, D. A., ed.,
Caudillo and Peasant in the Mexican Revolution. Cambridge, 1980.
Brading, D. A., and C. Wu.
"Population Growth and Crisis: León, 1720–1860," *JLAS* 5:1 (1972), pp. 1–36.
Braudel, F.
The Structures of Everyday Life: The Limits of the Possible (Civilization and Capitalism, 15th–18th Century. Part One). trans. from the French. London, 1985.
Bravo Ugarte, J., ed.
Conde de Revilla Gigedo, instrucción reservada al Marqués de Branciforte (1794). Mexico City, 1966.
Brenner, R.
"Agrarian Class Structure and Economic Development in Pre-industrial Europe." *PaP* 70 (1976), pp. 30–74.
"Agrarian Class Structure and Economic Development in Pre-industrial Europe: The Roots of European Capitalism." *PaP* 97 (1982), pp. 16–113.
Brewer, J.
"Commercialization and Politics." In McKendrick, ed., *Birth,* pp. 197–262.
Briggs, R.
Early Modern France, 1560–1715. Oxford, 1977.
Brinckmann S. L.
"Natalidad y mortalidad en Tecali (Puebla): 1701–1801." *Siglo XIX Revista de Historia* 4:7 (1989), pp. 219–69.
Bronner, F.
"Urban Society in Colonial Spanish

America: Research Trends." *LARR* 31 (1986), pp. 1–77.

Brooks, F. J.
"Parish and Cofradía in 18th Century Mexico." Ph.D. diss., Princeton University, 1976.

Brown, K.
Bourbons and Brandy. Imperial Reform in Eighteenth-Century Arequipa. Albuquerque, 1986.

Brown, L. R., et al.
State of the World 1990. New York, 1990.

Browning, D. G.
"Preliminary Comments on the 1776 Population Census of the Spanish Empire." *Bulletin SLAS* 19 (1974), pp. 5—13.

Brunner, K., and G. Joritz.
Landherr, Bauer, Ackerknecht. Der Bauer im Mittelalter, Klischee und Wirklichkeit. Cologne, 1985.

Brunner, O., W. Conze, and R. Kosseleck, eds.
Geschichtliche Grundbegriffe: Historisches Lexikon zur politischen-sozialen Sprache in Deutschland. Volume 3. Stuttgart, 1982.

Bryson, R. A. and C. Padoch.
"On the Climates of History." *JIH* 10:4 (1980), pp. 583–97.

Bullock, W.
Seis meses de residencia y viajes en México. trans. from the English. Mexico City, 1983. first published in London, 1825.

Bunker, S.
Underdeveloping the Amazon. Extraction, Unequal Exchange, and the Failure of the Modern State. Urbana and Chicago, 1985.

Burke, P.
Popular Culture in Early Modern Europe. London, 1978.
Historical Anthropology in Early Modern Italy. Cambridge, 1987.
Stadscultuur in Italië tussen renaissance en barok. trans. from the English. Amsterdam, 1988.

Burkholder, M. A., and D. S. Chandler.
From Impotence to Authority. The Spanish Crown and the American Audiencias,

1687–1808. Columbia, 1977.

Butlin, R. A.
The Transformation of Rural England, c. 1580–1800: A Study in Historical Geography. Oxford, 1982.

Buve, R.
"Peasant Mobilization and Reform Intermediaries During the Nineteen Thirties. The Development of a Peasant Clientele Around the Issue of Land and Labor in a Central Mexican Highland Municipio: Huamantla, Tlaxcala." *JbLA* 17 (1980), pp. 350–95.
"Agricultores, dominación política y estructura agraria en la Revolución mexicana: el caso de Tlaxcala (1910–1918)." In Buve, ed., *Haciendas*, pp. 199–271.

Buve, R., and R. Falcón.
"Tlaxcala and San Luis Potosí under the Sonorenses (1920–1934): Regional Revolutionary Power Groups and the National State." In Pansters and Ouweneel, eds., *Region*, pp. 110–33.

Buve, R., ed.
Haciendas in Central Mexico from Late Colonial Times to the Revolution. Amsterdam, 1984.

Calderón Quijano, J. A.
El Banco de San Carlos y las comunidades de indios en Nueva España. Seville, 1963.

Calvento Martínez, M. C.
"Intereses particulares y política de abastecimiento en México." *RdI* 36 (1976/143–144), pp. 159–211.

Calvo, Th.
"Démographie historique d'une paroisse mexicaine: Acatzingo (1606–1810)." *CAL* 6 (1972), pp. 7–42.
Acatzingo. Demografía de una parroquia mexicana. Mexico City, 1973.

Camacho Rueda, E.
Propiedad y explotación agraria en el Aljarafe sevillano: el caso de Pilas (1760–1925). Seville, 1984.

Canby, Th. Y.
"The Year the Weather Went Wild." *NG* 152:6 (1977), pp. 799–829.
"El Niño's Ill Wind." *NG* 165:2 (1984),

pp. 145–83.

Canudas Sandoval, E.
"Transición de un sistema de castas a un sistema de clases—el caso de México." *Estudios Políticos* 5 (1979/18–19), pp. 13–80.

Carmagnani, M.
El regreso de los dioses. El proceso de reconstitución de la identidad étnica en Oaxaca. Siglos XVII y XVIII. Mexico City, 1988.

Carrasco, P.,
"Social Organization of Ancient Mexico." In Wauchope, ed., *HMAI*, X, pp. 349–75.

Carrasco, P., et al.
La sociedad indígena en el Centro y Occidente de México. Zamora, 1986.

Carrasco, P., and J. Broda et al.
Estratificación social en la Mesoamérica prehispánica. Mexico City, 1976.
Economía política e ideología en el México prehispánico. Mexico City, 1978.

Carrera Stampa, M.
"The Evolution of Weights and Measures in New Spain." *HAHR* 29 (1949), pp. 2–24.
"Las ferias novohispanas." *HMex* 2 (1953/7), pp. 319–42.

Carroll, P.
"Estudio sociodemográfico de personas de sangre negra en Jalapa, 1791." *HMex* 23 (1973/89), pp. 111–25.
"Mandinga. The Evolution of a Mexican Runaway Slave Community, 1735–1827." *CSSH* 19 (1977), pp. 488–505.

Casado, H.
Señores, mercaderes y campesinos. La comarca de Burgos a fines de la Edad Media. Valladolid, 1987.

CASART,
Guía artesanal del estado de México. Toluca, 1984.

Castañeda, P., and J. Marchena.
"Las ordenes religiosas en América: propiedades, diezmos, exenciones y privilegios." *Anuario dEA* 35 (1978), pp. 125–58.

Castells, M.
The City and the Grassroots. A Cross-Cultural Theory of Urban Social Movements. Berkeley, 1984.

Castilleja, A.
"Asignación del espacio urbano: el gremio de panaderos, 1770–1793." In Moreno Toscano, ed., *Ciudad*, pp. 37–46.

Castoriadis, C.
The Imaginary Institution of Society. Oxford, 1987.

Castro Morales, E.
"Los cuadros de castas de la Nueva España." *JbLA* 20 (1983), pp. 671–90.

Chase, M.
"Can History be Green? A Prognosis." *Rural History*, 3:2 (1992), pp. 243–51.

Chamoux, M.-N.
Nahuas de Huauchinango. Transformaciones sociales en una comunidad campesina. Mexico City, 1987.

Chance, J. K.
Race and Class in Colonial Oaxaca. Stanford, 1978.
"On the Mexican Mestizo." *LARR* 14:3 (1979), pp. 153–68.
"The Ecology of Race and Class in Late Colonial Oaxaca." In Robinson, ed., *Studies*, pp. 93–117.
"Social Stratification and the Civil Cargo System among the Rincón Zapotecs of Oaxaca: The Late Colonial Period." In Garner and Taylor, eds., *Iberian Colonies*, pp. 143–59.
Conquest of the Sierra. Spaniards and Indians in Colonial Oaxaca. Norman, 1989.
"Indian Elites in Late Colonial Mesoamerica." Paper, Arizona State University, Tempe, 1990.
"The Barrios of Colonial Tecali: Patronage, Kinship, and Territorial Relations in a Central Mexican Community." Paper, Annual Meeting of the American Anthropological Association, Washington 1993.

Chance, J. K., and W. B. Taylor.
"Estate and Class in a Colonial City:

Oaxaca in 1792." *CSSH* 19:3 (1977), pp. 454–87.

"Estate and Class, A Reply." *CSSH* 21:3 (1979), pp. 434–42.

"*Cofradías* and *Cargos*: An Historical Perspective on the Mesoamerican Civil-Religious Hierarchy." *American Ethnologist* 12 (1985), pp. 1–26.

Charlton, Th.H.
"Land Tenure and Agricultural Production in the Otumba Region, 1785–1803." In Harvey, ed., *Land*, pp. 223–63.

Chaussinand-Nogaret, G.
The French Nobility in the Eighteenth Century: From Feudalism to Enlightenment. Cambridge, 1985.

Chávez Orozco, L.
Las cajas de comunidades indígenas de la Nueva España. Mexico City, 1934.
Las instituciones democráticas de los indígenas mexicanos en la época colonial. Mexico City, 1943.

Chayanov, A. V.
The Theory of the Peasant Economy. D. Thorner et al., eds. Homewood, 1966.

Chevalier, F.
La formation des grands domaines au Mexique: terre et société aux xvie–xviie siècle. Paris, 1952.
La formación de los grandes latifundios en México. Tierra y sociedad en los siglos xvi y xvii. trans. from the French. Mexico City, 1956.

Chevalier, J.
Civilization and the Stolen Gift. Capital, Kin, and Cult in Eastern Peru. Toronto, 1982.

Chirot, D.
"The Growth of the Market and Service Labor Systems in Agriculture." *JSH* 8:3 (1975), pp. 67–81.

Chisholm, M.
Rural Settlement and Land Use. London, 1979.

Chorley, G. P. H.
"The Agricultural Revolution in Northern Europe, 1750–1880: Nitrogen, Legumes and Crop Productivity." *EcHR* 34 (1981), pp. 71–93.

Cipolla, C. M.
Before the Industrial Revolution. European Society and Economy, 1000–1700. rev. ed. London, 1976.

Clark, C.
Population Growth and Land Use. London, 1967.

Clark, P.
"Migration in England during the Late Seventeenth and Early Eighteenth Centuries." *PaP* 83 (1979), pp. 57–90.

Clark, P., ed.
The Transformation of English Provincial Towns, 1600–1800. London, 1984.

Clarkson, L. A.
Proto-industrialisation. The First Phase of Industrialisation? London, 1985.

Clendinnen, I.
"Landscape and Worldview: The Survival of Yucatec Maya Culture Under Spanish Conquest." *CSSH* 22 (1980), pp. 374–93.

Cline, H.
"Civil Congregations of the Indians in New Spain, 1598–1606," *HAHR* 29 (1949), pp. 349–69.

Cline, S. L.
Colonial Culhuacan, 1580–1600. A Social History of an Aztec Town. Albuquerque, 1986.

Coe, M. D.
"The Chinampas of Mexico." *Scientific American* 211 (1964/1), pp. 90–98.

Cohen, A. P.
The Symbolic Construction of Community. London, 1985.
Whalsay: Symbol, Segment and Boundary in a Shetland Island Community. Manchester, 1987.

Cohen, A. P., ed.
Symbolising Boundaries: Identity and Diversity in British Cultures. Manchester, 1986.

Cole, J., ed.
Church and State in Latin America. New Orleans, 1984.

Coleman, D. C.
"Labour in the English Economy of the Seventeenth Century." *EcHR* 8 (1956), pp. 280–95.

Colín, M.
  *Antecedentes agrarios del municipio de
  Atlacomulco, Estado de México.
  Documentos.* Mexico City, 1963.
Collier, G. A., R. J. Rosaldo, and J. D. Wirth,
  eds.
  *The Inca and Aztec States 1400–1800.
  Anthropology and History.* New York,
  1982.
Collomp, A.
  "Alliance et filiation en Haute-Provence
  au 18e siècle." *Annales ESC* 32 (1977),
  pp. 445–77.
  "Tensions, Dissensions, and Ruptures
  Inside the Family in Seventeenth- and
  Eighteenth-Century Haute-Provence."
  In Medick and Sabean, eds., *Interest*,
  pp. 145–70.
  "From Stem Family to Nuclear Family:
  Changes in the Coresident Domestic
  Group in Haute-Provence between the
  End of the Eighteenth and the Middle
  of the nineteenth Centuries." *CaC* 3:1
  (1988), pp. 65–81.
Connell, K. H.
  Irish Peasant Society. Four Historical Essays.
  Oxford, 1968.
Cook, S. F.
  *The Historical Demography and Ecology of
  the Teotlalpan.* Berkeley, 1949.
Cook, S., and W. Borah.
  *The Indian Population of Central Mexico,
  1531–1610.* Berkeley, 1960.
  "Indian Food Production and
  Consumption in Central Mexico
  Before and After the Conquest." In
  their *Essays*, 3, pp. 129–76.
  Essays in Population History. 3 vols.
  Berkeley, 1971, 1974, 1979.
Cooper, D. B.
  *Epidemic Disease in Mexico City
  1761–1813: An Administrative, Social
  and Medical Study.* Austin, 1965.
Cooper, J. P.
  "In Search of Agrarian Capitalism." *PaP*,
  80 (1978), pp. 20–65.
Cope, R. D.
  "The Limits of Racial Domination:
  Plebeian Society in Colonial Mexico

City, 1660–1720." Ph.D. diss.,
  University of Wisconsin, Madison,
  1987.
Corbin, A.
  *Le territoire du vide, l'Occident et le désir du
  rivage (1740–1840).* Paris, 1988.
  Het verlangen naar de kust. trans. from the
  French. Nijmegen, 1989.
Costeloe, M. P.
  *Church Wealth in Mexico. A Study of the
  'Juzgado de Capellanías' in the
  Archbishopric of Mexico, 1800–1856.*
  Cambridge, 1967.
Couturier, E. B.
  "Hacienda of Hueyapán. The History of a
  Mexican Social and Economic
  Institution, 1550–1940." Ph.D. diss.,
  Columbia University, 1965.
  "Micaela Angela Carrillo: Widow and
  Pulque Dealer." In Sweet and Nash,
  eds., *Struggle*, pp. 362–75.
  "Pedro Romero de Terreros: ¿comerciante
  o empresario capitalista del siglo
  XVIII?" In Florescano, ed., *Orígenes*,
  pp. 17–32.
Croot, P. and D. Parker.
  "Agrarian Class Structure and Economic
  Development." *PaP* 78 (1978), pp.
  37–47.
Crosby, A.
  *Ecological Imperialism. The Biological
  Expansion of Europe, 900–1900.*
  Cambridge, 1986.
Cross, H. E.
  "Living Standards in Rural Nineteenth-
  Century Mexico: Zacatecas,
  1820–1880." *JLAS* 10:1 (1978), pp.
  1–19.
Crouch, D. P.
  "Roman Models for Spanish
  Colonization." In Hurst Thomas, ed.,
  Columbian Consequences, ed., 3, pp.
  21–35.
Cruz Villalón, J.
  *Propiedad y uso de la tierra en la Baja
  Andalucía. Carmona, siglos XVIII–XX.*
  Madrid, 1980.
Cuello, J.
  "El mito de la hacienda colonial en el

norte de México." In Ouweneel and
Torales, comps., *Empresarios*, pp.
186–205.

Cuenca Esteban, J.
"Statistics of Spain's Colonial Trade,
1792–1820: Consular Duties, Cargo
Inventories, and Balance of Trade."
HAHR 61 (1981), pp. 381–428.

Damen, M., et al., eds.
*Geschiedenis, psychologie, mentaliteit.
Negen discussiebijdragen.* Amsterdam,
1982.

Darnton, R.
*The Great Cat Massacre and Other Episodes
in French Cultural History.* New York,
1985.

Davies, W.
*Small Worlds. The Village Community in
Early Medieval Brittany.* Berkeley and
Los Angeles, 1988.

Dealy, G.
"Prolegomena on the Spanish American
Political Tradition." *HAHR* 48 (1968),
pp. 37–58.
"The Tradition of Monistic Democracy in
Latin America." *JHId* 34:4 (1974), pp.
625–46.

Deans-Smith, S.
"The Money Plant: The Royal Tobacco
Monopoly of New Spain, 1765–1821."
Jacobsen and Puhle, eds., *Economies*,
pp. 361–87.

Dehouve, D.
"The 'Secession' of Villages in the
Jurisdiction of Tlapa (Eighteenth
Century)." Ouweneel and Miller, eds.,
Indian Community, pp. 162–82.
"El pueblo de indios y el mercado: Tlapa
(Guerrero) en el siglo xviii." Ouweneel
and Torales, comps., *Empresarios*, pp.
86–102.
*Quand les banquiers étaient de Saints. 450
ans de l'histoire économique et sociale
d'une province indienne de Mexique.*
Paris, 1990.

Delgado Ribas, J.
"La integración de Hispanoamérica en el
mercado mundial." *BolAm* 23 (1981/
31), pp. 41–52.

Delort, R.
Les Animaux ont une histoire. Paris, 1984.

Denevan, W. M., ed.
*The Native Population of the Americas in
1492.* Madison, 1976.

Derrida, J.
*The Post Card: From Socrates to Freud and
Beyond.* trans. from the French.
Chicago, 1987.
Margins of Philosophy. trans. from the
French. Chicago, 1982.

Devine, Th. M., ed.
*Farm Servants and Labour in Lowland
Scotland, 1770–1914.* Edinburgh, 1984.

Díaz Palacios, J.
*El Perú y su medio ambiente. Southern Peru
Copper Corporation, una compleja
agesión ambiental en el sur del país.*
Lima, 1988.

Dirks, R.
"Social Responses During Severe Food
Shortages and Famine." *Current
Anthropology* 21:1 (1980), pp. 1–44.

Domínguez, J. I.
*Insurrection or Loyalty. The Breakdown of
the Spanish American Empire.*
Cambridge, 1980.

Dorfman, A.
*Some Write to the Future. Essays on
Contemporary Latin American Fiction.*
Durham and London, 1991.

Duby, G.
Early Growth of the European Economy.
trans. from the French. London, 1974.
*Les trois ordres ou l'imaginaire du
féodalisme.* Paris, 1978.

Dumont, L.
Religion, Politics and History in India. The
Hague, 1970.

Duncan, K., and I. Rutledge, eds.
*Land and Labour in Latin America. Essays
on the Development of Agrarian
Capitalism in the Nineteenth and
Twentieth Centuries.* Cambridge, 1977.

Dunn, E.S.
The Location of Agricultural Production.
Gainesville, 1967.

Dyckerhof, U.
"Colonial Indian Corporate

Landholding: A Glimpse from the
Valley of Puebla." In Ouweneel and
Miller, eds., *Indian Community*, pp.
40–59.

Dyer, C.
"The Past, the Present and the Future in
Medieval Rural History." *Rural History.
Economy, Society, Culture* 1:1 (1990),
pp. 37–49.

Eco, U. and Th. A. Sebeok, eds.
The Sign of Three: Dupin, Holmes, Peirce.
Bloomington, 1983.

Eddy, J. A.
"Climate and the Role of the Sun." *JIH*
10:4 (1980), pp. 725–47.

Eerenbeemt, H. F. J. M. van den.
"De 'Rode Dood' in stad en Meierij van
's-Hertogenbosch; een dysenterie-
epidemie in de jaren 1779–1783." *ESHJ*
36 (1973), pp. 75–101.

Elias, N.
The Civilizing Process. 2 vols. New York,
1978 and 1982.
The Symbol Theory. London, 1991. Earlier
published in three parts in *Theory,
Culture and Society,* 6:2 (1989), pp.
169–217; 6:3 (1989); pp. 339–83; and
6:4 (1989), pp. 499–537.

Enge, K. I., and S. Whiteford.
*The Keepers of Water and Earth. Mexican
Rural Social Organization and Irrigation.*
Austin, 1989.

Ennew, J., P. Hirst, and K. Tribe.
"'Peasantry' as an Economic Category."
JPS 4:4 (1977), pp. 295–322.

Ewald, U.
"Versuche zur Änderung der
Besitzverhältnisse in den letzten
Jahrzehnten der Kolonialzeit.
Bestrebungen im Hochbecken von
Puebla-Tlaxcala und seiner Umgebung
zur Rückführung von *Hacienda*-land an
Gutsarbeiter und indianische
Dorfgemeinschaften." *JbLA* 7 (1970),
pp. 239–51.
"Das Poblaner Jesuitenkollegium San
Francisco Xavier und sein
Landwirtschaftlicher Grossbesitz."
JbLA 8 (1971), pp. 39–73.

*Estudios sobre la hacienda colonial en
México. Las propiedades rurales del
Colegio Espíritu Santo en Puebla.*
Wiesbaden, 1976.
"The von Thünen-principle and
Agricultural Zonation in Colonial
Mexico." *Journal of Historical Geography*
3:2 (1977), pp. 123–33.
*The Mexican Salt Industry 1560–1980. A
Study in Change.* Stuttgart, 1985.

Eysberg, C. D.
"Gebruik en misbruik van het model van
von Thünen in de geografie."
Geografisch Tijdschrift 13 (1979), pp.
15–31.

Farriss, N. M.
"Indians in Colonial Yucatán: Three
Perspectives." In MacLeod and
Wasserstrom, eds., *Spaniards*, pp. 1–39.
*Maya Society under Colonial Rule: The
Collective Enterprise of Survival.*
Princeton, 1984.

Favre, H.
"The Dynamics of Indian Peasant Society
and Migration to Coastal Plantations
in Central Peru." In Duncan and
Rutledge, eds., *Land*, pp. 253–67.

Fenoaltea, S.
"The Rise and Fall of a Theoretical
Model: The Manorial System." *JEH* 35
(1975), pp. 386–409.

Fernández, R., ed.
*España en el siglo XVIII. Homenaje a Pierre
Vilar.* Barcelona, 1985.

Fernández de Lizardi, J. J.
El Periquillo Sarniento. Mexico City, 1918;
repr. 1959.

Fischer, D. H.
*Historians' Fallacies. Toward a Logic of
Historical Thought.* New York, 1970.

Fischer, W.
"Rural Industrialization and Population
Change." *CSSH* 15 (1973), pp. 158–70.

Florescano, E.
"El abasto y la legislación de granos en el
siglo xvi." *HMex* 14 (1965), pp.
567–630.
*Precios del maíz y crisis agrícolas en México
(1708–1810).* Mexico City, 1969.

Orígen y desarrollo de los problemas agrarios de México, 1500–1821. Mexico City, 1976.
"The Hacienda in New Spain." CHLA (1984), 2, pp. 153–88.
Florescano, E., coord.
Haciendas, latifundios y plantaciones en América Latina. Mexico City, 1975.
Orígenes y desarrollo de los problemas agrarios de México, 1500–1821. Mexico City, 1976.
Florescano, E., et al.,
La clase obrera en la historia de México. Volúmen I: de la colonia al imperio. Mexico City, 1980.
Florescano, E., and I. Gil, comps.
Descripciones económicas generales de Nueva España, 1784–1817. Mexico City, 1973.
Descripciones económicas regionales de Nueva España. Provincias del Centro, Sudeste y Sur, 1766–1827. Mexico City, 1973.
Florescano, E., and I. Gil.
"La época de las reformas borbónicas y el crecimiento económico, 1750–1808." HGdM, 2, pp. 183–301.
Florescano, E., and V. San Vicente, eds.
Fuentes para la historia de la crisis agrícola (1809–1811). Mexico City, 1985.
Flynn, M.
Sacred Charity. Confraternities and Social Welfare in Spain, 1400–1700. New York, 1989.
Forster, R.
"Obstacles to Agricultural Growth in Eighteenth-Century France." AmHR 75 (1970), pp. 1600–15.
"Achievements of the Annales School." JEH 38 (1978), pp. 58–76.
Forster, R, and O. Ranum, eds.
Rural Society in France. Selections from the Annales Economies, Sociétés, Civilisations. Baltimore, 1977.
Fortmann, H. M. M.
Wat is er met de mens gebeurd? Over de taak van een vergelijkende cultuurpsychologie. Utrecht and Antwerpen, 1959.

Foster, G. M.
Culture and Conquest. America's Spanish Heritage. Chicago, 1960.
"Peasant Society and the Image of Limited Good." American Anthropologist 67 (1965), pp. 293–315.
Foss, D. A., and R. Larkin.
Beyond Revolution. A New Theory of Social Movements. South Hadley, Mass., 1986.
Foucault, M.
The History of Sexuality. Volume One: An Introduction. trans. from the French. New York, 1980.
Fox, B., ed.
Hidden in the Household: Women's Domestic Labour Under Capitalism. Ontario, 1980.
Frank, A. G.
Capitalism and Underdevelopment in Latin America. New York, 1969.
Latin America: Underdevelopment or Revolution. New York, 1969.
World Accumulation, 1492–1789. New York, 1978.
Mexican Agriculture 1521–1630. Cambridge, 1979.
Fremantle, A., ed.
Latin American Literature Today. New York, 1977.
Freudenberger, H.
"Das Arbeitsjahr." In Bog, Strukturen, 3, pp. 307–20.
Friedlander, J.
Being Indian in Hueyapan. A Study of Forced Identity in Contemporary Mexico. New York, 1975.
Friedmann, H.
"Household Production and the National Economy: Concepts for the Analysis of Agrarian Formations." JPS 7:2 (1980), pp. 158–84.
Frijhoff, W.
"Cultuur en mentaliteit: over sporen, tekens en bronnen." In Van Besouw et al., eds., Balans, pp. 189–204.
Frost, E. C., M. C. Meyer, and J. Z. Vázquez, eds.
El trabajo y los trabajadores en la historia de México. Mexico City and Tucson, 1979.

Garavaglia, J. C.
  Mercado interno y economía colonial.
  Mexico City, 1983.
Garavaglia, J. C., et al.
  Modos de producción en América Latina.
  Mexico City, 1973.
Garavaglia, J. C., and J. C. Grosso.
  "La región de Puebla-Tlaxcala y la
  economía novohispana (1670–1821)."
  HMex 35 (1986/140), pp. 549–600.
  "De Veracruz a Durango: un análisis
  regional de la Nueva España
  borbónica." *Siglo XIX. Revista de
  Historia* 2:4 (1987), pp. 9–52.
  "Mexican Elites of a Provincial Town:
  The Landowners of Tepeaca." *HAHR*
  70:2 (1990), pp. 255–93.
García, C.
  "Sociedad, crédito y cofradía en la Nueva
  España. El caso de Nuestra Señora de
  Aránzazu." *Historias* 3 (1983), pp.
  53–68.
García Acosta, V.
  "Manufactura y colonia. Las panaderías
  de la ciudad de México en el siglo
  XVIII." Tesis Maestría, Universidad
  Iberoamericana, Mexico City, 1985.
  "Oscilación de los precios y de la
  producción: el trigo y el pan." In
  Ouweneel and Torales, comps.,
  Empresarios, pp. 116–37.
  *Las panaderías, sus dueños y trabajadores.
  Ciudad de México, Siglo XVIII.* Mexico
  City, 1989.
García-Baquero González, A.
  *Cádiz y el Atlántico. El comercio colonial
  español bajo el monopolio gaditano.* 2
  vols. Seville, 1976.
García-Baquero, A., and L. C. Alvarez
  Santaló.
  "El utilaje agrícola en la tierra de Sevilla,
  1700–1833." *ArchHisp* 193–194 (1980),
  pp. 235–68.
García de Cortázar, J. A.
  La sociedad rural en la España medieval.
  Madrid, 1988.
García de Cortázar, J. A., et al.
  *Organización del espacio en la España
  medieval. La Corona de Castilla en los
  siglos viii a xv.* Barcelona, 1985.

García Martínez, B.
  *El Marquesado del Valle. Tres siglos de
  régimen señorial en Nueva España.*
  Mexico City, 1969.
  Historia de México. León, 1985.
  *Los pueblos de la Sierra. El poder y el
  espacio entre los indios del norte de
  Puebla hasta 1700.* Mexico City, 1987.
  "*Pueblos de Indios, Pueblos de Castas*: New
  Settlements and Traditional Corporate
  Organization in Eighteenth-Century
  New Spain." In Ouweneel and Miller,
  eds., *Indian Community*, pp. 103–16.
  "Jurisdicción y propiedad: una distinción
  fundamental en la historia de los
  pueblos de indios del México
  colonial." *ERLACS* 53 (1992), pp.
  47–60.
García Sanz, A.
  *Desarrollo y crisis del antiguo régimen en
  Castilla la Vieja. Economía y sociedad en
  tierras de Segovia, 1500–1814.* 2d ed.
  Madrid, 1986.
  "El interior peninsular en el siglo XVIII:
  un crecimiento moderado y
  tradicional." In Fernández, ed.,
  España, pp. 630–80.
Garner, R. L.
  "Silver Production and Entrepreneurial
  Structure in Eighteenth-Century
  Mexico." *JbLA* 17 (1980), pp. 157—86.
  "Exportación de circulante en el siglo
  XVIII (1750–1810)." *HMex* 31 (1982/
  124), pp. 544–98.
  "Price Trends in Eighteenth-Century
  Mexico." *HAHR* 65 (1985), pp.
  279–326.
  *Economic Growth and Change in Bourbon
  Mexico.* Gainesville, 1993.
Garner, R. L., and W. B. Taylor, eds.
  *Iberian Colonies, New World Societies:
  Essays in Memory of Charles Gibson.* 2d
  ed. private printing, 1985.
Gaskin, K.
  "Age at First Marriage in Europe before
  1850: A Summary of Family
  Reconstitution Data." *JFH* 3 (1978),
  pp. 23–36.
Geertz, C.
  Peddlers and Princes: Social Development

and *Economic Change in Two Indonesian Towns*. Chicago, 1963.
Agricultural Involution. The Process of Ecological Change in Indonesia. Berkeley, 1971.

Gemelli Careri, G. F.
Viaje a la Nueva España. ed. Francisca Perujo. Mexico City, 1976.

Georgescu-Roegen, N.
"The Institutional Aspects of Peasant Communities: An Analytical View." In Wharton, ed., *Subsistence Agriculture*, pp. 61–93.

Gerhard, P.
A Guide to the Historical Geography of New Spain. Cambridge, 1972.
"La evolución del pueblo mexicano: 1519–1975." *HMex* 24 (1975/96), pp. 566–78.

Germani, G.
"Stages of Modernization in Latin America." In Halper and Sterling, eds., *Latin America*, pp. 1–43.

Gibson, Ch.
Tlaxcala in the Sixteenth Century. New Haven, 1952.
The Aztecs under Spanish Rule. A History of the Indians of the Valley of Mexico, 1519–1810. Stanford, 1964.
"Indian Societies under Spanish Rule." In the *CHLA* (1984), II, pp. 381–419.

Giddens, A.
The Constitution of Society. Outline of the Theory of Structuration. Cambridge, 1984.

Gil, J.
Mitos y utopías del descubrimiento. 3 vols. Madrid, 1989.

Ginzburg, C.
I Benandanti. Torino, 1966.
The Night Battles. trans. from the Italian. London, 1983.
Il Formaggio e i Vermi. Il Cosmo di un Mugnaio del '500. Torino, 1976.
The Cheese and the Worms. The Cosmos of a Sixteenth-Century Miller. trans. from the Italian. New York, 1982.
De kaas en de wormen. Het wereldbeeld van een zestiende-eeuwse molenaar. trans. from the Italian. Amsterdam, 1982.

Glaser, R., and R. Walsh, eds.
Historical Climatology in Different Climatic Zones. Würzburg, 1991.

Glass, D. V., and D. E. C. Eversley, eds.
Population in History. London, 1965.

Goldsmith, J. L.
"The Agrarian History of Pre-Industrial France. Where Do We Go From Here?" *JEEH* 13 (1984), pp. 175–99.

González, L.
Pueblo en vilo. Microhistoria de San José de Gracia. Mexico City, 1968.

González Angulo Aguirre, J.
"Los gremios de artesanos y la estructura urbana." In Moreno Toscano, ed., *Ciudad de México*, pp. 25–36.
Artesanado y ciudad a finales del siglo XVIII. Mexico City, 1983.

González Sánchez, Isabel.
Los trabajadores alquilados de Tlaxcala para las haciendas foráneas, siglo XVIII. Mexico City, 1976.

Goodman, D., and M. Redclift.
From Peasant to Proletarian. Capitalist Development and Agrarian Transitions. Oxford, 1981.
Environment and Development in Latin America. The Politics of Sustainability. Manchester, 1991.

Goody, J., J. Thirsk, and E. P. Thompson, eds.
Family and Inheritance. Rural Society in Western Europe, 1200–1800. Cambridge, 1976.

Goody, J.
The Development of the Family and Marriage in Europe. Cambridge, 1983.

Gormsen, E.
"Wochenmärkte im Bereich von Puebla. Struktur und Entwicklung eines traditionellen Austauschsystems in Mexiko." *JbLA* 8 (1971), pp. 366–400.

Gortari Krauss, L. de.
Pueblos indios en la jurisdicción de la alcaldía mayor de Yahualica. Mexico City, 1986.

Goubert, P.
Beauvais et le Beauvaisis de 1600 à 1730. Paris, 1960.
The Ancien Régime. French Society,

1600–1750. trans. from the French. New York, 1973.

Gould, J.
Economic Growth in History. London, 1972.

Goy, J., and E. LeRoy Ladurie, eds.
Prestations paysannes, dîmes, rente foncière et mouvement de la production agricole a l'époque préindustrielle. 2 vols. Paris, 1982.

GRAL.
El valle de Toluca. Raíces indígenas, luchas campesinos y suburbanización. Toulouse, 1978.

Greenleaf, R.
"Land and Water in Mexico and New Mexico, 1700–1821." *New Mexico Historical Review* 47 (1972), pp. 85–112.

Greenow, L.
"Marriage Patterns and Regional Interaction in Late Colonial Nueva Galicia." In Robinson, ed., *Studies*, pp. 119–47.
Credit and Socioeconomic Change in Colonial Mexico. Loans and Mortgages in Guadalajara, 1720–1820. Boulder, 1983.

Gregson, N.
"The Multiple Estate Model: Some Critical Questions." *Journal of Historical Geography* 11 (1985), pp. 339–51.

Grieshaber, E.
"Hacienda-Indian Community Relations and Indian Acculturation: An Historiographical Essay." *LARR* 14:3 (1979), pp. 107–28.

Grigg, D.
Population Growth and Agrarian Change: An Historical Perspective. Cambridge, 1980.
The Dynamics of Agricultural Change. The Historical Experience. London, 1982.

Gruzinski, S.
Les Hommes-dieux de Mexique. Pouvoir indien et société, XVIe-XVIIIe siècles. Paris, 1985.
"La mère dévorante: alcoolisme, sexualité, et déculturation chez les Mexicas (1500–1550)." *CAL* 20 (1979), pp. 5–36.
"La 'segunda aculturación': el estado ilustrado y la religiosidad indígena en Nueva España (1775–1800)." *Estudios Novohispana* 8 (1985), pp. 175–201.
"La red agujerada. Identidades étnicas y occidentalización en el México colonial (Siglos XVI–XIX)." *AI* 36:6 (1986), pp. 411–33.
El poder sin límites. Cuatro respuestas indígenas a la dominación española. trans. from the French. Mexico City, 1988.
"Indian Confraternities, Brotherhoods and *Mayordomías* in Central New Spain. A List of Questions for the Historian and the Anthropologist." In Ouweneel and Miller, eds., *Indian Community*, pp. 205–23.
La colonización de lo imaginario. Sociedades indígenas y occidentalización en el México español. Siglos XVI–XVIII. trans. from the French. rev. ed. Mexico City, 1991.

Guerra, F.-X.
Le Mexique de l'Ancien Régime a la Révolution. 2 vols. Paris, 1985.

Guerrero, R.
El pulque. Religión, cultura, folklore. Mexico City, 1980.

Gullickson, G. L
Spinners and Weavers of Auffay: Rural Industry and the Sexual Division of Labor in a French Village, 1750–1850. New York, 1986.

Gunn, J., and R. E. W. Adams.
"Climatic Change, Culture, and Civilization in North America." *World Archaeology*, 13:1 (1981), pp. 87–100.

Gusfield, J. R.
Community: A Critical Response. Oxford, 1975.

Gutman, H.
"Work, Culture, and Society in Industrializing America, 1815–1819." *AmHR* 78 (1973), pp. 531–87.

Gutmann, M. P.
Toward the Modern Economy. Early Industry

in Europe, 1500–1800. New York, 1988.

Hagen, W. W.

"Working for the Junker: The Standard of Living of Manorial Laborers in Brandenburg, 1684–1810." *JMH* 58 (1986), pp. 143–58.

Hajnal, L.

"European Marriage Patterns in Perspective." In Glass and Eversley, eds., *Population*, pp. 101–43.

Halper, S.A., and J. R. Sterling, eds. *Latin America. The Dynamics of Social Change.* London, 1972.

Halperin, R., and J. Dow, eds. *Peasant Livelihood: Studies in Economic Anthropology and Cultural Ecology.* New York, 1977.

Hamill Jr., H. M.

"Early Psychological Warfare in the Hidalgo Revolt." *HAHR* 41 (1961), pp. 206–35.

Hamnett, B.

"The Appropriation of Mexican Church Wealth by the Spanish Bourbon Government. The Consolidación de Vales Reales, 1805–1809." *JLAS* 1:2 (1969), pp. 85–113.

"Dye Production, Food Supply and the Laboring Population of Oaxaca, 1750–1820." *HAHR* 51 (1971), pp. 51–78.

Politics and Trade in Southern Mexico, 1750–1821. Cambridge, 1971.

The Mexican Bureaucracy Before the Bourbon Reforms, 1700–1770: A Study in the Limitations of Absolutism. Glasgow, 1979.

"Mexico's Royalist Coalition: The Response to Revolution, 1808–1821." *JLAS* 12 (1980), pp. 55–86.

"Royalist Counterinsurgency and the Continuity of Rebellion: Guanajuato and Michoacán, 1813–1820." *HAHR* 62 (1982), pp. 19–48.

Social Structure and Regional Elites in Late Colonial Mexico, 1750–1824. Glasgow, 1984.

Roots of Insurgency. Mexican Regions, 1750–1824. Cambridge, 1986.

Hanawalt, B. A.

The Ties That Bound. Peasant Families in Medieval England. Oxford, 1986.

Haring, C. H.

The Spanish Empire in America. New York, 1947; repr. 1975.

Harris, C., ed.

The Sociology of the Family: New Directions for Britain. Keele, 1979.

Harris III, Ch.

A Mexican Family Empire. The Latifundio of the Sánchez-Navarros, 1765–1867. Austin, 1975.

Harrison, P.

The Third Revolution. Environment, Population and a Sustainable World. London and New York, 1992.

Harvey, H. R.

"Aspects of Land Tenure in Ancient Mexico." In Harvey and Prem, eds., *Explorations*, pp. 83–102.

Harvey, H. R., ed.

Land and Politics in the Valley of Mexico. A Two Thousand Year Perspective. Albuquerque, 1991.

Harvey, H. R., and H. J. Prem, eds. *Explorations in Ethnohistory. Indians of Central Mexico in the Sixteenth Century.* Albuquerque, 1984.

Harvey, M.

"Planned Field Systems in Eastern Yorkshire: Some Thoughts on Their Origin." *AgHR* 31:2 (1983), pp. 91–103.

Haskett, R. S.

"A Social History of Indian Town Government in the Colonial Cuernavaca Jurisdiction, Mexico." Ph.D. diss., University of California, Los Angeles, 1985.

"Indian Town Government in Colonial Cuernavaca: Persistence, Adaptation, and Change." *HAHR* 67 (1987), pp. 203–31.

"Indian Community Land and Municipal Income in Colonial Cuernavaca. An Investigation through Nahuatl Document." In Ouweneel and Miller, eds., *Indian Community*, pp. 130–41.

"'Our Suffering with the Taxco Tribute':
Involuntary Mine Labor and
Indigenous Society in Central New
Spain." *HAHR* 71:3 (1991), pp. 447–75.
*Indigenous Rulers. An Ethnohistory of Town
Government in Colonial Cuernavaca.*
Albuquerque, 1991.
Hassig, R.
*Trade, Tribute, and Transportation. The
Sixteenth-Century Political Economy of
the Valley of Mexico.* Norman, 1985.
Heath Constable, H. J.
*Lucha de clases. La industria textil en
Tlaxcala.* Mexico City, 1982.
Henao, L. E.
Tehuacán. Campesinado e irrigación.
Mexico City, 1980.
Hernández Palomo, J. J.
*La renta del pulque en Nueva España,
1663–1810.* Seville, 1979.
Herrera García, A.
*El aljarafe sevillano durante el antiguo
régimen.* Seville, 1980.
Hewitt, C.
"Boundaries and Paradigms: the
Anthropological Study of Rural Life in
Post-Revolutionary Mexico."
Proefschrift Rijksuniversiteit Leiden,
1982.
Hilgard, E. R., R. C. and R. L. Atkinson.
Introduction to Psychology. New York,
1975, 6th ed..
Hilton, R. H.
*The English Peasantry in the Later Middle
Ages.* Oxford, 1975.
"A Crisis of Feudalism," *PaP* 80 (1978),
pp. 3–20.
"Medieval Market Towns and Simple
Commodity Production." *PaP* 109
(1985), pp. 3–23.
Hoberman, L.
"Hispanic American Political Theory as a
Distinct Tradition." *JHId* 41:2 (1980),
pp. 199–218.
Hoberman, L. S., and S. M. Socolow, eds.
*Cities and Society in Colonial Latin
America.* Albuquerque, 1986.
Hobsbawm, E., and T. Ranger, eds.
The Invention of Tradition. Cambridge,
1983.

Hochstadt, S.
"Migration in Preindustrial Germany."
Central European History 16:3 (1983),
pp. 195–224.
Hoekstra, R.
"A Different Way of Thinking:
Contrasting Spanish and Indian Social
and Economic Views in Central
Mexico (1550–1600)." In Ouweneel
and Miller, eds., *Indian Community*, pp.
60–86.
"A Changing Order. Congregation
Politics in Mexico (1550–1605)." Ms.,
Amsterdam, 1990.
"Profit from the Waste Lands. Social
Change and the Formation of
Haciendas in the Valley of Puebla
(1570–1640)." *ERLACS* 52 (1992), pp
91–123.
*Two Worlds Merging. The Transformation
of Society in the Valley of Puebla,
1570–1640.* Amsterdam, 1993.
Hoetink, H.
*Caribbean Race Relations. A Study of Two
Variants.* Oxford, 1967.
Hoffman, Ph. T.
"The Modern Economic Theory of
Sharecropping in Early Modern
France." *JEH* 44:2 (1984), pp. 309–19.
*Church and Community in the Diocese of
Lyon, 1500–1789.* New Haven, 1984.
Hollander, P.
*Political Pilgrims. Travels of Western
Intellectuals to the Soviet Union, China
and Cuba (1928–1978).* Oxford, 1981.
Holton, R. J.
*The Transition From Feudalism to
Capitalism.* London, 1985.
Howell, C.
*Land, Family and Inheritance in Transition:
Kibworth Harcourt 1278–1700.*
Cambridge, 1983.
Hoyt, R. S., and S. Chodorow.
Europe in the Middle Ages. 3d ed. New
York, 1976.
Hufton, O. H.
*The Poor of Eighteenth-Century France,
1750–1789.* Oxford, 1974.
Humboldt, A. von.
Ensayo político sobre el reino de la Nueva

España. Mexico City, 1822; repr.,
Mexico City, 1978.

Hunt, D.
"Chayanov's Model of Peasant
Household Resource Allocation." *JPS*
6:3 (1979), pp. 247–85.

Hurtado, F.
"Dolores Hidalgo en el siglo XVIII. Una
aproximación cuantitativa." *HMex* 27
(1978/108), pp. 507–40.

Hurst Thomas, D., ed.
*Columbian Consequences. Volume Three:
The Spanish Borderlands in Pan-
American Perspective*. Washington,
1991.

Hutton, P. H.
"The History of Mentalities: The New
Map of Cultural History." *HaT* 20
(1981), pp. 237–59.

Ingham, J. M.
*Mary, Michael and Lucifer. Folk Catholicism
in Central Mexico*. Austin, 1986.

Inglehart, R.
Culture Shift in Advanced Industrial Society.
Princeton, 1990.

Izard, M.
"Metropolitanos, Criollos y Reformistas.
La Nueva España de Revillagigedo
(1789–1794)." *BolAm* 22 (1980/30), pp.
181–222.
"Reformismo borbónico e insurgencias
indianas." *JbLA* 21 (1984), pp. 155–70.

Jackson, S.
"Population and Change. A Study of the
Spatial Variations in Population
Growth in North East Somerset and
West Wiltshire, 1701–1800." Ph.D.
diss., University of Liverpool, 1980.

Jacobs, I.
*Ranchero Revolt. The Mexican Revolution in
Guerrero*. Austin, 1982.

Jacobsen, N., and H.-J. Puhle, eds.
*The Economies of Mexico and Peru During
the Late Colonial Period, 1760–1810*.
Berlin, 1986.

Jacquart, J.
La crise rurale en Ile-de-france, 1550–1670.
Paris, 1975.

Jarquín Ortega, Ma.T.
Formación y desarrollo de un pueblo

*novohispano: Metepec en el valle de
Toluca*. Zinacantepec, 1990.

Jarquín Ortega, Ma.T., J. F. Leal y
Fernández, P. Luna Marez, R. Rendón
Garcini, Ma.E. Romero Ibarra, coords.
*Origen y evolución de la hacienda en
México: siglos XVI al XX. Memorias del
Simposio Realizado del 27 al 30 de
Septiembre de 1989*. Zinacantepec,
1990.

Johnson, L.
"Artisans." In Hoberman and Socolow,
eds., *Cities*, pp. 227–50.

Jones, G. D.
*Maya Resistance to Spanish Rule. Time and
History on a Colonial Frontier*.
Albuquerque, 1989.

Jones, P. M.
*Politics and Rural Society. The Southern
Massif Central, c. 1750–1880*.
Cambridge, 1985.

Joseph, G.M.
*Revolution from Without. Yucatán, Mexico
and the United States, 1880–1924*.
Durham, 1988.

Kagan, S.
*Penal Servitude in New Spain: The Colonial
Textile Industry*. Ann Arbor, 1977.

Kamen, H.
European Society, 1500–1700. London,
1984.

Kaplan, S.
*Provisioning Paris. Merchants and Millers in
the Grain and Flour Trade during the
Eighteenth Century*. Ithaca, 1984.

Karremans, J. A. J.
*Zon, water en vruchtbaarheid in de
volkskunst van Izúcar de Matamoros. Een
structuralistische analyse van
cultuurverandering en cultuurcontact*.
Leiden, 1983.

Katz, F.
"Labor Conditions on Haciendas in
Porfirian Mexico: Some Trends and
Tendencies." *HAHR* 54 (1974), pp.
1–47.
"Rural Uprisings in Preconquest and
Colonial Mexico." In Katz, ed., *Riot*,
pp. 65–94.

Katz, F., ed.
  Riot, Rebellion, and Revolution. Rural Social Conflict in Mexico. Princeton, 1988.
Katzman, M.T.
  "The von Thünen Paradigm, the Industrial-Urban Hypothesis, and the Spatial Structure of Agriculture." *AJAE* 56 (1974), pp. 683–96.
Kay, C.
  El sistema señorial europeo y la hacienda latinoamericana. Mexico City, 1980.
  Latin American Theories of Development and Underdevelopment. London, 1989.
  "The Development of the Hacienda System." In Kay and Silva, eds., *Development,* pp. 33–53.
Kay, C., and P. Silva, eds.
  Development and Social Change in the Chilean Countryside. From the Pre-Land Reform Period to the Democratic Transition. Amsterdam, 1992.
Kaye, H. J.
  The British Marxist Historians. An Introductory Analysis. Oxford, 1984.
Keith, R. G.
  "Encomienda, Hacienda and Corregimiento in Spanish America: A Structural Analysis." *HAHR* 51 (1971), pp. 431–46.
  Conquest and Agrarian Change. The Emergence of the Hacienda System on the Peruvian Coast. Cambridge, 1976.
Keith, R. G., ed.
  Haciendas and Plantations in Latin American History. New York, 1977.
Kellog, S.
  "La supervivencia cultural de los indígenas en el México central desde 1521 hasta 1600: una nueva interpretación." *Mesoamérica* 5 (1984/8), pp. 304–20.
Kicza, J.
  "The Pulque-Trade of Late Colonial Mexico City." *TAm* 37 (1980), pp. 193–221.
  Colonial Entrepreneurs. Families and Business in Bourbon Mexico City. Albuquerque, 1983.

Kingston, J.
  The Weather of the 1780s over Europe. Cambridge, 1988.
Kirchhoff, P.
  "Land Tenure in Ancient Mexico, a Preliminary Sketch." *Revista Mexicana de Estudios Antropológicos,* 14 (1954), pp. 351–61.
Kinsbrunner, J.
  Petty Capitalism in Spanish America. The Pulperos of Puebla, Mexico City, Caracas and Buenos Aires. Boulder, 1987.
Klages, K. H. W.
  Ecological Crop Geography. New York, 1942.
Klein, H. S.
  "La economía de la Nueva España, 1680–1809: un análisis a partir de las Cajas Reales." *HMex* 34 (1985/136), pp. 561–609.
Klima, A.
  "Agrarian Class Structure and Economic Development in Pre-Industrial Bohemia." *PaP* 85 (1979), pp. 49–67.
Kloos, P.
  Door het oog van de antropoloog. Botsende visies bij heronderzoek. Amsterdam, 1988.
Knight, A.
  The Mexican Revolution. Volume 1: Porfirians, Liberals and Peasants. Cambridge, 1986.
  The Mexican Revolution. Volume 2: Counter-revolution and Reconstruction. Cambridge, 1986.
Knowles, D.
  The Evolution of Medieval Thought. New York, 1962.
Knowlton, R. J.
  Church Property and the Mexican Reform, 1856–1910. De Kalb, 1976.
  "La división de las tierras de los pueblos durante el siglo XIX: el caso de Michoacán." *HMex* 40:1 (1990/157), pp. 3–25.
Kochanowicz, J.
  "The Peasant Family as an Economic Unit in the Polish Feudal Economy of the Eighteenth Century." In Wall,

Robin, and Laslett, eds., *Family Forms*, pp. 153–66.

Köhler, U.
"Estructura y funcionamiento de la administración comunal en San Pablo Chalchihuitan." *AI* 42:1 (1982), pp. 117–45.
"Ciclos de poder en una comunidad indígena de México: política local y sus vínculos con la vida nacional." *AI* 46:3 (1986), pp. 435–51.

Kollonitz, P., Gravin.
De eerste dagen van het Mexicaanse Keizerrijk. Amsterdam, 1867.

Konrad, H. W.
"Life in A Jesuit Hacienda in Colonial Mexico: Santa Lucía, 1576–1767." *ACTAS ICA* 42 (1976), II, pp. 460–76.
A Jesuit Hacienda in Colonial Mexico. Santa Lucía, 1576–1767. Stanford, 1980.

Kriedte, P.
Peasants, Landlords and Merchant Capitalists. Europe and the World Economy, 1500–1800. trans. from the German, 1980. Leamington Spa, 1983.

Kriedte, P., H. Medick, and J. Schlumbohm, eds.
Industrialization Before Industrialization. Rural Industry in the Genesis of Capitalism. Cambridge, 1981.

Kuhn, Th.
The Structure of Scientific Revolutions. Chicago, 1972.

Kuperus, J. A.
"Honderd jaar bedrijfsresultaten van de Wilhelminapolder (1814–1913)." *Historia Agriculturae* 6 (1962), pp. 117–273.
"Boekhoudingen op Nederlandse landbouwbedrijven vóór 1900." *Ceres en Clio* (Wageningen, 1964), pp. 79–110.

LaCapra, D.
"Is Everyone a *Mentalité* Case? Transference and the 'Culture' Concept." *HaT* 23 (1984), pp. 296–311.

Ladd, D. M.
The Mexican Nobility at Independence, 1780–1826. Austin, 1976.
The Making of a Strike. Mexican Silver Workers' Struggles in Real del Monte 1766–1775. Lincoln, 1988.

Lafaye, J.
Quetzalcoatl y Guadalupe. La formación de la conciencia nacional en México. Mexico City, 1977.

Lamb, H. H.
Climate, History and the Modern World. London, 1982.

Langdon, J.
"The Economics of Horses and Oxen in Medieval England." *AgHR* 30 (1982), pp. 31–40.

Langenberg, I.
"Urbanización y cambio social. El traslado de la Ciudad de Guatemala y sus consecuencias para la población urbana al fin de la época colonial (1773–1824)." *Anuario dEA* 36 (1979), pp. 351–74.
Urbanisation und Bevölkerungsstruktur der Stadt Guatemala in der ausgehenden Kolonialzeit. Cologne, 1981.

Langer, E. D.
"Labor Strikes and Reciprocity on Chuquisaca Haciendas." *HAHR* 65 (1985), pp. 255–78.

Larson, B.
"Economic Decline and Social Change in an Agrarian Hinterland: Cochabamba (Bolivia) in the Late Colonial Period." Ph.D. diss., Columbia University, 1978.
"Caciques, Class Structure, and the Colonial State in Bolivia." *Nova Americana* 2 (1979), pp. 197–235.
"Rural Rhythms of Class Conflict in Eighteenth-Century Cochabamba." *HAHR* 60 (1980), pp. 407–30.
Colonialism and Agrarian Transformation in Bolivia. Cochabamba, 1550–1900. Princeton, 1987.

Laslett, P.
The World We Have Lost—Further Explored. 3d ed. London, 1983.

Lauer, W.
"The Altitudinal Belts of the Vegetation

in the Central Mexican Highlands and
their Climatic Conditions." *Arctic and
Alpine Research* 5:3 (1973), pp. 99–113.
"Medio ambiente y desarrollo cultural en
la region de Puebla-Tlaxcala."
Comunicaciones Puebla-Tlaxcala, 16
(1979), pp. 29–53.
Lauer, W., and D. Klaus.
"The Thermal Circulation of the Central
Mexican Meseta Region within
Influence of the Trade Winds." *Arch.
Met. Geoph. Biokl. ser. B.* 23 (1975), pp.
343–66.
Lavrin, A.
"The Execution of the Law of
Consolidación in New Spain: Economic
Aims and Results." *HAHR* 53 (1973),
pp. 27–49.
"Mundos en contraste: cofradías rurales y
urbanas en México a fines del siglo
XVIII." Paper, Mexico City, 1983.
"Rural Confraternities in the Local
Economies of New Spain. The
Bishopric of Oaxaca in the Context of
Colonial Mexico." In Ouweneel and
Miller, eds., *Indian Community*, pp.
224–49.
Lavrin, A., and E. Couturier.
"Dowries and Wills: A View of Women's
Socioeconomic Role in Colonial
Guadalajara and Puebla, 1640–1790."
HAHR 59 (1979), pp. 280–304.
Leal, J. F., and M. Huacuja.
*Economía y sistema de haciendas en México.
La hacienda pulquera en el cambio siglos
XVIII, XIX y XX.* Mexico City, 1982.
Leet, D. R., and J. A. Shaw.
"French Economic Stagnation,
1700–1960. Old Economic History
Revisited." *JIH* 8 (1978), pp. 531–44.
Lefèbvre, G.
*The Great Fear of 1789. Rural Panic in
Revolutionary France.* London, 1973.
Le Goff, J.
*De woekeraar en de hel. Economie en religie
in de middeleeuwen.* trans. from the
French. Amsterdam, 1987.
Lemaire, T.
De Indiaan in ons bewustzijn. De

*ontmoeting van de Oude met de Nieuwe
Wereld.* Baarn, 1986.
LeRoy Ladurie, E.
The Peasants of Languedoc. trans from the
French. Urbana, 1974.
*Montaillou. Cathars and Catholics in a
French Village, 1294–1324.* trans. from
the French. Harmondsworth, 1980.
"Family Structures and Inheritance
Customs in Sixteenth-Century
France." In Goody, Thirsk, and
Thompson, eds., *Family*, pp. 37–70.
"A Reply to Professor Brenner." *PaP* 79
(1978), pp. 55–60.
LeRoy Ladurie, E., and M. Baulant.
"Grape Harvests from the Fifteenth
through the Nineteenth Centuries."
JIH 10:4 (1980), pp. 839–50.
LeRoy Ladurie, E., and J. Goy.
*Tithe and Agrarian History from the
Fourteenth to the Nineteenth Century An
Essay in Comparative History.*
Cambridge, 1982.
Levi, G.
Inheriting Power. The Story of an Exorcist.
trans. from the Italian. Chicago, 1988.
Levine, D.
*Family Formation in an Age of Nascent
Capitalism.* London, 1977.
*Reproducing Families. The Political
Economy of English Population History.*
Cambridge, 1987.
Lewis, J. A.
"New Spain during the American
Revolution, 1779–1783: A Viceroyalty
at War." Ph.D. diss., Duke University,
Durham, 1975.
"Nueva España y los esfuerzos para
abastecer La Habana, 1779–1783."
Anuario dEA 33 (1976), pp. 501–26.
Lewis, L.
"In Mexico City's Shadow. Some Aspects
of Economic Activity and Social
Processes in Texcoco, 1570–1620." In
Altman and Lockhart, eds., *Provinces*,
pp. 125–36.
Lewis, W. A.
Theory of Economic Growth. London,
1955.

Licate, J.
Creation of a Mexican Landscape. Territorial Organization and Settlement in the Eastern Puebla Basin (1520–1605). Chicago, 1981.

Liehr, R.
Stadtrat und städtische Oberschicht von Puebla am Ende der Kolonialzeit (1787–1810). Wiesbaden, 1971.
"Die Grundherrschaft der Herzöge von Atlixco im kolonialen Mexico." *JbLA* 9 (1972), pp. 137–72.
"Entstehung, Entwicklung und sozialökonomische Struktur der hispanoamerikanischen Hacienda." In Puhle, ed., *Lateinamerika*, pp. 105–46.
"Endeudamiento estatal y crédito privado: la Consolidación de Vales Reales en Hispanoamérica." *Anuario dEA* (1984), pp. 553–78.

Lienhard, M.
"La legitimación indígena en dos novelas centroamericanas." *Cuadernos Hispanoamericanos* 414 (1984), pp. 110–20.

Lindert, P. van.
"Agrarische commercialisatie." *Geografisch Tijdschrift (nwe.r.)* 12:5 (1978), pp. 442–51.

Lindert, P. H., and J. G. Williamson.
"English Workers' Living Standards during the Industrial Revolution." *EcHR* 36 (1983), pp. 1–25.

Lindley, R. B.
Haciendas and Economic Development. Guadalajara, Mexico, at Independence. Austin, 1984.

Lindzey, G., C. S. Hall, and R. F. Thompson. *Psychology.* New York, 1975.

Lipsett, S.
"Water and Social Conflict in Colonial Mexico. Puebla 1680–1810." Ph.D. diss., Tulane University, 1988.

Lis, C., and H. Soly.
Poverty and Capitalism in Pre-Industrial Europe. Atlantic Highlands, 1979.

Liss, P.
"México en el siglo XVIII. Algunos problemas e interpretaciones cambiantes." *HMex* 27 (1977/106), pp. 273–315.

Littman, R.
The Greek Experiment. Imperialism and Social Conflict (800–400 BC). London, 1974.

Lockhart, J.
"Encomienda and Hacienda: The Evolution of the Great Estate in the Spanish Indies." *HAHR* 49 (1969), pp. 411–29.
"The Social History of Colonial Spanish America: Evolution and Potential." *LARR* 7:1 (1972), pp. 6–45.
"Capital and Province, Spaniard and Indian: The Example of Late Sixteenth-Century Toluca." In Altman and Lockhart, eds., *Provinces*, pp. 99–124.
"Views of Corporate Self and History in Some Valley of Mexico Towns: Late Seventeenth and Eighteenth Centuries." In Collier, Rosaldo and Wirth, eds., *Inca and Aztec States*, pp. 367–93, as well as in Lockhart, *Nahuas and Spaniards*, pp. 39–64.
"Social Organization and Social Change in Colonial Spanish America." *CHLA* (1984), 2, pp. 265–320.
Charles Gibson and the Ethnohistory of Postconquest Central Mexico. Melbourne, 1988.
Nahuas and Spaniards. Postconquest Central Mexican History and Philology. Los Angeles, 1991.
"Postconquest Nahua Society and Culture Seen Through Nahuatl Sources." In his *Nahuas and Spaniards*, pp. 2–22.
"A Vein of Ethnohistory: Recent Nahuatl-Based Historical Research." In his *Nahuas and Spaniards*, pp. 183–200.

Lockhart, J., and S. B. Schwartz.
Early Latin America. A History of Colonial Spanish America and Brazil. Cambridge, 1983.

Loera, M.
"Calimaya y Tepamaxalco. Tenencia y transmissión hereditaria de la tierra en

dos comunidades indígenas. Época
colonial." Tesis Lic., Universidad
Iberoamericana, 1977.
*Economía campesina indígena en la colonia.
Un caso en el valle de Toluca.* Mexico
City, 1981.
Loewenberg, P.
"The Psychohistorical Origins of the Nazi
Youth Cohort. *AmHR* 76 (1971), pp.
1,457–1,502.
Lombardo de Ruíz, S.
*Antología de textos sobre la ciudad de
México en el período de la Ilustración
(1788–1792).* Mexico City, 1982.
Long, N.
"From Paradigm Lost to Paradigm
Regained? The Case for an Actor-
oriented Sociology of Development."
ERLACS 49 (1990), pp. 3–24.
"Commoditization: Thesis and
Antithesis." In Long, Van der Ploeg,
Curtin, and Box, eds., *Commoditization
Debate*, pp. 8–23.
Long, N., J.-D. Van der Ploeg, C. Curtin,
and L. Box, eds.
*The Commoditization Debate: Labour
Process, Strategy and Social Network.*
Wageningen, 1986.
Loomis, R. S.
"Agricultural Systems." *Scientific
American* 235:3 (1976), pp. 99–105.
López Sarrelangue, D.
Una villa mexicana en el siglo XVIII.
Mexico City, 1957.
"La hacienda de San José de Coapa." In
Florescano, ed., *Haciendas*, pp. 223–41.
"Santa Ana Aragón. Una hacienda
comunal indígena de la Nueva
España." *HMex* 32:1 (1982), pp. 1–38.
Lösch, A.
The Economics of Location. New Haven,
1954.
Love, E.
"Marriage Patterns of Persons of African
Descent in a Colonial Mexico City
Parish." *HAHR* 51 (1971), pp. 79–91.
Lovell, W. G.
*Conquest and Survival in Colonial
Guatemala. A Historical Geography of the
Cuchumatán Highlands, 1500–1821.*

Kingston and Montreal, 1985.
"Surviving Conquest: The Maya of
Guatemala in Historical Perspective."
LARR 23:2 (1988), pp. 25–57.
Lovell, G., and W. R. Swezey.
"Indian Migration and Community
Formation: An Analysis of
Congregación in Colonial Guatemala."
In Robinson, ed., *Migration*, pp. 18–40.
Lowry, M.
Under the Volcano. New York, 1947.
Lucassen, J.
"Naar de kusten van de Noordzee.
Trekarbeid in Europees perspektief,
1600–1900." Proefschrift,
Rijksuniversiteit Utrecht, 1984.
Luria, K. P.
*Territories of Grace. Cultural Change in the
Seventeenth-Century Diocese of Grenoble.*
Berkeley, 1991.
McCaa, R.
"*Calidad*, Clase, and Marriage in Colonial
Mexico: The Case of Parral, 1788–90."
HAHR 64 (1984), pp. 477–501.
McCaa, R., and M. M. Swann.
*Social Theory and the Loglinear Approach:
The Question of Race and Class in
Colonial America.* Discussion Paper,
Syracuse, 1982.
McCaa, R., S. B. Schwartz, and A.
Grubessich.
"Race and Class in Colonial Latin
America: A Critique." *CSSH* 21:3
(1979), pp. 421–33.
McCloskey, D. N.
"The Persistence of English Common
Fields." In Parker and Jones, eds.,
European Peasants, pp. 73–119.
Macfarlane, A.
*The Origins of English Individualism: The
Family, Property and Social Transaction.*
Oxford, 1978.
The Culture of Capitalism. Oxford, 1987.
Macfarlane, A., et al.,
Reconstructing Historical Communities.
Cambridge, 1977.
McFarlane, A.
"Civil Disorders and Popular Protest in
Late Colonial New Granada." *HAHR* 6
(1984), pp. 17–54.

McGovern-Bowen, C. G.
Mortality and Crisis Mortality in Eighteenth-Century Mexico: The Case of Pátzcuaro, Michoacán. Syracuse, 1983.

McIntosh, M. K.
Autonomy and Community: The Royal Manor of Havering, 1200–1500. Cambridge, 1986.

McKendrick, N.
"Commercialization and the Economy." In McKendrick, Brewer, and Plumb, *Birth*, pp. 9–145.

McKendrick, N., J. Brewer, and J. H. Plumb, eds.,
The Birth of a Consumer Society. The Commercialization of Eighteenth-Century England. London, 1982.

McKitterick, R.
The Frankish Kingdoms under the Carolingians, 751–987. London, 1983.

MacLachlan, C. M.
Criminal Justice in Eighteenth-century Mexico: A Study of the Tribunal de Acordada. Berkeley, 1974.

MacLachlan, C. M., and J. E. Rodríguez.
The Forging of the Cosmic Race: A Reinterpretation of Colonial Mexico. Berkeley, 1980.

MacLeod, M. J.
Spanish Central America. A Socioeconomic History, 1520–1720. Berkeley, 1973.
"Aspects of the Internal Economy of Colonial Spanish America: Labour, Taxation, Distribution and Exchange." *CHLA* (1984), 2, pp. 219–64.

MacLeod, M. J., and R. Wasserstrom, eds.
Spaniards and Indians in Southeastern Mesoamerica: Essays on the History of Ethnic Relations. Lincoln and London, 1983.

McMillen, N.
"Alfarería. Hispanic Ceramics in New Spain: Origins, Evolution and Social Significance." Ph.D. diss., Texas A & M University, 1983.

Malthus, Th.
An Essay on the Principle of Population or a View of Its Past and Present Effects on Human Happiness. ed. by G. T. Bettany. London, 1890.

Malvido, E.
"Factores de despoblación y de reposición de la población de Cholula (1641–1810)." *HMex* 23 (1973/89), pp. 52–110.
"El abandono de los hijos. Una forma de control del tamaño de la familia y del trabajo indígena. Tula (1683–1730)." *HMex* 29 (1980/116), pp. 521–61.

Mann, M.
The Sources of Social Power. Volume I: A History of Power from the Beginning to A.D. 1760. Cambridge, 1986.

Manning, R. B.
Village Revolts. Social Protest and Popular Disturbances in England, 1509–1640. Oxford, 1988.

Margolies, B. L.
Princes of the Earth. Structural Diversity in a Mexican Municipality. Washington, 1975.

Marshall, C. E.
"The Birth of the Mestizo in New Spain." *HAHR* 19 (1939), pp. 161–84.

Martin, C. E.
"Haciendas and Villages in Late Colonial Morelos." *HAHR* 62 (1982), pp. 407–27.
Rural Society in Colonial Mexico. Albuquerque, 1985.

Martin S J, N. F.
Los vagabundos en la Nueva España, Siglo xvi. Mexico City, 1957.
"La desnudez en la Nueva España del siglo XVIII." *Anuario dEA* 29 (1972), pp. 261–94.

Martínez-Alier, J.
Labourers and Landowners in Southern Spain. London, 1971.
Haciendas, Plantations and Collective Farms. Agrarian Class Societies. Cuba and Peru. London, 1977.
"Ecology and the Poor: A Neglected Dimension of Latin American History." *JLAS* 23 (1991), pp. 621–39.

Mason, P.
Deconstructing America: Representations of the Other. London, 1990.

Matthews, S. W.
"What's Happening to Our Climate?" *NG*

150:5 (1976), pp. 576–615.

Mauzi, R.
L'idée du bonheur au XVIIIe siècle. Paris, 1960.

Maya Ambia, C. J.
"Tres ensayos sobre la hacienda mexicana del siglo XIX." Tesis Lic., Universidad Autónoma de México, 1974.
"Estructura y funcionamiento de una hacienda jesuita: San José Acolman (1740–1840)." *IAAnf* 8 (1982), pp. 329–59.

Mecham, J. L.
Church and State in Latin America. Chapel Hill, 1966.

Medick, H.
"The Proto-Industrial Family Economy: The Structural Function of Household and Family during the Transition from Peasant Society to Industrial Capitalism." *Social History* 3 (1976), pp. 291–315.

Medick, H., and D. W. Sabean, eds.
Interest and Emotion. Essays on the Study of Family and Kinship. Cambridge and Paris, 1984.

Medina Rubio, A.
La iglesia y la producción agrícola en Puebla, 1540–1795. Mexico City, 1983.

Meer, P. L. G. van der.
"Suikerrietcultures in koloniaal Mexico. Bedrijf en beheer van Xochimancas en Barreto." Doctoraalscriptie, Rijksuniversiteit Leiden, 1986.
"Jezuïetenhaciendas in koloniaal Mexico." *Leidschrift* 8 (1987), pp. 35–50.
"El Colegio de San Andrés y la producción del azúcar en sus haciendas de Xochimancas y Barreto (1750–1767)." In Ouweneel and Torales, comps., *Empresarios,* pp. 138–64.

Melville, R.
Crecimiento y rebelión. El desarrollo económico de las haciendas azucareras en Morelos (1880–1910). Mexico City, 1979.

Mendels, F. F.
"Proto-Industrialization: The First Phase of the Industrialization Process." *JEH* 32 (1972), pp. 241–61.

Menegus, M.
"Ocoyoacac: Una comunidad agraria en el siglo XIX." *Estudios Políticos* 5:18–19 (1979), pp. 81–112.
"La parcela de indios." In Carrasco, et al., *Sociedad indígena,* pp. 103–28.

Mentink, G. J.
"De rode loop in Gelderland." part 1 in *BMVG* 64 (1970), pp. 124–44; part 2 in *BMVG* 65 (1971), pp. 29–38.

Mentz, B. von.
"La militarización de la sociedad prusiana en el siglo xviii." *Humanidades* 3 (1979), pp. 89–113.
Pueblos de indios, mulatos y mestizos 1770–1870. Los campesinos y las transformaciones protoindustriales en el poniente de Morelos. Mexico City, 1988.

Merquior, J. G.
"The Other West: On the Historical Position of Latin America." *International Sociology* 6:2 (1991), pp. 149–64.

Messenger Jr., L. C.
"Ancient Winds of Change. Climatic Settings and Prehistoric Social Complexity in Mesoamerica." *Ancient Mesoamerica,* 1 (1990), pp. 21–40.

Mewett, P. G.
"Boundaries and Discourse in a Lewis Crofting Community." In Cohen, ed., *Symbolising Boundaries,* pp. 71–87.

Meyer, J.
"Haciendas y ranchos, peones y campesinos en el porfiriato. Algunas falacias estadisticas." *HMex* 35 (1986/139), pp. 477–510.

Meyers, A., and D. E. Hopkins, eds.
Manipulating the Saints. Religious Brotherhoods and Social Integration in Post-conquest Latin America. Hamburg, 1988.

Miño, M.
"Espacio económico e industria textil: los trabajadores de Nueva España,

1780–1810." *HMex* 32 (1983/128), pp. 524–53.

"El camino hacia la fábrica en Nueva España: el caso de la 'Fábrica de Indianillas' de Francisco Iglesias, 1801–1810." *HMex* 34 (1984/ 133), pp. 135–48.

Obrajes y tejedores de Nueva España, 1700–1810. La industria urbana y rural en la formación del capitalismo. Madrid, 1990.

Miño, M., ed.
Haciendas, pueblos y comunidades. Los valles de México y Toluca entre 1530 y 1916. Mexico City, 1991.

Mingay, G. E.
"The Size of Farms in the Eighteenth Century." *EcHR* 14 (1962), pp. 469–88.

Mitrany, D.
Marx Against the Peasant. A Study of Social Dogmatism. New York, 1961.

Mitteis, H.
Der Staat des hohen Mittelalters. Grundlinien einer Verfassungsgeschichte des Lehnzeitalters. 3d. ed. Weimar, 1948.

Mitzman, A.
"Sociability, Creativity and Estrangement: A Psychohistorical Approach to Michelet and Flaubert, or History as Epos and Anti-Epos." In Damen, et al., eds., *Geschiedenis*, pp. 101–16.

Mokyr, J.
Industrialization in the Low Countries, 1795–1850. New Haven and London, 1976.

Molina Enríquez, A.
Los grandes problemas nacionales. Mexico City, 1909; repr. 1978.

Momigliano, A.
The Classical Foundations of Modern Historiography. Los Angeles, 1990.

Moore, J. W.
The Changing Environment. New York, 1986.

Moore Jr., B.
Social Origins of Dictatorship and Democracy. Lord and Peasant in the

Making of the Modern World. Harmondsworth, 1966.

Moral Ruíz, J. del.
La agricultura española a mediados del siglo XIX, 1850–1870. Resultados de una encuesta agraria de la época. Madrid, 1979.

Morel, A.
"Power and Ideology in the Village Community of Picardy: Past and Present." In Forster and Ranum, eds., *Rural Society*, pp. 107–25.

Moreno, R.
Joaquín Velázquez de León y sus trabajos científicos sobre el Valle de México. Mexico City, 1977.

Moreno Cebrían, A.
El corregidor de indios y la economía peruana del siglo XVIII. Madrid, 1977.

Moreno García, H., ed.
Después de los latifundios. Zamora, 1982.

Moreno Ollero, A.
Sanlucar de Barrameda a fines de la Edad Media. Cádiz, 1983.

Moreno Toscano, A.
"Economía regional y urbanización: tres ejemplos de relación entre ciudades y regiones en Nueva España a finales del siglo XVIII." *ACTAS ICA* 39 (1970), II, pp. 191–217.

"Los trabajadores y el proyecto de industrialización, 1810–1867." In Florescano, ed., *Clase obrera*, pp. 302–50.

Moreno Toscano, A., ed.
Ciudad de México. Ensayo de construcción de una historia. Mexico City, 1978.

Moreno Yáñez, S.
Sublevaciones indígenas en la Audiencia de Quito, desde comienzos del siglo XVIII hasta finales de la colonia. Bonn, 1976.

Morfi, A. de, Fray.
Viaje de Indias y diario de Nuevo México. Vito Alessio Robles, ed. Mexico City, 1935.

Morin, C.
Santa Inés Zacatelco (1646–1812). Contribución a la demografía histórica del México Central. Mexico City, 1973.

Michoacán en la Nueva España del siglo
XVIII. Crecimiento y desigualdad en una
economía colonial. Mexico City, 1979.
"Techniques et productivité sur les
haciendas mexicaines au XVIIIe siècle."
NS 4 (1979/7), pp. 1–20.
Morineau, M.
Les faux-semblants d'un démarrage
économique. Agriculture et démographie
en France au XVIIIe siècle. Paris, 1970.
Mörner, M.
Race Mixture in the History of Latin
America. Boston, 1967.
"The Spanish American Hacienda: A
Survey of Recent Research and
Debate." *HAHR* 53 (1973), pp.
183–216.
Estado, razas, y cambio social en
hispanoamérica colonial. Mexico City,
1974.
Perfil de la sociedad rural de Cuzco a fines
de la colonia. Lima, 1978.
"Economic Factors and Stratification in
Colonial Spanish America with Special
Regard to Elites." *HAHR* 63 (1983), pp.
335–69.
"Research on Latin American History
Today: New Challenges." *Boletín ELC*
37 (1984), pp. 9–18.
The Andean Past. Land, Societies, and
Conflicts. New York, 1985.
Morris, A.
Latin America. Economic Development and
Regional Differentiation (London,
1981).
Muchembled, R.
Culture populaire et culture des élites dans
la France moderne (xve–xviiie siècle).
Paris, 1978.
L'invention de l'homme moderne. Paris,
1988.
Muir, E.
"Introduction: Observing Trifles." In
Muir and Ruggiero, eds., *Microhistory*,
pp. vii–xxviii.
Muir, E., and G. Ruggiero, eds.
Microhistory and the Lost Peoples of Europe.
Baltimore, 1991.

Munch, G.
El cacicazgo de San Juan Teotihuacán
durante la colonia (1521–1821). Mexico
City, 1976.
Murphy, M.
Irrigation in the Bajío Region of Mexico.
Boulder, 1988.
Museo de América.
El mestizaje Americano. Madrid, 1985.
Nadal, J., and G. Tortella, eds.
Agricultura, comercio colonial y crecimiento
económico en la España contemporánea.
Barcelona, 1974.
Navarro y Noriega, F.
Memoria sobre la población del reino de
Nueva España. Mexico City, 1820;
repr., 1954.
Nickel, H. J.
Soziale Morphologie der Mexikanischen
Hacienda. Wiesbaden, 1978.
North, D. C.
Structure and Change in Economic History.
New York, 1981.
Norris, C. R.
What's Wrong with Postmodernism. Critical
Theory and the End of Philosophy.
London, 1990.
Nusteling, H.
Welvaart en werkgelegenheid in Amsterdam,
1540–1860. Amsterdam, 1985.
Nutini, H. G.
San Bernardino Contla. Marriage and
Family Structure in a Tlaxcalan
Municipio. Pittsburgh, 1968.
Nutini, H. G., and B. Bell.
Ritual Kinship. The Structure and Historical
Development of the Compadrazgo System
in Rural Tlaxcala. Princeton, 1980.
Ritual Kinship, Vol. 2., Ideological and
Structural Integration of the
Compadrazgo System in Rural Tlaxcala.
Princeton, 1984.
Ogilvie, S. O.
"Proto-industrialization in Europe." *CyC*
8:2 (1993), pp. 159–79.
Olivera, M.
Pillis y macehuales. Las formaciones
sociales y los modos de producción de
Tecali del siglo xii al xvi. Mexico City,
1978.

O'Neill, B. J.
Social Inequality in a Portuguese Hamlet. Land, Late Marriage, and Bastardy, 1870–1978. Cambridge, 1987.
O'Neill, K.
Family and Farm in Pre-Famine Ireland. The Parish of Killashandra. Madison, 1984.
Orlove, B. S.
"Inequality Among Peasants: The Forms and Uses of Reciprocal Exchange in Andean Peru," in Halperin and Dow, eds., Peasant Livelihood, pp. 201–214.
Orozco, W. L.
Legislación y jurisprudencia sobre terrenos baldíos. Mexico City, 1895.
Los ejidos de los pueblos. Mexico City, 1915; repr. 1975.
Orr, A.
"Farm Servants and Farm Labour in the Forth Valley and the South-east Lowlands." In Devine, ed., Farm Servants, pp. 29–54.
Ortega, M.
La lucha por la tierra en la Corona de Castilla. Madrid, 1986.
Ortíz de la Tabla, J.
Comercio exterior de Veracruz, 1778–1821. Crisis de dependencia. Seville, 1978.
Osborn, W. S.
"A Community Study of Metztitlán, New Spain, 1520–1810." Ph.D. diss., University of Iowa, 1970.
"Indian Land Retention in Colonial Metztitlán." In Ouweneel and Miller, eds., Indian Community, pp. 142–61.
Oss, A. C. van
"Architectural Activity, Demography and Economic Diversification: Regional Economies of Colonial Mexico." JbLA, 16 (1979), pp. 97–145.
"Catholic Colonialism. A Parish History of Guatemala, 1524–1821." Ph.D. diss., University of Texas at Austin, 1982.
"Church and Society in Spanish America. Historical Essays ed. B. H. Slicher van Bath." Manuscript, Wageningen, 1985.

"A Far Kingdom: Central American Autarky at the End of the Eighteenth Century." In Van Oss, "Church and Society."
Catholic Colonialism. A Parish History of Guatemala, 1524–1821. Cambridge, 1986.
Oss, A.C. van, and B. H. Slicher van Bath.
"An Experiment in the History of Economy and Culture." JEEH 7 (1978), pp. 407–27.
Outhwaite, R.B., ed.
Marriage and Society. Studies in the Social History of Marriage. New York, 1982.
Ouweneel, A.
"De hacienda als landbouwbedrijf. Centraal-Mexico in de achttiende eeuw." Doctoraalscriptie, Rijksuniversiteit Leiden, 1983.
"Eighteenth-Century Tlaxcalan Agriculture: Diary 9 of the Hacienda San Antonio Palula, 1765–1766." In Buve, ed., Haciendas, pp. 1–83.
"Schedules in Hacienda Agriculture: The Cases of Santa Ana Aragón (1765–1766) and San Nicolás de los Pilares (1793–1795), Valley of Mexico." Boletín ELC 40 (1986), pp. 63–97.
"Don Claudio Pesero y la administración de la hacienda de Xaltipan (1734–1737)." In Ouweneel and Torales, comps., Empresarios, pp. 165–85.
"De gobernador de indios en de gesloten boerengemeenschap in Centraal-Mexico in de achttiende eeuw." ESHJ 53 (1990), pp. 253–304.
"Altepeme and Pueblos de Indios. Some Comparative Theoretical Perspectives on the Analysis of the Colonial Indian Communities." In Ouweneel and Miller, eds., Indian Community, pp. 1–37.
"Growth, Stagnation, and Migration: An Explorative Analysis of the Tributario Series of Anáhuac (1720–1800)." HAHR 71:3 (1991), pp. 531–77.
"From Tlahtocayotl to Gobernadoryotl: A Critical Examination of Indigenous

Rule in Eighteenth-Century Central
Mexico." *American Ethnologist* 22:4
(1995), pp. 756–85.
Ouweneel, A., and C. Torales Pacheco,
comps.
*Empresarios, indios y estado. Perfil de la
economía mexicana (Siglo XVIII).*
Amsterdam, 1988; repr. Mexico City,
1994.
Ouweneel, A., and S. Miller, eds.
*The Indian Community of Colonial Mexico.
Fifteen Essays on Land Tenure, Corporate
Organizations, Ideology and Village
Politics.* Amsterdam, 1990.
Ouweneel, A., and C. Bijleveld.
"The Economic Cycle in Bourbon Central
Mexico: A Critique of the *Recaudación
del diezmo líquido en pesos.*" *HAHR* 69:3
(1989), pp. 479–530.
Ouweneel, A., and R. Hoekstra.
"Tierras concejiles and propiedad
indígena. Una hipótesis de la
evolución del pueblo mexicano
(1520–1920)." Manuscript,
Amsterdam, 1992.
Ouweneel, A., and W. Pansters.
"Capitalist Development and Political
Centralization Before and After the
Revolution: An Introduction." In
Pansters and Ouweneel, eds., *Region,*
pp. 13–14.
Overton, M.
"Estimating Crop Yields for Probate
Inventories: An Example from East
Anglia, 1580–1740." *JEH* 39 (1979),
pp. 363–78.
Palerm, A.
Antropología y marxismo. Mexico City,
1980.
Pansters, W.
"Paradoxes of Regional Power in Post-
Revolutionary Mexico: The Rise of
Avilacamachismo in Puebla,
1935–1940." In Pansters and
Ouweneel, eds., *Region,* pp. 134–57.
Pansters, W., and A. Ouweneel, eds.,
*Region, State and Capitalism in Mexico.
Nineteenth and Twentieth Centuries.*
Amsterdam, 1989.

Papousek, D. A.
"The Openness of a Closed Community."
IAAnf 1:3 (1975), pp. 245–52.
*Op eigen houtje . . . Aanpassingsprocessen
onder de peasant-potters van enkele
dorpen in het Mazahuagebied in Midden-
Mexico.* Amsterdam, 1978.
Parker, A. E.
*San Mateo Huiscolotepec a Piedras Negras.
Historia de una hacienda Tlaxcalteca,
1580–1979.* Mexico City, 1979.
Parker, W. N., and E. L. Jones, eds.
European Peasants and their Markets.
Princeton, 1975.
Parry, J. H.
The Spanish Seaborne Empire.
Harmondsworth, 1973.
Pastor, R.
*Campesinos y reformas: la Mixteca,
1700–1856.* Mexico City, 1987.
Patch, R. W.
"Agrarian Change in Eighteenth-Century
Yucatán." *HAHR* 65 (1985), pp. 21–49.
Peachey, K. D.
"The Revillagigedo Census of Mexico,
1790–1794: A Background Study."
Bulletin SLAS 25 (1976), pp. 63–80.
Peet, R.
"Von Thünen-Theory and the Dynamics
of Agricultural Expansion." *EEH* 8
(1970–71), pp. 181–201.
Peeters, H. F. M.
*Historische gedragswetenschap. Een bijdrage
tot de studie van menselijk gedrag op de
lange termijn.* Meppel, 1978.
Percheron, N.
*Problèmes agraires de l'Ajusco: sept
communautes agraires de banlieu de
México (XVIe–XXe siècles).* Mexico City,
1983.
Pérez Rocha, P.
"Comercio y precios en la Nueva España.
Presupuestos teoricos y materiales para
una discusión." *RdI* 44 (1984/174), pp.
467–90.
Pérez-Rocha, E.
*La tierra y el hombre en la Villa de Tacuba
durante la época colonial.* Mexico City,
1982.

Pérez Zevallos, J. M.
"El gobierno indígena colonial en Xochimilco (siglo XVI)." *HMex* 33 (1984/132), pp. 445–62.

Pfister, C.
Agrarkonjunktur und Witterungsverlauf im westlichen Schweitzer Mittelland, 1755–1797. Bern, 1975.

Pfister, C., and P. Brimblecombe, eds.
The Silent Countdown. Berlin and Heidelberg, 1990.

Phelan, J. L.
The People and the King. The Communero Revolution in Colombia, 1781. Madison, 1978.

Phipps, H.
Some Aspects of the Agrarian Question in Mexico. A Historical Study. Austin, 1925.

Pietschmann, H.
"Die Reorganisation des Verwaltungssystems im Vizekönigreich Neu-Spanien im Zusammenhang mit der Einführung des Intendantensystems in Amerika (1763–1786)." *JbLA* 8 (1971), pp. 126–220.
"*Alcaldes Mayores, Corregidores* und *Subdelegados.* Zum Problem der Distriktsbeamtenschaft im Vizekönigreich Neuspanien." *JbLA* 9 (1972), pp. 173–270.
Die Einführung des Intendantensystems in Neu-Spanien im Rahmen der allgemeinen Verwaltungsreform der Spanischen Monarchie im 18. Jahrhundert. Cologne, 1972.
"Der *Repartimiento*-Handel der Distriktsbeamten im Raum Puebla im 18. Jahrhundert." *JbLA* 10 (1973), pp. 236–50.
"Dependencia-Theorie und Kolonialgeschichte. Das Beispiel des Warenhandels der Distriktbeamten im kolonialen Hispanoamerika." In Puhle, ed., *Lateinamerika*, pp. 147–67.
Staat und staatliche Entwicklung am Beginn der Spanischen Kolonisation Amerikas. Münster, 1980.

Lateinamerika: die staatliche Organisation des kolonialen Iberoamerika. Stuttgart, 1980.
"Burocracía y corrupción en hispanoamérica colonial. Una aproximación tentativa." *Nova Americana* 5 (1982), pp. 11–37.
"Agricultura e industria rural indígena en el México de la segunda mitad del siglo XVIII." In Ouweneel and Torales, comps., *Empresarios*, pp. 71–85.
El estado y su evolución al principio de la colonización española de América. trans. from the German. Mexico City, 1989.

Piñeiro, M., and E. Trigo, eds.
Technical Change and Social Conflict in Agriculture. Latin American Perspectives. Boulder, 1983.

Plumb, J. H.
"Commercialization and Society." In McKendrick, ed., *Birth*, pp. 265–334.

Poitrineau, A.
La vie rurale en Basse-Auvergne au XVIIIe siècle (1726–1789). 2 vols. Paris, 1965.

Popkin, S.
The Rational Peasant. The Political Economy of Rural Society in Vietnam. Berkeley, 1979.

Post, J. D.
The Last Great Subsistence Crisis in the Western World. Baltimore, 1977.
"Climatic Variability and the European Mortality Wave of the Early 1740s." *JIH* 15:1 (1984), pp. 1–30.

Postan, M. M.
Essays on Medieval Agriculture and General Problems of the Medieval Economy. Cambridge, 1973.

Postan, M. M., and J. Hatcher.
"Population and Class Relations in Feudal Society." *PaP* 78 (1978), pp. 24–37.

Prem, H. J.
Milpa y hacienda. Tenencia de la tierra indígena y española en la cuenca del alto Atoyac, Puebla, México (1520–1650). Wiesbaden, 1976.

Press, V.
"Herrschaft, Landschaft und 'Gemeiner

Mann' in Oberdeutschland vom 15.
bis zum frühen 19. Jahrhundert."
Zeitschrift für die Geschichte des
Oberreihns 123 (1975), pp. 169–214.
Priestley, H.
José de Gálvez. Visitor-General of New Spain
(1765–1771). Berkeley, 1916.
Puhle, H.-J., ed.
Lateinamerika. Historische Realität und
Dependencia-Theorien. Hamburg, 1977.
Pulido Bueno, I.
La tierra de Huelva en el Antiguo Régimen,
1600–1750. Un analisis socioeconómico
comarcal. Huelva, 1988.
Rabell Romero, C.
"San Luis de la Paz. Estudio de economía
y demografía histórica (1645–1810)."
Ph.D. diss., Universidad Nacional
Autónoma de México, 1983.
Randall, R. W.
Real del Monte. A British Mining Venture in
Mexico. Austin, 1972.
Razi, Z.
"Family, Land and the Village
Community in Later Medieval
England." *PaP* 93 (1981), pp. 3–36.
Real Díaz, J. J., and M. Carrera Stampa.
Las ferias comerciales de Nueva España.
Mexico City, 1976.
Rebel, H.
Peasant Classes. The Bureaucratization of
Property and Family Relations under
Early Habsburg Absolutism, 1511–1636.
Princeton, 1983.
Redclift, M. R.
Agrarian Reform and Peasant Organization
on the Ecuadorian Coast. London, 1978.
Sustainable Development. Exploring the
Contradictions. London and New York,
1987.
Redclift, N., and E. Mingione, eds.,
Beyond Employment: Household, Gender
and Subsistence. Oxford, 1985.
Reed, M.
"'Gnawing It Out': A New Look at
Economic Relations in Nineteenth-
Century Rural England." *Rural History.*
Economy, Society, Culture 1:1 (1990),
pp. 83–94.

Reed, N.
The Caste War of Yucatán. Stanford, 1964.
Rees, P.
Transportes y comercio entre México y
Veracruz, 1519–1910. Mexico City,
1976.
Reher, D.
"Old Issues and New Perspectives:
Households and Family Within an
Urban Context in Nineteenth-Century
Spain." *CaC* 2 (1987), pp. 103–43.
Familia, población y sociedad en la
provincia de Cuenca, 1700–1970.
Madrid, 1988.
Rendón Garcini, J. R.
"Tenencia de la tierra y organización
agraria de dos centros de producción
pulquera en el estado de Tlaxcala:
Mazaquiahuac y El Rosario
(1876–1941)." Ms., Mexico City, 1983.
"Paternalism and Moral Economy in Two
Tlaxcalan *Haciendas* in the *Llanos de*
Apan (1857–1884)." In Pansters and
Ouweneel, eds., *Region*, pp. 37–46.
Dos haciendas pulqueras en Tlaxcala,
1857–1884. Tlaxcala, 1989.
Reyes, A.
Visión de Anáhuac y otros ensayos. Mexico
City, 1983; repr. of essays.
Reyes García, L.
Cuauhtinchan del siglo xii al xvi. Formación
social y desarrollo histórico de un señorío
prehispánico. Wiesbaden, 1977.
Reynolds, S.
Kingdoms and Communities in Western
Europe, 900–1300. Oxford, 1984.
Ridder, R. de, and J. A. J. Karremans, eds.
The Leiden Tradition in Structural
Anthropology. Essays in Honour of P. E.
de Josselin de Jong. Leiden, 1987.
Riley, J. C.
"Insects and the European Mortality
Decline." *AmHR* 91 (1986), pp.
833–58.
Riley, J. D.
"Santa Lucía: desarrollo y administración
de una hacienda jesuita en el siglo
XVIII." In Florescano, ed., *Haciendas,*
pp. 242–73.

Hacendados jesuitas en México. El Colegio Máximo de San Pedro y San Pablo, 1685–1767. Mexico City, 1976.
"The Wealth of the Jesuits in Mexico, 1670–1761." *TAm* 33 (1976), pp. 226–66.
"Landlords, Laborers and Royal Government: The Administration of Labor in Tlaxcala, 1680–1750." In Frost, Meyer, and Zoraida, eds., *Trabajo*, pp. 221–41.
"Crown Law and Rural Labor in New Spain: The Status of Gañanes during the Eighteenth Century." *HAHR* 64 (1984), pp. 259–85.

Ringrose, D. R.
"Transportation and Economic Stagnation in Eighteenth-Century Castile." *JEH* 28 (1968), pp. 51–79.
"Madrid and the Castilian Economy." *JEEH* 10 (1981), pp. 481–90.

Robinson, D. J.
"Indian Migration in Eighteenth-Century Yucatán: The Open Nature of the Closed Corporate Community." In Robinson, ed., *Studies*, pp. 149–73.

Robinson, D. J., ed.
Social Fabric and Spatial Structure in Colonial Latin America. Syracuse, 1979.
Studies in Spanish American Population History. Boulder, 1981.
Migration in Colonial Spanish America. Cambridge, 1990.

Robinson, D. J., and C. G. McGovern.
"La migración regional yucateca en la época colonial. El caso de San Francisco de Umán." *HMex* 30:1 (1980), pp. 99–125.

Robisheaux, Th.
Rural Society and the Search for Order in Early Modern Germany. Cambridge, 1989.

Rodríguez, C.
Comunidades, haciendas y mano de obra en Tlalmanalco (Siglo XVIII). Mexico City, 1982.

Rodríguez O., J. E., ed.
The Independence of Mexico and the Creation of the New Nation. Los Angeles, 1989.

Roessingh, H. K.
"The Veluwe." *AAG Bijdragen* 12 (1965), pp. 90–112.

Rogers, E. M.
"Motivations, Values, and Attitudes of Subsistence Farmers: Toward a Subculture of Peasantry." In Wharton, ed., *Subsistence Agriculture*, pp. 111–35.

Rojas, B.
La destrucción de la hacienda en Aguascalientes, 1910–1931. Mexico City, 1981.

Romano, R.
"American Feudalism." *HAHR* 61 (1984), pp. 121–34.

Romero, M. E.
"Hipótesis de trabajo para el análisis de la hacienda de San José Acolman y anexas, 1743–1840." *RMCPS* 91 (1978), pp. 47–58.

Romero, M. E., and E. Villamar.
"San José Acolman y anexas (1788–1798)." In Semo, ed., *Siete*, pp. 151–87.

Romero Frizzi, Ma. A.
Economía y vida de los españoles en la Mixteca Alta: 1519–1720. Oaxaca, 1990.

Romero de Solís, P.
La población española en los siglos XVIII y XIX. Estudio de sociodemografía histórica. Madrid, 1973.

Rorty, R.
Irony, Contingency, Solidarity. Cambridge, 1989.
Solidariteit of objectiviteit. trans. from the English. Meppel, 1990.

Ros, M. A.
"La Real Fábrica de puros y cigarros: organización del trabajo y estructura urbana." In Moreno Toscano, ed., *Ciudad de México*, pp. 47–55.

Rosenblat, A.
La población indígena de América desde 1492 hasta la actualidad. Buenos Aires, 1945.

Roux, B.
Crisis agrícola en la Sierra Andaluza. Seville, 1975.

Rudé, G.
The Crowd in History. New York, 1964.
Ideology and Popular Protest. New York,
1980.
Rulfo, J.
El llano en llamas. Mexico City, 1953.
Ruvalcaba Mercado, J.
"Agricultura colonial temprana y
transformación social en Tepeapulco y
Tulancingo (1521–1610)." *HMex* 33
(1984/132), pp. 424–44.
Sabean, D. W.
*Landbesitz und Gesellschaft am Vorabend
des Bauernkrieges. Eine Studie der
sozialen Verhältnisse im südlichen
Oberschwaben in den Jahren vor 1525*.
Stuttgart, 1972.
"Aspects of Kinship Behaviour and
Property in Rural Western Europe
before 1800." In Goody, Thirsk, and
Thompson, eds., *Family*, pp. 96–111.
*Power in the Blood. Popular Culture and
Village Discourse in Early Modern
Germany*. New York, 1984.
*Property, Production, and Family in
Neckarhausen, 1700–1870*. Cambridge,
1990.
Sahlins, M.
Stone Age Economics. Chicago, 1972.
Saltman, M.
"Feudal Relationships and the Law: A
Comparative Enquiry." *CSSH* 29
(1989), pp. 514–32.
Salvucci, L. K.
"Costumbres viejas, 'hombres nuevos':
José de Gálvez y la burocracia fiscal
novohispana (1754–1800)." *HMex* 33
(1983/130), pp. 224–64.
Salvucci, R. J.
"Enterprise and Economic Development
in Eighteenth-Century Mexico: The
Case of the Obrajes." Ph.D. diss.,
Princeton University, 1982.
"Entrepreneurial Culture and the Textile
Manufactures in Eighteenth-Century
Mexico." *Anuario dEA* 39 (1982), pp.
397–419.
*Textiles and Capitalism in Mexico. An
Economic History of the Obrajes,
1539–1840*. Princeton, 1987.

Salvucci, R. J., and L. K. Salvucci.
"Crecimiento económico y cambio de la
productividad en México, 1750–1895,"
HISLA 7:10 (1987), pp. 67–89.
Sánchez Albornoz, N.
The Population of Latin America, A History.
Berkeley, 1974.
Sánchez Díaz, G.
"La transformación de un régimen de
propiedad en un pueblo: conflictos
agrarios en Churumuco, 1869–1900."
In Moreno García, ed., *Después de los
latifundios*, pp. 63–78.
Sánchez Salazar, F.
"Los repartos de tierras concejiles en la
España del Antiguo Régimen." In
Anes, ed., *Economía española*, pp.
189–258.
Sarrablo Aguareles, E.
*El Conde de Fuenclara. Embajador y virrey
de Nueva España (1687–1752)*. 2 vols.
Seville, 1955–1966.
Sartorius, C.
Mexico About 1850. Stuttgart, 1961.
Sayer, C.
Mexican Costume. London, 1985.
Scardaville, M.
"Alcohol Abuse and Tavern Reform in
Late Colonial Mexico City." *HAHR* 60
(1980), pp. 643–71.
Schama, S.
*Dead Certainties (Unwarranted
Speculations)*. New York, 1991.
Schejtman, A. Z.
"Elementos para una teoría de la
economía campesina: pequeños
propietarios y campesinos de
hacienda." *El Trimestre Económico* 42
(1975), pp. 487–508.
Schell Jr., W.
*Medieval Iberian Tradition and the
Development of the Mexican Hacienda*.
Syracuse, 1986.
Schenk, F.
"Dorpen uit de Dode Hand. De
privatisering van het grondbezit van
agrarische gemeenschappen in het
district Sultepec, Mexico
(1856–1893)." Doctoraalscriptie,
Rijksuniversiteit Leiden, 1986.

"Jornaleros y hacendados. La distribución de la propiedad de la tierra en el sur-oeste del Estado de México hacia 1900." In Miño, ed., *Haciendas*, pp. 230–69.

Schmidt, G. A. *Mexiko*. Berlin, 1921.

Schremmer, E. "Proto-Industrialisation: A Step Towards Industrialisation." *JEEH* 10:3 (1981), pp. 653–70.

Schroeder, S. *Chimalpahin and the Kingdoms of Chalco*. Tucson, 1991.

Schryer, F. J. "A Ranchero Economy in Northwestern Hidalgo, 1880–1920." *HAHR* 59 (1979), pp. 418–43.

The Rancheros of Pisaflores. The History of a Peasant Bourgeoisie in Twentieth Century Mexico. Toronto, 1981.

Una burguesía campesina en la revolución mexicana. Los rancheros de Pisaflores. trans. from the English. Mexico City, 1986.

"Ethnicity and Politics in Rural Mexico: Land Invasions in Huejutla." *Ms/EM* 3:1 (1987), pp. 99–126.

"Class Conflict and the Corporate Peasant Community: Disputes over Land in Nahuatl Villages." *Journal of Anthropological Research* 43:2 (1987), pp. 99–120.

"Peasants and the Law: A History of Land Tenure and Conflict in the Huasteca." *JLAS* 18 (1987), pp. 283–311.

"A *Ranchero* Elite in the Region of Huejutla (The Career of General Juvencio Nochebuena of Atlapexco)." In Pansters and Ouweneel, eds., *Region*, pp. 158–73.

"Peasant Quiescence in the Huasteca." Paper read at the 45th International Conference of Americanists, Amsterdam, 1988.

Ethnicity and Class Conflict in Rural Mexico. Princeton, 1990.

Schulte, R. "Infanticide in Rural Bavaria in the Nineteenth Century." In Medick and Sabean, eds., *Interest*, pp. 77–102.

Schultz, T. W. *Transforming Traditional Agriculture*. New Haven, 1964.

"New Evidence on Farmer Responses to Economic Opportunities from the Early Agrarian History of Western Europe." In Wharton, ed., *Subsistence Agriculture*, pp. 105–110.

Schuurman, A. J. "Historische demografie en sociale geschiedenis. Enkele nieuwe ontwikkelingen." *TvSG* 11 (1985), pp. 375–86.

Schwaller, J. F. *Origins of Church Wealth in Mexico. Ecclesiastical Revenues and Church Finances, 1523–1600*. Albuquerque, 1985.

Schwartz, S. B. *Sugar Plantations in the Formation of Brazilian Society. Bahía, 1550–1835*. Cambridge, 1986.

Scott, J. "Exploitation in Rural Class Relations. A Victim's Perspective." *Comparative Politics* (1975), pp. 489–532.

The Moral Economy of the Peasant. Rebellion and Subsistence in South East Asia. New Haven, 1976.

Weapons of the Weak. Everyday Forms of Peasant Resistance. New Haven, 1985.

Scribner, B., and G. Benecke. *The German Peasant War of 1525. New Viewpoints*. London, 1979.

Searle, C. E. "Custom, Class Conflict and Agrarian Capitalism: The Cumbrian Customary Economy in the Eighteenth Century." *PaP* 110 (1986), pp. 106–33.

Seccombe, W. "Marxism and Demography." *New Left Review* 137 (1983), pp. 22–47.

Seed, P. "Parents Versus Children. Marriage Oppositions in Colonial Mexico, 1610–1779." Ph.D. diss., University of Wisconsin, 1980.

"Social Dimensions of Race: Mexico City 1753." *HAHR* 62 (1982), pp. 569–606.

Seed, P., and Ph. F. Rust.
"Estate and Class in Colonial Oaxaca
    Revisited." *CSSH* 25:4 (1983), pp.
    703–9.
Seele, E., and K. Tyrakowski.
*Cuescomate y zencal en la región Puebla-
    Tlaxcala, México. (Comunicaciones
    Suplemento).* Mexico City, 1985.
Seers, D., ed.
*Dependency Theory, A Critical
    Reassessment.* London, 1981.
Segalen, M.
"'Avoir Sa Part': Sibling Relations in
    Partible Inheritance Brittany." In
    Medick and Sabean, eds., *Interest*, pp.
    129–44.
Semo, E.
Historia del capitalismo. Mexico City,
    1973.
Semo, E., ed.
*Siete ensayos sobre la hacienda mexicana,
    1780–1880.* Mexico City, 1977.
Semo, E., and Pedrero, G.
"La vida en una hacienda-aserradero
    mexicana a principios del siglo XIX."
    In Florescano, ed., *Haciendas*, pp.
    273–306.
Sempat Assadourian, C.
*El sistema de la economía colonial: mercado
    interno, regiones y espacio económico.*
    Lima, 1982.
Sen, A.
*Poverty and Famines. An Essay on
    Entitlement and Deprivation.* Oxford,
    1981.
Sepúlveda, M. T.
*Los cargos políticos y religiosas en la región
    del Lago de Pátzcuaro.* Mexico City,
    1974.
Serrera Contreras, R.
*Guadalajara ganadera. Estudio regional
    novohispana, 1760–1805.* Seville, 1977.
Shaffer, J. W.
*Family and Farm. Agrarian Change and
    Household Organization in the Loire
    Valley, 1500–1900.* New York, 1982.
Shanin, T., ed.
*Peasants and Peasant Societies: Selected
    Readings.* Harmondsworth, 1971.

Sheail, J.
"Green History: The Evolving Agenda."
    Rural History, Economy, Society, Culture,
    4:2 (1993), pp. 209–23.
Simpson, L. B.
*Exploitation of Land in Central Mexico in
    the Sixteenth Century.* Berkeley, 1952.
The Encomienda in New Spain. Berkeley,
    1966.
Singelmann, P.
*Structures of Domination and Peasant
    Movements in Latin America.* Columbia,
    1981.
Skipp, V.
*Crisis and Development. An Ecological Case
    Study of the Forest of Arden, 1570–1674.*
    Cambridge, 1978.
Skocpol, T.
*States and Social Revolutions. A
    Comparative Analysis of France, Russia,
    and China.* Cambridge, 1979.
Slater, D.
"On Development Theory and the
    Warren Thesis: Arguments against the
    Predominance of Economism." *Society
    and Space* 5:3 (1987), pp. 263–82.
"Development Theory at the
    Crossroads." *ERLACS* 48 (1990), pp.
    116–26.
"Fading Paradigms and New Agendas—
    Crisis and Controversy in
    Development Studies." *ERLACS* 49
    (1990), pp. 25–32.
"Power and Social Movements in the
    Other Occident: Latin America in an
    International Context." Paper CEDLA
    Workshop, Amsterdam, 1991.
Slater, D., ed.
*New Social Movements and the State in
    Latin America.* Amsterdam, 1985.
Slicher van Bath, B. H.
*Een samenleving onder spanning.
    Geschiedenis van het platteland in
    Overijssel.* Assen, 1957; repr., Utrecht,
    1977.
*De agrarische geschiedenis van West-
    Europa, 500–1850.* Utrecht, 1960, repr.,
    1977.
"Accounts and Diaries of Farmers Before
    1800 as a Source for Agricultural

History." *AAG Bijdragen* 8 (1962), pp. 1–33.

"Yield Ratios, 810–1820.," *AAG Bijdragen* 10 (1963), pp. 1–264.

"Les problèmes fondamentaux de la société pré-industrielle en Europe occidentale. Une orientation et un programme." *AAG Bijdragen* 12 (1965), pp. 3–46.

"Eighteenth-Century Agriculture on the Continent of Europe: Evolution or Revolution?" *AH* 43 (1969), pp. 169–79.

"Feudalismo y capitalismo en América Latina." *Boletín* 17 (1974), pp. 21–41.

"Agriculture in the Vital Revolution." *CEHE, Vol. 5: The Economic Organization of Early Europe*, pp. 42–132. E. Rich and C. H. Wilson, eds. Cambridge, 1977.

"Twee sociale stratificaties in de agrarische maatschappij in de pre-industriële tijd." In his *Geschiedenis*, pp. 301–13.

"De economische toestand van de Republiek in de 17de eeuw." In his *Geschiedenis*, pp. 360–74.

Geschiedenis: theorie en praktijk. Utrecht, 1978.

"Vrijheid en lijfeigenschap in agrarisch Europa." In Slicher van Bath and Van Oss, *Geschiedenis*, pp. 93–117.

"The Calculation of the Population of New Spain, especially for the Period Before 1570." *Boletín* 24 (1978), pp. 67–96.

Spaans Amerika omstreeks 1600. Utrecht, 1979.

"Economic Diversification in Spanish America around 1600: Centers, Intermediate Zones and Peripheries." *JbLA* 16 (1979), pp. 53–95.

"De historische demografie van Latijns Amerika; problemen en resultaten van onderzoek." *TvG* 92 (1979), pp. 527–56.

Bevolking en economie in Nieuw Spanje (ca. 1570–1800). Amsterdam, 1981.

"Het Latijns-Amerikaanse goud en zilver in de koloniale tijd." *ESHJ* 47 (1984), pp. 177–94.

"Dos modelos referidos a la relación entre población y economía en Nueva España y Perú durante la época colonial." In Ouweneel and Torales, comps., *Empresarios*, pp. 15–44.

Indianen en Spanjaarden. Een ontmoeting tussen twee werelden. Latijns Amerika 1500–1800. Amsterdam, 1989.

"Geschiedenis tussen kritiek en illusie." In his *Indianen en Spanjaarden*, pp. 53–67.

"Spanje en de Peruaanse Andes na de Conquista, een botsing tussen twee sociale en economische systemen." In his *Indianen en Spanjaarden*, pp. 117–37.

Slicher van Bath, B.H., and A. C. van Oss. *Geschiedenis van maatschappij en cultuur.* Baarn, 1978.

Smith, C. A.
"Ideologies of Social History." *Critique of Anthropology* 7:2 (1987), pp. 51–60.

"El estudio económico de los sistemas de mercadeo: modelos de la geografía económica." *Nueva Antropología* 6 (1982/19), pp. 29–80.

Smith, G. A.
"Reflections on the Social Relations of Simple Commodity Production." *JPS* 13 (1986), pp. 99–108.

Smith, M. E.
"El sistema de mercado azteca y patrones de asentamiento en el Valle de México: un análisis de lugares centrales." *Cuicuilco* 2:5 (1981), pp. 18–26.

Smith, R. M.
"Some Reflections on the Evidence for the Origins of the 'European Marriage Pattern' in England." In Harris, *Sociology of the Family*, pp. 74–112.

"Some Issues Concerning Families and their Property in Rural England 1250–1800." in Smith, ed., *Land*, pp. 1–86.

Smith, R. M., ed.
Land, Kinship and Life-Cycle. Cambridge, 1984.

Smith, W. D.
"The Function of Commercial Centers in the Modernization of European Capitalism: Amsterdam as an Information Exchange in the Seventeenth Century." *JEH* 44:4 (1984), pp. 958–1,005.

Solórzano Fonseca, J. C.
"Pueblos de indios y explotación en la Guatemala y El Salvador coloniales." *Anuario ECA* 8 (1982), pp. 125–33.
"Haciendas, ladinos y explotación colonial: Guatemala, El Salvador y Chiapas en el siglo XVIII." *Anuario ECA* 10 (1984), pp. 95–123.

Southern, R. W.
The Making of the Middle Ages. London, 1953.

Spalding, K.
"Social Climbers: Changing Patterns of Mobility Among the Indians of Colonial Peru." *HAHR* 50 (1970), pp. 645–64.
"The Colonial Indian: Past and Future Research Perspectives." *LARR* 7 (1972), pp. 47–76.
"Exploitation as an Economic System: The State and the Extraction of Surplus in Colonial Peru." In Collier, Rosaldo, and Wirth, eds., *Inca and Aztec States*, pp. 321–42.
Huarochirí. An Andean Society under Inca and Spanish Rule. Stanford, 1984.

Spalding, K., ed.
Essays in the Political, Economic and Social History of Colonial Latin America. Newark, 1982.

Spillman, R. C.
"The Disaster Complex of 1785–1786 in New Spain: Prologue to a Geographical Analysis." Paper presented at the 75th Annual Meeting of the Association of American Geographers, Philadelphia, 1979.

Spores, R.
The Mixtecs in Ancient and Colonial Times. Norman, 1984.

Spufford, M.
Contrasting Communities. English Villagers in the Sixteenth and Seventeenth

Centuries. Cambridge, 1974.

Stavig, W.
"Ethnic Conflict, Moral Economy, and Population in Rural Cuzco on the Eve of the Thupa Amaro II Rebellion." *HAHR* 68:4 (1988), pp. 737–70.

Stearns, P.N., and C. Z. Stearns.
"Emotionology: Clarifying the History of Emotions and Emotional Standards," *AmHR* 90 (1985), pp. 813–36.

Stein, S. J.
"Bureaucracy and Business in the Spanish Empire, 1759–1804: Failure of a Bourbon Reform in Mexico and Peru." *HAHR* 61 (1981), pp. 2–28.

Stein, S. and B.
The Colonial Heritage of Latin America. Essays on Economic Dependence in Perspective. New York, 1970.

Stern, S. J.
Peru's Indian Peoples and the Challenge of Spanish Conquest, Huamanga to 1640. Madison, 1982.
"Latin America's Colonial History. Invitation to an Agenda." *LAP* 12 (1985/44), pp. 3–16.
"New Directions in Andean Economic History: A Critical Dialogue with Carlos Sempat Assadourian." *LAP* 12 (1985/44), pp. 133–48.
"Feudalism, Capitalism, and the World-system in the Perspective of Latin America and the Caribbean." *AmHR* 93:4 (1988), pp. 829–72, with comments by Wallerstein and a reply by Stern on pp. 873–97.

Stevens, D. F.
"Agrarian Policy and Instability in Porfirian Mexico." *TAm* 39:2 (1982), pp. 153–66.

Stone, L.
The Causes of the English Revolution, 1529–1642. London, 1972.
The Family, Sex and Marriage in England, 1500–1800. New York, 1979.

Suárez Argüello, C. E.
La política cerealera en la economía novo-hispana: el caso del trigo. Mexico City, 1985.

Sunkel, O., and N. Gligo, eds.
Estilos de desarrollo y medio ambiente en la América Latina. Mexico City, 1981.

Super, J.
"The Agricultural Near North: Querétaro in the Seventeenth Century." In Altman and Lockhart, eds., *Provinces,* pp. 231–51.
"Pan, alimentación y política en Querétaro en la última década del siglo XVIII." *HMex* 30 (1980/118), pp. 247–72.
"Bread and the Provisioning of Mexico City in the Late Eighteenth Century." *JbLA* 19 (1982), pp. 159–82.
La vida en Querétaro durante la colonia, 1531–1810. Mexico City, 1983.

Super, J. C., and Th. C. Wright, eds.
Food, Politics, and Society in Latin America. Lincoln, 1985.

Suttles, G. D.
The Social Construction of Communities. Chicago, 1972.

Swaan, A. de.
In Care of the State: Health Care, Education and Welfare in Europe and the USA in the Modern Era. New York, 1988.
Zorg en de staat. Welzijn, onderwijs en gezondheidszorg in Europa en de Verenigde Staten in de nieuwe tijd. Amsterdam, 1989.

Swan, S. L.
"Climate, Crops and Livestock: Some Aspects of Colonial Mexican Agriculture." Ph.D. diss., Washington State University, 1977.

Swann, M. M.
"The Spatial Dimensions of a Social Process: Marriage and Mobility in Late Colonial Northern Mexico." In Robinson, ed., *Social Fabric,* pp. 117–80.
Tierra Adentro. Settlement and Society in Colonial Durango. Boulder, 1982.
Migrants in the Mexican North: Mobility, Economy and Society in a Colonial World. Boulder, 1989.

Sweet, D. G., and G. B. Nash, eds.,
Struggle and Survival in Colonial America. Berkeley, 1981.

Swift, J.
Economic Development in Latin America. New York, 1978.

Tajfel, H.
"Instrumentality, Identity and Social Comparison." In Tajfel, ed., *Social Identity,* pp. 483–507.

Tajfel, H., ed.
Social Identity and Intergroup Relations. Cambridge, 1982.

Tanck de Estrada, D.
"La abolición de los gremios." In Frost, Meyer, and Zoraída Vázquez, eds., *Trabajo,* pp. 311–31.

Tandeter, E., and N. Wachtel.
"Conjunctures inverses. Le mouvement des prix a Potosí pendant le XVIIIe siècle." *Annales ESC* 38 (1983), pp. 549–613.

Tannenbaum, F.
The Mexican Agrarian Revolution. Washington, 1928.

Tansley, A. G.
"The Use and Abuse of Vegetational Concepts and Terms." *Ecology,* 16 (1935), pp. 284–307.

Tata, R. J., ed.
Latin America: Search for Geographical Explanations. Boca Raton, 1974.

Taylor, W. B.
Landlord and Peasant in Colonial Oaxaca. Stanford, 1972.
"Land and Water in the Viceroyalty of New Spain." *New Mexico Historical Review* 50 (1975), pp. 189–212.
"Town and Country in the Valley of Oaxaca, 1750–1812." In Altman and Lockhart, eds., *Provinces,* pp. 63–96.
Drinking, Homicide, and Rebellion in Colonial Mexican Villages. Stanford, 1979.
"Indian Pueblos of Central Jalisco on the Eve of Independence." In Garner and Taylor, eds., *Iberian Colonies,* pp. 161–83.
"Conflict and Balance in District Politics: Tecali and the *Sierra Norte de Puebla* in the Eighteenth Century." In Ouweneel and Miller, eds., *Indian Community,* pp. 270–94.

Tawney, R. H.
The Agrarian Problem in the Sixteenth Century. London, 1912.
Tedde, P., eds.
La economía española al final del antiguo régimen. Vol. II. Manufactura. Madrid, 1982.
Thomas, K.
Religion and the Decline of Magic. Studies in Popular Beliefs in Sixteenth- and Seventeenth-Century England. Harmondsworth, 1973.
Man and the Natural World. Changing Attitudes in England, 1500–1800. Harmondsworth, 1973.
Thompson, E. P.
Making of the English Working Class. New York, 1963.
"Time, Work-Discipline and Industrial Capitalism." *PaP* 38 (1967), pp. 56–97.
"The Moral Economy of the English Crowd in the Eighteenth Century." *PaP* 50 (1971), pp. 76–136.
The Poverty of Theory. London, 1978.
Thomson, G.
"The Cotton Textile Industry in Puebla during the Eighteenth and Nineteenth Centuries." In Jacobsen and Puhle, eds., *Economies*, pp. 169–202.
Puebla de los Angeles. Industry and Society in a Mexican City, 1700–1850. Boulder, 1989.
Thorner, D.
"Old and New Approaches to Peasant Economies." In Wharton, ed., *Subsistence Agriculture*, pp. 94–99.
Thorpe, R., and G. Bertram.
Peru 1890–1977. Growth and Policy in an Open Economy. New York, 1978.
Tichy, F.
"Siedlung und Bevölkerung im Raum Puebla-Tlaxcala am Ende des 18. Jahrhunderts dargestellt im Kartenbild." *JbLA* 10 (1973), pp. 207–35.
Titow, J.
"Evidence of Weather in the Account Rolls of the Bishopric of Winchester." *EcHR* 12 (1960), pp. 361–407.

Torales Pacheco, C.
"Francisco Ignacio de Yraeta. Comerciante novohispano del siglo XVIII." Tesis Lic., Universidad Iberoamericana, Mexico City, 1983.
"A Note on the *Composiciones de Tierra* in the Jurisdiction of Cholula, Puebla (1591–1757)." In Ouweneel and Miller, eds., *Indian Community*, pp. 87–102.
Torales Pacheco, C., et al.
La compañía de comercio de Francisco Ignacio de Yraeta (1767–1797). Cinco ensayos. 2 vols. Mexico City, 1985.
Toulmin, S.
Cosmopolis. The Hidden Agenda of Modernity. New York, 1990.
Tovar Pinzón, H.
"Elementos constitutivos de la empresa agraria jesuita en la segunda mitad del siglo XVIII en México." In Florescano, ed., *Haciendas*, pp. 132–222.
Insolencias, tumultos e invasiones de los naturales de Zacoalco (México) a fines del siglo XVIII. Mexico City, 1982.
Tranfo, L.
Vida y magia en un pueblo otomí del Mezquital. Mexico City, 1974.
Trautmann, W.
Las transformaciones en el paisaje cultural de Tlaxcala durante la época colonial. Una contribución a la historia de México bajo especial consideración de aspectos geográfico-económicos y sociales. Wiesbaden, 1981.
Tribe, K.
Land, Labour and Economic Discourse. London, 1982.
Trumbach, R.
The Rise of the Egalitarian Family. Aristocratic Kinship and Domestic Relations in Eighteenth-Century England. New York, 1978.
Tulchin, J.
"Emerging Patterns of Research in the Study of Latin America." *LARR* 18:1 (1983), pp. 85–94.
Turner, M.
"Agricultural Productivity in England in the Eighteenth Century Evidence from

Crop Yields." *EcHR* 35 (1982), pp. 489–510.

Tutino, J. M.

"Hacienda Social Relations in Mexico: The Chalco Region in the Era of Independence." *HAHR* 55 (1975), pp. 496–528.

"Provincial Spaniards, Indian Towns and Haciendas: Interrelated Sectors of Agrarian Society in the Valleys of Mexico and Toluca, 1750–1810." In Altman and Lockhart, eds., *Provinces*, pp. 177–94.

"Creole Mexico: Spanish Elites, Haciendas and Indian Towns, 1750–1810." Ph.D. diss., University of Texas, Austin, 1976.

"Life and Labor on North Mexican Haciendas: The Querétaro-San Luis Potosí Region, 1775–1810." In Frost, Meyer and Zoraída Vázquez, eds., *Trabajo*, pp. 339–77.

"Power, Class, and Family: Men and Women in the Mexican Elite, 1750–1810." *TAm* 39 (1983), pp. 359–81.

From Insurrection to Revolution in Mexico. Social Bases of Agrarian Violence, 1750–1940. Princeton, 1986.

"Agrarian Social Change and Peasant Rebellion in Nineteenth-Century Mexico: The Example of Chalco." In Katz, ed., *Riot*, pp. 95–140.

Université de Toulouse, ed.

El valle de Toluca. Raíces indígenas, luchas campesinas y suburbanización. Toulouse, 1978.

Valdes, D. N.

"The Decline of the Sociedad de Castas in Mexico City." Ph.D. diss., University of Michigan, 1978.

Valk, J. van der.

"Vrouwen en criminaliteit in koloniaal Mexico. Een case-study naar de rol van vrouwen in de criminele rechtspraak in Indiaanse dorpen van de provincie Tetepango, Mexico (1750–1800)." Doctoraalscriptie, Erasmusuniversiteit Rotterdam, 1991.

Van Young, E.

"Rural Life in Eighteenth-century Mexico: The Guadalajara Region, 1675–1820." Ph.D. diss., University of California, Berkeley, 1978.

"Urban Market and Hinterland: Guadalajara and Its Region in the Eighteenth Century." *HAHR* 59 (1979), pp. 593–635.

Hacienda and Market in Eighteenth-century Mexico. The Rural Economy of the Guadalajara Region, 1675–1820. Berkeley, 1981.

"Mexican Rural History Since Chevalier: The Historiography of the Colonial Hacienda." *LARR* 18:3 (1983), pp. 5–62.

"Conflict and Solidarity in Indian Village Life: The Guadalajara Region in the Late Colonial Period." *HAHR* 64 (1984), pp. 55–79.

"Recent Anglophone Scholarship on Mexico and Central America in the Age of Revolution (1750–1850)." *HAHR* 65 (1985), pp. 725–43.

"Millennium on the Northern Marches: The Mad Messiah of Durango and Popular Rebellion in Mexico, 1800–1825." *CSSH* 28:3 (1986), pp. 385–413.

"The Age of Paradox: Mexican Agriculture at the End of the Colonial Period." In Jacobsen and Puhle, eds., *Economies*, pp. 64–90.

"The Rich Get Richer and the Poor Get Skewed: Real Wages and Popular Living Standards in Late Colonial Mexico." Paper Meeting of the All-UC Group in Economic History, Los Angeles, 1987.

"A modo de conclusión: el siglo paradójico." In Ouweneel and Torales, comps., *Empresarios*, pp. 206–31.

"Moving Toward Revolt: Agrarian Origins of the Hidalgo Revolt in the Guadalajara Region, 1810." In Katz, ed., *Riot*, pp. 176–204.

"The Raw and the Cooked: Elite and Popular Ideology in Mexico,

1800–1821." In Ouweneel and Miller, eds., *Indian Community*, pp. 295–321.
La crisis del orden colonial. Estructura agraria y rebeliones populares de la Nueva España, 1750–1821. Mexico City, 1992.

Vanderwood, P. J.
"Comparing Mexican Independence with the Revolution: Causes, Concepts, and Pitfalls." In Rodríguez, ed., *Independence*, pp. 311–22.

Vasconcelos, J.
Obras completas. 4 vols.; Mexico City, 1961.

Vassberg, D. E.
Tierra y sociedad en Castilla. Señores, 'poderosos' y campesinos en la España del siglo XVI. trans. from the English. Barcelona, 1986;

Verrips-Roukens, K.
"Pachtrelaties en patronage: machtsbalansen op een Sallands landgoed." *TvSG* 18 (1980), pp. 139–61.
Over heren en boeren. Een Sallands landgoed, 1800–1977. Den Haag, 1982.

Viazzo, P. P.
Upland Communities. Environment, Population and Social Structure in the Alps since the Sixteenth Century. Cambridge, 1989.

Vigil Batista, A.
Catálogo del archivo de tenencia de la tierra en la provincia de Puebla. Sección de manuscritos Fondo Reservado Biblioteca Nacional. Puebla, 1992.

Vigneaux, E. de.
Viaje a México. trans. from the French, originally published in 1854. Mexico City, 1982.

Vilar, P.
La Catalogne dans l'Espagne moderne. Paris, 1962.
"La economía campesina." *Historia y Sociedad 2da época* 15 (1977), pp. 5–31.
Iniciación al vocabulario del análisis histórico. Barcelona, 1980.

Vives Azancot, P. A.
"Región e historia en la América Hispano-colonial. Ensayo de método e

hipótesis sobre regionalización." *Quintocentenario* 5 (1983), pp. 131–208.

Vivó Escoto, J.
"Weather and Climate of Mexico and Central America." In Wauchope, ed., *HMAI*, I, pp. 187–215.

Vollmer, G.
"La evolución cuantitativa de la población indígena en la región de Puebla (1570–1810)." *HMex* 23 (1973/89), pp. 43–51.

Vries, J. de.
The Economy of Europe in an Age of Crisis, 1600–1750. Cambridge, 1976.
"Measuring the Impact of Climate on History: The Search for Appropriate Methodologies." *JIH* 10:4 (1980), pp. 599–630.
European Urbanization, 1500–1800. Cambridge, 1984.

Wachtel, N.
La vision des vaincus. Les Indiens du Pérou devant la conquête espagnole, 1530–1570. Paris, 1971.
The Vision of the Vanquished. The Spanish Conquest of Peru Through Indian Eyes, 1530–1570. trans. from the French. New York, 1977.
"The Indian and the Spanish Conquest." *CHLA* (1984), 1, pp. 207–48.

Wall, R.
"Leaving Home and the Process of Household Formation in Pre-Industrial England." *CaC* 2 (1987), pp. 77–101.

Wall, R., J. Robin, J., and P. Laslett, eds.
Family Forms in Historic Europe. Cambridge, 1983.

Walter, J. and R. Schofield, eds.
Famine, Disease and the Social Order in Early Modern Society. Cambridge, 1989.

Warman, A.
. . . Y venimos a contradecir. Los campesinos de Morelos y el estado nacional. Mexico City, 1976.

Wasserstrom, R.
Class and Society in Central Chiapas. Berkeley, 1983.

Wauchope, R., gen. ed.
Handbook of Middle American Indians. sev. vols.; Austin, 1971.

Weir, D. R.
"Fertility Transition in Rural France, 1740–1829" Ph.D. diss., Stanford University, 1983.
"Life Under Pressure: France and England, 1670–1870." *JEH* 44:1 (1984), pp. 27–48.

Wells, A.
Yucatán's Gilded Age. Albuquerque, 1985.

Werner, G.
"Las consecuencias de la agricultura de los últimos tres mil años en los suelos de Tlaxcala." *Historia y sociedad en Tlaxcala. Memorias del 1er Symposio Internacional de Investigaciones Socio-históricas sobre Tlaxcala. 16 al 18 de octubre 1985* (Tlaxcala/Mexico City, 1986), pp. 222–24.

Wharton, C., ed.
Subsistence Agriculture and Economic Development. Chicago, 1969.

Whetten, N. L.
Rural Mexico. Chicago, 1948.

Wiles, R. C.
"The Theory of Wages in Later English Mercantilism." *EcHR* 21 (1968), pp. 113–26.

Wilken, G.
"Drained-Field Agriculture. An Intensive Farming System in Tlaxcala, Mexico." *Geographical Review* 59 (1969), pp. 215–41.
"Management of Productive Space in Traditional Farming." *ACTAS ICA* 42 (1976), 2, pp. 409–19.
Good Farmers. Traditional Agriculture and Resource Management in Mexico and Central America. Berkeley, 1987.

Wilkinson, R.
Poverty and Progress. An Ecological Model of Economic Development. London, 1973.

Williams, B. J.
"The Lands and Political Organization of Rural Tlaxilacalli in Tepetlaoztoc, c AD 1540." In Harvey. ed., *Land*, pp. 187–208.

Wilson, S.
Feuding, Conflict and Banditry in Nineteenth-Century Corsica. Cambridge, 1988.

Withers, Ch. W. J.
"Kirk, Club and Culture Change: Gaelic Chapels, Highland Societies and the Urban Gaelic Subculture in Eighteenth-Century Scotland." *Social History* 10:2 (1985), pp. 171–92.

Wobeser, G. von.
San Carlos Borromeo. Endeudamiento de una hacienda colonial (1608–1729). Mexico City, 1980.
La formación de la hacienda en la época colonial. El uso de la tierra y el agua. Mexico City, 1983.
"El uso del agua en la región de Cuernavaca-Cuautla durante la época colonial." *HMex* 32 (1983/128), pp. 467–97.
"Mecanismos crediticios en la Nueva España. El uso del censo consignativo." *MS/EM* 5:1 (1989), pp. 13–18.
"Los concursos de acreedores y los remates de las haciendas durante los siglos xvii y xviii." In Jarquín, et al., eds., *Orígen*, pp. 86–91.

Wolf, E. R.
"Types of Latin American Peasantry: A Preliminary Discussion." *American Anthropologist* 57 (1955), pp. 452–71.
"Closed Corporate Peasant Communities in Mesoamerica and Central Java." *SwJA* 13 (1957), pp. 1–18.
Sons of the Shaking Earth. Chicago, 1959.
Peasants. Englewood Cliffs, 1966.
Europe and the People without History. Berkeley, 1982.
"The Vicissitudes of the Closed Corporate Peasant Community." *American Ethnologist* 13 (1986), pp. 325–29.

Wolf, E., and S. W. Mintz.
Haciendas and Plantations." repr. in Keith, ed., *Haciendas*, pp. 36–62.

Womack, J.
Zapata and the Mexican Revolution. New York, 1969.

Wood, S. G.
"Corporate Adjustments in Colonial Mexican Indian Towns: Toluca Region, 1550–1810." Ph.D. diss., University of

California, Los Angeles, 1984.
"The *Fundo Legal* or Lands *Por Razón de Pueblo*: New Evidence from Central New Spain." In Ouweneel and Miller, eds., *Indian Community*, pp. 117–29.

Woodward, D
"Wage Rate and Living Standards in Pre-Industrial England." *PaP* 91 (1981), pp. 28–46.

Wordie, J. R.
"Social Change on the Leveson Gower Estates, 1714–1832." *EcHR* 27 (1974), pp. 593–609.

World Commission on Environment and Development (Brundtland Report), *Our Common Future*. Oxford, 1987.

Wrightson, K.
English Society 1580–1680. London, 1982.

Wrightson, K., and D. Levine.
Poverty and Piety in an English Village: Terling 1525–1700. London, 1979.

Wrigley, E. A.
"A Simple Model of London's Importance in Changing English Society and Economy, 1650–1750." *PaP* 37 (1967), pp. 44–70.
"Urban Growth and Agricultural Change: England and the Continent in the Early Modern Period." *JIH* 15:4 (1985), pp. 683–728.

Wrigley, E. A., and R. S. Schofield.
The Population History of England,

1541–1871. A Reconstruction. Cambridge, 1981.

Wu, C.
"The Population of the City of Querétaro in 1791." *JLAS* 16:2 (1984), pp. 277–305.

Wunder, H.
"Peasant Organization and Class Conflict in East and West Germany." *PaP* 78 (1978), pp. 47–55.
Die bäuerliche Gemeinde in Deutschland. Göttingen, 1986.

Wykstra, R. A.
Introductory Economics. New York, 1971.

Yacher, L.
Marriage, Migration and Racial Mixing in Colonial Tlazazalca (Michoacán), 1750–1800. Syracuse, 1977.

Zanden, J. L. van.
Arbeid tijdens het handelskapitalisme. Opkomst en neergang van de Hollandse economie, 1350–1850. Bergen NH, 1991.

Zavala, S.
La encomienda indiana. Madrid, 1935.
"Orígenes coloniales del peonaje en México." *El Trimestre Económico* 10 (1944), pp. 711–48.
Estudios Indianos. Mexico City, 1948.

Zunz, O., ed.
Reliving the Past. The Worlds of Social History. Chapel Hill, 1986.

Index

About the Book and Author

Shadows over Anáhuac

An Ecological Interpretation of Crisis and Development in Central Mexico, 1730–1800

Arij Ouweneel

The majority of the population of colonial New Spain resided in the central Mexican region of Anáhuac. Drought, overpopulation, and the Bourbon Reforms eroded Anáhuac prosperity during the eighteenth century. After a famine in 1786, both Indians and Spaniards sought to reverse this economic decline. These efforts are analyzed using an ecological approach to the interrelationship among population density, landscape, climate, and culture in shaping the rural economy.

The result is a book with an interpretive breadth as large and multifaceted as the very phenomena it studies. Ouweneel argues that Indians actively and astutely countered the downward spiral of the economy through emigration and urbanization, proto-industrialization, and charity solicited from the state, hacendados, and their own caciques. He also shows how Indian caciques and Spanish entrepreneurs collaborated for mutual benefit.

"I consider this work among the most original and important ever to appear on the economy of colonial Latin America."—Eric Van Young, University of California at San Diego

Arij Ouweneel is senior lecturer at the Center for Latin American Research and Documentation in Amsterdam.